WileyPLUS Learning Space

An easy way to help students learn, collaborate, and grow.

Designed to engage today's student, WileyPLUS Learning Space will transform any course into a vibrant, collaborative learning community.

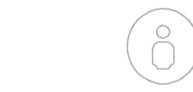

Identify which students are struggling early in the semester.

Educators assess the real-time engagement and performance of each student to inform teaching decisions. Students always know what they need to work on.

Facilitate student engagement both in and outside of class.

Educators can quickly organize learning activities, manage student collaboration, and customize their course.

Measure outcomes to promote continuous improvement.

With visual reports, it's easy for both students and educators to gauge problem areas and act on what's most important.

www.wileypluslearningspace.com

WILEY

ECONOMICS

Theory & Practice

ELEVENTH EDITION

ECONOMICS

Theory & Practice

ELEVENTH EDITION

Patrick J. Welch

St. Louis University

Gerry F. Welch

*St. Louis Community College
at Meramec*

VICE PRESIDENT & DIRECTOR	George Hoffman
EXECUTIVE EDITOR	Mike McDonald
SPONSORING EDITOR	Mary O'Sullivan
PROJECT SPECIALIST	Nichole Urban
ASSISTANT MARKETING MANAGER	Puja Katariwala
ASSOCIATE DIRECTOR	Kevin Holm
SENIOR CONTENT SPECIALIST	Nicole Repasky
PRODUCTION EDITOR	Rajeshkumar Nallusamy
COVER PHOTO CREDIT	©Marilynne Bradley, "Sculpture Garden"

This book was set in Palatino LT Std by SPi Global and printed and bound by Quad/Graphics.

This book is printed on acid free paper. ∞

Founded in 1807, John Wiley & Sons, Inc. has been a valued source of knowledge and understanding for more than 200 years, helping people around the world meet their needs and fulfill their aspirations. Our company is built on a foundation of principles that include responsibility to the communities we serve and where we live and work. In 2008, we launched a Corporate Citizenship Initiative, a global effort to address the environmental, social, economic, and ethical challenges we face in our business. Among the issues we are addressing are carbon impact, paper specifications and procurement, ethical conduct within our business and among our vendors, and community and charitable support. For more information, please visit our website: www.wiley.com/go/citizenship.

APPLICATION ICON. Jigsaw Puzzle. ©Andrew Johnson/iStockphoto

UP FOR DEBATE. Buttons with Yes and No. ©3d_kot/iStockphoto

TEST YOUR UNDERSTANDING. Check Mark. ©cogal/iStockphoto

CRITICAL THINKING CASE. Question Cube. ©skystardream/iStockphoto

ISBN: 978-1-118-94973-3 (BRV)

ISBN: 978-1-119-23942-0 (EVALC)

Library of Congress Cataloging in Publication Data:

Names: Welch, Patrick J., author. | Welch, Gerry F., author.
Title: Economics : theory & practice / Patrick J. Welch, St. Louis
   University, Gerry F. Welch, St. Louis Community College at Meramec.
Description: 11th edition. | Hoboken, NJ : John Wiley & Sons, Inc., [2016] |
   Includes index.
Identifiers: LCCN 2015045231 | ISBN 9781118949733 (looseleaf)
Subjects: LCSH: Economics.
Classification: LCC HB171.5 .W3935 2016 | DDC 330—dc23 LC record available at http://lccn.loc.gov/2015045231

Printing identification and country of origin will either be included on this page and/or the end of the book. In addition, if the ISBN on this page and the back cover do not match, the ISBN on the back cover should be considered the correct ISBN.

Printed in the United States of America

V10011008_061219

Dear Student,

Welcome to the study of economics and to the eleventh edition of *Economics: Theory & Practice*. This course may well be among the most valuable you will take for application to and enrichment of your everyday life. We are excited to join you in this learning experience.

What can you expect from this textbook and your course?

- ◆ Economic topics are given a great deal of attention in daily news reports. Unemployment numbers, banking issues, health-care programs, gasoline price changes, the stability of global economies, and so many more topics are frequently featured. This textbook will provide basic information that helps you to understand economic issues in a knowledge-based context.
- ◆ In the first few pages of Chapter 1, you will learn that economics is rooted in scarcity and choice: The scarcity of resources, time, and money forces everyone, including businesses and governments, into making choices, or decisions, about how to use these limited resources, or how to deal with scarcity. Economics introduces us to tools used in decision-making and to thought processes that are valuable in our own problem solving and in thinking through issues.
- ◆ Other than mathematics and parts of the natural sciences, very little in fields of study is indisputable. Instead, in most areas such as economics, the subject matter is gray and lends itself to varied points of view. Every chapter in this textbook has an "Up for Debate" where issues are viewed from different perspectives. For example, the issue of banning the use of cell phones while driving (the Up for Debate in Chapter 11) has both pro and con arguments.
- ◆ Today's focus on environmental issues is a significant example of the basic economic problem, and the decisions that surround these concerns are perfect examples of the application of the study and tools of economics in our everyday world. Throughout this edition, you will find environmental applications and debates in almost every chapter. This text will make you smarter about thinking through global warming, recycling, carbon emissions, and a host of other green and sustainable issues as well as the new career opportunities they bring.

We have worked to maintain and improve the reputation of this textbook for its student-friendly style. For the student who needs extra support, there is online help. We know that economics has a reputation as a difficult and dense subject area, but we ask that you put this notion aside as you work through this accessible textbook—you will find it most readable and interesting. We are always open to your ideas and questions.

Enjoy!
Patrick Welch
Gerry Welch

PREFACE

We are pleased to introduce the eleventh edition of *Economics: Theory & Practice*. Over the decades, many students have learned the basic fundamentals of economics through class work and this textbook, and have come to appreciate the relevancy of the field in their everyday life. The study of basic economic principles and institutions is an important endeavor. It enables us to sort through a daily barrage of information to identify issues and understand them in a knowledge-based framework. Basic economics also introduces us to decision-making tools and thought processes that make us smarter about problem solving. And, importantly, economics shows us that choices made at all levels, from personal to global, are based on values and points of view that differ with decision makers and contexts.

Economics: Theory & Practice is appropriate for a variety of courses from the one-semester introduction or survey course to the one-semester principles of economics course to the economics refresher in an MBA program. Its balanced coverage of microeconomics and macroeconomics, flexibility in topic coverage order, and the use of appendices and chapter sections to shorten or deepen course material give an instructor a choice of levels and sequences for a course.

Through the 10 editions and now the 11th, *Economics: Theory & Practice* has never lost its focus on student learning, the very foundation of this text. Known as a student-friendly, readable, and understandable textbook, the title has stayed true to its original intention—connecting theory to the practice of economics and the everyday world through examples and applications, debates, and critical thinking cases: some that are classics in the field and others that are fresh and up-to-date.

The eleventh edition of *Economics: Theory & Practice* builds on the substantial changes in the 10th edition with updated and new data, examples, applications, and critical thinking cases. It also continues its emphasis on the environment and green and sustainability issues. We believe that currently there is no better area to illustrate the basic problem of scarcity and choice, to connect economic concepts to the world around us, to understand the process of decision making and its consequences, and to recognize the varying points of view that underlie policy recommendations.

OBJECTIVES OF THE BOOK

This textbook has three primary objectives: (1) to introduce and survey basic economic concepts and institutions in a way that provides students with a solid understanding of key economic relationships and terms; (2) to give students exposure to economic thinking and an understanding of some fundamental processes used in decision making that can be applied to their own decision making as well as an evaluation of opinions, news reports, and other sources of economic information; and (3) to engage students through a writing style, applications, and examples that connect economics to everyday life.

Economic Concepts and Institutions

Economics: Theory & Practice, 11th edition, includes a broad overview of what economists label the principles of macroeconomics and microeconomics. A scan through the Table of Contents provides information about topics that range from supply and demand, to total spending and economic fluctuations, to the behavior of firms in different market settings, to comparative advantage in international trade.

The text also introduces data and institutions with which students should be familiar to understand the operation of the economy. These range from measures of unemployment and gross domestic product (GDP), to the Federal Reserve, to poverty guidelines, to foreign exchange markets. This institutional information helps to link the conceptual world to the real world and encourages economics to be viewed in a broader perspective.

FEATURES OF THE BOOK

Several key features of *Economics: Theory & Practice* contribute to the successful teaching and learning of introductory economics.

Balance of Macroeconomic and Microeconomic Coverage

Economics: Theory & Practice offers a balanced presentation of macroeconomic and microeconomic topics. The book is divided into four parts: Part One covers basic concepts and definitions, economic systems, and supply and demand. Part Two covers macroeconomics in six chapters. Part Three covers microeconomics in six chapters. Part Four covers international economics.

Flexibility in Sequencing of Macroeconomics and Microeconomics

The text can be used in a macroeconomic–microeconomic sequence by going directly through the chapters, or in a microeconomic–macroeconomic sequence by reversing the order of Parts Two and Three. Basic tools and definitions are covered in Part One, and extreme care has been taken to ensure that Parts Two and Three are independent units and can stand alone. In fact, one author has taught using the text's micro–macro sequence, and the other with the text's macro–micro sequence.

Flexibility to Shorten Course Coverage

Instructors who want to shorten material coverage will find it easy to do with *Economics: Theory & Practice*. Entire chapters, such as Chapter 9 on macroeconomic viewpoints and models, Chapter 14 on government and the markets, or Chapter 17 on international finance, can be eliminated because they stand alone. Instructors can also eliminate portions of chapters such as the section on the historical development of the U.S. economy in Chapter 2, price elasticity of demand and supply in Chapter 3, or portions of labor-related topics in Chapter 15. The authors are available to work with text users in fine tuning coverage.

Flexibility to Lengthen or Deepen Course Coverage

Instructors who want to add to course coverage, perhaps for use in a graduate level survey course, can do so in several ways. Instructors can work through all of the chapters in the text, ensuring, for example, that students have complete coverage of antitrust and government regulation by assigning Chapter 14. Several appendices have also been added to extend coverage: for example, an appendix to Chapter 3 on measuring price elasticity, to Chapter 12 on additional cost calculations, and to Chapter 13 on determining the profit-maximizing price and output in various market structures.

There are also several lengthy footnotes that explain material such as the marginal utility/price rule for maximizing utility that can be included.

Flexibility in Course Level and Content

Economics: Theory & Practice has been used in a variety of courses and course levels over the years. Its flexibility allows the text to be used effectively in basic introductory survey courses, more rigorous one-term principle courses, and even in basic graduate level MBA coursework. The range of traditional core topics combined with up-to-date topics, friendly reading style, flexibility of course coverage, and student aids have contributed to the success of this text for a wide variety of student audiences for over three decades.

Student Engagement and Learning

Economics: Theory & Practice provides examples, applications, issue debates, and critical thinking cases to enable students to connect economic concepts to everyday life: from decision making about a wedding, to driving while using a cell phone, to exploring factors that affect the price of peanut butter, to the global reach of Starbucks. In addition to these connections to everyday life, there are a number of learning aids in each chapter to foster active student learning.

APPLICATIONS, UP FOR DEBATES, TEST YOUR UNDERSTANDINGS, CRITICAL THINKING CASES, AND OTHER LEARNING AIDS

Each chapter in *Economics: Theory & Practice* provides a set of tools to enhance learning of the material in the chapter and to tie the text to the real world: applications, an up for debate, a critical thinking case, a test your understanding, and study and discussion features.

> *Applications:* The applications included with each chapter are lively, relevant, and up-to-date. For example, the issue of future funding of the Social Security system comes through Application 6.2, "How Much Do We Love Granny?" the opportunities for careers in new green labor markets come in Application 15.1, "Go Green," and Application 5.4, "Unconventional Indicators of Economic Health," points out some of the studies and factors such as the number of abandoned boats along waterways associated with macroeconomic changes. Other applications deal with the growing export of college educations for foreign students, modern day Luddites, the real cost of smoking, and customer service responses.

> *Up for Debate:* Each chapter includes an Up for Debate that shows students the varying perspectives on issues that underlie policy decisions. For example, the Up for Debate in Chapter 11, "Should Drivers Be Banned from Using Cell Phones While Operating a Vehicle?" includes arguments on both the yes and no sides of the issue. Several of the Up for Debates focus on environmental issues: mandatory recycling, nonprice competition and resource waste, banning international trade that may harm the environment, and a possible relationship between environmental damage and economic growth.

Critical Thinking Cases: The Critical Thinking Case at the end of each chapter concentrates on a problem/situation designed to strengthen the understanding of economic concepts in the chapter and to develop some critical thinking skills. Questions are included with each case. The cases cover a wide range of issues from the health care allocation dilemma, to the markets for haircuts, to Frederic Bastiat's famous *Petition* that a law be passed to protect French industry from ruinous competition from the sun.

Test Your Understanding: The Test Your Understanding in each chapter provides a review of some typically difficult material in the chapter and usually requires some calculations or graphic analysis. For example, in Chapter 3 students tackle a set of events that allows them to strengthen their understanding of supply and demand, and in Chapter 15 students calculate marginal revenue product and graph a labor demand curve.

Study and Discussion Support: Each chapter helps students to organize their studies and reinforces student learning through a variety of learning aids. These include objectives for each chapter, margin definitions, a carefully constructed chapter summary, a list of key definitions and concepts, review questions, discussion questions, and a Test Your Understanding.

NEW TO THE ELEVENTH EDITION

Economics: Theory & Practice, eleventh edition, has been thoroughly updated. All data, both macroeconomic and microeconomic, are the latest available at the time of publication. In addition, students can locate even newer data by referring to the sources of the information.

Many changes have occurred in the U.S. macroeconomy in less than a decade. We have been through a recession with high and prolonged unemployment figures, followed by a modest recovery. Substantial budget deficits have created a sizeable federal debt that is now larger than GDP. In the money and banking arena, there was a serious financial crisis in 2007–2009 that brought new legislation, such as Dodd–Frank, that has been complicated and challenged. In addition to these major macro issues, there are concerns about the environment, income distribution, government regulation, and much more. Today, there is an edginess about policy issues and decisions, especially at the federal level. Probably more than ever, it is important that students understand some economic basics.

In keeping with the text's reputation for connecting economic theory to practice, this edition includes new and updated applications, debates, and critical thinking cases to add more recent examples of concepts. Products that consumers have rejected, updated profiles of Starbuck's and Kraft, an updated real cost of smoking, connecting diseconomies of scale to poor customer service, and pointing out the power of Janet Yellen's words, are just some of the new changes and updates.

The eleventh edition continues to emphasize environmental examples, issues, and policies throughout the text. Chapter 1, for example, includes recycling, concerns over global warming, the ozone layer, greenhouse gas emissions, sustainability, carbon emissions, energy efficient appliances, and fuel efficiency requirements in the language of the chapter. Other chapters include topics and examples such as environmental damage in planned economies, toxic waste, landfills, and more.

Several Up for Debates provide weighty looks at current environmental debates. Among the questions are the following: Should trade be restricted if it results in environmental damage? Does nonprice competition waste resources? Should St. Louis County, Missouri, impose mandatory trash pickup and recycling?

This edition, similar to the others, helps to make students aware that policy decisions are based on values and information that are not cast in certainty. The up for debates and the critical thinking cases help to illustrate that there is no correct answer in public policy, but rather there usually are many facets to an issue. As students read through the cases on eminent domain or on the allocation of health-care expenditures or the up for debate on government regulation of fuel efficiency requirements, the lack of certainty about positions should become clear.

SUPPLEMENTARY MATERIALS

A dedicated companion website with extensive resources for both students and professors can be found at http://www.wiley.com/college/welch. This website includes all of the resources listed here. The student Study Guide includes for each chapter a listing of objectives and terms from the textbook, a study organizer identifying important concepts, a self-test review, computational exercises, and practice examination questions. Answers to the exercises and practice questions are included at the end of the Study Guide. The Test Bank contains approximately 3,000 multiple-choice, true/false, and short essay questions, many requiring students to make computations. A computerized Test Bank containing all test questions from the test bank is also available. This version of the Test Bank allows instructors to customize exams for their courses. The Instructor's Manual provides a teaching overview, which is particularly useful to new instructors, and a sample syllabus giving information about topic coverage, assignments, examinations, and such. Also included for each chapter is a restatement of objectives, teaching suggestions, and recommendations on incorporating the discussion and review questions and critical thinking cases into a course. Suggested answers for the discussion and review questions are also provided. A set of PowerPoint presentations consists of chapter outlines and enlarged versions of all the figures and tables contained in the text. This set can be used to create overhead transparencies for viewing in the classroom, or they can be copied and used as handouts for students.

ACKNOWLEDGEMENTS

We are especially grateful to the reviewers whose invaluable comments and suggestions have helped improve our title over its many editions.

Over the years many editors, book reps, and design staff have worked with creating this textbook that has been a part of the economics textbook publishing world for over three decades. It began with encouragement from Russ Boersma, a sales representative from Dryden Press that was the initial publisher. Through mergers and other decisions the text moved to Harcourt, Brace Jovanovich, and then to John Wiley & Sons. We are grateful to these companies and their staffs for support, good advice, and commitment to this text.

It has been our good fortune to work with a great Wiley staff that is talented and committed to professional excellence. We have appreciated being part of the Wiley team.

Many thanks are due to Mary O'Sullivan—Sponsoring Editor, Nichole Urban—Project Specialist, and Rajeshkumar Nallusamy—Production Editor.

We have also benefitted from the support of many colleagues at St. Louis University and St. Louis Community College who have been generous with their comments and informal reviews. So many students at these two institutions have given us the passion to strive for a textbook that would put basic economics into a context and language that would enable them to carry the relevancy of economics with them far beyond the classroom. Without a doubt, comments about enjoying the text or wanting to take more economics or no longer believing that economics is irrelevant continue to be the impetus to produce this textbook.

Patrick Welch
Gerry Welch
October 2015

BRIEF CONTENTS

CONTENTS

Introduction to Economics

CHAPTER OBJECTIVES

Define economics, scarcity and choice, opportunity cost, efficiency, and equity.

Identify the four factors of production and the income return to each type of factor.

Differentiate between economic theory and economic policy, and discuss the components of model building.

Define the tools economists use to express theories and policies.

Use the production possibilities model to illustrate scarcity and model building.

Define the differences between the study of macroeconomics and microeconomics.

Explain how to construct a graph and interpret the illustrated relationship.

WHAT IS ECONOMICS?

We are always making choices. We constantly choose how to spend our time and our money. We make simple choices like whether to take the time to eat lunch rather than work or whether to spend money for bottled water rather than drink from a water fountain. We make complex choices about careers, where to live, and colleges. And, as members of society, we make choices about voting, supporting public policy issues, recycling, and volunteering to clean up the local park.

Choices are a part of everyday life because our wants exceed our ability to satisfy them. You may want to achieve a high grade point average (GPA) and maintain a job that gives you enough money for clothes, a car, and decent housing during a semester that does not provide enough time for both. People in a community may want a recreation complex, street repairs, an ambulance, and other services but do not have enough tax dollars to pay for it all. It is this scarcity of time and things and the resulting choices that must be made that bring us to the study of economics.

Economics

The study of how scarce, or limited, resources are used to satisfy unlimited wants and needs; the study of decision making in a world of scarcity.

Economics is the study of how scarce, or limited, resources are used to satisfy people's unlimited wants and needs. In other words, economics is concerned with how people make decisions in a world of scarcity. Much of the study of economics is focused on satisfying people's wants and needs for material "things"—shoes, cars, medical services, entertainment, and the like. And, although happiness, sorrow, beauty, and integrity are not direct concerns of the discipline of economics, we know that often these values underlie the economic decisions that people make. Many of us have given our time and money to a person or cause rather than spend it on ourselves because it gives us greater happiness.

The field of economics is extensive and it is always growing. While you may hear economists voicing opinions about unemployment, inflation, interest rates, poverty, energy, the environment, and international trade, this just scratches the surface. This textbook introduces you to some of the major areas of study in economics, some key institutions and relationships, and some controversial policy issues. A quick glance through the table of contents will give you an idea of the breadth of topics included in the discipline of economics.

Why study economics? What can it do for you? Economics permeates our lives. Many of our own personal decisions are obviously rooted in economics: how we pay next semester's tuition or whether we should take a job halfway across the country. But economics is also at the root of decisions made with far-reaching impacts: what programs to fund in a congressional budget or how much support to provide for concerns over global warming.

A course in economics not only provides valuable information, but it also develops reasoning and analytical skills that enable you to think smarter. Through the study of economics, you will be introduced to important institutions, such as the Federal Reserve and foreign exchange markets, which play a key role in the unfolding of economic events. You will also be introduced to analytical techniques that develop your critical thinking and reasoning skills, enabling you to better understand, for example, why the price of a product you want keeps rising, why the benefits of a job move outweigh its costs, or why you support the position of a candidate for public office.

Once you are armed with economic institutional information and skills—skills you will be developing for the rest of your life—you will be better prepared to evaluate and respond to news reports, promises of aspiring politicians, crises at work, personal decisions, and other situations. In short, an understanding of economics helps make you a better-informed citizen and decision maker and is important for success in your career—be it law, health care, journalism, or anything else.

Economics and Scarcity

Scarcity

Too few goods and services to satisfy all wants and needs.

Scarcity is the reason for the study of economics. **Scarcity** means that there are not enough, nor can there ever be enough, goods and services to satisfy the wants and needs of all individuals, families, and societies. Look at your own situation. Do you own the car you would most like to have? Do you have enough money for the concerts, e-reader, and boots you want? Does the recent car insurance bill mean ramen and peanut butter this month? Societies face the same scarcity problem on a larger scale. Money spent for roads is money not available for hospitals or schools. Gasoline and oil used now will not be available in the future.

The root of the scarcity problem is in the definition of economics—that people have limited resources to satisfy their unlimited wants and needs. People seem to continually require more goods and services and to become dissatisfied with what they have. When this psychological drive for more is considered for all members of society, wants and needs become so great in number that they can be viewed as virtually unlimited. For example, your instructor could devote one class period to listing everything everyone in the class wanted both for themselves and for society in general. By the next class period, and in all later periods, the list would increase as students added goods and services originally forgotten or introduced to them throughout the semester. The list would never be completed! Ten years ago the average American did not need a smartphone, 4G capability, organic carrots, a juicer, or an electric car.

All of these unlimited wants and needs cannot be satisfied because the resources available to produce goods and services are limited. These resources include all the people, materials, machinery, and other items that contribute to the production of goods and services. For example, to provide pizzas, a business needs cheese and other ingredients, people to cook and serve, electricity, water, ovens, refrigerators, a manager, and a building. Every resource available for production is limited in amount: There is not an infinite supply of labor, energy, or any other resource.

The problem of limited resources also occurs for individuals. We never seem to have enough money to purchase everything we want and need, and never have enough time to accomplish everything we want to do. Limited resources keep many students from taking a trip over spring break, upgrading a cellphone, or buying a new car instead of repairing an old one. Many students would like to produce a high GPA, work at a part-time job, and enjoy an active social life but cannot achieve all of these due to time constraints.

In recent years, we have become more conscious than ever of our limited resources as we face worldwide environmental issues. We are keenly aware of the limits of air, water, energy, and the ability of the earth to sustain itself. Global warming, holes in the ozone layer, greenhouse gas emissions, fracking for natural gas, and water shortages throughout the world have become topics of regular discussion and concern.

Scarcity and Choice

Since it is impossible to satisfy all of the wants and needs of individuals, businesses, nonprofits, government units, and societies, decisions must be made about what to satisfy and how to use limited resources. A student, for example, who is pressed by the demands of a job and the need to study for an exam must make a decision about how to use limited available time. A state university that is facing a reduction in funds must make choices about what programs, staff, and services to cut. And, as a society, we must choose the degree to which we will pollute our air and water.

Trade-off
Giving up one thing for something else.

Anytime we make a choice, there are **trade-offs** and consequences. Suppose that a student has $100 (a limited sum) and wants to use the money for either e-supplements in a tough course or a weekend visit with an old friend. The visit is the trade-off for the course supplements, and the supplements are the trade-off for the visit. In choosing between these, the student will evaluate the consequences of each alternative. The supplement purchase might result in a good grade in a course; the visit might mean renewing a friendship.

In making choices, a decision maker's values play a very important role and underlie most choices. Values are those principles and standards that a person considers to be worthwhile and are the ideals that drive people and organizations. Try the exercise in Table 1.1 to determine your own core values.

TABLE 1.1	*Values Exercise*

Each of us has several core values that drive us. They are at the heart of our decisions and the actions that we take. Sometimes it is helpful to identify these core values so that we understand what is at the root of our actions. The following lists some possible values. Circle the five that best represent your core values.

Love	Happiness	Money	Respect
Security	Freedom	Truth	Power
Peace	Health	Learning	Thrift
Honesty	Responsibility	Change	Dependability
Safety	Family	Stability	Artistry
Religion	Friendship	Independence	Creativity
Success	Faith	Cleanliness	Knowledge
Work	Individualism	Authority	Intelligence
Integrity	Education	Community	Analysis

Value judgment
The relative importance one assigns to an action or alternative.

Decisions usually involve a **value judgment**, which is the relative importance that a person assigns to an action or alternative. If the student faced with the choice of course supplements or a weekend with a friend decides that a good grade is more important, the course supplements will be purchased with the $100; if friendship is valued more than a good grade, the student will choose the visit.

Scarcity also forces business owners and managers to make decisions based on value judgments. Companies might have to decide between raises for employees and equipment updates, or whether or not to continue a costly health insurance program at the expense of another need, such as a building renovation. In some business-related choices, employees are highly valued and wage increases are important; in others, stockholder profit is the primary value.

Society faces the same scarcity-related trade-off problem. Take a look around your community to see the value judgments of its residents. Public decisions about how well schools, parks, roads, and fire and police are funded—or not funded—reflect the values of the community. At the national level, balancing a federal budget may require reduced government spending elsewhere and laws that permit gas-guzzling and carbon-emitting vehicles may have future environmental consequences.

Each trade-off made is necessary, because we cannot have everything, and each trade-off reflects the value judgments of the decision makers.

Opportunity Cost
The cost of a purchase or decision measured in terms of a forgone alternative; what was given up to make a purchase or carry out a decision.

Opportunity Cost   In making choices, people evaluate both the benefits and the costs of their choices. Because of scarcity, every decision to acquire a good or service or to spend time or money in a certain way has a cost attached to it. Economists call this **opportunity cost**. An opportunity cost is the cost of a purchase or a decision measured in terms of a forgone alternative—that is, what was given up to make the purchase or carry out the decision. Once time or money is devoted to one thing, the opportunity to use that time or money for something else is lost.

Everything that someone can purchase or do has an opportunity cost attached to it. If you spend $40 to put gas in your car, the opportunity cost of that gas is what was given up to buy it—perhaps a few decent meals. What was the opportunity cost of the last purchase you made? What is the opportunity cost of cutting a class in this course?

| FIGURE 1.1 | *Scarcity, Choice, and Influences on Decision Makers* |

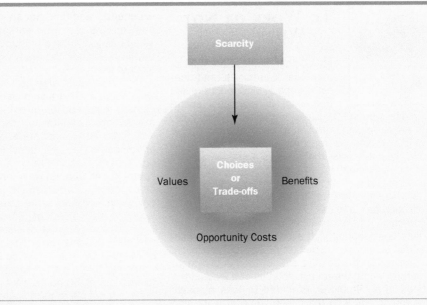

Scarcity imposes choices on decision makers who are influenced by the benefits and opportunity costs of the alternatives, as well as by their own values.

The opportunity cost of choosing to acquire more shoes or food, rather than supporting an increase in a school tax, could be an inferior education for children in a community. The opportunity cost of balancing a government budget could be forgone educational and health benefits due to reduced spending. Because of scarcity, individuals, families, businesses, and societies make choices based on both the benefits and the opportunity costs of their decisions. Figure 1.1 shows the relationship between scarcity and choice, and the influences on a decision maker.

Application 1.1, "To Work or Not to Work," deals with the opportunity costs faced by teenagers who work long hours while going to school. What are students trading off to work more and earn more income?

Efficiency and Equity

In dealing with the basic problem of scarcity—not enough goods and services to satisfy everyone's wants and needs—there are two important concepts to consider: efficiency and equity.

Efficiency is concerned with using resources effectively or getting the most from scarce resources. **Efficiency** occurs when a given good or service is produced at the lowest possible cost. If all goods and services were produced efficiently, society would experience the greatest possible lessening of the scarcity problem. Producing efficiently does not eliminate scarcity, but it does allow for the production of the maximum amount of goods and services to satisfy unlimited material wants and needs. This is important in a world of scarcity and is a major economic goal.

When is a student efficient? Most students set a goal for a grade, and then need to commit the time to achieve that grade. (While most instructors think this should be

Efficiency
Producing a given good or service at the lowest possible cost; getting the most output from resources.

To Work or Not to Work

After-dinner visits to the mall or the local Starbuck's and late night stops at McDonald's reveal that a lot of teenagers spend their evenings working at close-to-minimum-wage jobs. Teens are driven to work late hours, especially during the school week, for various reasons: unemployment for a good family income earner that creates a critical need to contribute to household expenses; escalating car insurance payments from multiple accidents; simply wanting cash for clothes and concerts; or just plain enjoyment from the socialization part of a job.

Understanding the impact of teen employment and long working hours during high school has been the subject of some economic, sociological, and psychological studies. Findings on the positive side of teen employment include learning about the responsibilities of a job and the expectations of an employer, exposure to time management, and interaction with the public. Time at work also means time staying out of trouble.

But what are the costs? Obviously, time spent at work is time given up for studying and engaging in activities that are part of the high school club and athletic experience, and time not spent with family and friends. In addition, the teen who works long hours may not get the sleep needed to be a productive learner during the school day. In one study, too many work hours often led to higher alcohol use.

There could also be long-run consequences. Those work hours and extra income could mean lower grades, the inability to gain acceptance into a competitive college, and missed opportunities for discoveries about cultural, athletic, and academic interests that ultimately drive and enrich one's life. Also, consider how this affects an economy that increasingly relies on mental rather than physical contributions from its work force for economic growth. One study found that 53 percent of American teens worked in any given week. In some other countries, this was much less: only 18 percent of Japanese students worked.

"There are a lot of benefits to students' working in moderation," says one sociology professor at the University of Minnesota. "But most sociologists and psychologists would say that it's an excessive load for full-time students to work 25 or 30 hours a week if you think it's important for young people to participate in extracurricular activities, develop friendships, and spend time with their families."[a]

[a]Quote and references to studies are from Steven Greenhouse, "Problems Seen For Teenagers Who Hold Jobs", *The New York Times*, January 29, 2001.

---

an A, in reality it might just be a C!) A student is efficient when this targeted grade is earned using the least amount of time possible. This could result from effective note taking, good study habits, careful textbook reading, and the like. Students who study efficiently have more time for other activities and get the most from their limited resource of time.

Likewise, a society gets the most from its limited resources when efficient techniques of production allow those resources to be used to the fullest. With the aid of good computer software, for example, professionals like architects, accountants, and others can be very efficient. As more household appliances are manufactured to operate with less energy usage, society can stretch its energy resources. Inefficient students waste their time, and an inefficient use of a society's resources wastes those resources. In both cases, the scarcity problem is worsened.

In a world of scarcity, where there are not enough goods and services to satisfy everyone's wants and needs, there is the issue of what is a fair, just, or equitable distribution of goods and services among the members of a society. **Equity**, or justice and fairness, raises two basic questions: Should a fair distribution of goods and services be an economic goal for a society? If it is, how is a fair distribution defined and achieved?

The concept of what constitutes an equitable distribution of goods and services is controversial because it is based on people's value judgments. To some people, equity occurs when goods and services are divided equally. To others, the distribution of goods and services should be made according to people's needs. And to some, equity results when people are rewarded according to what they

Equity

Justice or fairness in the distribution of goods and services.

contribute to production: Those who contribute more or better resources should receive more. This last view—that people should be rewarded for their contribution to production—is the philosophical basis of a market system. Market and other economic systems are discussed in Chapter 2.

The issue of how to define and achieve equity is not easily resolved because there are so many diverse viewpoints. In the United States, for example, there is a continuing debate over how much the government should provide for those who are in need. This debate has received extensive media coverage in recent years over issues such as health care, tax breaks, welfare payments, and unemployment compensation.

FACTORS OF PRODUCTION

Think about all of the thousands of different types of **resources**, or **factors of production**, that are used to produce goods and services, from the shelving in a big box store, to the skilled hands of a neurosurgeon, to the air filters on a plane. To bring order to a discussion about resources, economists classify them into four groups: labor, capital, land, and entrepreneurship.

- ◆ **Labor** includes all human effort, both physical and mental, going into the production of goods and services. It encompasses the efforts of everyone from lawyers to lifeguards—all who work to produce goods and services.
- ◆ **Capital** includes warehouses, machinery and equipment, computers, office furniture, and all other goods that are used in the production of goods and services.
- ◆ **Land** includes all inputs into production that originate in nature and are not human-made—oil, iron ore, and fertile acreage to name a few.
- ◆ **Entrepreneurship** is the function of organizing or bringing other factors together and taking the risk of success or failure. Without this function, economic activity would not occur. A small business owner usually performs this function and is called an entrepreneur, and in corporations, managers organize and stockholders take the risk.

The relationship between productive resources and society's material wants and needs is summarized in Figure 1.2.

Resources (Factors of Production)
Persons and things used to produce goods and services; limited in amount; categorized as labor, capital, land, and entrepreneurship.

Labor
Physical and mental human effort used to produce goods and services.

Capital
Items, such as machinery and equipment, used in the production of goods and services.

Land
Productive inputs that originate in nature, such as coal and fertile soil.

Entrepreneurship
The function of organizing resources for production and taking the risk of success or failure in a productive enterprise.

FIGURE 1.2   *Relationship between Resources and Wants and Needs*

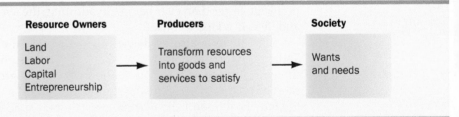

Resource Owners	Producers	Society
Land Labor Capital Entrepreneurship	Transform resources into goods and services to satisfy	Wants and needs

Producers transform factors of production that they get from resource owners into goods and services to satisfy society's wants and needs.

Factors and Income

People who own resources provide them for production because they expect a return. Although the return may be personal satisfaction, such as a positive feeling from community service, most often people expect to be paid, or to receive an income. While money is money, and $100 received by a worker is no different from $100 received by the owner of a building, it is helpful to label the incomes received from selling different types of resources. These are

Wages
Income return to labor.

Interest
Income return to owners of capital.

Rent
Income return to owners of land resources.

Profit
Income return to those performing the entrepreneurial function.

- ◆ **wages**—income for labor,
- ◆ **interest**—income for capital,
- ◆ **rent**—income for land resources, and
- ◆ **profit**—income for carrying out the entrepreneurial function.

While it might appear trivial to give a separate name to the income received by each of the different groups of resources, the distinction can be significant. For example, various legislative and public policy initiatives are aimed at particular income groups. Consider the Social Security program. Payments into this program come from wages as well as income, or profit, earned by the individual entrepreneur. Rent, interest, and corporate profit are incomes that are not part of the Social Security system.

The classification of people into different earning groups has also had interesting social connotations. As the economist Robert Heilbroner put it, "It is not just Labor on the one hand and Land or Capital on the other; it is the Bronx on the one hand and Park Avenue on the other."[1] In addition, Marxian theory, which is critical of capitalism, is based on the premise that a conflict exists between wage and profit earners that is inherent in capitalistic systems.

Scarce Resources

How scarce are resources, or factors of production? In the U.S. economy alone, there are over 155 million people working or looking for work, almost a billion acres of farmland, and billions of barrels of petroleum reserves. The list of available resources goes on and on.[2]

While large numbers of resources may be available in an *absolute* sense, they are scarce *relative* to the wants and needs that their use attempts to satisfy. People's wants always continue to outrun the economy's ability to satisfy them.

If we cannot solve the scarcity problem, can we ease it? Over the last few decades has the scarcity problem eased or worsened? On the positive side, we have made much progress: Medical advancements have increased life expectancies; technological changes in transportation allow us to travel rapidly; fashionable clothing is available to buyers of all income levels; and we can prepare food, process information, and communicate faster than ever before. In addition, the average person has more belongings and lives in a larger house.

But there is also evidence to suggest that the scarcity problem has worsened. Today, we worry about the availability of clean air and water, while earlier generations thought of these as free and abundant. There is growing concern about our current rates of production and disposal of goods, and the resulting effects on our quality of life, our health, and the earth's forests, open spaces, and ozone layer. Some people argue that today we are more acutely aware of the limits of our productive capability than we have ever been.

[1] R. L. Heilbroner, *The Limits of American Capitalism*, Harper Torchbook ed. (New York: Harper & Row, 1967), p. 71.
[2] ProQuest Statistical Abstract of the U.S. 2015 Online Edition, Tables 605 and 842; www.eia.gov.

APPLICATION 1.2

DOES MONEY BUY HAPPINESS?

In recent decades, much research in the fields of economics and psychology has focused on the ties between money and happiness. And the answer to the question "Does money buy happiness?" is maybe yes, maybe no.

Money allows people to buy more, and better-quality, goods and services. On the surface, it appears that the basic economic problem of scarcity is lessened by having more money, and that this should lead to higher levels of happiness. We might think that people who drive new luxury cars and live in big homes are happier than people who ride a bus and live in a small apartment. A few researchers might say yes, the richer are happier, but many say the opposite, and a few say that happiness is increased very slightly with more money.

Psychologist Richard E. Lucas of Michigan State University thinks there is evidence to answer yes to three interesting happiness questions: Does money make you happier? Does being happier in the first place allow someone to earn more, perhaps through increased creativity or energy? Is there another factor that brings more of both money and happiness?

Happiness is certainly a subjective state of mind influenced by a person's values, experiences, future prospects, and a host of other factors. There is also a difference between short, even momentary, periods of happiness and a longer-term level of sustained satisfaction. Winning the lottery or receiving a year-end bonus can provide immediate happiness, but whether or not it will have a sustained impact is another consideration.

There is also some thought that extra money for someone who is very poor might account for higher levels of happiness because it has a greater positive effect on negative circumstances. News stories of families who receive homes built through volunteer efforts or children who attend a summer camp that they could not afford without donors often focus on the intense happiness of the recipients.

So, if there is no evidence to suggest that people who live in Virginia are happier than those who live in Oregon because their average household income is greater ($67,620 for Virginia and $56,307 for Oregon in 2013), what does make us happier? A clear answer to this question would certainly land us on the talk show circuit. Professor George Lowenstein of Carnegie Mellon University suggests that people are not good at figuring out what to do with their money and might overestimate the pleasure from something they buy. Professor Daniel Gilbert suggests that human relationships, time with family and friends, and experiences are the key to happiness. And others suggest that altruistic spending is the answer.

Sources: Malcolm Ritter, "Study: Money-Happiness Link Is Complex," Associated Press, November 26, 2006, www.sfgate.com; Matthew Herper, "Now It's a Fact: Money Doesn't Buy Happiness," *Forbes*, moneycentral. msn.com; "The Smiling Professor," *The New York Times*, April 22, 2008, www.nytimes.com; U.S. Census Bureau, Table H-8. Median Household Income by State: 1984 to 2013, www.census.gov.

Application 1.2, "Does Money Buy Happiness?," takes a look at some research on the ties between money and happiness. Many people think that a larger income lessens scarcity by providing more personal opportunities to satisfy wants and, therefore, makes people happier. This may not be the case. After reading this application, how would you answer the question "Does money buy happiness?"

ECONOMIC THEORY AND POLICY

As households, businesses, and governments go about conducting their economic affairs, it is helpful to have an understanding of some basic economic cause-and-effect relationships. Knowing about the drivers behind consumer behavior and spending and the causes of changing interest rates, income levels, and job growth fosters better decision making. Some economic relationships are complex, and gaining an appreciation for them is important. This task of sorting out and understanding cause-and-effect relationships falls to economic theory.

While theory tells us about relationships, economic policy deals with guidelines and actions. Policy decisions are made at many levels—from an instructor setting a grading policy, to a corporation setting policy about executive salaries, to a city setting its annual budget. When a decision maker sets parameters for actions, policy is made.

When the media speak of an economic policy for dealing with rising prices or unemployment, they are referring to the course of action that has been chosen to deal with the economic problem. Ideally, theories and policies are related. Before committing to a particular course of action, a person should make an effort to order and understand the basic relationships with which he or she is dealing.

Economic Theory

Economic Theory
A formal explanation of the relationship between economic variables.

An **economic theory** is a formal explanation of the relationship between economic variables.[3] A theory gives a reason why something happens, offers a cause-and-effect interpretation for a set of events, or shows the effect on one variable when another changes. There are economic theories to explain unemployment, inflation, price movements in the soybean market, wage rates paid to teenagers, changes in foreign exchange rates, and almost any other economic condition. For example, one important economic theory deals with the relationship between changes in the price of an item and the quantity of the item demanded by consumers.

Model
The setting within which an economic theory is presented.

In order to obtain a valid and predictable relationship between economic variables, theories are explored within the framework of a **model**. This model framework includes several elements:

♦ variables to be explored,
♦ assumptions concerning the model,
♦ data collection and analysis, and
♦ conclusions.

Variables   A theory is created to provide an explanation for something. This is why the first step in developing a model is the selection of two variables that have a potential cause-and-effect relationship to explore. For example, suppose that students in a class agree that it was unusually hard to find a job last summer and are interested enough in the problem to explore it further. One student theorizes that it was hard to find a job because a major employer left the area, another student thinks that the number of 16- through 22-year-olds wanting summer jobs increased, and another says that the economy in general had weakened. From this discussion, three separate sets of variables have been identified, and each set could be selected for exploration within the context of a model: the change in the number of employers and the number of summer jobs, the changing demographics of the student population and the number of summer jobs, and the state of the economy in general and the number of summer jobs.

In developing theories, disputes may occur because a variety of factors can be considered in analyzing a problem, and only one or a few of those factors are chosen as variables when developing a theory to explain the problem. In exploring reasons for a slow-growing economy, for example, some economists focus on the relationship between the money supply and growth, some on spending and growth, and some on the price level.

Assumptions
Conditions held to be true within a model.

Assumptions   **Assumptions** are the conditions held to be true while exploring the relationship between variables. For example, if our students were to develop an economic theory about the relationship between changes in the number of employers

---

[3]A dictionary definition of a theory is "systematically organized knowledge applicable in a relatively wide variety of circumstances; especially, a system of assumptions, accepted principles, and rules of procedure devised to analyze, predict, or otherwise explain the nature or behavior of a specified set of phenomena." From *The American Heritage Dictionary of the English Language*, ed. William Morris (New York: American Heritage Publishing Co., 1973), p. 1335.

and the number of available summer jobs, assumptions could be made about demographics, the economy in general, and the number of students wanting to enroll in summer school.

Frequently, an assumption is made to hold constant everything other than the variables under consideration. For example, if we were exploring the relationship between the price of coffee and the quantity demanded by consumers, an assumption to hold constant everything that affects the demand for coffee other than its price could be made. That is, it would be assumed that there would be no newly published health report extolling the virtues of coffee drinking, no shift in people's taste toward tea, and no change in income earned while the effect of a change in the price of coffee on the quantity demanded was explored.

Whether an assumption is "true" is not absolutely necessary within the context of a theory. For purposes of developing the theory, it is treated as if it were true. For example, in examining the effect of a change in the number of employers on available summer jobs, one could assume an annual growth rate in the 16- through 22-year-old population group of 0 percent, 3 percent, 12 percent, or any other rate. Whatever rate was assumed would be held constant while the theory was developed.

Data Collection and Analysis   When developing a theory, researchers collect and analyze data to determine how the variables are related. This is easy to understand with medical theories: Someone proposes a cause of a disease and then data are collected and analyzed to support or deny that cause-and-effect relationship. In other words, a theory can be supported by showing that the relationship between the variables is logically or statistically valid.

In economics, theories are often demonstrated to be statistically valid by examining real-world numbers concerning the variables. For example, if we wanted to evaluate the relationship between changes in the price of coffee and the amount consumers buy, statistics regarding coffee prices and sales could be used. When data are not readily available, a model builder might conduct a study to gain the necessary information. Offices of institutional research at colleges often conduct studies to determine levels of student satisfaction, completion rates, and such. The federal government, private research groups, and others collect and provide valuable information and extensive data on many facets of economic life, and the computer has made possible speedier and more sophisticated testing of ideas. **Econometrics**, which is the use of statistical techniques to describe the relationships between economic variables, is an important subfield in economics.

Econometrics
The use of statistical techniques to describe the relationships between economic variables.

Conclusions   The conclusion in a model gives the resulting relationship between the variables based on the assumptions, logic, and data analysis that went into the model. For example, by assuming buyers' tastes and incomes to be constant, and by examining past sales records, an economist could statistically show that consumers will decrease the quantity of coffee demanded as the price rises. The variables—price of coffee and quantity demanded—have an inverse relationship.

It is important to understand that different assumptions, data collection methods, or statistical techniques can cause the conclusions of studies to vary. Over the past two decades, we have become obsessed with coffee: drinking lattes and macchiatos, scheduling visits with friends and meetings in coffee shops, and conversing about coffee brands and brews. As this interest grows, so do the studies on the effects of caffeine on our health. And, these studies come with a wide variation in their conclusions.

Some studies say that caffeine causes dehydration; other studies indicate little or no evidence that it serves as a diuretic. Some studies suggest that it holds off baldness, lowers the risk of Parkinson's, and may be beneficial in the prevention of type 2 diabetes. Other studies have shown that caffeine raises blood pressure and that boiled unfiltered coffee (such as French-pressed) may raise cholesterol levels.[4] So, what is a person to believe? Why are there so many conflicting results on the pros and cons of caffeine? As one delves into these studies, there are obvious differences in the assumptions and data collection methods. The number of observations, the conditions held constant in the study, and the choice of analytical techniques all contribute to the conclusion.

Serious controversy has always existed among economists concerning their theories. Scholarly publications sometimes devote many pages to running disputes among practitioners in the field. Questions arise as to the assumptions underlying a theory, the significance and appropriateness of the variables studied, the data collection and analysis, and the possibility that a more influential factor has not yet been tested. Controversies such as these are not limited to economics and are a healthy sign. They are found in all serious inquiry—be it in the social sciences, natural sciences, or humanities—where people are not satisfied with what they now know. Application 1.3,

---

APPLICATION 1.3

OK, WHAT ARE THEY?

For most of us, our only contact with UFOs—unidentified flying objects—is watching films such as Steven Spielberg's hit, *Close Encounters of the Third Kind*. Do you know that the movie's title is actually a technical term—CE-3—used by people, called "ufologists," who study UFOs?

UFOs may have caught people's attention since ancient times. But it is only since the late 1940s that serious investigation and efforts to document the phenomenon have occurred.

Someone who wants to understand exactly what a UFO is will have to be ready to work through a not-too-short list of competing theories. One theory is that UFOs are objects flown by aliens from outer space or by some type of being who is smart enough to move back and forth in time and space. Another theory is that UFOs are simply images in the atmosphere caused by things such as "ball lightning," glowing ionized gas, or light refraction.

A further theory says that UFOs are highly advanced military aircraft undergoing testing in absolute secrecy. And yet another theory claims that people who have "seen" UFOs are simply not seeing clearly enough to recognize that they are actually looking at conventional aircraft or natural atmospheric conditions. Finally, there is speculation that people "seeing a UFO" might be searching for something to save them from today's world.

If building arguments to support an economic theory seems difficult, imagine what it must be like building supporting arguments for a UFO theory! Just think, what data would you use? There is nothing comparable to the widely accessible numbers available to explain the effect of a tax increase on spending or a drop in business sales on unemployment rates. Also, like economics, for every argument there could be a counterargument. The argument that Einstein's theory of relativity raises serious doubts about whether aliens from outer space could make it to earth can be countered by the argument that his theory, while brilliant, may not capture something we have yet to learn.

So, just like someone who pulls an economic theory apart to decide whether it is realistic, a person looking into a UFO theory should want to know about the credibility of the person making the argument, the reliability of the evidence (e.g., whether the photograph of the UFO has been doctored), the consistency of the arguments, and other details. In other words, we should not be surprised by a relatively large similarity in the rules to evaluate theories across fields of inquiry.

Based on: "Frequently Asked Questions about UFOs," http://www.cufos.org/Faq_English_P1.html; "Frequently Asked Questions about UFOs Part II," http://www.cufos.org/Faq_English_P2.html; "BBC—Science & Nature—Space—UFOs," http://www.bbc.co.uk/science/space/life/aliens/ufos/index.shtml; "Northern UFOs—Theories," http://www.ssimicro.com/~ufoinfo/theories.html.

---

[4] Anahad O'Connor, "The Claim: Caffeine Causes Dehydration," *The New York Times*, March 4, 2008, www.nytimes.com; Anna Jane Grossman, "Black for Me, Light for My Hips," *The New York Times*, July 12, 2007, www.nytimes.com; Jane E. Brody, "Personal Health: You Are Also What You Drink," *The New York Times*, March 27, 2007, www.nytimes.com.

| FIGURE 1.3 | *Economic Theory and Models* |

An economic theory is generally explored within the context of a model.

"OK, What Are They?," further explores problems and controversies surrounding theories by looking at an area of inquiry where alternative points of view are likely more hotly contested than in economics: explaining UFOs (unidentified flying objects).

In summary, economic theories explain the relationships between economic variables. By focusing on one or a few key relationships, economic theories simplify reality so that it can be better understood. Figure 1.3 summarizes the components of a model.

Economic Policy

Economic Policy
A guide for a course of action.

An **economic policy** sets a guide for a course of action. Usually, an economic policy is created to address an economic problem or change an economic condition. A legislated tax decrease to speed up the economy, mandatory clean air measures, and restrictions on imports of foreign-produced food are all examples of economic policies.

Economic policy is the result of a decision by a policymaker, whether a business manager, a local city council, the Congress, or voters. Usually, policymakers can choose among several courses of action and may even have several available policy tools. For example, board members of a university that is facing a serious budget crisis could put policies in place that raise tuition, hire fewer faculty members and increase class size, or postpone maintenance or new building construction.

Making policy is not always easy because of the need to weigh the consequences of various courses of action. Consider rising gasoline prices due to increased usage of gasoline coupled with a decreased supply of it. There are several possible policies to keep gas prices from rising: adopting fuel efficiency requirements for trucks and SUVs; banning vehicles with low gas mileage; funding mass transit projects; and opening up oil reserves in the Alaskan wilderness. Each of these policies carries consequences ranging from a loss of truck and SUV sales and jobs, to environmental issues.

Policy decisions are heavily influenced by the values of the policymaker. Someone who values the environment would likely not support destruction of the Alaskan wilderness, while a Congressperson from a state that depends on the production of trucks and SUVs for significant employment would likely not support policies that negatively affect that industry. Take the question of granting tax credits for college tuition. Families who are facing financial difficulties sending their children to college will likely favor this type of tax break, and those who think that existing programs for tuition relief are adequate may oppose it.

Because economic theories explain how economic variables interact, and because economic policies involve the manipulation of those economic variables, it is crucial that policymakers have some knowledge of these theories and their complexities. Without that knowledge, the consequences of policy decisions could be unfortunate. One benefit of a course in economics is that it enables you to better evaluate the consequences of policies and to judge how well or how poorly policymakers are informed.

Up for Debate, "Should St. Louis County, Missouri, Impose Mandatory Trash Pickup and Recycling?" provides a real-world example of an economic policy decision before a county council. Arguments that St. Louis County Council members heard in support of and against this mandated service are given. Can you identify the economic analysis in the arguments as well as the value judgments of those supporting and those opposing this program?[5]

UP FOR DEBATE

SHOULD ST. LOUIS COUNTY, MISSOURI, IMPOSE MANDATORY TRASH PICKUP AND RECYCLING?

Issue   *Recently, St. Louis County, Missouri, established trash districts in its unincorporated, nonmunicipal areas and mandated a subscription service that would provide trash pickup and curbside single-stream recycling. Every household was required to participate and pay a monthly fee for the service. The program sparked substantial public support, but also created a great deal of opposition. Should the program have been approved?*

Yes   Recycling should not be optional. It is the right thing to do to address growing environmental issues. Every citizen needs to participate. Furthermore, curbside pickup encourages recycling by making it easy. Communities with mandatory recycling, especially with large wheeled carts, have experienced significant increases in the volume of recycled materials and decreases in items going to landfills.

There are substantial economic benefits for a district from using one trash hauling company, rather than many private haulers. With one company there is less trash traffic. Rather than many trash trucks using residential streets every day, there is just one service in the neighborhood on pickup day. This saves on street pavement conditions, noise, and gas. Typically, bills are also less for each household.

No   The government should not mess with people's garbage. It is another example of government interference with private property and the right of property owners to make their own decisions. People have a right to choose what to throw away, where to throw it, and who to haul it away. Also, by going with a government-contracted trash hauler, smaller trash companies may be put out of business.

Many people produce little trash, especially single-person households. Why should these people pay the same price as all other households? Sometimes people find other means to dispose of their trash. These include taking it to work, using a neighborhood business's dumpster, or placing it in a public trash can. Why should these people be forced to now pay a monthly trash bill?

---

[5] In St. Louis County, some areas are organized as cities, or municipalities, and some are unincorporated. In the unincorporated areas, the county provides municipal services.

TOOLS OF THE ECONOMIST

Words, Graphs, and Mathematical Equations

There are several ways to express economic theories and policies. The first and most basic method is a verbal presentation, or descriptive statement. Earlier we noted that the quantity of coffee demanded falls as its price increases. This is a simple verbal statement about the relationship between coffee prices and the amount people will buy. Using such verbal statements to convey theories is easy, but provide no information about actual numbers. Adding numbers can make verbal descriptions lengthy and clumsy.

A second method for expressing theories and policies is graphing. A **graph** is a picture illustrating the relationship between two variables, one shown on the horizontal axis and the other on the vertical axis. For instance, returning to our coffee example, the graph in Figure 1.4 shows a relationship between the price of a pound of coffee and the number of pounds of coffee demanded by consumers over a certain period of time.

We frequently use graphs because numbers can easily be incorporated and relationships are visualized. For example, the graph in Figure 1.4 demonstrates that at a price of $8 per pound 600 pounds of coffee are demanded, and at a price of $4 the quantity demanded increases to 1,200 pounds. Or, if you are interested in selling 900 pounds of coffee, the price will need to be $6 per pound.

Once you have had some practice in reading graphs, you will discover that a line or curve illustrates at a glance the relationship between the variables. In a **direct relationship**, the variables move in the same direction and the line slopes upward. In an **inverse relationship**, the variables move in opposite directions and the line slopes downward. If you are uncomfortable working with graphs, you should stop at this point and read the appendix to this chapter, where direct and inverse relationships and other information on constructing and interpreting graphs are presented.

Graph
An illustration showing the relationship between two variables that are measured on the vertical and horizontal axes.

Direct Relationship
Two variables move in the same direction: when one increases, so does the other; graphs as an upward-sloping line.

Inverse Relationship
Two variables move in opposite directions: when one increases, the other decreases; graphs as a downward-sloping line.

FIGURE 1.4   *Relationship between Coffee Prices and the Amount of Coffee Demanded*

The downward-sloping line in this graph illustrates the various amounts of coffee demanded at different coffee prices.

A third way to express economic theories is through mathematical equations. While some people lack confidence in using mathematics, equations have an important advantage. They are very specific about how economic variables are related. Let us return to our coffee example.

Suppose we find that the relationship between the price of coffee and the amount demanded is shown by the equation

$$Q_c = 1,800 - 150P_c$$

Here, Q_c represents the quantity of coffee demanded, and P_c represents the price of coffee. By substituting different prices in place of the P_c term, you can see how much coffee buyers would want. For example, if the price were $6 per pound, buyers would want 900 pounds of coffee [$900 = 1,800 - 150(6)$]. If the price fell to $4, they would want 1,200 pounds [$1,200 = 1,800 - 150(4)$].

SCARCITY, MODEL BUILDING, AND GRAPHS

Because economists frequently illustrate concepts and theories through models and graphs, we use these tools to explore scarcity in greater detail.

Modeling Scarcity

As we know, theories are explored within the context of a model that includes variables, assumptions, data, and conclusions. Here, we develop a model to explore scarcity in an economy by examining the production of two goods using that economy's resources. Although this hypothetical economy has the potential for producing a large assortment of goods and services, in this model all the economy's resources will be diverted to the production of only two goods: cell phones and garden tractors. These two goods are the variables in our model.

In the example that follows, the hypothetical economy will be viewed over a short period of time using the following assumptions.

1. All resources, or factors of production, are held constant. There are no changes in the available amounts of the economy's labor, machinery, trucks, or other factors.
2. All resources are fully employed. Everyone who wants a job has one, and all other resources (such as factories and transportation equipment) available for use are being used. There is no involuntary unemployment of resources.
3. The existing technology is held fixed; no new inventions or innovations occur.

Production Possibilities Table (or Curve)
Gives the various amounts of two goods that an economy can produce with full employment and fixed resources and technology.

The data for this model are provided in the table in Figure 1.5, which lists some possible combinations of cell phones and garden tractors that could be produced in the economy given the assumptions made. Because the table provides possible levels of production, it is termed a **production possibilities table**. The data show that if all resources are fully employed in the production of cell phones, then 25 million cell phones can be made, but no garden tractors. If some garden tractors are manufactured (e.g., 200,000), then some resources employed in the production of cell phones must be diverted to making tractors, and fewer cell phones will be produced. If all factors are used in the manufacture of garden tractors, no cell phones can be made.

The production possibilities listed in the table in Figure 1.5 can be graphed to illustrate the same relationship. In Figure 1.5, the different cell phone and garden

FIGURE 1.5	*Possible Combinations of Cell Phones and Garden Tractors*

Cell Phones (Millions)	Garden Tractors (Hundreds of Thousands)
25	0
24	2
20	4
15	6
9	8
0	10

A production possibilities table and curve illustrate the various combinations of two goods that an economy could produce with full employment and fixed resources and technology. Under these conditions, more of one good can be produced only by giving up some of the other.

tractor combinations from the table are plotted on a graph and the points are connected with a line to form a **production possibilities curve**.

Interpreting the Model

The basic conclusion of the production possibilities model is a restatement of the scarcity problem: Even with full employment, limited resources allow only limited production of goods and services. In our hypothetical economy, it would be impossible to produce 15 million cell phones and 800,000 garden tractors (shown by point A in Figure 1.5) in the time allowed, even if desired, because there are not enough factors of production to do so. In other words, scarce resources impose a boundary, or limit, on an economy that is illustrated by a production possibilities curve. Our hypothetical economy cannot produce beyond (to the right of) the curve in Figure 1.5.

The production possibilities model also emphasizes the concepts of trade-off and opportunity cost. When an economy operates at full employment, more of one good can be produced only by giving up some amount of another good. If this economy were producing 20 million cell phones and 400,000 garden tractors, and households demanded 600,000 tractors, then households could have the additional tractors only by giving up some cell phones. This trade-off concept is a restatement of the principle of opportunity cost, which was introduced earlier: The cost of additional garden tractors can be measured by the number of cell phones given up, and vice versa. The opportunity cost of going from 400,000 to 600,000 tractors is 5 million cell phones. What is the opportunity cost of going from 800,000 to 1,000,000 tractors?[6]

---

[6] The production possibilities table and curve show that this economy is producing 9 million cell phones when it produces 800,000 tractors, and no cell phones when it produces 1 million tractors. Therefore, the opportunity cost of moving from 800,000 to 1 million tractors is 9 million cell phones because cell phone production goes from 9 million to zero.

Several other economic concepts can be illustrated with the production possibilities model by changing the model's assumptions. If the assumption of full employment is dropped and it is assumed that some resources available for production are not used, or there is **unemployment**, then the economy cannot produce as much as it does under the condition of full employment. With full employment, one production combination was 15 million cell phones and 600,000 garden tractors. If some labor, machinery, or other resource is idle, then less will be produced—perhaps only 10 million cell phones and 400,000 tractors. The result of unemployment is illustrated graphically by a point inside, or to the left of, the production possibilities curve, such as point B in the left-hand graph in Figure 1.6.

When we drop the assumptions of fixed resources and fixed technology, this model can also be used to illustrate **economic growth**, which is an increase in an economy's full employment level of output over time. Economic growth can result from additional resources and/or better methods of production (technology). In this case, more labor and other resources or a newly automated manufacturing process would allow an increase in cell phone and garden tractor production. Economic growth can be illustrated graphically by a shift of the production possibilities curve to the right, as shown in the right-hand graph in Figure 1.6. Point A, which was unattainable under the original assumptions, is now within reach of the economy.

Test Your Understanding, "Production Possibilities," provides an opportunity to examine your command of the concepts illustrated by the production possibilities model. Here the model is used to evaluate the choices an economy can make between producing **capital goods**, such as machinery and equipment, which are used to produce other goods and services, and **consumer goods**, such as food and household furniture, which are produced for final buyers.

Unemployment
Resources available for production are not being used.

Economic Growth
An increase in an economy's full employment level of output over time.

Capital Goods
Goods, such as machinery and equipment, that are used to produce other goods and services.

Consumer Goods
Goods, such as food and household furniture, that are produced for final buyers.

| FIGURE 1.6 | *Unemployment and Economic Growth in a Production Possibilities Model* |

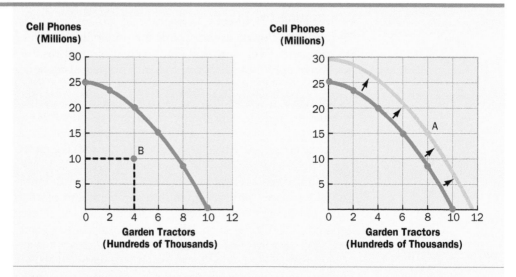

With unemployment, an economy is unable to reach the combinations of goods and services that it could produce if resources were fully employed. Point B in the left-hand graph represents production with unemployment. An increase in the number of available resources or an improvement in technology allows the production of goods and services to increase, and the economy's production possibilities curve shifts to the right as indicated in the right-hand graph.

PRODUCTION POSSIBILITIES

All economies are subject to a trade-off between the production of capital goods, which are used to produce other goods and services, and consumer goods, which are produced for final buyers. Assume that in a hypothetical economy with full employment and fixed resources and technology, the following amounts of consumer and capital goods can be produced.

Consumer Goods (Millions of Units)	Capital Goods (Millions of Units)
0	45
10	40
20	32
30	20
40	0

Create a production possibilities curve from this table on the accompanying graph and answer the following questions.

1. What is the opportunity cost of increasing the production of consumer goods from 20 million to 30 million units? What is the opportunity cost of increasing the production of capital goods from 40 million to 45 million units?
2. On the accompanying graph, illustrate the effect of a small amount of unemployment with a point labeled A, and a large amount of unemployment with a point labeled B.

Consumer Goods (Millions of Units)

Capital Goods (Millions of Units)

3. Where, in your opinion, is the ideal point on the production possibilities curve for this economy to operate? Label this as point C. On what value judgment about the importance of capital goods and consumer goods did you base your location of point C? What would cause another student to locate point C elsewhere on the production possibilities curve?
4. What would life be like in this economy 10 years from now if today it produced only consumer goods? What would life be like in the economy today if it produced only capital goods?
5. Demonstrate graphically what would happen if new technology were created for producing both capital goods and consumer goods.

Answers can be found at the end of the book.

MACROECONOMICS AND MICROECONOMICS

Macroeconomics
The study of the operation of the economy as a whole.

Microeconomics
The study of individual decision-making units and markets within the economy.

The study of economics is organized under two major headings: macroeconomics and microeconomics. **Macroeconomics** focuses on the operation of the economy as a whole and the interactions of the major groups (called the household, business, government, and foreign sectors) in the economy. It includes topics such as inflation, unemployment, taxes and government spending, and money and banking. Part 2 of this textbook deals with "The Macroeconomy."

Microeconomics focuses on the behavior of individual businesses and households and on specific product and resource markets. It includes topics such as consumer behavior, cost–benefit analysis, the determination of business profits, and pricing in specific markets. Part 3 of this textbook, "The Microeconomy," is concerned with understanding the behavior of these individual decision-making units in the economy.

Both macroeconomic and microeconomic concepts have global applications and are relevant to international topics. Part 4 of this textbook, "The International Economy," which deals with international trade and finance, uses both macroeconomics and microeconomics.

Summary

1. Economics is the study of how limited resources are used to satisfy unlimited wants and needs. The basis of economics is a scarcity of goods and services caused by people's insatiable wants for goods and services coupled with a limited amount of resources to produce them.

2. Since individuals and societies cannot have everything they want, they must make choices, or trade-offs. These trade-offs are influenced by the decision maker's value judgments. Trade-offs carry an opportunity cost, which measures the cost of a decision or purchase in terms of a forgone alternative.

3. Efficiency and equity are important considerations when dealing with the problem of scarcity. Efficiency results when a given good or service is produced at the lowest cost. It allows the greatest attainable lessening of scarcity because resources are used to their fullest. Equity refers to fairness in the distribution of goods and services. The determination of equity differs according to people's value judgments.

4. Resources, or factors of production, are those things used in the production of goods and services. All resources are scarce, or limited, in amount. Economists classify these limited factors into four categories: land, labor, capital, and entrepreneurship. When sold, they generate incomes termed, respectively: rent, wages, interest, and profit.

5. There is a distinction between economic theory and policy. Economic theory explains why an event occurs, or gives a generalized interpretation of the relationship between economic variables. Economic theories are explored within the framework of a model that includes variables, assumptions or conditions held to be true, data collection and analysis, and conclusions. Economic policy is a guideline for a course of action. Value judgments are important in the selection of economic policies.

6. In expressing theories and policies, economists use verbal statements, graphs, and mathematical equations. An upward-sloping line in a graph illustrates a direct relationship between variables, and a downward-sloping line indicates an inverse relationship.

7. A production possibilities table and curve can be used to illustrate scarcity. These show that, with assumptions of full employment and constant resources and technology, more of one good can be obtained only by giving up some of another good, making trade-offs necessary. The effect of unemployment, which causes an economy to produce fewer goods and services than with full employment, is shown by a point inside, or to the left of, the production possibilities curve. Increases in technology and/or resources allow for economic growth, permitting a shift of the curve to the right.

8. Macroeconomics is concerned with the operation of the economy as a whole and with the interactions of its major sectors. Microeconomics deals with individual operating units and markets within the economy.

Key Terms and Concepts

Economics
Scarcity
Trade-off
Value judgment
Opportunity cost
Efficiency
Equity
Resources (factors of production)
Labor
Capital
Land
Entrepreneurship
Wages
Interest
Rent
Profit

Economic theory
Model
Assumptions
Econometrics
Economic policy
Graph
Direct relationship
Inverse relationship
Production possibilities
   table (or curve)
Unemployment
Economic growth
Capital goods
Consumer goods
Macroeconomics
Microeconomics

Review Questions

1. What are the definition of and the root of the study of economics? How does a combination of scarce resources and unlimited wants force people to make economic decisions? How are value judgments and opportunity costs important in the making of these decisions?

2. Classify each of the following factors of production into one of the four resource categories used in economics, and identify the income return to the owners of each factor.
   a. The scanner used to check out groceries in a supermarket
   b. The instructor of this course
   c. A pasture used for grazing a herd of cattle
   d. A coffee urn used by a catering service
   e. The person who just started her own lawn service company
   f. The manager of a restaurant that is part of a national chain
   g. The green field site ready for construction of a new big box store

3. What is meant by a direct and an inverse relationship between economic variables? Illustrate, using the accompanying graphs, how you think each of the following relationships would appear, and indicate whether each relationship is direct or inverse.
   a. Inches of snow and sales of mittens
   b. Tuition and students demanding to enroll in a university
   c. Consumers purchasing the same amount of gasoline regardless of its price
   d. Salaries and years of education

4. Distinguish between economic theory and economic policy. What are some reasons for economic theory controversies and economic policy controversies? Give a recent example of economic policy.

5. Identify and briefly explain the four elements of a model used to explore an economic theory. How can the choice of assumptions and data used affect the conclusions?

6. Draw a production possibilities curve and explain how it illustrates the trade-offs, or choices, that must be made when an economy is operating at full employment. How can unemployment and economic growth be shown on this graph?

7. What is a capital good and what is a consumer good? How does an economy's choice about how many of its resources to devote to capital goods production as compared to consumer goods production affect its current standard of living and its future standard of living?

8. The following production possibilities table gives the various combinations of hours that can be worked and GPAs that can be earned by a particular college student who holds a job and takes 12 credit hours of courses a semester. Draw a production possibilities curve based on the information in this table on the graph provided and answer the following questions.
    a. What is the opportunity cost for this student of increasing the hours worked per week from 10 to 20?
    b. What factors could cause this curve to shift to the right?
    c. What factors could cause this student to operate inside, or to the left, of this production possibilities curve?

Hours Worked per Week	GPA
50	0.00
40	1.00
30	1.90
20	2.60
10	3.25
0	3.75

    d. What would determine the student's best location on this curve?

    e. Are there any similarities between the choices that this student makes concerning hours worked and GPA and the choices an economy makes between the production of consumer goods and capital goods?

9. (*From the appendix*) Think about the relationship between driving at higher speeds and the likelihood of injury in an automobile accident. How can this relationship be illustrated in one graph to make it appear that the likelihood of injury increases relatively little at higher speeds, and in another graph to make it appear that the likelihood of injury increases dramatically at higher speeds? What warning does this sound about basing a decision on a quick scan of the appearance of a line in a graph?

10. Distinguish between macroeconomics and microeconomics, and identify some topics relevant to each.

Discussion Questions

1. If resources are scarce and if people are always wanting more than the economy can provide, how is it possible that we would have unemployment?

2. Suppose that you are an advisor to a health team working in a poor country. In that country, 20 percent of the children below the age of five die of a particular disease each year. If the health team were to inoculate the population, the disease would cease to be a problem. However, with more people surviving, the country's food supply would become grossly inadequate, and it is estimated that about 20 percent of the children below the age of five would die of starvation each year. Which policy would you follow: inoculation or no inoculation? What are the trade-offs with each policy? Why would you follow your chosen policy, and how are your values important in reaching a decision?

3. How do the popular expressions "you can't have your cake and eat it, too" and "there is no such thing as a free lunch" relate to the basic economic problems of scarcity, choice, and opportunity costs?

4. Is there a trade-off between efficiency and equity, or are these two goals mutually compatible for an economy? Why?

5. In your opinion, what would be an equitable, or fair, distribution of goods and services in a society? Why would this be an equitable distribution and what value judgments underlie your opinion? Do you think your opinion would be shared by your friends and family? Why?

6. Should national defense-related goods, such as submarines and nuclear weapons, be classified as capital goods or consumer goods? Why?

7. Individuals and societies evaluate both the benefits and costs of their choices when making decisions. Can you think of a recent decision you made where you consciously weighed the benefits and costs of possible courses of action? Can you think of a decision where you did not consciously weigh the benefits and costs but wish now that you had?

Critical Thinking Case 1

DIFFICULT CHOICES IN THE EXTREME[a]

Critical Thinking Skills

Defining a problem and possible solutions

Identifying values that underlie a problem

Economic Concepts

Scarcity

Choice

Americans today would identify the cost and availability of health care as a major concern. In 2013, health-care spending was close to $3 trillion or about $9,250 per person.[b] Rising expenditures for the Medicare and Medicaid programs as well as the costs for private health insurance continue to be a source of uneasiness about how much Americans can afford for health care.

Advanced technology that keeps critically ill people alive, the increasing incidence of expensive diseases, the aging of the population, the growth in diabetes and heart disease, costly disease detection tests, high-priced medications, and overtreatment from rising malpractice suits have all contributed to the escalation in costs.

The philosophy in the United States has long been to pursue all medical procedures necessary to prolong life. These include life-support equipment, treatments, and intensive hospitalization for all persons regardless of their prognosis. Medicare reports, for example, that a large portion of its funding goes to people who are in the last few days of their life.

A concern for people who are unable to afford routine and necessary medical care and basic

medication has given impetus to health care reform. However, despite recent plans passed by Congress the debate coutinues. Mandatory coverage, increased regulation on hospitals and doctors, the Medicare program, and more continue to meet opposition.

Regardless of where one falls in the health care debate, lurking behind the medical care issue is a major, unavoidable decision imposed by scarcity. If it is impossible to fund every person's medical needs and provide the latest in treatment for all conditions, then decisions must be made as to who gets medical treatment and what treatment is provided. Does treatment beyond basic care go to those who are adequately insured? To younger people? To those who are productive? However we choose to reallocate scarce resources to medical care, we must question whether we can continue to operate under the current premise that all medical procedures must be used at all times for everyone.

Economic decisions rarely exist in a vacuum, but are influenced by social, ethical, and other values. The decisions about the allocation of scarce medical resources are perfect examples about the role that value judgments play in making hard choices. What should Americans consider in the debate about health care?

[a]At the end of each chapter, a Critical Thinking Case is presented. These cases have two objectives: the development of critical thinking skills and the application of economic concepts. The skills and concepts associated with each case are identified. Suggested questions for discussing each case are included. If an instructor makes no assignment regarding a case, you might want to try answering the questions on your own.
[b]Centers for Medicare & Medicaid Services, "National Health Expenditures 2013 Highlights," www.cms.gov.

Questions

1. What is the basic economic problem in this case?
2. What values underlie a solution to this problem? What values are deeply rooted? What values seem to be more political?
3. What reasonable choices can be made to deal with this problem? Are there unreasonable choices? What solutions would be totally off the table?

CHAPTER 1 APPENDIX

GRAPHING

Constructing a Graph

A graph is a picture of a relationship between two variables. The variables are given on the vertical and horizontal axes of the graph, and the line in the graph provides a visual image of how those variables are related. Table 1A.1 provides data about two variables that will be used to construct a graph in Figure 1A.1: Various hourly wage rates in a market for day camp assistants and the numbers of teenagers applying for a job at each rate.

The first step in constructing or reading a graph is to identify the variables on the vertical and horizontal axes. In Figure 1A.1, wage rates are represented on the vertical axis and applicants for jobs on the horizontal axis. (It is conventional in economics to put money data on the vertical axis.)

The second step in graphing is to assign numbers along the axes. The numbers assigned to the axes of a graph are important for proper interpretation of the graph. In assigning numbers to a graph, several rules need to be remembered: (1) Always use zero at the origin (the point where the horizontal and vertical axes meet); (2) work up the number scale as you go out on each axis; and (3) when moving along an axis, use equal spaces for equal amounts.[1] Notice the application of these rules in Figure 1A.1. Zero is used at the origin, numbers along each axis move up the number scale, the vertical axis is labeled in equal series of $1.50, and the horizontal axis is labeled in equal series of 50 applicants.

The third step in constructing a graphic relationship is to plot data points. Each data point gives a specific combination of the two variables observed. Each point in Figure 1A.1a, for example, indicates a wage rate–applicant combination given in Table 1A.1. Point A shows that when the wage rate is $6, the number of applicants is 150, and point B shows that at a wage rate of $12, 350 teenagers apply.

TABLE 1A.1	Hourly Wage Rates and Numbers of Applicants for a Job

This table illustrates a relationship between hourly wage rates and the number of teenagers applying for a job.

Hourly Wage Rate	Number of Teenagers Applying for a Job
$ 3.00	50
4.50	100
6.00	150
7.50	200
9.00	250
10.50	300
12.00	350

[1]For those students who are familiar with graphing techniques, we might point out that only the first, or northeast, quadrant of a graph is used in most examples in this text.

FIGURE 1A.1   *Hourly Wage Rates and Numbers of Applicants for a Job*

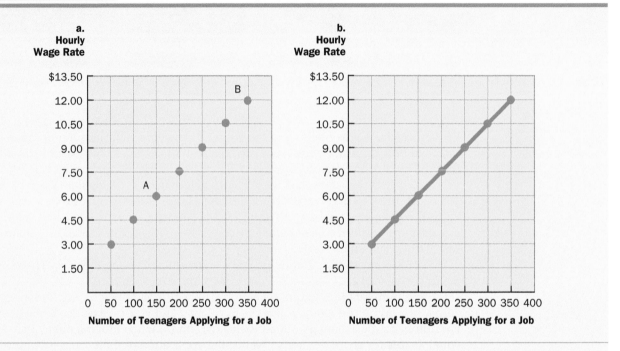

A line in a graph is a series of connected points; each point represents a particular combination of the two variables.

Finally, a line in a graph is nothing more than a series of connected data points. In Figure 1A.1b, the wage rate–applicant combinations from Figure 1A.1a are connected. Joining these points allows us to visualize the relationship between the variables and to "read between" the points. For example, we could conclude that if the wage offered were $6.75, the number of applicants would be approximately 175.

Direct and Inverse Relationships

Earlier in the chapter, it was pointed out that the slope of a line in a graph indicates whether a direct or an inverse relationship exists between the variables. A direct relationship exists when both variables move in the same direction; that is, as one gets larger or smaller, so does the other. We can conclude that the relationship between wage rates and the number of job applicants just discussed is direct. Graphically, a direct relationship is illustrated by a line that slopes upward. An inverse relationship exists when the variables move in opposite directions; that is, as one becomes larger, the other becomes smaller, and vice versa. Graphically, an inverse relationship is illustrated by a line that slopes downward.

The upward-sloping line in Figure 1A.2a illustrates a direct relationship between the price of average-size hot fudge sundaes and the number of sundaes some ice cream stores would be willing to sell at different prices. At a price of $3.75 per sundae, the number supplied would be 1,500, and if the price fell to $1.25, they would like to sell only 500 (preferring instead to sell other, perhaps more profitable, items).

The downward-sloping line in Figure 1A.2b illustrates an inverse relationship between the price of pistachios and the number of pounds of pistachios demanded at

FIGURE 1A.2   *Direct and Inverse Relationships*

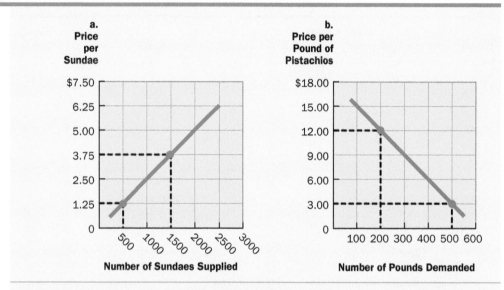

A direct relationship is illustrated by an upward-sloping line in a graph, and an inverse relationship is illustrated by a downward-sloping line.

each price. At a price of $12 a pound, consumers would demand 200 pounds, and when the price fell to $3, they would demand 500 pounds.

Students often have trouble reading a graph when there are no numbers given on the axes. If this occurs with you, just put a few hypothetical numbers along each axis and try reading it again. (Remember the rules for numbering when you do this.) After you have some practice in reading graphs, this problem should disappear. Figure 1A.3 gives you an opportunity to test your ability to recognize graphic relationships. What does each graph say about the relationship between the variables identified?

FIGURE 1A.3   *Examples of Direct and Inverse Relationships*

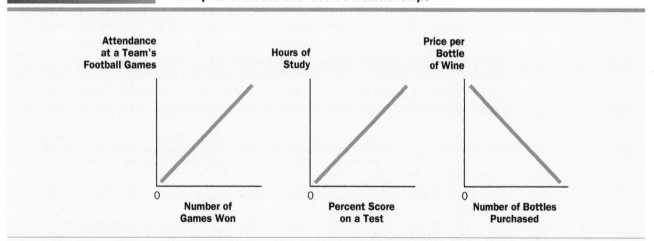

What type of relationship (direct or inverse) is illustrated in each of these graphs?

| FIGURE 1A.4 | *Undergraduate Tuition and Required Fees for Full-time Students in Degree-Granting Institutions, Public and Private Schools* |

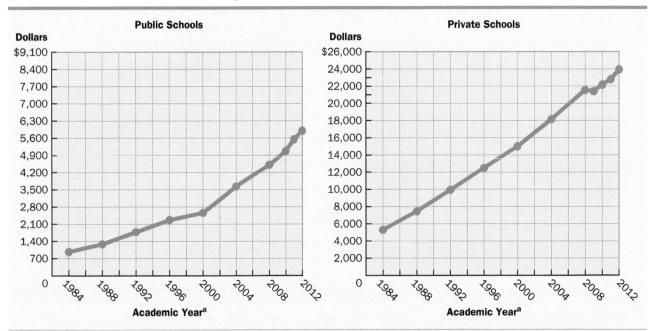

The appearance of data in a graph and the impression created for the reader can be affected by how the axes of the graph are numbered.

ᵃEach year is an academic year. For example, 1984 represents the 1984–1985 academic year.
Source: National Center for Education Statistics, *Digest of Education Statistics: 2013*, Table 330.10, www.nces.ed.gov.

In considering information given in graphs, one needs to be careful that a quick glance might lead to misinterpretation. In addition, sometimes graphs are used to present a point of view that is not always apparent to the reader. Figure 1A.4 gives two graphs that show information about college tuition and fees for students in public and private institutions. In the graph on the left, the increases are less severe than they are on the right, giving the impression that private school tuition over the years has increased more steeply than public tuition. Yet, when the numbers are calculated, private tuition and fees increased by 350 percent while public tuition increased by 508 percent from 1984 through 2013. What accounts for this differing display? Who might want to use the graph on the left rather than the right? Information about manipulating statistics to present a point of view is available in many books and articles.[2]

[2] The difference between the two graphs in Figure 1A.4 is the spacing used for the numbers on the vertical axes. The graph on the left uses each vertical mark to represent $700, and the graph on the right uses each vertical mark to represent $2,000. By choosing each vertical mark on the left graph to represent $700, rather than a larger number, it exaggerated the rise in the line. The line would have been much less steep if $1,000, for example, had been used. On the right hand graph, the line could have been steeper with vertical marks used to represent something less than $2,000 or more shallow with vertical marks of less than $2,000. In other words, we can deliberately create a different impression for the reader through a selection of units of measure on the axes.

The percentage increases in tuition and fees are found by taking the change in the tuition and dividing it by the base tuition. For private tuition, it is $18,628 divided by $5,315; for public tuition it is $4,928 divided by $971.

Economic Decision Making and Economic Systems

CHAPTER OBJECTIVES

Introduce the basic economic decisions that must be made in every society because of scarcity and how those decisions are made in various economic systems.

Explain the basic philosophy, structure, and operation of a market economy and its strengths and weaknesses.

Describe how economic decisions are made in a planned economy and its strengths and weaknesses.

Explain mixed economies and some of the changes in the world's planned economies.

Consider how the U.S. economic system was influenced by its British foundations and major periods in U.S. history.

Chapter 1 introduced the basic concept of scarcity that underlies the study of economics. No economy, no matter how large or sophisticated, can provide all the goods and services to satisfy every member's wants and needs. Thus, people in every economy must make decisions about what goods and services to produce, how to produce them, and who will receive the goods and services that are produced. In this chapter, we focus on these decisions and how they are made in different economies.

SCARCITY, THE BASIC ECONOMIC DECISIONS, AND ECONOMIC SYSTEMS

All economies continually produce goods and services, whether they are simple agricultural products or complex surgical equipment. The U.S. economy, for example, currently produces in excess of $18 trillion of cars, new construction, health care, and other goods and services over the course of a year. Unfortunately, even this seemingly huge output satisfies only part of people's wants and needs; the U.S. economy cannot satisfy every want.

How do we decide what collection of goods and services the economy will produce? How do we decide who gets what and how much they get? Why can some households buy steak while others can afford only hamburger? This economic predicament resembles the myth that Santa Claus faces—millions of cherubic boys and girls dreaming of endless toys but only one workshop, a few elves, and just one sleigh to carry the goodies. What does Santa put in his bag?

In every society, regardless of its wealth and power, certain choices about production and distribution must be made. Specifically, every society faces three **basic economic decisions:**

Basic Economic Decisions
The choices that must be made in any society regarding what to produce, how to produce, and to whom production is distributed.

♦   What goods and services to produce and in what quantities?
♦   How to produce goods and services, or how to use the economy's resources?
♦   Who gets the goods and services?

The first economic decision, what to produce, addresses the dilemma that every society's members voice endless wants but economies can produce only limited varieties and amounts of goods and services. As a result, in every society choices must be made about the types and quantities of goods and services to produce: Are cars or SUVs or trucks to be produced? How many? What models?

The second economic decision, how to produce goods and services, or how to use an economy's resources, reflects the reality that products can be made in any number of different ways, and different methods require different resources and processes. In producing cars, a company must decide what technology to use, how many workers to hire, whether to use sheet metal or plastic, and whether to add GIS systems and leather seats.

The third decision is a distribution issue: Who will get the goods and services produced? Who will receive the hybrid SUVs, running shoes, medical services, homes, and premium ice cream?

Economic Systems and the Basic Economic Decisions

The way that a society makes the three basic economic decisions depends on its **economic system.** An economic system is a particular way of organizing the relationships among businesses, households, and the government to make basic choices about what goods and services to produce, how to produce them, and who will get them. Economists often classify economic systems into three basic types or models:

Economic System
The way in which an economy is organized to make the basic economic decisions.

♦   market economies,
♦   planned economies, and
♦   mixed economies.

In market economies, individual buyers and sellers make the basic economic decisions as they communicate through prices in marketplaces. Planned economies emphasize collective decision making: Government planners represent economic participants. A mixed economy combines elements of planned and market economies.

While today all economies are mixed economies, it is helpful to understand the basic model that underlies a particular mixed economy. Figure 2.1 summarizes the relationship among scarcity, the basic economic choices, and economic systems.

FIGURE 2.1   *Scarcity, the Basic Economic Decisions, and Economic Systems*

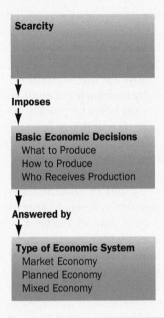

Scarcity imposes three basic economic decisions on a society. A society's economic system determines how the decisions are made.

Traditional Economies

Before studying the three basic models, it is useful to understand that most economies started out as **traditional economies**. A traditional economy generally relies on tradition, custom, or ritual to decide what to produce, how to produce it, and to whom to distribute the results. As traditional economies grow, they usually move to market, planned, or mixed systems.

Traditional economies rely on historical, social, political, or religious arrangements and traditions to decide what to produce. Typically, these economies are focused on some kind of agricultural commodity (like cotton, corn, or cattle) or mineral commodity (like copper).

Traditional systems usually stay fairly small and rural, with economic decisions closely tied to hierarchies and work roles tied to traditional family and gender roles. People use the same production methods that their families used for generations. Traditional economies often resist change and only slowly adopt new production techniques. Resources like land and labor are generally not very specialized, so production is less than if resources were used more efficiently.

The decision of how to distribute goods and services is also made through tradition. Sometimes what people get is determined by their place in society. For example, landowners may fare better than others. Sometimes groups work to support all members.

People in traditional economies often rely on **barter**—the direct exchange of goods or services for other goods or services—to meet their needs. As people's economic needs become complicated and varied, they inevitably need to create money to facilitate trade. This is one reason that traditional systems evolve into more developed economies.

Traditional Economy
An economy that relies largely on tradition, custom, or ritual when making the basic economic decisions.

Barter
The direct exchange of goods or services for other goods or services.

MARKET ECONOMIES

Market Economy

An economy in which the basic economic decisions are made by individual buyers and sellers in markets using the language of price.

Price System

A market system; one in which buyers and sellers communicate through prices in markets.

Private Property Rights

Individual rights to possess and dispose of goods, services, and resources.

Free Enterprise

The right of a business to make its own decisions and to operate with a profit motive.

Capitalism

An economic system with free enterprise and private property rights; economic decision making occurs in a market environment.

Circular Flow Model

A diagram showing the real and money flows between households and businesses in output, or product, markets and input, or resource, markets.

Output Markets (Product Markets)

Markets in which businesses are sellers and households are buyers; consumer goods and services are exchanged.

A **market economy** is rooted in the belief that decisions are best made by individuals, or in a philosophy of individualism. In a market economy, individual buyers and sellers interacting in markets[1] make the basic economic choices. Also called **price systems**, market economies rely on prices as the language through which buyers and sellers communicate their intentions. For example, Starbucks expresses its intention to sell lattes by making them available at a particular price, and consumers tell Starbucks that they want lattes by paying the price asked. The exchange of the latte is made because the price is suitable to both buyer and seller.

Essential to this system is **private property rights**, which give individuals and businesses the right to own resources, goods, and services and to use them as they choose. In a pure market economy, individuals are free to form businesses, operate with a profit motive, and make their own decisions about price or product-related matters or to engage in **free enterprise**.

Pure market systems, where individual buyers and sellers make *all* economic decisions with no government intervention, have virtually disappeared. But price systems are extremely important for us to understand because they provide the philosophical and operational bases for economies like the U.S. market economy. The United States has kept the key features of a market economy, although it is more of a mixed system because of government's role.

Markets have existed in different types of economies throughout the history of the world. In some instances, markets have served simply as an allocation mechanism to aid people in making the basic economic decisions. Even planned economies have used markets in modern times to help allocate goods and services. For example, the former Soviet Union used markets even prior to the economic restructuring of the 1990s.

Market economies are usually associated with **capitalism**, an economic system in which private individuals own the factors of production and operate on a free-enterprise basis. Pure capitalist economies leave little room for government interference.

The Operation of a Market Economy

We can best illustrate the operation of a pure market economy with no government intervention by a **circular flow model**, such as that in Figure 2.2. This model shows how businesses and households relate to one another as buyers and sellers. In one part of this relationship, shown in the lower half of Figure 2.2, businesses are the sellers of goods and services, and households are the buyers. Here there are a real flow of goods and services from businesses to households and a money flow of dollars from households to businesses. For example, sweaters, televisions, fajitas, and furniture flow to households, which give businesses dollars for these items.

Transactions of this type, where businesses sell goods and services and households buy them, occur in **output markets**, or **product markets**. In these markets, buyers and sellers may deal with one another face-to-face, as in automobile showrooms or restaurants, or through more impersonal negotiations, such as catalog orders, Internet purchases, or vending machines.

In the second part of the household–business relationship, businesses are the buyers and households are the sellers. Businesses need resources, or factors of production, which belong to households, to produce goods and services. In the upper half of

---

[1] A market is defined as a place or situation in which the buyers and sellers of a product interact for the purpose of exchange. Markets are discussed in detail in the following chapter.

FIGURE 2.2	*The Circular Flow of Economic Activity*

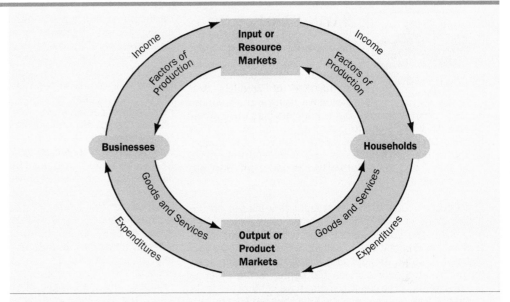

Households sell factors of production to businesses in input markets, and businesses sell goods and services to households in output markets.

Figure 2.2, a real flow of labor, capital, land, and entrepreneurship goes from households (sellers) to businesses (buyers). In return for these resources, businesses send a money flow of wages, interest, rents, and profits to households. For example, Ford Motor must hire machinists, design engineers, and line workers to produce vehicles. In return, these employees receive wages. Ford also pays dividends to its stockholders in return for their entrepreneurial role. Transactions involving resource purchases occur in **input markets**, or **resource markets**.

Input Markets (Resource Markets)

Markets in which households are sellers and businesses are buyers; factors of production are bought and sold.

A market economy's basic structure can be fully explained by focusing on the two buyer–seller relationships of businesses and households at the same time, or on Figure 2.2 as a whole. Businesses and households relate to one another through both input markets and output markets. Households sell labor, capital, land, and entrepreneurship to businesses in return for income in input markets. That income is then used to buy goods and services from businesses in output markets.

Economic Decisions in a Market Economy

How are the basic economic choices of what, how, and to whom made in a market system?

What to Produce?   In a market economy, what and how many goods and services are produced is the result of millions of independent decisions by individual households and businesses in marketplaces. A business will produce something if it thinks that enough households will purchase the item at a price that will make its production profitable. If people do not want a good or service or will not pay a price that allows a profit, businesses will not produce that item. This is why some products like microwaves and the Ford Mustang continue to appear, while some clothing styles and

APPLICATION 2.1

SAYING NO!

Companies can exert great power in markets through the research, development, and introduction of products and their advertising and promotion. But consumers also wield power through their decisions to purchase—or not purchase—a product. Over the years, there have been products brought to the market, sometimes by very large and well-known businesses, and consumers have rejected them. Here are a few examples.

The Edsel   One of the most legendary misses on the auto market was Ford's Edsel, named after Henry Ford's only child. The Edsel was introduced in 1957 with great fanfare and expectations to sell more than 200,000 annually. But in 1958, its best year, barely 63,000 were sold. Its push-button gear shift on the center of the steering wheel and the horse-collar grill may have contributed to its demise. It was reported that the Edsel caused Ford to lose more than $300,000 a day before the announcement in November 1959 that production of this car would cease.

New Coke   Coke drinkers around the country rebelled against the New Coke introduced by Coca-Cola in the mid-1980s. Even marketing campaigns could not assuage the anger of Coke drinkers who wanted the original taste to return. It took less than three months for the company to announce the return of the original formula—as Classic Coke.

Food Products   The world of food products provides a plethora of examples of items that consumers said no to, sometimes despite substantial expenditures for product development and advertising. These include some interesting items. Colgate at one time introduced Kitchen Entrees—eat a Colgate meal and then brush with Colgate tooth paste. Jimmy Dean's chocolate chip pancakes wrapped around a sausage on a stick disappeared. Kellogg's Breakfast Mates with cereal, milk, and a spoon didn't quite appeal to people who don't like room-temp milk on their cereal, and purple and green ketchup, frozen stuffing, garlic cake, aerosol spray toothpaste, and Dunk-a-Balls Cereal (designed to be something kids could play with before eating) are all gone from the market. Thirsty Dog, water for cats and dogs that was infused with flavors like beef and fish, also went away.

Football   Two attempts were made to launch a new football league. The U.S. Football League (USFL) was introduced in 1983 to provide football during the spring and summer seasons with both ABC and ESPN contracting to televise games of the initial twelve teams. In 1985, the decision to bring the USFL into fall competition caused its collapse, and the League played its last game in spring 1985. The XFL, another off-season football attempt, lasted for one season in 2001. The XFL was a joint venture of NBC and the World Wrestling Federation to allow a rougher, fewer rules game.

Other Near and Total Misses   Harley-Davidson perfume didn't appeal to their loyal fans. The DeLorean car with its stainless steel exterior and wing doors saw a production of just 9,000. Smith & Wesson, the noted gun maker, couldn't transfer its appeal to the mountain bikes it decided to produce. Lululemon's expensive yoga pants were pulled from the market when the fabric was determined to be too sheer. Some new BlackBerry products found a rocky market, and Disney's remake of the Lone Ranger fell short of expectations.

recording artists disappear from the market. New products such as tablets and mobile apps emerge because individuals want them and businesses see profit opportunities in producing and selling them.

In a world of large corporate producers like car and cola companies, can individuals actually bring about product change? A single buyer acting alone may be powerless, but together consumers "vote" by virtue of spending or not spending their money on a product. Products disappear from the market when consumers do not buy them.[2] Application 2.1, "Saying No!" describes cases where consumers decided against a company's product.

---

[2] An important question must be raised: To what extent are individuals' decisions influenced by advertising and other promotional activities? If businesses exert a strong influence on people's attitudes and tastes, do the dollars consumers spend reflect their independent choices, or do they represent something else? Put differently, do businesses respond to consumers' preferences, do they shape those preferences, or is there some mixture of the two? The independence of consumer economic decision making is a controversial issue. What is your position on this question?

TABLE 2.1	*Costs of Different Methods for Producing a Guitar*

Method 3 illustrates the least-cost method of production.

Method of Production	Cost to Company per Unit
1. Machine assembled	$650.00
2. Hand assembled	900.00
3. Hand-and-machine assembled	530.00

How to Produce?   In a market economy, businesses decide how to produce goods and services through their choices of production methods. Generally, a business can produce a good or service in more than one way, so businesses must decide which of the available techniques and resources or factors should be used for production. For example, suppose that a company identifies three different methods for producing a type of guitar: by machine, by hand, or by a combination of labor and machinery. The cost for each of the three methods is given in Table 2.1. Which method of production will the company choose in a market economy?

Least-Cost (Efficient) Method of Production
The method of production that allows a given good or service to be produced at the lowest cost.

The company's owners will choose the **least-cost method of production**, or the most **efficient** method, as we discussed in Chapter 1. Since the owners' profit on the guitars is the difference between the product's price and its production costs, the lower the cost, the greater the profit. By using both labor and machinery (method 3), the company's owners stand to earn more profit than they would if they chose one of the other methods.

In a market system, factor prices determine the most efficient production method and are the basis for a firm's decisions about production techniques. In the United States, for example, agriculture is highly mechanized. Given the market prices of farm machinery and labor and available technology, U.S. farmers find it cheapest to use more machinery and less labor to produce a given output. In other parts of the world, abundant and cheap labor encourages farmers to use production methods that emphasize human effort.

Who Gets Goods and Services?   The price system determines who receives goods and services in a market economy. The circular flow model in Figure 2.2 shows a flow of goods and services going from businesses to households in output markets, matched by a flow of dollars going from households to businesses. In a market economy, people get goods and services only if they can pay for them. In other words, in a market economy, goods and services are distributed to those who can afford them.

In market systems, people earn money to buy goods and services by selling factors of production in resource markets. The amount and quality of labor, entrepreneurial skills, capital, or land that people sell determine the amount of income they have to spend on goods and services. People lacking marketable skills are not paid well in resource markets, so they cannot afford many goods and services. People who have many resources, or resources that are highly valued, may enjoy a substantial income, enabling them to buy the items they want in output markets. In a market system, people's abilities to purchase mountain cabins, original works of art, and cellars full of French wine—or peanut butter, one-room apartments, and bus tickets—are determined by the number and value of the resources they offer for sale.

Evaluating Market Economies

Like all economic systems, market economies have both strengths and weaknesses.

Strengths: Efficiency, Consumer Choice, and the Opportunity for Success   On the plus side, market economies tend to produce goods and services efficiently because profit and income act as incentives to guide production. Profit causes businesses to produce efficiently, and income incentivizes households to effectively use and improve their resources. Many students, for example, invest in education to become more productive and obtain higher salaries. (Table 15.5 provides data on the relationship between education and income.)

Market systems also encourage efficiency because the information required for production and distribution decisions passes directly between buyers and sellers via price. The market coordinates business and household actions and through prices responds fairly quickly to their decisions.

Market systems also provide a wide range of choices in the variety and quality of goods and services for consumers. Market systems sometimes provide goods and services even before consumers realize that they want them. Market economies also offer significant opportunities for growth and change. Stories about the "local boy or girl makes good" abound in market systems. Many immigrants and Americans born into poverty have ascended the economic ladder through talent and hard work.

Market Failure
A market system creates a problem for a society or fails to achieve a society's goals.

Weaknesses: Market Power, Equity, and Information   There are several problems inherent in a market economy. Typically these are called **market failures**, a term economists use to describe problems created by a market-based system, or the inability of the system to achieve a society's goals.

The competition at the foundation of a market economy can be lessened when competition drives out sellers and the market becomes dominated by one or a few sellers. When this happens, the interaction between buyers and sellers becomes lopsided, with undesirable consequences for buyers including higher prices, fewer choices, and less attention to quality. Consider an airport or stadium with just one food service: Here people likely pay a high price and have fewer menu choices.

Market systems provide no protection for those who cannot provide for themselves. There is no means to acquire goods and services by people, such as the elderly, disabled, or children living in poverty, who cannot contribute to production. Pure market systems do not protect people who lack the knowledge to make informed decisions about purchases or employment. Market systems have no organized way to ensure that products offered for sale, such as medications and processed foods, or work environments are safe. The information required to assess every item a person could buy or the health and safety of a work place would be expensive, technical, and time consuming.

Market failure can also occur when age, race, or gender discrimination results in unequal treatment for some workers. Such discrimination leads to the inefficient use of labor resources.

Finally, market failure can result when the profit-driven, cost-minimizing efforts of businesses lead to costs that must be absorbed by all of society. Hazardous products, poor working conditions, or degradation of the environment could result from the efforts of producers to find less expensive means to operate. A hog farm that lowers its costs by allowing raw sewage to drain into a stream benefits through throwing some of its costs onto society. Table 2.2 summarizes the strengths and weaknesses of a market economy.

TABLE 2.2	Strengths and Weaknesses of Market Economies

A market economy has both strengths and weaknesses, which are termed market failures.

Strengths	Weaknesses
Strong efficiency incentives	People without marketable skills may not get needed goods and services
Prices allow direct signals between buyers and sellers	Market power in hands of few sellers
Economic freedom	No protection for people with inadequate knowledge about products and jobs
Wide selection of goods and services	
Incentives for innovation and growth	Business cost-minimizing efforts can lead to social costs
Choices/prices of goods and services reflect buyers' and sellers' values and priorities	Age, race, or gender discrimination

Government Intervention in a Market Economy: A Mixed Economy

Not surprisingly, society frequently turns to the government for help when it wants to address its economy's market failures. When government intervenes, the economy moves from its "pure" status to what we call a mixed economy. In simple terms, government law intervene in the business sector, the household sector, output markets, and input markets when markets fail.

There are some general ways in which government influences decision making:

Government Regulation
Government commissions
and boards are involved in
business decision making.

- Government establishes the legal framework within which businesses and households operate. This involves the definition of property rights, contracts, standards of fair competition, court procedures, and other matters.
- While keeping business ownership in private hands, government sometimes intervenes through **government regulation**. Government commissions may oversee decisions that range from pricing and availability of service in certain industries, such as natural gas, to addressing specific problems, such as product safety, that cross many industries.
- Sometimes government intervenes in resource markets to protect workers and wages. There are laws relating to the minimum wage, collective bargaining, worker health and safety, and other labor-related issues.
- Government taxing and spending policies influence inflation, unemployment, and the overall level of economic activity. The size of some government expenditures, such as those in defense-related industries, affects certain markets.
- The U.S. government provides several income support programs such as Social Security, job-training programs, and Medicare.

**Planned Economy
(Command Economy)**
An economy in which the
basic economic decisions
are made by planners rather
than by private individuals
and businesses.

PLANNED ECONOMIES

A **planned economy**, also termed a **command economy**, is based on a philosophy of collectivism. In this type of economy, decisions are made by planning authorities, not by individuals. In this system, there are no private property rights. Rather, resources are owned collectively or by the government.

Government agencies, bureaus, or commissions may be the official planners in a planned economy. These economies allow no market activity and rely on extensive bureaucracies to make millions of detailed economic decisions and deal with the vast numbers of problems that invariably arise. Planned economies usually operate according to blueprints, termed plans, that establish general objectives, both economic and noneconomic, for the economy to accomplish over a period of time.

Today, few planned economies operate without some market orientation. As we move further into the twenty-first century, the large purely planned economies of the former Soviet Union and China are undergoing significant changes. The Soviet Union rushed into a quick abandonment of its planning system in the late 1980s and had problems adjusting to a new philosophy and institutional mechanisms. The Chinese, on the other hand, have adopted a slower, systematic approach to using market mechanisms.

Planned, or command, economies are often associated with **socialism**. In a socialist system, there may be no private property rights, since governments or collective groups of citizens officially own all resources. Socialist societies often attempt to make income distribution more equal among their members, at least in theory. A socialist system may depend heavily on planning or may, as in the case of market socialism, employ some planning but also rely heavily on markets.[3]

Socialism
An economic system in which many of the factors of production are collectively owned, and an attempt is made to equalize the distribution of income.

Economic Decisions in a Planned Economy

In planned economies, planning authorities decide what types and amounts of goods and services to produce. Planners use the planning objectives and their value judgments to determine how many submarines, corn silos, shoes, and other items the system will produce.

Government planners also decide how to allocate resources to produce goods and services. Here, the authority's influence is generally less direct and comes through determining which factors of production and processes will be made available to producers. For example, cars can be produced by manual labor or the use of robotics. If planners want to keep people employed, they will not plan for robotic equipment. In a purely planned economy, a producer cannot order a machine, part, or piece of equipment if the authority has not permitted it to be produced. Planners determine who will work in what jobs; how to use land, buildings, and productive equipment; and where economic opportunities lie.

Predictably enough, planning officials decide who will have access to goods and services. A rationing system may be used to distribute specific items or services, or planners may give individuals freedom to purchase what has been produced. If individuals can choose, then planners face the problem of income determination. That is, planners must decide how much income goes to the various production factors or to individuals.

Evaluating Planned Economies

What advantages do planned economies offer? These economies may achieve certain societal goals faster than in a less formally organized economy. The development of a high-tech industry or increased agricultural products might be accomplished more rapidly when a central authority coordinates efforts. Planned economies should also find it easier to eliminate unemployment when producers can simply be forced to use more labor in their processes. In addition, the ability to control the distribution of goods and services can alter shares in the economy's output. For example, a planning authority could ensure adequate heating fuel for all homes.

---

[3] In market socialism, some goods and services (such as those used by households) are allocated through markets, while others (such as machinery and equipment used by businesses) are allocated by the planners.

TABLE 2.3	*Strengths and Weaknesses of Planned Economies*

Planned economies have both strengths and weaknesses, called planning failures.

Strengths	Weaknesses
Ability to accomplish social goals quickly	Creation of production problems due to complexity of planning
Reduce unemployment by using more labor in production	Few incentives to create quality products or services, operate efficiently, or meet consumer demand
Can provide for an equal distribution of income and goods and services	Few incentives to protect the environment
Possible provision for more economic security and safety nets	Few economic choices for most participants

Planning Failure
Centralized planning creates a problem for a society or fails to achieve a society's goals.

Just as market economies do not work perfectly, planned economies may experience **planning failures** when they create problems for a society or fail to achieve its goals. It is difficult for planned economies to match consumer wants and needs with production. The value judgments of planners about what to produce may not coincide with consumers' value judgments. Furthermore, the time lapse between a plan's creation and actual production may be so lengthy that items once considered desirable are no longer appropriate.

The sheer complexity of production where government planners determine which resources, technology, and processes will be used creates issues. Shortages of a key resource can stop production. Mistakes and delays come with a slowed flow of information and decision making. With no incentives for producers or workers, the result can be inferior products and inefficient processes.

The environmental damage that can and has occurred with planning is a serious issue. In Eastern Europe and China, air and water pollution problems are consequences of planners' failures to take the environment into account in many of their decisions. In 2013, environmental awareness in China was raised to new heights when Beijing experienced air pollution that turned day into night, and there was acknowledgment of "cancer cluster villages" that were downstream from plants with industrial waste discharged into water. Table 2.3 summarizes the strengths and weaknesses of a planned economy.

MIXED ECONOMIES

Mixed Economic
An economic system with some combination of market and centralized decision making.

Technically, all economies are **mixed economies** because the three basic choices are addressed by some combination of market and centralized decision making. Pure market and pure planned economies are polar cases that help us order our thinking but have no real-world counterparts. An important factor giving the different economies their unique styles is the manner and degree to which individual and collective decision making are combined. As discussed earlier, pure market and pure planned economies are not perfect. Market failures and planning failures cause the movement to mixed economies.

Figure 2.3 provides a helpful way to think about economic systems, which can be visualized as lying along a continuum. At one end are pure market economies, and at

---

FIGURE 2.3   *Continuum of Economic Decision Making*

| | United States   Britain   China   Cuba | |
| Pure Market ═══════════════════════════════════════ Pure Planned |

| Individualism | | Collectivism |

Economies can be classified according to their dependence on planned versus market decision making.

TEST YOUR UNDERSTANDING

ECONOMIC DECISION MAKING AND THE CIRCULAR FLOW

1.   Indicate for each of the following situations whether it would most likely occur in a pure market economy, a pure planned economy, or a mixed economy:

a.   Businesses in an industry are free to produce however they want and are constantly looking for cost-reducing techniques since every dollar saved in cost means more profit.

b.   An economics instructor in a particular country does not bother to explain the circular flow model because it has no relevance to how the basic economic decisions are made in that country.

c.   Union and management representatives submit a deadlocked labor contract negotiation to the government for mediation.

d.   Workers who have lost their jobs and incomes cut back their spending because there is no alternative source of emergency financial support once their savings run out.

e.   Consumers can't get car windshield wipers and tires because they are not being produced, yet accordions are plentiful and not in demand and continue to be produced.

f.   A catering business goes bankrupt, but its employees receive unemployment compensation while they look for other jobs.

2.   Suppose that, because of uncertainty about future jobs and incomes, households decide to increase their savings and reduce their current purchases of goods and services from businesses. With the aid of the circular flow diagram below, answer each of the following:

a.   Identify the flows on the bottom half of the circular flow model and explain what impact these household decisions will have on each of those flows.

b.   Identify the flows on the upper half of the circular flow model and explain what impact the actions taken on the bottom half of the model will have on the flows on the upper half.

c.   Based on the changes in the flows in the entire model, what should be the effect of this decision by households on future jobs and incomes?

Answers can be found at the back of the book.

the other end are pure planned economies. The world's economies lie between these extremes and combine elements of market, or individual, decision making and planned, or collective, decision making. Where an economy falls on the continuum depends on its core philosophy about decision making and the degree to which it deviates from this core. For example, the United States lies closer to the market end of the continuum because of its reliance on markets, and Cuba lies closer to the planned end of the continuum because of its reliance on planning.

Test Your Understanding, "Economic Decision Making and the Circular Flow," allows you to practice distinguishing among the different economic systems and to review the key relationships in a market economy.

Changing Economic Systems

Over the past few decades, dramatic changes have occurred in many of the world's planned economies. The former Soviet Union, Poland, China, and other nations have been moving toward greater use of free markets and individual decision making. Described in terms of Figure 2.3, these and other planned economies have been shifting to the left along the continuum of economic decision making. In several of these countries, economic reform has been accompanied by greater political freedom.

Privatization

The granting to individuals of property rights to factors of production that were once collectively owned or owned by the state.

An essential element for planned economies to move toward market economies is **privatization**. Individuals are granted property rights to factors of production that were once collectively owned or owned by the state. Without the protection of private ownership and the right to profit that it secures, individuals have few incentives to carry out the entrepreneurial functions that drive a market economy. Successful privatization is key to the actual transformation of a planned to a market economy.

Today we watch China, a country of more than 1.3 billion people (the U.S. population is slightly more than 320 million) with a landmass slightly less than that of the United States, experience exceptionally rapid economic growth. Once considered to be a closed planned economy, China has moved slowly and carefully toward a more market-oriented system and has become an important player in world markets. China has quickly become a major consumer of energy and other resources, as well as the world's largest exporter. Application 2.2, "The People's Republic of China," gives some background on changes in the economy of China.

THE U.S. ECONOMIC SYSTEM

The U.S. economy has been described as a mixed economic system that largely depends on markets and individual decision making. The government plays a somewhat lesser but vitally important role in the U.S. system. We can trace the evolution of the U.S. economy into its present form by focusing on the British foundations of the U.S. economy and on major historical events in the United States.

The British Foundations of the U.S. Economy

In 1776, a Scottish philosophy professor named Adam Smith (1723–1790) published a book entitled *The Wealth of Nations*. This book was to have a profound impact on economic thinking in his generation and future generations as well. Even today Adam Smith's book is frequently quoted as it provided an intellectual justification for an economic system based on individualism.

THE PEOPLE'S REPUBLIC OF CHINA

If you put China into your search engine, a huge number of sites for information will be identified. The World Factbook *provides some basic demographic data and information, such as the geography, language, government, economy, and religions of China. Other sites provide historical and cultural information as well as political commentary.*

For centuries, China stood as a leading civilization, outpacing the rest of the world in the arts and sciences, but in the nineteenth and twentieth centuries, the country was beset by civil unrest, major famines, military defeats, and foreign occupation.

This huge country, which borders India, Pakistan, and Vietnam, among others, experienced a serious change in government after World War II. The Communists under Mao Zedong, better known as Chairman Mao, established an autocratic socialist system that, while ensuring China's sovereignty, imposed strict controls over everyday life and took the lives of tens of millions of people.

After 1978, Mao's successor Deng Xiaoping and other leaders began moving China from a centrally planned economy to a more market-oriented system. Reforms included the phasing out of collectivized agriculture, the gradual liberalization of prices, fiscal decentralization, development of stock markets, a push to grow the private sector and foreign trade, and more.

For much of the population, living standards have improved dramatically, and the room for personal choice has expanded, yet political controls remain tight. China since the early 1980s has increased its global outreach and participation in international organizations. In 2010, China became the world's largest exporter. In 2011, the government adopted the Twelfth Five-Year Plan, which continues to reform the economy.

But, like other countries, China faces some serious problems. The one-child policy leaves China with one of the most rapidly aging countries in the world. Deterioration in the environment, especially air pollution from reliance on coal production, soil erosion, and the steady fall of the water table bringing water shortages along with a loss of arable land are other long-term issues.

Changes in China's economy and the impact it has on its own population as well as other world economies as it moves from a planned to a market-oriented system provide us with an interesting scenario to watch.

Source: United States Central Intelligence Agency, "China," *The World Factbook, 2013–2014*, www.cia.gov.

Laissez-Faire Capitalism
Capitalism with a strong emphasis on individual decision making; little or no government interference.

Mercantilism
An economic system or philosophy that subordinates individual interests and decisions to those of the state.

Invisible Hand Doctrine
Adam Smith's concept that producers acting in their own self-interest will provide buyers with what they want and thus advance the interests of society.

Smith's thesis, put simply, was this: *The best way to increase the wealth of a nation is through individual decision making with minimal government interference.* The system he proposed, called **laissez-faire (French for "let it alone") capitalism**, stood in sharp contrast to **mercantilism**, the then reigning economic philosophy. Mercantilism held that the state is the best judge of what is good for the economy. Mercantilist policies stood for the subordination of individual interests to the collective interests of the state and the belief that economic decisions should not be left to individuals acting in their own interest.

Central to Smith's argument for an economic system based on individual decision making was his **invisible hand doctrine**. According to this doctrine, it is foolish to expect people to base their business dealings with others on altruism or benevolence. Rather, people carry on their business in a way that serves their own best interests. In a system of free and open competition where buyers have a wide range of businesses with which they can deal, it is in the producer's or seller's best interest to try to give the buyer what he or she wants on terms that are acceptable to both parties. In this way, Smith believed, by pursuing one's own best interest, one is guided "as if by an invisible hand" to advance the interests of all society. Government does not need to closely oversee the operation of the economy, since people working for their personal gain will achieve the most desired results.

Industrial Revolution
A time period during which an economy becomes industrialized; characterized by such social and technological changes as the growth and development of factories.

At the same time as the rise of economic individualism, the British **Industrial Revolution** with its significant technological and social changes was transforming England and Scotland into modern industrial economies. Prior to the mid-1700s, economic activity in Britain was primarily agricultural with some simple cottage or home industries. Then a series of inventions and innovations like massive mechanical weaving looms changed the emphasis of economic activity from agriculture and home production to a system fostering the growth of factories. Many new and different products and new production techniques increased overall output. Great strides were made in providing goods and services.

Industrialization, however, also had a dark side. With factories often came poor working conditions, low pay, long hours, and a reliance on women and children who would work for less and were easier to control. In 1818, Mary W. Shelley wrote about the threatening relationship between people and science in a well-known work entitled *Frankenstein*. The poem "The Factory Girl's Last Day," also written in the early 1800s and excerpted in Application 2.3, makes a strong statement about the factory system. What can you learn from this poem?

APPLICATION 2.3

THE FACTORY GIRL'S LAST DAY

The art and poetry of a particular time period often reflect the social attitudes of the day. Several poems written during the British Industrial Revolution make strong statements about the poor working conditions in factories. Below is an excerpt from "The Factory Girl's Last Day," written in the early 1800s and attributed to various authors.

"'Twas on a winter morning,
　　The weather wet and mild,
Two hours before the dawning
　　The father roused his child:
Her daily morsel bringing,
　　The darksome room he paced,
And cried: 'The bell is ringing;
　　My hapless darling, haste!'

"'Dear father, I'm so weary!
　　I scarce can reach the door;
And long the way and dreary:
　　O, carry me once more!'
Her wasted form seems nothing;
　　The load is on his heart:
He soothes the little sufferer,
　　Till at the mill they part.

"The overlooker met her
　　As to her frame she crept;
And with his thong he beat her,
　　And cursed her when she wept.

It seemed, as she grew weaker,
　　The threads the oftener broke;
The rapid wheels ran quicker,
　　And heavier fell the stroke.

"She thought how her dead mother
　　Blessed her with latest breath,
And of her little brother,
　　Worked down, like her, to death:
Then told a tiny neighbor
　　A half-penny she'd pay
To take her last hour's labor,
　　While by her frame she lay.

"The sun had long descended
　　Ere she sought that repose:
Her day began and ended
　　As cruel tyrants chose.
Then home! but oft she tarried;
　　She fell and rose no more;
By pitying comrades carried,
　　She reached her father's door.

"At night, with tortured feeling,
　　He watched his sleepless child:
Though close beside her kneeling,
　　She knew him not, nor smiled.
Again the factory's ringing
　　Her last perceptions tried:
Up from her straw bed springing,
　　'It's time!' she shrieked, and died!"

Source: Robert Dale Owen, *Threading My Way* (New York: Augustus M. Kelley, 1967), pp. 129–130. Original publication, 1874. Reprinted with permission.

Historical Highlights in the Development of the U.S. Economy

In the early history of the United States, the economy was closer to a pure market system, or laissez-faire capitalism, than it is today. Over the years, several key events and historical periods have helped to shape the U.S. economy and are noteworthy in understanding how a basic market system can adapt to change but retain its fundamental characteristics.

After the Civil War, through the early 1900s, significant changes occurred in the United States similar to the British Industrial Revolution. Growth in transportation and communications (primarily the railroads and telephone) opened new markets; new energy sources such as oil and electricity permitted mass production; and a factory system grew. There were great numbers of inventions introduced, such as the light bulb, more efficient new machinery, and people moving to cities to seek work and opportunity. Immigrants from Europe came to the United States in droves.

In the midst of this industrial boom came new government intervention. Some businesses, such as U.S. Steel and Standard Oil, were becoming large and powerful corporations capable of monopolizing an entire market. Other companies were joining together to form trusts (such as sugar and tobacco). As a result, in 1890 Congress attempted to preserve competition and prevent monopolies by passing the Sherman Antitrust Act. In 1914, the Clayton Act was passed to prohibit some anticompetitive business practices. (See Chapter 14 for additional information on these acts.)

With this growth, the living and working conditions for many Americans were becoming inordinately harsh. Many worked long hours for low wages in intolerable conditions; child labor was permitted; city slums flourished; and attempts to form unions were often met with violence. As a result, legislation was passed to address these issues. However, there was not one single sweeping law; rather, change came from bits and pieces of new federal and state legislation that began in the early 1900s.

Muckrakers

Authors, journalists, and others who sensationalized American social problems in the early twentieth century.

The **muckrakers**, a group of authors, journalists, photojournalists, and others, stirred the public through their exposés of the harsh and dispiriting side of the industrial age. For example, Upton Sinclair, probably the best-known muckraker, wrote of conditions in the meat packing industry in *The Jungle*. The following excerpt shows the sensationalist manner in which Sinclair and other muckrakers wrote. It is no wonder that one response to this book was the Meat Inspection Act of 1907.

> This is no fairy story and no joke; the meat would be shovelled into carts, and the man who did the shoveling would not trouble to lift out a rat even when he saw one—there were things that went into the sausage in comparison with which a poisoned rat was a tidbit. There was no place for the men to wash their hands before they ate their dinner, and so they made a practice of washing them in the water that was to be ladled into the sausage. There were the butt-ends of smoked meat, and the scraps of corned beef, and all the odds and ends of the waste of the plants, that would be dumped into old barrels in the cellar and left there. Under the system of rigid economy which the packers enforced, there were some jobs that it only paid to do once in a long time, and among these was the cleaning out of the waste barrels. Every spring they did it; and . . . cart load after cart load of it would be taken up and dumped into the hoppers with fresh meat, and sent out to the public's breakfast.[4]

---

[4] Upton Sinclair, *The Jungle* (New York: Signet Classics, The New American Library), pp. 136–137. Original publication, 1906.

Other legislation of this period included the Food and Drug Act of 1906, state legislation limiting the hours and ages of working children, laws setting maximum hours and minimum wages for women, state workers' compensation insurance for injury on the job, and many other laws affecting matters that ranged from fire regulations to mandatory schooling.

The Great Depression and the New Deal   The stock market crash of 1929 signaled the beginning of the Great Depression—a severe economic decline that began in October 1929 and lasted for more than a decade. The Great Depression led to a series of programs and legislative reforms termed the **New Deal**.

These programs had various objectives. Some gave substantial aid to specific sectors of the economy such as agriculture. Programs were established to help the unemployed by providing jobs building public infrastructure such as bridges and roads, and by working in forestry and parks. The Social Security Act was passed in 1935 to provide income for older adults, the blind, and others.

Some programs were designed to regulate or bolster businesses and financial markets, such as the creation of the Securities and Exchange Commission (SEC) to establish safeguards in securities markets. The Federal Deposit Insurance Corporation (FDIC) provided some banking assurances, and the National Labor Relations Act gave workers the right to bargain collectively.

In the Depression years, the federal government began to run deficit budgets on a regular basis, typically spending more than it took in from taxes and other revenues. This practice was a significant break from the past and began a new direction in government budget policy.

World War II Era   The Great Depression came to an abrupt halt with the entry of the United States into World War II in December 1941. The extent and magnitude of the war effort brought many government agencies to oversee production, human resources, wages, prices, and such. While most of these agencies were dismantled after the war, they created a precedent for future reestablishment.

Following World War II, one of the most significant steps toward more government involvement in economic activity occurred with the passage of the **Employment Act of 1946**. This act gave the federal government the right and responsibility to provide an environment in which full employment, full production, and stable prices could be achieved. Under this act, Congress could manipulate taxes and government spending and run deficit budgets in an effort to enhance the economy. Such power had not been legislated before this period.

Recent Decades   Over the past few decades, the United States has gone through cycles of regulation and deregulation. In the 1960s and 1970s, there were numerous (about 25) government regulatory agencies established including the Environmental Protection Agency and the Consumer Product Safety Commission. This trend, however, was reversed in the late 1970s and 1980s when deregulation of various industries, such as trucking and natural gas, occurred. But that was followed by another round of regulation.

Another significant change in recent decades has been the dramatic rise in the federal public debt which occurs when the U.S. government borrows to finance its budget deficits. Chapter 6 deals with the size and impact of borrowing and debt on the economy.

New Deal
A series of programs and legislative reforms instituted during the administration of Franklin D. Roosevelt in the Great Depression of the 1930s.

Employment Act of 1946
Legislation giving the federal government the right and responsibility to provide an environment for the achievement of full employment, full production, and stable prices.

Other issues have dominated public attention: the cost and payment for health care, regulation of banking and financial services, the environment, Social Security funding, Medicare funding, immigration, the environment, and more. The pressure to tackle some of these issues comes with a larger population of aging boomers that puts pressure on some government programs. Other pressures have come with a rising immigrant population and with a greater awareness of environmental issues.

Today there is a contentious atmosphere in Washington as various groups and parties weigh in on the role of government in economic activity. There are some who favor increased participation by government and increased oversight. They support government's role in ensuring health care for all, increased regulation of banking and financial institutions and the environment, and continued funding of programs such as Medicare. There are some who favor a lessening or dismantling of government regulation and would revert toward a more laissez-faire system. They would like to see more privatization of programs such as Social Security and fewer environmental regulations. The unbending positions of many in Washington feed an inability to reach compromise and has left many Americans frustrated with the federal government.

Up for Debate, "Are U.S. and Western European Economic Institutions Appropriate for Other Nations?" provides some interesting discussion about whether the roots of the U.S. economic system and its institutions provide the best path for growth in nonmarket economies.

UP FOR DEBATE

Are U.S. and Western European Economic Institutions Appropriate For Other Nations?

Issue   *People living in the United States and Western Europe enjoy high standards of living, especially compared to many other countries. Does this mean that policies that stimulate growth in these nations will be just as effective for people living in other nations?*

Yes   Some experts believe the answer to this question is "yes" and recommend the adoption of U.S. and Western European legal systems, political structures, and free markets as the basis for making the three economic choices. Societies that are rooted in individual choice and markets have strong economies. Proof of this can be found by comparing indicators of economic well-being in Western-type economies with other economies. For example, the life expectancy is estimated to be about 80 years in 2014 in the United States, Germany, France, and most other Western European countries. The life expectancy in Angola, Nigeria, or Zimbabwe is about 55 years. Also, while the estimated 2014 per capita GDP was over $44,000 for the United States, Canada, Sweden and others, the per capita GDP in Ukraine was $8,200 and for Haiti and Ethiopia it was less than $2,000.

In many Western nations free-market economic institutions have also helped to lead to political freedoms and democracy. A striking example of this is the conversion of some former Soviet-bloc countries to market capitalism as well as democratic political systems.

No   Some experts argue that "grafting" Western institutions onto other nations, some of which have vastly different histories and cultures, may fail to improve living standards and may conflict with traditional cultural norms. For example, many former Soviet-bloc countries had little experience with political freedom and the institutions of free markets, and transplanting these institutional structures did not result in Western-style growth. Inserting Western institutions into countries may force them to make hard decisions between the familiar social orders of the past and new political and economic freedoms.

In addition, the desirability of imposing Western values on non-Western nations can be questioned. Even the goal of economic development—with its emphasis on increasing output—can be controversial when it conflicts with very different collectively oriented value systems in many parts of the world. Some of the values that those living in Western-style economies take for granted—for example, the emphasis on consumerism and material progress—are themselves foreign to some other cultures.

Sources: Jasen Castillo, "The Dilemma of Simultaneity: Russia and Georgia in the Midst of Transformation," *World Affairs*, June 22, 1997; Mike Dowling, http://www.Mrdowling.com/8oclife.html; U.S. Central Intelligence Agency, *The World Factbook*, www.cia.gov, 04/27/2015.

Summary

1. All individuals and economies in the world experience scarcity; no economy can completely satisfy all of its members' wants and needs for goods and services.

2. Because of scarcity, every society must make three basic economic decisions: what goods and services to produce and in what quantities, how to produce goods and services, and who gets the goods and services that are produced.

3. Societies develop economic systems in order to deal with the three basic economic decisions. Societies usually evolve beyond traditional economies as they become more complex and move toward more formal economic systems, which we usually classify as market, planned, or mixed economies.

4. Market economies rely on individual buyers and sellers to make the economic decisions. These systems are rooted in private property rights and free enterprise and are usually associated with capitalism.

5. In a market economy, buyers and sellers communicate their wants and needs through prices in markets. A market economy produces goods and services if buyers demand them at a price that allows sellers to produce them at a profit.

6. In a market system, businesses produce goods and services efficiently by seeking least-cost production methods to maximize profits. The value of resources—land, labor, capital, and entrepreneurship—that individuals sell determines how many goods and services they can afford to buy.

7. Economists use a circular flow model to illustrate the basic structure of a market economy. This model shows how businesses and households relate to one another as buyers and sellers in output and input markets.

8. Market economies have advantages: They provide incentives to produce and use resources efficiently, allow direct communication between buyers and sellers, and reflect individual value judgments in production and distribution choices.

9. Market economies have problems called market failures. They may leave the uninformed unprotected, allow discrimination among workers in input markets, not provide goods and services to those unable to contribute to production, foster monopolies, and create environmental problems.

10. In a planned, or command, economy, government planners make the basic economic decisions. These systems are usually rooted in a philosophy of collectivism. Planned economies can allow societies to achieve noneconomic goals more easily, limit unemployment, and provide for a more equal distribution of goods and services. Planning failures may also arise: poor quality products, production stoppages, a lack of worker incentives, problems coordinating production with consumer choices, and pollution problems. Planned economies are often associated with socialism.

11. Mixed economic systems combine elements of market and planned economies. Mixed economies arise in response to planning and market failures. Countries around the world fall on a continuum between pure market and pure planned economies: Pure types no longer exist.

12. The U.S. economy can be better understood by examining its British foundation which includes the rise of a philosophy of individualism advocated in Adam Smith's *The Wealth of Nations* and the British Industrial Revolution.

13. Important events in U.S. history have helped to shape the U.S. economy including the industrial boom, the Great Depression, World War II, and recent concerns over health care, Social Security, the environment, and other issues that relate to the role of government in economic activity.

Key Terms and Concepts

Basic economic decisions
Economic system
Traditional Economy
Barter
Market economy
Price system
Private property rights
Free enterprise
Capitalism
Circular flow model
Output markets (product markets)
Input markets (resource markets)
Least-cost (efficient) method of production
Market failure

Government regulation
Planned economy (command economy)
Socialism
Planning failure
Mixed economy
Privatization
Laissez-faire capitalism
Mercantilism
Invisible hand doctrine
Industrial Revolution
Muckrakers
New Deal
Employment Act of 1946

Review Questions

1. What are the three basic decisions every economy must make? Why must these decisions be made?

2. How do market, planned, and mixed economies make the three basic economic decisions?

3. Draw a simple circular flow diagram to illustrate the structure of a market economy. Include businesses and households, input and output markets, and real and money flows.

4. Below are listed seven activities. Indicate whether each one is a real flow through a product market, a money flow through a product market, a real flow through a resource market, or a money flow through a resource market.

a. Receiving a paycheck at the end of each month
b. Delivering a specially ordered hybrid car to a buyer
c. Receiving patient care in a hospital
d. Using a credit card to buy a meal in a restaurant
e. Earning profit over the summer from your own ice cream stand
f. Obtaining college credits
g. Working overtime

5. Identify three strengths of a market economy. Define and give a current example of a market failure.

6. Identify the strengths and weaknesses of a planned economy. Explain what we mean by planning failure.

7. What is the invisible hand doctrine, and why is it important for laissez-faire capitalism? How are the British Industrial Revolution and the U.S. industrial boom similiar?

8. Indicate how each of the following had an impact on the development of the U.S. economy.
a. The Sherman Antitrust Act of 1890 and the Meat Inspection Act of 1907
b. The New Deal programs of the 1930s
c. World War II programs
d. Health-care legislation during the Obama administration

Discussion Questions

1. Suppose that you have been chosen to be on a blue-ribbon panel of experts to determine how well or poorly the economies of the world are operating. Your task is to come up with a checklist of five criteria by which different economies can be judged. Which five factors would you pick as criteria? Why?

2. What considerations might cause one nation to choose to operate as a market economy and another as a planned economy?

3. Many people today are asking what the U.S. government should do when people who need health care cannot afford it. Is lack of access to health care an example of a market system allocating scarce resources efficiently, or is it an example of market failure? Can it be both?

4. This chapter illustrates how economic systems change over time. What forces might lead to the evolution of an economic system, and how would these forces cause an economy to change?

5. Do you think that China will someday have an economic system that leans more toward laissez-faire capitalism than the U.S. economy?

6. Would mercantilism, the economic system that was important in Europe in the seventeenth and eighteenth centuries, be more consistent with a market economy,

a planned economy, or a mixed economy? Do you know of any economic activity occurring at the present time that reflects a mercantilist philosophy?

7. Based on your general knowledge of U.S. history and current events, how active a role do you think government will be playing in the economy 20 years from now compared to the role it plays today?

8. Environmental concerns are increasingly global as we realize that the careless use of the world's resources influences the entire globe. The impact of global warming, excessive energy use, and polluting rivers and streams is not confined to any one nation. What type of economic system do you think would best address environmental concerns? Will global concerns push more nations toward similar systems?

9. Chapter 1 introduced the importance of efficiency and equity as they affect economic decisions. Discuss how each of the three basic decisions are related to efficiency and equity.

Critical Thinking Case 2

JUDGING ECONOMIES

Critical Thinking Skills

Getting to conclusions

Recognizing value judgments in decision making

Economic Concepts

Varied economic systems

Measuring standards of living

Familiarity with countries throughout the world has increased significantly. The emergence of easy, rapid communication, global travel opportunities, international corporations, the presence of large numbers of foreign students on U.S. college campuses, and much more have helped to expand our knowledge of each other's cultures and economies.

But how do we judge the health of various economies throughout the world? If we were to step back and assess places like Russia, Indonesia, India, Japan, and Bhutan, how would we label their economies? How would we decide whether they are successful and growing or just the opposite?

Over the last half of the twentieth century, it was the "isms" that drove judgments about an economy: capitalism, communism, and socialism. There was a fundamental philosophical belief that issues like property rights and individual decision making formed the basis for judging an economy. Clashes among the "isms" went a long way toward explaining the Cuban Missile Crisis in the early 1960s and certainly the Vietnam War in the late 1960s and early 1970s.

Today we appear to be less concerned about philosophical beliefs and more concerned about other different measurements for judging an economy. We seem to search for criteria and data that offer a picture of the well-being of people in an economy. This focus on well-being has contributed to the growing interest in the Gross National Happiness (GNH) Index, a measure proposed in 1972 by King Wangchuck of Bhutan for his country. The GNH goes beyond measurements of production and jobs and looks at environmental conservation, cultural preservation, sustainable economic development, and good governance.

In the search for new measures of economic success, consider the following questions as criteria for evaluating an economy. These questions call for different evaluation data and standards:

♦ What measures other than jobs and production should be included in assessing the standard of living in an economy?
♦ What is the current and expected future standard of living in the economy?
♦ How is income distributed? How many families live in poverty? In the middle class? Have high incomes?
♦ How does the economy affect people's civil rights?
♦ How well educated are people in the economy? Is there access to physical and mental health care?
♦ How happy are people?

[a] For more information about Bhutan's Gross National Happiness Index as well as the focus by other nations and organizations on happiness, just put Gross National Happiness in your search engine. The Bhutan government has created "A Short Guide to GNH Index" that is easily accessible and will give you more specific information about the index and its findings.

Questions

1. Do you agree that we have moved from a more philosophical and political evaluation of an economy to more specific economic and social indicators? If so, what has accounted for this change? Will the philosophical evaluation always be part of the judgment of economic health?

2. Of the six questions for evaluating an economy, which ones should rank first, second, and third? What is missing from this list?

3. It might seem a bit of a reach to judge economies in terms of civil rights, happiness, and people's health. In your opinion, is it appropriate to pay attention to these factors?

4. Should the Gross National Happiness Index be adopted in the United States? Should the United States focus on the four areas of importance to this Index rather than production and employment?

Demand, Supply, and Price Determination

CHAPTER OBJECTIVES

Explain how demand and supply work using schedules and graphs.

Demonstrate how demand and supply interact in markets to determine prices and to show equilibrium price and quantity, shortages, and surpluses in a market.

Explain how changes in nonprice factors cause changes in demand and changes in supply.

Illustrate how changes in demand and changes in supply affect equilibrium prices and quantities in markets.

Illustrate how government-imposed price ceilings and price floors influence market conditions.

Introduce the concept and calculation of price elasticity, which measures buyers' and sellers' sensitivities to price changes.

Explain how to measure price elasticity.

As we noted in Chapter 2, one way societies can make the basic economic decisions is through individual buyers' and sellers' actions in markets. Many societies, such as the United States and some countries in Western Europe and Asia, base their economic systems on such market decision making. There are two basic economic tools to study buyers and sellers and their behaviors in the marketplace: demand and supply. Together these tools help us understand the forces at work in a market economy. In this chapter, we explore demand and supply in detail and put the two together to see how they interact to determine the prices of goods and services.

DEMAND AND SUPPLY

Demand: The Buyer's Side

Demand, in economic terms, refers to buyers' plans concerning the purchase of a good or service. For example, you might demand an airplane ticket to London, tennis lessons, or a chemistry lab book. A business might demand workers, raw materials, machinery, or any other factor of production. Many considerations go into determining the demand for a good or service. These include the product's price as well as nonprice factors such as the buyer's income and attitude toward the item and available substitute products.

Demand, Defined   In formal terms, we define a buyer's **demand** for a good or service as the different amounts of the good or service that the buyer would be willing and able to purchase at different prices over a given period of time with all nonprice factors held constant. Therefore, when we speak of a buyer's demand for baseball tickets, gasoline, or whatever, we are speaking of the different amounts of the item that the buyer would purchase at different prices over some period of time, such as a day, a week, or a year, with all nonprice factors unchanged. In determining demand, note that only the product's price is allowed to change: All nonprice factors that affect demand, such as the buyer's income, are held constant in order to highlight the relationship between the product's price and the amount of the product a person would be willing and able to buy.

We can illustrate the relationship between the amount of a product that a consumer would buy and the product's price in two ways: through a **demand schedule** (or table) and through a graph (called a demand curve). Table 3.1 is a demand schedule that shows Zach's weekly demand for fresh-baked bagels.[1] Note the relationship between the price per bagel and the number of bagels that Zach is willing and able to buy. As the price per bagel goes up from $0.20 to $0.40, the number of bagels Zach

Demand
The different amounts of a product that a buyer would purchase at different prices in a defined time period when all nonprice factors are held constant.

Demand Schedule
A list of the amounts of a product that a buyer would purchase at different prices in a defined time period when all nonprice factors are held constant.

TABLE 3.1   *Zach's Weekly Demand for Fresh-Baked Bagels*

This demand schedule lists different amounts of bagels that Zach would purchase each week at various prices and illustrates the Law of Demand: It shows the inverse relationship between price and quantity demanded.

Price per Bagel	Number of Bagels Demanded Weekly
$0.20	15
0.40	12
0.60	10
0.80	8
1.00	6
1.20	4
1.40	2
1.60	1

---

[1]Examples in this chapter are hypothetical.

would buy falls from 15 to 12; as the price increases from $0.40 to $0.60, the amount demanded falls from 12 to 10. Each additional $0.20 increment further reduces the number of bagels Zach would buy. In other words, as the price increases, Zach would buy fewer fresh-baked bagels. We could have used any other consumer and any other good or service—restaurant meals, plastic pink flamingos, digital cameras, or jeans—with the same result: The quantity demanded falls as the price rises, and the quantity demanded rises as the price falls.

Law of Demand   Zach's buying behavior, illustrated in Table 3.1, reflects a typical buyer's plan to purchase a good or service. It shows a relationship between price and quantity demanded that we know to be generally true. This relationship is called the **Law of Demand**. It states that, holding all nonprice factors constant, as a product's price increases, the quantity of the product demanded decreases, and as a product's price decreases, the quantity demanded increases. In other words, the Law of Demand states that a product's price is inversely related to the quantity of that product that consumers demand.

Why do consumers react this way to price changes? Behind the Law of Demand is the fundamental problem of economics: scarcity and choice. Consumers purchasing goods and services face a scarcity problem: Their incomes are always limited. Consumers—even very wealthy consumers—can afford only so much. So as the price of an item goes up, buyers may not be able to afford as much of it as they could at the lower price. On the other hand, when the price of a good or service falls, consumers will likely increase their purchases of the item because they can satisfy more wants and needs with their limited incomes.

Choice also influences demand because consumers can always purchase alternative (or substitute) products. As the price of fresh-baked bagels increases, Zach can choose to eat other foods—doughnuts, cereal, or fruit, to name a few—in place of bagels. As the price of bagels decreases, he may choose to eat more of them and less of other items.

Graphing Demand   Typically, economists display demand in graphs rather than in schedules or tables. Figure 3.1 shows Zach's demand for bagels exactly as it appeared in Table 3.1 but presented graphically. On this graph, price appears on the vertical axis (measured in 20-cent intervals) and quantity demanded appears on the horizontal axis (in two-bagel increments). When we plot each price–quantity combination from the demand schedule in Table 3.1 and then connect those points with a line, we call the resulting downward-sloping line a **demand curve**. Recall from Chapter 1 that downward-sloping lines such as this demand curve represent inverse relationships. Since the Law of Demand predicts this type of inverse relationship between price and quantity demanded, we can generalize that demand curves slope downward: Consumers normally demand more at lower prices and less at higher prices.

Supply: The Seller's Side

Economists refer to supply as a seller's plan to make a good or service available in the market. Like demand, supply depends on the product's price and any nonprice factors that influence the seller, such as the cost of producing the product and the seller's expectation of future market conditions.

Supply, Defined   Economists define **supply** as the different amounts of a good or service that a seller would make available for sale at different prices in a given time

---

Law of Demand
There is an inverse relationship between the price of a product and the quantity demanded.

Demand Curve
A line on a graph that illustrates a demand schedule; slopes downward because of the inverse relationship between price and quantity demanded.

Supply
The different amounts of a product that a seller would make available for sale at different prices in a defined time period when all nonprice factors are held constant.

| FIGURE 3.1 | *Zach's Weekly Demand for Fresh-Baked Bagels* |

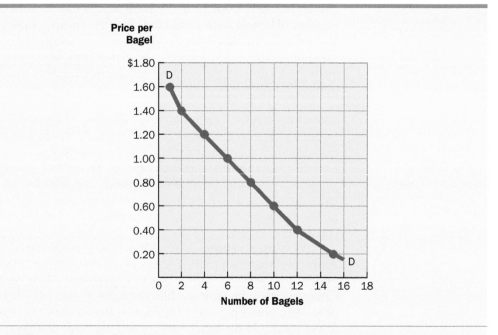

The downward-sloping demand curve illustrates the Law of Demand, showing that Zach demands fewer bagels at higher prices and more bagels at lower prices.

period, holding constant all nonprice factors that affect the seller's plans for the product. In other words, supply indicates how many hot fudge sundaes, haircuts, tires, or any other product a supplier would be willing to sell at different prices during a week, a month, or a year, with all nonprice factors unchanged. As with demand, we hold all nonprice factors affecting supply constant to highlight the relationship between a product's price and the quantity of the product supplied.

Supply Schedule
A list of the amounts of a product that a seller would offer for sale at different prices in a defined time period when all nonprice factors are held constant.

We can illustrate the relationship between the amount of a product a seller would make available for sale and the product's price in a **supply schedule** (or table). Table 3.2 shows the number of bagels of a particular size and quality that City Bakery is willing to sell each week at various prices. Observe the direct relationship between price and the quantity supplied. At a low price, the bakery would offer no or few bagels for sale, but it is willing to offer more bagels for sale as the price increases. If we were to choose to illustrate the supply of another good or service as an example, the same relationship would appear: The quantity supplied would increase as the price increased, and the quantity supplied would decrease as the price decreased.

Law of Supply
There is a direct relationship between the price of a product and the quantity supplied.

The Law of Supply   The direct relationship between price and quantity supplied illustrates the **Law of Supply**. This law states that, holding nonprice factors constant, the quantity of a good or service that a supplier is willing to offer on the market relates directly to price. Why does the bakery react this way? Seller behavior and the Law of Supply are based on a seller's ability to cover costs and earn a profit. At very low prices, a seller may not be able to cover costs and would likely not be interested in

TABLE 3.2	*City Bakery's Weekly Supply of Bagels*

The Law of Supply is illustrated in this supply schedule, which shows that more bagels are supplied at higher prices.

Price per Bagel	Quantity Supplied per Week
$0.20	0
0.40	0
0.60	200
0.80	350
1.00	500
1.20	650
1.40	750
1.60	800

supplying the product. But as the price increased, a supplier could cover costs and perhaps earn a small profit. If a seller produced many products (as does City Bakery), it might produce some of the product for a small profit but concentrate on producing other items that yield more favorable returns. At higher prices, a seller would want to further increase the quantity supplied as it could cover additional costs from producing more and make greater profits.[2] The bakery, for example, might be willing to decrease its production of birthday cakes, danishes, eclairs, and other products in order to increase its production of bagels if the price and profit on bagels were extremely high.

We can easily understand the Law of Supply in relationship to our own labor that we supply in labor markets. Take campus tutoring as an example. If you were offered a job in the Economics Tutoring Center for $3 an hour, how many hours a week would you be willing to work? How much would you be willing to work if the wage were $10 an hour? $20 an hour?

Graphing Supply   Economists usually present supply, like demand, graphically, with price measured on the vertical axis and the quantity supplied measured on the horizontal axis. Each price–quantity combination from Table 3.2 appears in Figure 3.2, and a **supply curve** is drawn by connecting those points. Note that a supply curve slopes upward, showing that higher prices correlate with larger quantities supplied. Recall that the Law of Supply indicates a direct relationship between price and quantity supplied. Because direct relationships appear in graphs as upward-sloping lines, we can generalize that supply curves slope upward to reflect that direct relationship.

You might be amazed at how often we are affected by the Laws of Demand and Supply. Application 3.1, "The Laws of Demand and Supply," focuses on gasoline and organic milk and gives some situations where price had an important impact on the decisions and behaviors of buyers or sellers.

Supply Curve
A line on a graph that illustrates a supply schedule; slopes upward because of the direct relationship between price and quantity supplied.

---

[2]Is it valid to assume that the cost per bagel might increase as the bakery produces more bagels? Yes. For example, the owner might incur extra expenses from additional repairs on equipment because it is used more often, or producing more bagels might require that the employees of the bakery work overtime at a higher wage rate. See Chapter 12 for details on rising costs associated with increased production.

| FIGURE 3.2 | *City Bakery's Weekly Supply of Bagels* |

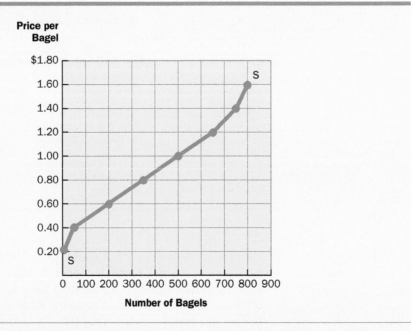

The upward-sloping supply curve illustrates the Law of Supply, showing that more is supplied at higher prices and less is supplied at lower prices.

MARKET DEMAND, MARKET SUPPLY, AND PRICE SETTING

Market Demand and Market Supply

Market
A place or situation in which the buyers and sellers of a product interact for the purpose of exchange.

Market Demand and Market Supply
The demand of all buyers and supply of all sellers in a market for a good or service; found by adding together all individual demand or supply schedules.

When buyers and sellers come together to exchange goods or services, they form **markets**. A market can arise anywhere—a store, eBay, used-car lot, stock exchange, or vending machine, for example. Once we speak of multiple buyers and sellers, we move from individual demand and supply to **market demand** and **market supply**. Market demand and market supply represent the sum of all individual quantities demanded and supplied of a product at each price in a market. For example, the market demand for an Academy Award-winning motion picture sums up all the individual demands to see the film. When we discuss markets, we are concerned with the sum of all buyers' and sellers' actions—rather than individual demand and supply decisions.

Markets and Price Setting

Markets perform the critical function of price setting as buyers and sellers interact and make economic choices. To see how markets operate to set prices, let's return to the bagel example, where we analyzed Zach's individual demand and City Bakery's individual supply of fresh-baked bagels.

Table 3.3 shows market demand and market supply schedules for fresh-baked bagels. We can find the market demand for bagels each week by adding together the number of bagels that Zach and all other buyers in this market would purchase at each price. Similarly, we can find market supply by adding together the quantity of

APPLICATION 3.1

THE LAWS OF DEMAND AND SUPPLY

Law of Demand

Gasoline   Gasoline prices often rise rapidly on the rumor of some event that will affect the supply of oil coming to refineries. And, if reality is attached to the rumor, there can be an extended period of high prices.

And when those prices rise, consumer frustration usually leads to altered behaviors in purchasing gasoline. Some people might drive a few miles to wholesale stores for discounted gas and some spend a lot of time waiting in line at the station with the cheapest price. People become more careful and consider the necessity of a trip to the mall or visits with friends and relatives, often forgoing them. One unfortunate result is the increase in thefts when prices go up by non-paying drivers pulling away from a gas pump.

If a price increase is sustained, more radical behavior changes occur. People car pool and use public transportation. They sell their gas guzzlers and search for and purchase vehicles with higher gas mileage. Sometimes people move to a neighborhood or suburb closer to work and the sports, cultural, and health amenities they frequent.

What drives these reactions to higher gas prices? We all have limited incomes, and paying more for gas means having less for other things like tuition, mortgage payments, and fresh produce. But, unlike many other consumer needs, the alternatives to putting gas in the tank aren't easy. It is not like switching to chicken when the price of beef increases. Can you just put a tank of corn-based ethanol in your vehicle or switch your internal combustion engine to an electric motor? Can you just zip over to the car dealership and switch out your car for a hybrid?

Law of Supply

Organic Milk   In the "olden" days, people went to the store and bought milk—milk was milk. Dairy farmers had few alternatives: They milked their cows and sent their product to the market. Today, we have choices about milk: whole, skim, 1 percent, 2 percent, and even chocolate. While these don't have a direct influence on dairy farmers, the latest opportunity for choice in milk selection—organic milk—certainly does.

Organic milk is a major product in the trend toward buying organic foods. To be labeled as organic milk, a set of federal standards must be met. These include guidelines about feed, soil, outdoor access for cows, processing operations, as well as a ban on antibiotics and growth hormones.

While the route to become an organic milk producer cannot be put in place overnight because time is needed to ensure that operations and herds meet the standards set to receive the organic label, dairy farmers now have an alternative to producing "regular" milk. This means that as the price of organic milk rises, farmers have an incentive to switch production from nonorganic to organic.

And, the price of organic milk is certainly higher than nonorganic milk. A visit to the Schnuck's supermarket in St. Louis in September 2015 revealed that a gallon of nonorganic 2 percent milk was $3.59. A gallon of organic 2 percent milk was $6.98.

There is evidence that the rise in price in organic milk is increasing the quantity supplied. A few years ago, organic milk could be found only in specialty health-food type stores. Today, supermarkets not only devote much shelf space to organic milk but, like the St. Louis grocery store, typically carry several labels or brands.

Shortage

Occurs in a market when the quantity demanded is greater than the quantity supplied, or when the product's price is below the equilibrium price.

bagels that City Bakery and all other sellers in this market would make available at each price. In the analysis of this market and those that follow, we assume that both buyers and sellers compete strongly with one another. No buyer or seller exerts any unusual or undue influence, and no price-controlling government regulation occurs.[3]

In the market shown in Table 3.3, the price for a fresh-baked bagel ranges from $0.20 through $1.60. What would happen in this market if the price were $0.20 per bagel? At $0.20, buyers would demand 30,000 bagels, and sellers would offer only 2,000 for sale. Thus, at a price of $0.20, the quantity supplied would fall short of the quantity demanded by 28,000 bagels (30,000 quantity demanded −2,000 quantity supplied): The market would experience a **shortage** of 28,000 bagels. In response to this

---

[3]A more technical definition of a market appears in Chapter 13. At this point, however, it is sufficient to know that a particular market is made up of a group of sellers that compete with each other for the same group of buyers. In other words, because of geographic distance, many separate markets for fresh-baked bagels arise. For instance, a market in Houston is not the same as a market in Seattle because each is composed of different buyers and sellers. In fact, in Houston, geographic distance causes many bagel markets to arise in various parts of the city.

TABLE 3.3	**Weekly Market Demand and Supply of Fresh-Baked Bagels**

Market demand and market supply illustrate the different amounts of a product that all buyers in a market would demand and all sellers in a market would supply at various prices.

Price per Bagel	Quantity Demanded	Quantity Supplied
$0.20	30,000	2,000
0.40	24,000	8,000
0.60	20,000	12,000
0.80	16,000	16,000
1.00	12,000	20,000
1.20	8,000	24,000
1.40	4,000	28,000
1.60	2,000	30,000

shortage, sellers who observed the number of buyers left unsatisfied in the market would raise the price and increase the quantity they would offer on the market (because of the Law of Supply). Once the price rose, the quantity demanded would fall (because of the Law of Demand), and the bagel shortage would shrink.

So, then, what would happen if the price were $0.40 per bagel? At $0.40, buyers would demand 24,000 bagels and suppliers would offer 8,000 bagels. The market would again experience a shortage, but of only 16,000 bagels (24,000 quantity demanded – 8,000 quantity supplied). Sellers would react to the shortage by raising prices above $0.40. As price increased, suppliers would offer more bagels and buyers would demand fewer bagels: The shortage would again shrink.

What would happen if sellers charged $1.60 per bagel? At $1.60, consumers would want to buy only 2,000 bagels, but sellers would offer 30,000 bagels for sale. The quantity supplied would exceed the quantity demanded by 28,000 bagels, or there would be a **surplus** of 28,000 bagels on the market. Sellers would react like any other seller with excess merchandise at a price consumers will not pay: They would lower their prices. As the price fell, the Law of Demand would go into operation, and some buyers who would not purchase bagels at $1.60 each would do so at the lower price. At the same time, because of the Law of Supply, the lower price would encourage suppliers to reduce the quantity supplied, and the surplus would diminish. If the price charged were $1.40, a surplus of 24,000 bagels would develop, sellers would again lower their price, and the surplus would again shrink.

Equilibrium Price and Equilibrium Quantity

The market in Table 3.3 appears to be moving automatically toward a price of $0.80, where the quantity demanded equals the quantity supplied at 16,000 bagels. If sellers charge $0.80 per bagel, no surpluses or shortages will arise and sellers will have no incentive to raise or lower price.

We call the price that sets buyers' plans equal to sellers' plans ($0.80) the **equilibrium price**. The quantity at which those plans are equal (16,000 bagels) is the **equilibrium quantity**. Thus, equilibrium price and equilibrium quantity are the price and quantity toward which a market will automatically move. At the equilibrium price, quantity demanded equals quantity supplied, and neither sellers nor buyers will

Surplus
Occurs in a market when the quantity supplied exceeds the quantity demanded, or when the product's price is above the equilibrium price.

Equilibrium Price and Equilibrium Quantity
The price and quantity where demand equals supply; price and quantity toward which a free market automatically moves.

Market Clearing Price

Equilibrium price; price at which the quantity demanded equals the quantity supplied.

want to change the price or the quantity. Economists often refer to the equilibrium price as the **market clearing price** because at this price the amount that buyers want exactly matches the amount that sellers offer, thereby clearing the market of the good or service.

If the price of a good or service is below its equilibrium level, a shortage will develop, and the price will be driven up toward equilibrium. If the price is above equilibrium, a surplus will develop, causing the price to fall toward equilibrium.

The bagel market shown in Table 3.3 is graphed in Figure 3.3. We draw the demand curve from the Price per Bagel and Quantity Demanded columns, and the supply curve from the Price per Bagel and Quantity Supplied columns. From the graph, we can easily see that the equilibrium price and quantity lie at the intersection of the supply and demand curves—in this case, at a price of $0.80 per bagel and a quantity of 16,000 bagels.

Shortages and surpluses can also be illustrated graphically. Figure 3.4a shows that at a price of $1.20 the quantity demanded is 8,000 bagels and the quantity supplied is 24,000 bagels, a surplus of 16,000 bagels. The difference between the demand and supply curves at $1.20 equals the amount of the surplus. Notice that as the price comes closer to the equilibrium level, the distance between the demand and supply curves narrows, and the surplus becomes smaller. Figure 3.4b measures the shortage of 8,000 bagels that would occur at a price of $0.60. Can you determine the shortage at a price of $0.20 per bagel?[4]

| FIGURE 3.3 | *Weekly Market Demand and Supply of Fresh-Baked Bagels* |

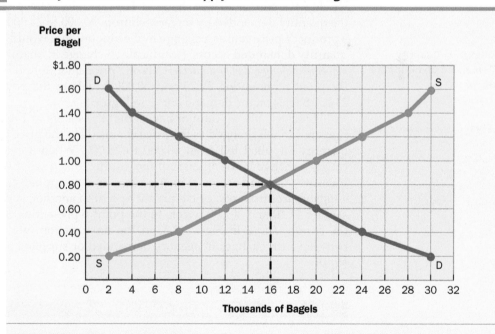

The equilibrium price and quantity in a market occur at the intersection of the market demand and supply curves. At equilibrium, the quantity demanded in a market equals the quantity supplied.

[4]A shortage of 28,000 bagels would result.

FIGURE 3.4   *Measuring Surpluses and Shortages on Demand and Supply Curves*

The surplus or shortage at a particular price is equal to the difference between the quantity demanded and the quantity supplied at that price.

Changes in Quantity Demanded and Quantity Supplied

When the price of bagels in Table 3.3 and Figure 3.3 changed, the amount that buyers would have purchased also changed. For example, as the price rose from $0.20 to $0.40, the quantity demanded by buyers fell from 30,000 to 24,000 bagels. When a change in a product's price causes a change in the amount that would be purchased, a **change in quantity demanded** occurs. Graphically, a change in quantity demanded appears as a *movement along a demand curve* from one price-quantity point to another, such as from the point representing $0.20 and 30,000 bagels to the point representing $0.40 and 24,000 bagels on the demand curve in Figure 3.3.

Change in Quantity Demanded and Quantity Supplied

A change in the amount of a product demanded or supplied that is caused by a change in its price; represented by a movement along a demand or supply curve from one price-quantity point to another.

Likewise, the amount of bagels that the sellers in Table 3.3 and Figure 3.3 were prepared to sell changed as the price changed. As the price fell from $1.60 to $1.40, the quantity supplied fell from 30,000 to 28,000. When a change in a product's price causes a change in the amount of the product that a seller would supply, a **change in quantity supplied** occurs. A change in quantity supplied appears as a *movement along a supply curve* from one price-quantity point to another, such as from the point representing $1.60 and 30,000 bagels to the point representing $1.40 and 28,000 bagels on the supply curve in Figure 3.3. In the next section, we emphasize the difference between such changes in *quantity* demanded or supplied and changes in demand or supply.

CHANGES IN DEMAND AND SUPPLY

When we introduced demand and supply, we emphasized that the buyers and sellers of a product respond both to the product's price and to nonprice considerations. Then, as we developed demand and supply schedules and curves, we held nonprice factors constant in order to focus on buyer and seller behavior in response to a price change. For example, when we derived Zach's demand for bagels, only the price of bagels was allowed to change. All nonprice factors such as Zach's income, the popularity of bagels, and the degree of substitutability between bagels and other foods were held constant.

Now it is time to no longer hold nonprice factors constant and to examine how nonprice factors influence buyer and seller behaviors—and ultimately how they influence market equilibrium.

Changes in Demand

A change in one or more nonprice factors influencing the demand for a product causes a **change in demand** for the product. Changes in nonprice factors cause demand schedules and curves to change as buyers develop new sets of plans. Someone's weekly demand for, say, a particular brand of cola could change because of a change in a nonprice factor influencing that demand. For example, suppose that Gwen, who has a demand for a particular cola, gets a raise. She might respond to the raise by buying more cola. We can illustrate this increase in Gwen's demand in Table 3.4, which shows Gwen's demand for the cola before and after a change in her income. Notice how the number of cans that Gwen demands in a week increases at each price. For example, at $1.00 a can the amount increases from 10 to 16.

Change in Demand

A change in the demand schedule and curve for a product caused by a change in a nonprice factor influencing the product's demand; the demand curve shifts to the right or left.

Nonprice Factors that Influence Demand

Nonprice factors such as income, taste, and expectations that help to determine the demand for a product.

Normal Good (or Service)

Income changes relate directly to the demand for the good or service.

Nonprice Factors That Influence Demand To help us see the key difference between price and nonprice factors, we can categorize major **nonprice factors that influence demand**.

♦ **Taste, fashion, and popularity**. The demand for "in" items typically increases; and when an item is "out," demand decreases. The recent focus on cupcakes, even fashioned as wedding cakes, has certainly shifted their demand to the right. A good, catchy advertising campaign that makes a product popular can increase demand.

♦ **Buyers' incomes**. Changes in can encourage people to buy more or less of an item. We label goods as **normal goods** when income changes relate directly to

---

TABLE 3.4   *Gwen's Weekly Demand Schedule for 12-Ounce Cans of Cola before and after an Increase in Income*

A change in a nonprice factor causes a change in the amount of an item demanded at each price. After an increase in Gwen's income, the number of cans of a particular cola she demands each week increases at every price.

Before		After	
Price per Can	Number of Cans Demanded Weekly	Price per Can	Number of Cans Demanded Weekly
$0.20	18	$0.20	24
0.40	16	0.40	22
0.60	14	0.60	20
0.80	12	0.80	18
1.00	10	1.00	16
1.20	8	1.20	14
1.40	6	1.40	12
1.60	4	1.60	10
1.80	2	1.80	8

changes in demand: Income increases generally lead to an increase in the demand for new cars. Goods are labeled as **inferior goods** when income changes relate inversely to changes in demand: Income increases generally lead to a decrease in the demand for used cars. While these categories can be subjective, some goods are easy to identify as normal or inferior. How would you label Ramen noodles, pro football game tickets, costume jewelry, fine watches, and vacation stays at a Marriott Resort or a Motel 6?

Inferior Good (or Service)
Income changes relate inversely to the demand for the good or service.

♦ **Buyers' expectations concerning future income, prices, or availabilities**. What people anticipate for the future affects behavior in the present. For example, if people think the price of gasoline will escalate in the coming weeks, they will fill their gas tanks as soon as possible and increase the current demand. What happens in local stores when a snowstorm is anticipated and news reports focus on a shortage of ice melt?

♦ **Prices of goods related as substitutes and complements**. Buyers' demand for a product can change when the price of an item they regard as a substitute or complement for that product changes. For example, people might buy more peanut butter to make sandwiches when the prices of cheese or processed turkey slices (substitutes for peanut butter) go up. And people might buy and send fewer holiday cards when the price of stamps (a complement to cards) increases.

♦ **Number of buyers in the market**. As the number of buyers in a market increases or decreases, so does demand. With people moving into newly renovated lofts in city neighborhoods, local restaurants and grocery stores have more customers. The reverse holds when residents begin to abandon a neighborhood.

Increases and Decreases in Demand   We can label a change in demand as either an increase in demand or a decrease in demand. An **increase in demand** means that buyers want to purchase more of a product at every price because one or more nonprice factors have changed. Graphically, an increase in demand causes the demand curve for a good or service to shift to the right.

Increase in Demand
A change in a nonprice influence on demand causes more of a product to be demanded at each price; the demand curve shifts to the right.

Such a shift is shown in Figure 3.5a, which illustrates Gwen's demand schedules for cola in Table 3.4. Curve D1 shows Gwen's original demand for cola before her change in income. When Gwen's income increases, and she wants to purchase more cola at each price, her demand schedule changes. When this new schedule is graphed in Figure 3.5a, the demand curve shifts to the right, to D2. Observe on the graph that at $0.80 she is now willing to buy 18 rather than 12 cans, and at $1.20 she is now willing to buy 14 rather than 8 cans. Clearly, she demands more at each price or has experienced an increase in demand.

Decrease in Demand
A change in a nonprice influence on demand causes less of a product to be demanded at each price; the demand curve shifts to the left.

A **decrease in demand** means that buyers want to purchase less of a product at every price because of a change in a nonprice factor. Graphically, a decrease in demand causes the demand curve to shift to the left. For example, U.S. consumers frequently change their vehicle preferences. At one time the large SUV was the choice of families. But today households are turning toward hybrids and away from large gas-guzzling SUVs. Figure 3.5b shows a change in the demand for large SUVs as consumer tastes change. Where 225,000 were demanded at a sticker price of $34,000 before the change in taste, only 125,000 are demanded after large SUVs become less popular.

In summary, an increase in demand means that more of a product is demanded at each price and the demand curve shifts to the right. A decrease in demand means that less is demanded at each price and the demand curve shifts to the left.

| FIGURE 3.5 | Increases and Decreases in Demand |

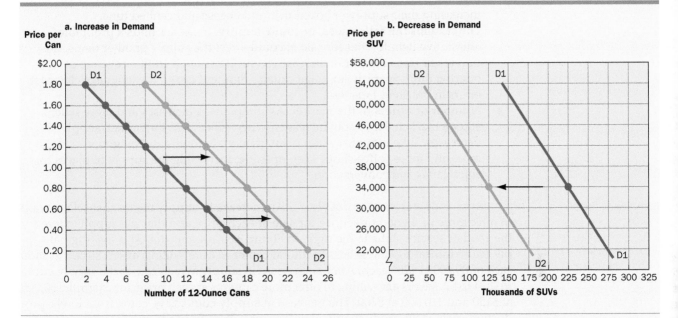

An increase in Gwen's demand for a cola causes the demand curve to shift to the right from D1 to D2, indicating that she now demands more cans of the cola at each price. A decrease in the demand for large SUVs causes the demand curve to shift to the left from D1 to D2, indicating that fewer are demanded at each price.

Changes in Supply

Changes in nonprice factors that influence supply cause entire supply schedules and curves to change, or cause **changes in supply**. Changes in these nonprice factors cause the supply curve to shift either to the right (an increase in supply) or to the left (a decrease in supply).

Change in Supply

A change in the supply schedule and curve for a product caused by a change in a nonprice factor influencing the product's supply; the supply curve shifts to the right or left.

Nonprice Factors Influencing Supply

Nonprice factors, such as the cost of production and the number of sellers in the market, that help to determine the supply of a product.

Nonprice Factors That Influence Supply   Just as for demand, we can categorize **nonprice factors that influence supply**.

♦ **Cost of producing an item**. When a seller experiences a change in the production costs of a good or service, more or less of that good can be made available at each price. Increases in production costs cause less to be made available. When the price of a barrel of crude oil (the basic material for refining gasoline) increases on the market, the supply of gasoline decreases. Decreases in production costs cause more to be made available. Technology has made it cheaper to produce many electronics on the market today.[5]

♦ **Expectations about future market conditions**. Just as with buyers, sellers can anticipate future conditions that affect their current behavior. When grocery

---

[5] Take care to distinguish between the terms *price* and *cost*. Price is the amount that an item can be sold for in the market. Cost is the expenditure required to produce the item.

managers anticipate that consumer incomes will fall, they may change their inventory and decrease their supply of fresh berries and imported cheeses while increasing their supply of boxed mac and cheese and canned tuna.

♦ **Other items the seller does, or could, supply**. If a seller finds a profitable alternative item to offer for sale, it could affect the supply of other items. If a university finds that it can increase its enrollment and tuition revenue by offering more Spanish language courses, it might lessen the language classes it offers in Polish or Japanese.

♦ **Number of sellers in the market**. As competition increases and more sellers enter a market, the supply increases. When sellers leave a market, supply decreases. Take the coffee shop phenomenon. In towns and neighborhoods, more and more coffee shops keep opening, increasing the supply of places to enjoy lattes and conversation.

Increase in Supply

A change in a nonprice influence on supply causes more of a product to be supplied at each price; the supply curve shifts to the right.

Increases and Decreases in Supply   An **increase in supply** means that sellers want to offer more of a good or service for sale at each price and that the supply curve for the good or service shifts to the right. In Figure 3.6a, assume that S1 is the original supply curve indicating that sellers of digital cameras were willing to sell 50,000 at $150 each or 80,000 at $200 each. After an increase in supply, which causes the supply curve to shift to S2, sellers are willing to offer more cameras at each price: for example, 80,000 at $150 and 110,000 at $200. The increase in supply could have come from lower production costs, new production technology, or sellers trying to increase sales now for fear of a weakening market in the future.

FIGURE 3.6   *Increases and Decreases In Supply*

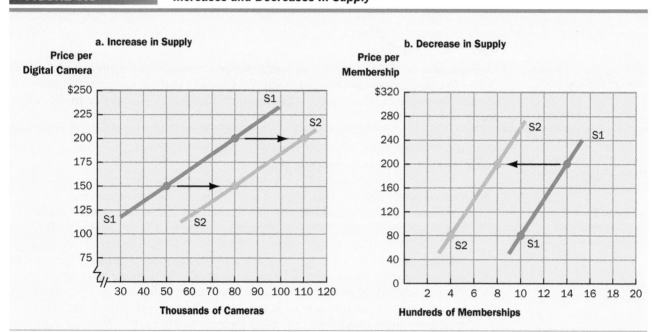

An increase in the supply of digital cameras causes the supply curve to shift to the right from S1 to S2, indicating that sellers offer more at each price. A decrease in the supply of health club memberships causes the supply curve to shift to the left from S1 to S2, indicating that fewer memberships are supplied at each price.

Decrease in Supply
A change in a nonprice influence on supply causes less of a product to be supplied at each price; the supply curve shifts to the left.

A **decrease in supply** means that sellers are willing to offer less of a product at each price because one or more nonprice factors have changed. Figure 3.6b shows the original supply curve for an area's health club memberships as S1, indicating that clubs were willing to sell 1,400 memberships at a price of $200 each. A decrease in supply, represented by a shift of the supply curve to S2, reveals that clubs are now willing to sell fewer memberships at each price, for example, only 800 at $200 each. Sellers could have decreased the supply because of increased wage, equipment, or liability insurance costs.

In summary, an increase in supply means that a larger quantity of a product is made available for sale at each price, causing the supply curve to shift to the right. A decrease in supply means that a smaller quantity is made available for sale at each price, causing the supply curve to shift to the left. Application 3.2, "Fads: Some In, Some Out," shows how nonprice factors influence the demand and supply of some items.

Changes in Quantity Demanded or Supplied and Changes in Demand or Supply: A Crucial Distinction

Be warned: We must maintain clear distinctions between *changes in quantity demanded and quantity supplied* and *changes in demand and supply*. Although the terms are similar, they refer to completely different concepts.

Changes in quantity demanded and quantity supplied arise *only* from changes in a product's price. Quantity is a variable tied to price. We illustrate the responses to price changes by movements along fixed demand or supply curves from one price–quantity combination to another. For example, the movement along the demand curve in Figure 3.7a from $20 and 100 units to $10 and 150 units illustrates an increase in quantity demanded caused by a decrease in price. The movement along the supply

---

APPLICATION 3.2

FADS: SOME IN, SOME OUT

Your professor might remember grandparents with kitchen appliances in harvest gold and avocado green. How exciting it was for them to be so "in" with refrigerators and stoves in the latest color.

All of us look back from time to time and laugh at ourselves as we wore clothing we wouldn't be caught in today—and certainly hope that no one has a photo of us in such an outrageous outfit. Yes, some folks will shudder in the future about wearing pajama bottoms to class.

And yet we get caught up in the latest clothing, the latest color of the year, and the latest food fad. We contribute mightily to changes in demand that inspire us to be trendy, or to abandon what is clearly out. Most of us are fortunate to be able to participate in the "good for you," "bad for you" environment that is set by health experts, fashion police, and corporate advertising budgets.

Take the pantone color of the year that is decided annually. In 2013, we had emerald green; in 2014, radiant orchid; and in 2015, the color of the year was marsala, said to be an earthy wine red. How many rooms were painted emerald green or orchid or marsala to be the latest? How many sweaters, ties, tote bags, and coordinating pillows showed up in one of these colors? By 2016, would all of that need to be replaced? Were paint cans or bottles of nail polish containing emerald green or orchid on sale in 2015?

But the most fickle trends can be found with the food we put in us. At one point, diets that promised better health were those that lowered "carbs" or carbohydrates, which are a source of energy found in bread, pasta, sugar, and other foods. Carbs became a no-no and college cafeterias, fast-food eateries, and homemakers were adjusting what they cooked and served. People turned to beef, pork, and other no-carb foods and shunned those baked goods and pasta. Some companies that produced carb-laden items struggled to find replacements. But have no fear. The low-carb replacements, like low-carb Doritos and Cheetos, and the rejection of pasta and bread didn't survive. We were on to no fat foods and the carbs were acceptable in the next diet fad. So, the question remains, how long we will put quinoa in us?

| FIGURE 3.7 | *Changes in Quantity Demanded and Quantity Supplied versus Changes in Demand and Supply* |

Changes in quantity demanded or quantity supplied are shown by movements along a fixed demand or supply curve, but with changes in demand or supply, the entire curve shifts.

curve in Figure 3.7b from $20 and 100 units to $10 and 50 units illustrates a decrease in quantity supplied caused by a decrease in price.

On the other hand, changes in demand and supply do not result from changes in a product's price. Rather, they result from changes in a nonprice determinant of demand or supply. Changes in demand or supply appear as shifts of the demand or supply curve to the right or left.

In Figure 3.7c, the demand curve shifts to the right from D1 to D2, or there is an increase in demand because of a change in a nonprice influence on that demand. For example, at a price of $20, the amount demanded increases from 100 to 150 units. These could be great super-sized pizzas that people might now order more often because word of their great taste has gotten around.

The shift of the supply curve in Figure 3.7d from S1 to S2 illustrates a decrease in supply. Fewer items are supplied at $20 and every other price because of a change in a nonprice factor. Perhaps this is a decrease in the supply of super-sized pizzas caused by a rise in the cost of cheese, a key ingredient.

You will find it easier to understand the behavior of buyers and sellers in markets, and how they react to various price and nonprice considerations, if you remember these distinctions.

CHANGES IN EQUILIBRIUM PRICE AND EQUILIBRIUM QUANTITY

We have seen that when nonprice factors affecting demand or supply change, demand or supply curves shift. Recall that the equilibrium price and quantity of a good or service appear at the intersection of its demand and supply curves. Therefore, whenever a product's demand or supply curve shifts, its equilibrium price and quantity change as well.

Can we analyze and predict how changes in buyer and seller behavior alter both the equilibrium price of a product and the quantity bought and sold? Yes, we can by using the following tools to order our thinking about such changes in market conditions. Let's consider separately how each change in demand and supply affects equilibrium price and quantity.

Effect of Increases and Decreases in Demand

Increase in Demand   How does an increase in demand affect a product's equilibrium price and quantity? Consider an item that becomes a fad. Suppose that volleyball becomes the "in" sport and that all over the country people are searching for volleyball nets to put in their yards and take to parks and beaches. Common sense would tell us that the volleyball net market might heat up with such an increase in demand, and price would rise. But even at this increased price, more nets would be sold. Let's examine the graphical analysis in Figure 3.8a to determine whether our common-sense analysis is correct.

S is the monthly market supply curve for volleyball nets, and D1 shows the monthly demand for volleyball nets before the sport becomes a fad. With supply curve S and demand curve D1, the equilibrium price is $40 per net, and the equilibrium quantity is 25,000 nets. As the game becomes really popular, the demand for volleyball nets increases, and the demand curve shifts to the right to D2. At the new equilibrium of S and D2, 35,000 nets are sold to buyers at a price of $80 each. Thus, an increase in the demand for a product causes both its equilibrium price and equilibrium quantity to increase.

Decrease in Demand   How does a decrease in demand affect a product's equilibrium price and quantity? Consider the market for mid-sized rental cars in a location popular with tourists during the summer months. Assume that S in Figure 3.8b is the weekly supply curve for mid-sized rental cars in this location and that D1 is the weekly demand curve for these cars during the summer. With S and D1, the equilibrium price is $300 per week and the equilibrium quantity is 1,200 cars.

But during the winter, fewer tourists visit this location and the demand for rental cars decreases. Figure 3.8b shows such a shift of the demand curve to the left from D1 to D2. As a result of this decrease in demand, the equilibrium price falls to $150 and the equilibrium quantity falls to 800. Thus, a decrease in the demand for a product causes both its equilibrium price and equilibrium quantity to fall. Consider the passing of a recent fad, like a singer who loses popularity with the young teen crowd. What happened to the price and quantity sold of that singer's recordings as the singer became less popular?

| FIGURE 3.8 | *Effect of Increases and Decreases in Demand* |

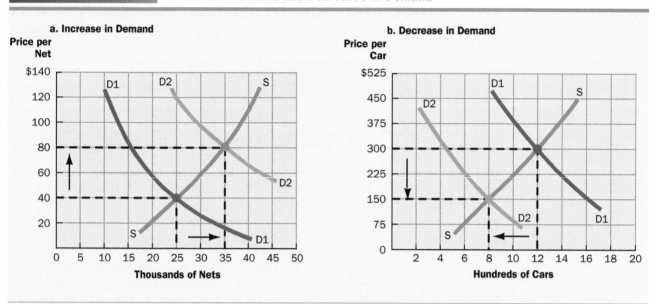

An increase in the demand for a product, such as volleyball nets, causes an increase in the product's equilibrium price and equilibrium quantity. A decrease in the demand for a product, such as rental cars, causes a decrease in the product's equilibrium price and equilibrium quantity.

Effect of Increases and Decreases in Supply

Increase in Supply   What effect does an increase in supply have on the equilibrium price and quantity of a product? We might respond immediately that an increase in the product's supply means that the price will fall and the amount sold will increase. Let's test this response.

Over the years, several products, such as cell phones, have become much more plentiful because technology has made them cheaper to produce and, hence, to supply. Many new companies have also entered the market. In Figure 3.9a, S1 and D are the original supply and demand curves for a type of cell phone. With this supply and demand, the equilibrium price is $100 a unit, and the equilibrium quantity is 2 million units. Later, as new technologies and new manufacturers impact the market, the supply curve shifts to S2. Following this increase in supply, the new equilibrium price is $60 per unit, and the equilibrium quantity is 6 million units. Thus, with an increase in supply, the equilibrium price falls and the equilibrium quantity increases.

Decrease in Supply   What will happen to a product's equilibrium price and quantity if supply falls? Assume that a virus is infecting chickens, causing fewer eggs to be produced, so that the supply of eggs decreases, but the demand for eggs does not change. D and S1 in Figure 3.9b are the demand and supply curves for eggs before the available amounts are reduced. With D and S1, the equilibrium price is $1.40 per dozen, and the equilibrium quantity is 12 million dozens. Suppose now that fewer eggs come to the market, causing the supply curve to shift to the left to S2. With this decrease in supply, the new equilibrium price is $2.10 per dozen, and the equilibrium quantity is 10 million dozens. Thus, a decrease in supply leads to an increase in the equilibrium price and a decrease in the equilibrium quantity of a product.

FIGURE 3.9   *Effect of Increases and Decreases In Supply*

An increase in the supply of a product, such as cell phones, causes a decrease in the product's equilibrium price and an increase in its equilibrium quantity. A decrease in the supply of a product, such as eggs, causes an increase in the product's equilibrium price and a decrease in its equilibrium quantity.

Test Your Understanding, "Changes in Demand and Supply," lets you evaluate your skill at analyzing the factors causing demand and supply curves to shift and the effects of those shifts on equilibrium price and quantity.

Effect of Changes in Both Demand and Supply

In each of the preceding examples, we held constant one side of the market—either demand or supply—to examine the effects of changes in nonprice factors. In reality, both demand and supply might change simultaneously. For example, both the demand and supply of volleyball nets or cell phones might increase at the same time. Although such simultaneous changes are not illustrated here, your graphing skills should enable you to arrive at some conclusions about them.[6]

[6] If you try graphing simultaneous changes in demand and supply, you should get the following results.

Change	Equilibrium Price Will	Equilibrium Quantity Will
Demand and supply both increase	Increase, decrease, or stay the same	Increase
Demand and supply both decrease	Increase, decrease, or stay the same	Decrease
Demand increases and supply decreases	Increase	Increase, decrease, or stay the same
Demand decreases and supply increases	Decrease	Increase, decrease, or stay the same

In the cases where equilibrium price or quantity can increase, decrease, or stay the same, the actual change depends on the size of the changes in supply and demand. For example, an increase in demand that is larger than an increase in supply will result in an increase in price, whereas an increase in demand that is smaller than an increase in supply will result in a decrease in price.

Changes in Demand and Supply

Complete the table by determining which of the following each example represents.
a. An increase in demand   d. A decrease in supply
b. A decrease in demand   e. No change in either demand or supply
c. An increase in supply

Example	Result	Graphic Change	Change in Equilibrium Price	Change in Equilibrium Quantity
1. Some peach growers drop out of the local farmers market.	d.	supply curve shifts to the left	increase	decrease
2. A clothing retailer increases the effectiveness of its advertising campaign without increasing its advertising costs.				
3. A waste hauler finds its costs increasing because of environmental regulations.				
4. Tuition and fees increase at a community college.				
5. Buyers in the upscale motorcycle market experience a decline in their incomes.				
6. Fans become more supportive of a pro football team because it has a winning season.				
7. Technology makes it cheaper to produce e-readers.				
8. Women decide that they no longer want very large purses.				
9. Buyers expect that incandescent light bulbs will be unavailable in the future.				
10. Local movie theaters raise their ticket prices.				
11. Secondhand, used clothing store buyers experience a rise in their incomes.				
12. Several new stores selling mountain bikes open in town.				
13. The price of apples goes down.				
14. A seller of a popular soft drink shifts more resources toward that product after discontinuing production of a less successful beverage.				

Answers can be found at the back of the book.

LIMITING PRICE MOVEMENTS

Up to this point, we have dealt with free-market conditions, where buyers and sellers interact independently without any kind of outside intervention. But sometimes governments step into certain markets and interfere with free pricing by setting upper or lower limits on prices. State governments, for example, have limited prices on utilities, home mortgage interest rates, and interest rates on credit cards. The federal government has propped up prices for other goods and services, such as labor (with the minimum wage law) and some farm products. We can use supply and demand analysis to explain how this type of government intervention affects market conditions.

Price Ceilings

Legally imposed **upper price limits**, called **price ceilings**, keep prices from rising above certain levels. Price ceilings have been placed on gas and electricity in some states, rental apartments, and the interest rates people pay to borrow money. If the market goes to equilibrium at a price below the government-established upper legal limit, or ceiling, the ceiling will have no impact on buyers and sellers: The ceiling will not take effect. But if the market tries to go to an equilibrium price above its upper legal limit, the price ceiling will take effect and a shortage will occur.

For example, suppose that a state law sets the maximum interest rate on student loans at 12 percent. Such laws that set maximum interest rates are called **usury laws**. Figure 3.10a gives the demand for and the supply of loans when the equilibrium interest rate is lower than the ceiling rate—so the ceiling has no impact. Here borrowers' and lenders' plans balance at an interest rate of 10 percent, and $10 million is loaned each month. Do you see that, because the government-imposed ceiling on interest rates lies above the equilibrium rate, the usury law is irrelevant in this case?

Suppose, however, that more students want to borrow money, causing the demand curve to shift to the right. This new situation appears in Figure 3.10b. If the market were free to go to equilibrium after this increase in demand, the new interest rate would be 14 percent. However, the upper legal limit is 12 percent, so lenders may charge no more. Rather than increasing from 10 to 14 percent, the interest rate can rise only to the legal limit of 12 percent. At the 12 percent rate, borrowers would like to have $16 million in loans, but lenders would provide only $12 million in funds. At the 12 percent usury limit, there would be a $4 million shortage of funds for borrowing. Thus, when the free-market equilibrium price is above the ceiling, a shortage develops.

Price Floors

Legally imposed **lower price limits**, called **price floors**, prevent prices from falling below certain levels. A good example of a price floor is the minimum wage law, which sets the minimum hourly payment that many workers can earn. As long as the equilibrium price of a good or service is above its price floor, the free market will not be affected by the limit. However, if the equilibrium price of a good or service falls below the floor, buyers will be forced to pay the government-set price. Because this legally imposed price is higher than the price the free market would have permitted, sellers offer more than buyers want to buy at the set price, and surpluses develop.

Consider the effect of a minimum wage law. Suppose that the minimum wage is set at $8 per hour. If the supply and demand for a certain type of labor are as shown in

FIGURE 3.10   *Effect of a Price Ceiling on a Market*

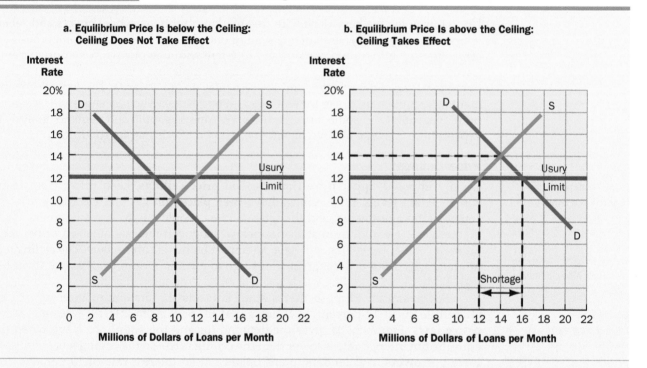

**a. Equilibrium Price Is below the Ceiling:
Ceiling Does Not Take Effect**

**b. Equilibrium Price Is above the Ceiling:
Ceiling Takes Effect**

When the equilibrium price for a product is below its legal upper limit, the price ceiling has no effect on the market. When the equilibrium price is above its legal upper limit, the price ceiling takes effect and a shortage develops.

Figure 3.11a, the minimum wage will have no impact on the market. The equilibrium wage of $9 per hour is greater than the minimum wage, and the number of available workers equals the number demanded.

Now suppose that the government raises the minimum wage from $8 to $10 per hour but that neither the supply nor demand for labor changes in this market. Because the equilibrium wage rate is $9, or less than the minimum wage, the $10 minimum wage will take effect. Figure 3.11b shows the market condition with the new minimum wage rate. At $10 per hour, the number of workers demanded falls to 1,000, and the number of willing and able workers rises to 1,200. The price floor has created a surplus of 200 people who cannot obtain a job in this market. Thus, when the free-market equilibrium price is below the government-imposed floor, a surplus develops.

In summary, price ceilings, when they take effect, keep prices lower than they would otherwise be and result in shortages. Price floors, when they take effect, keep prices higher than they would otherwise be and result in surpluses. Price ceilings and price floors benefit some groups and hurt others. Application 3.3, "Is Rent Control a Good Thing or a Bad Thing?" explores some issues around the setting of ceilings on rents for apartments in New York City. Hopefully, the application will help you recognize why it is difficult to arrive at a clear answer to questions like who gains and who loses from rent control.

Up for Debate, "Is It a Mistake to Raise the Minimum Wage?" applies this same question to labor markets. Who gains and who loses from an increase in the minimum wage?

FIGURE 3.11   *Effect of a Price Floor on a Market*

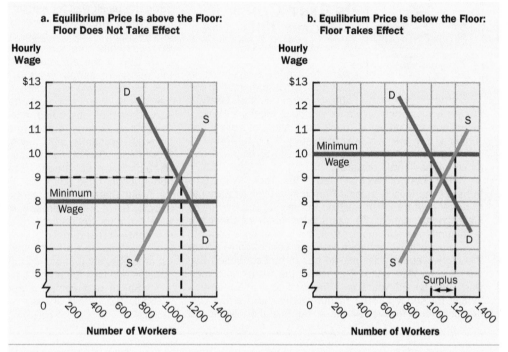

a. Equilibrium Price Is above the Floor:
Floor Does Not Take Effect

b. Equilibrium Price Is below the Floor:
Floor Takes Effect

When the equilibrium price for a resource or a product is above its legal lower limit, the price floor has no effect on the market. When the equilibrium price is below its floor, the floor takes effect and a surplus develops.

We should note that government can also affect markets by influencing the supply side of the market. For example, local governments can limit the number of trash haulers in an area and the Food and Drug Administration controls the flow of new medications onto the market.

PRICE ELASTICITY OF DEMAND AND SUPPLY

One message in this chapter should be clear: The quantity of a good or service that consumers demand relates inversely to its price, and the quantity of a good or service that sellers supply relates directly to its price. But there is another piece of the buyer and seller puzzle. How much will quantities demanded and supplied change as buyers and sellers respond to a particular price change? If a bike shop offered a huge sale—say, 50 percent off—on its finest bicycles, would people line up around the block to buy top-of-the-line bikes for $2,000 (half off of the usual retail price of $4,000)? Would they more likely show up for a store's 50 percent sale on designer purses? When the price of an item—say, peanut butter—increases, do consumers respond weakly, demanding just a little less of the item, or strongly, demanding much less? What about their response when the price of steak or fine wine increases?

We can ask similar questions about sellers. Would automobile manufacturers respond weakly or strongly if the price of luxury cars dropped by 10 percent? How much corn would farmers plant next year if the price of corn rose 50 percent this year?

APPLICATION 3.3

Is Rent Control a Good Thing or a Bad Thing?

Want to start an argument in New York City? Just bring up the subject of rent control. Likely, if there are two people within earshot, one will think it's wonderful and the other will think that, short of selling the Yankees, it is the best way to destroy the City. And what can begin as a civil discussion on the topic may well end as an intense battle of words.

Rent control was instituted in New York City in 1943 to help keep local residents from losing their apartments to better-paid transient wartime workers who could afford higher rents. Almost 75 years later, many of the city's rental units are still subject to some type of price control.

Part of the argument over rent control comes from the stories about what people pay in rent-controlled versus uncontrolled units. There was the 80-year-old man who lived for 50 years in a four-bedroom in Greenwich Village for about $330 a month, where the average two-bedroom rents for over $4,700 a month and a town house down the block was for sale at $5 million. And there was the woman who lived for over 30 years in a rent-controlled one-bedroom suite in a hotel overlooking Central Park for $8 a day while hotel guests paid up to $1,600 a day.

One of the arguments against rent control is that the rents are simply too low. One landlord complained that people in his neighborhood pay more to park than they pay to rent. Landlords often say that it is difficult to survive as their costs rise. Another argument is that rent control has nothing to do with need. Many well-to-do people who can comfortably pay more live in rent-controlled apartments. Sometimes a lone person lives in a spacious three-bedroom apartment because moving to a smaller non-rent-controlled unit would be more costly.

But there are arguments on the other side of the debate. There are renters who might be living on the street were it not for the controlled rate. A number of people in rent-controlled and rent-stabilized units have low incomes. Rent controls can also be credited for providing people with the stability that comes from being able to raise their families and develop a network of friends in one location.

So, is rent control a good thing or a bad thing? Probably the safest answer is "it depends on who you talk to."

How would computer hardware and software companies respond to a decrease in the price of their products?

Price Elasticity

A measure of the strength of buyers' or sellers' responses to a price change.

Price Elastic

A strong response to a price change; occurs when the percentage change in the quantity demanded or supplied is greater than the percentage change in price.

Price Inelastic

A weak response to a price change; occurs when the percentage change in the quantity demanded or supplied is less than the percentage change in price.

Price elasticity measures the strength of buyers' or sellers' responses to a price change. If buyers or sellers respond strongly to a price change, we say that their demand or supply is price elastic. More specifically, demand or supply is considered to be **price elastic** when a given percentage change in price (say, 5 percent) results in a *larger* percentage change in quantity demanded or supplied (say, 6 percent or 10 percent). If buyers or sellers are less sensitive to a price change—that is, if their response is weak—we say that their demand or supply is price inelastic. Again, more specifically, demand or supply would be **price inelastic** if a given percentage change in price (say, 8 percent) resulted in *a smaller* percentage change in quantity demanded or supplied (say, 7 percent or 3 percent). The mechanics of calculating elasticities of demand and supply are explained in the appendix to this chapter.

Price Elasticity of Demand

Why do consumers respond strongly to some price changes and weakly to others? In other words, what determines whether demand will be relatively price elastic or inelastic?

Factors Affecting Price Elasticity of Demand   Several categories of factors affect price elasticity of demand.

- ♦ **Necessities versus luxury goods**. Generally, people respond more strongly when the price of a luxury good changes than they do when the price of a necessity changes. You would expect a fairly strong response by buyers to a price change on dinners at an upscale restaurant or cruises to Alaska. However, when a product is absolutely essential, people do not change their purchases very much, even when a price rise is substantial. Typically, consumers respond weakly to price changes on necessities like trips to the ER, water, gasoline, electricity, and prescription drugs. It is a lot easier to cut back on vacation plans than antibiotics.

◆ **Substitutes**. The availability of acceptable substitutes influences consumer responses to product price changes. If buyers can switch to alternative products when prices rise, they respond more elastically to a price change. If movie theater ticket prices increase, you can go to a concert or use Netflixs. On the other hand, if prices increase for a good or service with no or few substitutes, buyers may have little choice but to pay the higher prices: a price-inelastic response. When the price of a required textbook increases, for example, students have little choice but to buy it.

◆ **Proportion of income**. The portion of income that a purchase requires influences buyer responses to price changes. A person with an average income will likely respond weakly to a 20 percent increase in the price of a birthday card but respond strongly to a 20 percent increase in college tuition. The greater the portion of income required for a good or service, the stronger the reaction will be to a price change for that good or service, or the more price elastic will be the response.

IS IT A MISTAKE TO RAISE THE MINIMUM WAGE?

Issue   *In recent years, the size of the minimum wage has brought protests around the country, especially by fast-food workers who were challenging the $7.25 per hour federal rate in 2015. Some states have raised their minimum wage above the federal level, some over $9.00 per hour, in support of a higher wage. Congress has raised the minimum wage many times since it was enacted in the 1930s. There are those who support raising the wage to provide more income for workers and those who oppose it because of the increased costs for businesses. So, we are left with the question, "is it a mistake to raise the minimum wage?"*

Yes   It is a bad idea to raise the minimum wage. The higher wage may help workers who will now take home more income, but it also raises the cost of doing business for a worker's employer. These increased costs may force some small or financially strapped businesses to rethink their workforce needs and hire fewer workers in the future—or even lay workers off now. An increase in the minimum wage might be enough to push an employer to finally buy the machine that will, once and for all, replace workers or to move its production operations to China, India, or some other country. And if a business cannot absorb the increased costs, it may be forced to close. What good does it do workers to be promised an increase in wages, only to lose their jobs as a result of that increase?

Also, if the new minimum wage falls above the equilibrium wage in a market, it will lead to an increase in the number of available workers at the very time that businesses are cutting back the number of workers demanded. Some people who would have had jobs at the lower equilibrium wage will now find themselves unable to obtain work. This may be a particular problem for college students looking for summer employment.

No   It is not a mistake to raise the minimum wage for several reasons. For one, a scan of job advertisements shows that many people, such as those working in fast-food restaurants and college students seeking summer jobs, are already earning more than the minimum wage. To say these people would have greater difficulty finding or keeping work may overstate the problem created by an increase in the minimum wage.

But perhaps the strongest argument for raising the minimum wage is the inability to subsist on this wage. A person working 8 hours a day, five days a week, 50 weeks a year at the minimum wage of $7.25 per hour would earn $14,500 for the year. By comparison, the official poverty-guidelines income in 2014 (when the minimum wage was $7.25) was $11,670 for the average one-person household. This reality is important for the minimum wage earner who is the only, or primary, source of income for a family. Not all minimum wage workers are high school or college students working part-time while living in a higher income household.

Source: The 2014 poverty level is from U.S. Department of Health and Human Services, "2014 Poverty Guidelines," http://aspe.hhs.gov/poverty/14poverty.

Price Elasticity of Demand and Total Revenue   The seller of a product needs to know whether buyers will react strongly or weakly to a price change. Without this information, a seller may be surprised by the impact that a price change has on the total revenue received from selling the product. This important concept could cause tremendous problems for the local transit authority, a theater, a homebuilder, a college, or any other seller that misgauges buyer reaction to a price change.

When customers react strongly, or there is an **elastic response to a price change**, total revenue moves in the opposite direction from the price change. If price is increased and consumers react strongly by demanding much less of a product, total revenue (price times quantity) will fall—the strong quantity response brings total revenue down with it. If price is decreased and consumers react strongly by demanding much more, total revenue will increase. If the owner of an Irish dance studio has 100 students who pay $50 a month for lessons, she receives $5,000 in revenue (100 × $50). If she raises the price to $60 a month and there is a strong student reaction causing a student drop to 75, her total revenue falls to $4,500 (75 × $60).

When buyers react weakly, or there is an **inelastic response to a price change**, total revenue moves in the same direction as the price change. If price is increased and consumers react weakly by demanding a little less, total revenue will rise with the price increase—the weak quantity response will not be enough to offset the effect of the price increase. If price is decreased and consumers react weakly by demanding just a little more, total revenue will decrease. Take the Irish dance studio with its 100 students paying $50 a month for lessons. If the owner increases the price to $60 and loses just 10 students, total revenue will increase to $5,400 (90 × $60).

Sellers need to know whether people will respond weakly or strongly to a price change. Think about your own college or university. When administrators ponder changing the price of tuition, they can make good decisions about their budgets and expenditures if they know whether students will respond elastically or inelastically to a given change. Imagine the surprise the finance office staff faces when they believe that students will not care about an increase they have made, but they do and react elastically.

Table 3.5 summarizes the effect on total revenue with elastic and inelastic price changes.

Elastic Price Change and Total Revenue
Total revenue moves in the opposite direction of a price change when consumers react strongly or elastically.

Inelastic Price Change and Total Revenue
Total revenue moves in the same direction of a price change when consumers react weakly or inelastically.

TABLE 3.5   *Price Elasticity of Demand and Total Revenue*

Total revenue moves in the opposite direction of the price change when demand is elastic, and total revenue moves in the same direction as the price change when demand is inelastic.

If the Price Change Is	
Elastic	Inelastic
Total revenue and price move in opposite directions	Total revenue and price move in the same direction
↑P → strong ↓Qd → ↓TR	↑P → weak ↓Qd → ↑TR
↓P → strong ↑Qd → ↑TR	↓P → weak ↑Qd → ↓TR

APPLICATION 3.4

PEANUT BUTTER: A YUMMY STAPLE

Families, food banks, and other organizations devoted to hunger relief began to notice significant increases in the price of peanut butter in the fall of 2011. As the price of a ton of peanuts increased to about $1,200 a ton from $450 a ton a year earlier, companies that produce well-known brands of this staple announced increases of up to 40 percent. And some folks jokingly said that children needed to hoard the Reese's Peanut Butter cups in their trick-or-treat bags.

Peanut butter is a necessity in the everyday life of many people. Not only do kids love the stuff—experts saying that the average kid will eat 1,500 PB&J sandwiches before high school—but it also provides an important and usually cheap source of protein. For some, peanut butter is the key ingredient in a meal; for others it is a snack.

Food banks rely on peanut butter for its popularity, long shelf life, and nutritional value. Moreover, the therapeutic food often used to treat malnourished children in poor countries, such as Haiti, is created from ground roasted peanuts.

The quick rise in the price of peanut butter in 2011 and 2012 is a classic example of the application of supply and demand. Nonprice factors drove changes in the market and price influenced the quantity demanded.

Clearly, the underlying problem of the rise in peanut butter prices was on the supply side. It began with a short crop in the summer of 2010 when a drought negatively affected the supply of good, usable peanut kernels. But the summer of 2011 was calamitous for peanut farmers. Record-breaking heat and drought in the two largest peanut growing states, Georgia and Texas, brought a small crop. Since the peanut plant flowers above ground but eventually grows downward into the soil, some plants were badly scorched by the sun and never developed while other plants produced a low-yielding, poor-quality crop. And, as the planting season approached, some farmers switched their fields to cotton or soybeans since the prices on these major crops were high.

As the supply of peanuts quite literally dried up, the price began to rise. And now there was concern about how families and food banks and hunger relief groups would deal with the rising price of this nutritional commodity. Moreover, a recession with its high unemployment increased the dependence on this cheap source of food by struggling families and also increased the number of clients reaching out to food banks.

Some food banks said they needed to buy less peanut butter to deal with their own limited budgets and that they were receiving fewer donations of peanut butter. This resulted in a cutback on the amount of peanut butter they gave out. Further limitations to supply came from the smaller amount of peanut butter available through U.S. agricultural commodity programs for schools and nonprofits.

Price Elasticity of Supply

Price elasticity also applies to sellers. How much more will sellers be willing to supply at a higher price, and how much less at a lower price? If sellers respond strongly to price changes, we say that supply is price elastic. If they respond weakly to changes in price, we say that supply is price inelastic.

Factors Affecting Price Elasticity of Supply   For most sellers, price elasticity of supply is primarily affected by time. The more time sellers have to react to a price change, the greater is the ability to change the quantity supplied, and the more elastic is the response. Suppose that a particular style of jeans becomes very popular and the increase in demand pushes up its price. Sellers of these jeans can initially supply only as many pairs as the inventory on hand allows. Thus, the immediate response to this increase in price is inelastic. But given more time, sellers can order more jeans and respond with a larger increase in the quantity supplied—a more elastic response. Given even more time, other sellers and manufacturers may see how popular this style has become and may offer many more for sale. The jeans supply becomes even more price elastic.

Application 3.4, "Peanut Butter: A Yummy Staple," looks at how supply and demand played out in the market for peanut butter. Can you explain how the relationship between demand and supply influenced price? How have nonprice factors and the elasticities of both demand and supply played a role?

Summary

1. Demand refers to a buyer's willingness and ability to purchase different amounts of a product at different prices in a given period of time when all nonprice factors are held constant. The relationship between a product's price and the quantity buyers plan to purchase at each price is typically shown in a demand schedule or graph called a demand curve, which slopes downward. Demand schedules and curves reflect an inverse relationship between price and quantity demanded, called the Law of Demand. The Law of Demand results from limited buyers' incomes and substitute products.

2. A supply schedule shows the different amounts of a product that a seller would offer in the market at different prices in a given time period when all nonprice factors are held constant. Graphically, a supply schedule appears as an upward-sloping supply curve because of the Law of Supply, which states that there is a direct relationship between price and quantity supplied. The Law of Supply follows from sellers' efforts to cover costs and earn profits.

3. The total amount of a product demanded by all buyers in a market at a particular price is market demand, and the total amount made available by all sellers at that price is market supply.

4. The price that equalizes buyers' and sellers' plans, and toward which a market automatically moves, is called the equilibrium price. Equilibrium price is at the intersection of the product's market demand and supply curves. If the market price of a product is above its equilibrium price, a surplus of the product will appear on the market, and forces will bring the price down to its equilibrium level. If the market price of a product is below its equilibrium level, a shortage will result, and forces will bring the price up to its equilibrium level.

5. Nonprice factors also influence buyers' and sellers' behaviors. Changes in these nonprice factors lead to shifts in demand and supply curves. An increase in demand or supply means that buyers are demanding or sellers are supplying more of a product at each price, and the demand or supply curve has shifted to the right. When less of a product is demanded or supplied at each price, demand or supply decreases, and the demand or supply curve shifts to the left. Because the equilibrium price and quantity of a product are shown by the intersection of its demand and supply curves, increases or decreases in demand and/or supply cause the product's equilibrium price and quantity to change.

6. It is important to understand the difference between changes in demand and/or supply, shown by shifts in the demand and/or supply curves, and changes in quantity demanded and/or quantity supplied, shown by *movements along* existing demand and/or supply curves. Changes in price cause *movements along* a demand or supply curve from one price–quantity point to another, or cause changes in quantity demanded or quantity supplied. Changes in nonprice influences cause shifts of demand or supply curves, or cause changes in demand or supply.

7. If government sets a price ceiling for a good or service, and the equilibrium price is above the ceiling, the ceiling price takes effect and a shortage develops. If

government sets a price floor for a good or service, and the equilibrium price is below the floor, the floor takes effect and a surplus develops.

8. Price elasticity measures buyers' and sellers' sensitivities to changes in the price of a product. Demand or supply is price elastic when the quantity demanded or supplied changes by a greater percentage than the percentage price change. Demand or supply is price inelastic when the quantity demanded or supplied changes by a smaller percentage than the percentage price change. Elasticity of demand is influenced by whether the product is a luxury or a necessity, the availability of substitutes, and the price of the product relative to the buyer's income. Time is the major determinant of a product's price elasticity of supply.

9. When the response by buyers to a price change is inelastic, total revenue moves in the same direction as the price change. When the response by buyers to a price change is elastic, total revenue moves in the opposite direction of the price change.

10. *(From the appendix)* Price elasticity of demand or supply is calculated by dividing the percentage change in quantity demanded or quantity supplied by the percentage change in price. If the resulting number is greater than 1, demand or supply is price elastic. If the resulting number is less than 1, demand or supply is price inelastic. And if the resulting number is exactly 1, demand or supply is unitary elastic.

Key Terms and Concepts

Demand
Demand schedule
Law of Demand
Demand curve
Supply
Supply schedule
Law of Supply
Supply curve
Markets
Market demand and market supply
Shortage
Surplus
Equilibrium price and equilibrium quantity
Market clearing price
Change in quantity demanded and quantity supplied
Change in demand
Nonprice factors influencing demand
Normal good (or service)

Inferior good (or service)
Increase in demand
Decrease in demand
Change in supply
Nonprice factors influencing supply
Increase in supply
Decrease in supply
Price ceiling (upper price limit)
Usury laws
Price floor (lower price limit)
Price elasticity
Price elastic
Price inelastic
Elastic price change and total revenue
Inelastic price change and total revenue

From the appendix
Elasticity coefficient
Unitary price elastic

1. Define the Law of Demand and Law of Supply. Draw a demand curve and a supply curve and explain how each curve illustrates the related law. Identify the factors underlying these laws.

2. Surpluses and shortages are temporary conditions in freely operating markets. Explain what causes each and how these temporary conditions resolve themselves in free markets.

3. Distinguish between a change in quantity demanded or quantity supplied and a change in demand or supply. How would you represent each change graphically?

4. Explain how each of the following would cause demand or supply to shift and how the equilibrium price and quantity for the good or service in question would change.
    a. A decrease in the number of builders in a housing market
    b. Expectations by automobile buyers that new, more efficient hybrids will be on the market next year
    c. An increase in the popularity of organic peanut butter
    d. A wage increase paid to a hospital's employees
    e. A cost-reducing innovation adopted by the manufacturers of washing machines
    f. The identification of a food as high in cholesterol
    g. A fall in income by buyers of fine antique jewelry

5. Plot the following demand and supply schedules on the accompanying graph, and answer questions a through e.
    a. What is the equilibrium price and equilibrium quantity?
    b. How much of a shortage or surplus would occur at $2.50?
    c. How much of a shortage or surplus would occur at $7.50?
    d. What would happen if the government established a price floor of $8.75 on this item?
    e. What would happen if the government established a price ceiling of $8.75 on this item?

Price per Item	Quantity Demanded	Quantity Supplied
$1.25	150	0
2.50	140	50
3.75	125	60
5.00	105	70
6.25	80	80
7.50	50	90
8.75	10	100
10.00	0	110

Price

$10.00
8.75
7.50
6.25
5.00
3.75
2.50
1.25

0 20 40 60 80 100 120 140 160

Quantity

6. What does price elasticity of demand and of supply measure? Identify factors that affect these price elasticities and give examples of each.

7. (*From the appendix*) Calculate the price elasticity coefficient of demand or supply for each of the following. Identify whether the response is elastic, inelastic, or unitary elastic.
    a. The number of cans of a soft drink demanded increases by 30 percent after its price decreases by 40 percent.
    b. The number of available apartments increases by 8 percent following a 6 percent increase in rents.
    c. The number of Cobb salads demanded at a restaurant increases from 60 to 80 per week when the price falls from $10.00 to $9.00.
    d. At a price of $200, 10,000 gas grills were supplied each month. Since the price increased to $250, 14,000 are supplied each month.
    e. The number of carpet cleaning machines rented each weekend falls from 50 to 40 following an increase in the rental charge from $20 to $24.

Discussion Questions

1. People pay attention to political upheavals in foreign countries, local and national elections in the United States, and environmental and other developments around the world because such events can directly affect their lives. But the functioning of markets may go relatively unnoticed because market effects are usually less obvious or dramatic. How does the functioning of markets affect your everyday life? If prices were not set in markets, how else could they be determined? How would this affect your life?

2. We placed great emphasis on the distinction between changes in quantity demanded and quantity supplied and changes in demand and supply. Why would an automobile dealership treat buyers' reactions to price changes differently than it would their reactions to changes in everything else that affects their purchasing decisions? Does that seller have any control over nonprice determinants of demand, such as buyer taste? How and why?

3. Both real and perceived differences arise among the kinds of entertainment, food, and clothing that are popular among buyers in different age groups. Pick one product from each of these three categories that is popular with your age group and explain how its demand and equilibrium price would change if it were marketed to people older than you. How would the cost of this increased marketing affect its equilibrium price and quantity?

4. Minimum wage laws keep many workers' hourly wages above what they would be in the absence of such laws. Do minimum wage laws help or hurt college students looking for summer work?

5. If a government-imposed price ceiling or floor helps some people but hurts others, what factors do you think the government should consider before deciding on such a policy?

6. Give some examples of goods and services where a consumer's response to a price change might typically be elastic and where it might typically be inelastic. Explain why the response would be elastic or inelastic.

7. How does price elasticity of demand determine whether a seller's revenue will increase or decrease following an increase in the price of its product? What impact might the cost of production have on a seller's decision to change its price?

Critical Thinking Case 3

How Do Supply and Demand Work in Health Care?

Critical Thinking Skills

Identifying exceptions to a norm

Comparing applications of a principle in different settings

Economic Concepts

Supply and demand

Pricing

About a year ago, John decided that, with 160,000 miles on his 2006 Volvo, the time had come to buy a new car. He was successful in his job and wanted to update his look. Because John knew this would be expensive, he spent a good bit of time reading reports about different models, shopping online, and going from dealer to dealer. Finally, after three weeks of visits to showrooms, John found a car he really liked. Its price tag was $31,000. John wanted the car, but this didn't stop him from trying to talk the dealer down from the $31,000 sticker price because he had done enough research to know this was possible. After a few days of phone calls back and forth, John bought the car for $22,000 plus his 2006 Volvo in trade.

About three weeks later, John called a doctor after having severe knee pain following a fall. The doctor told him to come in for a checkup as soon as possible. After an exam and some tests, John's doctor recommended surgery. With John's agreement, the doctor scheduled all of the routine presurgery testing as well as the surgery at South City Hospital where he is on staff. There are other hospitals closer to John's home, but John didn't bother to ask about going to one of them. He also did not ask about the costs involved with the testing and surgery.

Shortly after arriving at the hospital, John was assigned to a room on the third floor. He was surprised to see how many beds on the floor were empty. After surgery and post-op recovery, John's doctor gave him two prescriptions, released him from the hospital, and set appointments for checkups and physical therapy. John collected his belongings, paid his co-payment for his health insurance, and hobbled out the door. On his way home, he filled and paid for his prescriptions. He didn't bother to ask the pharmacist if there were cheaper generic drugs he could use in place of his prescriptions. He was just happy to be on his way home.

Later in the month John totaled up the bills for his doctor's visits, hospital treatment, medications, and therapy. They came to $31,000.

Questions

1. Contrary to conventional economics, physicians (the suppliers) typically decide the quantity and type of health care services their patients (the demanders) will purchase. What is it about medical services that usually allows the supplier to determine the demand?

2. Suppose a person who knows nothing about auto maintenance takes a car in for its 30,000-mile checkup. The service manager reads off a list of repairs that need to be done. In your opinion, will this person act like John did on learning the doctor's diagnosis? Does the market for auto repairs behave like the market for medical care? Should it?

3. Most people have a large part of their health care expenses paid by an insurance provider. Explain how this might lead patients to pay little attention to the price of their treatment. Other than insurance coverage, what other factors would cause a patient to pay little attention to the price of a treatment?

4. Conventional economics suggests that a business with unsold, or surplus, merchandise will lower its price to attract buyers. Do you think that a physician would lower the price of a procedure or a hospital would lower its daily bed rate to attract patients?

Goals and Problems of the Macroeconomy: Employment, Prices, and Production

CHAPTER OBJECTIVES

Introduce the problem of unemployment—its causes, consequences, and related data and concepts—and the goal of full employment.

Discuss inflation—its causes, consequences, and measures.

Define full production and economic growth and introduce GDP, the primary measure of production.

Describe problems associated with simultaneously reaching full employment, full production, and price stability.

This chapter begins the section of the textbook devoted to macroeconomics, which is the study of the economy as a whole, or the "big picture." Macroeconomics brings us such topics as aggregate (total) employment and production, unemployment, inflation, economic growth, money, and government stabilization policies. (Microeconomics, which focuses on decision making by individual units in the economy, is covered in Part 3 of this textbook.) The study of macroeconomics will help you to understand the roles the household, business, and government sectors play in the economy, and how the sectors relate to each other. We will also learn about problems that arise in the big picture economy and how those problems can be resolved.

Before we begin any analysis, we need to become familiar with some basic terms and concepts involving employment, production, and prices. These three areas are the sources of the major problems of the macroeconomy: unemployment, falling production, and inflation. They are also the basis for the major goals of the macroeconomy: full employment, full production and economic growth, and stable prices. These problems and goals will be explored in this chapter.

In the United States, full employment, full production and economic growth, and stable prices are regarded as important economic goals. As noted in Chapter 2, Congress enacted the Employment Act of 1946 to permit the government to help in creating an economic environment that would lead to the achievement of these goals. In this act, the government does not ensure that these goals will be achieved. Rather, it commits to providing an environment that will lead to their achievement.

UNEMPLOYMENT AND FULL EMPLOYMENT

Unemployment
Resources available for production are not being used.

One of the primary macroeconomic goals in the United States is employment for all available factors of production, or the minimization of unemployment. **Unemployment** means that a resource available for production is not being used. While machines, raw materials, warehouses, and trucks can all be unemployed, our primary concern is the unemployment of people who would like to be working but are not. This concern results because the consequences of unemployment among people are obviously more striking.

The most dramatic siege of unemployment the United States has ever witnessed occurred in the Great Depression of the 1930s. From 1932 through 1935, the unemployment rate stayed at 20 percent or more of the civilian labor force, and, in 1933, it reached almost 25 percent.[1]

Consequences of Unemployment

There is concern about unemployment, especially among workers, because of several undesirable consequences.

Recall that economics is about scarcity: not enough resources to satisfy unlimited wants and needs. When resources are unemployed, fewer goods and services are produced, and scarcity is intensified. Think about how many more goods and services could be produced if all resources were put to work.

In addition to the impact of unemployment on society's levels of output, unemployment causes hardships for people who would like to be working but are not. Without a job and an income, spending levels must be cut back, causing adversity that could be dramatic if unemployment is prolonged. In 2010 and 2011 as the economy stalled and decent income producing jobs declined, housing foreclosures rose and food pantries and free lunch recipients increased.

There is also ample evidence that there are psychological and physiological costs associated with unemployment. A number of studies have shown that depression, suicide, mental hospitalization, ulcers, and even the common cold can be affected by being out of work. Application 4.1, "What's at Stake When a Job is Lost?" goes into more detail about the adverse economic and social consequences that can befall the unemployed and those around them.

Types of Unemployment

Before unemployment can be remedied, we need to understand its cause. There is no single cause of unemployment; instead there are three main sources: (1) friction in the labor market, (2) cyclical or periodic changes in the demand for goods and services, and (3) changes in the structure of the economy. These three sources provide a framework for us to define the primary types of unemployment:

- ◆ frictional unemployment,
- ◆ cyclical unemployment, and
- ◆ structural unemployment.[2]

---

[1] U.S. Bureau of the Census, *Historical Statistics of the United States, Colonial Times to 1957* (Washington, DC: U.S. Government Printing Office, 1960), Series D 46–47, p. 73.

[2] A fourth type of unemployment, called seasonal unemployment, is not discussed here. The seasonally unemployed are those who lose their jobs at the same time each year because of weather changes or tradition. Farmworkers unemployed in the winter when land is out of production and teachers unemployed in the summer because of traditional school-year schedules are examples of the seasonally unemployed. Because it occurs predictably each year and can be planned for well in advance, seasonal unemployment need not be a problem.

APPLICATION 4.1

WHAT'S AT STAKE WHEN A JOB IS LOST?

What causes a person to feel good? According to Sigmund Freud, two main anchors of mental health are love and work. The impact of love on mental health should come as no surprise, but work? People like to complain about work: so-and-so at the office, the meeting that refused to end, the surprise "I need it now" visit from the boss, and other annoyances.

All these complaints notwithstanding, work can have a huge positive impact on a person's sense of well-being. Regrettably, this sometimes becomes apparent only after a job has been lost.

What do people lose when their jobs disappear and the world they've taken for granted is replaced by something much less certain? One important dimension of loss and uncertainty is obviously economic. The loss of a job can dramatically heighten a household's economic insecurity. Now that the job is gone, how much will spending need to be cut? Will we be able to meet our rent or mortgage and auto payments? What's going to happen to our credit card debt? Will we be able to afford our daughter's tuition?

And the economic concerns are not just about right now. The loss of a job can make the future very cloudy.

The length of unemployment and its impact on a household's savings and borrowing are unknown, as is the income from a future job.

But the impact of job loss can go far beyond economics. The everyday structure and routine provided by going to work are gone. This, in turn, can disrupt and dramatically change household responsibilities, authority, and schedules. Also gone is the status conferred by employment, and along with it may go a person's sense of self-esteem, confidence, and contribution to the household or community. Finally, it can be hard to maintain friendships if they are with people with whom a person used to work and no longer frequently sees.

What personal and social consequences can come from job loss? Studies indicate that job loss can cause depression, increased anxiety, and a greater risk for suicide, alcohol abuse, traffic accidents, and criminal or violent behavior. Those close to people who have lost their jobs can suffer as well. Spouses of people who have lost their jobs have been shown to have a higher incidence of psychiatric disorders than do spouses of people who are working. Not surprisingly, unemployment has been linked to spouse and child abuse, and it is a contributing factor to separation and divorce.

Based on: Richard H. Price, Daniel S. Friedland, and Amiram D. Vinokur, "Job Loss: Hard Times and Eroded Identity," in *Perspectives on Loss: A Sourcebook*, ed. John H. Harvey (Philadelphia: Brunner/Mazel, 1998), pp. 303–310.

Frictional Unemployment　　Some job seekers have voluntarily quit a job to search for another one. Some may be entering the job market for the first time or after a period of not looking for work. These job seekers will likely experience a short period of unemployment while they send out applications, follow up leads, and interview with prospective employers. The inability to make quick and smooth transitions from old employment situations to new jobs comes from "friction" in the labor market. Thus, the **frictionally unemployed** are job seekers voluntarily out of work for a short period of time while they job search.

Frictional Unemployment
Occurs when people are voluntarily out of work for a short period of time while searching for a job.

In a large, complex economy like the United States, people are always voluntarily unemployed: We always have some frictional unemployment. These job seekers may have quit a job because they were unhappy with it, want to relocate or change their occupation, or have some other reason. Because frictional unemployment always exists, when we say that the economy is at full employment, we do *not* mean that 100 percent of the labor force is working. Rather, **full employment** means that everyone in the labor force except the frictionally unemployed is working.

Full Employment
Occurs when only those voluntarily out of work are unemployed, or the unemployment rate includes only frictional unemployment.

Cyclical Unemployment　　Market economies go through upswings and downswings in production called business cycles. Periodically, the economy falls into a downswing, or recession, during which the demand for goods and services decreases. When this happens, workers producing those goods and services may be involuntarily laid off.

Cyclical Unemployment
Involuntary unemployment that results from a downswing in a business cycle, or a recession.

This type of unemployment is termed **cyclical unemployment** because it is the result of a recession, or a downswing in the business cycle.

Cyclical unemployment is a matter of serious concern because, unlike frictional unemployment, it is involuntary and continues until the economy breaks out of the recession. A downturn could last a few months and involve a relatively small number of workers, or it could last for several years and extend to millions of households. As we noted earlier, the unemployment rate was at 20 percent or more for several years during the Great Depression. More recently, the unemployment rate rose from 4.6 percent in 2007 to 9.6 percent in 2010 due largely to a cyclical downswing in the economy.[3]

Some industries are more sensitive to changes in general economic conditions, and workers in these industries are particularly vulnerable to cyclical unemployment. When a recession is looming, consumers may postpone purchases of durable goods, such as new homes and automobiles, and businesses may postpone, or even cancel, purchases of capital goods, such as heavy machinery and buildings. As sales decline, workers in these industries may be laid off. Auto, heavy manufacturing, and construction workers are among those especially susceptible to cyclical unemployment.

Structural Unemployment
Involuntary unemployment that results when a worker's job is no longer part of the production structure of the economy.

Structural Unemployment   Like cyclical unemployment, **structural unemployment** is involuntary. It occurs when a worker loses a job because that job is no longer a part of the structure of the economy. The good or service the worker produced may no longer be demanded or may now be made in a way that eliminates that particular job. Unlike cyclical unemployment, structural unemployment offers no prospect for rehire in the future.

In today's fast-paced economy, there are many examples of structural unemployment. With up-to-date computers and software, fewer people are needed to perform clerical tasks in offices. High-tech automated equipment is replacing manufacturing workers in industries like automobiles; reorganizations are eliminating administrators and mid-level managers; the ability to produce goods cheaply in another country has caused the closure of many domestic manufacturing facilities; banking transactions online lessen the need for tellers; and in the arts, studio musicians and graphic artists are being replaced by sophisticated software.

A structurally unemployed person may need to find a new occupation, or retrain, or relocate. It may also impose a hardship on older workers who face competition with younger workers available at a lower salary.

Continued technological advancements, efforts by firms to operate more efficiently, and foreign competition promise to bring about more structural changes in the U.S. economy and to threaten many types of blue-collar and white-collar jobs. There is also some concern that the middle class is shrinking as semiskilled jobs are eliminated, leaving a workforce of highly paid, highly skilled workers and poorly paid, unskilled workers. Retraining workers and lifelong education are essential to meet changing job requirements in the U.S. economy.

Employment and Unemployment Measures and Statistics

In this section as well as others in this chapter and the textbook, there are references to important economic performance measures. These are often used by the media but most certainly by those who try to gauge the current state of the economy or to study it over a longer historical trend.

---

[3]See Table 4.1.

This text provides the latest available data at the time of its publication and gives you an indication of how those data have changed over time. If you want the current, latest data or if you want to delve deeper into the history of a data set, it is easy to do. The federal government collects this information and makes it available on websites that various bureaus maintain:

♦ The annual *Economic Report of the President*, released each February, contains extensive data appendices of a large number of economic indicators. The tables typically contain data over some time span, and the format is easy to read. You can access the *Economic Report* through www.whitehouse.org or www.gpo.gov/fdsys.

♦ The Bureau of Labor Statistics gathers and publishes employment and overall price level information such as the Consumer Price Index. There is a wealth of national and regional information as well as aggregated and subset numbers. You can access these at www.bls.gov.

♦ The Bureau of Economic Analysis (BEA) collects and publishes data regarding production, such as the Gross Domestic Product (GDP), and related areas like consumer spending, as well as regional and international product and income data. You can access these at www.bea.gov.

The data tables in this text are sourced so that you can easily find additional current or historical data relevant to that table. See the footnotes in each table for the data source.

Labor Force, Participation Rates, and Unemployment   When we talk about the labor force, the employed, and the unemployed, whom do we include, and how do we arrive at the numbers we use?

Labor Force

All persons 16 years of age and older who are working or actively seeking work.

The **labor force** is defined as all persons 16 years of age and older who are working or actively seeking work. If a person is capable of working but is not working and not interested in seeking work, then that person is not included in the labor force. It is the activity directed toward employment, not the capability of holding a job, that determines whether a person is or is not in the labor force.

Table 4.1 gives some frequently reported statistics on the labor force for selected years. The second and third columns of the table give, respectively, the number of people eligible for, and the number actually in, the labor force.[4] It is important to appreciate how many millions of people are in the U.S. labor force: almost 156 million in 2014.

Participation Rate

The percentage of some specified group that is in the labor force.

Participation rates for the labor force are given in the fourth column of Table 4.1. The term **participation rate** refers to the percentage of some group that is in the labor force. The group could be the entire eligible population, women, persons in different age groups, and so on. According to Table 4.1, in 2014, 62.9 percent of those eligible for the labor force were in the labor force. That is, approximately 156 million people out of a population group of approximately 248 million were employed or seeking work.

Unemployment Rate

The percentage of the labor force that is unemployed and actively seeking work.

The fifth and sixth columns of Table 4.1 give some data on the unemployed. Column five shows the number of unemployed persons in the labor force, and column six gives the **unemployment rate**, which is the percentage of the labor force that is unemployed and actively seeking work. For example, the unemployment rate of

[4]All figures in this table are for the noninstitutional civilian population, which is all people 16 years of age and older who are living in the United States and are not confined to penal, mental, senior-nursing, or other institutions and are not on active duty with the armed forces.

| TABLE 4.1 | | *The Labor Force, the Participation Rate, and Unemployment*[a] |

Many labor-related statistics are collected in the United States. Some of the most important are the labor force, the participation rate, and the unemployment rate.

Year	Population Eligible for Labor Force[b]	Civilian Labor Force	Participation Rate	Unemployed Persons	Unemployment Rate
1929	—	49,180,000	—	1,550,000	3.2%
1933	—	51,590,000	—	12,830,000	24.9
1940	99,840,000	55,640,000	55.7%	8,120,000	14.6
1945	94,090,000	53,860,000	57.2	1,040,000	1.9
1950	104,995,000	62,208,000	59.2	3,288,000	5.3
1955	109,683,000	65,023,000	59.3	2,852,000	4.4
1960	117,245,000	69,628,000	59.4	3,852,000	5.5
1965	126,513,000	74,455,000	58.9	3,366,000	4.5
1970	137,085,000	82,771,000	60.4	4,093,000	4.9
1975	153,153,000	93,775,000	61.2	7,929,000	8.5
1980	167,745,000	106,940,000	63.8	7,637,000	7.1
1985	178,206,000	115,461,000	64.8	8,312,000	7.2
1990	189,164,000	125,840,000	66.5	7,047,000	5.6
1995	198,584,000	132,304,000	66.6	7,404,000	5.6
2000	212,577,000	142,583,000	67.1	5,692,000	4.0
2001	215,092,000	143,734,000	66.8	6,801,000	4.7
2002	217,570,000	144,863,000	66.6	8,378,000	5.8
2003	221,168,000	146,510,000	66.2	8,774,000	6.0
2004	223,357,000	147,401,000	66.0	8,149,000	5.5
2005	226,082,000	149,320,000	66.0	7,591,000	5.1
2006	228,815,000	151,428,000	66.2	7,001,000	4.6
2007	231,867,000	153,124,000	66.0	7,078,000	4.6
2008	233,788,000	154,287,000	66.0	8,924,000	5.8
2009	235,801,000	154,142,000	65.4	14,265,000	9.3
2010	237,830,000	153,889,000	64.7	14,825,000	9.6
2011	239,618,000	153,617,000	64.1	13,747,000	8.9
2012	243,284,000	154,975,000	63.7	12,506,000	8.1
2013	245,679,000	155,389,000	63.2	11,460,000	7.4
2014	247,947,000	155,922,000	62.9	9,617,000	6.2

[a]Some adjustments in the population definitions that affect the year-to-year comparability of the data have been made over time. For additional information concerning these adjustments, see the source for this table.

[b]This and all other columns refer to the noninstitutional civilian population.

Source: *Economic Report of the President* (Washington, DC: U.S. Government Printing Office, 2012), Table B-35; Table B-11, 2015 *Report*.

8.9 percent in 2011 indicates that 13,747,000 persons in a labor force of 153,617,000 were unemployed and actively seeking work.

Participation rates are important because when examined over time they show us changes in the labor force. For example, we can see in Table 4.1 that the overall participation rate has been dropping since 2000, a matter for concern and speculation about the causes of this decline. Table 4.2 shows participation rates for various groups.

TABLE 4.2	*Participation Rates: Civilian Labor Force and Subgroups, Selected Years*

Participation rates differ among subgroups in the labor force. Changes in participation rates affect the composition of the labor force over time.

Group[a]	1992	2002	2012
Overall	66.4%	66.6%	63.7%
Men	75.8	74.1	70.2
Women	57.8	59.6	57.7
Teenagers (16–19 years)	51.3	47.4	34.3
Workers 55 years and older	29.7	34.5	40.5

[a] Includes persons 16 years of age and older in the civilian population.

Source: http://data.bls.gov/cgi-bin/print.pl/emp/ep_table_303.htm.

For example, it indicates that 57.7 percent of women over 16 were in the labor force in 2012.

While this table provides some indication of falling participation rates, it does not show that prior to 1970 the participation rate of women grew substantially, while the rate for men slowly declined. One interesting observation from Table 4.2 is the sizeable drop by teenagers in the labor force and the considerable rise by older workers in recent years. We could surmise that many jobs typically filled by teenagers, such as grocery checkers and baggers, are now filled by older workers who have experienced structural unemployment in their previous higher-paying positions.

Table 4.3 gives unemployment rates for various groups in the labor force. Notice the disparity in the unemployment rate among these groups. Married men and those with a college degree tend to fare better in the job market. Teenagers and those with less education tend to fare worse. These data raise an important policy question: Should government unemployment programs be directed toward the unemployed generally or toward specific groups?

TABLE 4.3	*Unemployment Rates: All Workers and Labor Force Subgroups*

Over the years, some groups in the labor force, such as teenagers, have faced more severe unemployment problems than other groups.

Group	Unemployment Rate in 2014
All workers	6.2%
Men	6.3
Women	6.1
Married men, spouse present	3.4
Women, widowed, divorced, or separated	6.6
Teenagers (16–19 years old)	19.6
High school graduates, no college	6.0
Bachelor's degree and higher	3.2

Source: Bureau of Labor Statistics, Household Data Annual Averages, Tables 3, 7, 24, www.bls.gov.

Calculating Unemployment Statistics   The U.S. Department of Labor, Bureau of Labor Statistics (BLS), calculates unemployment rates and other labor force data on a monthly and annual basis.[5] Each month's calculations are published by the BLS, and the overall unemployment rate is given wide coverage by the media. Contrary to what many people think, unemployment statistics are not based on numbers reported to the U.S. government by state employment offices. Rather, they are derived from a survey conducted for the BLS, called the Current Population Survey.

Each month a scientifically developed sample of households from across the United States is surveyed through interviews. On the basis of their responses, persons are classified as employed, unemployed, or not in the labor force.

Many people find the requirements to be classified as employed a surprise. A person is classified as employed if, during the survey week, that person

- did *any* work—even just 1 hour—as a paid employee, or in his or her own business, profession, or on his or her own farm;
- worked without pay for 15 or more hours in a family-operated business; or
- was temporarily away from a job or business due to illness, weather, vacation, labor-management disputes, or personal reasons.

As a result of the way in which we officially classify the employment status of people, many who are seeking to work more hours or full-time while doing limited work for themselves or others (even just 1 hour of work per week) show up as "employed" in government data.

Interpreting Unemployment Statistics

There are some subtle, but important, details we should keep in mind when evaluating unemployment statistics.

Sometimes people become **discouraged workers**: They search unsuccessfully for a job for a long time, then lose hope for employment, give up the job search, and drop out of the labor force. Because the unemployment rate measures only those who are unemployed and *actively* seeking work, discouraged workers are excluded from the statistic: They are not counted as unemployed. By excluding discouraged workers, the unemployment rate understates the true level of unemployment in the economy. The number of discouraged workers changes with economic conditions. It is higher when the economy is in a downswing and work is harder to find than when the economy is close to full employment and work is easier to find.

The overall unemployment rate is a national figure and does not tell us the unemployment situation in various parts of the country. With such a diversity of industries in the United States, it is possible that a slowdown in one of them, such as defense-related airplane manufacturing, will have a significant regional impact that is greater than the national numbers indicate. Think about the region in which you live. What impact would a slowdown in one of your major regional industries have on your area?

The overall unemployment rate provides no information about the jobs held by the employed. It does not indicate how many people classified as employed are

---

[5]For additional information see Bureau of Labor Statistics, "How the Government Measures Unemployment," http://www.gls.gov/cps/cps_htgm.htm.

working part-time but are seeking permanent full-time work. Recall that even 1 hour of work can label a person as employed. With the increasing costs of health insurance and other benefits, there has been substantial growth in temporary and part-time employment.

Underemployment

A resource is not used to its fullest productive capability.

The overall unemployment rate does not provide information about those who are underemployed. **Underemployment** occurs when the full capabilities and skills of a resource are not utilized. Many people with valuable skills and good educations will accept unskilled jobs rather than be unemployed. When times are tough due to a prolonged downturn in the economy, people will often "take what they can get" in order to pay the rent and put food on the table. Sometimes college graduates or those with years of professional employment spend time as food servers because it pays the bills.

The Goal of Full Employment

As stated earlier, full employment is a major macroeconomic goal. However, full employment does *not* mean that 100 percent of the labor force is working. It means that only those who are voluntarily out of work are unemployed.

What is the unemployment rate at which full employment occurs? What percentage of the labor force tends to be voluntarily, or frictionally, unemployed? There are no hard-and-fast answers to these questions.

The rate of unemployment associated with full employment has changed over time. Over the past few decades, we have thought full employment was anywhere between 4 percent and 6 percent. As changes in the structure of the economy have occurred, we have periodically reevaluated the unemployment rate associated with full employment. Changes in the composition of the labor force brought about by the increased participation of women and changes in government unemployment compensation payments have contributed to this reevaluation. But, importantly, finding the unemployment rate associated with full employment has been complicated by the growth in temporary and part-time work where there tends to be more work and where people who accept these types of jobs are counted as employed, even though they want to work full-time.

Conceptually, full employment means that all resources available for production are *fully* utilized. Thus, the statistic called "full employment" may not perfectly represent the economic concept of full employment.

The ultimate test of where the full employment rate is may be inflationary pressure. As you will soon learn in the next section, a market economy that is operating at full employment, or at capacity, has a tendency to experience inflation.

Natural Rate of Unemployment

The unemployment rate that includes the frictionally and structurally unemployed; occurs when cyclical unemployment is eliminated.

The Natural Rate of Unemployment Some economists believe that achieving the **natural rate of unemployment**, a different measure than full employment, should be the goal of the macroeconomy. The natural rate of unemployment includes the frictionally and structurally unemployed or is the rate at which there is no cyclical unemployment. Because it includes the structurally unemployed, the natural rate is higher than the full employment rate and can be achieved with more unemployed workers. The natural rate of unemployment has become a popular goal with some policymakers because traditional macroeconomic stabilization tools, which will be introduced in the next few chapters, are more suited to dealing with cyclical than with structural unemployment. Also, cyclical unemployment is typically of shorter duration than structural unemployment.

INFLATION AND STABLE PRICES

Inflation
An increase in the general level of prices.

Another major macroeconomic goal in the United States is to maintain stable prices, or to control inflation. Like unemployment, inflation can have serious consequences. **Inflation** occurs when there is an increase in the general level of prices. It does not mean that prices are high, but rather that they are increasing. For example, assume that over the past two years the price of a certain collection of goods has been stable at $100 in country A and has gone up from $10 to $30 in country B. Country B, not country A, faces a problem with inflation. Inflation refers to price movements, not price levels.

Since inflation refers to an increase in the *general level* of prices, the price of every good and service need not increase. An inflation rate of 7 percent does not mean that all prices are increasing by 7 percent. Rather, it means that, on average, prices are going up by that amount. Also, an increase in the general level of prices is not necessarily a matter of concern. An economy with an inflation rate of 2 or 3 percent a year does not have a problem. But, when prices increase quickly by a large percentage, such as 8 percent to 10 percent or more per year, inflation becomes a serious issue. When inflation rages out of control and prices increase by enormous amounts such as a million or more percent as was the case in Germany in the 1920s and Yugoslavia in the 1990s, it is termed **hyperinflation**.

Hyperinflation
Extremely rapid increases in the general level of prices.

Consequences of Inflation

When an economy experiences inflation, several problems emerge. Inflation can

- ♦ intensify scarcity when income does not rise as quickly as prices;
- ♦ penalize some groups, such as savers and lenders receiving low interest rates;
- ♦ change the value of assets; and
- ♦ be politically and socially destabilizing.

Money (Nominal) Income
Income measured in terms of current dollars.

Inflation and Income   Unemployment intensifies scarcity by reducing or even terminating the incomes of some people. Inflation can also reduce a person's income—by reducing the purchasing power of money. With inflation, a given amount of **money**, or **nominal**, **income**—income measured in terms of current dollars—buys fewer goods and services. Expressed differently, inflation causes **real income**, or income measured in terms of the goods and services that a sum of money income can purchase, to fall. As a result, people's scarcity problems increase when money incomes do not rise as rapidly as prices.

Real Income
Income measured in terms of the goods and services that can be purchased with a particular amount of money income.

How much must money income increase in the face of inflation to sustain the same purchasing power, or real income, from year to year? Figure 4.1 shows a person who had $35,000 in 1990 to spend (or save) *after* all income-based taxes including Social Security and Medicare were paid. By 2015, that person needed $63,395 after taxes just to keep pace with 1990.

Inflation hits some income groups harder than others, such as people living on a fixed income like a pension. If the size of a pension check remains unchanged while prices keep rising, the purchasing power of that check keeps shrinking. Over time, persons dependent on fixed incomes may suffer greatly from a declining standard of living. For example, if Figure 4.1 applied to a person who retired in 1990 and began receiving a fixed $35,000 a year pension, that person would have serious problems as inflation rose and there was no adjustment in the pension.

FIGURE 4.1   *The Purchasing Power of Income*

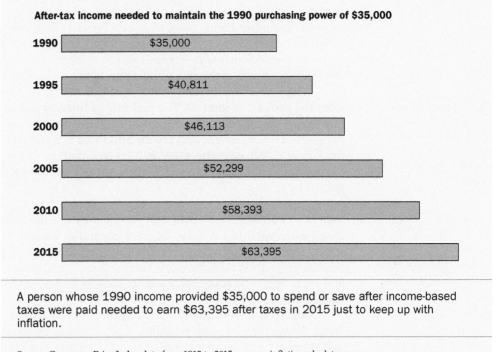

After-tax income needed to maintain the 1990 purchasing power of $35,000

Year	Amount
1990	$35,000
1995	$40,811
2000	$46,113
2005	$52,299
2010	$58,393
2015	$63,395

A person whose 1990 income provided $35,000 to spend or save after income-based taxes were paid needed to earn $63,395 after taxes in 2015 just to keep up with inflation.

Source: Consumer Price Index data from 1913 to 2015, www.usinflationcalculator.com.

Contract workers may also be hurt by inflation if their contracted wage increases are less than the inflation rate. For example, the teachers in a school district might sign a contract that provides for an annual wage increase of 4 percent and then encounter an inflation rate of 9 percent. To avoid this situation, many contracts provide **cost-of-living adjustments (COLAs)**, which are automatic wage or payment increases when prices go up.

Cost-of-Living Adjustment (COLA)
An arrangement whereby an individual's wages automatically increase with inflation.

Inflation and the Interest Rate   Lenders, borrowers, and savers refer to the price of money as an **interest rate**. Interest rates determine how much savers receive for their money, how much borrowers pay for loans, and how much lenders receive for making a loan.

Interest Rate
The price of money; determines the return to savers and lenders of money, and the cost to borrowers.

Those who save can be hurt by inflation if the interest rate they receive is less than the rate of inflation. For example, if you put $10,000 in a three-year certificate of deposit that earns 3 percent interest a year and the inflation rate averages 5 percent a year during this time, at the end of the three years, the $10,000 plus interest is worth less in terms of its purchasing power than it was when you put it in the bank. Also, the income tax on the interest earned from the money further reduces its buying power.

Lenders may also be hurt by inflation if the interest rate they charge is less than the rate of inflation and if the terms of the loans are fixed and cannot be altered to allow interest rate increases. This problem sometimes occurs when a lender makes a long-term loan commitment.[6] Experience has taught many lenders to transfer risks to borrowers. Many home mortgages are currently made with variable rates and flexible terms.

On the other hand, borrowers can benefit from low interest rates, especially if inflation occurs. Lower interest rates mean lower monthly loan payments. When homeowners lock in low mortgage rates or students lock in low rates on student loans, they transfer much of the risk of inflation to the lenders of such loans.

When we evaluate how inflation affects savers and borrowers, we need to consider the real rate of interest. The **real rate of interest** is the nominal, or stated, interest rate minus the inflation rate. For example, if the nominal interest rate on a certificate of deposit (CD) is 6 percent and the inflation rate is 8 percent, the real rate of interest on the CD is –2 percent: The saver is hurt by inflation. If the inflation rate is 3 percent during the term of a 6 percent CD, the real rate of interest is 3 percent: The saver has gained by saving.

Real Rate of Interest

The nominal, or stated, rate of interest minus the inflation rate; a nominal interest rate adjusted for inflation.

Inflation and Wealth   Although people may use the terms *income* and *wealth* interchangeably, each has a very different meaning. Income is a flow of earnings from selling factors of production. **Wealth** measures the value of people's tangible assets, or what they own. Wealth includes stocks, bonds, real estate, cash, diamonds, fine art, and such. Someone could have a large income and little wealth, or great wealth and a small income.

Wealth

A measure of the value of tangible assets; includes such items as real estate and corporate securities.

During inflation, many assets appreciate, or increase in value, as prices rise. Thus, the wealthy become wealthier. Consider real estate. A home valued at $100,000 in 2000 might well be worth $200,000 today largely as a result of inflation.

While inflation often benefits people who have wealth, it penalizes people who are looking to make asset purchases. Again, consider real estate. As prices rapidly increase, people who want to purchase a home—the largest asset purchase for most people—find it more difficult. Young adults who are trying to purchase that first home pay a high penalty for inflation.

Social and Political Consequences of Inflation   In addition to its economic consequences, inflation may have social and political implications as well. Inflation-related issues often form planks in election campaigns as candidates trade blame and offer solutions.

If prolonged or severe enough, inflation might lead not only to changes in leadership but also to changes in social and political institutions. The eminent British economist John Maynard Keynes wrote, "There is no subtler, no surer means of overturning the existing basis of society than to debauch the currency."[7] The rise of Adolf Hitler and Nazism can be traced in part to the discontent and social disruption caused by the German hyperinflation of the early 1920s.

Table 4.4 summarizes who gains and who loses from inflation.

Causes of Inflationary Pressure

Since inflation is an upward movement in the general level of prices and prices result from the interaction of buyers' and sellers' decisions, economists have created a logical way of classifying the causes of inflation. Inflation that originates from pressure on

[6]A fixed rate means that the interest rate does not change during the loan repayment period. A long-term loan means that the borrower has a considerable period of time for repayment, perhaps as much as 30 years.
[7]John Maynard Keynes, *The Economic Consequences of the Peace* (New York: Harcourt, Brace and Howe, 1920), p. 236.

| TABLE 4.4 | *Winners and Losers from Inflation* |

For some people inflation creates opportunities and for others it creates problems.

Winners	Losers
People with after-tax income rising faster than the rate of inflation	People on fixed incomes or working under contracts with wage increases below the inflation rate
Borrowers paying back loans at an interest rate less than the inflation rate	Savers and lenders earning interest rates below the inflation rate
Owners of assets that increase in value with inflation	People who want to buy assets that are rapidly increasing in price
Politicians gaining support because of their position on inflation	Politicians losing popular support because of their inability to control inflation

prices from the buyers' side of the market is termed demand-pull inflation. Inflation that originates from pressure on prices from the sellers' side of the market is called cost-push inflation.

Demand-Pull Inflation   When buyers' demands to purchase goods and services outstrip sellers' abilities to supply them, prices on available goods and services rise, and **demand-pull inflation** occurs. When this demand-based spending subsides, so does the pressure on prices.

Demand-Pull Inflation
Pressure on prices from the buyers' side of the market; tends to occur when spending is greater than the productive capability of the economy.

     Demand-pull inflation has a tendency to occur when the economy is close to or at full employment. Recall that at full employment the economy is at full capacity. Since it is producing the maximum amount of goods and services possible, production cannot be easily expanded. At the same time, consumer demand for goods and services is high because more people are working and have money to spend. Businesses may now also find it profitable to expand and begin to spend on investments in new buildings and machinery. This spending pressure by households and businesses, coupled with production at or near capacity, sets off demand-pull inflation.

     Demand-pull inflation is also related to the amount of money in the economy. The ability of households and businesses to spend depends in part on the amount of money available for spending. If the supply of money in the economy increases at a faster rate than production, upward pressure on prices can result. If the economy is at full employment and more money is put into the hands of businesses and consumers, the result will be inflationary. Thus, too much money in the economy and in the hands of businesses and consumers can contribute to demand-pull inflation.

Cost-Push Inflation   When price pressure comes from the sellers' side of the market, **cost-push inflation** occurs. In this case, increases in sellers' costs are wholly or partially passed on to buyers, who will then face higher prices. Anything that is a cost to a business is a potential source of price increases and, if significant enough, of cost-push inflation. Upward pressure on prices could come from increased costs of labor, raw materials, fuels, machinery, borrowing, and even attempts to increase profit.

Cost-Push Inflation
Pressure on prices from the sellers' side of the market, particularly from increases in costs of production.

     Classic examples of cost-push inflation have come from oil price increases. In the 1970s and 1980s, energy prices contributed to serious inflation when a barrel of oil that sold for $3.18 in 1970 jumped to $31.77 in 1981. In 2008, oil-induced inflation again surfaced when the price of a barrel of oil increased from $69.61 in July 2007 to $137.11 in July 2008.[8]

More likely, cost-push inflation results when costs push up the prices of businesses that play a large role in the economy, such as car manufacturers, or when the costs push up the prices of a significant number of firms. Increases in the costs of energy, for example, have an impact on almost every seller, large or small, in the economy. There have also been fears that the increasing costs of health care will contribute to inflation.

Cost-push and demand-pull inflation can come simultaneously and have a potential to spiral. An increase in overall spending that leads to demand-pull inflation could cause people to negotiate higher wages to compensate for the inflation. Employers who now face increased wage costs may pass them on to buyers through higher prices. It is easy to see the escalating pattern of inflation as rising prices from increased spending can fuel increased wages that can fuel increased prices to cover them. Application 4.2, "The $4 Summer of 2008," focuses on cost-push inflation. Can you see from this application the potential for a spiraling of prices as people seek higher wages to cope with the inflation?

The Role of Expectations   Expectations about inflation can cause inflation to occur. On the demand-pull side, buyers' fears of higher prices in the future may lead them to increase their current spending before the expected higher prices become reality. At full

---

APPLICATION 4.2

THE $4 SUMMER OF 2008

It seemed that the United States needed to add a $4 bill to its currency during the summer of 2008. Quite suddenly the price of two staples of ordinary life—gas and milk—hit $4 a gallon. The $4 price of these key necessities wrecked family budgets, summer vacation plans, and trips to visit grandma. For some businesses, from pizza delivery to household moving companies, these price increases caused huge havoc. Even cities suffered as they gassed up their three-mile-per-gallon fire trucks.

We knew an oil-based energy problem was looming. Americans became used to gas-guzzling SUVs and trucks as these vehicles zoomed in popularity. We neglected to fund good public transportation. China and India were growing quickly and putting huge demands on energy sources. There was disruption in oil supplies with the war in Iraq. But what we didn't anticipate was the suddenness and severity of the rise in oil and gasoline prices.

We also didn't think that another staple of ordinary life—milk—would take such a large price jump. Yet, it was another consequence of the energy crisis. As alternatives to fueling vehicles with gas were pursued, there was a turn toward ethanol. Ethanol is produced primarily from corn, a key ingredient in the diet of farm animals. Farmers who paid $2.04 for a bushel of corn in 2006 were suddenly faced with prices in excess of $5.70 per bushel in June of 2008 as the demand for corn increased.[a]

There are not many good alternatives to a gallon of gas or a gallon of milk. In the summer of 2008, families were stuck with figuring out how to purchase these necessities and live within their means. But, for many businesses to survive, there was no choice but to raise the price of their products. This included farmers in the dairy business and food suppliers who had to haul goods by truck.

Here is a tale of cost-push inflation. By late summer 2008, the $4 gallon was certainly fueling inflation. Data indicated that prices increased over the summer by 7.2 percent and that energy increased by a whopping 32.9 percent.[b] Inflation—cost-push inflation—reared its ugly head.

[a] "Monthly Average Corn Farm Price Received in Illinois for the 1960–2008 Calendar Year(s)", www.farmdoc.uiuc.edu, August 14, 2008.
[b] Bureau of Labor Statistics, "Economic News Release, Consumer Price Index Summary," http://www.bls.gov/news.release/cpi.nr0.htm. Figures are percent changes in CPI for all urban consumers (CPI-U) for June, July, and August 2008.

---

[8] U.S. Bureau of the Census, *Statistical Abstract of the United States: 1990*, 110th ed. (Washington, DC: U.S. Government Printing Office, 1990), p. 692; "All Countries Spot Price FOB Weighted by Estimated Export Volume (Dollars per Barrel)," http://tonto.eia.doe.gov, August 15, 2008.

employment, this increased spending puts additional pressure on an economy already operating at productive capacity and results in inflation. On the sellers' side, firms that expect increasing costs might raise prices in anticipation of those higher costs. Thus, a curious situation results in which the expectation of rising prices can trigger inflation.

Measures of Inflation

We measure changes in price levels by using a scale called a price index. Price indexes use percentages and provide an easy method to compare and evaluate price changes. The government maintains three primary price indexes to measure inflation, each focusing on the prices of a collection of goods and services important to a particular segment of the economy. These are

♦ the Consumer Price Index (CPI), which focuses on goods and services typically purchased by households;
♦ the Producer Price Index (PPI), which focuses on production inputs purchased by businesses; and
♦ the GDP Price Index, which measures price changes in the economy as a whole.

Before we examine these indexes, we will work through an exercise that will help you understand what a price index is, how it is constructed, and how it is interpreted.

Price Index

Measures changes in the price of an item or a group of items using a percentage scale.

Constructing a Price Index   A **price index** is a measure of price changes using a percentage scale. A price index can be based on the prices of a single item or a selected group of items, called a market basket. For example, several hundred goods and services, such as housing, electricity, and automobiles, are used to calculate the CPI. Because a market basket includes a range of goods and services, it is a more comprehensive measure of inflationary pressure than a single item.

Table 4.5 demonstrates how to calculate a simple price index. The column headed Dollar Outlay for Market Basket gives the expenditure required to purchase the same items in years 1 through 6. Notice that this expenditure increases each year: The same goods and services that cost $475 in year 1 cost $600 in year 4.

Base Year

The year against which prices in other years are compared in a price index; given the index number 100.0.

Actual dollar outlays for the market basket are converted to a percentage scale, the price index, which is shown in the right-hand column of Table 4.5. To create an index, a **base year** is selected to serve as the year against which all other years' prices

---

TABLE 4.5   *A Price Index*

The annual dollar outlays over time for a market basket of goods and services are converted to a percentage scale called a price index. Year 2 is the base year of this index.

Year	Dollar Outlay for Market Basket	Price Index
1	$475	95.0
2	500	100.0
3	550	110.0
4	600	120.0
5	625	125.0
6	750	150.0

are compared. The base year is given the number of 100.0, or 100 percent, in the index. In Table 4.5, year 2 is the base year.

The index numbers for the other years represent, in percentages, how many more or fewer dollars than base year dollars are needed to buy the same items. The equation for calculating an index number for a given year is

$$\frac{\text{dollar outlay for a given year}}{\text{dollar outlay for the base year}} \times 100 = \text{price index number for a given year.}$$

For example, in year 4, $600 is needed to buy what $500 bought in the base year. Putting these numbers into the equation yields

$$\frac{\$600}{\$500} \times 100 = 120.0.$$

The price index number of 120.0 indicates that prices have gone up by 20 percent from year 2 to year 4. Expressed differently, a person must spend an additional $100, or 20 percent more, in year 4 to buy what $500 bought in year 2, the base year.

The same goods and services that cost $500 in year 2 cost $475 in year 1. Using the price index equation, this means that the index number for year 1 is ($475 / $500)× 100 = 95.0. Only 95 percent of the dollars used in year 2 were needed in year 1 to buy the same basket of goods. Prices were 5 percent lower in year 1 than in the base year.

We read the index numbers for each of the remaining years in the same way as years 1 and 4. The index number of 125.0 for year 5 indicates that prices are 25 percent higher in year 5 than in the base year, and the dollar outlay of $750 in year 6 is 50 percent higher than the outlay required in the base year.

Consumer Price Index (CPI)

Measures changes in the prices of goods and services that consumers typically purchase, such as food, shelter, clothing, and medical care.

The Consumer Price Index   The **Consumer Price Index (CPI)** measures changes in the prices of goods and services typically bought by consumers. In Table 4.6 we see, for selected years, the overall CPI as well as separate indexes for various categories of goods and services within the CPI, such as medical care and household energy. In this table, the base year comes from averaging prices over three years: 1982, 1983, and 1984.[9]

We can make some interesting observations about the CPI from this table. In the All Items column, notice the movement in overall consumer prices over the years. What households could purchase for $100 on average in the base period cost $38.80 in 1970 and $234.80 in 2014. Also observe in Table 4.6 that the prices in some categories of goods and services increased by less or by more than the overall index. In the Apparel category, the index numbers are less than the overall CPI and fell for many years listed. Medical Care, however, is much higher than the overall index and grew much faster. There should be no surprise that healthcare costs are an ongoing concern.

Because a price index compares price changes between a given year and a base year, rather than year-to-year, annual percentage changes in prices, or inflation rates, are not obvious. Figure 4.2 traces the annual percentage change in the CPI from 1976

---

[9] These numbers are not shown in Table 4.6. This average is calculated by adding the numbers for the three years together, dividing by 3, and then using the average of the three years for the base dollar outlay. This further means that the index numbers for these three years average 100.0.

TABLE 4.6	Consumer Price Index: All Items and Various Categories for Selected Years (1982–1984 = 100.0)

The Consumer Price Index measures changes in the prices of goods and services that consumers typically purchase. Increases in prices for some components in the index, such as medical care, have been greater than the increase in the overall index.

Year	All Items	Food	Household Energy	Apparel	Medical Care
1970	38.8	39.2	25.5	59.2	34.0
1975	53.8	59.8	42.1	72.5	47.5
1980	82.4	86.8	86.0	90.9	74.9
1985	107.6	105.6	101.6	105.0	113.5
1990	130.7	132.4	102.1	124.1	162.8
1995	152.4	148.4	105.2	132.0	220.5
2000	172.2	167.8	124.6	129.6	260.8
2005	195.3	190.7	177.1	119.5	323.2
2006	201.6	195.2	196.9	119.5	336.2
2007	207.3	202.9	207.7	119.0	351.1
2008	215.3	214.1	236.7	118.9	364.1
2009	214.5	218.0	193.1	120.1	375.6
2010	218.1	219.6	211.4	119.5	388.4
2011	224.9	227.8	243.9	122.1	400.3
2012	229.6	233.8	246.1	126.3	414.9
2013	233.0	237.9	192.2	126.5	427.1
2014	234.8	246.0	197.1	123.9	439.7

Source: *Economic Report of the President* (Washington, DC: U.S. Government Printing Office, 2013), Table B-60; Bureau of Labor Statistics, CPI Detailed Reports, Table 1, January 2014, December 2014, www.bls.gov.

through 2014.[10] Notice that in recent decades inflation has been much less of a problem for households.

Changes in the CPI and other indexes are calculated monthly. These monthly changes must be compounded to arrive at an annual figure for comparison. That is, if a 1.1 percent monthly change in the prices of all items were to persist throughout the year, it would lead to an annual inflation rate of 14.0 percent.

Other Price Indexes   As noted earlier, two other indexes, in addition to the CPI, are watched when measuring inflation in the economy: the Producer Price Index and the GDP Price Index.

[10] To determine an annual percentage change in prices between two consecutive years, 1 and 2, in a price index, use the following equation:

$$\frac{\text{year 2 index number} - \text{year 1 index number}}{\text{year 1 index number}} \times 100 = \text{annual percentage change.}$$

For example, using the numbers in the All Items column in Table 4.6, the price change from 2010 (year 1) to 2011 (year 2) would be

$$\frac{224.9 - 218.1}{218.1} \times 100 = 3.12\%.$$

FIGURE 4.2   *Annual Percentage Changes in the Overall CPI*

The United States experienced serious inflation problems in the late 1970s and early 1980s.

Source: *Economic Report of the President* (Washington, DC: U.S. Government Printing Office, 2015), Table B-10.

Producer Price Index (PPI)

Measures changes in the prices of goods and services that businesses buy, either for further processing or for sale to a consumer.

GDP Price Index

The price index used when calculating price changes for the entire economy.

The **Producer Price Index (PPI)** measures changes in the prices that businesses pay for materials they consume, such as energy and supplies, and goods and services they buy for further sale. Just as with the Consumer Price Index, the government calculates and announces the Producer Price Index monthly. The PPI has an important connection to the CPI and is watched carefully. Changes in the prices that businesses pay now often contribute to changes in the prices that consumers pay later. As a result, changes in the PPI may lead to future changes in the CPI.

The **GDP Price Index** is used to measure price changes for the entire economy and is calculated in a slightly different way from the CPI and PPI. The use of this index is discussed later in this chapter.

Importance of Indexes   Academics, businesspeople, and government officials do not study price indexes out of idle curiosity. Rather, they have an important impact on policymakers' decisions and on the operation of the economy. They directly affect wages of workers who receive cost-of-living adjustments based on the CPI. Employers and employees often look to these indexes in determining fair salary increases. Some government programs, such as Social Security, base changes in recipients' checks on a variation of one of these indexes. Private business contracts may provide for price adjustments based on the Producer Price Index, and, in some instances, other payments such as child support and rent have been tied to one of these indexes.

Deflation and Disinflation

Deflation

A sustained decrease in the general level of prices.

We must note two important terms before leaving the discussion of inflation: deflation and disinflation. **Deflation** occurs when there is a sustained decrease in the general level of prices. This does not mean that a few items decrease in price or that there is a decrease for a short period of time. In the United States, deflation has not occurred since the 1930s.

Although a sustained decrease in the general level of prices might sound attractive, deflation, like inflation, can create problems for households and businesses. For example, homeowners who want to move could be forced to sell their houses for less than they paid for them, and businesses could suffer losses if their products' prices dropped to a level that did not cover previously incurred production costs. Also, people might be less enthusiastic about deflation when one of the prices that drops is the price they get for their labor.

Disinflation

A slowing of the inflation rate.

We refer to a reduction of the inflation rate as **disinflation**. Disinflation does not mean that prices are falling; rather it refers to a slowing of the inflation rate. For example, when the line is falling in Figure 4.2, disinflation is illustrated. When Congress and the Federal Reserve try to slow inflation through their actions, they are pursuing disinflation. Tools available for pursuing disinflation are discussed in Chapters 6 and 8.

PRODUCTION

Production

The creation of goods and services.

Production is the creation of goods and services. Productive activities range from the construction of a piano to the repair of a dented car door. Shipping goods from wholesalers to discount houses constitutes production, as do the grocery store services of renting carpet cleaners and making floral arrangements. Because production is linked to an economy's standard of living and employment, it is important to measure an economy's overall output and its capacity to produce. Any discussion of setting and reaching macro goals and working through macro problems is based on having data about an economy's production.

Full Production and Economic Growth

Full Production

Occurs when an economy is producing at its maximum capacity, or when it is experiencing full employment.

An economy achieves the macroeconomic goal of **full production** when it produces as much as possible with its available resources or operates at its maximum capacity. Although the problem of scarcity always exists, full production permits an economy to minimize its impact. Production and employment are interrelated: When an economy reaches full employment, it also reaches full production. When resources are unemployed, full productive capacity is not met.

Economic Growth

An increase in an economy's full production output level over time.

In addition to full production, this macroeconomic goal calls for **economic growth**, which means that the economy's full production–full employment level of output grows over time. A good way to evaluate economic growth is to observe per capita output over time for an economy.

These data for the United States from 1986 through 2014 are illustrated in Figure 4.3. (Real output measures output with the effects of inflation removed and is explained in the next few pages.) Although the figure shows actual production rather than full employment production, it indicates that real output per person has grown substantially

| FIGURE 4.3 | *U.S. Economic Growth: Real Output per Capita*[a] |

Real output per person in the United States has grown substantially since 1986.

[a] Real output is in chained 2005 dollars; 2014 figure is preliminary.

Source: *Economic Report of the President* (Washington, DC: U.S. Government Printing Office, 2013), Table B-31; 2015, Table B-3; U.S. Census Bureau, Population Estimates.

over the years. In 1986, when the U.S. population was approximately 240 million, the economy produced $29,418 of real output per person. By 2014, when the population was approximately 319 million, real output per person had grown to $44,614.[11]

Achieving Economic Growth   An economy's production levels are based on the amount of available resources and how they are used. Economic growth can occur with more resources or more efficient resource use: labor force expansion through immigration; new sources of oil and gas; more entrepreneurial efforts; or new machinery, for example. Government can encourage economic growth through its policies that impact new resources and efficiency, such as changes in the tax code or interest rates.

Technology
Increase in knowledge about production and its processes.

The state of knowledge about production and its processes, or **technology**, is probably the most important force for economic growth. In today's world, technology is influencing production in rapid and dramatic ways as it impacts everything from medical breakthroughs to communications to even the production of this textbook.

Human Capital Investments
Investments, such as formal education, that increase the productivity of people.

In addition, investments in people through education, training, wellness, and other ways, or through **human capital investments**, also increase economic growth. Investments in people strengthen the quality of a workforce, make individuals more productive, and raise the overall level of knowledge in the economy. This, in turn,

[11] See sources in Figure 4.3.

ensures that technological change continues. An economy of healthy, educated people is critical to economic growth.

Costs of Economic Growth   Not everyone agrees that a high rate of economic growth is desirable. Today, more than ever, people argue that significant costs are attached to a push for continually increasing production. The growth of the U.S. economy that has brought its annual output to over $18 trillion has resulted in billions of tons of garbage including nuclear waste, full and closed landfills, toxic chemicals seeping into soil, and health problems. We are also aware that the rapid economic growth in countries like China has brought severe air pollution and that global warming is another consequence of rapid growth.

Some people argue that it may be better to produce a smaller output and better deal with the waste and other problems that are created. There is also concern about the depletion of resources that are not easily regenerated and will become a problem of the future.

"Up For Debate: Will Policies to Protect the Environment Slow Economic Growth?" addresses the debate over the relationship between environmental regulatory policies and economic growth.

UP FOR DEBATE

WILL POLICIES TO PROTECT THE ENVIRONMENT SLOW ECONOMIC GROWTH?

We are keenly aware of the impact of our current style of living and production on the world's natural resources: global warming, deterioration in air and water quality, and rapid depletion of the limited supply of oil and other energy sources. There is recognition that policies must be put in place to protect the earth for future generations and global support for doing so. On the other hand, opposition to these protective policies is coming from those who believe that such policies will slow down the world's economies and cause economic stagnation. Will policies to protect the environment actually slow economic growth?

YES   It's obvious that in order to "clean" the environment, production all over the world must be lessened. Just consider the 2008 summer Olympics in Beijing, China, when in order to clear the air for the athletes, China shut down a large number of its production facilities. Closing many of the world's factories and other polluting facilities will send hundreds of thousands of workers into unemployment. Economies will stagnate.

Cleaner air requires that people drive less. This will have a huge impact on individual lifestyles as they find ways to lessen their discretionary driving. People will likely patronize restaurants and entertainment venues less and not drive to shopping malls and stores with as much frequency. This has the potential to cause many small businesses and retail outlets to fail.

There are many other negative economic consequences of environmental regulations. As people are forced to lessen the use of resources, there will be an associated loss of jobs from mail carriers to truck drivers to workers in SUV plants. Government entities that provide police and fire protection and code enforcement may have to lessen their service levels to meet environmental regulations.

NO   Policies to protect the environment will encourage economic growth. While there could be some disruption without time to adjust to regulations, a well-planned transition will result in many new types of industries, businesses, and jobs. People are smart and will conquer the challenge of producing and living in a world that protects the environment.

We know the advantages of new technology, accessible information, and better communication. These will move us toward a different kind of production and lifestyle. Take building as an example. Today, many businesses and educational institutions are seeking LEED certification[a] of their new construction. This certification promotes efficiencies in the use of resources—from green roofs to solar energy to water runoff. LEED does not bring a decrease in economic growth, rather it is inspiring changes in the way architects and builders do business.

The future is promising for economic growth as life, careers, and production change—not stop. Single-stream recycling, hybrid cars, rainwater reuse, and so much more are already contributing to growth, with so much more to come.

[a] The LEED (Leadership in Energy and Environmental Design) Green Building Rating System is a certification program with nationally accepted benchmarks for the design, construction, and operation of high-performance green buildings. http://www.usgbc.org.

Measures of Production

Gross Domestic
Product (GDP)

A dollar figure that measures
the value of all finished
goods and services
produced in an economy in
one year.

The United States, as well as most other countries, calculates on a regular basis how much its economy has produced. **Gross domestic product**, or **GDP**, is the dollar figure that measures the value of all the *finished* goods and services produced in an economy in one year. GDP counts only finished goods and services, which are those ready for sale to their final users: Products in a stage of production, or not yet completed, are not included. If we included an item in the process of production, say, the flour for pasta, and then included it again when the product was completed, say, linguini noodles, production would be overstated.

It is also important to understand that GDP measures goods and services produced, not sold. We do not count goods involved in secondhand sales, such as a student's purchase of a 2008 car, because these goods were counted in GDP when they were originally produced. We also do not count purchases of "paper," such as stocks and bonds, because they do not represent production, but rather a transfer of assets.

Money GDP (Current,
or Nominal, GDP)

Measures the value of
production in terms of prices
at the time of production.

GDP figures are usually given in two forms: money GDP and real GDP. **Money GDP**, sometimes called **current GDP** or **nominal GDP**, measures the value of production in terms of prices at the time of production. Money GDP is affected by both changes in production and changes in prices. **Real**, or **constant**, **GDP** is money GDP adjusted to eliminate inflation. It measures actual (real) production and shows how actual production, without price increases, has changed. People who "watch the economy" prefer real GDP rather than money GDP figures for gauging the state of the economy.

Real GDP
(Constant GDP)

Money GDP adjusted to
eliminate inflation; measures
real production.

Calculating Real GDP   Table 4.7 shows why real GDP is a better measure of production than money GDP. This table presents a hypothetical economy that produces only automobiles. Notice in the column Output of Autos that this economy was stagnant from year 1 to year 2, producing 60 cars in each year; had real growth in year 3 when production increased to 65 cars; and experienced a decline in production during year 4 with a drop to 55 cars. During this period, the economy also experienced inflation: The price of autos increased year after year, as shown in the column Price per Auto.

We calculate money GDP, or the current dollar value of production, by multiplying output times price for each year. In year 1, when the 60 cars produced were $16,000 each, money GDP was $960,000, and in year 2 when the 60 cars produced were $18,000 each, money GDP was $1,080,000. This is given in the fourth column.

Notice that the price increases caused money GDP to climb for each of the four years. If we relied solely on the money GDP numbers, we could mistakenly believe

---

TABLE 4.7   *Determining Money GDP and Real GDP*

Money GDP can give a misleading impression of the output of an economy when the level of prices is changing over time.

Year	Output of Autos	Price per Auto	Money GDP	Auto Price Index	Real GDP
1	60	$16,000	$960,000	100.0	$960,000
2	60	18,000	1,080,000	112.5	960,000
3	65	20,000	1,300,000	125.0	1,040,000
4	55	24,000	1,320,000	150.0	880,000

that production increased from year to year when it did not. Inflation has distorted these production data.

To assess real levels of production, we need to calculate real GDP. To do so, we need a measure of the price changes over the years. In Table 4.7, the prices of the autos over the four years are translated to a price index, given in the Auto Price Index column, using year 1 as the base year. This price index provides the mechanism for converting money GDP to real GDP.

The equation for determining real GDP is

$$\frac{\text{money GDP for a given year}}{\text{price index number for that year}} \times 100 = \text{real GDP for the given year.}$$

The real GDP, for example, for year 2 in Table 4.7 is calculated by dividing the money GDP of $1,080,000 by the index number of 112.5 and multiplying that answer by 100.

It is important to notice in Table 4.7 that real GDP did not change from year 1 to year 2 and that it increased in year 3 and decreased in year 4. Real GDP, not money GDP, reflects the actual annual output for this economy.

Assessing U.S. Production   Table 4.8 gives money GDP and real GDP for the U.S. economy since 2000. Notice the sheer magnitude of the numbers: Money GDP was over $17 trillion in 2014, putting the average daily output of the U.S. economy over $46 billion.

Table 4.8 includes the GDP price index for the entire economy, which was mentioned earlier in this chapter. The government calculates this index as a measure of

---

| **TABLE 4.8** | *Money GDP, Real GDP, and the GDP Price Index* |

Real GDP is a much more accurate measure of the economy's performance over time than is money GDP.

Year	Money GDP (Billions)	Real GDP (Billions)	GDP Price Index (2009 = 100)
2000	$10,284.8	$12,559.7	81.890
2001	10,621.8	12,682.2	83.755
2002	10,977.5	12,908.8	85.040
2003	11,510.7	13,271.1	86.735
2004	12,274.9	13,773.5	89.118
2005	13,093.7	14,234.2	91.985
2006	13,855.9	14,613.8	94.812
2007	14,477.6	14,873.7	97.340
2008	14,718.6	14,830.4	99.218
2009	14,418.7	14,418.7	100.000
2010	14,964.4	14,783.8	101.226
2011	15,517.9	15,020.6	103.315
2012	16,163.2	15,369.2	105.174
2013	16,768.1	15,710.3	106.739
2014[a]	17,420.7	16,089.8	108.309

[a]Numbers for 2014 are preliminary.

Source: *Economic Report of the President* (Washington, DC: U.S. Government Printing Office, 2015), Tables B-2, B-3.

overall inflation and uses it to convert money GDP to real GDP. Just as we did in the auto example, we find real GDP for a given year by dividing that year's money GDP by that year's GDP price index number and then multiplying by 100.[12]

In the base year of the price index, money GDP equals real GDP since the price index value is 100.0. In 2009, the base year in Table 4.8, money GDP and real GDP are equal at $14.4 trillion. In years when a dollar buys more than in the base year, the GDP price index number is less than 100.0, and real GDP is greater than money GDP. Observe that in 2000 real GDP is greater than money GDP. In years when a dollar buys less than in the base year, the GDP price index number is greater than 100.0, and real GDP is less than money GDP. In 2014, real GDP is less than money GDP.

In Table 4.8, we find the reason for using real GDP rather than money GDP to evaluate the economy. Look at the GDP data for 2007 through 2010. During that time money GDP constantly grew except for 2009. The real GDP figures, however, show the extended slowdown in the economy that occurred over these years. It was not until 2011 that GDP grew again to its pre-slowdown years. Money GDP can give a false impression of the economy and mislead people who are unaware of how price changes, or inflation, can distort output measures.

The government calculates and publicly announces GDP figures on both a quarterly and an annual basis. Quarterly figures are used to gauge the health of the economy and are usually reported by the media. Concern is generated when little or no growth occurs in GDP from quarter to quarter.

Test Your Understanding, "Calculating Price Indexes and GDP," provides an opportunity to practice calculating and evaluating price indexes and GDP figures.

Does GDP Tell the Whole Story?

Although we rely on GDP data to evaluate production, those data do not give us a complete picture. GDP figures actually understate our output levels because many goods and services that are produced are never included in the calculation. The U.S. economy is more productive than is reported because nonmarket productive activities, unreported work, and swapped services are not included.

Some goods and services are not included in GDP because they are not bought and sold in a market. Many people maintain their own cars, paint their own homes, cook meals, volunteer in hospitals and camps, or spend hours a day "working" without being paid. These activities result in the actual production of goods and services and improve the economy's well-being but are not included in GDP because no pay is involved. If someone were paid to do this work, the dollar value of the output would be included in the accounts. For example, if you teach yourself to use Excel, it is not included in GDP, but if you pay for a course and an instructor teaches you Excel, the value of this service is included in GDP.

When people work for cash and do not report this income to the federal government, the work is not included in GDP. Young people often cut grass or sit with children, accept their wages in cash, and do not report the income on their tax forms. Sometimes, major work is not reported, such as full-time housecleaning, tip income, or moonlighting by plumbers or electricians. On occasion, people will swap services: A dentist maintains the teeth of a lawyer in return for legal advice. Also, people who are engaged in illegal activities likely don't report that income, causing illegal production not to be included in GDP.

---

[12]If you try to check your understanding of the conversion of money GDP to real GDP by applying the conversion formula to the numbers in Table 4.8, some of your real GDP figures may be slightly different than those given there—partly because the numbers in the table have been rounded and partly because of some properties of the index.

CALCULATING PRICE INDEXES AND GDP

The following problems provide an opportunity to calculate price indexes, money GDP, and real GDP.

1. Calculate two price indexes for the market basket in the following table. Use year 2 as the base year for the index in column 3 and year 4 as the base year for the index in column 4.

Year	Price of Market Basket	Price Index	Price Index
1	$176		
2	220	100.0	
3	242		
4	275		100.0
5	286		
6	330		

2. Assume that a hypothetical economy produces only motor scooters, as given in the following table.

Year	Output (Number of Scooters)	Price per Scooters
1	500	$10,000
2	550	11,000
3	500	12,500
4	450	13,000
5	600	15,000
6	600	15,500

Determine this economy's money GDP, GDP price index, and real GDP assuming that year 1 is the base year. Record these in the appropriate columns of the following table.

Year	Money GDP	GDP Price Index	Real GDP
1			
2			
3			
4			
5			
6			

3. Below are money GDP and GDP price index numbers over several years for a hypothetical economy. Calculate real GDP for each of the years given in the table below and record your answers in the appropriate column. Answer the questions following this table.

Year	Money GDP (Billions)	GDP Price Index	Real GDP (Billions)
2006	$900.0	90.0	
2007	1,000.0	100.0	
2008	1,260.0	105.0	
2009	1,500.0	120.0	
2010	1,600.0	128.0	
2011	1,800.0	150.0	
2012	2,000.0	160.0	

a. On the basis of real GDP, how has this economy performed from year to year?
b. Generally, for the entire period, how does the picture of the economy's performance using real GDP compare with the picture using money GDP?

Answers can be found at the back of the book.

Underground Economy
Productive activities that are not reported for tax purposes and are not included in GDP

We use the term **underground economy** to refer to productive activities that are not reported for tax purposes and are, therefore, not included in GDP. While economists care that these goods and services are not included in GDP, most of the concern about the underground economy centers on the lost tax revenue and the social harm resulting from some of these activities.

We must also note that GDP fails to measure the impact of production and consumption on the environment. It also does not account for future costs that may be incurred from current production. And sometimes GDP is not a sure indicator of the

APPLICATION 4.3

A Tale of Two Families

Here is the tale of two productive families. While each family has the same goal of providing a healthy and happy home life for its children and is successful at that goal, each family's contribution to the U.S. economy, or to GDP, is starkly different.

Joe and Lydia

Joe and Lydia and their three children are part of a small like-minded, rural community. They live simply in a three-bedroom house heated by a wood-burning stove and depend on a well for their water needs. Joe and Lydia raise much of the food the family consumes; their garden and orchard are abundant with fruits, berries, and vegetables and Lydia cans and bakes. The goats provide milk for drinking as well as cheese making. Between feeding the animals and creating compost, they produce very little trash.

All of their clothing is sewn by Lydia, who visits some secondhand shops for items with good fabric that can be refashioned. Sometimes she trades her pies and donuts for fabric that someone in the community has purchased. Lydia wants her children to be well educated, and they visit the local lending library frequently.

Joe is an excellent carpenter. When work is available, he will join a building crew (sometimes for no pay if it is a community need) or other carpenters that make tables and chairs for custom orders. Since Joe has an old, unreliable pickup truck which he repairs himself, sometimes he hires a driver who will take him and the family to a city farmers market where they sell some of their bountiful produce and birdhouses that he and the children make.

Even though this family lives well and works hard to produce the goods and services that they need, trade, and sell, they contribute little to the GDP calculations. They spend little on food and clothing, utilities, and transportation. Their sales at the farmers market, wages earned as a carpenter, payments to a driver, and small purchases are about all that they contribute to the official calculation of GDP.

Angie and Rob

Angie and Rob and their three children live in a three-bedroom house in a suburb of a big city. Like all suburban residents, they depend on the local water, gas, electric, sewer, and trash companies for their everyday utilities.

Angie and Rob shop at the local grocery chain for the family's food, and the family sometimes enjoys a meal at a restaurant or grabs something at a fast-food establishment. Angie likes to cook and bake and depends on the good-quality flour, vanilla beans, and natural cocoa that she can buy in a local specialty shop. Sometimes Angie visits the local farmers market where she buys fresh berries, vegetables, and cheese.

Rob is an accountant and works as a loan officer for a bank. Sometimes during tax season he will work weekend hours on his own by doing taxes for a few paying clients. Angie teaches math to junior high students.

Angie and Rob own an old sedan and bought a new SUV this year. Their kids are active in a few local sports leagues and spend time in the community's ice arena. Angie likes to ensure that she has at least a few clothing pieces that are in fashion and there are plenty of new books in the house.

This family lives well and contributes much to the GDP calculations. Angie and Rob have jobs that produce services that are added to the country's GDP, and they spend money on things that add to the officially calculated production levels of the economy: utilities, food, clothes, a new car, and more.

quality of people's lives. Application 4.3, "A Tale of Two Families," shows that we can be led astray by relying solely on high GDP figures as a testament to a good life.

Productivity

In addition to measuring real GDP, we also periodically evaluate the productivity of our resources. The amount of goods and services that an economy produces is influenced by the way in which its resources are used. Efficient labor usage, technology in production processes, and updated equipment contribute to productivity.

The concept of assessing the amount of output produced by an economy's resources is called **productivity**. Basically, productivity measures output per worker. This measure takes labor plus other factors of production into consideration. Productivity does not measure how hard a person works, but rather the output that results when labor is combined with other inputs. For example, the product per hour of someone who is building a wall for a landscape contractor depends not just on the

Productivity
Concept of assessing the amount of output produced by an economy's resources; often measured specifically by output per worker.

person but also on the equipment that is used. The number of hybrids that roll off an assembly line at an auto plant each day depends on workers, machinery, management style, energy, and other resources. Productivity increases when the equipment used on the job is technologically advanced and efficient.

Not surprisingly, productivity in the U.S. economy has increased dramatically over the past few decades. Increased productivity provides benefits for the economy because we get more goods and services from available resources. More immediate to the goals of macroeconomic policy, improved productivity can ease inflationary pressure by allowing firms to meet rising costs through increased output rather than through higher prices. Increased productivity can change employment opportunities by stimulating new, higher-skilled jobs.

A POSSIBLE POLICY PROBLEM

The federal government is officially committed to help create an environment conducive to reaching full employment, full production, and price stability. While each of these goals is desirable, it may be difficult to simultaneously reach them all.

We know that when the U.S. economy reaches full production and full employment, pressures from increased spending power on the buyers' side of the market can combine with the inability of the economy to expand its output to cause demand-pull inflation. We also know that removing the upward pressure on prices by curbing buyers' demands could lead to unemployment and less than full production.

This dilemma sometimes faces policymakers and may force them to choose to seek full employment and full production accompanied by inflation, or stable prices accompanied by unemployment and less than full production. In the next few chapters, you will learn about policies that can change economic conditions and who is responsible for pursing these policies. You will learn about Congress and fiscal policy and the Federal Reserve and monetary policy. While there are disputes about what goals to seek, how to reach them, and who benefits, we are fortunate to have some options available.

Summary

1. The three fundamental goals of the U.S. economy are full employment, stable prices, and full production and economic growth. The three fundamental problems are unemployment, inflation, and falling production. To help create an environment in which these goals can be reached, Congress enacted the Employment Act of 1946.

2. Unemployment intensifies the scarcity problem for society and creates personal hardships for individuals who are out of work. Unemployment can be frictional, cyclical, or structural. Frictional unemployment is voluntary, short term, and primarily due to the time required to locate work. Cyclical unemployment is involuntary and caused by downswings in the general level of economic activity. Structural unemployment is involuntary and occurs when a particular job is no longer in demand in the economy.

3. The labor force includes all persons 16 years of age and older who are employed or actively seeking work. A participation rate measures the percentage of a group that is in the labor force. The overall unemployment rate is the percentage of the

labor force that is unemployed and actively seeking work. Unemployment rates and participation rates can be calculated for subgroups within the labor force and differ from group to group.

4. The government calculates unemployment rates from a monthly sample survey. People who work even 1 hour per week while looking for full-time employment are considered to be employed. When people quit looking for work because they have been unsuccessful in their search, they become discouraged workers. Discouraged workers and part-time workers seeking full-time work may cause the unemployment rate to understate the extent to which labor resources are underutilized.

5. Full employment occurs when everyone in the labor force except the frictionally unemployed is working. The unemployment rate associated with full employment is not universally agreed upon and has changed over time. The natural rate of unemployment is the rate that includes the frictionally and structurally unemployed.

6. Inflation refers to an increase in the general level of prices. It reduces the purchasing power of money, hurts some groups in society more than others, and may lead to social and political instability.

7. When inflation is caused by upward pressure on prices from the buyers' side of the market, it is termed demand-pull inflation. When it comes from the sellers' side of the market, it is termed cost-push inflation. Expectations of future economic conditions can influence demand-pull and cost-push inflation.

8. Three widely used indicators of inflation are the Consumer Price Index, Producer Price Index, and GDP Price Index. Price indexes express the prices for a collection of goods and services in different years as a percentage of the prices for those same goods and services in a base year. A price index number of 120.0 means that prices in a certain year are 20 percent higher than prices for the same items in the base year.

9. Deflation occurs when there is a sustained decrease in the general level of prices. Disinflation occurs when there is a slowing of the inflation rate.

10. An economy's levels of production and employment are related. Full production is reached when an economy operates at maximum capacity or at full employment. Economic growth is an increase in the full employment level of output over time. Economic growth is based on the number and use of resources available to an economy. Technological change and human capital investments are important in achieving growth.

11. Gross Domestic Product (GDP) is a dollar figure that measures the value of all finished goods and services produced in an economy in one year. Money GDP is the value of output in prices at the time production occurs and is affected by changes in both output and price levels. Real GDP is money GDP adjusted to eliminate inflation, and it changes only as the level of output changes. Real GDP is a better measure of production than money GDP. GDP understates actual output because some production is never included in the calculation.

12. It is important to measure the productivity of an economy's resources. Productivity is measured by output per worker, which combines the results of production from labor and other inputs.

13. It may not be possible to reach full employment, full production, and price stability at the same time. As the economy approaches full employment, increased spending causes demand-pull inflationary pressure. The reduction of spending to dampen demand-pull inflationary pressure can cause employment and production to fall.

Key Terms and Concepts

Unemployment	Demand-pull inflation
Frictional unemployment	Cost-push inflation
Full employment	Price index
Cyclical unemployment	Base year
Structural unemployment	Consumer Price Index (CPI)
Labor force	Producer Price Index (PPI)
Participation rate	GDP Price Index
Unemployment rate	Deflation
Discouraged workers	Disinflation
Underemployment	Production
Natural rate of unemployment	Full production
Inflation	Economic growth
Hyperinflation	Technology
Money (nominal) income	Human capital investments
Real income	Gross domestic product (GDP)
Cost-of-living adjustment (COLA)	Money (current, or nominal) GDP
Interest rate	Real (constant) GDP
Real rate of interest	Underground economy
Wealth	Productivity

Review Questions

1. Define the three major goals and the three major problems of the macroeconomy. What is the significance of the Employment Act of 1946 with regard to these goals and problems?

2. Identify which of the following individuals would be classified as unemployed and, if they are, the type of unemployment that each is experiencing.
   a. A student who decides at midsemester to devote the rest of the term to studying and quits her part-time job
   b. A graphic artist who is out of work because a computer now does her job
   c. A waiter who quits his job and is applying for the same type of work in a restaurant where the working conditions are better

    d. The son of a local farmer who works 20-hour weeks without pay on the farm while waiting for a job at a nearby factory

    e. A travel agent who is laid off because the economy is in a slump and vacation travel is at a minimum

    f. A plumber who works 5 hours per week for his church (on a paid basis) until he can get a full-time job

3. Define labor force, unemployment rate, participation rate, full employment, and the natural rate of unemployment. Explain what each measure tells us about the economy.

4. What is the difference between demand-pull inflation and cost-push inflation? Must the economy experience only one type of inflation at a time, or can these types occur simultaneously? How might inflation tend to spiral?

5. Calculate price index numbers for the following table assuming that year 3 is the base year, and put your results in the last column.

Year	Market Basket Dollar Outlay	Price Index
1	$170	_____
2	180	_____
3	200	_____
4	200	_____
5	224	_____
6	250	_____
7	280	_____

6. What is the difference between deflation and disinflation? Although the United States has not experienced deflation since the 1930s, what problems could result if deflation occurred over the next five years?

7. In each of the following examples, identify whether the person or institution will be penalized by inflation and, if so, why.

    a. Mosie borrows $5,000 for her college expenses at an interest rate of 4 percent to be paid off over five years, during which time the inflation rate averages 6 percent.

    b. Oscar invests $3,000 in securities that pay 5.3 percent annually for 10 years, and the inflation rate during that time averages 6.4 percent.

    c. The Lilyton National Bank commits to $10 million in 15-year mortgages at an average mortgage rate of 4.5 percent. The inflation rate averages 6 percent over this 15-year period.

    d. Barney bought a house in 2006 for $100,000 that he is now selling for $200,000. During this time the inflation rate has averaged 3 percent.

8. What are the primary factors responsible for economic growth? How are they related?

9. Complete the following table for a hypothetical economy assuming that year 1 is the base year for the price index. How does the completed table illustrate that real

GDP is a better measure of the performance of an economy over time than is money GDP?

Year	Real Output (units)	Price per Unit	Money GDP	GDP Price Index	Real GDP
1	100	$4.00	_____	_____	_____
2	120	4.40	_____	_____	_____
3	110	5.00	_____	_____	_____
4	110	5.20	_____	_____	_____
5	135	5.20	_____	_____	_____
6	140	5.60	_____	_____	_____

Discussion Questions

1. Suppose that you are a candidate for the U.S. Congress. National Public Radio, which attracts an educated and sophisticated audience, interviews you about the economy. How will you answer each of the following questions?
   a. Since it is fairly apparent that the economy cannot sustain full employment and stable prices at the same time, which of these two goals would you choose?
   b. Do you favor using the full employment rate of unemployment or the natural rate of unemployment as a macro goal?
   c. How would you reduce cyclical and structural unemployment? How far would you be willing to intervene in the operations of businesses to control unemployment?

2. Can you identify someone you know who is working part-time but would like to be working full-time or is working in a job that is not fully using the person's skills? In your opinion, is listing this person as employed a serious flaw in the way unemployment statistics are gathered and reported? What changes, if any, would you make in the way we calculate unemployment?

3. Each of the following allows you to integrate this chapter into your everyday life. Choose one from this list to complete.
   a. Interview someone who has been out of work for over a month. Is this person classified as unemployed, and, if so, what type of unemployment is this person experiencing? What are the costs of unemployment to this person?
   b. How has inflation affected the tuition you pay at the college or university you are currently attending? What was the tuition in 2005, 2010, and the current year? How have changes in your school's tuition compared to changes in the overall Consumer Price Index?
   c. Compile a list of all the goods and services that you have produced in the last month that would not be counted as part of GDP. Why would they not be counted? Can you estimate the value of this production?

4. What are some economic, social, and political reasons that make economic growth important to a nation? How could a population increase contribute to economic growth, and how could it hinder growth?

5. An argument can be made that the aggressive pursuit of economic growth may impose costs on people today and in future generations. Is growth important enough that these costs should be ignored, or should they be balanced against the gains from economic growth when making decisions about the path the economy should follow in the future?

6. In recent years, the annual rate of growth in productivity in the United States has increased. What do you think is most responsible for this increase?

7. Create three separate lists showing the groups that you think are hurt most by unemployment, inflation, and declining production.

8. As the Up for Debate on page 105 indicates, many people oppose regulations that address environmental concerns because they believe that they harm businesses and the economy. Others join this position because they think that studies showing deteriorating air and water quality are fabricated or that there is too much government intervention. On the other hand, there is evidence that new business opportunities and products, such as the growth in wind and solar energies, are emerging and new careers will result. Where do you fall in this discussion?

Critical Thinking Case 4

STATISTICS AND DECISION MAKING

Critical Thinking Skills

Understanding the statistical concepts of population and sampling

Determining whether data support a generalization

Evaluating the reliability of a statistic used to make a judgment

Economic Concepts

Relationship between statistical measures and economic decision making

Factors underlying the calculation of the unemployment rate

"The average age of smokers has fallen by 3 percent." "Prices are expected to increase by 9.9 percent this year." "The unemployment rate has dropped to 5.8 percent." "Corporate profits rose by 8 percent."[a] We are constantly bombarded with statistics about economic and noneconomic phenomena. Statistics are often used because they add precision to statements that might otherwise be vague and authority to the positions people take. People like to hear and use statistics.

Statistics often provide the incentive for making a decision. For example, many people have chosen to quit smoking because of statistics on the health and longevity of smokers and nonsmokers. And the prediction of a high unemployment rate—say, 10 percent—could induce some households to save more, cause some businesses to spend less on investments, and lead to the enactment of certain government stabilization policies.

Too often, though, numbers are accepted without question. We do not stop to consider where a statistic comes from, how it is calculated, or how accurately it represents the statement it supports. Consider an announcement that the unemployment rate in a large metropolitan area has increased from 5.4 percent to 6.2 percent in the last 3 months. Does this statistic accurately reflect this area's unemployment? What data were collected, how were they collected, and how were they analyzed in order to arrive at this statistic?

The concepts of population and sampling are important in understanding what lies behind a statistic. Population identifies the group from which the statistic is drawn. On learning the unemployment rate for this particular metropolitan area, many questions about the population that statistic represents could be asked. For example, does it have the same characteristics as the population used to determine the national unemployment rate? Does it include the city and all its suburbs, or does it extend to adjacent rural counties?

The sample for the statistic is the group selected from the population for actual measurement. Both the size of the sample and the method of selecting the sample are important because a statistic based on a poorly drawn sample could misrepresent the larger population. If your college makes the statement that graduates earn on average $70,000 the first year after receiving their degrees, you might be curious about how many graduates were sampled and how they were selected. This statistic could be based on a response to a questionnaire by only five graduates, all of whom are proud of their high salaries and who worked for several years before graduating.

Unfortunately, we usually do not have ready access to information on the population and sample from which a statistic is drawn. However, a simple awareness of these concepts reminds us that a statistic is only as good as its population and sample and that decisions based on faulty statistics can lead to poor results.

[a] The numbers are hypothetical.

Questions

1. The population and sample for deriving the overall unemployment rate in the United States are given in this chapter. What are the population and sample for this statistic?

2. If you could change the current procedures for calculating some key economic statistics, how would you redefine the term unemployed, and who would you include in the population and sample for measuring the unemployment rate? What would you include when determining the Consumer Price Index?

3. In the next few days, locate the population and sample for three publicly issued statistics. These could be on the sports page in your local paper, in a news report on a website, or in this textbook.

4. Assume it was reported today that "the interest rate on car loans is expected to jump by 5 percentage points in the next year." What types of economic decisions might be made as a result of this statement? What serious consequences could occur if this statistic were inaccurate?

Foundations of the Macroeconomy

CHAPTER OBJECTIVES

Explain the pattern of changes in macroeconomic activity.

Understand how total spending or the spending behavior of households, businesses, government units, and the foreign sector, drives the economy's levels of employment and production, and influences prices.

Introduce the multiplier effect.

Discuss the relationships between total spending and inflation and total spending and expectations, and the role of macroeconomic policies on total spending.

Part of the daily news coverage on the Internet, CNN, major television and cable networks, and newspapers is devoted to the state of the economy. There are stories on the stock market, jobs, and inflation; forecasts of recovery or recession; updates on the status of foreign trade; and numerous other topics devoted to reporting the pulse of the economy. What should be clear from the media is that the U.S. economy continually changes: It goes through upswings and downswings, or periods of expansion and contraction, and never stays at a particular level of activity. Two data series discussed in Chapter 4 attest to this movement: the unemployment rate and real GDP, both of which change on a regular basis.

This chapter deals with fluctuations in the level of production, or economic activity, in the macroeconomy. It identifies the pattern of these fluctuations and provides a foundation for understanding why they occur.

CHANGES IN MACROECONOMIC ACTIVITY

Generally, when people say that the economy is getting better or worse, going into an upswing or downswing, or expanding or contracting, it is because the economy's real GDP is increasing or decreasing. Sometimes, however, people focus on changes in the unemployment rate as their gauge of changes in the economy. Regardless, these two indicators are related: Changes in real GDP cause changes in unemployment. Increases in production bring about reductions in unemployment, and decreases in production increase unemployment.

Figure 5.1 shows changes in real GDP from 1990 through 2014 in the upper graph and changes in the unemployment rate over the same period in the lower graph. In the top graph, notice that real GDP constantly changes and that it does not change at the same rate from year to year. In some years, growth or decline was more rapid than in other years. In the bottom graph, notice the change in unemployment that results from changes in real GDP. For example, unemployment began to grow when real GDP began to slow down in 2008.

FIGURE 5.1   *Real Gross Domestic Product and the Unemployment Rate, 1990–2014[a]*

A market economy, such as that of the United States, constantly goes through upswings and downswings in its level of output. There is a generally inverse relationship between the economy's level of output and the rate of unemployment: As output decreases or increases, unemployment tends to rise or fall, respectively.

---

[a] GDP is given in chained 2005 dollars and the unemployment rate is seasonally adjusted for civilian workers.

Source: *Economic Report of the President* (Washington, DC: U.S. Government Printing Office, 2015), Table B-11; Bureau of Economic Analysis, "Current-Dollar and 'Real' Gross Domestic Product," www.bea.gov.

While the connection between production and employment is fairly straightforward, the connection between production and price levels is not. We learned in the last chapter that when real GDP approaches its full production level and people continue to spend, demand-pull inflation may occur. However, when real GDP increases, but is well below the full-production level, or when real GDP decreases, price levels may remain relatively stable. Since price levels may or may not be affected by production levels, we use the expression "changes in economic activity" to refer to changes in production and employment and not prices.

Business Cycles

Business Cycles
Recurring periods of growth and decline (or expansion and contraction) in an economy's real output, or real GDP.

Recovery, Peak, Recession, Trough
The phases of the business cycle during which real GDP, or output, increases, reaches its maximum, falls, and reaches its minimum, respectively.

Changes in economic activity do not occur randomly or haphazardly, but rather in wavelike patterns called business cycles. These patterns provide some degree of predictability that enables us to better use macroeconomic policy tools to address downswings. **Business cycles** are recurring periods of growth and decline in real output, or real GDP. A business cycle goes through four phases: a **recovery**, which is an expansionary phase during which real GDP increases; a **peak**, where maximum output occurs; a **recession**, during which real GDP falls; and a **trough**, where real GDP reaches its minimum.[1] Figure 5.2 illustrates the wavelike movement of business cycles and shows how the phases of the cycle are repeated.

The economy is always in some phase of a business cycle. It does not remain stationary at a particular level of output until some force causes it to increase or decrease. Instead, the economy is always expanding, contracting, or at a turning point in activity.

Cyclical Behavior of the U.S. Economy   Figure 5.3 gives us a good historical view of business cycles in the United States by tracing these wavelike patterns since the early 1920s. It also points out some important properties of business cycles. First, the

---

FIGURE 5.2   *Phases of the Business Cycle*

The economy is always in one of the four phases of the business cycle. Activity is either at a peak, in a recession, at a trough, or in a recovery.

---

[1] The terms *recession* and *depression* do not have the same meaning. A recession is a downswing in economic activity. The Great Depression was a historical event in the 1930s when the United States and other economies experienced sharp reductions in output and increases in unemployment.

FIGURE 5.3   *Economic Activity: A Long-Term View*

The length of each phase and the intensity of the change in output differ from cycle to cycle.

phases of business cycles are not of equal length: Some phases last just a few months, whereas others last for years. Notice also that after the 1940s, periods of expansion outweigh periods of contraction and there is less severity in the cycles. This might be due in part to the federal government's commitment to a healthy economy, a better understanding of the economy, and improved information to make economic decisions. A second important property of business cycles is the unequal intensity, or strength, of expansions and contractions. For example, the output declines from 1929 to 1932 and in 1945 were dramatic, whereas others, like the decline in 2008, are not as severe.

Every business cycle is unique in the lengths of its phases and the intensity of its recovery and recession. Regardless of the messages of some financial gurus, as you can see, there is no exact rule for determining the duration and magnitude of recessions and recoveries or for defining the exact amount of time required for each business cycle.

Causes of Economic Fluctuations

What causes the economy to expand and contract? This is likely the most important macroeconomic question to be asked. If we understand why we have recessions and recoveries, we can foster the upswings and control the downswings.

For centuries, people have pondered the causes of economic fluctuations. Over the years, some theories, like one attributing business cycles to sunspots, have emerged and disappeared, while others have been accepted and refined. And some, like the conspirators theory in Applications 5.1, "What's Causing the Economy to Change?" go beyond what one typically expects to hear.

Today, there are several theories about what causes economic activity to change. When considering the merits of these theories, it is helpful to remember what we learned in Chapter 1: Theories are abstractions that are based on assumptions and

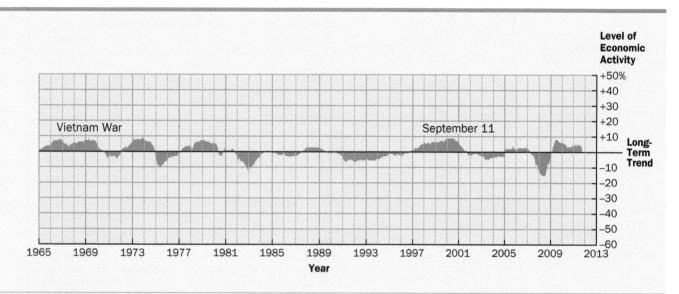

Source: Tom King, "Industrial Production Index," Board of Governors of the Federal Reserve System, G.17 Industrial Production and Capacity Utilization, updated 09/14/2012.

focus on the relationship between two variables. That is, different macroeconomic theories use different assumptions and variables and explain the economy's behavior from different perspectives.

There are several popular theories today that deal with causes of recessions and recoveries. In addition to this chapter, Chapter 9 presents several other generally accepted theories. However, to fully appreciate and understand the working of the macroeconomy, as well as these macroeconomic theories, it is important to have a solid grasp of some basics. That is the goal of this chapter.

TOTAL SPENDING AND MACROECONOMIC ACTIVITY

Analyzing the macroeconomy is not easy: Sometimes it is difficult to bring orderly relationships to such a large picture. To ease our study, economists tend to think of the macroeconomy as having four large groups or sectors: households, businesses, government, and the foreign sector. All macroeconomic activity falls into one of these groups, and each group makes decisions that play an important role in the health of the economy.

Economists have also identified an important macroeconomic relationship that we need to understand: Changes in total (aggregate) spending in the economy cause changes in total (aggregate) production and employment. **Total, or aggregate, spending** is all of the spending for all new goods and services that occurs in the economy. Total spending is the spending of each of our major groups—households, businesses, government units, and foreign buyers—together.

In a market economy, spending is the driver. As long as buyers spend their money, producers will continue to produce goods and services and hire people to do

Total, or Aggregate, Spending
The total combined spending of all units in the economy (households plus businesses plus government plus foreign) for new goods and services.

WHAT'S CAUSING THE ECONOMY TO CHANGE?

Over the years there have been some interesting explanations for changes in the macroeconomy that are not based on reasons one would describe as "economic." Let's take a brief look at a few of them.

Sunspots   In 1837, 1847, and 1857 the British economy went through a series of downswings. William Stanley Jevons, a highly regarded economist at that time, argued that these downswings may have been caused by sunspots—which show up about every 10 years. Actually, now we know that a connection between sunspots and economic activity is not that farfetched. Sunspots can adversely affect weather, which in turn can reduce crop yields. The British depended on India to buy exported British products. But since a major source of income for India was its crops, when the crops failed (presumably due to sunspots), India had less income to buy British exports. In turn, the British economy suffered.

Conspirators   During the Great Depression and the administration of President Franklin D. Roosevelt, a theory emerged that downswings are caused by conspirators. Some people said that a group was conspiring to do damage to the economy and that these conspirators were using a popular comic strip to openly communicate with each other. One of the characters in this comic strip was a cigar smoker. According to the conspiracy theorists, smoke coming up from his cigar in a given day's comic signaled one thing to the conspirators, and ashes falling from his cigar signaled something else.

Psychology and Theology   Explanations for movements in the economy have also been built on psychological and theological foundations. It has been suggested by some that people go through waves of optimism and pessimism, and that these emotional waves in turn cause the economy to go through waves of expansion and contraction. Others have argued that downswings in the economy are punishment for sins committed while the economy was prospering.

so. If total spending decreases—people quit buying homes, the government cancels a major aircraft order, and developers quit building shopping centers—producers respond by decreasing production, which in turn results in a decrease in employment and in incomes. If total spending increases, producers respond by increasing output, which in turn results in an increase in employment and in incomes. Thus, a reduction in spending leads to a recession because of its dampening effect on output, employment, and income. An increase in spending leads to a recovery because of its expansive effects. The relationship between spending and output, employment, and income is summarized in Figure 5.4.

Obviously the spending behavior of households, businesses, the government, and foreign buyers is critical to the health of the macroeconomy. In the next few pages, we will examine each group and the factors that significantly influence its spending behavior.

The Household Sector

Households constitute the largest spending group in the economy and buy far more goods and services than do businesses, government, and foreign purchasers combined. For example, households purchased almost $12 trillion of the approximately $17.5 trillion output produced in 2014.[2] Furthermore, individuals do not radically alter their spending patterns from year to year, making this spending fairly stable as it

---

[2] *Economic Report of the President* (Washington, DC: U.S. Government Printing Office, 2015), Table B-2; numbers are preliminary.

FIGURE 5.4   *Total Spending and the Level of Economic Activity*

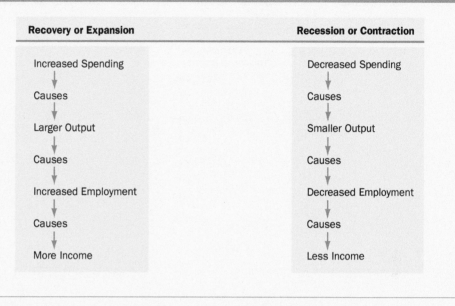

Recovery or Expansion	Recession or Contraction
Increased Spending	Decreased Spending
↓	↓
Causes	Causes
↓	↓
Larger Output	Smaller Output
↓	↓
Causes	Causes
↓	↓
Increased Employment	Decreased Employment
↓	↓
Causes	Causes
↓	↓
More Income	Less Income

Changes in total, or aggregate, spending lead to changes in output, employment, and income.

generally increases. It is fortunate for the economy that the largest spending group is so steady in its spending patterns.

Technically speaking, we call aggregate household spending on new goods and services **personal consumption expenditures**. Figure 5.5 plots real personal consumption expenditures for 2000 through 2014.[3] Notice that the line almost always slopes upward with little fluctuation.

The Household Sector and the Circular Flow   Most of the spending that we do comes from income that we earn. We deliver pizzas, work as CEOs, own and run bed-and-breakfasts, and do a host of other activities to earn money. In the macroeconomy, then, we know that the majority of spending by the household sector on new goods and services comes from the income earned by households, or is **income-determined spending**.

Figure 5.6 builds on the circular flow model introduced in Chapter 2; it illustrates some of the important factors that influence household spending and how they are related. For now, observe lines 1, 2, 3, and 4. Line 1 shows a flow of earned income from selling factors of production to businesses (line 2), and line 4 shows a flow of personal consumption expenditures for goods and services (line 3). You can see that earned income provides the spending power to purchase goods and services.

While earned income is the major source of household spending, it is not the only source. Households can also spend from funds that they borrow through bank loans,

Personal Consumption Expenditures
Household spending on new goods and services.

Income-Determined Spending
Household spending on new goods and services that comes from income earned from providing resources to producers.

---

[3] The numbers in Figure 5.5 as well as Figures 5.7, 5.10, and 5.12 are given in real terms. That is, the numbers are adjusted for price increases, or inflation.

| FIGURE 5.5 | *Real Personal Consumption Expenditures, 2000–2014*[a] |

Total spending by households does not fluctuate widely from year to year, and the growth of personal consumption expenditures is relatively stable over time.

[a] Numbers are in chained 2009 dollars; 2014 number is preliminary.

Source: *Economic Report of the President* (Washington, DC: U.S. Government Printing Office, 2015), Table B-2.

Transfer Payments
Money from the government for which no direct work is performed in return.

Nonincome-Determined Spending
Spending that is generated from sources other than household earned income.

Injections into the Spending Stream
Spending that comes from a source other than household earned income; nonincome-determined spending.

credit card purchases, or such, and from government **transfer payments**, which are payments from the government for which no direct work is performed in return. Social Security payments, unemployment compensation, and agricultural subsidies are examples of transfer payments. Checks from working for a government are not transfer payments.

When households make personal consumption expenditures from money that they borrow or receive in transfers, we call that **nonincome-determined spending**. It is important to separate income- and nonincome-determined spending. Since nonincome-determined expenditures are based on sources other than earned income, they become **injections into the spending stream**. That is, they are expenditures over and above what household earned income alone would allow. Injections into the spending stream are important because they lead to an expansion of output, employment, and income in the economy as businesses produce more to meet this additional demand. In Figure 5.6, transfers and borrowing are shown as injections into the circular model.

We also know that households do not spend all of their income: Some is used to pay taxes and some is saved. Households pay a variety of taxes to various government units. Households also save in a variety of ways through the use of

| FIGURE 5.6 | *Household Spending, Borrowing, Transfers, Saving, and Taxes* |

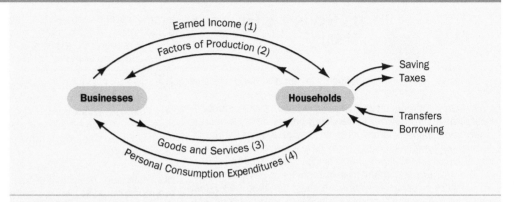

Household spending, which is influenced mainly by the size of earned income, is also affected by transfers and borrowing, which provide injections into the spending stream, and by saving and taxes, which are leakages from the spending stream.

Financial Institutions
Organizations such as banks, credit unions, and insurance companies that provide a means for saving and borrowing.

Leakages from the Spending Stream
Uses for earned income other than spending, such as paying taxes and saving.

financial institutions such as banks, brokerage houses, credit unions, and insurance companies. Both saving and taxes are **leakages from the spending stream** because they are income that households are not spending. Leakages from the spending stream cause output, employment, and income in the economy to shrink as businesses cut back production in response to a reduced demand.

In summary, the amount that households spend is influenced by

♦   earned income,
♦   borrowing,
♦   transfers,
♦   saving, and
♦   taxes.

When people earn more or less, change their saving habits, or change any of the other factors just listed, total personal consumption expenditures and the economy as a whole can be affected. For example, fear of a recession could cause people to increase saving, with a resulting decline in spending; or a decrease in interest rates could encourage people to borrow for new cars, home remodeling, and other spending purposes.

Although personal consumption expenditures is the largest component of total spending, the impact on the economy of changes in the household sector is affected by spending in the business, government, and foreign sectors. As a result, we need to examine the other sectors and consider all of them together before drawing any conclusions about the economy.

Up for Debate, "Is Saving a Healthy Habit?" examines conflicting messages about saving. Do you agree with the underlying message that what may be good for the individual may not be good for the group?

The Business Sector

Businesses play an extremely important role in the macroeconomy because of their spending habits. The size of business spending on new goods is huge: Each year they put hundreds of billions of dollars into new machinery and equipment, replacement

Is Saving a Healthy Habit?

Issue *From the time we are children, we are encouraged to save. Grandparents often give savings bonds and accounts to celebrate a birthday, banks frequently provide penny accounts, and some parents attempt to encourage savings habits by matching amounts saved. By the time a person enters adulthood, regularly saving money may be a lifestyle habit.*

But the argument that it is smart to save seems to contradict a basic economic relationship that we've just explored: Increased spending leads to more output and employment, and decreased spending—or more saving— leads to declines in output and employment. In other words, for the good of the economy, it is healthier to spend than to save? Faced with these contradictory messages, we need to ask: Is saving a healthy habit?

Yes People should save on a regular basis. Good planning for the future involves good financial planning, which encourages saving. The ability to qualify for a mortgage, send kids to college, or retire comfortably is affected by the amount a person has saved. In addition, the peace of mind afforded by a cushion of certificates of deposit, stocks, mutual funds, and other assets may lessen everyday stress.

Saving also provides a means for increasing income through interest and dividends. As one saves more, the income earned from saving increases and affords additional funds for more saving or spending.

It is also important to develop good savings habits and build up a reserve of funds because life throws us curves that can be better negotiated if we have money. Job loss, illness, or an auto accident could be disastrous without money to assist us through such a crisis. Life can also throw us opportunities that can be seized if we have the funds—traveling, an interesting nonpaying internship, a stock tip, and a partnership in a business, to name a few.

No People need to be careful that they do not save too much because, while saving may be good for the individual, the health of the economy depends on the overall level of spending. And, since ordinary consumers like us are part of the largest spending group, it is important that we buy goods and services and not save too much money.

When we increase our saving, businesses respond by cutting back on production. For example, if we all decided to wait to buy a car until we have saved enough to pay cash, car sales and production would fall dramatically, jobs would be lost in the auto and related industries, and the economy would slow down. This applies to services also. Saving rather than going to the dentist or even taking piano lessons causes a reduction in some incomes.

Increases in saving could kick off a downward spiral into a recession, with resulting job losses. Without jobs, there is no income to save. If we all listen to the adages about the value of saving, we could hurt ourselves.

Investment Spending
Business spending on new goods, such as machinery, equipment, buildings, and inventories; nonincome-determined spending.

parts, buildings, inventories, and the like. Technically, we term this **investment spending**, and we label it nonincome-determined spending because investment spending does not come from household earned income.

Investment spending is not steady and tends to fluctuate from year to year. Figure 5.7 plots real gross investment for 2000 through 2014 and shows how this spending fluctuates. This figure gives us an excellent picture of a very important piece of macroeconomic reality: *Changes in investment spending are a primary cause of changes in economic activity.* When business spending declines, it can bring about a slowdown or recession; when it increases, it can help pull the economy into a recovery. Figure 5.7 shows declines in investment spending that began in 2007. The United States experienced a serious recession and increasing unemployment rates at this time.

Business Spending and Profit Expectations Why does business spending fluctuate? Business spending habits in the aggregate are very different from household habits because the motivation for spending is different. Householders look to their earned income as the basis for spending to support a lifestyle. Households tend to have fairly stable expenditures for housing, food, and other necessities and/or luxuries. Businesses look for the potential to make a profit as their basis for spending. Businesses invest in new buildings and equipment and larger inventories if they expect to earn

| FIGURE 5.7 | *Real Gross Investment, 2000–2014[a]* |

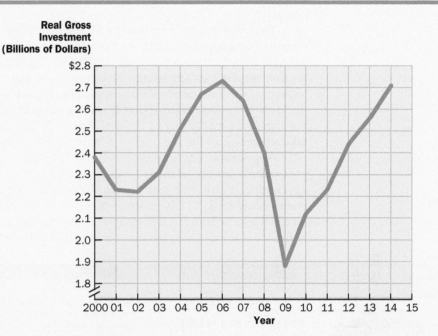

Investment spending can fluctuate widely from year to year and is a major cause of changes in economic activity.

[a]Numbers are in chained 2009 dollars; 2014 number is preliminary.

Source: *Economic Report of the President* (Washington, DC: U.S. Government Printing Office, 2015), Table B-2.

enough profit from the investment to make it worthwhile. The reason Wal-Mart constructs a new Sam's Club or Ford retools a truck plant is that these companies expect to increase their profit levels with these expenditures.

Sometimes businesses plan for new investment spending—perhaps a technology upgrade—but "hold on" to those plans and postpone them because the timing is not right. Most investment spending is postponable: Building a new box store, constructing a new ride at a theme park, remodeling corporate headquarters, or even buying a new pizza oven by a mom-and-pop operation are likely not expenditures that must be made for day-to-day operations to continue. Since most businesses can delay major capital expenditures until profit expectations increase, this adds to the reasons for fluctuations in business spending.

An important factor that influences expected profit and investment spending is expectations of future overall levels of economic activity. Fear of a recession can discourage investment spending as businesses speculate that falling demand and growing inventories of unsold goods will make their operations unprofitable. Likewise, expectations of healthy sales and a surge in economic activity can bring about an increase in business spending. Predictions of economic doom and gloom coupled with the reality of falling demand and rising unemployment from 2008 through 2010 helped to scare businesses into postponing investment spending plans. The economy was so skittish that the stock market reacted to many announcements, even the possible spread of swine flu.

The price tag on a business's investment plans can be staggering. Imagine the construction costs for a new stadium for one of the major league baseball teams or even for a medical center in your hometown. Since most businesses borrow the funds for their investment spending, the interest rate that they must pay to borrow greatly influences the level of investment spending. If the interest rate is high, businesses may decide that it is best to postpone spending because the high cost of borrowing reduces the expected profitability of the investment. If the interest rate is low, businesses may take advantage of the reduced cost of funds and increase their borrowing.

Application 5.2, "Interest Rates and Investment Spending," provides a very simple example of how an investment decision can be affected by the interest rate. In this application, a five-year loan for $200,000 at an 18 percent interest rate would cost a business owner $1,212.10 more in monthly payments or a total of $72,726 more than would the same loan at a 6 percent interest rate. The importance of the effect of changes in the interest rate on economic activity will be discussed further in Chapter 8.

APPLICATION 5.2

INTEREST RATES AND INVESTMENT SPENDING

Quite a few young adults are combining a passion for healthy food with an entrepreneurial spirit that is bringing fresh, wholesome breads, baked goods, and more to markets. Usually, a motivating factor for opening a business is the possible money that can be made. But, sometimes, the passionate baker is looking first for the ability to cover costs and not lose money on a risky venture.

Let's take the case of Serious Bread and its owners. They have been selling some varieties of their wonderful bread at the local farmers market and to a number of restaurants and are receiving rave reviews. The owners/bakers would very much like to combine a bread baking facility with a retail space so that their customers have ready access to their bread.

Serious Bread has determined that it needs to borrow $200,000 to make the dream a reality. But one of the critical considerations in going forward is whether or not

they can make payments on the principal and interest for this $200,000 loan. Can they afford these payments every month to retire this loan?

In simple terms, an annual interest rate of 6 percent means that the interest payment alone for one year on $200,000 is $12,000 (0.06 × $200,000). An interest rate of 12 percent means an annual interest cost of $24,000, and an 18 percent interest rate is $36,000. And, as a small business without established credit, the owners know that a higher rate is likely.

Assume now that the owners decide to go for it and explore taking out a loan for $200,000 that they will repay over five years. The following table summarizes the payments they will need to make each month. (The calculations in this table are complex because loan payments are based on a declining principal.)

Notice the substantial difference in monthly payments that must be made on this loan as well as the total interest paid over five years as the interest rate rises. The owners must be able to assess whether their bread baking operation and sales are capable of making these monthly payments. Also, you can understand why they will search for someone who will loan them money at the lowest interest rate.

Monthly Payments and Total Interest Paid for a $200,000 Loan with a Five-Year Repayment

	Interest Rate		
	6%	**12%**	**18%**
Monthly payment	$3,866.60	$4,448.90	$5,078.70
Total interest paid	$31,996.00	$66,934.00	$104,722.10

FIGURE 5.8   *Business Investment Spending, Saving, and Taxes*

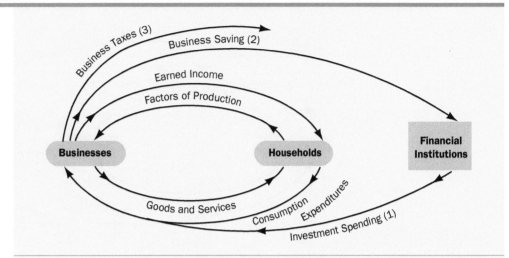

Business investment spending is an injection into the spending stream, and business saving and taxes are leakages from the spending stream.

Retained Earnings

The portion of a business's accumulated profits that has been retained for investment or other purposes.

The Business Sector and the Circular Flow   The circular flow model in Figure 5.8 shows the role of the business sector in economic activity. Line 1 is business investment spending, which is an injection into the spending stream because it is nonincome-determined spending. Line 2 represents business saving, called **retained earnings**. Line 3 represents business taxes: corporate income tax, sales tax, and license fees, to name a few. Both business saving and taxes are leakages from the spending stream.

Notice the addition of financial institutions to Figure 5.8. These are important for business saving and investment borrowing. Businesses use financial institutions to hold their savings through deposits, stocks, bonds, or some other security that earns money until the funds are needed. Financial institutions also provide the means for financing investment spending through loans, new shares of stock, or simply redeeming the retained earnings.

Saving–Borrowing Relationship

The relationship between the amount saved by households and businesses and the amount returned to the spending stream through investment and household borrowing.

The Saving–Borrowing Relationship   This is a good time to point out a critical flow in the macroeconomy: the **saving–borrowing relationship**. Figure 5.9 adds household saving and borrowing back into the circular flow and allows us to see a fuller picture of saving and borrowing. Through financial institutions, dollars saved by households and businesses—dollars that are leakages from the spending stream—can be borrowed and spent by other households and businesses and thereby returned to the spending stream. In other words, financial institutions are vehicles for changing leakages from the spending stream into injections.

Since the motivations for saving and for borrowing are not the same, it is important to understand that the amount saved may not equal the amount borrowed. In other words, the economy could experience conditions where savings are greater than borrowing, savings are less than borrowing, or savings equal borrowing.

Because saving is a leakage from the spending stream and spending from borrowing is an injection into the stream, overall spending in the economy and the resulting levels of output and employment are influenced by this relationship. When saving is

| FIGURE 5.9 | *Saving, Investing, and Borrowing by Households and Businesses* |

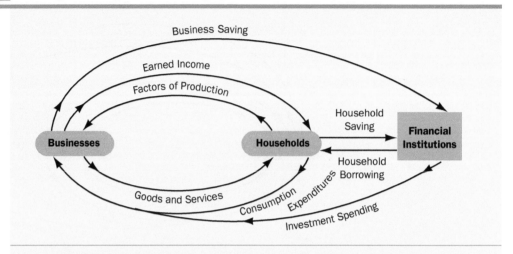

The relationship between saving and investment spending and household spending from borrowing can cause the economy's levels of output, employment, and income to increase, decrease, or remain unchanged.

greater than borrowing, the relationship will foster a decrease in total spending and a downturn in the economy. When saving is less than borrowing, the relationship will foster an increase in total spending and an upturn in the economy. We need to understand that, at this point, we have isolated this saving–borrowing relationship. Before we draw any big picture conclusions, we need to put other relationships into the model.[4]

The Government Sector

The government—federal, state, and local—is another sector that has a major impact on the economy because of its own spending as well as its power to influence spending in the other sectors through the taxes that are imposed. And, as we will soon learn in Chapter 6, the federal government can use its spending and taxing to change the direction of the economy. We classify government spending into two major categories: purchases of goods and services, and transfer payments.

Government Purchases of Goods and Services
Government spending on new goods and services; nonincome-determined spending.

Governments provide us with many needed services and, as a result, make **government purchases of goods and services** to do so: fire trucks, police radar detectors, defense systems, park benches, paper, and the services of government employees to fix roads and maintain a court system, to name a few. Technically, we classify government purchases of goods and services as nonincome-determined spending because they do not come directly from household earned income. Government purchases have the same impact on the economy as does other spending: Increases in government purchases can increase economic activity, and decreases can decrease output, employment, and income.

In most years, government spending for new goods and services is the second largest component of total spending. Figure 5.10 plots real government purchases of

---

[4] We are simplifying the saving–borrowing relationship by assuming that 100 percent of borrowed funds are spent. While this may not always be true, it does allow us to understand the impact of this important relationship. To be precise, we would compare saving with spending from borrowing.

| FIGURE 5.10 | *Real Government Purchases of Goods and Services, 2000–2014ᵃ* |

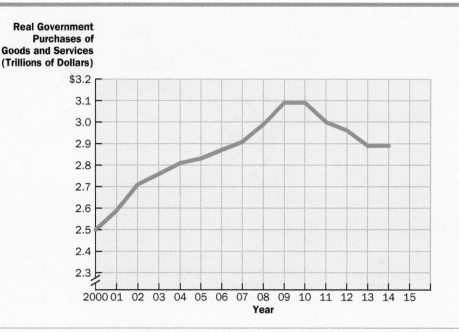

The growth in government purchases of goods and services has been relatively stable.

ᵃNumbers are in chained 2009 dollars; 2014 number is preliminary.

Source: *Economic Report of the President* (Washington, DC: U.S. Government Printing Office, 2015), Table B-2.

goods and services for 2000 through 2014. This figure shows that, like household spending and unlike business spending, except for the serious 2008–2010 recession, government purchases tend to be stable and increase over time.

Government also uses a substantial portion of its funds for transfer payments, such as Social Security and unemployment compensation, which go to individuals or households that perform no direct work in return. These transfer payments can then be used to buy groceries, pay for prescriptions or rent, or make other personal consumption expenditures. Household spending from transfers is nonincome-determined spending because it does not come from household earned income.

We want to point out the importance of thinking of government spending in terms of the two categories just discussed: government purchases and transfer payments. This distinction will help you to better understand the material in this chapter and the following one.

The Government Sector and the Circular Flow   The government sector is added to the basic circular flow model in Figure 5.11. Line 1 shows the flow of transfer payments, which can be used for consumption spending; line 2 represents government purchases of goods and services; and lines 3 and 4 show taxes going from households and businesses to government. This model shows that government purchases are a direct injection into the spending stream, transfers provide an injection through households, and taxes are a leakage.

FIGURE 5.11   *The Government Sector and the Circular Flow*

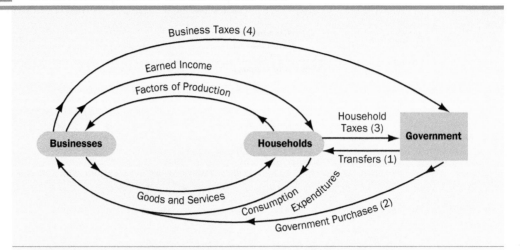

Government purchases of goods and services and spending from transfer payments are injections into the spending stream, and taxes paid to government by businesses and households are leakages from the spending stream.

The Government Taxing–Spending Relationship   There is another relationship like the saving–borrowing one that is important to economic activity: the government taxing–spending relationship. This one, however, is slightly more complicated because while government taxing and spending may be equal, the amount leaked from the spending stream may not equal the amount injected because of saving. That is, taxpayers may pay their taxes using part of their incomes that would have been saved and part that would have been spent, and transfer recipients may save part of their payments. For readers who want to explore the details of this complication, footnote 6 gives that information.[5] For our purposes here we will discuss the amounts leaked from and injected into the spending stream through the government sector, rather than taxes and spending.

---

[5] We are being careful to compare the amount put into the spending stream through government purchases and transfers with the amount taken from the spending stream through taxes. This is because not all transfer payments are used to purchase goods and services and not all taxes are paid with money that would have been spent. When households receive transfer payments, a portion of what they receive from the government may be saved. When households pay taxes, part of that payment may come from money that would have been used for personal consumption expenditures, and part may come from money that would have been saved. For this reason, assessing the impact of government expenditures and taxes becomes somewhat complex. Let us illustrate with the following example.

Suppose that the government taxes households $100 billion and uses that money to purchase $100 billion of goods and services. Suppose also that $70 billion of that tax is paid with dollars that households would have used for personal consumption expenditures and $30 billion is paid with dollars they would have saved. Because of this, the tax of $100 billion reduces household spending by only $70 billion. Thus, the net effect of the tax of $100 billion and the expenditure program of $100 billion is to enlarge the spending stream by $30 billion, and the economy grows. In this example, if the government wanted the effect of its spending and taxes to be neutral, it would spend $70 billion and tax $100 billion.

This example could be further complicated by assuming that out of the $100 billion in government expenditures, only $50 billion is spent for the purchase of goods and services and that the other $50 billion goes for transfer payments. The $50 billion spent on goods and services goes directly into the spending stream, but part of the $50 billion in transfers could go into savings. If households saved $15 billion and spent $35 billion, then only $85 billion of the government's total expenditures would go into the spending stream.

Sometimes the amount that flows into the government in taxes does not equal the amount that is returned to the spending stream through government purchases and spending from transfers. When the amount that is leaked through taxes is greater than the amount returned through these injections, a downswing in economic activity is fostered. When the amount that is leaked in taxes is less than the amount returned through these injections, an upswing in economic activity could result. When they offset each other, there is no change in economic activity from this relationship.

When we complete our discussion of all four economic sectors, we will put the government sector relationships together with the others to get a complete picture.

The Foreign Sector

The fourth major sector that has an impact on the direction of the macroeconomy is the foreign sector. While it is the smallest of the four, it has been growing in importance. Most of us interface daily with some aspect of today's global economy: We buy electronics manufactured in Asia, work on farms that have corn sold to Mexico, wear shoes from Brazil and China, read foreign papers, and go to college credit programs in Europe. In short, the lines between domestic and foreign products and services have become increasingly blurred.

Exports
Goods and services that are sold abroad.

Imports
Goods and services purchased from abroad.

Net Exports
Exports minus imports; is positive when exports exceed imports and negative when imports exceed exports.

We term goods and services produced in the United States and sold abroad as U.S. **exports** and goods and services produced in foreign countries and sold in the United States as U.S. **imports**. Generally speaking, exports increase spending in the economy and imports take spending out of the economy. As a result, we tend to think of exports as injections and imports as leakages. In 2014, exports were 12.9 percent of GDP and imports were equal to 15.8 percent of GDP.[6]

The real values of U.S. exports and imports from 2000 through 2014 are plotted in Figure 5.12a. Notice that the values of exports and imports have generally grown over the years and that the value of U.S. imports has been more than U.S. exports. When we subtract imports from exports, we get the difference between their values or **net exports**. Net exports is positive when exports are greater than imports and negative when exports are less than imports. Net exports of goods and services for 2000 through 2014 is plotted in Figure 5.12b. Negative net export years fall below the zero line on the graph. It is easy to observe that for these years net exports is negative—and exceptionally negative in 2005 and 2006.

The Foreign Sector and the Circular Flow   Figure 5.13 uses a variation of the circular flow model to show the effect of exports and imports on the U.S. economy. Line 1 represents the injections into the U.S. economy that result from expenditures by foreign buyers on exported goods and services. Line 2 represents the leakages from the U.S. economy that result from expenditures by U.S. buyers on imported goods and services. Imports and exports have the same effect as the other leakages and injections: Purchases of imports deflect spending from the economy and foster a downswing, and purchases of exports by foreign buyers increase spending and foster an upswing. Spending on exports is another example of nonincome-determined spending since it does not come from U.S. household earned income.

Here, once again, is another important relationship—the export–import relationship—to consider. And, again, as with the other sectors, injections and leakages may not be equal. Exports can be greater than imports, which makes net exports

[6] *Economic Report of the President* (Washington, DC: U.S. Government Printing Office, 2015), Table B-2. Numbers are preliminary.

FIGURE 5.12 *Real U.S. Exports, Imports, and Net Exports of Goods and Services, 2000–2014[a]*

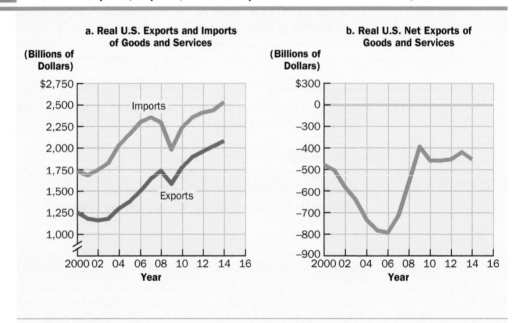

In general, real U.S. exports and imports of goods and services have increased since 2000, and imports have been greater than exports.

[a]Numbers are in chained 2009 dollars; 2014 number is preliminary.

Source: *Economic Report of the President* (Washington, DC: U.S. Government Printing Office, 2015), Table B-2.

positive, causing injections to be greater than leakages and overall spending in this sector to grow. Imports can be greater than exports, which makes net exports negative, causing leakages to be greater than injections and overall spending in this sector to decline. This relationship needs to be considered with the others in evaluating the direction of the overall economy.

Summary of Aggregate Spending, Leakages, and Injections

Let us review. Total, or aggregate, spending drives the economy's production, employment, and income levels. When total spending increases, the economy expands as output, employment, and income increase; when total spending decreases, the economy contracts as output, employment, and income fall. We compute total spending by aggregating the spending of households, businesses, governments, and foreign buyers. It is important to remember that of these four groups, business investment spending, because of its size and instability, is a major cause of changes in economic activity.

Some actions in each of the four spending sectors cause leakages from the spending stream. These include

♦ saving by households and businesses,
♦ paying taxes by households and businesses, and
♦ importing foreign goods and services.

FIGURE 5.13   *The Foreign Sector and the Circular Flow*

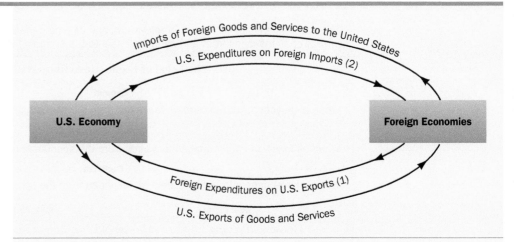

Exports of goods and services generate injections into the U.S. economy's spending stream, and imports cause leakages from the U.S. economy's spending stream.

Other actions in the four sectors cause injections into the spending stream. These include

♦ household spending from borrowed dollars,
♦ household spending from government transfer payments,
♦ business investment spending,
♦ government purchases of goods and services, and
♦ foreign purchases of exported goods and services.

The relationship between leakages and injections influences aggregate spending and, in turn, the economy's production and employment levels. Up to this point in our discussion, we have identified three important relationships: the saving–borrowing, the tax–government expenditures, and the import–export relationships. To assess the economy as a whole, we must consider these relationships together. For example, while saving could exceed borrowing, causing a downswing, government expenditures could exceed taxes, causing an upswing.

In looking at the big picture, we know that

♦ if all leakages from the spending stream are equal to all injections, the economy will not change;
♦ if leakages are greater than injections, the economy will fall into a recession; and
♦ if injections are greater than leakages, the economy will expand into a recovery.

These cause-and-effect relationships are summarized in Table 5.1.

Each of the pieces of the macroeconomic puzzle that we have just created is extremely important because of the impact that each can have on the economy. Even a ban on genetically altered grain and seed exports could have macroeconomic implications. As a result, these various pieces are watched closely by those concerned with the

TABLE 5.1	*Leakages, Injections, and Changes in Economic Activity*

The economy's levels of output, employment, and income depend on the combined impact of all leakages from and all injections into the spending stream.

The Level of Economic Activity Will

Expand

When all injections into exceed all leakages from the spending stream

Remain Unchanged

When all injections into equal all leakages from the spending stream

Contract

When all injections into are less than all leakages from the spending stream

Leakages	Injections
Household saving	Household spending from borrowing
Business saving	Household spending from transfer payments
Household taxes	Business investment spending
Business taxes	Government purchases of goods and services
Import expenditures	Export expenditures

state of the economy. And the media are particularly interested in reporting consumer confidence indexes, saving patterns, transfer payment changes, investment declines, and such.

THE MULTIPLIER EFFECT

In this chapter, we have identified spending as either income-determined or nonincome-determined. There is just one example of income-determined spending: the spending on goods and services that comes from people's earned incomes. All of the other spending that we discussed—from borrowing and transfer payments, investment spending, government purchases, and spending on U.S. exports—is nonincome-determined spending.

It is important to make a distinction between income-determined and nonincome-determined spending. This is because nonincome-determined spending, when it is injected into the economy, is subject to a **multiplier effect**. An increase or decrease in nonincome-determined spending causes changes in output and employment that are far greater than the initial change in spending. An increase, for example, of $100 million in nonincome-determined expenditures will cause the economy to grow by much more than $100 million because of the multiplier effect.

Why is there a multiplier effect? How does it work? Nonincome-determined spending is not part of the "basic circle" of the circular flow model. That is, it is spending that does not come from income earned from production that is taking place. Instead, it comes from outside the core circle of the economy, or is injected into the economy. Once the injection enters the economy, it becomes part of the basic circle and these dollars are spent over and over again.

Multiplier effect
The change in total output and income generated by a change in nonincome-determined spending is larger than, or a multiple of, the spending change itself.

Let's work through an example. Suppose that a developer borrows $10,000,000 to invest in building homes. As the homes are constructed, the developer uses the $10,000,000 to hire people and buy materials and other resources. This spending by the developer puts $10,000,000 into the economy that was not previously there. In other words, this investment injection of $10,000,000 initially creates $10,000,000 in output (the homes) and incomes.

People who receive the $10,000,000 in income from this injection will now take part of it and spend it—they can buy cars, go on vacation, and eat in trendy restaurants—and use part for saving and taxes. We will assume that they spend $8,000,000. Since this $8,000,000 is "new" to the economy, it will result in $8,000,000 of new production and incomes. The income earners of the $8,000,000 will now take part of that, say, $6,400,000, and spend it.

The process does not stop here but continues through the economy in a circular pattern, creating more output and income along the way. In the end, the initial injection of $10,000,000 in the economy creates a substantial amount of output and income. Table 5.2 illustrates this example of the multiplier process through several rounds. When this example is carried through enough successive rounds to approach a zero increase in the last round, and the output and income created in each round are summed, $50,000,000 in total output and income results. This means that the initial injection of $10,000,000 has been multiplied, or magnified, to $50,000,000 of output and income; there has been a multiplier effect equal to five times the initial change in spending.

| TABLE 5.2 | **Effect on Total Output and Income from a Nonincome-Determined Spending Injection of $10,000,000** |

Because of the multiplier effect, an injection of nonincome-determined spending into the spending stream causes total output and income to increase by more than the amount of the nonincome-determined spending itself.

	New Output	New Income	New Personal Consumption Expenditures
Round 1 ($10,000,000 nonincome-determined expenditure)	$10,000,000 →	$10,000,000 →	$8,000,000
Round 2	→8,000,000 →	8,000,000 →	6,400,000
Round 3	→6,400,000 →	6,400,000 →	5,120,000
Round 4	→5,120,000 →	5,120,000 →	4,096,000
Round 5	→4,096,000 →	4,096,000 →	3,276,800
Rounds 6, 7, and so on	•	•	•
	•	•	•
	•	•	•
Total	$50,000,000	$50,000,000	

Calculating the Multiplier Effect   There is an easier way to calculate the multiplier effect than to go through each round of spending, as in Table 5.2. To do so, divide the initial change in nonincome-determined spending by the percentage of the additional income received by households that is *not* spent. Expressed as a formula, the multiplier effect is

$$\frac{\text{initial change in nonincome} - \text{determined spending}}{\text{percentage of additional income not spent}} = \text{total change in output and income.}$$

In the preceding example, the initial change in nonincome-determined spending was $10,000,000 with householder spending 80 percent of income and saving 20 percent throughout the example. Accordingly, the initial change in nonincome-determined spending of $10,000,000 would be divided by 0.20, the percentage of additional income *not* spent in each round, to result in an answer of $50,000,000, the total change in output and income.[7]

The multiplier effect is dependent on how much is spent and not spent from each successive round of income and output that is created: The more that is spent, the greater the multiplier effect; the less that is spent, the smaller the multiplier effect. If households in the preceding example had spent only 75 percent and not spent 25 percent of each successive round of newly created income, the level of economic activity would have grown by $40,000,000 ($10,000,000/0.25 = $40,000,000) rather than $50,000,000.

The multiplier effect also applies when nonincome-determined expenditures are cut back. For example, a decrease in investment spending of $10,000,000, by the time it works its way through the economy, will cause the level of economic activity to decline by more than the initial $10,000,000 decrease.

The multiplier effect is frequently used in local impact studies. Sometimes colleges and universities, for example, will conduct economic studies and use a local multiplier to show how they bring positive economic benefits to a community. Students can be regarded as bringing injections into a local economy as they buy courses, housing, food, books, and such. In addition, multipliers are used to justify large public projects like stadiums. The case is frequently made that a new stadium brings more fans into an area, becomes a tourist magnet, encourages spending for hotels and food, and thus creates additional employment and income for the area.

In summary, changes in nonincome-determined spending, such as investment spending, government and foreign purchases, and household expenditures from transfer payments or borrowing, will cause changes in economic activity that are a multiple of the initial change in spending.

Application 5.3, "Ripples through the Economy," provides three examples of the multiplier effect. The first deals with slumps experienced in western Pennsylvania because of coal and steel, the second with rewards from attracting conventions and sporting events to a city, and the third with recent problems in the auto industry. Keep in mind that the multiplier effect applies to both increases and decreases in spending.

---

[7] Be careful when calculating the multiplier effect to always express the percentage of additional income not spent as a decimal. That is, if 20 percent of additional income is not spent, then the multiplier effect is determined by dividing the initial change in nonincome-determined spending by 0.20, not by 20.

APPLICATION 5.3

RIPPLES THROUGH THE ECONOMY

Western Pennsylvania   Certainly the older generation in western Pennsylvania, home to coal mining and steel making for over a hundred years, experienced the ripple effect caused by the multiplier principle. Most families in this area knew what it meant when these two industries began to lay off workers.

All one needed was a visit to Pittsburgh or one of the smaller towns like Monessen or Uniontown to see how the slump in steel or coal affected the entire community. As steelworkers or coal miners no longer clocked in to their jobs, the lines formed at the unemployment offices for some relief.

But being out of work meant little or no spending at car lots, restaurants, and local shops, and even church collections fell. These establishments then had no choice but to lay off workers, too. As the flower shops, shoe stores, restaurants, remodeling companies, and even churches laid off some of their employees, families had little choice but to cut back on their spending. And you could see it as towns lost their vibrancy. The ripple effect hit almost everyone.

Bring on the Visitors   Cities and towns today know the value of attracting tourists, conventions and conferences, and major sporting events. Dynamic communities are funding visitor and convention bureaus, websites, and magazine ads designed to bring people to their towns.

Why are they doing this? It is very simple—the multiplier principle. Consider a major convention like the American Medical Association annual meeting in June 2015 in Chicago. This largest association of medical doctors brought people from all over the United States to Chicago who rented hotel rooms, ate three meals a day, shopped, visited museums, or, in short, spent a lot of money in Chicago. This provided more jobs and income for many Chicagoans, from hotel to museum staff. This convention, like others in Chicago, boosted that city's economy.

This also explains the competition to attract major sporting events like the Super Bowl and the Final Four or for cities to cheer their baseball teams on to the World Series. Think about the money that flows into a local economy from four World Series games. Visitors to a city, from the media folks to out-of-town baseball fans, leave the community with millions of dollars that would not have been injected without the event.

The Snowball Effect   In the spring of 2009, the economy continued a downward decline that began in the fall of 2008. This downhill spiral was exacerbated by a substantial drop in car sales and uncertainty over the future of General Motors and Chrysler.

When Chrysler announced in May 2009 that it would close a large number of car manufacturing plants in the United States as part of its bankruptcy plan, near panic occurred in cities like Fenton, Missouri, the home of two large Chrysler assembly plants. This would mean a job loss of another 1,000 employees at facilities that just a few years ago employed more than 7,000 people.

Without the plants, suppliers of parts for the Fenton facility—like a nearby car seat company—feared the possibility of going out of business, causing even more workers to be unemployed. And businesses that grew because of the Chrysler plants—from bars and restaurants to grocery stores—worried that their customer base would be gone and they, too, would be forced to shut down.

In addition, the city and the local school district were concerned. How many employees would have to be "let go" because the taxes generated by these facilities would no longer be collected? The plants provided for about 10 percent of the Fenton city budget and paid $5.7 million annually to the school district.

Fenton officials and business owners were not optimistic about the downward spiral that this old river town could now face. The owner of a local tea house and gift shop was worried about declining customers as spouses of plant workers pinch pennies. "I'm afraid of the snowball effect," she said.

INFLATION, EXPECTATIONS, AND MACROECONOMIC POLICIES

A Word about Inflation

We must be careful to understand that it is not always to the benefit of the economy to encourage more spending. When the economy expands, the full production–full employment level of output sets a limit on how far spending can cause production and employment to increase. If spending continues to grow when the economy is at or close to the full production–full employment level of output, demand-pull inflation may result.

Inflation may occur if injections into the spending stream are greater than leakages when the economy is at or near full employment. Too much spending through investment, household borrowing, exporting, and/or government expenditures, or too little saving, importing, and/or taxing could cause prices to rise.

A Word about Expectations

Expectations

Anticipations of future events; can affect current actions by households and businesses and the likelihood that the future events will occur.

Earlier we noted that **expectations** of a recession might induce businesses to cut back investment spending in anticipation of a decline in sales. Expectations of a recession could also cause households to increase their saving because they fear possible job losses. Such actions prompted by the fear of a recession can actually trigger a recession. Fear-induced increases in saving bring about a greater leakage from the spending stream, and a reduction in investment lessens this injection into the spending stream. As saving is increased and investment is reduced, the resulting decrease in spending causes output, employment, and income to fall, and the economy slips into a recession.

Expectations can also cause or worsen inflation. If households and businesses expect prices to rise, they may try to beat the price increases by buying now what they want and need in the future. This surge in spending may serve only to cause or worsen the inflation that is feared.

It is important to maintain good, positive expectations about the economy. Recovery from a recession is more difficult when households and businesses are unwilling to spend because they are pessimistic about the prospects of recovery. Controlling inflation is more difficult if households and businesses believe that prices will continue to go up in the future and that they will be penalized for postponing their expenditures.

You can check your knowledge of the impact of spending, leakages, injections, the multiplier, the full employment ceiling, and expectations on the economy by completing Test Your Understanding, "Changes in Economic Activity."

Macroeconomic Predictors and Policies

Chapters 4 and 5 have provided a wealth of basic information about the macroeconomy, from data to key terminology to an understanding of the forces that impact how the economy behaves. You now know the indicators of good and bad health in the economy and how that is defined. The constant coverage of economic conditions by the media and the expressions that are used should make you smart about evaluating that coverage.

Part of the interest in economic conditions is in predicting the future, or where the economy is headed. Is it moving into or out of a recession or a recovery? Some of the economic data we have examined give the state of the economy: unemployment and GDP figures, for example. Other data such as consumer spending and interest rates serve more as predictors. When consumers are fearful of times ahead and cut back on their spending, it has a negative impact on economic activity. Likewise, an increase in interest rates makes investment spending less profitable and inclines businesses toward postponement. The list of predictors, however, is not limited to these data as people also watch many other indicators such as changes in business inventories and measures of consumer confidence. You might enjoy Application 5.4, "Unconventional Indicators of Economic Health," which gives some of the more unique and quirky predictors that various people have found.

TEST YOUR UNDERSTANDING

CHANGES IN ECONOMIC ACTIVITY

In the following examples, explain the effect on output and employment that would result from each action taken alone. Unless specifically indicated, the economy is not at full employment when the action occurs.

1. Businesses install new telecommunications systems.
2. Congress increases personal income tax rates by 5 percent.
3. A decrease in mortgage loan rates and a continued strong demand for housing cause a boom in the home construction business.
4. Overseas buyers purchase a large amount of road-building equipment manufactured in the United States.
5. Newspaper headlines continually carry predictions of a recession in the months to come.
6. Because the economy is at full employment, several major credit card companies successfully campaign to increase the number of, and usage by, cardholders.
7. The interest rates for borrowing money increase.
8. Net exports of goods and services changes from a negative to a positive number.
9. Social Security benefit payments are increased by 2.3 percent.
10. Households, fearing that prices will spiral upward because the economy is at full employment, immediately purchase big-ticket items such as cars and furniture.
11. Businesses postpone their expansion plans while they wait for better economic times.
12. Political pressure prompts Congress to cut its spending on highway projects.
13. Each U.S. taxpayer receives a tax rebate check when the economy is at full employment.
14. A law is passed limiting the number of new foreign automobiles that can enter the country each year.
15. U.S. citizens begin to change their attitudes toward thrift and start to save more.

The following examples relate to the multiplier effect. Determine the direction and size of the change in total output and income that will result from each change in nonincome-determined spending.

16. After several years of drought, farmers in central Illinois spend $50 million on irrigation equipment at a time when households do not spend 25 percent of the additional income they receive.
17. The federal government cuts defense expenditures by $35 billion at a time when households are not spending 40 percent of the additional income they receive.
18. Developers borrow $120 million for new home construction in northern Virginia at a time when households are spending 70 percent of the additional income they receive.
19. Business spending for machinery and equipment falls by $6 billion after predictions of a recession. Households spend only 50 percent of the additional income they receive due to these predictions.
20. Exports increase by $20 million at the same time that imports increase by $25 million. Households spend 60 percent of the additional income they receive.
21. (Be careful!) Government transfer payments increase by $100 million at a time when households spend 80 percent of the additional income they receive.

Answers can be found at the back of the book.

Fiscal Policy

Influencing the levels of aggregate output and employment or prices through changes in federal government purchases, transfer payments, and/or taxes.

Monetary Policy

Influencing the levels of aggregate output and employment or prices through changes in interest rates and the money supply.

Regardless of where the economy is moving, the goals continue to be full employment, price stability, and full production and economic growth. Since total spending is the fundamental driver of production and employment and sometimes price levels, policies have been designed to affect spending in the economy.

Fiscal policy modifies spending by changing government taxes, transfer payments, and purchases of goods and services. Fiscal policy can increase spending to redirect the economy into an expansion or decrease spending to slow it down. The workings of this strategy for influencing the economy will be discussed in the next chapter.

Monetary policy focuses on changing borrowing and, to a lesser degree, saving, or the injections and leakages that flow through financial institutions. This policy falls into the domain of the Federal Reserve, whose actions can change interest rates and the amount of funding available for loans. The Federal Reserve can create conditions that encourage borrowing and spending by households and businesses or tighten credit

UNCONVENTIONAL INDICATORS OF ECONOMIC HEALTH

Over the years, there have been a number of "studies" of unusual predictors of the state of the economy. Here are a few. What do you think might be missing from this list?

Hemline Index
This index is attributed to Wharton Professor George Taylor in 1926, who observed that in good times, like the Roaring Twenties, hemlines were short. When the Depression came in the 1930s, hemlines fell. Thus came the conclusion that has fascinated many over the decades: hemlines are short in good times and long in bad times. The mini made its debut in good times; the long hippy skirts in bad times. Explanations of this trend have varied, including the idea that women couldn't afford stockings during the Depression.

Men's Underwear and Neckties
It is said that these two male wardrobe items are good predictors. Since men's underwear sales tend to be relatively flat, a decline in sales foretells a recession where an increase in sales is just the opposite. A new necktie is a relatively inexpensive way to improve one's appearance when seeking a new job or living in fear of losing one: necktie sales up, economy down.

Lipstick Index
This index was proposed by Estee Lauder's chairman who found that lipstick sales go up in a down economy, which was even true in the Great Depression. It was thought that this is a small luxury when women have less discretionary spending.

The Movies
In bad times, people tend to escape to the movies. Both movie attendance and home movie rentals tend to go up when times are tough. Do you think popcorn sales trend the same way?

Diesel Fuel Sales
An economist at UCLA believes that truckers' diesel purchases are a leading indicator of economic activity. More sales mean more goods and services are being moved; a decline indicates production is going down.

Urban Forecasts
Several urban economists and planners have unusual data they scour. In San Francisco, one looks at Rapid Transit passenger numbers and cars in parking garages closest to a major shopping area. In New York, a measure of Broadway ticket sales tells a story about tourism. In Jacksonville, Florida, it is social services usage that provides needed information. Another economist is eager to find a way to monitor Craigslist for prices on various items, while another wants to measure web searches on various topics.

Abandoned Boats
While there does not appear to be a statistical study, there is indication that during a recession people tend to abandon more boats along coastal waterways. When people can't afford the payments on boats, or to maintain or fuel them, or to pay for the costs of proper disposal, they tend to abandon them, leaving local or state governments to deal with the issue.

Urban Farming
Indications are that people are taking up urban farming to save money on groceries, not just because it is trendy.

and discourage borrowing and spending. The Federal Reserve, loan making, interest rates, and monetary policy are covered in Chapters 7 and 8.

Strong opinions and disagreements exist about which policies are best for dealing with problems in the macroeconomy. Various points of view on the proper method for reaching objectives or dealing with problems in the macroeconomy will be covered in the upcoming macroeconomic chapters.

Summary

1. Market economies, such as that of the United States, are constantly experiencing expansions and contractions in their levels of real GDP. These recurring upswings and downswings in production are called business cycles. Business cycles affect not only output but also employment and income. Business cycles have four phases: recovery, peak, recession, and trough. The length of time in each phase and its intensity differ from cycle to cycle.

2. There are several theories about the causes of economic fluctuations. These different theories are based on differing sets of assumptions and variables.

3. Changes in total, or aggregate, spending on new goods and services cause changes in economic activity. An increase in total spending increases output, employment, and income, and the economy grows until it reaches full employment. A decrease in total spending decreases output, employment, and income, and the economy contracts. Total spending is the spending by the household, business, government, and foreign sectors together.

4. Household spending on new goods and services, called personal consumption expenditures, is fairly stable as it increases from year to year and is greater than the combined purchases of businesses, government units, and foreign buyers. Most household spending originates from income earned from producing goods and services. Households can also make purchases from borrowed funds and transfer payments, which are labeled nonincome-determined spending because they do not come from household earned income. These nonincome-determined expenditures are injections into the spending stream. In addition to buying goods and services, households can use income for saving or paying taxes, which are leakages from the spending stream.

5. The purchase of new goods such as machinery and equipment by businesses is called investment spending and is a form of nonincome-determined spending. Of the major components of total spending, investment is the least stable and a major source of fluctuations in output, employment, and income. Investment spending is influenced by profit expectations that are affected by the outlook for future economic activity and the interest rate for borrowing funds. Investment spending is an injection into the spending stream: Increases in investment spending stimulate the level of economic activity, and reductions in investment spending lead to reductions in output, employment, and income. Business saving and taxes are leakages from the spending stream.

6. Government can influence spending in three areas: the purchase of goods and services, transfer payments, and taxes on households and businesses. Government purchases of goods and services are a form of nonincome-determined spending and are direct injections into the spending stream. Transfer payments provide injections, and taxes are a leakage.

7. Expenditures by U.S. buyers on imported goods and services are leakages from the spending stream. Purchases of exported U.S. goods and services by foreign buyers are injections and classified as nonincome-determined expenditures. Net exports is exports minus imports and indicates whether the foreign sector had a net positive or negative impact on total spending. Net exports has tended to be negative over the past few decades.

8. Leakages from the spending stream include saving and paying taxes by households and businesses as well as purchases of imports. Injections include household spending from borrowing and transfer payments, business investment spending, government purchases of goods and services, and purchases of exports.

9. If all leakages from the spending stream equal all injections, the level of economic activity will continue unchanged. If leakages exceed injections, spending decreases, and the level of economic activity falls. If injections are greater than leakages, the spending stream expands, and the level of economic activity grows.

10. An increase or decrease in nonincome-determined household expenditures, investment spending, government purchases, or foreign spending leads to a multiple increase or decrease in the levels of output, employment, and income. The multiplier effect is calculated by dividing the initial change in nonincome-determined spending by the percentage of additional income received by households that is not spent.

11. If the economy is operating at or near full employment, increases in spending may lead to demand-pull inflation rather than to increases in output and employment. For this reason, increasing total spending does not always cause the economy to expand.

12. Expectations can influence total spending and therefore complicate the job of stabilizing the economy. Because of the effect of expectations on spending, fears can cause self-fulfilling prophecies: The fear of a recession can lead to a recession, and the fear of inflation can lead to inflation.

13. The objectives of full production and economic growth, full employment, and stable prices can be accomplished through increasing or decreasing total spending. Fiscal policy influences total spending through changes in government purchases of goods and services, transfers, and taxes. Monetary policy influences spending through changes in the interest rate and money supply, or changes in lending and borrowing.

Key Terms and Concepts

Business cycles
Recovery
Peak
Recession
Trough
Total, or aggregate, spending
Personal consumption expenditures
Income-determined spending
Transfer payments
Nonincome-determined spending
Injections into the spending stream
Financial institutions

Leakages from the spending stream
Investment spending
Retained earnings
Saving–borrowing relationship
Government purchases of goods and services
Exports
Imports
Net exports
Multiplier effect
Expectations
Fiscal policy
Monetary policy

<table>
<tr><td>

Review Questions

</td><td>

1. Identify the four phases of a business cycle and describe the changes in economic activity that occur during each phase.

</td></tr>
</table>

2. What is the basic cause of a recession?

3. What is the difference between income-determined spending and nonincome-determined spending? What are the different types of nonincome-determined spending? Why are all nonincome-determined expenditures injections into the spending stream?

4. Changes in the level of economic activity are related to changes in the spending of households, businesses, government units, and buyers in the foreign sector.
   a. How do personal consumption expenditures, investment spending, government purchases of goods and services, and net exports compare in terms of relative size and stability?
   b. How are personal consumption expenditures affected by taxes, transfer payments, saving, and borrowing?
   c. How is investment spending affected by changes in the interest rate?
   d. Why are government expenditures on goods and services a direct injection and government expenditures on transfer payments not a direct injection into the spending stream?
   e. What effects do transactions in the foreign sector have on domestic levels of output, employment, and income?
   f. Under what circumstances would an increase in total spending lead primarily to an increase in output, and when would it lead primarily to an increase in prices?

5. Identify the various leakages from and injections into the spending stream in a circular flow model of the economy. What is the relationship between leakages and injections when the level of economic activity is expanding, contracting, or remaining unchanged? What role do financial institutions play in the relationship between leakages and injections?

6. What is the multiplier effect, and how is it related to nonincome-determined spending and the circular flow of economic activity? What happens to the multiplier effect when the percentage of additional earned income not spent increases? Why does this happen?

7. In each of the following cases, calculate the change that occurs in the level of output as a result of the multiplier effect.
   a. Government purchases of goods and services increase by $600 million, and 20 percent of additional income received is not spent.
   b. Household spending from borrowing declines by $1 billion, and 30 percent of additional income received is not spent.
   c. Investment spending increases by $800 million, and 75 percent of additional income received is spent.
   d. Investment spending increases by $20 billion at the same time that U.S. net exports decrease by $15 billion, and 60 percent of additional income received is spent.

e. Household purchases from transfer payments increase by $500 million when the economy is at full employment, and two-thirds of additional income received is spent.

f. (Be careful.) Government purchases decrease by $200 million and transfer payments increase by $100 million when people are spending 75 percent of income received.

8. Take a large sheet of paper and construct a circular flow model that illustrates all of the leakages and injections in the macroeconomy.

Discussion Questions

1. Figure 5.1 shows that since 1990, business cycles in the U.S. economy have had long recovery and relatively short recession phases. Why do you think this has happened? Do you think this pattern is typical of what we can expect from the economy in the future?

2. Suppose the economy were in a recession and someone said to you, "If we simply started producing more, the recession and unemployment problems would go away." How would you evaluate this statement?

3. Personal consumption expenditures grow at a relatively constant rate over time, while investment spending fluctuates widely. What reasons might explain why personal consumption expenditures are more stable than investment spending?

4. Suppose the economy is in a recession and a member of Congress sponsors a bill to limit imports of vehicles, clothing, and other manufactured goods. The bill, if passed into law, would allegedly ensure that some of the dollars currently leaving the spending stream for imports would instead be spent on domestic products, thereby increasing output, employment, and income and reversing the recession. Is this bill a realistic solution to reversing the recession? How would you vote for this bill if you were in Congress?

5. Expectations play an important role in determining the level of economic activity and how the level of activity will change. What events might cause people to expect a recession? What events might cause people to expect inflation? What could be done to make the economy more predictable and help stabilize expectations?

6. Do you think there will be a positive or negative impact on economic activity as the United States pursues more "green" efforts? Consider a move toward more fuel-efficient vehicles and buildings in your answer.

7. The multiplier effect is larger or smaller depending on whether households spend more or less of their additional income. What effect might the expectation of a recession have on the multiplier? What effect might the expectation of inflation have on the multiplier?

8. Fiscal and monetary policies are designed to influence the level of economic activity through their impacts on total spending. Using the circular flow model, identify the leakages and injections each of these policies affects.

Critical Thinking Case 5

GETTING SMARTER

Critical Thinking Skills

Identifying valid predictors of future behavior

Determining reliable data to form an opinion

Economic Concepts

Indicators of economic activity

Interpretation of economic data

President Harry S. Truman (1945–1953), frustrated with advisors taking one position on the state of the economy and then backing away to another position, finally reached the point of asking if he could find a one-armed economist who wouldn't say, ". . . but on the other hand."

Data are data. It is how they are presented and interpreted that provides differing impressions of the impact of the data in the present and for the future. It is like a half glass of water: One person might see the glass as half full, and another person might see it as half empty.

Take the example of a release of data about U.S. manufacturing for September 2012. The *Wall Street Journal* online excerpted an article by Josh Mitchell on "U.S. Manufacturing Expanded in September." Mitchell reported that factory activity expanded and said that "Details in the report were encouraging, with higher readings for new orders and employment. That could point to a rise in hiring and production in coming months." Included on the site was a video titled "Finally, Some Good News for the Economy."[a]

On the same day, with the same data, a headline in *The Washington Post* read "The manufacturing recovery that wasn't." Neil Irwin reported that ". . . the most recent evidence, including survey data released Monday morning, has been a disappointment. The U.S. manufacturing sector isn't collapsing, but it is definitely flatlining." Further in the article, he asked, "Manufacturing recovery? What manufacturing recovery?"[b]

There are many sources of data about the economy as you have seen in Chapters 4 and 5, from aggregate unemployment to production to price levels to consumer and investment spending to net exports and more. Few people, however, go directly to these data and interpret them themselves as they try to figure out what the future holds. Instead, they go to forecasts about the economy, perhaps plugging "U.S. economic forecast" into a search engine, or going to the business section in a newspaper, or listening to reports on a major television network or on cable, or reading one of the many financial newsletters that investment bankers compile.

And the half-full or half-empty news could focus on any data that the reporters think are most relevant. They could be applications for unemployment payments, business profitability, the Consumer Confidence Index, actions of the Federal Reserve, changes in inventories, manufacturing numbers, or any other consideration. And even the unusual indicators of economic activity given in Application 5.4 could be the focus of a news report.

So, what is a good rule when confronting information on the state of the economy? Think about what you are reading and the source of the information. How valid is the information? Is it a "real" predictor? Does the source reporting the information tend to be optimistic or pessimistic?

Think about how much smarter you are after working through Chapters 4 and 5. By now you should be feeling really great about taking a course in economics!

[a] http://online.wsj.com/article, 10/1/2012.
[b] http://www.washingtonpost.com/business/economy, 10/1/2012.

Questions

1. Why would someone be interested in locating indicators to predict the future behavior of the economy?

2. What are some current data that you would consider important in finding valid, reliable indicators of the state of the economy? How could these data help someone predict whether the economy is headed into a recovery or a recession?

3. Can you name some sources of economic information that you think have an optimistic outlook? What are some sources that have a pessimistic outlook? Do you think that the political leanings of a news source influence its reports? How?

The Role of Government in the Macroeconomy

CHAPTER OBJECTIVES

Identify the major expenditures and revenues of federal, state, and local governments.

Distinguish among types of taxes—progressive, proportional, and regressive—and discuss tax reforms.

Explain fiscal policy, its mechanics, and differentiate between discretionary and automatic fiscal policy.

Define a surplus, balanced, and deficit budget, and identify their economic impacts.

Explain the national debt, its financing, size, and burden on taxpayers, and introduce crowding out.

Let's begin this chapter with a quick civics lesson. As the world becomes more global and we are far more influenced by the activities of other nations and cultures, differences in the types of governments under which people live become more relevant. Global concerns have also fostered an increased awareness of, and interest in, the democratic form in the United States. Here people elect other people to represent them and make decisions on their behalf; decisions are not made by dictators, military or religious leaders, or kings.

The philosophy underlying a representative form of government has fostered multiple political subdivisions in the United States: Authority and functions are dispersed through many government units. There is a federal jurisdiction along with state and local jurisdictions. As a result, we elect and give decision-making authority to a president, congresspersons, a state governor and state legislators, and local mayors, council members, county and township representatives, school board members, and others. Try to fill in Table 6.1 by identifying the elected officials who represent you.

While governments wrestle with everything from national security at airports to summer recreational camps for kids, our focus is on the role of the government sector in the macroeconomy. We know from Chapter 5 that total spending influences the

TABLE 6.1	*Government Representatives*

Use the following table to identify the persons who represent you.

U.S. CONGRESS

My state senators are _____ and _____.

My congressional district representative is _____.

STATE

My governor is _____.

My district's state senator is _____.

My district's state representative is _____.

LOCAL

My head of county government is _____.

I am represented at the local level (could be a mayor, council member, township representative, school board member) by

_____, who is a _____ (title);

_____, who is a _____ (title); and

_____, who is a _____ (title).

direction of the economy and that government impacts this spending through its purchases of goods and services, transfer payments, and the taxes it collects. This is a sizable role: The sheer magnitude of expenditures and taxes makes government extremely important in the functioning of the economy.

Not surprisingly, the largest single purchaser of goods and services in the United States is the federal government. A decision made at the federal level to initiate or cancel an interstate highway project or defense system, or to increase or decrease taxes, can have a far-reaching impact on the economy. Similar, but smaller, effects are felt when state and local governments change their tax and expenditure patterns. Enacting a local sales tax to fund park trails, building a new high school gym, and buying a few street sweepers have an impact on the economy.

Since government spending and taxing can affect the economy's levels of output, employment, income, and, sometimes, prices, government can modify the direction of the economy through its impact on total, or aggregate, spending. An important outcome for you from working through the material in this chapter is the foundation that you will gain for critically evaluating government tax and spending policies. These policies constantly receive widespread attention because we are always debating some related issue: the size of the national debt, appropriate government programs, tax cuts, the Social Security system, school funding, and many others. Government taxing and spending issues always play an important role in political campaigns. After learning the material in this chapter, you should be better able to tell whether the 30-second campaign sound bite of a candidate is accurate or even realistic.

GOVERNMENT EXPENDITURES AND REVENUES

Government Expenditures

In 2014, all government units together spent almost $6 trillion for a huge variety of purposes ranging from military aircraft to the construction of sewage plants to police salaries. Table 6.2 lists the total expenditures of all government units combined as well

TABLE 6.2

Total, Federal, and State and Local Government Expenditures, and Total Government Expenditures as a Percentage of GDP, Selected Years (Billions of Dollars)

Over the years, government expenditures have increased in absolute terms and remained relatively stable as a percentage of GDP.

	Government Expenditures			
Year	Total[a]	Federal	State and Local	Total as a Percentage of GDP
1995	$2,490.6	$1,653.7	$1,011.4	32.8%
2000	2,966.7	1,906.6	1,293.2	29.2
2005	4,034.9	2,602.8	1,775.4	31.3
2010	5,451.0	3,720.8	2,235.8	36.8
2014	5,843.9	3,900.9	2,453.3	33.9

[a]Some duplication of spending may occur since federal grants-in-aid to state and local governments are included in all expenditures.

Source: *Economic Report of the President* (Washington, DC: U.S. Government Printing Office, 2015), Tables B-19, B-23; 2014 from www.bea.gov, 05/15/2015.

as the federal government and state and local governments for selected years. In addition to the magnitude of government expenditures, notice that federal expenditures exceed state and local spending by a wide margin.

People frequently express concern over increases in government spending and the size of the government sector. Is this concern justified? One way to evaluate the size of government is to measure total government expenditures as a percentage of GDP. This is done in the last column of Table 6.2. A scan down this column shows that, over the years, government spending as a percentage of GDP has been relatively stable.

Government Purchases of Goods and Services
Government spending on new goods and services.

Public Good
A good (or service) provided for all of society; no one is excluded from use of a public good.

Quasi-Public Good
A government-provided public good that could be offered in a private market.

Transfer Payments
Money from the government for which no direct work is performed in return.

Categories of Government Expenditures   We can classify government expenditures into several categories. Some spending is for **government purchases of goods and services**, such as the services of people who work for government in many jobs from military careers to public pool lifeguards, and goods ranging from bridges to paper clips. Many government purchases are for **public goods**, which are those provided for everyone and which exclude no one from their use. Lighthouses, public parks, and flood control dams are all examples of public goods. When government provides a public good or service that could also be offered in a private market, such as education or an ambulance haul, it provides a **quasi-public good**. The provision of public and quasi-public goods is an important function of government.

Another category of government spending is **transfer payments**, which are payments from the government for which nothing is required in return. That is, people who receive monthly Social Security payments, veterans' benefits, unemployment compensation, or public assistance receive transfer payments, unlike people who receive wages for working as government employees.

Interest paid on borrowed funds is another government expenditure category. Since government units sometimes finance some of their spending through borrowed

TABLE 6.3	*Federal Government Expenditure Categories, Selected Years*

The composition of federal spending has changed over the years. Transfer payments constitute the largest expenditure category.

Expenditure Category	Percentage of Total Expenditures[a]				
	1995	**2000**	**2005**	**2010**	**2014**
Purchases of goods and services	26%	25%	28%	27%	25%
Transfer payments	51	54	57	61	62
Interest payments	21	19	13	10	11
Financial assistance	2	2	2	1	1
Total	100%	100%	100%	100%	100%

[a] Percentages may not add to 100 percent due to rounding.

Source: Office of Management and Budget, "Fiscal Year 2015 Historical Tables," Budget of the U.S. Government, www.whitehouse.gov. 2014 figures are estimated.

funds, the interest on that money is an expense that the government unit must pay.[1] Finally, the federal government may also provide financial assistance to state and local governments and others for additional police, road construction, and such.

Table 6.3 shows how the federal government has allocated money among the various expenditure categories just identified. Notice that the largest federal category is for transfer payments—and that it has been growing. The transfer category of spending presents challenges for assessing how federal money is spent and for any recommendations to reduce federal expenditures. It is popular today to advocate for less government spending which on the surface appears simple, yet the growing percentages associated with transfer payments lead to a complex issue. What transfer income do we cut? As you will read later in this chapter, Social Security is a large part of the equation. It is a separate trust fund yet payments made from this fund are calculated into the overall budget. In addition, during a recession certain transfer payments automatically increase to fill in spending gaps. By the end of this chapter, you will be smart about these issues.

There is also another way to look at spending by the federal government and by state and local governments: by assessing the function or purpose of using these funds. The largest functional spending categories for federal funds are Social Security, Medicare, national defense, and veterans. The largest category for state and local governments is education. These government units spend funds for a variety of services including teachers, police, fire and EMS personnel, court employees, and more.

Government Revenues

In 2014, governments received over $5 trillion in revenue. For very man, woman, and child in the United States this amount was, on average, $15,894.[2] Most of the revenue that governments receive comes from taxes, and we pay many different kinds: federal and state income taxes; local earnings taxes; sales tax; property tax on a residence;

[1] Borrowing at the federal level is done through various securities issued by the U.S. Treasury and at the state and local levels with municipal bonds or other instruments.

[2] "Government Current Receipts and Expenditures," "Bureau of Economic Analysis," www.bea.gov, 05/15/2015. 2014 population figure was used to calculate per capita number.

TABLE 6.4		*Sources of Federal Government Revenue, Selected Years*			

Individual income taxes and social insurance payments are the primary sources of revenue for the federal government.

| | Percentage of Total Revenue per Year[a] | | | | |
Source	1995	2000	2005	2010	2014
Individual income taxes	44%	50%	43%	42%	46%
Social insurance[b]	36	32	37	40	34
Corporation income taxes	12	10	13	9	11
Excise taxes	4	3	3	3	3
Other[c]	5	5	4	7	6
Total	100%	100%	100%	100%	100%

[a] Percentages may not add to 100 percent because of rounding.

[b] Includes social insurance and retirement contributions.

[c] Includes customs, estate, and gift taxes and other receipts.

Source: Office of Management and Budget, "Fiscal Year 2015 Historical Tables," Budget of the U.S. Government, www.whitehouse.gov. 2014 figures are estimates.

personal property tax; capital gains tax; inheritance and gift taxes; utility tax; gasoline, liquor, and cigarette taxes; tariffs on imports; corporate income tax; various business taxes; and others.

Governments also receive revenue from sources other than taxes. For example, the federal government's Social Security program is a **social insurance program**. Although payment is required from participating individuals, the payment is considered to be a contribution to a retirement and welfare fund rather than a tax. In addition, many local governments count on fees for revenue: building permits, rentals for the local ice rink, and fines for speeding, to name a few.

Social Insurance Program

Contributions from an individual's wages are made to a fund from which that individual may draw when eligible for benefits.

Revenue Sources   Table 6.4 gives the major sources of federal government revenue. The largest source of funds, and a fairly stable source, is the individual income tax; other taxes, such as the corporate income tax and excise taxes, typically provide less than 20 percent of federal revenue. The second largest source of revenue, at about one-third, is social insurance, primarily contributions to Social Security. The federal government's reliance on household income as a source of revenue, through the individual income tax and contributions to social insurance, helps to stir agitation about the tax burden imposed on individuals.

State and local government revenues come from a wider variety of sources than do federal revenues. Taxes include property, sales, and individual income taxes. Nontax sources include license fees, tuition from public colleges and universities, some recreation and other fees, and interest, as well as funds—typically grants—received from the federal government.

A wide disparity exists in the types of taxes and tax rates (percentages) imposed by different state and local government units. For example, it was recently estimated that a family in Philadelphia, Pennsylvania, earning $50,000 per year pays 17.6 percent of their income to state and local taxes, whereas a family in Jacksonville, Florida, earning $50,000 pays 6.5 percent. In Indianapolis, Indiana, the effective tax on residential property is $3.05 per $100, and in Honolulu, Hawaii, it is $0.35 per $100.[3] Some states have had unusual revenue sources: for example, a tax on income earned by "persons expounding religious doctrines" in Hawaii, a tax on raw fish in Alaska, and a fee for each parachute jump in New Hampshire.

TAXES: TYPES AND REFORM

Progressive, Proportional, and Regressive Taxes

There are always issues around the payment of taxes. Even though voters may elect to raise a tax, few people welcome an additional tax burden. The burden of paying a tax is not the same for all individuals. The proportion of one's income that goes to a tax differs with each specific tax and with the level of income. To help us understand how a tax impacts income, we classify taxes as progressive, proportional, or regressive.

Progressive Tax

A tax reflecting a direct relationship between the percentage of income taxed and the size of the income.

With a **progressive tax** there is a direct relationship between the percentage of income taxed and the size of the income: The percentage of income taxed increases as income increases and decreases as income decreases. The federal personal income tax is progressive. For 2014, taxpayers had seven income steps. For a single taxpayer, there was a 10 percent rate on income up to $9,075 with progressing rates and steps that ended with a 39.6% rate on income over $406,750.[4] Some states also have income taxes with progressive rates.

Proportional Tax (Flat Tax)

A tax equal to the same percentage of income regardless of the size of the income.

With a **proportional tax**, or **flat tax**, the percentage of income taxed is the same for any income, large or small. A city wage tax of, say, 1 percent means that an individual earning $10,000 per year would pay 1 percent, or $100, to the city and an individual earning $100,000 would also pay 1 percent, or $1,000. In each case, the same percentage of income is taken as tax. Proposals to change the federal income tax from a progressive to a flat tax often surface. Up for Debate, "Should the Federal Income Tax Be Changed to a Flat Tax?" raises some interesting points for both sides of this issue. Which position do you favor, and why?

Regressive Tax

A tax reflecting an inverse relationship between the percentage of income taxed and the size of the income.

With a **regressive tax**, the percentage of income taxed varies inversely with the size of the income: The percentage increases as income decreases and decreases as income increases. In other words, a regressive tax hits those with low incomes the hardest. Sales taxes are considered to be regressive, particularly the sales tax on food. On the surface, sales taxes may not appear to be regressive because they are a specified percentage of a product's price or the amount sold. But remember that it is the relationship between the tax paid and *income*, not between the tax paid and the purchase, that makes a tax regressive. For example, with a sales tax of 6 percent on food, an annual grocery bill of $8,000 means that a tax of $480 must be paid. For a family earning $24,000 a year, that $480 tax amounts to 2 percent of their income. For a family earning $80,000 a year, it amounts to just 0.6 percent of their income. The person with a low income likely thinks about the $6 that must be paid with every $100 grocery order and what must be given up to pay it.

Tax Reform and Issues

Our elected government representatives frequently find themselves in a tug-of-war. On one side are those constituents who want more from government—a better equiped military, prescription drug coverage, more police patrols, and local leaf pickup—and on

---

[3] ProQuest Statistical Abstract of the U.S. 2015 Online Edition, Tables 465, 466. Earnings percentages are for 2012; property tax rates are for 2013.

[4] "Tax Brackets," http://taxes.about.com.

SHOULD THE FEDERAL INCOME TAX BE CHANGED TO A FLAT TAX?

Issue   There have been several proposals to change the U.S. federal personal income tax from its current progressive structure to a flat tax, where everyone pays a tax equal to the same percentage of income regardless of the size of the income. Should we adopt a flat tax?

Yes   The current federal income tax system should be abandoned in favor of a flat tax because the current system is complicated and not as progressive as it might appear. This system has hundreds of tax forms and schedules, and it is estimated that nearly 5 billion person-hours are required to "do taxes." With these complications, people make mistakes or may not find the tax protection to which they are entitled. With a flat tax, a one-page form may be all that is needed.

   Although in principle the current tax system is progressive, it is a system riddled with shelters and exemptions that favor special groups. Once people take advantage of various tax-reducing opportunities, such as home mortgage, business expense, and retirement account reductions, some of the progressiveness of the system may be reduced. In the end, some higher-income earners may not pay much more than lower-income earners. Also, the federal income tax is only progressive up to a point. While a larger percentage of income will be taxed for a person earning $500,000 than for

a person earning $50,000, a person earning $5 million or even $50 million will pay no higher a percentage than the person earning $500,000. Where has the progressiveness gone?

No   The current progressive tax structure should be maintained because of the uncertainty about who actually benefits from a flat tax and the possibility that a greater tax burden will be placed on people with lower incomes. While a flat tax system would be easier to understand and administer, the equalized tax rate could result in lower taxes for those with higher incomes and higher taxes for those with lower incomes. The real issue is whether a flat tax treats everyone the same or whether it puts a greater tax burden on those least able to pay the tax.

   In other words, at the heart of the issue is the burden that will be placed on low-income earners. If everyone is taxed at a flat rate of say, 25 percent, this means that someone making a minimum wage of $7.25 per hour would need to contribute $1.81 of that wage to federal income taxes. Subtract FICA and any state taxes or local earnings taxes and that person takes home very little income. There would not be much incentive to work for this type of wage; businesses would need to pay much higher wages to attract needed labor, perhaps forcing some small businesses to close. A high flat tax might also provide the incentive to find ways to work for unreported cash.

   Think about this. A 25 percent flat rate tax on someone earning $200,000 a year leaves $150,000 for other taxes, spending, and saving. A 25 percent flat tax on someone earning $20,000 a year leaves $15,000 for those alternatives. A high flat tax would intensify the struggle that low-income earners already face.

Tax Reform

Changes in tax policies and structures.

the other side are those who want a reduction in taxes. As a consequence, changes in tax policies and structures, or **tax reform**, is the subject of much discussion and action at all levels of government. Sometimes tax reform reflects a need for more revenues to meet needs like school buildings for increasing numbers of school-age children or to purchase more fire equipment as new homes and apartments are built. But sometimes tax reform is rooted in politics. For example, candidates running for public office often make taxes a campaign issue as they attempt to win voters.

   Value judgments and political considerations enter into all discussions of tax reform. If a state, for example, needs more funding for its highways, should it tax everyone equally, should a progressive tax that places a greater burden on people earning higher incomes be imposed, or should the tax be levied on those who directly benefit from using the highways?

   Changes in the federal income tax provide good examples of how historical developments, value judgments, and political considerations lead to tax reform. Application 6.1, "A Chronology of Federal Income Tax Policies," highlights some major changes in federal corporate and individual income tax rates and rules that have occurred since the beginning of the twentieth century. What values or political

APPLICATION 6.1

A CHRONOLOGY OF FEDERAL INCOME TAX POLICIES

- **1909**   A federal corporate income tax of 1 percent with a $5,000 exemption is adopted.
- **1913**   A federal individual income tax is enacted; applies mainly to a small number of high incomes—the lowest bracket is 1 percent on taxable income up to $20,000; taxes are paid in quarterly installments in the year following the receipt of the income.
- **World War I Era**   The corporate income tax rate is raised to a high of 12 percent in 1918; the individual rate is raised to 6 percent on taxable income up to $4,000; and the top bracket rate is raised to 77 percent on taxable income over $1 million.
- **The 1930s**   The corporate tax rate changes several times, ranging between 7 percent and 27 percent; no significant individual rate changes for most average-size incomes.
- **World War II**   The need to raise revenue for the war effort causes significant increases in tax rates and a lowering of brackets and exemptions. Corporate rates reach as high as 25 percent on the first $25,000 of profit, 53 percent on the second $25,000, and 40 percent on profit over $50,000. Individual income tax rates reach as high as

23 percent on taxable income up to $2,000 and 94 percent on taxable income over $200,000.
- **1943**   The tax payment system is changed so that individual income taxes are paid when income is earned, rather than in quarterly installments in the following year.
- **1952**   The tax on corporate profit over $25,000 is raised to 52 percent and remains at approximately that level until 1974; however, other changes, such as rules for determining depreciation, occur over this same time period.
- **1964**   The first significant cut in individual income taxes since the 1940s occurs; rates are cut on lower income brackets and the highest rate is dropped to 77 percent.
- **1968**   A 10 percent additional charge is applied to all individual and corporate income taxes to help reduce inflationary pressure caused by spending on the Vietnam War effort.
- **1982**   As a result of legislation in 1981, individual income tax rates are significantly lowered; the highest rate drops to 50 percent.
- **1987**   Corporate tax rates, which have continuously declined during the 1980s, are lowered to 15 percent for the first $50,000 of profit and 34 percent on profit over $335,000.
- **1988**   A new tax law takes effect that lowers the highest marginal rate on individual income to 33 percent.
- **1990–2014**   The highest marginal tax rate fluctuates between 31 and 39.6 percent.

considerations might explain some of the changes recorded in this application? How does armed military conflict tend to affect the structure of taxes?

Tax Base
The particular thing on which a tax is levied.

Tax Base   An important decision for those imposing a tax is the **tax base**, or the particular thing on which the tax will be levied. For example, the tax base for an income tax is income, for a sales tax it is the price of the item sold, and for a property tax it is the value of the property. Often the choice of a tax base is determined by legislation, and some government units are limited in the selections they may make. The other important decision concerns the **tax rate**, or the amount that is levied on the base.

Tax Rate
The amount that is levied on a tax base.

Among the many concerns of state and local governments is dealing with a declining tax base or competing for a possible new one. When a city faces a decline with deteriorating neighborhoods and businesses exiting the city, local officials become concerned about decreasing revenue as the tax base erodes. On the other hand, many communities enter competition with other cities to gain the big-box stores, shopping centers, and corporate headquarters that increase a tax base and tax revenue. Sometimes governments try to lure companies and retailers through substantial tax incentives

Tax Abatement
A policy of reducing or eliminating a tax that would normally be charged.

such as **tax abatement**, which reduces or eliminates a tax that is normally charged. Usually, these incentives provide tax relief for some period of time in the hope that the local economy can be stimulated and tax revenue will increase in the long run.

FISCAL POLICY

We know that the amount of money that government spends and taxes affects the economy's levels of output, employment, and income. And a change in either spending or taxes can cause the economy to move into an expansion, or recovery, or move into a contraction, or recession. When the federal government changes its spending and/or taxing to control unemployment or demand-pull inflation, it is putting **fiscal policy** into play.

Fiscal Policy
Influencing the levels of aggregate output and employment or prices through changes in federal government purchases, transfer payments, and/or taxes.

Fiscal policy has evolved largely from the theories of John Maynard Keynes, who focused on the relationship between aggregate spending and the level of economic activity, and suggested that the government could fill in a spending gap created by a lack of private spending. The theories of John Maynard Keynes and other economists are discussed in greater detail in Chapter 9.

The Mechanics of Fiscal Policy

If you remember the material in Chapter 5 (the role of spending, the circular flow, the relationship between leakages and injections), the mechanics of fiscal policy should be easy. Remember the basic principle of that chapter: Increases in spending cause the economy to expand and decreases in spending cause it to contract.

When the economy experiences unemployment because of a decline in spending, Congress could help to reverse that unemployment through fiscal policy actions that increase the level of aggregate spending and, consequently, the level of economic activity. Increased spending could come from

♦ increased government purchases of goods and services, and/or
♦ increased transfer payments, and/or
♦ decreased taxes.

These three actions could be taken separately or in combination.

Although each of these actions can cause economic activity to grow, the expansionary impact of increasing government purchases by a particular amount is greater than the expansionary impact of increasing transfers or decreasing taxes by the same amount. All of the dollars spent on government purchases are injected directly into the spending stream, whereas increased transfers and decreased taxes provide additional income, part of which will be spent but part of which will be saved. In other words, there would be a stronger economic impact from spending $10 million to improve trails in national parks than from giving taxpayers a $10 million tax break.

If the economy is experiencing demand-pull inflation from too much spending, the appropriate fiscal policy action for lowering the inflation rate is to decrease aggregate spending. Excess spending could be removed from the economy by

♦ decreasing government purchases of goods and services, and/or
♦ decreasing transfer payments, and/or
♦ increasing taxes.

Again, a more pronounced decrease in spending results from a decrease in government purchases because some of the reduced transfers and increased taxes would affect saving rather than spending.

Government expenditures and taxes affect nonincome-determined spending, and, as a result, they are subject to a multiplier effect. (Again, review this material in

Chapter 5 if you have forgotten it.) This means, for example, if the government injected $50 billion into the spending stream through increased purchases or transfers, or through decreased taxes, the level of economic activity would increase by more than $50 billion. Alternatively, if the government withdrew $50 billion from the spending stream, output, income, and employment would decrease by more than $50 billion.

Discretionary and Automatic Fiscal Policy

Fiscal policy can be either discretionary or automatic.

Discretionary Fiscal Policy

Deliberate changes in government expenditures and/or taxes to control unemployment or demand-pull inflation.

Economic Stimulus

A term used for fiscal policy actions to counteract a recession by stimulating spending through government purchases of goods and services, increased transfer payments, and/or decreased taxes.

Automatic Fiscal Policy (Automatic Stabilization)

Changes in government expenditures and/or taxes that occur automatically as the level of economic activity changes; helps to control unemployment or demand-pull inflation.

Discretionary Fiscal Policy   The members of Congress, sometimes with the leadership of the president, exercise **discretionary fiscal policy** when they deliberately adjust government spending or taxing in response to a problem with unemployment or demand-pull inflation. Congress has significant fiscal powers: It can cut or raise taxes, change tax exemptions or deductions, grant tax rebates or credits, initiate or postpone transfer programs, and initiate or eliminate direct spending projects.

Congress has used discretionary fiscal policy several times. The classic example was a 10 percent surcharge levied on all income taxes to reduce inflation in 1968 that was caused by the Vietnam War. More recently, an effort was made for a tax cut to offset a threatening recession in 2001. Beginning in 2008, Congress used a variety of discretionary fiscal policy tools to deal with an economy that was in a severe downward slide. A tax rebate program gave individuals who paid taxes in 2007 up to $600. In 2009, Congress passed what has been known as an **economic stimulus** package. This included a substantial amount of government spending for infrastructure projects, schools, and other areas and a number of tax cuts through a variety of programs. The value of the economic stimulus program has been debated as some point to the budget deficits and debt that resulted while others believe that it kept the economy from sliding into a deeper recession.

Automatic Fiscal Policy   At the federal level, we have built-in automatic changes in government spending and taxing that help us to challenge a recession or demand-pull inflation. Without any deliberate action by Congress, **automatic fiscal policy**, or **automatic stabilization**, increases aggregate spending in a recession and dampens aggregate spending when the economy expands. Two automatic fiscal policy stabilizers are important: transfer payments, especially unemployment compensation, and the personal income tax.

Let's consider a recession to understand how automatic stabilization works. During an economic downturn, when people lose their jobs and earned incomes fall, some important changes in government expenditures and taxes occur automatically. Some of the unemployed become eligible for transfer payments, particularly unemployment compensation. In addition, some unemployed people may realize lower tax payments, or even a tax refund. Because the federal personal income tax is structured as a progressive tax with several rate steps, unemployment and the resulting decline in income could drop a person into a lower tax bracket. Both the increased transfer payments and lower tax rates are automatic and provide additional spending dollars. Without these built-in stabilizers, or automatic responses, household spending would drop more dramatically and the economy would likely slide into a deeper recession.

When the economy expands, unemployment falls, and incomes rise, the built-in stabilizers automatically remove spending from the economy to dampen demand-pull inflationary tendencies. As more people are employed, the government provides less in transfer payments, and higher incomes push some individuals into higher tax

| TABLE 6.5 | *Fiscal Policy Summary* |

Discretionary fiscal policy and automatic stabilization can be used to control unemployment or demand-pull inflation by changing the size of the spending stream.

Problem

| Unemployment | Demand-pull inflation |

Remedy

| Increase total spending | Decrease total spending |

Fiscal Policy Response

Discretionary

Congress can	Congress can
increase government purchases	decrease government purchases
increase transfer payments	decrease transfer payments
decrease taxes	increase taxes

Automatic Stabilization

| Automatic increases in some transfer payments (especially unemployment compensation), decreases in federal personal income taxes | Automatic decreases in some transfer payments (especially unemployment compensation), increases in federal personal income taxes |

Effect

| Puts more dollars into the spending stream | Withdraws dollars from the spending stream |

brackets. Without this automatic removal of spending power as the economy heats up, particularly toward full employment, inflation could be worse.

Automatic stabilizers soften the impact of cyclical expansions and contractions. Without the help of any deliberate legislative action, they pump spending into the economy during a downswing and decrease aggregate spending during an upswing. However, in the face of a severe recession or inflation, automatic stabilizers alone would not be sufficient to correct the problem. The role of fiscal policy in economic stabilization is summarized in Table 6.5.

GOVERNMENT BUDGETS

Every year, elected officials who are responsible for determining how a political unit's money is spent—from a trustee of a small village in Illinois to a state legislator in California to your own congressperson—forecast their government's revenues and expenses and lay out a plan for the year ahead. Typically, there is a formal passage of this plan, or budget. Unfortunately, unpredictable events occur that can alter that budget. These range from economic slowdowns that lessen tax collections to disasters of extreme magnitude. Even a $4 per gallon gas that wrecks family budgets hurt governments that have to fuel police cars, street sweepers, and trucks.

It is the resulting actual, not planned, year-end budget that is important for assessing how a government unit has influenced economic activity over the year. Here is where actual leakages from and injections into the spending stream are tallied. This figure indicates whether the government spent an amount equal to, less than, or greater than its revenues, or, putting it more technically, whether the government ran a balanced budget, a surplus budget, or a deficit budget.

Types of Budgets

Balanced Budget
A government's total expenditures equal its total revenues.

Surplus Budget
A government's revenues are greater than its expenditures.

Deficit Budget
A government's expenditures are greater than its revenues.

When a government's total expenditures equal its total revenues, it has run a **balanced budget**. A **surplus budget** occurs when a government does not spend all of its revenues, or when total expenditures are less than total revenues. A government with a surplus budget can pay off past loans or save the surplus and earn interest on the funds. A **deficit budget** occurs when a government's total expenditures are greater than total revenues. When a government operates with a deficit budget, it must either borrow and go into debt or use its reserve fund (savings) if one exists.

It is the federal government budget that is of most interest when considering macroeconomic activity because of its size and its relationship to fiscal policy. Table 6.6 lists federal government receipts, outlays, and resulting surpluses or deficits for the years 1970 through 2014.

The Surplus or Deficit column of Table 6.6 shows that the federal government typically operates with a deficit budget. The budget surpluses from 1998 through 2001 were the exception. Notice that the budget deficits that began in 2008 are stunning. Financing the troops, equipment, and veterans' medical care for the multiyear conflicts in Iraq and Afghanistan played a role in escalating government spending. But the real culprit was the slowdown in economic activity that began in 2008. The automatic stabilizers brought less in tax revenues and more in transfer payments. And added to that was the economic stimulus spending and tax cut programs that were enacted.

Unified Budget
A budget that assembles all federal government receipts and outlays, and the resulting overall deficit or surplus, in one report.

Trust Fund
A restricted fund; payments from this fund are specified as to recipients and/or uses.

Entitlements
Programs set up by the government to pay benefits to people who meet the eligibility requirements of the programs.

Beyond the Budget Figures   The "watchdogs" of the federal government budget are keenly aware of issues that are masked by using the basic reported surplus and deficit numbers to evaluate the federal budget, as we have just done. Since 1969 the federal government has used a **unified budget** to report its surplus and deficit figures. That is, all federal government transactions for the year are reported in one lump sum. The unified budget figures, those used in Table 6.6, give no details about trust fund balances, the sizes of payments through entitlement programs, and government operations such as the U.S. Postal Service.

The federal government has created several trust funds to administer some of its programs. A **trust fund** is an account earmarked for a specific purpose or program: Contributions to the fund and distributions from it are used solely for the program. Social Security and Medicare are the best-known trust funds. With Social Security, for example, contributions from employers and employees go directly to the fund, and all payments to beneficiaries are made from the fund.

The term **entitlements** refers to programs set up by the government to pay benefits to people who meet the eligibility requirements for the programs. Spending for entitlement programs tends to be less controllable than other types, such as funding for airport runways or national parks. Social Security and Medicare are examples of entitlement programs, as are veterans' benefits and the federal government employees' retirement program.

To identify the effects of some of these government programs on the overall budget, the unified budget figures have been broken into two categories: on-budget and off-budget. Although Congress has not been consistent about identifying the types of programs in each category, the general guideline is that **on-budget** figures are for programs, such as interstate highway construction, that are more controllable and can

TABLE 6.6	*Federal Budget Receipts, Outlays, and Surpluses or Deficits for Fiscal Years 1970–2014 (Billions of Dollars)*

The federal government has operated with a budget deficit for 41 of the 45 years from 1970 through 2014.

Fiscal Year	Receipts	Outlays	Surplus or Deficit (−)	Fiscal Year	Receipts	Outlays	Surplus or Deficit (−)
1970	$192.8	$195.6	−$2.8	1993	$1,154.3	$1,409.4	−$255.1
1971	187.1	210.2	−23.0	1994	1,258.6	1,461.8	−203.2
1972	207.3	230.7	−23.4	1995	1,351.8	1,515.7	−164.0
1973	230.8	245.7	−14.9	1996	1,453.1	1,560.5	−107.4
1974	263.2	269.4	−6.1	1997	1,579.2	1,601.1	−21.9
1975	279.1	332.3	−53.2	1998	1,721.7	1,652.5	69.3
1976	298.1	371.8	−73.7	1999	1,827.5	1,701.8	125.6
1977	355.6	409.2	−53.7	2000	2,025.2	1,789.0	236.2
1978	399.6	458.7	−59.2	2001	1,991.1	1,862.8	128.2
1979	463.3	504.0	−40.7	2002	1,853.1	2,010.9	−157.8
1980	517.1	590.9	−73.8	2003	1,782.3	2,159.9	−377.6
1981	599.3	678.2	−79.0	2004	1,880.1	2,292.8	−412.7
1982	617.8	745.7	−128.0	2005	2,153.6	2,472.0	−318.3
1983	600.6	808.4	−207.8	2006	2,406.9	2,655.1	−248.2
1984	666.4	851.8	−185.4	2007	2,568.0	2,728.7	−160.7
1985	734.0	946.3	−212.3	2008	2,524.0	2,982.5	−458.6
1986	769.2	990.4	−221.2	2009	2,105.0	3,517.7	−1,412.7
1987	854.3	1,004.0	−149.7	2010	2,162.7	3,457.1	−1,294.4
1988	909.2	1,064.4	−155.2	2011	2,303.5	3,603.1	−1,299.6
1989	991.1	1,143.7	−152.6	2012	2,450.2	3,537.0	−1,087.0
1990	1,032.0	1,253.0	−221.0	2013	2,775.1	3,454.6	−679.5
1991	1,055.0	1,324.2	−269.2	2014	3,021.5	3,506.1	−484.6
1992	1,091.2	1,381.5	−290.3				

Source: *Economic Report of the President* (Washington, DC: U.S. Government Printing Office, 2015), Table B-19.

On-Budget/Off-Budget Categories of the unified budget established by Congress; generally refers to programs that have immediately controllable and noncontrollable receipts and expenses, respectively.

be better used for fiscal policy actions. **Off-budget** figures are for programs, such as Social Security, that are less controllable. Table 6.7 provides the unified, on-budget, and off-budget surplus and deficit figures for 2000 through 2014.

Notice that the off-budget figures have been positive. This is because of annual surpluses in the Social Security trust fund. That is, more Social Security contributions have been taken in each year than have been paid out. Building up the fund has been deliberate, since fewer working adults will support retirees in the years ahead. However, these annual surpluses can lead to a misrepresentation about federal government deficits and surpluses. Without the Social Security surpluses, unified budget deficits would have been much larger and surpluses smaller each year.

Even with the surplus in the Social Security trust fund, there is concern about the coming retirement of huge numbers of people in the baby-boom generation. Current entitlement programs—especially Social Security and Medicare—as they now exist, even with a surplus, will not be able to support this large population. Application 6.2,

TABLE 6.7	*Federal Government Unified, On-Budget, and Off-Budget Balances, 2000–2014 (Billions of Dollars)*

In recent years, off-budget surpluses have reduced the size of the unified budget deficit.

Year	Unified Surplus or Deficit	On-Budget Surplus or Deficit	Off-Budget Surplus or Deficit
2000	$236.2	$86.4	$149.8
2001	128.2	−32.4	160.7
2002	−157.8	−317.4	159.7
2003	−377.6	−538.4	160.8
2004	−412.7	−568.0	155.2
2005	−318.3	−493.6	175.3
2006	−248.2	−434.5	186.3
2007	−160.7	−342.2	181.5
2008	−458.6	−641.8	183.3
2009	−1,412.7	−1,549.7	137.0
2010	−1,294.4	−1,371.4	77.0
2011	−1,299.6	−1,366.8	67.2
2012	−1,087.0	−1,148.9	61.9
2013	−679.5	−719.0	39.5
2014	−484.6	−514.1	29.5

Source: *Economic Report of the President* (Washington, DC: U.S. Government Printing Office, 2015), Table B-19. Figures are for fiscal years.

"How Much Do We Love Granny?"offers some background about this predicament. Over the next few years, we can expect proposals for dealing with this impending demographic problem. What would you suggest as a change in public policy to deal with retirement entitlements?

The Budget and Fiscal Policy: Tying Them Together

All of our discussions concerning government spending and taxing, budgets, and fiscal policy can be tied together.

A surplus budget occurs when government revenues exceed government expenditures. Generally, a surplus budget will slow the economy as the amount removed from the spending stream is greater than the amount returned.[5] In other words, a surplus budget dampens aggregate spending.

Discretionary fiscal policy suggests that the corrective action for managing demand-pull inflation is a reduction in government spending on its purchases and transfer payments and/or an increase in taxes. Each of these measures leans toward a surplus budget. And, in terms of automatic stabilization, in good times when spending is up, automatically tax collections increase and transfer payments fall. These, again, favor a surplus budget.

With a deficit budget, government expenditures exceed revenues, or more is pumped into the spending stream than is taken out. Unless the economy is at full

---

[5] The expression *generally* is used because the ultimate impact of the budget depends on the types of taxes collected, the percentage of those taxes that would have been saved, the percentage of expenditures that goes directly into purchases of goods and services, the percentage of transfers that is saved, and so forth.

HOW MUCH DO WE LOVE GRANNY?

Granny loves her grandkids; the grandkids love their grandparents. So, is there any concern about these familial relationships? Why do some people see the possibility of real tension in the years ahead?

It's the Social Security system. This system is on its way to paying out way more than it takes in and creating a huge financial burden on the younger generation—today's grandkids. Some estimate that the program will start losing money in 2018, and if it continues like it is today, it will lose over $760 billion a year by 2030.

Workers pay into the system when they work and get money from it when they retire. It's a big fund. People do not have individually managed accounts in their names. Instead, what people pay into the fund is used to help support people receiving payments. So the system needs workers to keep paying into the fund in order to make payments to recipients from the fund. The fund does have a reserve. It is just not enough.

The problem is a demographic one caused largely by the composition of the U.S. population. The number of people approaching retirement age is growing at a faster rate than the number of working people who will be making Social Security contributions. And the fund's reserve is not large enough to compensate.

The number of Americans 65 and older is expected to grow by over 70 percent from 2010 through 2030, while the number of workers 20 through 64 paying into Social Security is expected to grow by less than 5 percent. In 1935, when the Social Security Act was passed, there were 25 workers to support each retiree. Today there are only three, and by 2020 the number is expected to fall to two workers per retiree.

Here is the possible tension. Any suggestion to simply cut Social Security benefits could have dire consequences for all of those grandparents. For about two-thirds of its recipients, Social Security accounts for half of their income. For about 15 percent of the recipients, it is their only source of income. On the other side of the issue, any suggestion to raise the amount withheld from workers' paychecks for Social Security contributions could have a negative impact on many grandkids' incomes, particularly those who live on wages barely above the minimum wage level. In so many cases it is an individual situation: Some older workers live better than their grandkids; some do not.

Almost all of us live in a household where someone is paying into or receiving money from Social Security. Because of this, the coming Social Security crisis will likely affect most of us. What can we expect? You can be sure that we will have a difficult and controversial debate.

employment and incapable of expanding, a deficit budget will increase economic activity. In other words, a deficit budget will increase aggregate spending as well as output, employment, and income.

If the economy is in a recession, fiscal policy measures that increase expenditures and/or reduce taxes can be used to aid in reversing the recession. These tools will push the budget toward a deficit position whether they are used deliberately or whether automatic stabilization, which causes tax collections to fall and transfer payments to increase in bad times, kicks in.

A balanced budget, contrary to common belief, does not have a neutral impact on economic activity. In determining the effect of a balanced budget, we must recall that dollars from income that has been taxed would otherwise have been used partly for spending and partly for saving. Thus, when the government spends those tax dollars on goods and services, it is taking some money that would have been saved and is spending it. As a result, a balanced budget has a slightly expansionary impact on the economy.

In summary,

- a surplus budget dampens aggregate spending and can aid in managing demand-pull inflation,
- a deficit budget increases aggregate spending and can help to reverse a recession, and
- a balanced budget can slightly expand the economy.

GOVERNMENT'S IMPACT ON THE MACROECONOMY

Indicate the effect of each of the following actions—taken alone—on the macroeconomy. That is, in each case determine the changes that would result in aggregate output, employment, or prices. Unless otherwise specified, in each case the economy is not operating at full employment.

1. The amount that households can deduct from their incomes when calculating their federal personal income tax increases.
2. Payments to Social Security recipients are increased, but there is an equal decrease in government purchases of military vehicles.
3. The federal government balances its budget when the economy is at full employment.
4. Congresspersons vote themselves a 20 percent pay increase.
5. A budget surplus occurs as the economy falls into a recession.
6. Taxes on cigarettes and alcohol are raised by 50 percent.
7. The federal government increases taxes with the intention of paying off its accumulated debt within 10 years.
8. Across-the-board increases are made in defense, highway, and education spending.
9. The economy is at full employment, and the Social Security surplus is so large that social insurance taxes are lowered.
10. The federal government runs a deficit budget while the economy is experiencing demand-pull inflation.
11. The number of people eligible for payments under an entitlement program decreases.
12. Government shuts down for a week because agreement cannot be reached on a new budget and funding authorization has expired under the old budget.
13. The United States enters a military conflict without any tax increase to pay for it.
14. The federal government decides to get out of the business of making loans and grants to college students.

Answers can be found at the back of the book.

Test Your Understanding, "Government's Impact On The Macroeconomy," gives you an opportunity to assess how various actions by the federal government influence the economy's output, employment, and price levels.

The Realities of Fiscal Policy and the Federal Budget

Let's lay aside the smooth, simple mechanics of fiscal policy and go to the real world where the federal budget doesn't always perform according to the ideal strategy for keeping the economy on track. There are several points to consider in assessing how well the economic concepts that we have just learned are translated into economic policy.

While economists like to think that full employment and stable prices are the primary goals of congressional tax and spending plans, in reality congresspersons may have other goals in mind. For example, even though economic conditions might call for a reduction in spending, concerns about homeland security or global warming could result in increased expenditures.

Fiscal policy and the federal budget are major components of the work of elected public officials. With proposed spending and taxing changes, elected persons tend to consider how these changes will impact their constituents. The economy may take a back seat to what is better for a congressperson's home district. For example, you would expect a congressperson from farm country in Illinois to support farm subsidies regardless of larger macro problems.

Fiscal policy takes time to enact: The statistical information that identifies the extent of an unemployment or inflation problem takes time to gather, and the political debate and discussion over policy tools and between Congress and the executive branch are again time consuming. Sometimes the problem can self-correct while Congress debates the issue.

There is one additional dimension: Since the government can easily borrow to cover budget deficits, from time to time we have seen examples of wasteful and extravagant expenditures. This has led to growing interest among economists in **public choice**, which is the study of the economic motives and attitudes of voters and public officials, and how those motives and attitudes affect government decision making. Public choice is discussed more fully in Chapter 11.

THE NATIONAL DEBT

In the past few decades, the federal government has had a habit of running deficit budgets: Table 6.6 shows persistent annual deficits from 1970 through 1997 and substantial deficits since 2009. Just like people and businesses that must borrow because they have no savings and are spending more than they earn, the federal government must borrow funds to finance its deficits. And, as more is borrowed each year, the federal government goes deeper and deeper in debt. A surplus budget, which allows some of this debt to be repaid, occurs infrequently. The accumulated total debt of the federal government is called the **national debt**.

Financing and Assessing the National Debt

When the federal government needs to raise money to finance its spending, it borrows at the lowest interest rate it can negotiate from anyone who is willing to lend it money. In return for funds, the lender receives a **U.S. Treasury security**: a formal IOU stating the federal government's promise to make specified interest payments and to repay the loaned funds on a particular date. The time span from issuance to the maturity, or repayment, date determines whether the security is a **U.S. Treasury bill** (often called a "T-bill"), which matures in one year or less; a **U.S. Treasury note**, which matures in less than 10 years; or a **U.S. Treasury bond**, which matures in 30 years.

The process for federal government borrowing is public and investors from the average family to highly sophisticated institutional fund managers participate in this process. When it wants to borrow funds, the government publicly announces the total amount it intends to borrow and the repayment date. A kind of auction occurs and the government borrows from those who offer funds at the lowest interest rates.

Who loans the federal government money or owns Treasury securities? The largest portion of the debt is currently held by the Federal Reserve and U.S. intragovernmental holdings. But individual investors, pension funds, mutual funds, insurance companies, and state and local governments hold substantial amounts of Treasury securities. Perhaps the U.S. Treasury is in debt to you or your family. If you own a U.S. Treasury security, you have provided the federal government with borrowed funds. Many people are curious about the process of saving money through Treasury securities. Application 6.3, "U.S. Treasury Securities," answers some frequently asked questions about this process.

Size of the National Debt

The size of the national debt is incomprehensible to most people. Table 6.8 gives the total national debt and the per capita debt for selected years beginning with 1970. Because the debt is linked to the federal budget, years in which deficit spending occurred were also years of an increase in the national debt. Notice

---

Public Choice
The study of the economic motives and attitudes of voters and public officials, and how those motives and attitudes affect government decision making.

National Debt
The accumulated total debt of the federal government due to deficit spending.

U.S. Treasury Security
Issued by the federal government in return for funds lent to it.

U.S. Treasury Bill, Note, and Bond
U.S. Treasury securities that mature, respectively, in 1 year or less; 2 to 10 years; and 30 years.

APPLICATION 6.3

U.S. TREASURY SECURITIES

The following are some commonly asked questions, and their answers, about buying and holding U.S. Treasury securities as savings.

Q: How much money do I need to purchase U.S. Treasury securities?

A: Treasury bills, notes, and bonds are issued in denominations of $100.

Q: Are Treasury bills, notes, and bonds the only securities I can buy?

A: There are other securities like some savings bonds and securities tied to inflation.

Q: Where can I purchase a U.S. Treasury security?

A: A security can be purchased directly from the Treasury when the government announces its intention to borrow. Once the security has been issued, it can be bought and sold on a secondary market, which is a market for "used" securities. Treasury securities are regularly traded through brokers and some banks in the secondary market for a fee.

Q: Tell me more about the secondary market.

A: Previously issued Treasury securities can be bought and sold at any time on the secondary market. For example, if you have a $1,000 Treasury note and need your money, you can go to a broker who will sell this security to someone else. When you sell your security, you may get more or less than its face value depending on the interest rate on your security and the current interest rate. If your security's interest rate is more than the current rate, you will receive more than the face value; if your security's interest rate is less than the current rate, you will receive less than the face value.

Q: How much interest do I get and when do I receive that interest?

A: When a Treasury security is issued, it carries a maturity date and a stated annual rate of interest. Interest on notes and bonds is paid every six months based on the stated rate. For example, a $1,000 Treasury note with an 8 percent rate of stated interest means the holder receives $40 every six months until the maturity date when the holder can claim the $1,000 principal. Treasury bills are sold for less than their face value. At maturity the holder gets the full amount.

Q: How safe are Treasury securities?

A: Because U.S. Treasury securities are backed by the U.S. government, most people consider them to be very safe.

Q: How can I learn more about Treasury securities?

A: A good source, used here, of information about Treasury securities can be found at www.treasurydirect.gov.

---

the rapid and substantial increases in the debt since 2008 when it was close to $10 trillion and grew to close to $18 trillion by the end of 2014.

The share of the national debt for every man, woman, and child in the United States is shown in the Per Capita Debt column of Table 6.8. These figures illustrate startling increases in recent years. To have fully paid off the debt in 2014, a family of four would have needed to contribute over $223,200 as its share.[6]

Assessing the Debt   How does the national debt affect the average person today? What does it mean for future generations? Has the debt become too large? Have the substantial increases in the debt in the past 10 years been worth it? Should the debt be paid off as soon as possible? The national debt is frequently a topic of conversations—academic, political, and those around the kitchen table—and questions like these are typically discussed. Let us focus on a few critical issues.

The interest that must be paid to borrow and maintain a debt of this magnitude is a significant burden. The amount of interest paid annually to sustain the national debt is given in Table 6.8 in the column Net Interest Paid. In 2014, for example, $229 billion in interest—almost $4.5 billion per week—was paid to the holders of federal debt. The opportunity cost of paying this interest is the many alternative uses for these dollars: education, the environment, the rebuilding of aging bridges and highways, and relief for areas hit by destructive weather to name a few.

---

[6] A word of caution is in order regarding comparisons of the burden of the debt from year to year. The figures in Table 6.8 are in current, not real, dollars, so inflation has not been factored into these numbers.

TABLE 6.8   *The National Debt, Selected Years 1970–2014[a]*

Over the years, the national debt and the burden of the debt per person have grown.

Year	Total Debt (Trillions of Dollars)	Per Capita Debt (Dollars)	Net Interest Paid (Billions of Dollars)
1970	$0.038	$1,853	$14.4
1975	0.054	2,500	23.2
1980	0.091	4,005	52.5
1985	1.817	7,637	129.5
1990	3.206	12,852	184.3
1995	4.921	18,725	232.1
1996	5.182	19,538	241.1
1997	5.369	20,050	244.0
1998	5.478	20,270	241.1
1999	5.606	20,558	229.8
2000	5.629	19,934	222.9
2001	5.770	20,224	206.2
2002	6.198	21,513	170.9
2003	6.760	23,245	153.1
2004	7.355	25,063	160.2
2005	7.905	26,689	184.0
2006	8.451	28,265	226.6
2007	8.951	29,639	237.1
2008	9.986	32,763	252.8
2009	11.876	38,629	186.9
2010	13.529	43,609	196.2
2011	14.764	47,134	230.0
2012	16.051	51,096	220.4
2013	16.719	52,825	220.9
2014	17.795	55,809	229.0

[a]Fiscal years.

Sources: *Economic Report of the President* (Washington, DC: U.S. Government Printing Office, 2015), Tables B-19, B-21; 1945 to 1999 population data from www.census.gov; 2000 to 2011 population data from *Statistical Abstract of the United States: 2012*, pp. 8, 9; 2012–2014 population data from http://factfinder.census.gov, 05/15/2015.

Debt Service

The cost of maintaining a debt; generally measured in interest costs.

The interest cost of the national debt, or the **debt service**, cumulates as additional debt is incurred each year and the debt is not paid off. While the interest that must be paid is a burden to current and future taxpayers, many U.S. citizens own government securities and count on the interest payments for income. Treasury securities provide a relatively easy and popular way to save money.

The issue of whether the national debt has become too large is a value judgment. At what point, even in the case of our own finances, do credit obligations become too high? One way to evaluate the size of the national debt is to examine it as a percentage of GDP, as is done in Figure 6.1. Notice that the percentage generally rose from the 1980s through the mid-1990s, declined, and then rose again with a very large rise in recent years as it has become a matter of concern. This way of evaluating the size of the

FIGURE 6.1	*National Debt as a Percentage of GDP, 1980–2014*[a]

One way to evaluate the size of the national debt is to compare it to GDP. The ratio of debt to GDP has generally been rising.

[a]Figures are for fiscal years.

Source: *Economic Report of the President* (Washington, DC: U.S. Government Printing Office, 2015), Table B-20.

debt is analogous to comparing an individual's debt and income. Obviously a person can sustain more dollars of debt at an annual income of $60,000 than at an annual income of $20,000. The problem is whether or not someone can sustain a debt that takes a rising percentage of income.

Should we, or could we, pay off the debt? It would be a huge, probably impossible, burden, even over several years, to raise through taxes and other revenues the amount needed to pay off the debt. (Recall that every person would need to contribute about $56,000.) With repayment of the debt, a significant income redistribution would occur as the average taxpayer had less income due to the increased tax burden and the holders of government securities had more income from their newly redeemed funds.

Also, some portion of the debt is external, or foreign-owned. While normally this is not a serious concern, in a period of accelerated repayment, it would mean a sizable flow of dollars out of the United States. Finally, in order to pay off the public debt, a series of surplus budgets would be needed. Recall from earlier in the chapter that a surplus budget has a contractionary impact on the economy: While the debt was being paid off, economic activity would decline. In short, the opportunity cost of paying off the national debt would be a substantial slowdown in the economy.

Crowding Out

One other consideration involving deficit spending and the national debt is the strain that government borrowing puts on funds available for loans. The federal government competes with households and businesses to borrow whatever funds are available for loan making. If government borrowing is sizable, two important effects result in the market for loans. First, because the borrowing and lending of money takes place in markets where the forces of supply and demand determine interest rates (the price of money), increases in government borrowing increase the demand for loans and cause interest rates to rise. When the federal government borrows substantial amounts, the impact on interest rates can be significant.

A second effect of sizable government borrowing is the **crowding out** of private borrowing. Because households and businesses are sensitive to the interest rate, increases in the interest rate cause them to borrow less. The result is that available funds are soaked up by the federal government, which is not sensitive to the interest rate in its borrowing. Businesses and households borrow less for capital improvements, plant expansion, homes, automobiles, and such. With crowding out, economic growth may be slowed as businesses postpone borrowing to buy the machinery and equipment necessary for growth.

In Chapter 8, you will learn how Federal Reserve policy can change the supply of loans and influence the interest rate as well as the degree of crowding out that might occur with government borrowing.

Crowding Out
Occurs when borrowing by the federal government reduces borrowing by households and businesses.

Summary

1. The two main categories of government expenditures are purchases of goods and services and transfer payments. Some government purchases are for public goods, which are provided for all of society and from which no one can be excluded.

2. Governments receive revenues from taxes and other sources, such as contributions for social insurance. The primary source of federal government revenue is the individual income tax. Taxes may be classified according to the relationship between the percentage of income taxed and the size of the income: A progressive tax has a direct relationship, a regressive tax has an inverse relationship, and the percentage stays the same for a proportional tax.

3. Tax reform sometimes occurs because of a need for additional government funding or for political reasons. A tax base is the thing on which a tax is levied, and the tax rate is the amount that is levied on the base.

4. Fiscal policy refers to changes in government expenditures and/or taxes for the purpose of influencing the levels of output, employment, or prices in the economy. Fiscal policy can be used to reduce unemployment by injecting more spending into the economy through increased government purchases, increased transfer payments, and/or decreased taxes. Demand-pull inflation is reduced through decreased government purchases, decreased transfer payments, and/or increased taxes.

5. Fiscal policy is either discretionary or automatic. Discretionary fiscal policy is the deliberate adjustment of government purchases, transfers, and/or taxes by Congress to control unemployment or inflation. Automatic stabilization is the automatic change in some government expenditures, like transfer payments, and some taxes,

such as the federal personal income tax, that stimulates or dampens aggregate spending as the level of economic activity changes. These changes in spending and taxes automatically help soften the impact of unemployment or inflation.

6. When a government's outlays are less than its revenues, it is operating with a surplus budget; when its outlays exceed revenues, it is operating with a deficit budget; and when its outlays and revenues are equal, it is operating with a balanced budget. Surplus budgets generally cause economic activity to contract, since the government is withdrawing more from the spending stream than it is returning. Deficit and balanced budgets are expansionary because the government is injecting more into the spending stream than is being taken out as taxes. A surplus budget would be proper policy for fighting demand-pull inflation, while a deficit budget would be appropriate for fighting unemployment.

7. There has been a tendency to run annual federal budget deficits. These deficits are generally reported in a unified budget format rather than differentiating between on-budget and off-budget balances. The Social Security trust fund has been operating with annual surpluses that have reduced the size of the unified budget deficit.

8. Fiscal policy considerations compete with other economic and noneconomic objectives in establishing the federal budget. The effectiveness of fiscal policy may be reduced by the time lag from the onset and discovery of a problem to the implementation of a remedy.

9. The national debt is the debt owed by the federal government from the financing of its deficit budgets. In raising funds, the government borrows at the lowest interest rates offered from anyone willing to lend funds and gives U.S. Treasury securities in return. The size of the national debt has grown substantially over the years, as has the debt as a percentage of GDP. In addition, as the federal government borrows more, it can crowd out private borrowing.

Key Terms and Concepts

Government purchases of goods and services
Public goods
Quasi-public good
Transfer payments
Social insurance program
Progressive tax
Proportional tax (flat tax)
Regressive tax
Tax reform
Tax base
Tax rate

Tax abatement
Fiscal policy
Discretionary fiscal policy
Automatic fiscal policy (automatic stabilization)
Economic stimulus
Balanced budget
Surplus budget
Deficit budget
Unified budget
Trust fund
Entitlements

On-budget   U.S. Treasury security
Off-budget   U.S. Treasury bill, note, bond
Public choice   Debt service
National debt   Crowding out

Review Questions

1. Identify the major spending categories and the major revenue sources of the
    federal government.

2. Determine whether each of the following taxes is progressive, proportional, or
    regressive.
    a. A sales tax of 7 percent on medicine
    b. A state income tax with three brackets: 3 percent for income under $20,000, 8
        percent for income between $20,000 and $100,000, and 15 percent for income
        over $100,000
    c. A property tax of $2.85 per $100 of assessed property value
    d. A tax of $8 on room occupancy in all hotels in a county
    e. A tax of 3 percent on all wages earned in a city
    f. A sales tax of 5 percent on utilities
    g. A federal tax of $2 per pack of cigarettes

3. Identify the tax base in each of the examples in Question 2.

4. Explain how automatic stabilization stimulates spending in a recession and
    dampens spending during periods of demand-pull inflation. How does
    automatic stabilization affect the federal budget?

5. Explain whether the economy will expand, contract, stay the same, or inflate
    with each of the following fiscal actions taken alone. Assume the economy is not
    at full employment unless stated otherwise.
    a. Congress votes and sends a $600 tax credit to each taxpayer.
    b. Households are taxed an extra 15 percent, and the government spends the
        entire amount on purchases of goods and services.
    c. Congress allows many new income tax deductions when the economy is at
        full employment.
    d. Although Congress intends to balance the budget, a deficit occurs.
    e. At the end of a war, defense expenditures drop dramatically but are replaced
        by domestic spending programs for health and education.
    f. Congress decides to decrease defense expenditures with no increase in other
        spending programs.
    g. Congress increases expenditures for transfer payments at the same time it
        reduces spending on highways and bridges by the same amount.
    h. Congress works to run a surplus budget and debt reduction during a serious
        recession.

6. If the U.S. economy fell into a serious recession, what could Congress do to counte-
    ract that recession? Specifically, how could it use each of its fiscal policy tools?

7. What effect would each of the following, taken alone, have on a federal budget that is currently balanced? How would the budgetary changes, where they occur, affect the national debt?
    a. An increase in the percentage of income taxed in each of the federal personal income tax brackets
    b. An increase in government expenditures for research on global warming
    c. An equal increase in government expenditures and income tax revenues
    d. An increase in defense expenditures and a decrease in corporate income tax revenues
    e. An increase in Social Security payments by the government matched by a decrease in a subsidy to a particular group in the economy, such as farmers
    f. An exemption from federal income tax for interest earned on small savings accounts in banks

8. Could the national debt be eliminated over the next 10 years? How? What are the opportunity costs of paying off the debt and not paying it off?

9. How does crowding out affect businesses?

Discussion Questions

1. Suppose that the legislators in a particular state are choosing among three strategies to raise revenue: (1) imposing a progressive income tax; (2) imposing a sales tax on food; and (3) imposing a 1 percent tax on all earnings within the state. How do you think residents of the state in the upper, middle, and lower income groups would react to each of these proposals? Which of the three strategies do you favor? Which of the three has the greatest likelihood of being passed?

2. Give some arguments for and against a federal personal income tax that would be proportional rather than progressive. Who stands to win and who stands to lose from a flat tax?

3. Suppose that government policymakers are concerned about a forecasted recession. As a consequence, they want to increase spending in the economy by $10 billion and can follow any one of three policies: (1) a $10 billion increase in government purchases of goods and services, (2) a transfer payment increase that would provide funds for households to spend $10 billion, or (3) a reduction in taxes by an amount that would put $10 billion into spending. Does it make any difference which of the three policies is chosen? How would each affect the federal budget? Why might policymakers choose one policy over another?

4. Do you favor legislation requiring the federal government to balance its budget? Why? What are the economic implications of your position?

5. Off-budget entitlement programs such as Medicare have grown in recent years. Could Congress reasonably limit spending for Medicare given the demographics of the country?

6. You are invited to participate in a commission that is exploring the future of the Social Security system. What recommendations might you make?

7. Locate the most recent figures for the national debt. Has it increased or decreased in recent years? What type of effect will this debt have on future generations?

8. Assume that you are a congressperson whose district may be awarded a multimillion-dollar rapid transit project. The economy, however, is in the throes of one of the more severe inflationary periods of the decade. How would you vote on the passage of funds for the project? What would you tell your colleagues? Your constituents?

9. Crowding out, where businesses and households are forced out of the market for borrowed funds by federal government borrowing, occurs because businesses and households are sensitive to interest rate changes while the federal government is not. Why is federal borrowing not sensitive to the interest rate? What would be the effect on federal programs if it were sensitive to the interest rate?

Critical Thinking Case 6

NIMBY (NOT IN MY BACKYARD)

Critical Thinking Skills

Ranking alternatives

Evaluating effects of decisions

Recognizing conflicting objectives

Economic Concepts

Balanced budget

Government expenditures and revenues

Budget determination process

Balancing the federal budget has been one of the most talked about economic agenda items for decades. Democratic and Republican lawmakers alike have been on record backing a balanced budget, and, in principle, there is much support for the proposal among U.S. citizens.

The problem is that a balanced budget, given the usual deficit position of the federal government, requires an increase in taxes and/or a decrease in spending. So, once the discussion of creating a balanced budget moves from generalities to specific needed changes in taxes and/or spending, the supportive position for a balanced budget frequently turns to one of opposition. There is a saying that may be appropriate here: "not in my backyard," or NIMBY.

NIMBY often results when people support an idea in general—like a reduction in some government programs or the construction of a big box store in their community—until they see negative consequences for themselves. Once there is a real or perceived negative individual impact from a government decision, support for that action evaporates.

This puts U.S. congresspersons in a tough situation as they try to find acceptable actions to balance the budget. The following is a list of possible proposals that would raise revenue or cut costs in an effort to find a balance. Review this list as if you were in Congress and had to vote on these various proposals. Then answer the questions below.

Proposals to Balance the Budget

1. Increase all individual income taxes by 10 percent.
2. Increase the corporate income tax by 20 percent.
3. Cancel the income tax deductions for home mortgage interest payments.

4. End all agricultural subsidies.
5. Reduce defense/military expenditures for troops and equipment.
6. Cut government spending on Medicare by 25 percent.
7. End scholarships, low-interest loans, and other financial support to college students.
8. Reduce expenditures on conservation and the environment.

Questions

1. What groups would be most affected by each of these proposals?
2. Rank the proposals according to the likelihood that each would be approved by Congress. Rank the most likely to be approved first and the least likely last. Why did you rank these proposals in this way?
3. Based on these proposals, what conflicts, if any, are there between the goal of a balanced budget and other goals that you as a congressperson might seek?
4. It has been said that it is easier to promise that the budget will be balanced than it is to balance the budget. Based on your experience with these proposals, what do you think is the likelihood that the budget will be balanced?

Money, Financial Institutions, and the Federal Reserve

CHAPTER OBJECTIVES

Define money and explain the functions of money.

Identify the various measures and components of the U.S. money supply and different monetary standards.

Introduce the financial institutions that are important for the maintenance and control of the U.S. money supply, commercial banks, and commercial bank regulation.

Explain the role of the Federal Reserve system, its organization, and the functions that Federal Reserve banks perform.

Discuss recent legislative and structural changes in financial institutions.

We have explored several topics that in one way or another involve money. For example, we learned that economic activity expands or contracts as the size of the spending stream increases or decreases and that with inflation the purchasing power of money deteriorates. Without money, modern economies as we know them could not exist. Even though money does not itself produce goods and services, as do land, labor, capital, and entrepreneurship, it makes large-scale production and distribution possible. If a nation's monetary system becomes unstable, adverse economic consequences can result.

In this chapter we will deal with some basics about money, banks and other financial institutions, and the Federal Reserve, which plays an extremely critical role in the functioning of the economy and is regularly covered in the media. While this chapter provides information that may correct some myths for you (for example, money is backed by gold and silver), more importantly, it lays the groundwork for Chapter 8, where we study how money is actually created and destroyed and the effects of money on economic activity.

In recent years, the development and growth of financial services that operate outside of the banking system have created a number of issues for the U.S. macroeconomy, including a serious financial crisis that began in 2007. This chapter touches on these entities and the crisis.

MONEY

The Definition and Functions of Money

Money
Anything that is generally accepted as a medium of exchange.

Medium of Exchange
Something that is generally accepted as payment for goods, services, and resources; the primary function of money.

Very simply, **money** is *anything* that is generally accepted as a medium of exchange. A **medium of exchange** is something that people are readily willing to accept in payment for purchases of goods, services, and resources because they know it can be easily used for further transactions. In the United States, a $10 bill is a medium of exchange because people are willing to take this bill in payment, knowing that it can be used for other purchases.

Many people believe that money must be made of precious metal or be backed by a tangible asset, such as gold or silver. This is not true. Because a medium of exchange can be anything, possibilities for money include precious metals, stones, beads, coins, cigarettes, pieces of paper, and electronically transferred numbers. The physical form that money takes makes no difference as long as it is the generally accepted means of payment for purchases in an economy. Some unusual types of money that have been used at different times and in different places are listed in Table 7.1.

Value of Money
Measured by the goods, services, and resources that money can purchase.

If anything can serve as money, how is the **value of money** determined? Because money is a medium of exchange, the value of any money—a $20 bill, for example—is measured by the goods, services, and resources that it can purchase. Inflation causes the value of money to decline because fewer goods, services, and resources can be purchased with the same amount of money. Small, incremental increases in the general level of prices or serious bouts of inflation will cause a decline in the value of money: The decline can happen gradually or be a quick, significant deterioration.

Barter System
System in which goods and services are exchanged for each other rather than for money.

What would happen if there were no money—no generally accepted means of payment? In the absence of a medium of exchange, a **barter system** would develop. With barter, a direct exchange of goods and services occurs: A student might exchange some camping gear in return for a psychology textbook. With barter, people have to expend a lot of energy locating someone willing to take what they offer in trade for what they want. In today's world, few people operate on a barter system since it is virtually impossible to have much economic development by trading in this manner. A medium of exchange, or money, removes the problems of barter.

Measure of Value
A function of money; the value of every good, service, and resource can be expressed in terms of an economy's base unit of money.

Method for Storing Wealth and Delaying Payments
A function of money; allows for saving, or storing wealth for future use, and permits credit, or delayed payments.

While money serves primarily as a medium of exchange, it also performs two additional functions: It is a **measure of value**, and it provides a **method for storing wealth and delaying payments**. Every nation's money is expressed in terms of a base unit. In the United States, the base unit is the dollar; in Japan, the yen; and in many countries belonging to the European Union, the euro. With a base unit, the value of every resource, good, and service can be expressed in terms of that unit: A house, for example, might be worth 220,000 times a dollar unit ($220,000) and a car 22,000 times the unit ($22,000). Money's function as a base unit makes it easy to create simple

| TABLE 7.1 | Different Forms of Money |

Anything can serve as money in a society, provided it is generally accepted as payment for goods, services, and resources.

Form	Location
Cowrie shells	Africa, India, South Seas (perhaps the oldest money in the world)
Snail shells	Queen Charlotte Islands
Porpoise teeth	Malaita (island in the Solomon Group)
Boar tusks	New Guinea
Red woodpecker scalps	Karok Tribe on the west coast of North America
Feathers	South Seas
Beer	English coal mines in the mid-nineteenth century
Bars of crystal salt	Ethiopia
Round stones with centers removed	Yap
Glass	Ancient Egypt
Wampum (polished beads)	
Animal skins	
Rice	
Sugar	
Rum	North American settlements and Colonial period
Molasses	
Indigo	
Tobacco	
Cowries	
Tortoise shells	Ancient China
Agricultural implements	

Source: Norman Angell, *The Story of Money* (Garden City, NY: Garden City Publishing Co., 1929), pp. 73–76, 78–80, 82, 84, 85, 88–90.

comparisons among the values of goods and services, and the ability to express those values in terms of a common measure greatly reduces the information needed to make economic decisions.

Money also provides a method for storing wealth: It allows us to accumulate wealth or income to use in the future. With money, we can save from our current income, and a system of lending and borrowing is possible. It is this function that is critical to a stable economy. If there is a question about the future acceptability of today's money, people might be unwilling to save and institutions unwilling to lend for investment or other purposes. A bank might be reluctant to make a student loan or lend a developer millions of dollars this year if there were questions about the usability of future repayments.

The functions of money, as well as some of the types of money described in this section, are illustrated in Application 7.1, "Fixed Assets, Or: Why a Loan in Yap Is Hard to Roll Over."

APPLICATION 7.1

FIXED ASSETS, OR: WHY A LOAN IN YAP IS HARD TO ROLL OVER

Yap, Micronesia—On this tiny South Pacific island, life is easy and the currency is hard.

Elsewhere, the world's troubled monetary system creaks along. . . . But on Yap the currency is as solid as a rock. In fact, it is rock. Limestone to be precise.

For nearly 2,000 years the Yapese have used large stone wheels to pay for major purchases, such as land, canoes and permission to marry. Yap is a U.S. trust territory, and the dollar is used in grocery stores and gas stations. But reliance on stone money . . . continues.

Buying property with stones is "much easier than buying it with U.S. dollars," says John Chodad, who recently purchased a building lot with a 30-inch stone wheel. "We don't know the value of the U.S. dollar." Others on this 37-square-mile island 530 miles southwest of Guam use both dollars and stones. Venito Gurtmag, a builder, recently accepted a four-foot-wide stone disk and $8,700 for a house he built in an outlying village.

Stone wheels don't make good pocket money, so for small transactions, Yapese use other forms of currency, such as beer. Beer is proffered as payment for all sorts of odd jobs, including construction. . . .

Besides stone wheels and beer, the Yapese sometimes spend gaw, consisting of necklaces of stone beads strung together around a whale's tooth. They also can buy things with yar, a currency made from large sea shells. But these are small change.

The people of Yap have been using stone money ever since a Yapese warrior named Anagumang first brought the huge stones over from limestone caverns on neighboring Palau, some 1,500 to 2,000 years ago. Inspired by the moon, he fashioned the stone into large circles. The rest is history.

Yapese lean the stone wheels against their houses or prop up rows of them in village "banks." Most of the stones are 2 1/2 to five feet in diameter, but some are as much as 12 feet across. Each has a hole in the center so it can be slipped onto the trunk of a fallen betel-nut tree and carried. It takes 20 men to lift some wheels.

By custom, the stones are worthless when broken. You never hear people on Yap musing about wanting a piece of the rock. Rather than risk a broken stone—or back—Yapese tend to leave the larger stones where they are and make a mental accounting that the ownership has been transferred. . . .

The worth of stone money doesn't depend on size. Instead, the pieces are valued by how hard it was to get them here. . . .

There are some decided advantages to using massive stones for money. They are immune to black-market trading, for one thing, and they pose formidable obstacles to pickpockets. In addition, there aren't any sterile debates about how to stabilize the Yapese monetary system. With only about 6,600 stone wheels remaining on the island, the money-supply level stays put. "If you have it, you have it," shrugs Andrew Ken, a Yapese monetary thinker.

But stone money has its limits. Linus Ruuamau, the manager of one of the island's few retail stores, won't accept it for general merchandise. And Al Azuma, who manages the local Bank of Hawaii branch, the only conventional financial institution here, isn't interested in limestone deposits or any sort of shell game. So the money, left uninvested, just gathers moss.

But stone money accords well with Yapese traditions. "There are a lot of instances here where you cannot use U.S. money," Mr. Gurtmag says. One is the settling of disputes. Unlike most money, stones sometimes can buy happiness, of a sort; if a Yapese wants to settle an argument, he brings his adversary stone money as a token. "The apology is accepted without question," Mr. Chodad says. "If you used dollars, there'd be an argument over whether it was enough."

THE U.S. MONEY SUPPLY

Every economy has a supply of money that is used to carry out transactions. What makes up the money supply of the U.S. economy, and how large is this supply? This is a more difficult question than it appears to be since people look at what is actually money in different ways. For example, some people think that a savings account is money while others do not. As a result, we have two different official definitions of the money supply, with one broader than the other because it includes additional components.

TABLE 7.2	The U.S. Money Supply: M1

M1 is the narrower definition of the U.S. money supply.

M1

Coins and paper money in circulation
Nonbank-issued traveler's checks
Demand deposits
Other checkable deposits

Source: Federal Reserve, "H.6 Money Stock Measures," www.federalreserve.gov, January 19, 2015.

M1
Narrower definition of the U.S. money supply; includes coins and paper money in circulation, some traveler's checks, most demand deposits, and other checkable deposits.

Token Money
Money with a face value greater than the value of the commodity from which it is made.

Federal Reserve Notes
Paper money issued by the Federal Reserve banks; includes almost all paper money in circulation.

Currency
Coins and paper money.

Demand Deposits
Checking account balances kept primarily at commercial banks.

Other Checkable Deposits
Interest-bearing accounts similar to demand deposits offered by financial depository institutions.

Components of M1   The narrower definition of the money supply is called **M1**. The components of this definition are listed in Table 7.2: coins and paper money in circulation, nonbank-issued traveler's checks, almost all demand deposits (checking accounts) at commercial banks, and accounts called other checkable deposits.[1] In the U.S. economy, coins, which are issued by the U.S. Mint, are **token money**: The value of the metal in the coin is less than the face value of the coin. If this were not the case, coins might disappear from circulation. For example, in the past, when the price of copper increased to a level where a penny contained almost one cent worth of copper, pennies became short in supply. Today, pennies are made almost entirely of zinc. Information about U.S. coins—history, composition, and more—can be found at www.usmint.gov.

Paper money constitutes a larger share of our money supply than coins. Almost all U.S. paper money is **Federal Reserve Notes**. (Notice the inscription on the top of a paper bill that states "Federal Reserve Note.") Federal Reserve banks, which will be discussed shortly, issue and back this paper money. Coins and paper money make up **currency**.

Traveler's checks, which can be used in the United States or abroad, are purchased from banking organizations as well as some companies. However, only traveler's checks from "nonbank issuers" are categorized separately in M1, and these constitute the smallest component of M1.

The **demand deposit** component of the money supply is checking account balances kept primarily at commercial banks. These deposits include small balances kept by individuals as well as large sums kept by businesses and nonprofit institutions for payroll and other payment purposes. Demand deposits are merely bookkeeping numbers. When a check or online payment is deposited or one is written and cleared, numbers are transferred from one account to another. Because demand deposits are a large portion of the U.S. money supply, we need to realize that much of the money supply is simply numbers in accounts. Checks themselves are not money. They are simply the means to transfer or access funds.

Other checkable deposits are similar to demand deposits but offer interest on the funds in these accounts. The distinction between these and demand deposits is made for technical reasons. Most of us pay almost no attention to the distinction among checks, drafts, withdrawal orders, or other technical names given to these accounts. These accounts were introduced in the early 1980s and are provided by banks and other depository institutions.

[1] Only coins and paper money in circulation are included in the money supply. Although a large amount of both of these items is "warehoused" in bank and Federal Reserve vaults for future use, it is not counted as money until it is in the hands of the public.

| TABLE 7.3 | | *Currency, Traveler's Checks, Demand Deposits, and Other Checkable Deposits (Billions of Dollars)*[a] | | | | | | |

Currency has surpassed demand deposits and other checkable deposits as the largest component of the M1 money supply.

Year	Currency (Coins and Paper Money)	Traveler's Checks	Demand Deposits	Other Checkable Deposits	Total (M1)[b]	Total (M1) as a Percentage of GDP	Velocity
1995	$372.8	$9.0	$389.0	$356.6	$1,127.5	15.2%	6.6
2000	531.3	8.3	309.6	238.7	1,087.8	10.6	9.4
2005	724.6	7.2	324.3	318.7	1,374.8	10.5	9.5
2010	918.8	4.7	519.3	399.0	1,841.8	12.3	8.1
2014	1,252.4	2.9	1,162.2	489.1	2,906.6	16.7	6.0

[a] Figures are seasonally adjusted for December of the given year.

[b] Components may not sum exactly to total (M1) due to rounding.

Source: "H.6 Statistical Release," www.federalreserve.gov, January 29, 2015; *Economic Report of the President* (Washington, DC: U.S. Government Printing Office, 2015), Table B.2. 2014 GDP is preliminary. 1995 GDP is from the 2012 *Economic Report of the President*.

Table 7.3 gives the amount of each component of the M1 money supply as well as other important money-related information. Prior to the year 2000 checking-type accounts (demand deposits and other checkable deposits together) were the largest part of M1. People tended to pay for expensive items with one of these types of accounts and employers typically paid their bills and employees with a check.

Data show that in recent decades the currency component of M1 has grown significantly and in some cases it has been the largest component. Some of the early impetus for the reliance on cash for payments came when people feared that a major computer crash would occur on January 1, 2000, and bank records would be lost. Since then a number of changes in banking have occurred: ATM machines are popular and can be easily found just about everywhere; bank money market accounts provide limited checking but pay interest; there is an increased reliance on credit cards for everyday spending; and businesses can keep their funds in interest-bearing accounts and transfer them to demand deposits when needed.

Notice the column in Table 7.3 that shows the total M1 money supply for each year as a percentage of that year's GDP. Every year the total amount spent on new goods and services exceeds the amount of money in circulation. For example, the money supply in 2010 was equal to only 12.3 percent of the total expenditures made on new goods and services that year. Obviously, so much output can be purchased with so few dollars because the same dollars are spent several times over during the course of the year.

Velocity of Money

Average number of times the money supply is turned over in a year in relationship to GDP.

The average turnover of the money supply in relationship to annual GDP is termed the **velocity of money**. That is, velocity measures the average number of times a dollar is spent during a year as it is used for the purchase of new goods and services. The far right-hand column of Table 7.3 gives the velocity of M1. Notice that while the velocity increased after 2000 that it has fallen again. Even with these changes velocity is fairly consistent without extreme fluctuations from year to year.

TABLE 7.4	*The U.S. Money Supply: M2*

M2 is the broader definition of the U.S. money supply

M2

M1
+
Savings deposits including money market deposit accounts
Time deposits of less than $100,000
Retail money funds

Source: "H.6 Money Stock Measures," www.federalreserve.gov.

We tend to have a fairly regular routine about receiving paychecks and making major payments.[2]

M2: The Broader Definition of the Money Supply   M1 is considered by many to be too narrow, especially with the growth of new types of accounts not included in M1 that can be used to buy goods and services or readily converted to payment instruments. According to the definition of M1, only funds deposited in a checking account are considered money. While the funds in a savings account are easily transferable to a checking account or cash and funds in a money market deposit account can be spent, they are not counted in M1.

The broader definition of the money supply, **M2**, is given in Table 7.4. Notice that it builds on M1, adding money market deposit accounts, savings deposits, certificates of deposit (time deposits) of less than $100,000, and some money funds. M2 is considered by many observers to be an important measure of the money supply because it includes accounts that allow limited checkable transactions and deposits that can be easily converted to spendable funds. In other words, many of the components have a high degree of **liquidity**. Not surprisingly, there is a substantial difference in the sizes of M1 and M2. At the beginning of 2015, M1 was $2.9 trillion and M2 was $11.7 trillion.[3]

Monetary Standards

People are often curious and sometimes concerned about what backs our money and that of other countries. Economies have monetary standards, or designations, for the backing of their money supply. An economy in which money is backed by something of tangible value, such as gold or silver, is on a **commodity monetary standard**. If the money is backed by gold, the economy is on a gold standard; if it is backed by silver, the economy is on a silver standard.

For much of its history, the U.S. economy was on a commodity standard. Prior to 1933 the United States had a gold-coin standard, where gold not only backed the money supply but also freely circulated in the hands of the public. The use of gold

M2
M1 plus savings and small-denomination time deposit accounts, money market deposit accounts, and other financial instruments.

Liquidity
Ease of converting an asset to its value in cash or spendable funds.

Commodity Monetary Standard
An economy's money is backed by something of tangible value such as gold or silver.

[2] There is a relationship between velocity and M1 as a percentage of GDP. That is, velocity = 1/M1 as a percentage of GDP. For example, the velocity of 8.1 in 2010 is equal to 1/0.123 = 8.1. (Be careful: The 12.3 percent is converted to a decimal 0.123 when used in this equation.)

[3] "H.6 Money Stock Measures," www.federalreserve.gov. Figures are for January 19, 2015 and are a seasonally adjusted week average.

pieces as money was common. Then U.S. citizens were asked to turn their gold in to the government, and in 1934 the United States went on a gold-bullion standard. This meant that gold backed the money supply but was no longer available to the general public. Under this gold-bullion standard, however, foreign holders of dollars were paid in gold. In the years after 1950, more and more international debts were paid in gold, and the U.S. gold supply gradually diminished. This brought about a reduction in the gold backing of the money supply. By 1971, official U.S. gold reserves had decreased to the point where the gold supply was frozen. U.S. gold was to be made available to no one, and the dollar was no longer to be converted to gold, not even to settle international transactions.

Paper Monetary Standard

An economy's money is not backed by anything of tangible value such as gold or silver.

Since 1971, the U.S. economy has been on a **paper monetary standard**. This means that money itself has little or no intrinsic value and that it does not represent a claim to any commodity, such as gold or silver. What backs paper money is the strength of the economy, the willingness of people to accept the money in exchange for goods and services, and faith and trust in the purchasing power of the money.

What is better for an economy, a paper standard or a commodity standard? It is easy to argue that there is more faith in money if it is backed by gold or silver, but history does not bear this out. In the past, panics and monetary crises have occurred even when money was backed by a precious metal. In fact, the knowledge that paper money can be converted into gold or silver can make people act more dramatically on their fears.

But the most important reason that advanced economies turn to a paper standard is that the amount of gold or silver a nation possesses generally has very little to do with its economic needs and potential. It is much more important that the amount of money in an economy be tied to the country's economic conditions rather than the availability of a commodity like gold or silver. But there is always a warning with a paper standard. The administrators of the money supply must be informed and impeccably trustworthy in the decisions they make concerning the money supply and carefully manage it. Without proper controls, serious economic problems can arise.

FINANCIAL DEPOSITORY INSTITUTIONS

Financial Depository Institution

Institution that accepts and maintains deposits, and makes loans; can create and destroy money.

In the United States, there are organizations called **financial depository institutions** (FDI) that play an extremely important role in the economy because of their association with the money supply. To be classified as an FDI, two functions must be performed: accept and maintain deposits, and make loans. Commercial banks are the most important of the financial depository institutions, but thrifts like savings associations and credit unions are also among these organizations. While they may seem similar to us, they are different in the kinds of deposits and loans they are permitted to offer and the degree of regulation they face.

Financial depository institutions are vital to the economy because they have the ability to create and destroy money. Here is one of our myths to correct. Many people think that money is created only when currency is printed. This is not so. *Money is created when loans are made by financial depository institutions and destroyed when loans are repaid.* The process for doing this will be thoroughly explored in the next chapter. For now we want to let you know that these institutions, with their special abilities to accept deposits and make loans, are central to expanding and contracting the money supply.

Commercial Banks

Commercial Bank

Institution that holds and maintains checking accounts (demand deposits) for its customers, makes commercial (business) and other loans, and performs other functions.

The primary financial depository institution is the **commercial bank**—where most individuals, businesses, and nonprofit organizations do their banking. A commercial bank attracts deposits by offering checking accounts, or demand deposits, as well as other deposit arrangements; makes loans to businesses and individuals; and performs a number of other functions. Banks earn profit for their owners by attracting deposits and converting them to interest-earning assets such as loans. In 2014, there were about 5,800 commercial banks in the United States.[4]

We saw in Table 7.3 that in 2014 approximately 40 percent of M1 was in demand deposits, or checking accounts, at commercial banks. In addition, commercial banks held some portion of other checkable deposits as well as trillions in savings and time deposits. The huge dollar value of these deposits makes commercial banks the most important of all financial depository institutions.

Commercial Bank Regulation   Commercial banks are unique: They are profit-driven businesses but play an essential role in maintaining and changing the size of the U.S. money supply. Since their actions are key to the economy, we must ensure that commercial banks be sound and secure and not abuse their money-creating abilities. To accomplish this aim, a number of agencies set standards and regulations for commercial banks that include, for example, the backing needed for deposits, the allowable riskiness of loans, and the money capital necessary to open a bank.

Dual Banking System

Label given to the U.S. banking system because both the federal and state governments have the right to charter banks.

All commercial banks must be incorporated, or have a corporate charter. Because both the federal and state governments have the right to charter banks, the United States has a **dual banking system**: That is, a bank may be chartered by the federal government or by a state government. Federally chartered banks are called **national banks**, and state-chartered banks are simply called **state banks**.

While bank regulation appears to be scattered among several agencies, there is order among them to prevent duplication of bank-examining tasks and an exacerbation of the disruption that comes with a visit from the examiners. The following gives the various agencies with which a bank may have to deal:

National Bank

Commercial bank incorporated under a federal rather than a state charter.

- *Charter Authority*. The charter sets up the first line of regulation: National banks are regulated by a federal agency and state banks by a state banking agency.
- *The Federal Reserve*. The Fed, which we will discuss shortly, has various levels of regulatory authority. The Federal Reserve regulates its own members, which include all national banks (they must belong) and state banks that choose to belong, or become "state member banks." The Federal Reserve also imposes some uniform regulations on all commercial banks.
- *Federal Deposit Insurance Corporation*. Additional regulation comes from the **Federal Deposit Insurance Corporation (FDIC)**, which was established in 1933 and insures deposits in commercial banks up to a specified amount. All national and state member banks are insured, and nonmember state banks may affiliate with the FDIC. Relatively few banks are nonmember noninsured state banks.

State Bank

Commercial bank incorporated under a state charter.

Federal Deposit Insurance Corporation (FDIC)

Government agency established in 1933 to insure deposits in commercial banks up to a specified amount.

Bank Failures   With such extensive regulation, can banks fail? Banks are no different from other businesses that no longer have the assets necessary to pay their debts. Despite regulation, banks and other financial depository institutions have found themselves in this same bankruptcy-prone position.

[4] Number is for FDIC-insured commercial banks. www2.fdic.gov, June 30, 2014.

Asset

Something that an individual or business owns; can be used to cover liabilities.

Liability

A claim on assets; an obligation or a debt of an individual or a business.

Net Worth

Assets minus liabilities; the monetary value of a business.

Bank failure is easy to understand with some basic accounting terminology. Recall that the two functions of a financial depository institution are to make loans and to hold deposits. The loans of a bank are a major **asset** (what the bank owns), and its deposits are a major **liability** (what the bank owes). The **net worth** of a bank is its assets minus its liabilities.

A bank fails when its assets are no longer sufficient to cover liabilities that must be paid. This is usually the result of heavy loan losses combined with deposit withdrawals. For example, if a bank loans a developer $50 million to build a subdivision of homes, the bank has an asset of $50 million. If the developer goes belly up, perhaps unable to sell the homes in various stages of construction, the bank becomes the new owner of those homes. It will likely not receive the full $50 million it loaned as it tries to dispose of this construction project. In short, the bank is "stuck" with an asset of less than $50 million, or has taken a loan loss. This has been the situation with banks that in recent years have had many houses and properties in foreclosure: They cannot recoup the amounts they loaned.

When a bank's assets decline, it has fewer funds available for depositors who want to withdraw their money from the bank; in other words, it cannot meet the demands of the holders of its liabilities. If a bank has made too many bad loans, it may simply not be solvent. With an insured bank in this position, the FDIC steps in and guarantees that depositors with accounts of less than a specified amount will receive their money. With an uninsured bank, depositors have no such promise, and their funds may be lost.

The number of bank failures in the United States took a serious upturn during the financial crisis that began in 2008 (which will be covered shortly). From 2001 until 2008, there were few failures with no failures in some years. But in 2009, 2010, and 2011, there were a total of 389 failures. As just explained, in these cases assets could not meet the liabilities. These banks were located throughout the country and in most instances were acquired by another bank. While these numbers are serious, they do not approach the record number of bank failures during the Great Depression—for example, 4,004 in 1933 alone.[5]

Application 7.2, "What Do I Do?" gives some information on FDIC protection of accounts in banks and notes some of the decisions people face in managing their money.

Other Financial Depository Institutions

Other financial depository institutions that play an important role with the money supply are thrift institutions, such as savings associations and banks, and credit unions. In 2013, there were 936 insured savings institutions and 6,554 credit unions. Although the number of these institutions is larger than the number of commercial banks, their total size is smaller. For example, in 2013 the assets of credit unions were a little over $1 trillion, while the assets of the FDIC-insured institutions were close to $15 trillion.[6]

In the early 1980s, significant changes were made in the legislation regulating these institutions to permit them to offer a greater variety of deposit accounts, to make different types of loans, and to bring some aspects of their operations under Federal Reserve control. The deregulation of deposits and loans, however, caused a serious crisis in the savings and loan industry, requiring financial intervention from the government.

The future of some of these financial depository institutions remains unclear. The number of thrifts and credit unions has fallen in recent years. The closing and merging

APPLICATION 7.2

WHAT DO I DO?

What a surprise! Jeff knew he was Aunt Millie's favorite nephew, but he was totally taken aback when a check for $25,000 came from settling her will and estate. It was in a simple white envelope from her attorney.

After the shock wore off, Jeff realized that his first step was to deposit this check in a bank account. But he worried. Would this be safe? There were several bank closings in his area, and he didn't want to risk his money in a bank that might close.

Most banks in the United States are insured by the FDIC (Federal Deposit Insurance Corporation) which began in 1933. Since it began, customers of failed banks with FDIC insurance have gotten their money back, usually within a few days. But there is a limit to the insured amount with a current recovery maximum of $250,000. Jeff doesn't have to worry about reaching that limit; he just needs to make sure that his deposit is in an FDIC-insured bank.

But, once that money is deposited in his account, Jeff faces many decisions about that inheritance. Does he spend it, perhaps buying a new car? Does he pay off his credit cards and student loans? Does he put it away and save it for future use? Does he do a combination of all of these options?

If Jeff decides to save this money for the future, he has another set of decisions to make. Where should he invest these funds? While the money in the bank is insured, there are other ways to save his money that might yield a higher return. But that money is likely not protected. While U.S. Treasury securities (covered in Chapter 6) are safe, they are not FDIC-insured. Mutual funds and stocks are another option—again not FDIC-insured.

How funny money is. We want and need it—and work for it. But it does bring some stress with the many decisions about how to use and protect it.

---

of failing savings banks, switches from a savings to a commercial bank charter, and the acquisition of savings institutions by commercial banks have all contributed to this movement.

THE FEDERAL RESERVE SYSTEM

While the Federal Reserve is familiar to us through media coverage, many people are unaware of the considerable power and authority that it has over our money and the economy. A paper monetary standard, like the one under which we operate, requires careful control. That job has been given to the Federal Reserve. And, as we will learn in Chapter 8, through its control of the supply of money, the Fed has the ability to influence levels of employment and prices and affect unemployment and inflation problems.

Federal Reserve System
Coordinates commercial banking operations, regulates some aspects of all depository institutions, and oversees the U.S. money supply.

Created in 1913, the **Federal Reserve system** has been charged to

♦ oversee the money supply and adjust its size to meet the needs of the economy;
♦ coordinate commercial banking operations; and
♦ regulate some aspects of all depository institutions.

Prior to the creation of the Fed, there was little central organization, a hodgepodge of state and federal banking laws, a history of questionable banking practices, and a recurrence of monetary panics.

---

[5] A bank closing is defined as either a permanent or temporary suspension of operations by order of the bank's supervisory authorities or its directors. Bank failure data are from www.fdic.gov. The 1933 bank failure figure is from Bruce R. Dalgaard, *Money, Financial Institutions, and Economic Activity* (Glenview, IL: Scott, Foresman & Company, 1987), p. 103.

[6] ProQuest Statistical Abstract of the U.S. Online Edition, Tables 1190, 1191, 1197.

| FIGURE 7.1 | *Functional Structure of the Federal Reserve System* |

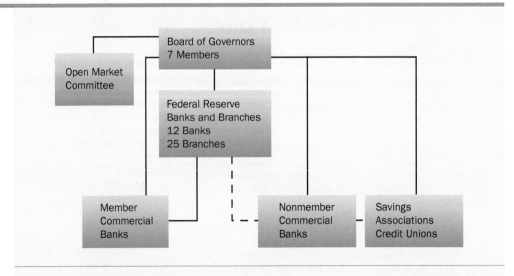

The Federal Reserve system is headed by the Board of Governors, and many system activities are carried out through the Federal Reserve banks and their branches.

Organization of the Federal Reserve System

The Federal Reserve system is organized on both a functional and a geographic basis. Figure 7.1 outlines the important features in the system's functional structure. The system is headed by the seven-member **Board of Governors**, each appointed by the president and confirmed by the Senate for a 14-year term.[7] One member is designated by the president as chairperson and serves as the spokesperson for Federal Reserve policy.

The Board of Governors has duties and responsibilities typical of a board of any organization: It sets goals and objectives for carrying out its charge and appropriate policies to meet them. The **Open Market Committee**, which includes the Board of Governors among its members, carries out the most important procedure for money supply control: It authorizes the buying and selling of government securities by the Federal Reserve.[8] You can go to the Federal Reserve website, www.FederalReserve. gov, for the pictures and biographies of the current members of the Board of Governors.

At the center of the Federal Reserve system are 12 **Federal Reserve banks** and their 24 branches, located throughout the country. These are not commercial banks: They deal with commercial banks and other financial depository institutions and perform a variety of functions that will be covered shortly. Each Federal Reserve bank is an independent corporation with its own board of directors, and each bank basically carries out the same functions. The remainder of the Federal Reserve system is the country's financial depository institutions, which are influenced by Federal Reserve policies and may depend on the Fed for certain services.

Board of Governors
Seven-member board heading the Federal Reserve system; develops policies concerning money, banking, and other financial institution practices.

Open Market Committee
Oversees the buying and selling of government securities by the Federal Reserve system.

Federal Reserve Banks
Twelve banks that deal with commercial banks and other financial institutions.

---

[7] The 14-year term was intended to keep any one president from appointing a majority of the Board of Governors. However, many appointees do not serve for 14 years, thus weakening the original intent of this arrangement.
[8] The operation of the Open Market Committee will be discussed in detail in Chapter 8.

FIGURE 7.2	*Federal Reserve Districts*

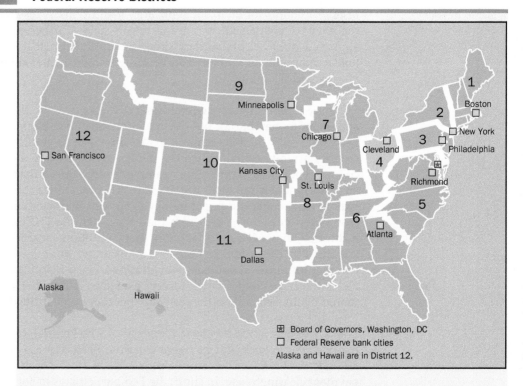

The United States is divided into 12 Federal Reserve districts, each with its own Federal Reserve bank.

Source: *Federal Reserve Bulletin,* Spring 2005, p. 312.

The Fed is also organized geographically. The United States is divided into 12 Federal Reserve districts, each represented by a Federal Reserve bank that is responsible for its own branch banks and the member commercial banks in its geographic area. Figure 7.2 illustrates the 12 Federal Reserve districts. In what district do you live, and how close are you located to one of these banks?

Functions of the Federal Reserve Banks

What do the Federal Reserve banks do? The Federal Reserve banks and their branches perform a variety of functions that do not directly involve the typical commercial bank customer. In fact, there is little reason for the average individual or businessperson to ever enter a Federal Reserve bank.

Supervise and Examine Member Banks   One function of each Federal Reserve bank is to supervise and examine member banks within its district. For this purpose, each Federal Reserve bank employs a staff of examiners who periodically check each member bank's financial condition and compliance with system regulations.

Maintain Reserve Accounts   Another Federal Reserve bank function is to maintain reserve accounts for financial depository institutions. A **reserve account** is a deposit in the name of a financial institution that is held at a Federal Reserve bank or other approved place. Financial depository institutions must have a reserve account and hold a minimum amount on reserve. However, the actual amount fluctuates daily and may exceed the minimum.

Currency Circulation   Federal Reserve banks provide the means for putting coins and paper money into or out of circulation. Each Fed bank maintains a warehouse of used and newly minted coins and paper money in its vaults (obviously with extensive security arrangements). When the public wants to carry more money in the form of coins and paper, as happens, for example, around the Christmas holidays, more checks are cashed, and more visits are made to ATM machines. And as financial institutions require more coins and paper money to convert their customers' deposits to currency, they order what they need from the Fed. When the Fed delivers cash to a financial institution, the cash is paid for out of that institution's reserve account. When less cash is wanted by the public, as happens, for example, after the Christmas holiday season, currency builds up at depository institutions. These institutions return their cash to the Fed and receive credit in their reserve accounts. Also, when currency is worn out, it is retired by the Fed and, in the case of paper money, destroyed.

Check and Electronic Payment Clearing   The Federal Reserve banks participate in the process of check and payment clearing. Each day the Federal Reserve processes millions of checks and electronic payments as financial institutions use the Fed as a payment clearinghouse. In short, the Fed participates in sorting checks and payments from deposits in financial institutions to be returned to the financial institution from which the deposit or check originated. For example, when you pay your tuition at your college with a check from your bank account, the Fed provides or oversees the means for transferring funds to your college from your bank.

When payment clearing is done within the same Federal Reserve district, the procedure is simple. However, if a check is drawn on an institution in another Federal Reserve district, it is forwarded to that district for further processing, or adds another step to the payments clearing mechanism.

Regardless of whether someone who has an account at a bank uses direct deposits, paper checks, or online banking, deposit and payment clearing causes a financial institution's reserve account to fluctuate. When a deposit is made at a financial institution and sent to the Fed for clearing, the full amount of that deposit is credited (added) to that institution's reserve account. When a check or other payment method is used by a customer with an account at a financial institution and that payment goes through the Fed clearing procedure, the full amount of that payment is subtracted from that institution's reserve account. This process causes a financial institution's reserve account to fluctuate daily, with the size of the fluctuation depending on the value of payments deposited and funds spent.

It is not necessary that all payments go through the Federal Reserve banks. Other clearinghouse arrangements exist. Regardless of the payments clearing mechanism, the effect on a financial depository institution's reserve account is the same: *Deposits increase a bank's reserves, and payments from an account held by a bank's customers decrease its reserves.*

Figure 7.3 shows how a $100 check sent from an aunt in San Francisco to a niece in Atlanta travels through the payments clearing system. When the niece deposits the

FIGURE 7.3   *Check Clearing through the Federal Reserve System*

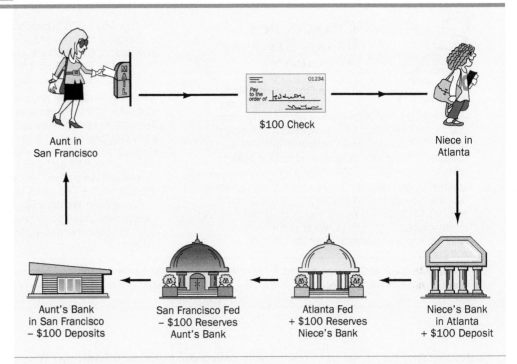

$100 Check

Aunt in
San Francisco

Niece in
Atlanta

Aunt's Bank
in San Francisco
– $100 Deposits

San Francisco Fed
– $100 Reserves
Aunt's Bank

Atlanta Fed
+ $100 Reserves
Niece's Bank

Niece's Bank
in Atlanta
+ $100 Deposit

Depository institution reserve accounts increase or decrease as checks move through the Federal Reserve's clearing system.

check, it increases deposits in her bank by $100. When the check is sent by the niece's bank to the Atlanta Federal Reserve bank for clearing, her bank receives $100 in reserves. From Atlanta the check goes to the San Francisco Federal Reserve bank, where the aunt's bank loses $100 in reserves. Finally, the check goes to the aunt's bank, which lowers the balance in her account by $100.

Technology has created many changes in the payments clearing process. **Check 21** went into law at the end of 2004 and legalizes an electronic picture of a check, allowing banks to use this picture in place of the canceled check. The process described in Figure 7.3 is the same, but the electronic picture, rather than the actual check, allows for a quicker movement through the payments clearing process and eliminates shipping checks. In addition, the growth of the **Automated Clearing House (ACH) Network** has facilitated electronic payments.

Fiscal Agents for the U.S. Government   The Federal Reserve banks act as fiscal agents for the U.S. government by performing a variety of chores, such as servicing the checking accounts of the federal government and handling many of the tasks associated with the maintenance of Treasury securities or the national debt.

Many of the functions performed by the Federal Reserve banks are necessary for the smooth operation of the banking system. However, sometimes commercial banks depend on each other instead of the Fed for these operational tasks. In this case, banks

Check 21
Law that allows electronic substitute checks for check-clearing purposes.

Automated Clearing House (ACH) Network
A large electronic payments network that facilitates a reliable, secure, and efficient payments system.

CHANGES IN A BANK'S RESERVE ACCOUNT[a]

1. The First National Bank of Latrobe starts its day with $18,993,560 in its reserve account. During the day $1,256,780 in checks is deposited and cleared, and $1,379,000 in checks written by the bank's customers is cleared. How much is in First National's reserve account at the end of the day? _____

2. California One begins its day with $35,664,440 in its reserve account at the Fed. During the day it returns $2,350,000 to the Fed in currency that has accumulated in its vaults. What is the bank's reserve account balance after the cash is returned? _____

3. The MBMB Bank of El Campo has $12,450,221 in its reserve account at the beginning of the day. During

the day, $644,970 in deposited checks and $788,450 in checks written by MBMB's customers are cleared. In addition, $350,000 in currency is delivered to the bank by the Fed. What is the bank's reserve account balance at the end of the day? _____

4. Westmoreland Bank ends a Wednesday with $14,544,500 in its reserve account. On Thursday its customers deposit $345,660 in checks, and on Friday they deposit $467,845 in checks, both clearing on the day deposited. On Thursday and Friday, $266,890 and $351,115, respectively, in checks written by the bank's customers are cleared. In addition, the Fed picks up $100,000 in currency on Friday from Westmoreland to return to the Fed's vaults. How much does Westmoreland Bank have in its reserve account at the end of business on Friday? _____

[a]All depository institutions in this exercise are hypothetical. Answers can be found at the back of the book.

Correspondent Banking
Interbank relationship involving deposits and various services.

set up a relationship called **correspondent banking**. Typically, in this arrangement a smaller bank keeps some deposits with a larger bank and receives advice and various services in return.

Be sure at this point that you understand how a reserve account is changed, especially by check clearing. This understanding is key to the material in Chapter 8. You can use the "Test Your Understanding: Changes in a Bank's Reserve Account," questions at the end of this chapter, and exercises in your Study Guide to explore some of the ways a bank's reserve account changes and to calculate reserve positions.

RECENT TRENDS IN FINANCIAL INSTITUTIONS

Since the early 1980s, after decades of traditional banking practices and strict government regulatory control over the banking system, U.S. financial institutions have changed significantly. We have seen increased similarities in the roles of financial institutions, consolidations and mergers that have created very large organizations, banks and other financial depository institutions move into new nonbank industries, and movement away from savings banks. More recently, we have been through a serious financial crisis, one of the most severe the United States has faced.

Legislative Changes

Depository Institutions Deregulation and Monetary Control Act (1980)
Legislation that increased the similarity among many financial institutions and increased the control of the Federal Reserve system.

In 1980, one of the most significant laws pertaining to money and banking was passed: the **Depository Institutions Deregulation and Monetary Control Act**. This law made financial depository institutions more similar in the deposit accounts they offer and the types of loans they make and eliminated much of the distinction between commercial banks and other financial depository institutions. The Monetary Control Act also increased the authority of the Federal Reserve and added a new relationship between the Federal Reserve and nonmember depository institutions.

In 1994 the **Riegle–Neal Interstate Banking and Branching Efficiency Act** was passed. This act opened the door for widespread **interstate banking**, or the ability for banking organizations to operate in more than one state. Today, we are used to large nationwide banks and likely don't remember that prior to the late 1970s, most banks were limited to operating facilities within a single state.

In 1999, significant new federal legislation that opened the door to the creation of huge financial institutions was passed: the **Gramm–Leach–Bliley Act**. This act tore down the strong firewall between commercial banking and other financial industries built in 1933 with the Glass–Steagall Act. Glass–Steagall had set an environment for control over banking by keeping banking apart from securities, insurance, and other financial industries. This separation would no longer hold.

The Gramm–Leach–Bliley Act influenced the activities of some **holding companies**, which are corporations formed for the purpose of owning, or holding, the controlling shares of stock in other corporations. Bank holding companies were permitted to become **financial holding companies**, and financial holding companies were now permitted to engage in a wide range of bank and nonbank activities. More specifically, these financial holding companies could now own corporations that engage in securities underwriting and dealing, and insurance agency and underwriting activities, as well as banking activities. Under Gramm–Leach–Bliley, the Federal Reserve was designated as the "umbrella" supervisor of the financial holding companies. Simply, a bank holding company could now add to its operation a variety of other types of corporations that it was not previously permitted to own.

In October 2008, the **Emergency Economic Stabilization Act** was passed in the middle of what we now label as "the financial crisis of 2007–2009" which will be covered shortly. The Act's purpose was to stem the possible collapse of a large number of banks and financial holding companies that began to fail. Housing was affected with rising numbers of foreclosures, credit was drying up, and there was much uncertainty over the future of the financial markets. This Act, which provided up to $700 billion for various relief programs, was not without controversy.

In July 2010, one of the most extensive acts regulating financial activities was passed: the Dodd–Frank Wall Street Reform and Consumer Protection Act, known simply as **Dodd–Frank**. This Act followed the financial crisis of 2007–2009 and has been extremely controversial: Some critics say it is too limited in its oversight, and others say it overly regulates the financial sector. Dodd–Frank has been mentioned frequently during recent political campaigns as candidates take positions about enforcing or repealing it.

Dodd–Frank is hundreds of pages and broad in scope. It strengthens consumer protection with new authority, heads off financial bailouts, creates an advance warning about systemic issues that threaten the economy, regulates exotic financial instruments, enforces regulations already in existence, and gives more oversight ability to the Federal Reserve among other regulatory reforms.

Structural Changes

All of the legislative changes in regulations concerning branch banking, interstate banking, and the ability to form financial holding companies have changed the face of banking during the past few decades. In addition, advances in technology have altered the way banks do business and made it easier to complete transactions.

Riegle–Neal Interstate Banking and Branching Efficiency Act (1994)
Allows banking organizations from one state to open or acquire banks, and to open branches, in other states.

Interstate Banking
The performance of services in more than one state by a single banking organization.

Gramm–Leach–Bliley Act
Passed in 1999 to allow bank holding companies to become financial holding companies and engage in securities and insurance activities.

Holding Company
A corporation formed for the purpose of owning, or holding, the controlling shares of stock in other corporations.

Financial Holding Company
A holding company that can own the controlling shares of stock of corporations in banking, securities, insurance, and other financial activities.

Emergency Economic Stabilization Act
Passed in 2008 to provide $700 billion to the U.S. Treasury for assistance in keeping financial companies from failing.

Dodd–Frank
Legislation passed in 2010 to increase accountability in and regulation over financial institutions and the instruments and products they provide.

TABLE 7.5	**The 10 Largest Commercial Banks**

The 10 largest banks are ranked by assets.

Rank	Bank Name	Location	Assets (in billions)	Number of Domestic Branches
1	JP Morgan Chase Bank	Columbus, OH	$2,002	5,656
2	Bank of America	Charlotte, NC	1,455	5,081
3	Wells Fargo Bank	Sioux Falls, SD	1,437	6,345
4	Citibank	Sioux Falls, SD	1,376	929
5	U.S. Bank	Cincinnati, OH	384	3,232
6	Bank of NY Mellon	New York, NY	319	3
7	PNC Bank	Wilmington, DE	317	2,816
8	State Street	Boston, MA	278	2
9	Capital One	McLean, VA	240	886
10	TD Bank	Wilmington, DE	220	1,306

Source: "Large Commercial Banks," Federal Reserve Statistical Release, June 30, 2014.

The size of a banking organization is largely determined by its ability to attract deposits, which, in turn, is influenced by location. Even with the growth in technology, people still want access to their banks. Banks in large urban areas with facilities in multiple locations have more potential to be large than banks located in small, rural communities with a few facilities. As a result, **branch banking**, where a bank operates more than one facility, is a significant factor in the size of a bank. In 2014, there were over 86,500 commercial banking offices.[9]

Branch Banking
Operation of more than one facility by a bank to perform its functions.

With the passage of Gramm–Leach–Bliley, there has been a growth in extremely large banking organizations. Table 7.5 gives the 10 largest commercial banks as of June 30, 2014. By the time you read this text, this list will have likely changed. Notice the size of the assets of these banks: The largest bank has over $2 trillion in assets and is over five times the size of the fifth largest bank. These banks also have rather large numbers of branches, over 6,000 in one case.

Mutual Fund Growth   A factor affecting the banking system is growth of the mutual fund industry. A **mutual fund** is a pool of dollars from depositors that is used to make financial investments in corporate stocks or bonds, government securities, or other instruments. Mutual funds compete with financial depository institutions for household savings and time deposits and for providing funds for business loans. In 2000, there were about $7 trillion of assets in mutual funds, and by 2013 assets more than doubled to $15 trillion.[10]

Mutual Fund
Pool of money from depositors that is used to make investments.

Mutual funds appeal to individual savers who want a higher return than they can get from CDs or passbook savings and who are willing to assume some degree of risk. Unlike savings and time deposits in banks, mutual funds are not insured, and the return to the owners of these funds fluctuates.

[9] Number is for FDIC-insured commercial banks. www2.fdic.gov, June 30, 2014.
[10] ProQuest Statistical Abstract of the U.S. 2015 Online Edition, Table 1226.

Savings and Loans   Before the late 1980s, saving and loan associations were a large part of the financial institutions landscape. Since that time most have been merged into other institutions or simply closed. The legislative and structural changes that altered traditional banking roles were the basis for a substantial number of savings and loan failures in the late 1980s and 1990s. Deregulation contributed to these failures as many institutions, no longer operating with interest caps, offered unprofitably high interest rates to attract deposits. Also, with new freedom to provide different types of loans, some institutions offered loans with little or no collateral and speculated on risky real estate.

The failures and insolvencies of these savings and loans caused the federal government to provide significant amounts of financial assistance in what might have been the first Congressional financial bailout. When the price tag was finally tallied, the bailout for cleaning up the insolvencies was $480.9 billion or about $2,000 for every man, woman, and child in the United States.[11]

The Financial Crisis of 2007–2009

This chapter and the next are concerned with traditional banking. Traditional banks are chartered by the federal or a state government, regulated in their operations and policies by the Federal Reserve, associated with agencies like the Federal Deposit Insurance Corporation (FDIC), and provide demand deposits and other checkable deposits. Traditional banking holds the key for controlling the money supply (as we will read in Chapter 8).

In recent years, there have been the development and growth of a host of financial entities we label as shadow banks. **Shadow banking** refers to the institutions and markets that provide many of the traditional banking functions but operate outside the regulated banking system. These can range from investment banks and mortgage companies to the provision of money market mutual funds. Shadow banks provide a means for investing money through a range of different opportunities.

It is important to understand that the shadow banking sector is not subject to the oversight, control, and regulation of traditional banks. These institutions have the ability to operate in a more creative fashion than traditional banks, even crafting financial instruments that may not be subject to control. Shadow banking companies and their traders are motivated to maximize profit like other businesses. In recent years, many of these shadow banking operations have grown to huge entities with a concentration of financial assets that can have an enormous impact on the economy, especially when they fail. It is the shadow banking sector that is primarily responsible for the financial crisis of 2007–2009.

During the financial crisis of 2007–2009, some financial institutions in the traditional and shadow banking sector found themselves in trouble. Some of the large investment banks had made investments that left them vulnerable and caused them to fail, like Lehman Brothers, or to be sold at low prices, or to need government bailouts to keep them afloat.

The mortgage market provides some insight into the crisis and gives you one example of the growth and operation of shadow banking. Mortgage market bundling was just one of the many creative financial instruments that were risky and began to fail, causing panic in shadow banking organizations as the crisis developed.

Shadow Banking
The institutions and markets that engage in some traditional banking functions but operate outside of traditional banking regulations.

---

[11] Robert A. Rosenblatt, "GAO Estimates Final Cost of S & L bailout at $480.9 Billion," *Los Angeles Times*, July 13, 1996, pp. D1, D2.

Subprime Mortgages
Borrowers have lower credit ratings and a greater risk of default; interest rates tend to be higher than prime mortgages.

Mortgage Bundling
Mortgages are packaged together and sold as a group; mixed mortgage bundles are a collection of prime and subprime mortgages.

During the years prior to the financial crisis, the price of housing in some markets increased rapidly, and the economy was in good shape. Many mortgage companies were eager to sell mortgages and offered deals to people who should not/could not qualify for the size of the mortgages they received. These shaky mortgages were labeled as **subprime mortgages**. Subprimes were attractive because they carried a high interest rate for the lender and frequently had a short time frame that required a rate redo of the mortgage in a few years. In short, the lenders of the mortgage money thought they had a good deal with the high interest rate, and the borrowers were happy to get a loan, sometimes counting on the rising value of the property as a speculative opportunity to "flip it" and make a nice profit.

Many mortgage companies began to bundle their prime and subprime mortgages and sell them as packages to institutions in the shadow banking sector. In the **mortgage bundle** was a mix of good, well-backed mortgages but also some subprime ones. The interest rate on the subprimes made the bundle attractive.

When the economy began to slide in 2007 and people lost their jobs, many were unable to pay their mortgages. In addition, the price of housing declined, sometimes severely, in many markets. As a result, many shadow banking institutions were left holding a bundle of mortgages that included many that were nonperforming. In addition, the value of the property in the bundle was declining. So, now that $500,000 mortgage couldn't be paid and, worse yet, the house was worth less than $500,000. In other words, what some thought was a good deal wasn't, and it left them holding a bag of declining value. This meant that a major asset of the holder was worth less and less. Now the organization faced a real issue: Do we panic and try to sell these bundles at a lesser price, or do we hold onto an asset that is worth much less? Each of these decisions means a decline in the value of the organization.

The mortgage situation was just one example of "what looked good on paper" having some underlying problems and issues. The underlying problems and the financial crisis were extremely complex, and even today we are still trying to sort it all out. Books are being written to try to analyze the situation and delve into the details of the crisis. Application 7.3, "Ben Bernanke's Reflections on the Financial Crisis," will give you some good information to understand the causes and problems that led to this significant financial crisis. Mr. Bernanke's speech is a good perspective and is available in its entirety on the web (see footnote of the application). If you are interested in learning more about the crisis, this speech is a good starting point.

APPLICATION 7.3

BEN BERNANKE'S REFLECTIONS ON THE FINANCIAL CRISIS

Mr. Bernanke's speech was given on April 13, 2012, and focuses on the causes of the 2007–2009 financial crisis. This speech pulls from talks and testimonies he gave on the crisis and provides a perspective in its aftermath.

[In analyzing the crisis, earlier testimony] drew the distinction between triggers and vulnerabilities. The *triggers* of the crisis were the particular events or factors that touched off the events of 2007–2009—the proximate causes, if you will. Developments in the market for subprime mortgages were a prominent example of a trigger of the crisis. In contrast, the *vulnerabilities* were the structural, and more fundamental, weaknesses in the financial system and in regulation and supervision that served to propagate and amplify the initial shocks. In the private sector, some key vulnerabilities included high levels of leverage; excessive dependence on unstable short-term funding; deficiencies in risk management in major financial firms; and the use of exotic and nontransparent financial instruments that obscured concentrations or risk. In the public sector, my list of vulnerabilities would include gaps in the regulatory structure that allowed systemically important

APPLICATION 7.3 *(Continued)*

firms and markets to escape comprehensive supervision; failures of supervisors to effectively apply some existing authorities; and insufficient attention to threats to the stability of the system as a whole (that is, the lack of a macroprudential focus in regulation and supervision).

[In regard to the subprime mortgage issue] judged in relation to the size of global financial markets, aggregate exposures to subprime mortgages were quite modest. By way of comparison, it is not especially uncommon for one day's paper losses in global stock markets to exceed the losses on subprime mortgages suffered during the entire crisis, without obvious ill effect on market functioning or on the economy. Thus, losses on subprime mortgages can plausibly account for the massive reaction seen during the crisis only insofar as they interacted with other factors—more fundamental vulnerabilities—that served to amplify their effects.

A number of the vulnerabilities . . . were associated with the increased importance of the so-called shadow banking system. . . . Indeed, the very foundation of shadow banking and its rapid growth before the crisis was the widely held view [that safeguards] would protect shadow banking activities against runs and panics. . . . When it became clear to investors that these alternative protections might not be adequate to protect against losses, widespread flight from the shadow banking system occurred, . . . [Other vulnerabilities can be viewed as a consequence of poor risk management by financial institutions and investors]. Unfortunately, the crisis revealed a number of significant defects in private-sector risk management and risk controls, importantly including insufficient capacity by many large firms to track firmwide risk exposures. . . . [that] led in turn to inadequate risk diversification, so that losses—rather than being dispersed broadly—proved in some cases to be heavily concentrated among relatively few, highly leveraged companies. . . .

In retrospect, it is clear that the statutory framework of financial regulation in place before the crisis contained serious gaps. Critically, shadow banking activities were, for the most part, not subject to consistent and effective regulatory oversight. Much shadow banking lacked meaningful prudential regulation. . . . The gaps in statutory authority had the additional effect of limiting the information available to regulators and consequently, may have made it more difficult to recognize the underlying vulnerabilities and complex linkages in the overall financial system. . . .

A broader failing was that regulatory agencies and supervisory practices were focused on the safety and soundness of individual financial institutions or markets—what we now refer to as microprudential supervision. In the United States and most other advanced economies, no governmental entity had either a mandate or sufficient authority—now often called macroprudential authority—to take actions to limit systemic risks that could result from the collective behavior of financial institutions and markets.

Source: Chairman Ben S. Bernanke, "Some Reflections on the Crisis and the Policy Response," given at the Russell Sage Foundation and The Century Foundation Conference on "Rethinking Finance," New York, New York, April 13, 2012. www.federalreserve.gov/newsevents/speech/bernanke20120413a.htm.

With all of the changes in the regulation of banking and the bailouts required to salvage many financial institutions in recent years, there remains a great deal of controversy over the extent to which the financial sector should be regulated. The passage of Dodd–Frank continues to be a major topic as some believe it is too stringent and should be repealed. Up for Debate, "Should Congress Enact More Stringent Regulations over the Banking System?" gives some of the arguments on each side of this issue.

UP FOR DEBATE

SHOULD CONGRESS ENACT MORE STRINGENT REGULATIONS OVER THE BANKING SYSTEM?

From 1980 to 2010, the banking industry became more deregulated. However, the near collapse of many large banks in 2008 caused Congress to provide a $700 billion bailout for the financial services industry and brought more regulation with Dodd–Frank. But the debate over the extent of regulation needed to ensure safety and stability in banking continues. Should Congress enact more stringent regulations over the banking system?

YES   The crisis of 2008 is certainly indicative of the need to return to more stringent banking regulation. From the Depression in the 1930s until more recent years, the United States enjoyed a fairly safe and secure banking industry. During that time, the banking industry was

(Continued)

UP FOR DEBATE (*Continued*)

regulated in terms of the activities that banks could undertake, and their size was limited because of various regulations. Banks were more personal places for customers such as business owners, who could turn to their local banker for loans.

While banks are profit-seeking corporations and their stockholders like to see the highest dividends possible, the banking industry is unlike others. Safe and secure banking is essential to a healthy economy. Once the banking system goes, the entire economy becomes dysfunctional. This reality became quite apparent with the quick approval in Congress of a substantial bailout of the financial services industry in the fall of 2008. The collapse of these institutions would have crippled the economy.

It may not be in the best interest of consumers to continue on the road of mergers, consolidations, and adding securities and insurance services to these large banking entities. For one, bank customers may end up with fewer choices, higher prices, and less responsiveness—all results of less competition in markets. In addition, the assumption of less risk with investments because they are bought through a bank, particularly among consumers who mistakenly believe that the FDIC is ensuring these transactions, could hurt the less–informed customer.

NO   Returning to an era of more stringent banking regulation because of the "sins" of a few is like punishing an entire classroom of children for the actions of one. Just because a few of the financial services holding companies engaged in poor, risky business practices, this is no reason to return to the old style of banking. The action that is needed is better audits and supervision of these financial services companies.

The ability of banks to become financial holding companies has benefits for consumers. Now bank customers can take advantage of a wider array of products in one place to meet their increasingly sophisticated needs. Rather than banking at one location, investing at a second, and taking care of insurance needs at a third, customers can conduct all of these activities at the same place. In addition, with all of these new opportunities, competition in these industries should increase, giving consumers more choices and better prices and services. It also can lead to more efficient operations.

Finally, banks and financial holding companies are profit-seeking corporations that thrive when their owners, the holders of their stock, see a profit from the company's operations. If banks are reregulated, this may come at the disadvantage of their stockholders. In addition, these financial holding companies have provided good jobs with excellent salaries to a large number of people who could now become unemployed.

Summary

1. Money is a medium of exchange, or something generally accepted as a means of payment for goods, services, and resources. Without money to facilitate transactions, an economy would need to rely on a barter system. Money also serves as a measure of value and as a method for storing wealth and delaying payment. The value of money is measured by the goods, services, and resources it can purchase. Inflation causes the value of money to fall.

2. There are two definitions of the U.S. money supply. M1, the narrower definition, includes coins and paper money in circulation, nonbank-issued traveler's checks, demand deposits (checking accounts) at commercial banks, and other checkable deposits. The other definition, M2, is important because it includes M1 plus accounts that have limited checkable features and accounts that are easily convertible to cash.

3. In any year, the economy's money supply is smaller than the value of goods and services produced, or GDP. The velocity of money measures the average annual turnover of the money supply in relation to GDP.

4. When money is backed by something tangible, such as gold or silver, the economy is on a commodity standard. At one time, U.S. money was backed by gold. Today, the United States is on a paper standard, where money is generally backed by people's willingness to accept it and by the strength of the economy. A paper standard has both advantages and disadvantages.

5. Financial depository institutions, such as commercial banks, savings associations, and credit unions, play a critical role in the economy because they can create and destroy money through their loan-making activities. Commercial banks are the most important of these financial institutions. Agencies, such as federal and state banking authorities, the Federal Reserve, and the Federal Deposit Insurance Corporation, regulate commercial banks.

6. The Federal Reserve system coordinates commercial banking operations, regulates other financial depository institutions, and oversees the U.S. money supply. The system, which is organized geographically into 12 districts, is headed by the Board of Governors. The 12 Federal Reserve banks and their branches provide services to financial institutions rather than directly to the general public. The functions of the Federal Reserve banks include supervising and examining the operations of member banks in their districts, maintaining reserve accounts, circulating coins and paper money, clearing checks and some electronic payments, and acting as fiscal agents for the federal government.

7. Significant changes have occurred in the U.S. banking system since the Monetary Control Act of 1980 made financial depository institutions more similar. In 1999, the Gramm–Leach–Bliley Act permitted the formation of bank and financial holding companies that allow banking organizations to conduct securities and insurance activities. Deregulation was reversed in 2010 with the Dodd–Frank Act.

8. Other significant banking changes include the financial bailout through the Emergency Stabilization Act, the increase in popularity of mutual funds, the elimination of most savings and loan associations, and the recent financial crisis of 2007–2009. The financial crisis brought attention to shadow banking operations.

Key Terms and Concepts

Money

Medium of exchange

Value of money

Barter system

Measure of value

Method for storing wealth and delaying payments

M1

Token money

Federal Reserve Notes

Currency

Demand deposits

Other checkable deposits

Velocity of money

M2

Liquidity

Commodity monetary standard

Paper monetary standard

Financial depository institution

Commercial bank

Dual banking system

National bank

State bank

Federal Deposit Insurance Corporation (FDIC)

Asset

Liability

Net worth

Federal Reserve system

Board of Governors

Open Market Committee

Federal Reserve banks

Reserve account

Check 21

Automated Clearing House (ACH)
network

Correspondent banking

Depository Institutions Deregulation
and Monetary Control Act (1980)

Riegle–Neal Interstate Banking and
Branching Efficiency Act (1994)

Interstate banking

Gramm–Leach–Bliley Act

Holding company

Financial holding company

Emergency Economic Stabilization Act

Dodd–Frank

Branch banking

Mutual fund

Shadow banking

Subprime mortgages

Mortgage bundling

Review Questions

1. List the basic functions of money and explain how a $20 bill fulfills each of these functions.

2. How much is a $20 bill worth? How is its value measured, and what causes that value to change?

3. What are the basic components of M1 and M2? How do these two measures differ? In your opinion, which is a better measure of the money supply? Why?

4. Answer the following questions concerning financial depository institutions.
    a. What distinguishes commercial banks from other financial depository institutions? Why are commercial banks so important?
    b. Give the various classifications of commercial banks and their regulating agencies. Why are commercial banks subject to extensive regulation?
    c. What circumstances might lead to the failure of a commercial bank?
    d. How much insured coverage does the FDIC provide for account holders in commercial banks?

5. What is the basic purpose of the Federal Reserve system? How is it organized functionally and geographically?

6. List and briefly describe the functions of a Federal Reserve bank.

7. The First National Bank of Anytown had $50,000,000 in its reserve account at the Fed one morning. Later that morning, $2,500,000 in checks that had been deposited at the Bank of Anytown was processed at the Fed, and the bank ordered $1,000,000 in currency. Later that day, $3,000,000 worth of checks written by the bank's customers cleared through the Fed. How much did the First National Bank of Anytown have in its reserve account at the Fed at the end of the day?

8. Define each of the following terms and explain how each has affected the financial institutions system in recent years.
    a. Branch banking
    b. Interstate banking
    c. Mutual funds

d. Financial holding company

e. Savings and loans

9. Explain the changes brought to banking and the significance of the following pieces of legislation: the Monetary Control Act of 1980, the Gramm–Leach–Bliley Act, and Dodd–Frank.

Discussion Questions

1. If demand deposits are a medium of exchange and if a medium of exchange is generally accepted as payment for goods and services, why is it sometimes difficult to pay with a check?

2. In the campaign to become the GOP candidate for president in 2012 Ron Paul suggested returning the U.S. economy to a gold standard. Do you agree with him? Are there any circumstances under which a commodity standard might be preferable to a paper standard?

3. "Regulation of financial depository institutions should be eliminated. These institutions should be free to sell their products like any other business in a free-enterprise system. As long as the government continues to insure deposits, regulation is unnecessary." What is your opinion of this statement?

4. Go to www.FederalReserve.gov and locate the name and a brief biography of each current member of the Board of Governors of the Federal Reserve system. What type of experience does each bring to the Board?

5. What is your position on a law that would place the Federal Reserve under the direct control of the President of the United States and that would allow each new president to completely replace the Board of Governors?

6. The Gramm–Leach–Bliley Act radically changed banking rules and the banking playing field that had been in place for over 60 years. In your opinion, did this abrupt change contribute to the financial crisis of 2007–2009 and the bailout made by the federal government?

7. Some people believe that taxpayers should not have footed the bill for the savings and loan crisis and bailout of large financial institutions in 2008, and that the government should not insure financial depository institutions. Do you think that the government should be involved in insuring deposits and providing bailouts?

8. Locate information on two or three mutual funds and explain how they differ from one another in terms of what is included in each fund, risk, and income growth potential.

9. If you had the power to reset the rules for financial institutions, would you change them? What would you change?

Critical Thinking Case 7

CIGARETTE MONEY

Critical Thinking Skills

Applying concepts in an unfamiliar setting

Recognizing conventional outcomes in unconventional circumstances

Economic Concepts

The functions of money

Monetary standards

This excerpt is from an article published shortly after World War II, which describes life in a German prisoner of war camp. It will help in reading this excerpt to know that prisoners received food and cigarettes from German rations and the International Red Cross. Some private parcels of personal items and cigarettes made their way into the camps as well.

Between individuals [prisoners] there was active trading in all consumer goods and in some services. Most trading was for food against cigarettes or other foodstuffs, but cigarettes rose from the status of a normal commodity to that of currency. RMk.s [German Reichsmarks] existed but had no circulation save for gambling debts, as few articles could be purchased with them from the canteen.

[W]hen we reached our permanent camp, there was a lively trade in all commodities and their relative values were well known, and expressed not in terms of one another . . . but in terms of cigarettes. The cigarette became the standard of value. In the permanent camp people started wandering through the bungalows calling their offers—"cheese for seven" (cigarettes). . . .

[E]veryone, including nonsmokers, was willing to sell for cigarettes, using them to buy at

another time and place. Cigarettes became the normal currency. . . .

The permanent camps in Germany saw the highest level of commercial organization. [A] shop was organised. . . . People left their surplus clothing, toilet requisites and food there until they were sold at a fixed price in cigarettes. Only sales in cigarettes were accepted—there was no barter—and there was no higgling. . . .

. . . Laundrymen advertised at two cigarettes a garment. . . . There was a coffee stall owner who sold tea, coffee or cocoa at two cigarettes a cup. . . .

[C]igarettes as currency . . . performed all the functions of a metallic currency as a unit of account, as a measure of value and as a store of value, and shared most of its characteristics. They were homogeneous, reasonably durable, and of convenient size for the smallest or, in packets, for the largest transactions. . . .

Source: Radford, R.A. "The Economic Organisation of a POW Camp," *Economica*, Blackwell Publishing, November 1945, pp. 189–201.

Questions

1. Were cigarettes really money? If so, how did they perform the functions that make something money? What backed the cigarettes used as money?

2. Reichsmarks were the official money of Germany, but they appear not to have been thought of as money by the prisoners in this camp. Why, in this camp, would Reichsmarks have been unable to perform the functions that make something money?

3. How would the homogeneity, durability, and convenient size of cigarettes help them perform the functions of money?

4. Cigarettes may have served as money in this camp, but do you think they could serve as money in a larger national economy if the official monetary system collapsed due to hyperinflation? Why?

CHAPTER 8

Money Creation, Monetary Theory, and Monetary Policy

CHAPTER OBJECTIVES

Explain the relationship between the economy's money supply and output, employment, and prices.

Explain how money is created and destroyed through the loan-making activities of financial depository institutions.

Show how interest rates affect borrowing from financial depository institutions and how they are influenced by changes in excess reserves.

Define monetary policy and the major tools for carrying out monetary policy by the Federal Reserve.

Show the relationship between government borrowing to cover deficit spending and to assess monetary policy.

For any economy, especially one that is on a paper monetary standard, careful control over the size of the money supply is extremely important. There is a strong relationship between an economy's money supply and the economy's production level, jobs, and overall price changes: Any change in the size of the money supply can change the economy's overall performance. Because of this relationship, changing the money supply is an important way to reach the economy's goals of full production and economic growth, full employment, and price stability. Monetary policy, or changing the money supply to address unemployment and inflation, is in the hands of the Federal Reserve.

You will learn a lot about how money affects the economy and the critical role interest rates play in economic activity in this chapter. You will also learn the processes for creating and destroying money, the tools that the Federal Reserve uses in its role as overseer and controller of the money supply, and how interest rates are determined and influenced through monetary policy. By the end of this chapter, you will have a good understanding of an area of the macroeconomy that seems mysterious to many

203

people but is critical to economic stabilization and growth. And, just a hint: some of the material in the first few pages of this chapter is less than exciting. But by working through these pages carefully and thoughtfully, the rest of the chapter and an area of the economy that plays a critical role in your life will be easy to understand.

THE MONEY SUPPLY AND THE LEVEL OF ECONOMIC ACTIVITY

Let's begin by summarizing some of the key lessons learned in Chapter 5.

- ◆ Total, or aggregate, spending drives the economy's levels of production, employment, and income and sometimes overall prices.
- ◆ Total spending is found by adding together the spending of all four major macroeconomic sectors: household, business, government, and foreign.
- ◆ Increases in total spending lead to increases in production, employment, and income unless the economy is at full employment.
- ◆ At (or near) full employment, increases in spending lead to overall price increases, or demand-pull inflation.
- ◆ Decreases in total spending result in a decline in production, employment, and income and may dampen inflation.

Household and business spending is related to the amount of money in the economy: An increase in the money supply increases spending, and a decrease in the money supply decreases spending. We learned in Chapter 7 that money is created when financial depository institutions, such as commercial banks, make loans. Because households typically borrow to finance the purchase of homes, automobiles, appliances, and other consumer products and businesses typically borrow to invest in buildings, machinery, equipment, and such, increased loan making results in increased spending.[1] So, increases in loans by financial depository institutions increase the money supply and spending, and when loan making falls, the money supply is decreased and spending declines. This significant relationship among loan making by financial depository institutions, money creation, and the level of spending is explained in detail as the chapter develops.

The Equation of Exchange

Equation of Exchange
$MV = PQ$: illustrates how changes in the supply of money (M) influence the level of prices (P) and/or the total output of goods and services (Q).

The relationship between money and economic activity is laid out in a simple, frequently cited equation called the **equation of exchange**:

$$MV = PQ.$$

On the left-hand side of this equation, M is the supply of money in the economy and V stands for the velocity of money or the number of times each dollar is spent for new goods and services in a year. The more frequently the money supply turns over each year, the higher the value of V. On the right-hand side of the equation, P represents the level of prices and Q the actual output of goods and services.

MV, the supply of money multiplied by the number of times it turns over each year, represents total spending on new goods and services in the economy. PQ, the

---

[1] Financial depository institutions also make loans to the government when they purchase government securities for their portfolios.

price level multiplied by the actual output of goods and services, can be interpreted as the dollar value of output produced in the economy or current GDP. Since the circular flow model tells us that a given level of spending brings forth an output of equal value, we know that MV and PQ are equal.[2] Thus, if the supply of money were $1.5 trillion and velocity were 9, MV (or total spending) would equal $13.5 trillion, as would PQ, the value of the economy's output.

Changing the Money Supply   What happens to the level of economic activity when the supply of money changes? The equation of exchange helps answer this question. To keep matters simple, assume that the velocity of money does not change. That is, let V be constant in the equation of exchange.[3]

First, we will deal with expanding the money supply. An increase in M causes the left-hand side of the equation of exchange, or total spending, to increase. Because the two sides of the equation must be equal, the right-hand side of the equation, the dollar value of output, must increase by the same amount. If the economy is not operating at full employment and production, the increase in the value of output comes primarily in the form of an expansion in production and employment. That is, the increase on the right-hand side of the equation of exchange would come mainly in the Q term. However, if the economy were at or near full employment, production and employment would be at or near their upper limits. Under these circumstances, Q in the equation of exchange could go up very little, if at all. At full employment, an increase in the money supply would lead primarily to an increase in the price level, the P term, or to inflation.

A decrease in M decreases total spending, the left-hand side of the equation of exchange. This, in turn, causes a decrease in the dollar value of output, the right-hand side of the equation. A decrease in the money supply typically results in a decrease in Q, or production and employment. P, or the overall price level, usually does not fall with a decrease in total spending. Businesses generally respond to decreases in spending by cutting production rather than by lowering prices. However, if the economy were operating at or near full employment and experiencing inflation, a decrease in the money supply would dampen some of the upward pressure on prices, causing prices to rise less rapidly.

In summary, the relationship between total spending and the economy's production, employment, and price levels is affected by changes in the economy's supply of money. Increasing the money supply facilitates spending and contributes to an expansion of economic activity. Whether this leads to increased production and employment or to inflation depends in large part on how close the economy is to full employment. Decreasing the supply of money inhibits the spending ability of businesses and households and in turn slows the level of economic activity.

MONEY CREATION

We know that money is created when financial depository institutions make loans, and money is destroyed when those loans are repaid. Although these loan-making institutions include savings associations and credit unions, it is the commercial banks that are primarily engaged in money creation and destruction. Because of the huge impact that

---

[2] Some economists write the equation of exchange as an identity: $MV \equiv PQ$. This equation is so classic that it was for years the license plate of a money and banking professor in St. Louis.

[3] In reality, the velocity of money (M1) does change over time. However, in looking at the effect on the economy of increasing or decreasing the money supply *at a particular moment in time*, the assumption that V is fixed is appropriate.

money supply changes have on the economy, it is important that the capacity of financial institutions to make loans be highly controlled. This is one of the functions of the Federal Reserve. However, in order to understand how the Fed exerts its control over money supply changes, we need to understand under what conditions a financial depository institution can make a loan and how those conditions change.

The Process of Money Creation

Actual Reserves

A financial depository institution's reserve account plus its vault cash.

Every financial depository institution has two assets that it counts as its **actual reserves**: the institution's reserve account and its vault cash. Every institution must have a reserve account, which, as we saw in Chapter 7, can be held at a Federal Reserve bank or at an approved designated institution. Vault cash is all the cash in the depository institution's vault and cash drawers.

Reserve Requirement

Specific percentage of deposits that a financial depository institution must keep as actual reserves.

Depository institutions have a **reserve requirement**, which is a specific percentage of *deposits* that must be kept as actual reserves. For example, a bank with a reserve requirement of 10 percent on demand deposits must have an amount on reserve equal to 10 percent of the value of the demand deposits it is holding. If a bank has $80,000,000 in checking accounts and a 10 percent reserve requirement, it must have at least $8,000,000 (0.10 × $80,000,000) in actual reserves. The amount of actual reserves that a financial depository institution must keep to back its deposits is called its **required reserves**. In this example, the bank's required reserves are $8,000,000.

Required Reserves

The amount of actual reserves that a financial depository institution must keep to back its deposits.

Every day each depository institution makes several calculations pertaining to its deposits and reserves. First, it computes the value of deposits held in the institution that day. Second, it calculates its required reserves. And, third, it determines how much it has in actual reserves. (Remember from Chapter 7: A depository institution's reserve account fluctuates daily due to check—paper or electronic—deposits and clearing and periodically due to currency orders and returns.) In short, the institution determines what it must have and what it actually does have on reserve.

Excess Reserves

Reserves of a financial depository institution over the amount it is required to maintain in actual reserves; actual reserves minus required reserves.

These calculations permit an institution to determine its **excess reserves**. Excess reserves are actual reserves minus required reserves, or reserves over and above those that an institution must maintain. If Hometown Bank has a reserve requirement of 10 percent and demand deposits of $60,000,000, its required reserves are $6,000,000 (0.10 × $60,000,000). If its actual reserves are $10,000,000, then its excess reserves are the actual reserves of $10,000,000 minus the required reserves of $6,000,000, or $4,000,000. In other words, the bank has $4,000,000 on reserve that it doesn't need to have. Table 8.1 summarizes these calculations.

Excess Reserves and Loan Making   Excess reserves are important because they are the foundation for a depository institution's loan-making abilities. Very simply, *a depository institution can make new loans up to the value of its excess reserves*. Why is this so?

When a financial depository institution makes a loan to a business or an individual, it usually gives the borrower those funds in either a cashier's check or through a direct deposit into the borrower's checking account. In either case, when the borrower spends these loaned funds and the payment for this spending is cleared through the payment-clearing mechanism, the lending bank loses reserves. For example, if Hometown Bank loans a baker $50,000 to buy and outfit a food truck to roam a city selling cupcakes and pastries, it will lose $50,000 in reserves when the payment for the truck is cleared through the payment-clearing mechanism.[4]

---

[4] The effect from lending to households, businesses, or the government is the same. When a financial depository institution lends money to the U.S. government by buying a Treasury security, it pays for that security out of its reserve account, causing the reserve account to decrease.

TABLE 8.1	*Hometown Bank's Reserve Calculations*

A financial depository institution's excess reserves are equal to its actual reserves minus its required reserves.

If Hometown Bank's

$$\text{Demand deposits} = \$60,000,000$$
$$\text{Reserve requirement} = 10 \text{ percent, or } 0.10$$
$$\text{Actual reserves} = \$10,000,000,$$

then Hometown Bank's excess reserves are found by the calculation

$$\text{Actual reserves} = \$10,000,000$$
$$\underline{- \text{ Required reserves} = \$6,000,000\,(0.10 \times \$60,000,000)}$$
$$\text{Excess reserves} = \$4,000,000.$$

Because a depository institution loses reserves when a loan is spent, it must be careful to make loans only up to the value of its excess reserves in order to meet reserve requirements. Return to the example of Hometown Bank, which had $10,000,000 in actual reserves, $6,000,000 in required reserves, and $4,000,000 in excess reserves. Given these figures, Hometown Bank could make new loans up to $4,000,000. If, however, Hometown Bank made loans over $4,000,000, say, $4,500,000, its $10,000,000 in actual reserves would drop to $5,500,000 when the loans were cleared. In this case, Hometown Bank would be $500,000 short on its required reserves. It is for this reason that an institution can make new loans only up to an amount equal to its excess reserves.

In making a loan, a depository institution does not take away one customer's money to give to another. Those who hold money at the institution (in demand deposits and other accounts) do not have their deposits altered; they retain all of their account balances and are free to spend their money when they so desire. Instead, in making a loan, a financial depository institution creates new money; that is, it provides dollars for spending that were not in the economy before the loan was made. If a bank maintains $60 million in demand deposits and makes new loans of $4 million, then the $60 million in demand deposits is still money, but it has been supplemented by the creation of an additional $4 million.

When a loan is repaid, money is destroyed. How is money destroyed? Repayment of a loan withdraws money from the economy by returning it to the lending institution, where it becomes reserves. Until the institution makes another loan based on these reserves, this money has disappeared from the system. Application 8.1 gives some typical questions and answers about reserves and loans.

It should be clear by now that excess reserves form the basis for loan making and thus for changing the money supply. The supply of money can be controlled, therefore, by controlling the amount of excess reserves in depository institutions. An increase in excess reserves is appropriate to increase the money supply, and a decrease in excess reserves is appropriate to decrease the money supply.

The Multiple Expansion of Money

So far, we have dealt with the money-creating ability of a single depository institution. However, to fully understand the relationship between changes in reserves and money creation and destruction in the economy as a whole, all such institutions must be considered together as a system.

QUESTIONS AND ANSWERS ABOUT RESERVES AND LOANS

Q: Do all financial depository institutions have the same reserve requirement?
A: There are uniform reserve requirements on all financial depository institutions, although the actual percentage requirement differs by type of account (for example, checkable versus time). These requirements are given later in the chapter in Table 8.4.

Q: What happens if an institution does not meet its reserve requirement?
A: Depository institutions in general have a 14-day computational period to satisfy their reserve requirements. The frequency of reporting could be weekly or quarterly and a 48-page *Reserve Maintenance Manual* (not too exciting) provides all of the technical rules associated with this reporting. If an institution has not met its reserve requirement on the average over its given time period, it will usually borrow the needed reserves rather than pay a deficiency charge.

Q: From whom can banks borrow reserves?
A: Banks can borrow reserves from a Federal Reserve bank or from other banks through the Federal Funds market. In the Federal Funds market, banks lend excess reserves to other banks, usually for a period of one day. The transfer of funds is completed electronically. Banks borrow in the Federal Funds market to cover reserve deficiencies or to obtain additional reserves with which to make loans.

Q: What is the prime rate and who determines it?
A: The prime rate is the interest rate banks charge on loans to their lowest-risk customers. It is a benchmark interest rate that a commercial bank sets for loan pricing. A prime rate is determined by each individual bank but is influenced by general credit conditions. The prime rate tends to be a few percentage points above the federal funds rate, a key interest rate discussed on page 219.

Q: How much do financial depository institutions keep in vault cash?
A: Financial depository institutions need enough paper money and coins to service their customers who want to cash a check or redeem savings or time deposits in cash. They do not want to keep excessive amounts of vault cash on hand, however, for security and storage reasons. These institutions also consider the amount of cash that is normally deposited daily by their customers in calculating the level of vault cash to maintain.

Source: Federal Reserve System, *Reserve Maintenance Manual*, November 2014.

Multiplier Effect (Money)
An initial change in excess reserves in the depository institutions system causes a larger change in the money supply.

When we make the transition from a single bank's excess reserve loan-making capability to consideration of the system as a whole, there is an interesting and important factor to consider. When excess reserves are changed in the system, a **multiplier effect** occurs: Any change in excess reserves in the system causes a multiple change in loans, or the money supply. That is, a $1 change in excess reserves in the system will create a change in loan making, or the money supply, that is a multiple of that $1. In other words, an initial increase in excess reserves in the system will cause the money supply to increase by some multiple of that increase in excess reserves, and an initial decrease in excess reserves in the system will cause the money supply to shrink by some multiple of that decrease. The following example illustrates this principle.

Assume that Hometown Bank experiences a $10,000 increase in excess reserves because of a policy change by the Fed. (Different methods for carrying out these policy changes will be discussed shortly.) Because a bank can make new loans up to the amount of its excess reserves, these new excess reserves permit Hometown Bank to make a new loan of $10,000. This is shown in the top row of Table 8.2.

Suppose the bank loans $10,000 to Mid Jones to build a small deck on the back of her house. Mid writes out a check in that amount to the contractor for the project, who deposits it in his account at Bank B. If Bank B, as well as each other bank in this example, has a reserve requirement of 10 percent, then that $10,000 deposit gives Bank B actual reserves of $10,000, of which $1,000 are required reserves and $9,000 are excess reserves (remember—check deposits, when cleared, increase a bank's reserves). On the basis of this check, Bank B can now make a new loan of $9,000. Bank B's situation is given in the second row of Table 8.2.

TABLE 8.2					

Multiple Expansion of Money (10 Percent Reserve Requirement)

An initial increase in excess reserves in the system causes the money supply to grow by a multiple of the initial excess reserve change.

	Demand Deposits	Actual Reserves	Required Reserves	Excess Reserves	Loans
Hometown Bank				$10,000.00	$10,000.00
Bank B	$10,000.00	$10,000.00	$1,000.00	9,000.00	9,000.00
Bank C	9,000.00	9,000.00	900.00	8,100.00	8,100.00
Bank D	8,100.00	8,100.00	810.00	7,290.00	7,290.00
Bank E	7,290.00	7,290.00	729.00	6,561.00	6,561.00
Bank F	6,561.00	6,561.00	656.10	5,904.90	5,904.90
Bank G	5,904.90	5,904.90	590.49	5,314.41	5,314.41
Bank H	5,314.41	5,314.41	531.44	4,782.97	4,782.97
Bank I	4,782.97	4,782.97	478.30	4,304.67	4,304.67
Bank J	4,304.67	4,304.67	430.47	3,874.20	3,874.20
Bank K	3,874.20	3,874.20	387.42	3,486.78	3,486.78
Banks L, M, N . . .	. . .	. . .	. . .	. . .	. . .
Total	$100,000.00				$100,000.00

Al Smith, who really wants a sailboat, goes to Bank B and borrows $9,000 for it. The boat dealer takes Al's check for that amount and deposits it in his account at Bank C, where it brings Bank C $9,000 in actual reserves, of which $900 are required reserves and $8,100 are excess reserves. On the basis of this $9,000 deposit, Bank C can now make a new loan of $8,100 that eventually will be deposited by someone in Bank D, and on and on. Table 8.2 shows this example through several more rounds, showing how new loans are made with each round. It is extremely important to realize that none of these loans could have been made without the initial increase in excess reserves at Hometown Bank. It is this initial increase in excess reserves that caused other banks to experience an increase in their excess reserves.[5]

When the full effect of this initial change in excess reserves is carried through the system, all the new loans can be added together to determine the total amount of money created. When we do this, it is apparent that the change in the money supply is some multiple of the initial change in excess reserves. In Table 8.2, a $100,000 increase in the money supply has resulted from an initial $10,000 increase in excess reserves. In this case, there has been a **money multiplier** of 10.

Money Multiplier
Multiple by which an initial change in excess reserves in the system can change the money supply.

Calculating the Money Multiplier   The money multiplier is determined by the reserve requirement. In fact, the money multiplier is the reciprocal of the reserve requirement. (The reciprocal of a fraction is the fraction "flipped over": The reciprocal of 1/3 is 3/1 or 3.) A 10 percent (1/10) reserve requirement means a multiplier of 10/1, or 10; a 25 percent (1/4) requirement means a multiplier of 4; and a 15 percent (3/20) requirement yields a multiplier of 20/3, or 6.67.

[5] The situation would be the same if any of these banks received multiple deposits: that is, if Hometown Bank or Bank B, C, or so on were repeated on the list in Table 8.2.

The initial change in excess reserves times the multiplier gives the total change that could result in the money supply, or stated in equation form:

initial change in excess reserves × money multiplier = total change in money supply.

An initial increase in the banking system of $8 million in excess reserves with a reserve requirement of 20 percent (multiplier of 5) could generate $40 million of new money, and an $8 million decrease in excess reserves with a 10 percent reserve requirement could decrease the money supply by $80 million. The multiplier can work in either direction: Increases or decreases in excess reserves are subject to its effect.[6]

The examples presented here show the maximum by which the money supply can grow or shrink following an initial change in excess reserves. In reality, the expansion of the money supply resulting from an increase in reserves can be dampened by actions such as converting some portion of the deposits to cash, putting some portion into mutual funds, or having institutions lend less than the maximum amount available. For instance, if the sailboat dealer in the example in Table 8.2 deposited $7,000 from Al Smith's $9,000 purchase in the dealership's checking account and took $2,000 in cash, the increase in the other banks' excess reserves and loans, and in the money supply, would have totaled to less than the $100,000 shown at the bottom of Table 8.2. In addition, if any of these banks loaned less than the total amount of their excess reserves, the effect on the money supply would also have been smaller than the $100,000 increase shown in Table 8.2.

It is important to understand that by controlling the amount of excess reserves in the system, the Federal Reserve has significant control over the money supply. It can put excess reserves into the system, enabling financial depository institutions to expand their loans and the money supply by a larger, or multiple, amount, or it can decrease excess reserves which multiplies the decrease in loans and money in the system.

EXCESS RESERVES, INTEREST RATES, AND THE LEVEL OF SPENDING

Let's summarize a few key points.

♦   Changes in the money supply are realized through changes in loan making by financial depository institutions.

---

[6] Another method for calculating the amount by which the money supply could change following an initial change in excess reserves in the system is to divide the initial change in excess reserves by the reserve requirement or

$$\frac{\text{initial change in excess reserves}}{\text{reserve requirement}} = \text{total change in money supply.}$$

Thus, if excess reserves increased by $8,000,000 when the reserve requirement was 20 percent (or 0.20), the total change in the money supply could be

$$\frac{\$8,000,000}{0.20} = \$40,000,000.$$

Be careful not to confuse this formula with the multiplier formula in Chapter 5. The formula given here is used to determine how much the *money supply* could change following an initial change in excess reserves in the depository institutions system. The formula in Chapter 5 determines how much *income* and *output* change as a result of an initial change in nonincome-determined spending.

♦ Increases in loan making lead to increases in spending and, ultimately, to increases in output and employment or to increases in prices if the economy is at or near full employment.

♦ Decreases in loan making lead to decreases in spending and output and employment.

These relationships among lending, the money supply, spending, and economic activity are summarized in Table 8.3.

Businesses and households take out loans with depository institutions because they choose to, not because they have been coerced into doing so. For this reason, simply having excess reserves available in depository institutions does not ensure that loans will be made and money will be created. This leads to two important questions. If borrowing is voluntary, how can businesses and households be stimulated to take out loans when an increase in the money supply and spending would help reduce unemployment? And how can businesses and households be encouraged to borrow less when the money supply should be reduced to dampen inflationary pressure?

Interest Rate

Price paid to borrow money; a percentage of the amount borrowed.

The answers are found in the role played by the **interest rate**, the price paid to borrow money. If $300,000 were borrowed for one year at an annual interest rate of 5 percent, at the end of the year the borrower would have to repay the $300,000 that was loaned plus $15,000 in interest, or $315,000. If the interest rate were 14 percent, at the end of one year the borrower would have to repay $342,000. As you can see, as the interest rate increases, so does the price that must be paid to borrow money. Since borrowed money, like any good or service, is subject to the Law of Demand (discussed in Chapter 3), the quantity of funds demanded for borrowing falls as the interest rate rises and rises as the interest rate falls.

Businesses are particularly sensitive to the interest rate when making decisions about borrowing for investment spending. (Recall this discussion in Chapter 5 on page 152 and Application 5.2.) The cost of borrowing funds to finance equipment,

---

TABLE 8.3   *Relationship among Loan Making, the Money Supply, Spending, and the Level of Economic Activity*

Changes in loan making lead to changes in spending, which in turn affect the economy's levels of output, employment, and/or prices.

Increases in the Money Supply	Decreases in the Money Supply
Increases in the money supply occur with increases in lending by financial depository institutions.	Decreases in the money supply occur with reductions in lending by financial depository institutions.
↓	↓
Increased loan making leads to increased spending.	Decreased loan making leads to decreased spending.
↓	↓
Increased spending leads to an increase in output and employment if the economy is at less than full employment and/or an increase in the price level if the economy is near or at full employment.	Decreased spending leads to a decrease in output and employment and a reduction of inflationary pressure if the economy is near or at full employment.

construction, and such must be recovered for any investment to break even, much less earn a profit. As the interest rate goes up, certain investment projects that would have been profitable at lower rates become unprofitable and are dropped from consideration. This in turn leads to a drop in the amount of funds demanded to finance such projects. Households are also sensitive to the interest rate when taking out loans. An increase in the interest rate on mortgages, auto loans, or other consumer loans leads to a decrease in the quantity of borrowed funds demanded by households to purchase houses and other goods.

Determining Interest Rates on Loans

How is the interest rate determined for loans made by financial depository institutions? What causes it to change? The interest rate is determined in the same way other prices are determined—through the interaction of demand and supply.

Recall that demand gives the various amounts of a product that someone will buy at various prices. The demand by businesses and households for loans from financial depository institutions is the different amounts they plan to borrow at different interest rates. A hypothetical demand for loans is given in Figure 8.1 by the demand curve D. As with other demand curves, D slopes downward to indicate an inverse relationship between the amount of planned borrowing and the interest rate.

On the other side of the transaction, the amount of loans that depository institutions are willing to make varies directly with the interest rate. Because a financial depository institution earns its profit from loan making and other sources, it is

| FIGURE 8.1 | *Determining the Interest Rate for Loans* |

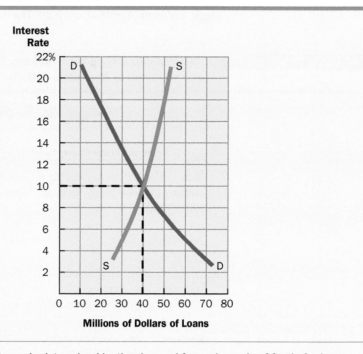

The interest rate for loans is determined by the demand for and supply of funds for loans.

motivated to use excess reserves in the way that brings the highest return. If the interest rate it can earn on loans is low, a depository institution may likely convert some of its excess reserves to higher-yielding assets. But when it can obtain a high interest rate for loaning funds, it will convert more of its excess reserves to loans. S in Figure 8.1 gives a hypothetical supply curve for loans by depository institutions. Because the base for loan making is excess reserves, there is a fairly steep supply curve: As the interest rate changes, the quantity of loans supplied cannot greatly vary.

Given D and S in Figure 8.1, the interest rate that emerges is 10 percent, with $40 million in loans resulting. This equilibrium condition occurs because at 10 percent, the amount of funds demanded equals the amount supplied. However, this equilibrium position can change. Recall from Chapter 3 that changes in demand and/or supply (shifts in the demand and/or supply curves) cause changes in market equilibrium. In the market for loans, factors that cause demand and/or supply to shift will change the equilibrium interest rate and quantity of loans made. For example, expectations of poor economic conditions could shift the demand curve to the left, causing a decrease in both the equilibrium interest rate and quantity of loans. When the economy slowed into a serious downturn from 2008 into early 2012, there was much hesitation about borrowing as predictions for the future became more dire. In this case, the demand curve took a noticeable shift to the left.

A change in the excess reserves of depository institutions alters their ability to make loans and shifts the supply curve. If excess reserves are decreased, institutions can make fewer loans, or the supply of loans decreases. This is shown in Figure 8.2a as

| FIGURE 8.2 | *Effect of Changes in Excess Reserves on the Interest Rate and the Quantity of Loans* |

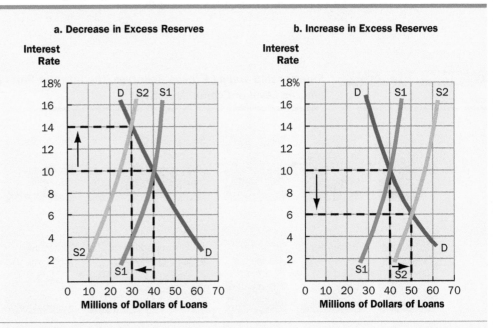

A decrease in excess reserves in the system will cause interest rates to rise and the amount of loans made to fall. An increase in excess reserves will cause interest rates to fall and the amount of loans made to rise.

a shift of the supply curve to the left from S1 to S2. As a result of this decrease in reserves, the equilibrium interest rate rises from 10 percent to 14 percent and the equilibrium quantity of loans made declines from $40 million to $30 million. In simple terms, a decrease in excess reserves causes interest rates to rise and the amount of loans made to fall.

An increase in excess reserves causes the supply of loans to increase and the supply curve to shift to the right, as shown in Figure 8.2b. When supply shifts from S1 to S2, the equilibrium interest rate falls from 10 percent to 6 percent and loans increase from $40 million to $50 million. This shows that an increase in excess reserves decreases the interest rate and increases the amount of loans made.

Figure 8.3 shows the relationship among loan making, the money supply, spending, and the level of economic activity summarized in Table 8.3 by including excess reserves and the interest rate.

An additional note of clarification about interest rates is in order. Although we frequently use the expression "the interest rate," in reality no singular interest rate exists. Instead, there are many different markets, each with its own interest rate, in which money is borrowed and lent: markets for home mortgages, secured corporate loans, student loans, and personal auto loans, for example. The interest rates in these markets differ because of differences in risk, loan size, length of repayment, and other factors. Therefore, when we refer to a rise in the interest rate because of declining excess reserves, we mean that interest rates *in general* are rising. Likewise, a fall in the interest rate due to increasing excess reserves in the system means that interest rates *in general* are falling. Application 8.2, "An Interest Rate Primer," provides additional information about how and why interest rates vary in different loan markets. Can you explain, after reading this application, why a medical student taking out a bank loan for 10 years might pay a higher interest rate than a local government taking out a 3-year loan to buy an ambulance?

FIGURE 8.3   *Relationship among Excess Reserves, the Interest Rate, Loan Making, and the Level of Economic Activity*

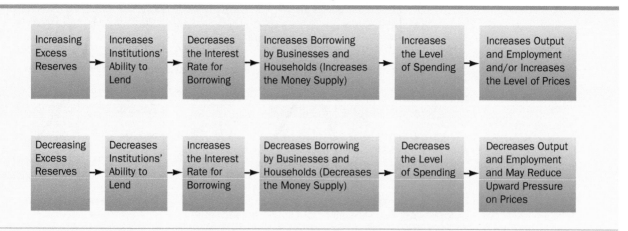

Changes in the level of excess reserves in the system influence institutions' lending abilities, interest rates, the money supply, total spending, and the economy's levels of output, employment, and/or prices.

APPLICATION 8.2

AN INTEREST RATE PRIMER

In May 2015, the U.S. Treasury was borrowing money at extremely low interest rates. The rate on its short-term bills (less than 1 year) ranged between 0.01 percent and 0.25 percent. Yes, that is just one-tenth and one-fourth of 1 percent. The 5-year notes were at about 1.5 percent and the 30-year bond rate was 3 percent. And, this was occuring when the U.S government was in debt for over $18 trillion.

In May 2015, a young couple with a household income of $80,000 signed a $175,000, 30-year mortgage to buy their first house. The interest rate on the mortgage was 4.0 percent. And then there was the college student who at that same time got his credit card bill where he was charged 20 percent interest on the $850 balance he had accumulated over a few months.

Why is the most deeply in-debt organization in the United States (and perhaps the world) paying the lowest rate on its loans, the couple that borrowed more than they make in two years paying the second lowest rate, and the student who "borrowed" just $850 on his credit card paying far and away the highest rate? There are several reasons, some more obvious than others.

Perhaps the most fundamental explanation for these varying rates is the risk of nonpayment by the borrower; that is, the likelihood that the lender won't get some or all of its money back either because the borrower can't afford to pay or intended not to pay. This is of little concern when lending money to the U.S. government, which is generally recognized as the safest borrower. The feds have an impeccable payback record, and if all else fails, the government can simply borrow more to pay off its debts. In fact, the feds have been considered so safe that people were loaning money to the government at about a 0 percent interest rate in late 2008 and early 2009, when some financial institutions were failing and people acted to ensure that their money was safe. And, this low interest has continued into 2015 even when the size of the federal debt was about the size of GDP.

Lending to homebuyers is riskier than lending to the government, but it is not an excessive risk. Certainly something like the loss of a job or an unexpected medical issue could mean an inability to make mortgage payments, but there are alternatives like refinancing. In the worst case, the lender would end up owning the house.

Then there is the student who is paying a high interest rate to borrow just $850 on a credit card—higher than is paid to borrow billions by the U.S. government or tens of thousands by the homeowners. But here the risk is fairly great for the lender. What if the student bought a backpack, some clothes, pizza, or other consumables? How feasible is it for the credit card company to locate the student and get back its $850 or the goods that the student bought if the loan is not repaid? Not only is there the risk of not paying back the loan, but here there is no collateral, or something that the lender can get in return for the loan. Collateral is another factor in determining interest rates.

Source: "Treasury Auction Results," www.treasurydirect.gov, 06/01/2015.

THE FEDERAL RESERVE AND MONETARY POLICY

Monetary Policy
Changing the money supply to influence the levels of output, employment, and/or prices in the economy.

Easy Money Policy
Policy by the Federal Reserve to increase excess reserves and decrease interest rates to increase spending.

Tight Money Policy
Policy by the Federal Reserve to reduce excess reserves and raise interest rates to reduce spending.

Several of the relationships we have covered are so important that we will repeat them one more time. The money supply is changed through loan making, and loan making depends on available excess reserves. As a result, control over the money supply comes from control over excess reserves. It is the Federal Reserve in its responsibility to oversee the money supply that influences the level of excess reserves in the economy. When the Fed acts to deliberately change excess reserves and interest rates (and, thus, the money supply) to influence the levels of output, employment, and/or prices in the economy, it is engaging in **monetary policy**.

If the economy has unacceptable rates of unemployment, total spending needs to be stimulated. To do so, the Federal Reserve would act to increase excess reserves in the system, decrease interest rates, and encourage borrowing. When the Fed takes steps to expand the money supply, it is said to be pursuing an **easy money policy**.

If the economy has demand-pull inflation, the appropriate policy prescription is to reduce spending. In this case, the Fed would act to decrease the level of excess reserves in the system, raise interest rates, and dampen borrowing. When the money supply is deliberately reduced, the Fed is said to be pursuing a **tight money policy**.

Monetary Policy Tools

The Federal Reserve has three major tools to change excess reserves in the financial depository institutions system and influence interest rates:

♦ the reserve requirement,
♦ the discount rate, and
♦ open market operations.

The Reserve Requirement   The Federal Reserve could reduce excess reserves and discourage borrowing by increasing the reserve requirement. Suppose that Hometown Bank has $50 million in demand deposits with a 10 percent reserve requirement: Hometown must keep $5 million on reserve. If the reserve requirement were raised to 11 percent, Hometown would need to keep $5.5 million on reserve for its $50 million in demand deposits. The bank would have $500,000 less in excess reserves and less loan-making ability. On the other hand, a decrease in the reserve requirement would increase excess reserves, giving Hometown the ability to make new loans.

A decrease in the reserve requirement would give institutions in the system more excess reserves and would be appropriate to stimulate the economy. An increase in the reserve requirement would give institutions in the system fewer excess reserves and would be appropriate to fight demand-pull inflation.

Table 8.4 shows the reserve requirements in effect on January 22, 2015. Notice in this table that the only requirement is on transaction or checkable accounts and that this requirement is three-tiered, ranging from 0 to 10 percent. The level at which each tier requirement takes effect is adjusted periodically. Notice also that there are no reserve requirements on time deposits. All depository institutions must meet the same reserve requirements.

The Federal Reserve usually does not radically change reserve requirements in carrying out monetary policy. Either an influx or a removal of an extremely large volume of excess reserves could be a shock to the depository institutions system. An increase of 1 or 2 percent in a reserve requirement on checkable accounts could cause banks and other institutions to have to "find" millions of dollars of reserves to meet that requirement.

TABLE 8.4	*Reserve Requirements[a]*

All depository institutions are subject to the same reserve requirements.

Type of Account	Reserve Requirement
Net transaction accounts including demand deposits and other accounts	
Balances up to $14.5 million	0%
Balances between $14.5 million and $103.6 million	3
Balances over $103.6 million	10
Time deposits and Eurocurrency liabilities	0

[a]In effect on January 22, 2015.

Source: Federal Reserve Board, "Reserve Requirements," www.federalreserve.gov/monetarypolicy/reservereq.htm, May 26, 2015.

The Discount Rate   All financial depository institutions may, under certain circumstances, borrow reserves from a Federal Reserve bank. Typically, when an institution borrows, its reserve account is increased with new reserves the Fed puts into the system. When the institution repays the Fed, its reserves are decreased and the Fed takes them out of the system. The interest rate that the Fed charges a depository institution for borrowing reserves is called the **discount rate**.[7] An increase in the discount rate, because it increases the price institutions must pay for reserves, is an attempt by the Federal Reserve to discourage reserve borrowing. A decrease in the discount rate is an attempt to encourage reserve borrowing.

Discount rate changes are always announced publicly and serve as an indicator of the intentions of the Fed. For example, an increase in the discount rate signals an attempt to tighten the money supply, which will probably lead to an increase in the interest rates that depository institutions charge their loan customers. This announcement would indicate that the Fed is pursuing a tight money policy to deal with demand-pull inflationary pressure. A decrease in the discount rate signals an attempt to loosen the money supply and will probably lead to a decrease in interest rates. This measure indicates that the Fed is concerned with a slowing economy and unemployment. Table 8.5 lists the various discount rates in effect from mid-2003 through the publication of this text.

Observe the rise from a discount rate of 2 percent in mid-2003 to a high of 6.25 percent in mid-2006. Then notice that the rate falls with especially low rates in late-2008, when the discount rate fell below 1 percent, and that it has continued to be low and unchanged since 2010. These rates reflect a money tightening as the economy grew and there were fears of inflation, followed by an easy money policy to deal with a slowing economy.

The Federal Reserve does not provide a limitless supply of borrowed reserves for depository institutions. It requires the borrowing institution to present a good reason for its loan request, such as an emergency or seasonal problem.

As noted in Application 8.1, banks can also borrow reserves from other banks in the **Federal Funds market**. However, the effect on the system is different when banks borrow reserves from one another rather than from the Fed. When banks borrow from other banks in the Federal Funds market, they are exchanging reserves that are already in the system. Thus, there is no potential for multiplying the money supply. When banks borrow from the Fed, new reserves are created in the system and the money multiplier can take effect.

Open Market Operations   Of the three monetary policy tools, open market operations is the one used most often for changing excess reserves in the financial depository institutions system. It is, however, one of the more difficult processes to understand because of the details involved in using this tool.

Very simply, **open market operations** is the buying and selling of securities, primarily U.S. government securities, on the open market by the Federal Reserve.[8] The actual physical operation is housed in the Federal Reserve Bank of New York, and buying and selling is carried on each business day. This means that adjustments in reserves can be made quickly. The **Open Market Committee**, consisting of the Board

Discount Rate
Interest rate that a Federal Reserve bank charges a financial depository institution for borrowing reserves.

Federal Funds Market
Market in which banks borrow reserves from other banks.

Open Market Operations
The buying and selling of securities, primarily U.S. government securities, on the open market by the Federal Reserve.

Open Market Committee
Committee that determines the general policy on Federal Reserve open market operations.

---

[7] Be careful to distinguish between the discount rate, which is the interest rate paid by banks to the Fed for borrowing reserves, and the prime rate, which is the benchmark interest rate banks use in setting interest rates on various types of loans.

[8] Recall that U.S. Treasury securities result from federal government borrowing to finance deficit spending.

TABLE 8.5	*Federal Reserve Discount Rates*[a]

Changes in the discount rate influence the borrowing of reserves by financial depository institutions from the Federal Reserve and serve as an indicator of the money supply intentions of the Fed.

Effective Date			Discount Rate[b]	Effective Date			Discount Rate
2003	June	25	2.00%		May	10	6.00%
2004	June	30	2.25		June	29	6.25
	Aug.	10	2.50	2007	Aug.	17	5.75
	Sept.	21	2.75		Sept.	18	5.25
	Nov.	10	3.00		Oct.	31	5.00
	Dec.	14	3.25		Dec.	11	4.75
2005	Feb.	2	3.50	2008	Jan.	22	4.00
	Mar.	22	3.75		Jan.	30	3.50
	May	3	4.00		Mar.	17	3.25
	June	30	4.25		Mar.	18	2.50
	Aug.	9	4.50		Apr.	30	2.25
	Sept.	20	4.75		Oct.	8	1.75
	Nov.	1	5.00		Oct.	29	1.25
	Dec.	13	5.25		Dec.	16	0.50
2006	Jan.	31	5.50	2010	Feb.	10	0.75
	Mar.	28	5.75				

[a]Each Federal Reserve bank determines the interest rate it will charge. Generally, the rates charged by all 12 banks are the same. However, there may be a lag of a few days when a rate adjustment is made. This table shows the rate charged by the Federal Reserve Bank of New York.

[b]Beginning in January 2003, the Federal Reserve made a distinction between depository institutions eligible for "primary credit" and less financially sound depository institutions eligible for "secondary credit." Higher rates are typically charged on secondary credit loans, and institutions receiving these loans cannot use them to expand their operations. The rates reported here are for primary credit institutions.

Source: Board of Governors of the Federal Reserve System, "The Discount Rate," www.federalreserve.gov/monetarypolicy/discountrate.htm, 02/10/2012; updated 06/01/2015.

of Governors and five Federal Reserve bank presidents, determines the general direction of open market policy. When the economy experiences more serious economic problems, extra attention is paid to the Open Market Committee meetings.

When the Fed buys securities on the Open Market, it can do so from banks or from dealers.[9] If a security is purchased by the Federal Reserve from a bank, the Fed takes the security for its own and credits the amount of the security to the selling bank's reserve account. For example, if the Fed wanted to buy government securities and if Hometown Bank were holding $1 million in Treasury notes in its portfolio that it wanted to sell, Hometown could exchange the securities for a $1 million increase in its reserve account.

When the Fed buys securities from a dealer, it pays the dealer. The dealer's proceeds are deposited in a financial institution, where, when they are cleared, the reserve

[9]The Federal Reserve cannot demand that a bank or dealer sell its securities to, or buy them from, the Fed. Rather, if the Fed intends to buy, it must offer a price high enough to induce a bank or dealer to sell. The reverse holds true if the Fed intends to sell. Most of the buying and selling by the Fed is done through dealers. In fact, many banks work through a dealer rather than directly with the Fed.

account of the institution is increased by that amount. A $1 million purchase of securities by the Fed from a dealer will increase reserves in the dealer's depository institution by $1 million. Thus, whether the Fed buys securities from a bank or from a dealer, the effect of its buying is an increase in reserves in the system.

When the Fed sells securities, it again trades with banks or dealers. If it sells to a bank, the bank exchanges its reserves for the securities, thus decreasing reserves. For example, if the Fed wants to sell Treasury notes and Hometown Bank wants to buy $2 million worth, Hometown could trade $2 million in its reserve account for these securities.

If the Fed sells to a dealer, the dealer pays for the securities. When the dealer's payment clears, the dealer's depository institution loses reserves. A $2 million sale to a dealer will decrease the reserve account of the dealer's depository institution by $2 million. Thus, when the Fed sells securities, reserves are removed from the system.[10]

It is important to understand that when reserves are increased or decreased because the Fed is buying securities from, or selling them to, banks and dealers on the open market, the Fed is not transferring reserves from one account to another. Rather, the Federal Reserve either creates new reserves for the system or destroys those that already exist. This process of reserve creation and destruction is one of the more mysterious powers of the Federal Reserve. Again, there is no transfer of reserves. They are simply created and destroyed in the system.

Open market operations provide a powerful tool for enacting monetary policy for two reasons. First, changes in reserves can be achieved quickly because operations are carried on every business day. Second, the quantity of reserves can be altered slightly or greatly depending on whether government securities are bought or sold in small or large quantities.

Open Market Operations and the Federal Funds Rate   Earlier we mentioned the Federal Funds market, which is the market in which banks lend to one another for a short period of time, usually overnight. This market allows banks that are short on meeting their reserve requirements to borrow from banks that have excess reserves. The interest rate charged in this market is called the **federal funds rate**.

Federal Funds Rate
The interest rate banks charge to lend reserves to other banks for a short period of time, usually overnight.

The federal funds rate is the most significant interest rate to observe in evaluating monetary policy. The Federal Reserve Open Market Committee targets a level for the federal funds rate and acts on this target in putting reserves into or out of the system. That is, once a direction is set for this rate, open market operations are used to move toward the target federal funds rate. If the federal funds rate needs to be lowered, open market operations are put in place to increase reserves in the system. If the rate needs to be raised, actions are taken to pull reserves out of the system.

Changes in the federal funds rate are a signal for the direction of interest rates and the course of monetary policy. Other interest rates, such as those on Treasury bills, tend to move parallel to the movement in the federal funds rate. It is important to note that the Fed does not "set" the federal funds rate but rather sets conditions in place to move toward a target. In mid-2015, the target rate was set between 0.0 percent and 0.25 percent.[11]

---

[10]Securities dealers' banks serve as "pass-throughs" for changes in excess reserves since dealers are buying and selling for clients throughout the country. For example, when a dealer in New York sells a security for a client who banks in Texas, ultimately the proceeds from the security sale pass through the dealer's bank to the client's bank in Texas. Thus, the impact of open market operations is felt throughout the banking system, not just at dealers' depository institutions.
[11]Federal Reserve Bank of New York, "Federal Funds Data," www.ny.frb.org/markets/omo/dmm/fedfundsdata.cfm, 06/01/2015.

TEST YOUR UNDERSTANDING

FINANCIAL DEPOSITORY INSTITUTION CALCULATIONS[a]

1. Fox Valley Community Bank, which has a reserve requirement of 10 percent on its deposits, has calculated the following numbers as of the end of business today: total deposits = $13,500,000; reserve account = $3,750,000; and vault cash = $2,250,000. Based on this information, determine the following for this bank:
   Required reserves = _____
   Actual reserves = _____
   Excess reserves = _____

2. How much in new loans can ABA National Bank make if its deposits are $45,000,000, vault cash is $5,550,000, and reserve account balance is $7,750,000? ABA's reserve requirement is 8 percent.
   New loans = _____

3. What is the amount that must be borrowed by Fresno Bank to cover its anticipated reserve shortfall if it has a reserve requirement of 12 percent, deposits of $27,500,000, vault cash of $2,500,000, and a reserve account of $3,250,000, and it has just made a new loan of $2,500,000 that has not yet cleared?
   New borrowing = _____

4. The Federal Reserve puts $50,000,000 in new excess reserves into the system when the reserve requirement is 8 percent. What is the money multiplier and the maximum amount by which the money supply can increase because of these new reserves?
   Money multiplier = _____
   Money supply increase = _____

5. The Fed decides to raise the reserve requirement from 10 percent to 11 percent. By how much will excess reserves decrease at Nashville Bank if Nashville has $33,500,000 in deposits and $5,750,000 in actual reserves?
   Decrease in excess reserves = _____

6. Lock Haven Bank has a reserve requirement of 6 percent, deposits of $8,500,000, vault cash of $1,255,000, a reserve account of $2,500,000, and $3,000,000 in government securities. How much in new excess reserves will be created at Lock Haven if it sells $2,000,000 of its government securities to the Fed?
   New excess reserves = _____

7. Carolina Coast Bank borrows $3,000,000 from California Coast Bank in the Federal Funds market. Inland Bank borrows $4,000,000 from its Federal Reserve bank. How much in new excess reserves has been put into the system by each transaction?
   New excess reserves by Carolina Coast = _____
   New excess reserves by Inland Bank = _____

8. The Federal Reserve buys $14,000,000 in securities in the open market at a time when the reserve requirement is 5 percent. What is the money supply increase that can result from this purchase?
   Money supply increase = _____

[a]All depository institutions in this exercise are hypothetical, and the figures are artificially low to ease calculations.

Answers can be found at the back of the book.

Tools and Policy Objectives   We have just learned how the Federal Reserve can use its major tools to change excess reserves (and the supply of money). If the Fed decided that the economy needed to expand, it would pursue lowered interest rates. It would increase reserves in the system by:

♦ buying securities from banks and dealers on the open market, and/or
♦ lowering the reserve requirement, and/or
♦ lowering the discount rate.

If the Fed decided to fight demand-pull inflation, it would pursue higher interest rates. It would remove excess reserves from the system and shrink the money supply by

♦ selling securities to banks and dealers on the open market, and/or
♦ increasing the reserve requirement, and/or
♦ increasing the discount rate.

Test Your Understanding, "Financial Depository Institution Calculations," provides an opportunity to practice some computations introduced in this chapter

WHO REALLY IS THE MOST POWERFUL PERSON IN THE UNITED STATES?

It's a fairly safe guess that people would identify the president of the United States as one of the most powerful persons in the world. Most folks would not give that kind of power designation to the Federal Reserve board chair. Yet, shortly before Janet Yellen was confirmed as the new chair of the Federal Reserve board in January 2014, *The Atlantic* published an article titled, "Why Janet Yellen Would Be the Most Powerful Woman in World History."

The Federal Reserve is tasked with ensuring that the U.S. economy keep unemployment and inflation in check through affecting interest rates. The Fed has an important role in stabilizing the economy while fostering healthy growth. This in itself is powerful. But it is not just the United States that is affected. Banks and money-related markets throughout the world respond to Federal Reserve actions. *The Atlantic* article opined that ". . . Janet Yellen will have more control over the global economy than any other living person once she's confirmed as Fed chair."[a]

History has proven that the Fed chair is powerful. People around the world pay attention to every word uttered by the chair. For example, Alan Greenspan, chair from 1987 to 2006, briefly expressed concern at a dinner speech about stock market prices being driven up by people's "irrational exuberance." The next morning stocks not only took a dive on the New York Stock Exchange but fell in Australia, Japan, and Europe.

Chairperson Ben Bernanke, Yellen's predecessor who served from 2006 to 2014, commented at a dinner speech about inflation and the Fed, and the following morning financial markets saw billions of dollars changing hands, falling stock prices, and a gain in the dollar against the euro.

As the economy develops problems, the Fed chair is often in the headlines as people watch for the direction the Fed is taking and the change in interest rates that will likely result. And the twice-a-year mandatory testimony before Congress may bring stock and bond fluctuations days ahead of the testimony as people try to anticipate what will be said and what policies are coming.

So, think about this power. Would people react as strongly with a few words from one of our presidents about inflation or irrational exuberance? Is Janet Yellen one of the most powerful women in world history as *The Atlantic* article suggests?

[a]Matthew O'Brien, "Why Janet Yellen Would Be The Most Powerful Woman in World History," *The Atlantic*, October 9, 2013, www.theatlantic.com.

that relate to depository institution reserves and lending, and monetary policy tools.

The actions of the Federal Reserve are closely watched because of the impact of policy decisions on interest rates and on economic activity. The public in general has become more aware of monetary terms such as M1 and M2, and of actions such as changes in the discount rate because of the way such matters affect jobs, mortgage rates, automobile loans, and other facets of everyday life. This raised awareness was quite evident in late 2008 and 2009 as the United States struggled with serious economic problems, many of which were related to financial institutions and loan making. Businesses, particularly those in financial areas, hire experts to anticipate Federal Reserve moves because changes in the interest rate by even a small percentage can cost them millions of dollars. The impact—and importance—of Federal Reserve policy can be seen in Application 8.3, "Who Really Is the Most Powerful Person in the United States?" This application shows the power of the Federal Reserve chair and the global reach of the chair's words and comments.

ASSESSING MONETARY POLICY

Government Deficits and Monetary Policy

When the federal government borrows to finance its deficit budgets, it impacts interest rates and the amount that households and businesses borrow. When the federal government enters the market for available loan monies, it puts upward pressure on interest rates and, when they rise, causes households and businesses to borrow less. The consequences of this federal action make it important to understand the relationship between government borrowing and monetary policy.

The downward-sloping demand curve for loans that was illustrated in Figures 8.1 and 8.2 came from the demand for loans by households and businesses, which are sensitive to interest rates. When the government, which is not sensitive to interest rates, plans to borrow to finance its deficit spending, its demand for borrowing is added to that of households and businesses. So, government borrowing shifts the demand curve for loanable funds to the right.

We can see the effect of government borrowing in Figure 8.4a. D1, which represents the demand for loanable funds by households and businesses, shifts to D2 when government borrowing is added to that of households and businesses. As a result of government borrowing, the interest rate rises from 10 percent to 16 percent and the quantity of loans made rises from $250 million to $300 million. The increase in the interest rate that results from government borrowing discourages business and household borrowing so that the growth in government borrowing is accompanied by a

FIGURE 8.4   ***Effect of Government Borrowing and Monetizing the Debt on the Interest Rate and Loan Making***

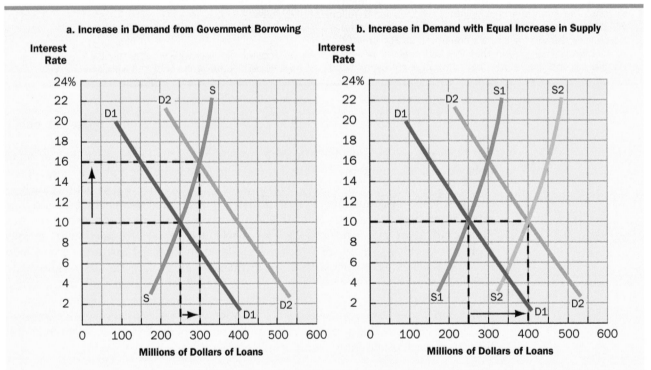

Government borrowing increases the demand for loans and the interest rate. When excess reserves are increased to meet this demand, the interest rate is lower and a larger quantity of loans is made than would otherwise occur.

Crowding Out
Occurs when borrowing by
the federal government
increases the interest rate
and reduces borrowing by
households and businesses.

Monetizing the Debt
Increasing the money supply
by the Federal Reserve to
accommodate federal
government borrowing and
reduce upward pressure on
the interest rate.

decrease in private borrowing. This is the **crowding out** problem that was introduced in Chapter 6.[12]

The rise in the interest rate from government borrowing could be prevented if the Federal Reserve would increase excess reserves in the system by an amount equal to the increase in the demand for funds by the government. Figure 8.4b illustrates a shift in the supply curve for loanable funds to the right, from S1 to S2, which is the amount necessary to compensate for the increase in demand. Notice that the increase in supply to S2 keeps the interest rate at the original level of 10 percent. This increase in excess reserves by the Federal Reserve to accommodate federal government borrowing plans and reduce upward pressure on the interest rate is referred to as **monetizing the debt**. By monetizing the debt, the Fed could hold the interest rate at its pregovernment borrowing level and offset the crowding out effect.

Why doesn't the Federal Reserve simply create enough reserves on a regular basis to cover the federal government's demand for funds, thereby eliminating the upward pressure that government borrowing puts on interest rates? The Federal Reserve has generally adhered to a philosophy of controlling the money supply and interest rates for the benefit of the macroeconomy, rather than accommodating government deficit spending. If it always increased reserves to meet government needs, the money supply could increase by an amount large enough to cause inflation and weaken the value of the dollar. Notice in Figure 8.4b that when the Fed increases excess reserves to meet increased government demand for borrowing, a $150 million increase in loans results. When demand and supply were at D1 and S1, $250 million was loaned, and when demand and supply increased to D2 and S2, $400 million was loaned. As illustrated in Figure 8.4a, were the Fed not to increase excess reserves to accommodate government borrowing, the quantity of loans would increase by only $50 million.

It should be reiterated that the Federal Reserve changes excess reserves to target interest rates: raising interest rates to slow down a possible problem with inflation and lowering interest rates to increase borrowing and spending to expand output and income or fight recessionary conditions. As the economy slowed in 2008 and for the next few years, the Federal Reserve put additional excess reserves into the system to bring the interest rate down. While the federal debt rose considerably, the intention of the Fed was not to monetize the debt, but rather to bring down interest rates.

Advantages and Disadvantages of Monetary Policy

Is monetary policy an effective tool for tackling inflation and unemployment? What are the advantages and disadvantages of using monetary policy? One of the major benefits of monetary policy is the speed with which it can be implemented. Unlike fiscal policy, which could take months to implement, the first steps toward changing the money supply can be taken the day the decision to do so is made. Another major benefit is its size flexibility: Reserves can be increased or decreased in small or large increments.

---

[12] The crowding out problem can also be seen in greater detail in Figure 8.4a. Demand curve D1, which represents planned borrowing by households and businesses, indicates that at an interest rate of 10 percent, households and businesses want to borrow $250 million, and at an interest rate of 16 percent, they want to borrow $150 million. Thus, when government borrowing forces the interest rate up from 10 percent to 16 percent, households and businesses borrow $100 million less than they otherwise would borrow.

Monetary policy is also largely removed from politics. The members of the Board of Governors, although appointed by a president, are not as subject to political pressure as are the members of Congress. This may be partially due to the fact that Board members are appointed for lengthy (14-year) terms and are not campaigning for re-election. The Board of Governors' motives in expanding and contracting the money supply are usually economic.

One of the major disadvantages of monetary policy is the loan-making link through which it is carried out. That is, the Fed can increase reserves to stimulate economic activity as much as it wants, but the reserves themselves do not alter the money supply. For the money supply (and spending) to increase, someone must be willing to borrow and a bank must be willing to lend. Because the Fed cannot force the loan-making process, it has only indirect control over increasing the money supply. This loan-making link may reduce the effectiveness of monetary policy in fighting unemployment during a deep and serious recession. If economic conditions are severe, no expansion of reserves and lowering of the interest rate may be enough to induce borrowers to take out loans.

Moreover, there is increasing concern that low interest rates can have a negative effect on those who count on interest income for spending. This ranges from retirees who use interest from CDs to school districts and local governments with reserve funds to colleges and universities with an endowment. For example, an interest rate of 6 percent on a $100,000 CD yields $6,000 a year as income, whereas an interest rate of 1 percent yields just $1,000. For a city or school district with a reserve fund of $3 million, that difference in the interest rate could be the salaries for a few police officers or teachers. For a college or university, it could be a major dent in available scholarships.

Another problem with monetary policy occurs during inflation. As the Federal Reserve tightens the money supply and forces the interest rate higher, it raises the price for borrowed money. Businesses that borrow at this high rate may in turn raise prices on their products to compensate. Thus, fighting inflation with monetary policy could worsen it.

Finally, there are those who feel that having the Federal Reserve and monetary policy removed from the political process is a disadvantage. Over the years there have been several proposals to place the Federal Reserve under more congressional control. Proponents of this action do not favor the independence of the Fed and presume that with control it would be more sensitive to public reaction in its policy making. Up for Debate, "Should the Federal Reserve Be Placed under the Direct Control of Congress?" provides arguments on each side of this issue. What is your position on this question?

A Note   Before concluding this chapter, two further considerations merit mention. First, it is possible for unemployment and inflation to occur simultaneously, and when this happens, there is no clearly appropriate monetary policy to follow. In late 1990, for example, this was the policy dilemma faced by the Federal Reserve when the economy was experiencing inflationary pressure while slipping into a recession. In 2008, as gasoline prices rose to extremely high levels and the economy was softening, the fear of simultaneous problems rose again.

Second, there is an economic philosophy called monetarism, and those who adhere to it are termed monetarists. Generally, monetarists believe that controlling the money supply is the main vehicle for controlling economic activity. Some monetarists favor increasing and decreasing the money supply to control unemployment and inflation, while others favor a constant annual increase in the money supply to promote stable growth and prices. Monetarism is discussed in Chapter 9.

UP FOR DEBATE

SHOULD THE FEDERAL RESERVE BE PLACED UNDER THE DIRECT CONTROL OF CONGRESS?

Issue   *Although the Federal Reserve is a creation of Congress and the Board of Governors is appointed by the president and confirmed by the Senate, policy decisions are made independent of congressional oversight. The policy decisions pursued by the Board of Governors have a significant impact on interest rates and economic activity. Some people argue that the Fed is too powerful to be so independent, while others strongly favor a monetary authority that is independent of the political process. Should the Fed be placed under more congressional control?*

Yes   The Federal Reserve should be placed under greater control of Congress. The actions of the Federal Reserve can change the direction of economic activity: Tools can be used to raise the interest rate and decrease spending in an effort to control inflation, or to lower the interest rate and increase spending in an effort to reduce unemployment. This ability gives the Board of Governors substantial power over the economy—power too great to be exercised independent of congressional approval.

Because Congress is part of the political process, members of Congress may be more responsive to the wishes of the electorate. Congress may prevent interest rates from rising to levels that negatively impact household and business borrowing, and may recommend that the federal debt be monetized when it is sizable.

Finally, the chairperson of the Board of Governors is a powerful force: Markets throughout the world react to the chair's statements. The person holding this position should be accountable to Congress.

No   The Federal Reserve should remain independent of congressional control. Effective control of the money supply, especially when it is based on a paper monetary standard, is a key to a stable economy. Allowing the money supply to increase too rapidly in order to hold down interest rates, for example, can cause significant inflation.

Putting the Federal Reserve under direct congressional control means putting the money supply in the hands of politicians whose motives in decision making may be to support partisan agendas and gain reelection. How likely is it that a politician will risk reelection to do what may be good for the economy, but not for the politician? For example, in order to hold down an interest rate increase caused by a budget deficit, a congressperson may decide that monetizing the debt is more politically expedient than trying to reduce the budget deficit.

The members of the Board of Governors are appointed by the president and confirmed by the Senate and are not, therefore, totally independent of the political process. The current arrangement provides some limited oversight but permits the Board to put the macroeconomy, not reelection, first in its decision making.

Summary

1. Since there is an important relationship between an economy's supply of money and its levels of output, employment, and prices, altering the money supply can help to reach the major macroeconomic goals.

2. The equation of exchange shows how money affects the level of economic activity. It illustrates that, operating through aggregate spending, changes in the supply of money lead to changes in output, employment, and/or prices. Generally, if the economy is at less than full employment, increases in the money supply expand output and employment. If the economy is at or near full employment, increases in the money supply cause increases in prices. A decrease in the money supply decreases output and employment and may dampen upward pressure on prices.

3. Changes in the money supply occur through lending by financial depository institutions: Money is created when loans are made and destroyed when they are repaid. Lending is not accomplished by transferring funds from one account to another. Loans represent newly created money.

4. A financial depository institution can make a loan if it has excess reserves, which is the difference between the institution's actual reserves and its required reserves. Required reserves, which is the amount of reserves that the institution must hold to back its deposits, is found by multiplying the institution's deposits by the reserve requirement. If new loan making exceeds the institution's excess reserves, actual reserves can drop below required reserves.

5. An initial increase or decrease in excess reserves in the depository institutions system will cause total lending and the money supply to change by a larger, or a multiple, amount. The money multiplier itself is the reciprocal of the reserve requirement, and the maximum change in the money supply is equal to the money multiplier times the initial change in excess reserves.

6. Having excess reserves available in financial depository institutions does not ensure that loans will be made by households and businesses. The stimulus for businesses and households to borrow when increased spending is desired, or to reduce borrowing when spending is excessive, is the interest rate, which is a cost of borrowing money. As the interest rate increases, the amount of borrowing by businesses and households and the amount of total spending based on borrowing decreases. When the interest rate is lowered, the reverse holds true.

7. The rate of interest on loans made by financial depository institutions is determined by the demand for loans and by the supply of available loanable funds, which is based on excess reserves. Increasing excess reserves increases the supply of available loanable funds, lowers the interest rate, and raises the amount of loans made. Decreasing excess reserves increases the interest rate and reduces the amount of loans made.

8. Adjusting the money supply to accomplish macroeconomic goals is a major responsibility of the Federal Reserve. The Fed uses three tools to change excess reserves in the system and influence interest rates: the reserve requirement, the discount rate, and open market operations.

9. Monetary policy to lower interest rates and stimulate spending calls for lowering the reserve requirement, and/or reducing the discount rate, and/or Federal Reserve purchases of securities on the open market. Monetary policy to raise interest rates and dampen spending calls for raising the reserve requirement, and/or raising the discount rate, and/or Federal Reserve sales of securities on the open market. Of the three policy tools, open market operations is the most important and the most frequently used.

10. The Federal Reserve could keep the interest rate stable in the face of government borrowing to finance deficit spending by increasing excess reserves to accommodate the government's demand for funds. However, such actions on a persistent basis, called monetizing the debt, could weaken the value of the dollar.

11. The use of monetary policy to correct unemployment or demand-pull inflation has the advantage of flexibility in timing and size. It has the disadvantages, however, of possible ineffectiveness in a severe recession and of the potential to make inflation worse in a tight money situation. Having the Federal Reserve removed from politics is viewed by some as an advantage and by others as a disadvantage.

Key Terms and Concepts

Equation of exchange

Actual reserves

Reserve requirement

Required reserves

Excess reserves

Creation and destruction
of money

Multiplier effect (money)

Money multiplier

Interest rate

Monetary policy

Easy money policy

Tight money policy

Discount rate

Federal Funds market

Open market operations

Open Market Committee

Federal funds rate

Crowding out

Monetizing the debt

Review Questions

1. Assuming that the supply of money in the economy is $3.2 trillion and velocity is 5, answer questions a through d.
   a. What is the dollar value of output produced in the economy?
   b. What would happen to the dollar value of output and the real value of output if $50 billion were added to the money supply when the economy was at full employment?
   c. What would happen to prices and to the level of output produced in the economy if the Fed reduced the supply of money to dampen inflationary pressure when the economy was at full employment?
   d. What would happen to the dollar value of output if people spent money faster (velocity increased) following a reduction in the money supply by the Fed?

2. What is the difference among a bank's actual reserves, required reserves, and excess reserves? How is each determined?

3. If a bank has $30,000,000 in demand deposits, a 15 percent reserve requirement, and $5,200,000 in actual reserves, what are its required and excess reserves and how much in new loans could it make?

4. What is the money multiplier and how is it related to the reserve requirement? If the Federal Reserve increases excess reserves in the system by $180 million with a reserve requirement of 12 percent, what is the maximum amount by which the money supply can increase as a result of the increased excess reserves?

5. Assume that the reserve requirement is 12.5 percent and that $500,000 is added to Hometown Bank's excess reserves as a result of a change in Federal Reserve policy.
   a. How much in new loans can Hometown Bank make as a result of this increase in excess reserves?
   b. If the entire amount of Hometown Bank's new loans is spent and the funds are deposited in Bank B, by how much can Bank B increase its loan making?

c. What is the maximum amount by which loan making can be increased in the financial depository institutions system as a result of the increase in Hometown Bank's excess reserves?

d. What is the maximum amount in new loans that could be made in the financial depository institutions system following the initial increase in Hometown Bank's excess reserves if the reserve requirement were 20 percent?

6. Suppose the Federal Reserve is concerned about demand-pull inflationary pressure that is building in the economy.

a. What would be the appropriate change in excess reserves to counteract this problem?

b. What would be the appropriate change in the reserve requirement, the discount rate, and open market operations to bring about this change in excess reserves?

7. Use the accompanying supply and demand graphs to explain how each of the following affects the supply of and/or demand for loans, the interest rate, and the actual amount of loans made.

a. The Federal Reserve sells securities on the open market.

b. The U.S. government borrows to finance its deficit, and the Fed does not monetize the debt.

c. The U.S. government borrows to finance its deficit, and the Fed monetizes the debt.

d. The Federal Reserve lowers the discount rate.

e. Private investment spending decreases because of fears of a recession.

a.	b.	c.	d.	e.
Interest Rate	Interest Rate	Interest Rate	Interest Rate	Interest Rate

    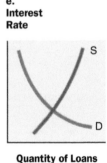

Quantity of Loans	Quantity of Loans	Quantity of Loans	Quantity of Loans	Quantity of Loans

8. What would be the effect of each of the following on Uptown Bank's excess reserves and loan-making ability if the bank had $600 million in deposits, a 5 percent reserve requirement, and actual reserves of $40 million?

a. The Federal Reserve sells $5 million in government securities to Uptown Bank.

b. The reserve requirement increases from 5 percent to 6 percent.

c. The discount rate is increased.

d. The reserve requirement is lowered from 5 percent to 4 percent, and the Federal Reserve buys $10 million in government securities from the bank.

1. It is assumed in the equation of exchange that the velocity of money is fixed or constant. Is this a safe assumption when applied to your own spending habits over the course of a month or a year? What would erratic and unpredictable velocity do to the usefulness of the equation of exchange?

2. In a discussion with a friend, you are told that it makes no difference whether the Federal Reserve uses open market operations, the reserve requirement, or the discount rate to change the supply of money because the impact of each policy is exactly the same. Do you agree or disagree with your friend's position?

3. Control by the Federal Reserve over the money supply and over total spending is weakened by the fact that borrowing by businesses and households is voluntary. How might the power of the Federal Reserve over borrowing be strengthened? Is this method consistent with the philosophy of capitalism?

4. Assume that the economy is at full employment and that the federal government needs to borrow $100 billion to finance a budget deficit. Should the Federal Reserve monetize the debt by putting an extra $100 billion in reserves into the system to finance this borrowing? If not, what action should the Fed take?

5. If you were trying to control inflation, would you depend on fiscal or monetary policy? Why? If you were trying to reduce unemployment, would you depend on fiscal or monetary policy? Why?

6. Suppose the economy is experiencing inflationary pressure because of rising food and energy costs at the same time that it is slipping into a recession because of cutbacks in defense spending. As the chairperson of the Board of Governors, how would you balance the attention you give to these two problems and what recommendations concerning the tools of monetary policy would you make to solve them? Would it make sense to use monetary policy to solve one of the problems while asking Congress to use fiscal policy to solve the other?

7. The tools of monetary policy are used to deal with the problems of unemployment, inflation, and slow economic growth. Could you make an argument that the Federal Reserve should concern itself only with problems relating to inflation and the price level and that other problems in the macroeconomy should be the responsibility of other policymaking groups?

8. From the end of 2008 to the time of the publication of this text, the price to borrow money was extremely low and savers were earning very little on CDs and other savings accounts. In your opinion, were Federal Reserve actions helping the economy or hurting it?

THE FED AND THE GREAT DEPRESSION OF THE 1930S

Critical Thinking Skills

Exploring similarities between historical and contemporary events

Identifying cause and effect

Economic Concepts

Monetary policy

The Federal Reserve

What caused the Depression? This question is a difficult one, but answering it is important if we are to draw the right lessons from the experience for economic policy. . . .

During the first decades after the Depression, most economists looked to developments on the real side of the economy for explanations, rather than to monetary factors. . . . However, in 1963, . . . [and in] contradiction to the prevalent view of the time, that money and monetary policy played at most a purely passive role in the Depression, [Milton] Friedman and [Anna] Schwartz argued that "the [economic] contraction is in fact a tragic testimonial to the importance of monetary forces."

. . . Friedman and Schwartz . . . identified a series of errors . . . by the Federal Reserve in the late 1920s and early 1930s [that] led to an undesirable tightening of monetary policy [and] sharp declines in the money supply. [These] could account for the drops in prices and output that subsequently occurred.

[One error] was the tightening of monetary policy that began in the spring of 1928 and continued until the stock market crash of October 1929. This tightening of monetary policy in 1928 did not seem particularly justified by the macroeconomic environment: The economy was only just emerging from a recession . . . and there was little hint of inflation. Why then did the Federal Reserve raise interest rates in 1928? The principal reason was the Fed's ongoing concern . . . that bank lending to brokers and investors was fueling a speculative wave in the stock market. When the Fed's attempts to persuade banks not to lend for speculative purposes proved ineffective, Fed officials decided to dissuade lending directly by raising the policy interest rate. . . .

According to Friedman and Schwartz, the Fed's tight-money policies led to the onset of a recession in August 1929. . . . The slowdown in economic activity, together with high interest rates, was in all likelihood the most important source of the stock market crash that followed in October. In other words, the market crash, rather than being the cause of the Depression, as popular legend has it, was in fact largely the result of an economic slowdown and the inappropriate monetary policies that preceded it. . . .

[Another] policy action highlighted by Friedman and Schwartz occurred in 1932. By the spring of that year, the Depression was well advanced, and Congress began to place considerable pressure on the Federal Reserve to ease monetary policy. The Board was quite reluctant to comply, but in response to the ongoing pressure the Board conducted open-market operations between April and June of 1932 designed to increase the national money supply and thus ease policy. These policy actions reduced interest rates on government bonds and corporate debt and appeared to arrest the decline in prices and economic activity. [But] Fed officials convinced themselves that the policy ease advocated by the Congress was not appropriate, and so when the Congress adjourned in July 1932, the Fed reversed the policy. By the latter part of the year, the economy had relapsed dramatically.

Source: Excerpted from remarks by Governor Ben S. Bernanke, member of the Fed Board of Governors, at the H. Parker Willis Lecture in Economic Policy, "Money, Gold and the Great Depression," March 2, 2004.

Questions

1. What is the significance of knowledge of Federal Reserve actions during the 1930s for the analysis of contemporary monetary policy?

2. In what ways did Federal Reserve policy in the early 1930s likely affect the U.S. economy?

3. What types of historical information (federal budgets, for example) would you want to know before you determined the extent to which monetary policy contributed to the Great Depression?

CHAPTER 9

Macroeconomic Viewpoints and Models

CHAPTER OBJECTIVES

Understand that various macroeconomic models have different assumptions and relationships, and an historical dimension.

Describe the classical school of thought, and the classical aggregate demand–aggregate supply model and its conclusions.

Understand the basic relationships in the Keynesian model and the policy implications of the model.

Explain the new classical model and its policy implications.

Define the basic relationships in the new Keynesian, monetarist, and supply-side models.

Define the relevance of macroeconomic theories for solving macroeconomic problems.

In Chapter 5, we discussed macroeconomic fluctuations: The macroeconomy is always expanding or contracting, or in some phase of a business cycle. Production increases and unemployment falls during a recovery, and production decreases and unemployment rises during a recession. The causes of these fluctuations have been pondered for centuries, as have the causes of another major macroeconomic problem: inflation.

The relationship between the amount of total spending in an economy and the economy's levels of production and employment was laid out in Chapter 5. Businesses respond to spending changes by households, other businesses, government, and foreign buyers by increasing or decreasing their levels of production.

The foundation built in Chapter 5 can be used to understand various viewpoints about the macroeconomy and different models that have been developed to explain how it operates. Some important questions can be answered by relying on our Chapter 5 foundation as well as these models. For example, while spending changes may trigger economic fluctuations, what triggers spending changes? Is there a difference in short-run and long-run macroeconomic relationships? Is there a level of activity that an economy automatically seeks?

We begin this chapter with an overview of macroeconomic model building and discuss the components of a model as well as how history has influenced the development of these models. We then introduce some of the major macroeconomic schools of thought—the classical, Keynesian, new classical, new Keynesian, and monetarist schools—and the basic model of each school.

MACROECONOMIC MODEL BUILDING

Much of the work of economists is model building; that is, economists look for explanations for relationships between economic variables or seek answers to why an economic problem or condition occurs. As explained in Chapter 1, model building involves four components: identifying variables, establishing assumptions, collecting and analyzing data, and interpreting conclusions.

Economic theory has an important historical dimension: Searches for explanations of economic problems are often related to historical events. For example, there was significant joblessness during the Great Depression in the 1930s, which gave rise to a need to determine the cause of unemployment and policies to remedy it. One of the great songs of the Depression era, "Brother, Can You Spare a Dime?," captures the extreme distress underlying the need to change the direction of the economy.

> "Once I built a railroad, I made it run, made it race against time.
> Once I build a railroad; now it's done. Brother, can you spare a dime?
> Once I built a tower, up to the sun, brick, and rivet, and lime;
> Once I built a tower, now it's done. Brother, can you spare a dime?"[1]

The severe inflations of the mid-to-late 1970s and early 1980s brought serious interest in determining the causes of inflation. Beginning in 2008, a deteriorating economy again brought significant interest in economic theory and policy. In addition, the rising role of the Federal Reserve and the bailout of financial institutions brought renewed interest in money and monetarism.

A Warning

Recall that a model examines the relationship between two variables. It is important to keep this in mind as we study the models in this chapter because not all macroeconomic models attempt to explain the same relationships. Rather, they focus on different problems and variables. In this chapter, one model explores the relationship between prices and output, another the relationship between spending and output, and a third the relationship between money and output.

The assumptions, or conditions held to be true, when building a model are important because they underlie the model and affect its conclusions. Assumptions can be influenced by the values of the model builder, and the role of these values in developing assumptions is often overlooked or difficult to identify. For example, if one values free markets, then free markets can become an underlying assumption of a model and in turn become important to policy recommendations that follow from the model. If one values government intervention, then this value can become important to the assumptions of a model and its resulting policy implications.

It is useful for students to identify the variables, assumptions, and data that go into the construction and presentation of a model. The interpretation of the conclusions

---

[1] Songs of the Great Depression, "Brother, Can You Spare a Dime?" lyrics by Yip Harburg, music by Jay Gorney (1931), http://www.library.csi.cuny.edu/dept/history/lavender/cherries.html.

of the model and its policy implications are affected by the choice of each of these parts of the model. This makes it important for students to be able to put models in their proper context in economics as well as in other classes. For example, in the social sciences, conclusions about people's behavior patterns are often based on research done in a model, so it is useful for students to understand how the model's assumptions and data collection affect those conclusions. Knowledge of the cultural setting of a model in sociology, the values of a teller of history, and the data collection method for a political science survey are all important for a fuller understanding of work in these fields.

Application 9.1, "Paying Close Attention to Models: It's Worth the Effort," provides some additional thoughts about economic model building and the impact of how the story in a model is presented. Can you think of a theory you studied in a social science course, such as psychology, sociology, or political science, that influenced history or the personal beliefs of a large number of people or policymakers?

Macroeconomic Schools of Thought   Over the years, different models have been developed by economists to explain the operation of the macroeconomy, and different policy prescriptions have been advocated to stabilize the economy. Alternative viewpoints about the macroeconomy often stem from the different assumptions on which the models are formulated. Also, sometimes a viewpoint loses popularity as new data

---

APPLICATION 9.1

PAYING CLOSE ATTENTION TO MODELS: IT'S WORTH THE EFFORT

Working your way through an economic model can be difficult, boring, and time consuming. The problem is that economic models have a significant impact on our lives. It is usually the conclusion of a model that is the starting point for policies that affect so many aspects of how we live, from our jobs to the kinds of things we can afford to buy. So, we should pay close attention to what is in a model.

The importance of economic forces is bluntly stated on the first page of a book by Alfred Marshall that played a major role in opening the door to what we think of as modern economics. Marshall wrote, "[M]an's character has been moulded by his every-day work, and the material resources which he thereby procures, more than by any other influence unless it be that of his religious ideals; and the two great forming agencies of the world's history have been the religious and the economic."[a]

While economic models might be difficult and boring, people (some of whom exert great power) take them very seriously. As John Maynard Keynes, one of the most influential economists of the twentieth century, put it, "[The] ideas of economists and political philosophers, both when they are right and when they are wrong, are more powerful than is commonly understood. Indeed, the world is ruled by little else. Practical men, who believe themselves to be quite exempt from any intellectual influences, are usually the slaves of some defunct economist. Madmen in authority, who hear voices in the air, are distilling their frenzy from some academic scribbler of a few years back."[b]

Sometimes the take on the story a model tells changes after its assumptions and data are explored in detail. For example, you probably know the story of the three little pigs. One lived in a house built of straw, the second in a house built of sticks, and the third in a house built of bricks. When the wolf came along, he blew down the houses of straw and sticks, but not the house of bricks. The usual moral of the story is that the pig in the brick house put in the effort to build a solid house, and the other two pigs were lazy. But how would the moral of the story change if the first pig worked an 80-hour week in the brick factory to get by and feed his kids, the second pig was disabled by an accident in the brick factory and unable to work, and the third pig was the brick factory owner's son?

What is the moral of the story in this application? The influence of economics is not to be taken lightly, and the models used to extend this influence should be thoroughly examined and understood. While we may not tolerate details well, it is the details of our economic models that tell the real story.

[a] Alfred Marshall, *Principles of Economics* (London: Macmillan and Co., 1890), p. 1.
[b] John Maynard Keynes, *The General Theory of Employment, Interest and Money* (New York: Harcourt, Brace and Co., 1936), p. 383.

and information provide better explanations of key economic relationships or solutions to problems.

These different macroeconomic theories and the policy prescriptions that follow from them can be better understood by placing them into categories, or "schools of thought." Several schools of thought are significant to the development of macroeconomic theory. These include the classical, Keynesian, new classical, new Keynesian, and monetarist schools.

CLASSICAL ECONOMICS

Classical Economics

Popularly accepted theory prior to the Great Depression of the 1930s; says the economy will automatically adjust to full employment.

The dominant school of economic thought before the 1930s was **classical economics**. This school, however, was largely rejected during the 1930s because it could not explain the cause of, or offer a successful remedy for, the prolonged and severe unemployment that developed during the Great Depression. The basic premise of the classical school, which dates from Adam Smith and his book *The Wealth of Nations* published in 1776, is that a free market economy, when left alone, will automatically operate at full employment. And, because a free market economy always automatically corrects itself to full employment, there is no need for government intervention to rectify its problems. Adam Smith is one of the economists featured in Application 9.2, "The Academic Scribblers."

The classical economists arrived at their position about the automatic self-correction to full employment because of several assumptions. First, they assumed that supply creates its own demand in a macroeconomy.[2] In other words, something that is produced will be bought by someone. As a result, there is no need for concern about operating at less than full employment and production: The goods and services that are produced will all be purchased.

A second assumption of the classical economists was that wages and prices are flexible and increase or decrease to ensure that the economy operates at full employment. This assumption is illustrated in Figure 9.1. The perfectly vertical aggregate, or total, supply curve (AS) in Figure 9.1a illustrates an economy producing at the full employment level of output, regardless of whether prices and wages are high or low. The aggregate demand curve (AD) in Figure 9.1a represents the spending plans of households and businesses in the economy. The curve slopes downward to indicate that an inverse relationship exists between prices and wages, and the amount of output demanded. When prices fall (which will also bring wages down in the classical model), households and businesses want to purchase a greater amount of output, and when prices increase, they want to purchase less. In Figure 9.1a, aggregate demand and supply are equal at the full employment level of output at price and wage level PW.

If there is a change in aggregate demand, as illustrated in Figure 9.1b by the decrease or increase in the aggregate demand curve from AD0 to AD1, or AD0 to AD2,

---

[2] "Say's Law," named after the French economist Jean Baptiste Say (1767–1832), states that supply creates its own demand. According to James Mill (1773–1836), one of the important popularizers of this position, whatever individuals produce over and above their own needs is done to exchange for goods and services produced by others. People produce in order to acquire the things that they desire, so what they supply and what they demand are equal. And if each person's supply and demand are equal, it follows that the supply and demand in the entire economy must be equal. Believing that demand and supply are equal for the entire economy, the classical economists saw surpluses in specific markets that would lead to unemployment as being offset by shortages in other markets that would lead to more employment. The surpluses would be removed by businesses following their own self-interest and guided by the profit motive. See James Mill, *Elements of Political Economy* (London: Baldwin, Cradock, and Joy, 1826), Chapter IV, Section III, especially pp. 228, 232, 234–235.

FIGURE 9.1   *Aggregate Supply and Aggregate Demand in Classical Economics*

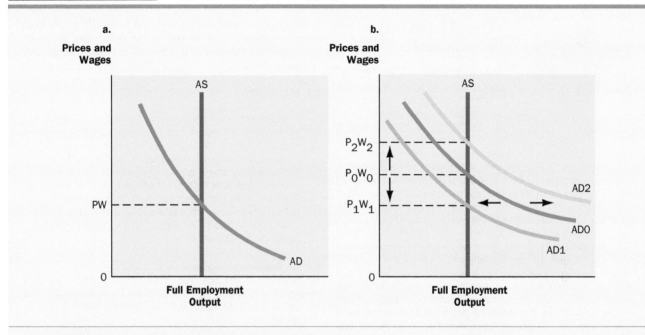

In the classical model, prices and wages adjust in order to maintain a full employment level of output.

respectively, there will be a change in prices and wages that allows the economy to continue to operate at full employment. For example, if initially in Figure 9.1b, aggregate demand were AD0, aggregate supply were AS, and the level of prices and wages were $P_0 W_0$, the economy would be operating at full employment. If aggregate demand were to decrease and the aggregate demand curve shifted to the left to AD1, less would be demanded than supplied at the original price and wage level ($P_0 W_0$), and the economy would experience some temporary unemployment. However, according to the classical assumptions, prices and wages would soon fall to $P_1 W_1$, and the economy would return to full employment. This lower price and wage level would permit full employment at the lower level of demand.

Likewise, if aggregate demand were to increase and the aggregate demand curve shifted to the right from AD0 to AD2 in Figure 9.1b, more would be demanded than could be supplied at the original price and wage level of $P_0 W_0$. Prices and wages would rise to $P_2 W_2$, with the economy continuing to operate at full employment. In the classical model, the adjustment to changes in aggregate demand is through changes in prices and wages, not output and employment. Production will seek the full employment level, regardless of changes in demand.

The classical economists also assumed that savings always equals investment: Everything leaked from the spending stream through savings is returned through the investment injection. This equality always occurs, they reasoned, because changes in the interest rate bring savings and investment into equality.

As indicated earlier, classical theory, with its hands-off attitude toward the economy, was largely abandoned in the 1930s when it could not explain the persistence of the Great Depression or offer a solution to the unemployment problem. In its

The Academic Scribblers

Adam Smith   Adam Smith, considered by many to be the "father" of market economics, or capitalism, was born in 1723 in Scotland. He lived during a time of tremendous change in Britain: The Industrial Revolution brought many economic and social changes.

Smith was a well-known philosopher and academic in his time. Smith's *The Theory of Moral Sentiments*, published in 1759, gave him recognition as he explored the philosophical question of how people, who are basically motivated by self-interest, consider the moral merits of an action.

Smith's most famous work, *The Wealth of Nations*, was revolutionary for its time because it represented a movement from mercantilist thinking to the idea that individual decision making would best serve a society's interests. In this text, Smith focused on the market mechanism and showed how individual self-interest operating through markets provides the greatest good for society. He also discussed the importance of competition in a market system and firmly stated that government should not intervene in the market mechanism. It is these assertions that strongly connect Smith to classical economics.

John Maynard Keynes   John Maynard Keynes, probably the most influential economist of the twentieth century, was born in 1883 in England. John Maynard was well educated, and his first interest was in mathematics. Urging by some distinguished professors sent him in the direction of economics.

Keynes led a full and active life intermingling different careers from a lectureship in economics at Cambridge to successful financial advisor. His interests were varied: He had close ties to the colorful Bloomsbury set of intellectuals, married a ballerina, financed a theater group, and had an extensive art collection.

Although Keynes is well known for his 1919 book, *The Economic Consequences of the Peace*, which discusses the economics of the Versailles Treaty of World War I, his major work is *The General Theory of Employment, Interest and Money*, published in 1936. This book focuses on Keynes' major contribution—that a market economy's

levels of output and employment are the result of the level of aggregate demand. It should be noted that although government interventionist policies are associated with Keynesian economics, Keynes' ideas were rooted in his regard for individualism. The following quote is from *The General Theory*.

> But, above all, individualism, if it can be purged of its defects and its abuses, is the best safeguard of personal liberty in the sense that compared with any other system, it greatly widens the field for the exercise of personal choice. It is also the best safeguard of the variety of life, which emerges precisely from this extended field of personal choice, and the loss of which is the greatest of all losses of the homogeneous or totalitarian state.[a]

Milton Friedman   The work of Milton Friedman is familiar to many Americans: He wrote and lectured in a wide variety of places and made appearances on television talk shows. In 1976, Milton Friedman received the Nobel Prize in economics.

Friedman was born in 1912 in New York to hardworking immigrants. He received his undergraduate degree from Rutgers, went to the University of Chicago for graduate study, and earned his Ph.D. from Columbia University. Friedman eventually returned to an academic post at the University of Chicago, where he remained until 1977.

Milton Friedman's many contributions to economics focused on the importance of money to the operation of the macroeconomy, and he was associated with renewing interest in money and macroeconomic policy. However, he was also known for strongly embracing a free market philosophy and for espousing the view, associated with the Chicago School, that a market economy works best when left alone. In many cases, such as public education, Friedman believed that a competitive market would do a better job and that the government has done more harm than good. Milton Friedman died in 2006.

[a] William Breit and Roger L. Ransom, *The Academic Scribblers*, rev. ed. (Hinsdale, IL: The Dryden Press, 1982), p. 68. Also see John Maynard Keynes, *The General Theory of Employment, Interest and Money* (New York: Harcourt, Brace and Co., 1936), p. 380.

place came Keynesian theory, which advocated managing total demand to attack the problems of unemployment and inflation. Like classical economics in the 1930s, however, Keynesian theory was not wholly successful in explaining the problems of the 1970s when the economy was experiencing high rates of both unemployment and inflation.

KEYNESIAN ECONOMICS

The ideas of the British economist John Maynard Keynes (1883–1946) form the basis for **Keynesian economics**. Keynes, one of the best-known economists of the twentieth century, came to the forefront of economics during the 1930s when prevailing classical theory could not provide a satisfactory explanation for the depression that most industrialized nations in the world faced. Keynes focused on the causes and cures for unemployment and low levels of output. His most famous work, *The General Theory of Employment, Interest and Money*, was published during the Great Depression.[3] Background on Keynes' life and thinking is given in Application 9.2.

Keynes revolutionized economic thinking by focusing on the role of aggregate, or total, spending in the economy. His major contribution was to link increases and decreases in output and employment with increases and decreases in spending. Keynes rejected the classical notion of an automatic adjustment to full employment, reasoning that an economy's output and employment would improve from less than full employment only if aggregate spending increased. Keynes also believed that the spending gap responsible for recessions and unemployment could be filled by the government.

Keynes introduced the idea that a macroeconomy seeks an equilibrium output level, or that there is a level of output toward which an economy moves. Macro-equilibrium could be at a low level of output, which results in unemployment and low incomes, or at a high and healthy level of output. During the Great Depression, conditions were such that the economy was moving toward an equilibrium level that was far below full employment.

Equilibrium in the Macroeconomy

An economy is in **macroeconomic equilibrium** when the amount that all households, businesses, government units, and foreign buyers plan to spend on new goods and services equals the total amount of output the economy is currently producing. At equilibrium there is no tendency for change in the level of economic activity because the planned spending of all buyers is just sufficient to purchase all the goods and services that are produced.

When the amount that households, businesses, government units, and foreign buyers plan to spend on new goods and services differs from the total output produced, the economy is not in equilibrium, and output, employment, and income will change. If the total planned spending of all buyers is greater than current production, then output, employment, and income will increase, assuming that full employment has not been reached. If the total planned spending is less than current production, then output, employment, and income will fall.

The key to understanding how spending can be more or less than current production is in the role played by **inventories**. Most businesses intentionally maintain an inventory of their products. When total spending in the economy is greater than current production, inventories begin to fall, signaling a need to increase output levels. When total spending is less than current production, unintentional inventories begin to accumulate, causing businesses to cut back on production.

Keynesian Economics
Based on the work of John Maynard Keynes (1883–1946), who focused on the role of aggregate spending in determining the level of macroeconomic activity.

Macroeconomic Equilibrium
Occurs when the amount of total planned spending on new goods and services equals total output in the economy.

Inventories
Stocks of goods on hand; can be intentional or unintentional.

[3] John Maynard Keynes, *The General Theory of Employment, Interest and Money* (New York: Harcourt, Brace and Co., 1936).

Illustrating Equilibrium   Table 9.1 illustrates possible levels of total output that a hypothetical economy could produce and the total planned spending of all households, businesses, government units, and foreign buyers that would occur at each level of output at a given point in time. For example, all buyers would purchase $2.5 trillion worth of goods and services at an output level of $2.0 trillion, or $3.5 trillion of goods and services at an output of $4.0 trillion. Total spending increases as output increases because with more output there is more earned income for households to spend.

Notice in Table 9.1 that there is one level of output, $3.0 trillion, where total planned spending equals total output. Here the economy is in equilibrium. At output levels less than $3.0 trillion, planned spending is greater than output; inventories fall, causing businesses to produce more; and the economy expands. At output levels greater than $3.0 trillion, planned spending is less than output; unintentional inventories build up causing businesses to produce less; and the economy contracts toward the equilibrium level of $3.0 trillion.

An important factor determining whether the economy is in equilibrium or expanding or contracting is the relationship between leakages from and injections into the spending stream. (Recall that leakages and injections were discussed in Chapter 5.) When leakages equal injections, the economy is in equilibrium. For example, suppose an economy produces $7 trillion of goods and services, which results in the creation of $7 trillion in income. Assume that from this $7 trillion income, households spend $5 trillion and the rest, $2 trillion, is leaked from the spending stream through saving, taxes, and the purchase of imports. In order to keep the production level unchanged at $7 trillion, or to maintain equilibrium, the entire amount that was leaked must be replaced by injections of an equal amount. That is, $2 trillion in business investment spending, government purchases of goods and services, household spending from transfer payments and borrowing, and/or foreign expenditures on exports must be put into the system.

If the amount that is leaked from the spending stream is greater than the amount injected into the spending stream, the economy will contract. Unintentional inventories

TABLE 9.1	**Total Output and Total Planned Spending (Trillions of Dollars)**

This macroeconomy is in equilibrium at $3.0 trillion, where total output is equal to total planned spending, and injections into the spending stream are equal to leakages.

Total Output	Total Planned Spending	Leakages	Injections	Economic Condition
$0.00	$1.50	$0.00	$1.50	Expansion
0.50	1.75	0.25	1.50	Expansion
1.00	2.00	0.50	1.50	Expansion
1.50	2.25	0.75	1.50	Expansion
2.00	2.50	1.00	1.50	Expansion
2.50	2.75	1.25	1.50	Expansion
3.00	3.00	1.50	1.50	Equilibrium
3.50	3.25	1.75	1.50	Contraction
4.00	3.50	2.00	1.50	Contraction
4.50	3.75	2.25	1.50	Contraction
5.00	4.00	2.50	1.50	Contraction

will build up, and businesses will respond by cutting back on output and employment. On the other hand, if injections are greater than leakages, the size of the spending stream will increase to a level greater than current output. Intentional inventories will fall and businesses will respond by expanding production, assuming that full employment has not yet been reached.

Observe in Table 9.1 the columns Leakages and Injections. Notice that the economy's injections are $1.5 trillion regardless of the level of output. Because injections are independent of earned income, they do not change as output and income change. Because leakages include saving, taxes, and purchases of imports, leakages are $0 when there is no output or income from which to save, pay taxes, or buy imports, and they increase as output and income increase. Notice in the right-hand column of Table 9.1 that the economy expands when injections are greater than leakages, and it contracts when leakages are greater than injections. At equilibrium they are equal.

Figure 9.2 illustrates the information given in Table 9.1. Total output is measured along the horizontal axis and total planned spending along the vertical axis. A 45-degree line is also plotted on this graph. Every point on this line matches a level of output with exactly the same level of spending. For this reason, the line is named the Spending Equals Output line.

The numbers from Table 9.1 showing total planned spending at each level of total output are illustrated by the Total Spending line in Figure 9.2. Notice that the Total Spending line crosses the Spending Equals Output line at exactly $3.0 trillion of output, which is the equilibrium level in Table 9.1. At output levels less than equilibrium, the Total Spending line is above the Spending Equals Output line. Because spending is greater than output, output will increase toward equilibrium. At output levels greater

| **FIGURE 9.2** | *Equilibrium in the Macroeconomy* |

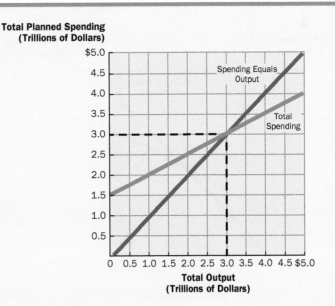

The macroeconomy is in equilibrium at the output level where the Total Spending line crosses the Spending Equals Output line.

than $3.0 trillion, the Total Spending line is below the Spending Equals Output line, causing output to fall toward equilibrium.

The difference between the 45-degree line and the Total Spending line at each level of output is equal to the difference between injections and leakages at that output level. When the Total Spending line is above the 45-degree line, injections are greater than leakages; when it is below, leakages are greater than injections. For example, the Total Spending line is $0.5 trillion above the 45-degree line at an output of $2.0 trillion because, at that output, injections exceed leakages by $0.5 trillion.

Keynesian Policy Prescriptions

Based on this model, Keynes pioneered the idea of using government expenditures and taxes to control the level of economic activity. According to Keynes, the appropriate policy prescription for counteracting a recession is to increase aggregate spending. This can be accomplished by increasing government expenditures on goods and services and/or transfer payments, and/or by lowering taxes. In other words, government can pump in the spending necessary to move the economy out of a recession.

Figure 9.3 illustrates Keynes' ideas about fiscal policy. In the economy in Figure 9.3, full employment would be reached at an output level of $5.0 trillion. Here the Spending Equals Output line becomes vertical to indicate that output cannot exceed $5.0 trillion, even though spending can continue to grow. In Figure 9.3a, the economy is moving toward an equilibrium level of $3.0 trillion, well below the full employment level of $5.0 trillion. In other words, this economy is moving toward an equilibrium with a significant amount of unemployment, or toward a recession.

FIGURE 9.3   *Changes in Macroeconomic Equilibrium*

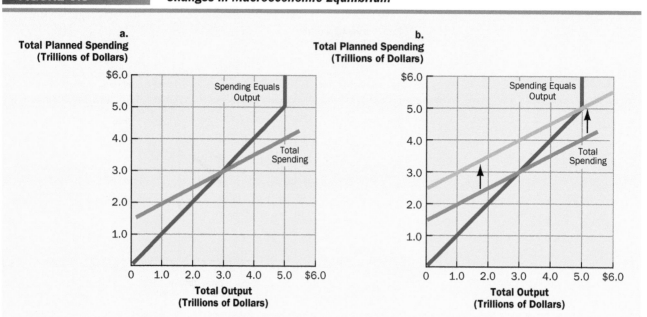

Government fiscal policy can be used to increase total spending in the economy and move equilibrium to a higher level.

To reach full employment, additional spending must be injected into the economy. This could be accomplished by increasing government purchases of goods and services, by increasing transfer payments to give households more money to spend, and/or by decreasing taxes, which also gives households more money to spend. Any of these actions could cause total spending to increase, or the Total Spending line to shift upward.

Figure 9.3b shows the result of fiscal policy actions to move the economy to full employment. In this case, government policies have shifted the Total Spending line upward so that the economy will move toward equilibrium at $5.0 trillion rather than $3.0 trillion, and the economy will experience a recovery rather than a recession.

Keynes believed that because an economy does not automatically seek a full employment level of output, it is appropriate from time to time for government to provide the spending boost that is needed. In other words, an upward shift of the Total Spending line could be government induced.

Keynesian economics reached its peak of popularity during the 1960s. In the early 1970s, however, it became a target for attack. Some argued that the problems of the 1970s could not be explained or remedied in Keynesian terms and that wasteful spending by government and increasing federal government deficits were linked to the Keynesian approach to economic policy.

During the 1980s, the political mood favored a movement away from government intervention in the economy, causing further attacks on Keynesian economics and a renewed interest in other approaches to macroeconomic policy, such as monetarism and new classical economics. In more recent years, there has been increased appreciation for, and application of, the fundamentals of Keynesian economics. In 2008, for example, the federal government sent tax rebate checks to qualifying taxpayers to help ward off a possible recession, and in 2009 an economic stimulus program was enacted. However, the substantial rise in the national debt as a result of the automatic stabilizers, a previous tax cut, the conflicts in Iraq and Afghanistan, as well as the 2008 and 2009 fiscal stimulus programs brought serious criticism over government spending.

NEW CLASSICAL ECONOMICS

Stagflation
Occurs when an economy experiences high rates of both inflation and unemployment.

In the mid-1970s, many of the world's economies began to experience serious inflationary problems. A sudden escalation in the price of oil caused a rapid increase in energy costs, which, in turn, kindled cost-push inflation. For example, fuel costing $17 in 1970 more than doubled in price by 1975 to $36.40 and peaked at $104.60 in 1981. In addition, the trade-off between price changes and unemployment that was traditionally acknowledged no longer applied. In the 1970s and early 1980s, the U.S. economy experienced **stagflation**, or high rates of both unemployment and inflation. In 1975, 1980, and 1981, the U.S. economy's rate of unemployment was between 7.1 and 8.5 percent, while the inflation rate was over 9.1 percent. By comparison, the unemployment and inflation rates in 2014 were 6.2 and 1.4 percent respectively.[4]

New Classical Economics
A return to the basic classical premise that free markets automatically stabilize themselves and that government intervention in the macroeconomy is not advisable.

These economic problems renewed an interest in exploring the relationship between price levels and output, or in returning to the views of the classical school. As a result, **new classical economics** was born.

Many of the basic elements of the classical school can be found in new classical economics. These include an underlying assumption of a free market economy, a

---

[4] *Economic Report of the President* (Washington, DC: U.S. Government Printing Office, 2015), Tables B-3 and B-11. The 2014 inflation rate is preliminary.

model that focuses on output and prices, a downward-sloping aggregate demand curve, and an emphasis on flexible prices. Also, while the classical economists said that the economy tends to operate at full employment, the new classical economists assert that, over the long run, the economy will operate at the **natural rate of unemployment**, or the rate at which there is no cyclical unemployment.[5] Expressed differently, the new classical position maintains there is no trade-off between unemployment and inflation over the long run.

Natural Rate of Unemployment

The rate of unemployment at which there is no cyclical unemployment.

The New Classical Model

Aggregate Demand in the New Classical Model   The aggregate demand curve in the new classical model is illustrated in Figure 9.4. Notice that it is basically the same as the aggregate demand curve in the classical model, with its emphasis on an inverse relationship between price levels and the amount of output demanded in the economy as a whole. With the new classical model, however, comes a more sophisticated explanation of the downward-sloping aggregate demand curve that has some important policy implications. The new classical economists provide three reasons for the downward-sloping curve: the interest rate effect, the wealth effect, and the foreign trade effect.

As overall prices change, the price of money, or the interest rate, also changes. When the interest rate increases along with an increase in overall prices, households and businesses borrow less and spend less, causing less output to be demanded. When the interest rate falls along with a decrease in the general level of prices, households and businesses borrow more and spend more, causing more output to be demanded. The downward slope of the aggregate demand curve is, therefore, shaped to a large

| **FIGURE 9.4** | *Aggregate Demand in the New Classical Model* |

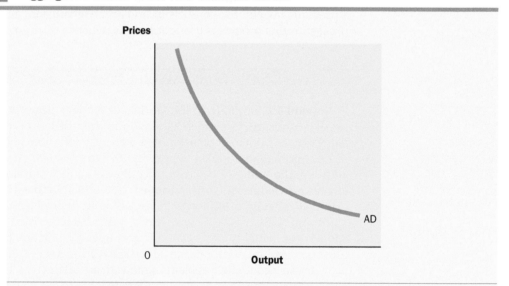

The aggregate demand curve in the new classical model is downward sloping and is based on the interest rate, wealth, and foreign trade effects.

[5] Be sure not to confuse the natural rate of unemployment with the full employment rate of unemployment, which includes only the frictionally unemployed. Review Chapter 4 for further information on these concepts.

extent by this relationship between the interest rate and spending, which is called the **interest rate effect** on aggregate demand.

Interest Rate Effect

The interest rate moves with changes in overall prices; there is an inverse relationship between the interest rate and the amount people borrow and spend.

People typically have some level of money wealth that they have accumulated and want to maintain. This includes, for example, cash, bonds, certificates of deposit, and such. When prices increase, the value of this accumulated wealth falls, and as prices decrease, the value of this accumulated wealth increases. In order to maintain the same value of money wealth, people will spend less when prices increase and more when prices fall. Again, the amount of output demanded increases with more spending and falls with less spending. The impact on the aggregate demand curve caused by changes in the value of money wealth is called the **wealth effect**.

Wealth Effect

In order to maintain the same amount of accumulated wealth, people spend less when prices rise and more when prices fall.

As prices rise in the economy, people may turn to lower-priced imports, and as prices fall, people will likely buy fewer imports. This **foreign trade effect** provides another reason for the downward-sloping aggregate demand curve: As prices rise, spending on the domestic output of goods and services falls because spending is diverted to imports; and as prices fall, spending on domestically produced goods and services rises because spending is diverted from imports.

Foreign Trade Effect

There is a direct relationship between changes in overall prices in an economy and spending on imports that diverts spending from domestically produced output.

Aggregate Supply in the New Classical Model   The aggregate supply curve in the new classical model can be viewed in two ways: short-run supply with three phases or long-run supply. Figure 9.5a gives the short-run aggregate supply curve in this model. At low levels of output, the aggregate supply curve is perfectly horizontal. In this range, output levels are so low that output will increase without any change in prices. At some point, however, a direct relationship between prices and output occurs: Increases in output are accompanied by increases in the overall price level. Finally, at a high level of output, where the economy is producing at its capacity, the supply

FIGURE 9.5   *Aggregate Supply in the New Classical Model*

Aggregate supply in the new classical model can be viewed in a short-run or a long-run time frame.

curve becomes perfectly vertical. Here the output level stays the same regardless of the level of prices.

The second view of the aggregate supply curve in the new classical model is the long-run view, illustrated in Figure 9.5b. Here the aggregate supply curve is similar to that of the classical school and is perfectly vertical at the natural rate of unemployment. In this long-run view, the economy moves toward the natural rate of unemployment and prices are flexible upward and downward.

Manipulating Aggregate Demand and Supply   The level of prices and output toward which an economy moves depends on whether aggregate demand and supply are viewed in the short run or the long run. In Figure 9.5a, where the short-run view is taken, a shift of the aggregate demand curve to the left, from AD0 to AD1, brings about a decrease in output and prices. If AD1 shifted farther to the left to the flat portion of the supply curve, output would decrease but prices would not be affected. A shift to the right, from AD0 to AD2, brings about an increase in prices and output. If AD2 shifted farther to the right and intersected the vertical portion of the supply curve, price levels would rise but output would not be affected.

In Figure 9.5b, where the long-run view is taken, a shift of the aggregate demand curve in either direction brings a change in the price level but no change in output. In the long-run view, output is at the natural rate of unemployment and prices are flexible in either direction.

The Long Run and Policy Implications   The policy implications of this long-run view are important because they suggest that the government should keep its hands off the economy. Any efforts to manipulate aggregate demand will, over the long run, result in no improvement in the level of unemployment but may cause the price level to rise. The ineffectiveness of government policies in reducing unemployment below its natural rate is called the **natural rate hypothesis**.

This long-run view of the new classical school is supported by the argument that households and businesses have expectations about how the economy should perform—especially with regard to inflation. The expectations may be **adaptive expectations** based on past and current experiences, or they may be **rational expectations** based on an understanding by households and businesses of how they would be affected by proposed government policies. Either way, because of these expectations, households and businesses act in ways that benefit themselves but undermine the intentions of policymakers.

Suppose, for example, that the government follows policies intended to lower unemployment below its natural rate. In the process of moving toward this goal, more demand is added to the economy, which only causes the price level to increase. In other words, government policies to shift the aggregate demand curve to the right result in no change in unemployment but increase the price level. This effect, shown in Figure 9.5b by a shift in aggregate demand from AD0 to AD2, results because households and businesses respond to the expectation of rising prices and weakening purchasing power by negotiating higher wages and raising their prices.

Test Your Understanding, "Classical, Keynesian, and New Classical Models," gives you an opportunity to strengthen your knowledge about these three important economic schools of thought.

Natural Rate Hypothesis
Over the long run, unemployment will tend toward its natural rate, and policies to reduce unemployment below that level will be ineffective.

Adaptive Expectations
Households and businesses base their expectations of the future on past and current experiences.

Rational Expectations
Households and businesses base their expectations of future policies on how they think they will be affected by those policies.

TEST YOUR UNDERSTANDING

CLASSICAL,
KEYNESIAN,
AND NEW
CLASSICAL
MODELS

1. Using the graph below, draw an aggregate demand
    curve and an aggregate supply curve that represent
    the classical model of an economy operating at full
    employment. Label these as D and S.
    a. Label the price and wage level at which the
        economy is operating as $P_0 W_0$.
    b. Draw a second aggregate demand curve
        showing a decrease in demand. Label that
        curve D1.
    c. Identify the level of output and level of prices
        and wages that would result when the economy
        fully adjusted to the decrease in demand. Label
        the new price and wage level $P_1 W_1$.
    d. Explain how the economy arrived at its new
        position.

Prices and
Wages

0   Full Employment
                 Output

2. Fill in the following table, indicating where equilibrium
    output occurs as well as where the economy expands
    and where it contracts. On the accompanying graph,
    illustrate two lines. First, draw a "Spending equals
    Output" line and label it. Second, illustrate the
    relationship between "Total Spending" and "Total
    Output" in the table. All figures are in billions.

Total Output	Total Spending	Leakages	Injections	Economic Condition
$0	$240	$0	$240	_____
200	360	80	240	_____
400	480	160	240	_____
600	600	240	240	_____
800	720	320	240	_____
1,000	840	400	240	_____

Total Spending
(Billions of Dollars)

Total Output (Billions of Dollars)

3. In the graphs below, draw the new classical aggre-
    gate supply in the short run and in the long run.
    a. Draw a new classical demand curve in each of
        the graphs. Explain the changes in prices and
        output that would result from a decrease in this
        demand curve.

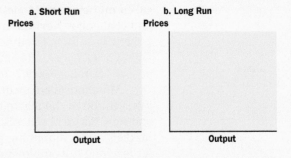

a. Short Run
Prices

Output

b. Long Run
Prices

Output

ADDITIONAL MACROECONOMIC MODELS

New Keynesian Economics

Keynesians, unlike the classical and new classical economists, saw the economy as not automatically returning to full employment once unemployment occurred. Building on this foundation, and responding to challenges to the Keynesian view that developed after the 1960s, economists known as new Keynesians went about explaining why the economy could persistently operate at less than full employment.

What distinguishes **new Keynesian economics** from its rival schools of macroeconomic thought—especially classical and new classical economics—is how each views the behavior of prices. While classical and new classical economists regard prices and wages as flexible, new Keynesian economists regard them as inflexible, or "sticky," downward. For this reason, new Keynesians do not think prices can be relied on to quickly drop and counter the adverse effects on employment that can result from a decrease in aggregate demand. Rather, because prices and wages are sticky downward, decreases in aggregate demand lead to adjustments on the supply side of the economy in the form of reductions in output and employment. Expressed differently, because prices do not drop, there is no mechanism to ensure that full employment will automatically be restored.

Another distinguishing feature of new Keynesian economics is the attention it pays to decision making by individual firms, or decision making in the microeconomy. One important explanation for the downward inflexibility of prices and wages is that firms set their prices based on what is necessary to maximize their own profits, not on the basis of what is occurring in the economy at large. The fact that individual sellers can resist pressures to lower their prices and may find it most profitable to decrease output when aggregate demand weakens helps explain why unemployment can persist in the economy.

Monetarism

Another school of thought significant to macroeconomic theory is **monetarism**. Those who focus on the money supply and advocate altering it to stabilize the economy are called **monetarists**. Monetarism was a popular viewpoint in the 1970s and early 1980s and challenges Keynesian fiscal policy prescriptions. Monetarism's best-known proponent is Milton Friedman (1912–2006), whose association with the University of Chicago leads some to label followers of his thinking as members of the "Chicago School." Application 9.2 provides some background on Friedman.

Monetarists are inclined to favor free markets and advocate limited government intervention in the macroeconomy. In this sense, they tend to align with the classical and new classical schools. Typically, a monetarist would suggest that allowing free markets and maintaining proper control over the money supply is the ideal strategy for reaching full employment or avoiding demand-pull inflation.

Supply-Side Economics

A discussion of alternative macroeconomic viewpoints would not be complete without some mention of **supply-side economics**, which was born in the late 1970s, popularized by its association with President Ronald Reagan and "Reaganomics," and resurfaces on occasion. The basic idea behind supply-side economics is to stimulate the supply side of economic activity by creating government policies that provide incentives for individuals and businesses to increase their productive efforts.

New Keynesian Economics
Builds on the Keynesian view that the economy does not automatically return to full employment; emphasizes downward sticky prices and individual decision making in the microeconomy.

Monetarism
School of thought that favors stabilizing the economy through controlling the money supply.

Monetarists
Persons who favor the economic policies of monetarism.

Supply-Side Economics
Policies to achieve macroeconomic goals by stimulating the supply side of the market; popular in the 1980s.

SHOULD GOVERNMENT'S ROLE IN INFLUENCING ECONOMIC ACTIVITY BE REDUCED?

Issue   *One place where classical and new classical economics on the one hand, and Keynesian and new Keynesian economics on the other, part company is the desirability of an active role by government in keeping the economy as close as possible to a noninflationary, full employment level of output. Should the federal government play a less active role in stabilizing the macroeconomy?*

Yes   Government should play a less active role in stabilizing the economy. A major point of classical and new classical economics should be heeded: The economy, if left alone, will tend to operate at its full (or natural) employment output level. Overall price and employment levels are of greatest concern in the economy. If government views its primary responsibility as keeping markets as free as

possible, the resulting movement of wages and prices should lead to the adjustments necessary to ensure natural or full employment levels.

A large, interventionist government, rather than solving macroeconomic problems, could add to them because it is reacting in an untimely way, or to the wrong signals, or on behalf of special interests rather than the overall interests of the economy.

No   Government should not play a less active role in stabilizing the economy. According to Keynesian theory, there is no reason to expect an economy, left alone, to automatically reach a full employment level of output. According to Keynes, unemployment, or a recession, arises from a lack of total spending.

Unless total spending increases, or a spending "kick" occurs, the economy can remain stagnant. Since there is nothing inherent in the economy to ensure that this spending increase will occur, government is the logical choice to take the actions necessary to increase spending. It is efficient to give government the authority to lead the way. The wait for millions of decisions by individual households and businesses to spend more could be endless.

The best-known supply-side argument is to lower taxes for businesses and individuals. Lowering taxes on businesses would make investments in buildings, equipment, and such more profitable, thereby stimulating growth in the economy. Lowering the tax burden on individuals is said to lead to greater savings (which could be channeled to businesses for investment purposes) and increased personal incentives to work. Government deregulation is also called for to increase productivity. Supply-side proposals have a political as well as an economic dimension. Reducing taxes and regulatory requirements lessens the presence of government in private economic decision making.

The issue of how much government intervention in the macroeconomy is appropriate is a source of continuous debate. The position taken on this issue is often rooted in one of the theories just discussed. Up for Debate, "Should Government's Role in Influencing Economic Activity Be Reduced?" presents some of the arguments for and against government intervention.

A FINAL WORD ON MACROECONOMIC VIEWPOINTS

By the end of this chapter, you have a good foundation for understanding macroeconomic theories and their relevance for solving macroeconomic problems. You have learned about past and present schools of economic thought that have made significant contributions to our understanding of the operation of the macroeconomy. Ideally, this chapter has provided the groundwork for informed judgments about past, present, and future efforts to understand and stabilize the economy.

It is helpful to keep in mind the discussion at the beginning of this chapter: An economic theory focuses on the relationship between two variables, and assumptions play an important role in the development of an economic theory. No theory is designed to explain all the complex relationships among the players and institutions in a macro-economy. Furthermore, the economy is not composed of a set of simple relationships that can be easily manipulated to neatly solve various problems as they arise. One can be misled into thinking that a simple policy choice can cure all economic problems. In reality, there are many ramifications to choosing an economic theory as the basis for remedying an economic problem. Accordingly, the assumptions that underlie the theory should be known, as should the consequences that could result from implementing policy based on the theory.

Macroeconomic theories and policy instruments must be updated and refined as conditions change and knowledge grows. The environment in which models are built and policy tools are employed is continually changing, and new data, questions, and issues constantly appear. Also, the task of assessing economic theories would be easier if we lived in **closed economies**, where events beyond a country's borders have no effect on its output, employment, prices, or policies. The reality is that we live in **open economies**, which are influenced by actions in countries around the world. Political unrest in the Middle East, reaction to the North American Free Trade Agreement (NAFTA), developments in China, and other circumstances outside the United States impact the U.S. economy and policies to stabilize it. As commercial relationships become more global and the economy becomes more open, the need to refine and update our knowledge becomes even greater. It is risky to assume that an understanding of the way things operate today will be sufficient to deal with the problems of the future.

Application 9.3, "The World According to . . . ," offers some additional thoughts about macroeconomic models and macroeconomists.

Closed Economy
An economy where foreign influences have no effect on output, employment, and prices.

Open Economy
An economy where foreign influences have an effect on output, employment, and prices.

APPLICATION 9.3

THE WORLD ACCORDING TO . . .

A major economy in today's global playing field is so complex that it can be mind-boggling to try to sort out the factors and relationships that provide for an economy's healthy growth and good jobs and incomes or spin it into a downward spiral. Trying to understand how the pieces of this gigantic and important puzzle called an economy fit together is the lifetime work of many macroeconomists as they explore and build theoretical relationships. Some of their research seems to be on target and has staying power in the profession's catalog of important contributions.

It is often the emergence of a major problem or issue, such as the Great Depression or prolonged high rates of inflation, that is the impetus for macroeconomic problem solving. And sometimes the discovery of and data proof of a cause-and-effect relationship holds up in the short-term but becomes debatable with time. The Phillips curve is one example.

In 1958, William Phillips popularized the idea that there was an inverse relationship between rates of inflation and rates of unemployment: low unemployment was associated with high inflation and vice versa. Over the years, this simplistic idea has shown to be true in some short-term data aggregations. But there have been many rebuttals by well-known economists who have created variations on the Phillips curve from their research and have framed both short-term and long-term alternative Phillips curves. Other economists are reviving the basic tenet of the relationship and incorporating it into new models.

What economists know in their theorizing is that short-term and long-term viewpoints and relationships can be different. What might be true over the period of a few years might not hold true if you take a long view. This further complicates the understanding of puzzle pieces and how to recommend policy proposals that might be needed to address short-term problems.

Finally, let us not forget that economists are just like the rest of us even though many folks believe that economists are wired a little differently. We are all driven by our values and those values play a role in what we regard as the ideal world. Beliefs about the importance of free markets versus government intervention, the rights of the individual versus the rights of society, and other beliefs influence how and what we think. We see those different thought processes in research, textbooks, and classroom presentations. During a stint as department chair, one of the coauthors of this text had to deal with a part-time faculty member who eliminated all material in his basic macroeconomics course but monetarism. When questioned about the narrow view given to his students, the response was simply "I don't believe that any other theories are valid."

Summary

1. Economic theory focuses on the relationship between two variables. Economic theories are explored within the context of a model that includes variables, assumptions, data collection and analysis, and conclusions. Because economic theories are often an attempt to identify the cause of an economic problem, macroeconomic theories frequently have an historical dimension.

2. There are several schools of thought important to the development and understanding of macroeconomics. These include classical, Keynesian, new classical, new Keynesian, and monetarism.

3. Classical economics was the prevailing school of thought prior to the 1930s and the Great Depression. The classical aggregate demand–aggregate supply model focuses on the relationship between price and wage levels and output levels. This model concludes that a free market economy's output level always self-corrects to full employment and that prices and wages increase and decrease with changes in aggregate demand. Increases in aggregate demand bring increases in prices and wages, and decreases in aggregate demand bring decreases in prices and wages.

4. Keynesian economics gained prominence during the 1930s when John Maynard Keynes introduced the ideas that a macroeconomy can move toward an equilibrium output level that is less than full employment and that no mechanism is built into the economy to automatically move it toward full employment. Keynes focused on the role of total spending in the economy, indicating that the equilibrium output level of an economy is a direct result of the level of total spending in the economy.

5. Macroequilibrium occurs in the Keynesian model when total spending equals total current output, or when the leakages from and injections into the spending stream are equal. When spending is greater than the current level of output, which is caused by injections exceeding leakages, the economy expands. When spending is less than the current level of output, which is caused by leakages exceeding injections, the economy contracts. Keynes advocated government intervention, or fiscal policy, to move the economy from equilibrium at low levels of output to equilibrium at a higher full employment level of output.

6. New classical economics was born in the 1970s when many of the world's economies experienced stagflation and Keynesian economics could not offer an explanation for the serious inflation. New classical economics focuses on an aggregate demand–aggregate supply model similar to the classical model. Aggregate demand is represented by a downward-sloping curve showing an inverse relationship between the levels of price and output demanded based on interest rate, wealth, and foreign trade effects.

7. New classical aggregate supply can be viewed in the short run or long run. In the short run, prices do not change at low levels of output, a direct relationship exists between prices and output in the intermediate range, and at high levels of output prices are flexible upward and downward and output does not change. The long-run view of aggregate supply is based on the natural rate

hypothesis: The economy moves toward the natural rate of unemployment as price changes bring aggregate demand into equality with aggregate supply. The new classical school advocates little government intervention in the economy because adaptive and rational expectations by households and businesses undermine the intentions of policymakers.

8. New Keynesian economics builds on the Keynesian view, emphasizes the inflexibility of prices and wages downward, and attempts to better connect macroeconomics to microeconomic decision making. New Keynesians also stress that the macroeconomy does not automatically adjust to full employment.

9. The monetarist school of thought focuses on the role of money in the economy and advocates changing the money supply to stabilize the macroeconomy. Supply-side economics focuses on policies to increase production and productivity.

10. In evaluating macroeconomic theories and policies, we must continually update our thinking to meet changing conditions. The economy is not composed of simple relationships that allow for neat solutions to economic problems. It must be remembered that individual economic theories focus on specific variables and that all theories are built on underlying assumptions.

Key Terms and Concepts

Classical economics
Keynesian economics
Macroeconomic equilibrium
Inventories
Stagflation
New classical economics
Natural rate of
  unemployment
Interest rate effect
Wealth effect

Foreign trade effect
Natural rate hypothesis
Adaptive expectations
Rational expectations
New Keynesian economics
Monetarism
Monetarists
Supply-side economics
Closed economy
Open economy

Review Questions

1. Identify the four basic components used to develop a model and explain how macroeconomic models can be influenced by history.

2. Show how the classical economists thought about aggregate supply by drawing a classical aggregate supply curve on the graph that follows. Explain why they believed that this represented the economy.

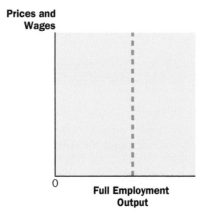

Prices and Wages

0

Full Employment Output

3. Draw an aggregate demand curve for the classical school on the graph above. Explain what happens in the economy when this demand increases and illustrate it on the graph above.

4. Fill in the column below (where all figures are in billions) by indicating whether the economy is expanding, contracting, or at equilibrium. On the graph following, draw a "Spending equals Output" line and a line showing "Total Spending." Explain the relationship between these lines at output levels of $600 and $1,800 billion.

Total Output	Total Spending	Leakages	Injections	Economic Condition
$0	$400	$0	$400	_____
300	600	100	400	_____
600	800	200	400	_____
900	1,000	300	400	_____
1,200	1,200	400	400	_____
1,500	1,400	500	400	_____
1,800	1,600	600	400	_____

Total Spending (Billions of Dollars)

$1,800
1,500
1,200
900
600
300

0   300   600   900   1,200 1,500 $1,800

Total Output (Billions of Dollars)

5. Using the information from number 4 above, explain how the relationship between Leakages and Injections influences the economic conditions in the last column.

6. Explain how interest rate, wealth, and foreign trade effects are important to aggregate demand in the new classical model.

7. What is the difference between short-run and long-run aggregate supply in the new classical model?

8. Fill in the following table by providing, for each listed school of thought, the variables on which the theory is built, the conclusions with regard to the macro-economy, and the role of government intervention advocated.

School of Thought	Variables	Conclusions	Government Intervention
Classical			
New classical			
Keynesian			

Discussion Questions

1. "When the economy is facing high rates of unemployment and inflation, policymakers must decide which of these problems to curb at the expense of the other." Is this statement accurate? What types of information should policymakers seek before deciding to sacrifice employment for price stability or price stability for employment?

2. Would you consider yourself to be classical, new classical, Keynesian, new Keynesian, monetarist, or other in your attitude toward macroeconomic policies? On what reasoning is your preference based?

3. What is the natural rate hypothesis and what problems does it cause for those wishing to pursue aggressive macroeconomic policies? What problems might adaptive and rational expectations cause for the government in its macroeconomic policymaking?

4. Macroeconomic policy proposals are frequently tied to political agendas. In your opinion, which of the policies that you have studied is politically the most desirable, and which is the least desirable? Explain.

5. Just as macroeconomic problems affect economic theory, they also affect the arts—visual art, music, and literature—of the day. Give an example of how a piece of visual art, a song, a novel, or a poem reflects the state of the macro-economy at the time it was created.

6. How do the assumptions underlying the various theories you have studied in this chapter help to explain why debates on the proper role of government in macro-economic activity can become so heated?

7. One lesson from this chapter is that the popularity of an economic theory depends in part on its ability to offer solutions for current, pressing problems. Because economic theories move in and out of fashion as conditions change, does this mean that they are not scientific after all?

Critical Thinking Case 9

DOES ANYONE CARE WHAT ECONOMISTS THINK?

Critical Thinking Skills

Identifying real-world implications from seemingly unreal-world concepts

Recognizing and evaluating values underlying technical arguments

Economic Concepts

Full employment—automatic or not

Government's role in managing the economy

We've just gone through several macroeconomic theories. In exploring these theories you have put up with graphs, theory-makers' assumptions, technical terms such as natural rate of unemployment, and radically differing views on how the world works. These theories are abstract and often contradictory. So much so that George Bernard Shaw said that if you laid all economists end to end you'd never arrive at a conclusion, and John Maynard Keynes hoped for the day when economists would be thought of as humble, competent people—like dentists.[a] Given all this, it is entirely reasonable to ask: "Why would policymakers or others in important decision-making positions pay any attention to what economists say?"

[a] John Maynard Keynes, *Essays in Persuasion* (New York: W.W. Norton, 1963), p. 373.

Questions

1. Do you think policymakers pay attention to ideas like those we have seen in this chapter?
2. Each of the theories in this chapter directly or indirectly takes a position on what public officials should or should not be doing about the macroeconomy. Which of these theories would be supported by an administration wishing to actively manage the economy? Which would be opposed?
3. Is it possible to develop a value-free economic theory? Is it possible to follow a policy that is compatible with all of the theories in this chapter?
4. Do you think policymakers are more likely to stick with long-accepted theories that they know or more likely to readily adopt new theories that address the problem at hand?

10

Households and Businesses: An Overview

CHAPTER OBJECTIVES

Provide a fundamental overview of household income and expenditures.

Explore the basic objective of economic decision making by individuals and the balancing process involved in spending and earning decisions.

Provide a fundamental overview of business including legal forms and business ownership of other businesses.

Discuss the goals and decisions of business firms around profit maximization.

This chapter begins the study of microeconomics. While microeconomics and macroeconomics are the two major divisions in studying the field and share the common language and model-building techniques of economics, their focus is quite different. Macroeconomics looks at the total economy and how it functions, and studies the economic behavior of groups such as households, businesses, and government units. Microeconomics looks at decision making and how it influences the behavior of individuals in households and businesses.

This chapter is designed to give you background information about households and businesses before we do an in-depth study of microeconomic concepts. It is helpful first to know some basic terminology, explore some data, and understand the economic objectives of decision making within households and businesses.

OVERVIEW OF HOUSEHOLDS

When economists and others collect and analyze information about the U.S. population, they often categorize these data by individuals, families, or households. For example, data tell us that in 2013, the population of the United States was about 316 million persons: 156 million men and 160 million women. The average age was 38 years old and most people lived in urban areas.[1]

People are included in family statistics only when two or more related individuals live together. As a consequence, many people are left out of family data. Household data are more inclusive, and usually preferable, since a **household** is made up of a person living alone or a group of related or unrelated persons who occupy a "housing unit," such as a house or an apartment. (Jails, military barracks, and college dorms do not count.)

In 2013, there were about 122 million households in the United States. The average size was about 2.5 persons (a slight decline in size over the past two decades) and about 27 percent of all households had just one person (a slight increase over the past two decades).[2]

Household Income and Expenditures

Do you remember the circular flow model in Chapter 2? In this model, households sell factors of production, like labor, for income, and use that income to buy goods and services. Since much economic decision making in household units revolves around these two areas, it is helpful to know something about the sources and sizes of household income and the types of expenditures that households make.

Household Income   Table 10.1 lists the sources of household pretax income, or **personal income**, on a percentage basis for selected years. The figures show that labor income is the primary source of household income and that fluctuations have occurred over the past few decades in the relative importance of all other income sources.

Table 10.1 also shows the importance of transfer payments in providing income: They were about 17 percent of personal income in 2015. Recall from Chapter 5 that **transfer payments** are money received from the government for which no direct work is performed in return. Government transfer payments include Social Security, unemployment, temporary disability, veterans' and public retirement benefits, public assistance, and others. A large amount of transfer payments in any given year goes to those covered under the Social Security Act.

How large is average household income? How much does it differ from household to household because of the gender, age, or education of the head of the household? The answers are in Table 10.2. The average income for all households in 2012 was $51,017, and there were significant differences among the average incomes for households when certain characteristics were observed. For example, family households headed by a married couple averaged $75,694, while families headed by a female (with no spouse present) averaged $34,002. Not surprisingly, household income was lower for older adults who may be retired from the labor force. It is also important to notice the effect of education on average income. Households headed by a person with a bachelor's degree on average earned twice as much as households headed by a high school graduate.

Household
A person living alone or a group of related or unrelated persons who occupy a house, an apartment, or other housing unit.

Personal Income
Household gross, or pretax, income; used to pay taxes, spend, and save.

Transfer Payments
Money from the government for which no direct work is performed in return.

---

[1] ProQuest Statistical Abstract of the U.S. Online Edition, Tables 6, 25.
[2] Ibid., Table 61.

TABLE 10.1   *Sources of Personal Income (Percentage Distribution for Selected Years)*

Since 1990 there have been slight changes in the relative importance of income sources. Labor income and transfer payments are the largest.

Source of Income	1990	2000	2010	2015
Earned income				
Wages, salaries, and other labor income	68.6%	67.6%	64.4%	62.8%
Proprietor's income	7.5	9.6	8.4	9.2
Rental income	1.0	2.5	2.8	4.4
Dividends	3.5	4.4	5.8	6.0
Interest	15.5	11.5	8.1	8.2
Unearned income				
Transfer payments	12.3	12.7	18.4	17.3
Personal contributions for social insurance[a]	−8.5	−8.2	−8.0	−8.0
Personal income[b]	100.0	100.0	100.0	100.0

[a] Contributions for social insurance are subtracted from earned income in calculating personal income.

[b] Columns may not total 100.0 because of rounding.

Source: *Economic Report of the President* (Washington, DC: U.S. Government Printing Office, 2012), pp. 352–353; Bureau of Economic Analysis, Table 2.1, Personal Income and Its Disposition, www.bea.gov, 05/29/2015. Figures are for the first quarter of 2015.

Household Expenditures   Basically, households use their incomes for three purposes: spending, paying taxes, and saving. The majority of income goes to spending: In early 2015 households used about 83 percent of their gross or personal income for personal outlays like goods and servcies, over 12 percent for personal taxes, and 5.5 percent for saving.[3] These figures, however, are on the aggregate and can be misleading. Households with higher incomes pay more taxes and save more, while households with lower incomes pay fewer taxes and may not save at all.

There is a wealth of data about the annual expenditures of consumer units which is frequently mined by researchers of consumer spending patterns, by macroeconomists, and by analysts for companies looking to increase their sales of a product. For example, data can be found to indicate how much the average consumer expends for food, transportation, housing pensions, and more.

When we look at how households spend their money, a popular way to classify expenditures is by whether they are for durable goods, nondurable goods, or services. A **durable good** has a useful lifetime of more than one year—a car, musical instrument, or furniture, for example. A **nondurable good** has a short span of use, such as food or gasoline. In recent years, the largest portion of household expenditures has gone for services—medical care, for example. In early 2015, people, on average, used about 68 percent of total expenditures for services, 21 percent for nondurable goods, and 11 percent for durable goods.[4] The percentages in these categories have not stayed constant over time; spending for services has been continually increasing.

Durable Good
A good that has a useful lifetime of more than one year.

Nondurable Good
A good that has a short useful lifetime.

[3] Bureau of Economic Analysis, Table 2.1, Personal Income and Its Disposition, www.bea.gov, 06/16/2015. Figures are for the first quarter of 2015.
[4] Ibid.

TABLE 10.2	*Average Money Income of Households*[a]

The average income of households differs according to the gender, age, and education of the household head.

Characteristic	Average Income
All households	$51,017
Family headed by a married couple	75,694
Family headed by a female—spouse absent	34,002
Household head aged 25–34 years	51,381
Household head aged 65 years or older	33,848
Household head, high school graduate	39,845
Household head with bachelor's degree	80,549

[a] The average used is the median.

Source: Proquest Statistical Abstract of the U.S. 2015 Online Edition, Table 714.

GOALS AND DECISION MAKING BY INDIVIDUALS

Maximizing Economic Well-Being

Think about all of the economic decisions that you make during a semester. Many of them are minor, like the choices between water and soda or chips and cookies from a vending machine; and many are major, like the choice of coursework, a place to live, or the kind of job to take on. During our lives all of us are constantly faced with decisions about how to use our money and our time. What is it that we are looking for as we make all of these decisions?

At first it might appear that there are a lot of different objectives that individuals could have when making economic decisions. But economists see all these decisions as ultimately coming down to one basic objective: Individuals try to obtain the most satisfaction possible from their decisions. In other words, people are out to maximize their economic well-being.

What do we mean by **maximizing our economic well-being**? Does it mean that we try to acquire all the goods and services that can possibly be obtained or that every waking hour is spent working in order to make lots of money? We derive satisfaction from the things we buy, the things we do, and the decisions we make. Some students really enjoy a cup of coffee in the morning; some dislike coffee. Some people enjoy their work; others find it mildly satisfying. Some students find economics fascinating; some find communications more attractive. And we can go on with many examples. The point is that everyone has things they enjoy more than others and things they dislike.

Maximizing economic well-being is a balancing process. It involves weighing the advantages, or benefits, and the disadvantages, or costs, of different courses of action and selecting the one that contributes most to economic satisfaction. In other words, people compare the satisfaction they get from various actions with the cost of those

Maximizing Economic Well-Being

Obtaining the greatest possible satisfaction, or return, from an economic decision.

actions in making their choices. This notion of balancing costs and benefits in order to maximize economic well-being should become clearer as we apply it to basic spending and earning decisions.

Maximizing Satisfaction from Consuming Goods and Services   With limited incomes, people can't have all of the goods and services they want. This is the individual's own version of the basic economic problem of scarcity: limited resources in comparison to the wants and needs to be satisfied. In Chapter 1, we learned that scarcity imposes decisions and choices: Individuals must choose how to use their limited incomes.

Economists refer to the satisfaction received from consuming (buying) a good or service as **utility**. When you buy a lunch or put gas in your car, for example, you receive utility. The goal of an individual in making spending decisions is to choose the combination of goods and services that gives maximum total satisfaction, or maximum **total utility**, for a given amount of income spent. To maximize total **utility**, a person must, for each good or service that could be purchased, weigh the satisfaction that can be obtained from consuming that good or service against its price. This decision-making process can be illustrated through some simple examples.

Suppose that you are at a sporting event and would like a large, hot pretzel and a soda. All you have is $3, and the pretzel costs $3 and the soda costs $3. What will you buy? Obviously, you will spend your money on the good that adds the greatest amount of satisfaction. If it's the pretzel, you spend $3 for the pretzel; if it's the soda, that is where your money goes. To maximize satisfaction, your $3 will be spent on the thing that adds the most for the money to your total utility.

In this example, the choice is easy because the prices are the same. But what happens when a person is choosing among goods with different prices? Suppose that someone has $100 to spend and would like to get a pizza for $20, go out to dinner for $25, buy $50 worth of hockey tickets, upgrade a cell phone for $100, and buy a $10 paperback. With so many choices and just $100, what should this person buy?

Before making a decision, this person will weigh the added satisfaction from each item *in comparison to the dollars spent on that item*. If the entire $100 is spent for a cell phone, satisfaction will be maximized only if that phone adds more than twice the satisfaction from the $50 hockey tickets, more than five times the satisfaction from the $20 pizza, more than four times the satisfaction from the $25 dinner, and so on.

The Utility–Price Rule   A simple rule emerges from the two preceding examples. To maximize total utility from spending a given income, a buyer must weigh the additional utility received from each good against the money spent on that good. In deciding between a pretzel and soda, you would have spent your $3 on the item that gave the greatest satisfaction for the money. In allocating $100 among the various alternative goods that could have been purchased in the previous example, the buyer would have weighed the added utility received from each item against its price.

Maximizing utility is not simply a matter of receiving more satisfaction from one item than another: It is a matter of receiving more satisfaction *for the money*. While a person who is car shopping might get a lot of satisfaction from a new hybrid, the price tag is likely higher than that of a used car. Total satisfaction might be greater by buying a used car plus all of the other goods and services that the lower-priced car allows the

Utility
Satisfaction realized from consuming a good or service.

Total Utility
Total satisfaction from consuming a particular combination of goods and services.

APPLICATION 10.1

FAMILY GOSSIP

We all know that collection of assorted relatives—aunts, uncles, grandparents, cousins—who come together for family holidays, birthdays, reunions, and, of course, weddings. Seldom are these events without a good dose of family discussion, or plain and simple family gossip. Take the recent wedding of Jennifer, daughter of Fred and Lynne who spent a year planning the "perfect" day, not to mention the small fortune—almost a year of Lynne's salary—they put out.

At a table of close relatives, enjoying that perfect wedding dinner and reception, the whispering commentary ranged from choices about clothing to food and, of course, the money that was wisely or unwisely (in their opinion) spent. That's the way with family gossip: The genes that make relatives somewhat biologically alike do not necessarily make them alike in their decision making.

"I can't believe that Jen's plain dress cost $4,000! This didn't even include the shopping weekend in New York so that she and Lynne could get a big name designer dress. She could have looked just as beautiful in a dress bought at our local bridal shop for a fraction of that price, and at least it would have had some lace and sequins," reported an observing aunt. "I could have found plenty of uses for that money. Fred and Lynne are always complaining about their old furniture. I say—they should have bought the furniture. It lasts for years. That dress is for one day."

Later the discussion turned to the reception. One cousin commented, "Those big baskets of roses and lilies on every table are a showy waste. Smaller arrangements would have been just as tasteful. It was enough that the church was decked out with enormous vases and sprays and garlands. Another cousin said, "I love, love, love the flowers. They have created the most perfect scene for the occasion."

And so it went. One uncle wished for cheaper fried chicken rather than the tenderloin and shrimp; someone else praised the champagne. The wedding cake was dry but delightfully decorated, a DJ would have worked rather than spending all that money on a live band, ... And everyone noted that when it was all over, the happy couple was moving into a small apartment. The price tag on this wedding was the equivalent of a huge down payment on a home.

The satisfaction we receive from various goods and services drives our spending decisions—and we are all different. Over our lifetime we will go to weddings big and small, some in parks, some in hotels. There will be fancy meal receptions and punch and cake in church halls. Sometimes guests will go home with a remembrance; sometimes with a dizzy head from good champagne. But, for sure, weddings are a great display of how people differ in their satisfaction levels, how they weigh costs and benefits, and how, ultimately, they use their scarce income.

person to purchase. Again, in making spending decisions, a maximizing person will consider both the added utility received from the item and the price of the item.[6]

Can this utility–price rule be seen at work in the real world? Do people really use this balancing principle in making purchasing decisions? The answer is absolutely yes, they do. The process might not be quite as precise as in the examples presented here,

---

[6] The utility-maximizing rule can be stated more precisely by comparing the added utility from consuming one more unit of each item to the item's price. Economists refer to the additional utility from consuming one more unit of an item as marginal utility. (Marginal utility is discussed more fully in Chapter 11.) If we divide the marginal utility from consuming one more unit of an item by the item's price, we can determine how much is added to total utility *per dollar spent on that item*.

Assume that a person is considering whether to buy Good X or Good Y. The marginal utility from consuming one more unit of Good X is 15 units of satisfaction and the price of Good X is $5.00. If MU_x and P_x stand for the marginal utility and price of Good X, then $MU_x/P_x = 15/\$5 = 3$ units of satisfaction for every dollar spent on that unit of Good X. One more unit of Good Y can be purchased for $8.00 and the marginal utility is 16 units of satisfaction. Comparing the marginal utility and price gives us $MU_y/P_y = 16/\$8 = 2$ units of satisfaction for every dollar spent on that unit of Good Y. Each dollar spent on the last unit of Good Y adds only two units of satisfaction, while every dollar spent on the last unit of Good X adds three. This person would be better off buying one more unit of Good X than Good Y.

When does a person pick exactly the right combination of goods and services to maximize total utility? Maximization occurs when the MU/P ratio is the same for the last unit of each of the items a person buys, or when:

$$MU_a/P_a = MU_b/P_b = MU_c/P_c = \ldots.$$

When all the MU/P ratios are equal for the last unit of each good or service purchased, the expenditure on the last unit of each item adds as much to total utility as is added by the expenditure on the last unit of each other item. If the MU/P ratio for an item is greater than that of other items, a person should buy more of that item because it adds more *per dollar* to total satisfaction. If the MU/P ratio for an item is less than that of other items, a person should buy less of that item because it adds less *per dollar* to total satisfaction than other items.

but basically consumers compare the price of an item with the expected addition to satisfaction from acquiring the item. Watch people at a vending machine or in line at a fast-food restaurant trying to choose the items that would give them the most satisfaction for their money. Or think of yourself as you grumble about, but do pay, the electric and other utility bills. Those bills are paid and the services continue because the satisfaction from having light, heat, and water is worth it. Can you see this balancing process at work in Application 10.1, "Family Gossip?"

Maximizing Satisfaction from Earning Income   As with spending decisions, maximizing satisfaction from working involves balancing benefits and costs. There are many considerations that go into the choice of a job: its mental and physical demands, pay, flexibility, location, and such. Each of these considerations carries benefits and costs: A flexible-time job that accommodates a decent semester course schedule might pay less than a job with inflexible hours.

Consider the decision to work overtime. Putting in more hours provides additional income for spending, but extra work hours mean less time for other activities. The choice is this: Is the extra income and satisfaction from working overtime enough to justify the dissatisfaction from forgoing other activities? For example, a student who works overtime might afford a better car or a trips over spring break, but at the cost of a higher GPA. Application 10.2, "You Decide," gives three examples of people doing the cost–benefit balancing act when making career decisions. What is your opinion of each of these choices?

APPLICATION 10.2

YOU DECIDE

Each of the following cases deals with career decision making. You decide: in your opinion, was this a good choice or a bad choice in each example?

Declaring a Major   John is a sophomore majoring in history because he really enjoys it. That changed when he had lunch with his friend Carrie, who is majoring in a technical computer field. John was amazed to learn that one of Carrie's friends with this technical major got a job paying $60,000 a year right after graduating last May. After lunch, John started thinking seriously about changing his major. It's true that he has no interest in computer technology. But who cares if he can get a salary like that. He thought that maybe after a few years on the job he'd find something to like about it. After all, a job is just a job. The next day John went into the student advising office and declared Carrie's field as his new major.

Dealing with a Dreadful Boss   Anna really liked her job. The pay was good, she'd travel to Europe a few times a year on business, and she spent most of her time working on projects that interested her. Then the new boss arrived. It soon became clear that never in his life had he made a mistake (at least in his own mind). The "Nightmare Boss," as he was quickly nicknamed by Anna's fellow workers, would walk into her office at 4:45 in the afternoon, put something on her desk, and say "Have this ready for me by tomorrow morning." Usually this meant about 5 or 6 hours of work that evening. Finally, Anna had enough. She started looking for other jobs and got some offers. While they paid well, they didn't interest her as much as her current work. After giving it a lot of thought, Anna decided that bosses come and go and kept her current job.

Making Music   Dan is a pianist who loves music and is very good at it. He typically earns over $40,000 playing jobs about 200 times a year. The thing is, while Dan loves music, his playing keeps him away from his family. The kids are usually asleep when he gets home, and he is usually asleep when they leave for school. And sometimes he and his wife are like two ships passing in the night: She's coming in from work and he's on his way out. Also, while the playing is great, it's unpredictable: Just because he played a lot of jobs this year doesn't mean the jobs will be there next year. Dan decided to make a career change. He was always interested in teaching music and will take coursework to get a teaching certificate. Dan hopes to teach music full time at the local high school and still play jobs—but many fewer times and only when he wants to play.

In summary, both spending and earning decisions involve the goal of maximizing economic well-being. The decision maker weighs the advantages, or benefits, and disadvantages, or costs, of different strategies to choose the one that comes closest to accomplishing that objective. This weighing, or balancing, which is at the heart of the individual decision-making process, is covered in detail in the next chapter.

OVERVIEW OF BUSINESS

Business

An organization established to produce and/or sell goods and services.

Since several of the following chapters focus on business decision making, it is important to have some basic knowledge about the business sector. A **business** is an organization established to produce and/or sell goods and services. In the United States there are over 32.5 million legally organized business firms. Well over one-half are small operations with annual receipts under $25,000; others are huge enterprises selling billions of dollars worth of goods and services each year.

Business decisions, especially about output and prices, have a powerful influence on the economy. A very large firm, like Wal-Mart, which employed more than 2 million people in 2015, or one of the other firms listed in Table 10.3, can have a significant impact on employment conditions in an industry or region. A few large firms with a substantial share of a market that accounts for a significant amount of consumer spending could contribute to inflation by raising their prices. Product development, concern for the environment, and community involvement are also areas that are affected by business decisions.

Before we explore the specifics of business decision making, let us examine the legal forms of business and some structural aspects of U.S. businesses.

TABLE 10.3   *The 10 Largest U.S. Corporate Employers: 2015*

The decisions of very large corporations that sell billions of dollars of output and employ hundreds of thousands of people can have a major impact on households, other businesses, government, and the economy in general.

Rank	Corporation	Number of Employees
1	Walmart	2,200,000
2	McDonald's	420,000
3	IBM	412,775
4	Kroger	400,000
5	Home Depot	371,000
6	Target	347,000
7	UPS	336,150
8	Berkshire Hathaway	316,000
9	General Electric	305,000
10	Yum Brands[a]	303,405

[a]Includes Taco Bell, KFC, and Pizza Hut.

Source: Fortune 500, http://fortune.com/fortune500/, 06/18/2015.

Legal Forms of Business

A business must take on a legal form before it can operate. It may be a

- proprietorship,
- partnership, or
- corporation.

Proprietorship   A one-owner business that is typically small—such as an antique shop or an independent consultant—is called a **proprietorship**. Usually in a proprietorship the owner is the manager and a jack-of-all-trades, performing the functions of a bookkeeper, financial analyst, and marketing specialist, among others. For the owner of the business, this legal form has two advantages: It is relatively easy to start a business that is organized as a proprietorship, and there is independence in decision making. The owner is not responsible or answerable to anyone.

A proprietorship, however, has several limitations: particularly, difficulty in raising money and unlimited liability. The sole proprietor who wants to raise money for expansion, remodeling, or other purposes can do so only by borrowing from private sources, such as family or friends, or from financial institutions like commercial banks, or through certain government programs. Because proprietorships cannot issue stocks and bonds, a large source of money capital cannot be readily tapped by the single-owner business.

A proprietorship is also subject to **unlimited liability**; that is, the owner's personal assets are subject to use as payment for business debts. If a creditor cannot be fully paid from the assets of the business, the courts may take the owner's personal property to satisfy such debts.

Partnership   A business similar to a proprietorship with two or more (perhaps hundreds of) owners is a **partnership**. This arrangement permits the pooling of money, experience, and talent. For example, a person killed in the kitchen and a person adept at management might create a successful restaurant. Unfortunately, partnerships often lead to dissension between partners and dissolution of the business.

Unless it is legally documented, all owners in a partnership are general partners. A **general partner** is one who has the burden of unlimited liability, and each partnership must typically have at least one general partner. If misunderstood, unlimited liability can create problems for a partner. In a partnership, each general partner is responsible for 100 percent of the business's debts. In case of default, liability is not necessarily divided in halves, thirds, or other equal amounts. Instead, the debts beyond those covered by the business's assets will be paid through the personal assets of whichever partners possess the means. If one general partner is penniless and the other wealthy, the partner with the assets will pay the debts.

Corporation   A **corporation** is a "legal person" created by law: It can sue or be sued, make contracts, pay fines, and carry on other aspects of business normally performed by individuals. Unlike humans, a corporation can continue indefinitely. To form a corporation, a charter, which involves some cost and red tape to acquire, must be obtained from a state.

As a corporation is established, shares of stock are sold (additional shares may be sold later), and the holders of those shares become the owners of the corporation. One major advantage for corporation owners is limited liability: Personal assets are *not* subject to payment for business debts. In case of bankruptcy, an owner can lose only the money used to purchase the stock. This sum, however, could be considerable.

Proprietorship
A one-owner business.

Unlimited Liability
A business owner's personal assets are subject to use as payment for business debts.

Partnership
The legal organization of a business that is similar to a proprietorship but has two or more owners.

General Partner
An owner in a partnership who is subject to unlimited liability.

Corporation
A legal entity, owned by stockholders; can carry on in its own name business functions normally performed by individuals.

The owners of a corporation receive profits through quarterly corporate dividend checks. How much profit a stockholder receives depends on the corporation's profitability, the type of stock the owner holds, and the amount of profit that is retained by the business. Corporations can issue both preferred and common stock. **Preferred stock** carries a stated dividend, and preferred stockholders are entitled to their dividends before common stockholders are paid. **Common stock** pays a dividend after creditors and preferred stockholders have been paid. A quarter with healthy sales and sizable profits might yield a healthy return on common stock, and a quarter with no profit will yield no dividend check.

Each share of common stock entitles its owner to one vote on some corporate policies and, most importantly, to elect a board of directors. The **corporate board of directors** is the governing body of a corporation and makes many major decisions, including the selection of the corporation's CEO (chief executive officer) and other top management. These managers run the corporation on a day-to-day basis. Figure 10.1 outlines the structure of a corporation.

Control of a corporation rests with those who hold a large portion of the stock. These stockholders have the power to elect themselves or their candidates to the board of directors. A person with a few thousand shares in a small corporation might have control over that business, but a few thousand shares in a company like Starbucks would be negligible. Test Your Understanding, "The Price of Stock Shares," discusses how the price of a share of stock is determined by supply and demand and provides an opportunity to evaluate how changes in supply and demand affect a stock's price.

No discussion of a corporation is complete without some mention of **bonds**. Corporations can borrow large amounts of money for building, expansion, and other purposes by selling bonds. Bonds provide a corporation with an avenue other than

Preferred Stock
Pays a stated dividend to its holder; preferred stockholders are entitled to receive dividends before common stockholders.

Common Stock
Pays a dividend dependent on the profit of a firm after all other financial obligations have been met.

Corporate Board of Directors
Governing body of a corporation; elected by stockholders.

Bond
A financial instrument through which a corporation can borrow funds and repay them over the long term.

FIGURE 10.1   *Structure of a Corporation*

The stockholders who own a corporation elect a board of directors that makes major decisions for the corporation and appoints top management to run the corporation.

TEST YOUR UNDERSTANDING

THE PRICE OF STOCK SHARES

A stock exchange is a facility for trading stocks. Only the stocks of corporations listed on a particular exchange may be traded there. The best-known exchanges are the New York Stock Exchange (NYSE) and the NASDAQ National Market. Easy access to quick, up-to-date stock information can be found on the Internet.

The price at which a share of a corporation's common stock is bought and sold may change daily, or hourly, or by the minute. This is due to changes in buyers' and sellers' plans that affect demand and supply. To illustrate, assume that a hypothetical company, the Grand Corporation, is

listed on the New York Stock Exchange and that the demand and supply for Grand common stock as of the opening of trading today is given in the figure shown here.

The downward-sloping demand curve indicates that as the price per share increases, buyers will decrease the quantity of shares demanded. The upward-sloping supply curve shows that as the price per share increases, sellers will be willing to sell more shares. In this market, the equilibrium price is $18.00 per share, and 3,000 shares are bought and sold.

What could cause this equilibrium price to change? Any factor that increases or decreases the supply and/or demand of Grand stock may do so. For example, a rumor that Grand is about to sign a lucrative government contract could increase the demand for Grand stock (shift the demand curve to the right) causing an increase in equilibrium price.

What would be the effect on demand, supply, and equilibrium price of each of the following?

1. A major pension fund holding a large amount of Grand stock sells its shares.
2. Corporate reports indicate that sales and profits are increasing.
3. Corporate sales and profits are on a slow, constant decline.
4. Returns on investment opportunities other than Grand stock are increasing.
5. Grand announces a two-for-one split of its stock in which each outstanding share is now worth two shares.
6. The stock market falls by a record amount, signaling a lack of investor confidence in the economy.

Answers can be found at the back of the book.

stocks to tap other corporations, private individuals, and organizations for funds. Corporate bonds are typically sold in $1,000 denomination blocks and have a specified interest rate and maturity date. A bondholder is a creditor of the company and not an owner.

Since the late 1970s, there has been growing interest in the United States in forming **Limited Liability Companies**, or **LLCs**, which combine characteristics of the three legal forms of business we have just discussed. Like corporations, LLCs protect their members with limited liability. But like proprietorships and partnerships, they also allow greater decision-making flexibility than is typically found in corporations. Depending on its legal form and for tax purposes, an LLC can be classified as a proprietorship, partnership, or corporation.

Limited Liability Companies (LLCs)
Businesses that combine the liability protection of corporations with the management flexibility of proprietorships and partnerships.

Numbers and Sizes of Businesses

How many businesses are there in the United States? How are they organized? Table 10.4 gives the number of legally organized businesses in the United States and the size of business receipts (sales) in 2011. There were about 32.5 million businesses,

TABLE 10.4	*Number and Receipts of Proprietorships, Partnerships, and Corporations: 2011*

Although the vast majority of U.S. firms are proprietorships, they account for a small percentage of business receipts. Most receipts go to corporations.

Business Firms	Number	Number as a Percentage of the Total	Receipts	Receipts as a Percentage of the Total
Total	32,535,000	100.0%	$30.9 trillion	100.0%
Proprietorships[a]	23,427,000	72.0	1.3 trillion	4.1
Partnerships	3,285,000	10.1	4.5 trillion	14.4
Corporations	5,823,000	17.9	25.2 trillion	81.5

[a]Includes only nonfarm businesses; figures are based on tax returns.
Source: ProQuest Statistical Abstract of the U.S. 2015 Online Edition, Table 762.

with the vast majority, about 72 percent, organized as proprietorships. Only 18 percent were corporations.

Table 10.4 also shows that most of the business receipts went to corporations. Of the $30.9 trillion in total sales, corporations accounted for about $25 trillion (or about 81.5 percent). Proprietorships received about 4 percent of the total sales. While the vast majority of businesses are proprietorships, they account for only a small percentage of the total sales of the economy. Corporations, which tend to be larger, account for most business sales.

Business Ownership of Business

Corporate stock is owned by funds, such as pension, endowment, and mutual funds, as well as directly by individuals. And in many cases the controlling shares of stock in one corporation are owned by another corporation. In these cases, the corporation that owns the stock is said to own the other corporation. It is often not readily apparent that one corporation owns another because both may retain separate identities and operate as separate businesses.

Merger or Acquisition
The acquiring of one company by another; can be accomplished by buying a controlling amount of stock.

Conglomerate Merger
A corporation acquires another corporation that produces unrelated goods and services.

The buying of controlling shares of stock in one corporation by another corporation is referred to as a **merger** or **acquisition**. Merger activity in the United States has been high since the 1980s but slowed down in recent years with a slowdown in the economy. The price tags on many corporate acquisitions are in the billions of dollars. For example, in 2014 Comcast acquired Time Warner Cable for $70 billion.[7]

When one corporation acquires another corporation and there is no relationship between the goods and services that the two corporations produce, the acquisition is called a **conglomerate merger**. General Electric, for example, has built a conglomerate that includes, in addition to its well-known household appliances, commercial lending, healthcare, mining, power systems, software, and more.[8]

[7]"10 Biggest Mergers and Acquisitions of 2014," http://investorplace.com/2014/12/mergers-and-acquisitions-biggest-deals-2014.
[8]All Products, www.ge.com/products.

In some cases, a corporation may acquire other corporations that are closely related to it or to each in some way. For example, NBC Universal was the result of a merger of two companies in the entertainment business. When a corporation merges with another in its market, a **horizontal merger** has occurred. When a corporation acquires another corporation that supplies its inputs or distributes its products, such as the merger between PayPal and eBay, a **vertical merger** has occurred.

Sometimes a corporation is formed specifically for the purpose of owning or holding stock in other corporations. This type of company, which produces nothing itself, is termed a **holding company**. Figure 10.2 shows a hypothetical example of a bank holding company, Alltown Bank Corporation, which exists only to own controlling shares of stock in Hometown Bank, Downtown Bank, and other banks.

There are many reasons why one firm may seek to merge with another: to fill out a product line or move into a new geographic market, to acquire a company with large amounts of cash, to diversify, to avoid a hostile takeover from yet another company, or some other reason. Mergers and acquisitions are covered in more detail in Chapter 14.

Application 10.3, "Two Profiles: Starbucks and Kraft Foods," provides short profiles of two corporations that all of us know, and are increasingly growing into major global companies. It is interesting to see how these two companies differ with regard to mergers, ownership, and growth. Notice the holding company arrangements with Kraft Foods and the growth of Starbucks without major acquisitions.

Horizontal Merger
A corporation acquires another corporation that competes in the same market.

Vertical Merger
A corporation acquires another corporation that supplies its inputs or distributes its products.

Holding company
A corporation formed for the purpose of owning or holding stock in other corporations.

GOALS AND DECISIONS OF BUSINESS FIRMS

A typical business, large or small, is faced with many decisions about how to legally organize, what products to sell, how to price, whether to expand, and such. What is a business really trying to accomplish? What is the ultimate purpose of its decisions?

In the study of economics, as well as other areas, it is generally assumed that the fundamental objective of business decision making is to maximize a firm's profit or minimize its loss. This doesn't mean just earn any profit or avoid a loss, but rather earn the largest profit possible or take the smallest loss.

| FIGURE 10.2 | *The Alltown Bank Holding Company* |

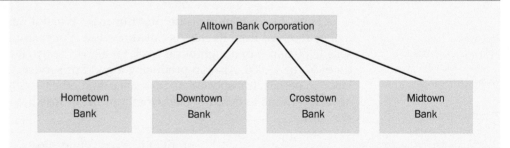

The purpose of a holding company, such as Alltown Bank Corporation, is to own shares of stock in other companies, such as Hometown Bank and Crosstown Bank.

TWO PROFILES: STARBUCKS AND KRAFT FOODS

Starbucks   Today Starbucks, named after the first mate in Melville's *Moby Dick*, is a household word and, for some, a necessity in life. And not just in the United States. People throughout the world—from China to Chile to Poland and over 50 other countries—count on the consistent Starbucks experience.

While Starbucks began in 1971 with one store in Seattle, it was the mid-1980s before the first Starbucks caffe latte was served and the Starbucks coffeehouse concept was born. It wasn't until 1992 that common stock in Starbucks was publicly issued and traded.

Starbucks' growth has been huge. This company had just 162 stores in 1992, growing to 1,412 stores in 1997, and over 21,000 worldwide in 2014. Its revenues were $1 billion in 1997 and about $16.4 billion in 2014. Close to 190,000 people were employed worldwide in 2014 in retail stores and the support, roasting, and warehousing of Starbucks' products.

Starbucks growth has not come from mergers with other companies, although it has purchased a few small companies like Tazo, an Oregon tea company, and Evolution Fresh, a juice company. It has, however, formed alliances and partnerships to extend its customer base. This includes agreements with some hotels and a relationship with Barnes & Noble. Starbucks also sells packaged coffee and tea in grocery and warehouse club stores.

Starbucks has built a reputation for social consciousness in doing business. It has set several goals toward which it works: produce 100 percent ethically sourced coffee; innovate and drive positive sustainability; and contribute to the neighborhoods in which Starbucks is located.

Kraft Foods   Oscar Mayer, Planters Peanuts, Velveeta, Kool-Aid, and more are foodstuffs that we all know. All of these—and more—are products offered for sale by Kraft Foods. Over a century old, Kraft Foods is one of the country's best-known consumer food and beverage companies with many of its current products, such as Jell-O, also over 100 years old.

Started in 1903 when James L. Kraft sold cheese from a horse-drawn wage, Kraft has grown to a North American presence with 22,000 employees and over $18 billion in revenues. Kraft has determined that its food and beverage brands can be found in 98 percent of U.S. and Canadian households.

The history and growth of Kraft is an interesting story. Over the past 100 years, the company has merged with other companies, changed its name a few times, been spun off from various owners, and bought and sold different products. Since 2000, it has been bought by Philip Morris Companies which changed its name to Altria Group, been spun off by Altria and become a fully independent company, acquired the $18-billion dollar Cadbury company, split the company in two, and merged with Heinz Foods.

In 2012, Kraft Foods split into two separate independent companies: Kraft Foods, which retained the basic grocery products, and Mondelez International, which was launched as a global snacks company. The Cadbury line, Nabisco with its oreos, and more became part of the Mondelez product line which had global net revenues of $34 billion in 2014.

In 2015, Kraft entered into a merger with H.J. Heinz and will now be known as the Kraft Heinz Company. Details of that merger, which will create the fifth largest food and beverage company in the world, are unfolding. Kraft Food is a member of the Standard & Poor's 500 and the NASDAQ-100 stock indices.

Sources: www.starbucks.com; www.kraftfoods.com; www.mondelez international.com; www.heinz.com.

Revenue
Money or income that a company receives from selling its product.

Profit or loss
What results when a business subtracts its costs from its revenue.

How does a firm measure profit or loss? When a business sells a product, the money received from its sales is called **revenue**. For example, when a doughnut shop sells 1,000 dozen of doughnuts a week for $7 per dozen, it receives a revenue of 1,000 times $7, or $7,000. Also, in producing a good or service, a business incurs costs for labor, materials, transportation, insurance, and other inputs. These costs are charged against revenue to determine whether a **profit or loss** has been made. So, for a business firm:

$$\text{profit or loss} = \text{revenue} - \text{costs}.$$

If revenue is $7,000 and costs are $5,000, the business earns a profit of $2,000. If revenue is $7,000 and costs are $7,500, there is a loss of $500.

SHOULD PROFITABLE BUSINESSES BE EXPECTED TO ACTIVELY PARTICIPATE IN IMPROVING THEIR COMMUNITIES?

Issue   *Because successful, profitable businesses are part of their local communities, should they be expected to channel some of their resources into projects that benefit their communities?*

Yes   A successful business should be expected to actively participate in its local community. While it is true that businesses bring much to their communities in the form of jobs and in other ways, it is also true that they are given much by their communities in return. When a business considers locating in a community, it evaluates the quality of the schools for its employees' children; the public safety and fire departments that will protect its assets; the recreation, entertainment, and other events available to enrich its employees' lives; and health care services.

Businesses should think of themselves as partners in their communities. Successful businesses have human and financial resources at their disposal to make lasting contributions to the communities that they call home. Sponsoring community events and lending talent to projects and boards are important. In the long run, these contributions could have a greater overall impact than that from providing a few extra dollars to each stockholder.

No   A successful business should not be expected to participate in its local community. The primary responsibility of a business is to its owners—not to its community. But even when a business is responsible to its owners, it automatically carries out activities that benefit its community as well. The contribution made by providing jobs for a community's citizens should not be undervalued. This is a contribution to which people give little thought until they learn that a local employer has fallen on hard times and may be forced to close its doors.

Businesses do actively support their communities by contributing tax dollars that are used for education, public safety, and streets, as well as paying off bonds for recreational or other community facilities. The tax revenue provided to a community by its businesses is significant to the financial health of that community. And finally, the question must be asked: Do we really want business managers to take larger social roles when, because of the resources at their disposal, their opinions may carry more weight than the opinions of other groups in the community?

Profit goes to the owners of a firm who bear the risk of its success or failure. In a proprietorship or partnership, profit goes to the owner(s) who organize and operate the business, and in a corporation it goes to the stockholders.

Profit maximization or loss minimization for a business is a balancing process, just as spending and earning decisions are for individuals. A firm weighs or balances the expected revenue and expected costs of each of the operating strategies from which it can choose, and then picks the strategy that contributes most to its profitability. This balancing of revenues and costs is covered in detail in the next chapter.

Questions about Profit Maximization   The goal of profit maximization or loss minimization raises some interesting issues and debates. What does profit maximization mean? Does maximizing mean that a business maintains the quality of its product, meets the needs of its workforce, and generally is a good citizen of the community as it seeks the largest profit possible? Or does it imply operating with minimum regard for quality, the environment, working conditions, and wages for the sake of a larger profit?

The relationship between profit-maximizing and socially responsible behavior is important and addressed in many political and legislative arenas. For example, today there are laws which penalize companies that in the quest for more profit destroy the environment, produce unsafe products, give misleading claims about their products, or disregard the rights of their workers.

Another issue centers on whether a business may actually seek some alternative goal other than profit maximization. For example, a company might sacrifice profits over the short run to introduce a new product or develop new technology or purchase another company. Is sacrificing profit in the short run in order to increase profit in the future inconsistent with the goal of profit maximization?

Debate also occurs over the importance of profit maximization to owners in the different forms of business. It is easy to see how profit maximization can motivate a sole proprietor or general partner, but it may be more difficult to understand in a large corporation, where stockholders are removed from decision-making and where managers who receive fixed salaries run the firm.

Why would the managers of a large corporation be motivated to maximize profit? If the profit performance of a company is unsatisfactory, stockholders can replace the corporation's top management. In addition, the fear of a hostile takeover by another corporation because of declining profits could motivate managers because with new ownership often comes new management of the acquired firm. Also, in some instances top managers might want to maximize profit because they have significant holdings of the company's stock.

Questions about profit-maximizing behavior are also raised in Up for Debate: "Should Profitable Businesses Be Expected to Actively Participate in Improving Their Communities?" What is your opinion of the arguments on each side, and which side do you think makes the better case? Do you have any examples of companies in your hometown that are active in community projects and events?

Summary

1. A household is made up of an individual living alone or several persons living in a group. The majority of household income comes from the sale of resources, particularly labor. Unearned income from government transfer payments is an important source of income. Of the different types of cash benefit transfer payments, Social Security is the largest.

2. The average income of all households taken as a group differs from the average incomes of various subgroups of households. This difference may be related to such factors as the education, age, or gender of the household head. Household income can be saved, used for paying taxes, or spent, with the vast majority going to purchase goods and services. Purchases of goods can be divided between expenditures on durable and nondurable goods.

3. The main economic objective of an individual's spending and earning decisions is to maximize economic well-being. Realizing this objective requires weighing alternatives and choosing the course of action that contributes most to economic satisfaction.

4. The satisfaction from buying a good or service is called utility. To maximize the total utility from spending a given sum of money, a purchaser must weigh the additional satisfaction from each unit of an item consumed against that item's price and compare that to the additional satisfaction and price of alternative goods and services.

5. Earning decisions involve weighing and balancing costs and benefits. Working means weighing the satisfaction from income against the dissatisfaction from forgoing alternatives to working.

6. A business is an organization established to produce and sell goods and services. A firm may be legally organized as a proprietorship, partnership, or corporation with each legal form having advantages and disadvantages. Numerically, there are more proprietorships in the U.S. economy than there are partnerships and corporations, but most receipts go to corporations.

7. Many corporations have a controlling share of their stock owned by another corporation. When a corporation buys the controlling shares of stock in another corporation, a merger or acquisition has taken place.

8. The basic objective of a business firm is to maximize profit or minimize loss. Profit or loss equals revenue minus costs. Business profit maximizing requires balancing the expected revenues and costs from different operating strategies.

9. There are some questions concerning the profit-maximizing objective. These include the relationship between profit-maximizing and socially responsible behavior, and the extent to which a firm's other short-term goals are compatible with long-term profit maximization.

Key Terms and Concepts		
Household	Corporation
Personal income	Preferred stock
Transfer payments	Common stock
Durable good	Corporate board of directors
Nondurable good	Bond
Maximizing economic well-being	Limited Liability Companies (LLCs)
	Merger or acquisition
Utility	Conglomerate merger
Total utility	Vertical merger
Business	Horizontal merger
Proprietorship	Holding company
Unlimited liability	Revenue
Partnership	Profit or loss
General partner	

Review Questions

1. What are the main sources of household income and the different uses to which household income can be put? How is household income affected by the head of household's age, gender, education, and other factors?

2. Would a person maximize satisfaction by buying a $15 product that adds twice as much satisfaction as a $5 product? Why? Would the person maximize satisfaction by buying the $15 product if the price of the other product was $10? Why? Explain the utility–price relationship that buyers use in maximizing their economic well-being.

3. An individual maximizes economic well-being by making spending and earning decisions, and a business maximizes profit by deciding how much of its product to produce and sell. These decisions are similar in that they involve a balancing process.
   a. Generally, what is common to the balancing processes in decisions made by households and businesses?
   b. How do their decisions differ in terms of what is balanced?

4. Explain differences in the three basic forms of business: proprietorship, partnership, and corporation. What are the advantages and disadvantages of each form for the owners?

5. What is the difference between a stock and a bond? Why might it be necessary for a firm to issue bonds in order to acquire another firm? What are some factors that would cause the price of a corporation's stock shares to fluctuate?

6. What is the difference among a conglomerate merger, horizontal merger, and vertical merger? Give some examples of each.

7. Suppose a coworker says, "What's required for a business to maximize profit is very simple: Produce the lowest-quality product you can, don't worry about the environment, and pay the lowest wages you can get away with." Do you think this is what profit maximizing is all about?

Discussion Questions

1. Students who rent apartments close to college campuses often complain that they have to pay a lot for what they get. Explain, in terms of what you have learned in this chapter, why students, despite a limited income, will continue to rent at these high prices.

2. Over the years, the amount of income spent on services in the United States has grown to the point where it is larger than the amount spent on both durable goods, such as automobiles, and nondurable goods, such as food, combined. What do you think is causing this growth in the demand for services?

3. Can you explain in economic terms why someone with a so-called sweet tooth might be more than willing to buy an expensive chocolate mousse cake but would not consider buying a high-quality steak?

4. What factors should a person consider when choosing between two job offers?

5. Suppose that you are a business organization consultant, and three people come to you, each wanting to start a business. The first person wants to start an organic vegetable farm with her sister, the second a store selling musical instruments, and the third a barge line for moving coal on rivers. Each is seeking your advice on whether to organize as a proprietorship, partnership, or corporation. How would you advise each of them?

6. "Paying higher salaries to its workers, or incurring higher costs to increase its share of the market, does not mean that a firm is giving up the objective of maximum profit. Instead, it means that the firm is taking steps now to ensure

that it will be able to maximize profit in the future." Do you agree or disagree with this statement? Explain your reasoning.

7. In a proprietorship, the owner is often the manager, but in a corporation the owners are often different from the managers. What advantages and disadvantages might there be in having a separation of ownership and management?

8. Companies sometimes provide funds to colleges and universities for buildings or stadiums. Do you think this is done because of a civic motivation or is it a marketing tool?

Critical Thinking Case 10

TIME TO MAXIMIZE

Critical Thinking Skills

Identifying criteria for decision making

Clarifying frameworks in which decisions are made

Economic Concepts

Maximizing behavior

Costs and benefits

U.S. business managers have been criticized for using a three month time frame—the interval between quarterly dividend payments to stockholders—to make decisions that affect corporate profitability. "Stockholders want profit now, so three months is the time frame that matters most," goes the argument for looking only this far ahead. A strategy that will dramatically improve profit five years down the road may not be seriously considered if it requires stockholders to forgo profit they are expecting today or in the near future. The unavoidable question is: How profitable would a company be today if five years ago its management committed to a long-term program of profit enhancement rather than planning from dividend payment to dividend payment?

How far to look into the future when forming plans and making decisions—especially about spending and earning—is also important to individuals. Noted economic and social theorist and author Jeremy Rifkin noted that people with larger incomes tend to have longer time horizons when planning than do people with smaller incomes.[a] A person who is not sure there will be enough income to buy groceries and pay the rent and utility bills this month may find it hard to focus on a plan that will pay off two years down the road.

Maximizing behavior involves balancing the costs and benefits of different courses of action in order to identify the one that gives the most desirable result. What is "most desirable" may, however, depend on the time period on which the decision maker is focused. And what is most desirable over one time period may be undesirable over another.

[a]Jeremy Rifkin, *Time Wars* (New York: Simon & Schuster, 1987), pp. 192–194.

Questions

1. Would a business trying to maximize its profits over three month intervals assign the same weights to specific costs and benefits as a business trying to maximize its profit over a three- or five-year period?

2. Would two college juniors make the same spending and earning decisions if one was planning to get a job after graduation and the other was planning to go to medical school? How would the criteria each uses for decision making differ?

3. If the results of a decision depend on what time frame is considered, how can it be determined which time frame is right for making a decision?

Benefits, Costs, and Maximization

CHAPTER OBJECTIVES

Explain how individuals measure costs and benefits in economic decision making and introduce marginal analysis.

Explain how businesses measure costs and revenues to maximize profit.

Introduce the concepts of externalities and social costs and benefits.

Explain how collective, or public, choices are made.

As we know, life is all about choices, big and small. Individuals and businesses are constantly making choices while weighing their costs and benefits to try to maximize some result. We choose how to spend our time and money; businesses choose products to sell and how to operate; and as a society we make collective choices that impact our lives.

Whether we are trying to figure out what to do on a Saturday night, or a developer is trying to decide about the best housing options for a project, or government officials are trying to set air quality standards, the thinking process in the decision making is the same. There are some simple thought mechanics used in balancing costs and benefits to find a best strategy. And the same processes are used by everyone: individuals, businesses, and society in general. This chapter introduces those mechanics.

In this chapter, we will learn how individuals, businesses, and society use some specific "rules" for maximizing as they go through the mechanics of weighing costs and benefits. You will also be introduced to marginal analysis, which is the basis of many microeconomic concepts. Marginal analysis will reappear in most of the following chapters.

The formal study of the process of balancing costs and benefits, referred to as cost–benefit analysis, is helpful in evaluating business investment and production decisions, government spending decisions, and individual decisions concerning major purchases. However, the principles of cost–benefit analysis are not limited in their usefulness to evaluating major economic and financial decisions. The principles can be applied to many more areas of human experience than those dealt with in modern economics. The story of Adam and Eve, and the choice to eat the apple in the Garden of Eden, is a lesson in balancing costs and benefits, as is an expression such as:

> 'Tis better to have loved and lost
> Than never to have loved at all.[1]

All rational decision making, be it economic or noneconomic, is based on the balancing of costs and benefits in order to, in the view of the decision maker, maximize something. This is true for the worker trying to maximize well-being by balancing the costs and benefits of working overtime for the child weighing the costs and benefits of lying to a parent, or for the painter deciding whether to move the ladder or stretch to reach the last few inches on a wall.

BALANCING BENEFITS AND COSTS: THE INDIVIDUAL

Defining Benefits and Costs

When people make decisions, from whether or not to carry an umbrella to class to whether or not to smoke, the goal of this decision making is to maximize, or to get the most from the decision. In doing so, an individual, usually subconsciously, uses a type of mathematical process, or applies certain mathematical rules, to weigh the costs and benefits of different courses of action. (Yes, even when trying to decide what to order at our favorite lunch spot, our brains are engaged in using mathematics to make a decision.) Before we thoroughly discuss the **cost–benefit analysis** process and these mathematical rules, let's understand how an individual measures benefits and costs.

Cost–Benefit Analysis
Weighing the costs and benefits of an action in order to maximize the net benefit from the action.

The benefit to a person from any action or purchase is the amount of satisfaction received from that action or purchase. This satisfaction, discussed in Chapter 10, is referred to as **utility**. In order to understand the behavior of utility, assume people have a small meter in their heads called a "Util-O-Meter." This meter measures total utility by clicking off points according to the amount of satisfaction received from each additional performance of an action or from the consumption of each additional unit of a good or service.

Utility
Satisfaction realized from the consuming of a good or service or taking an action.

Any measurement of satisfaction is highly subjective, as are the numbers registered on a Util-O-Meter for the benefits received from any action or purchase. Because of this, it is extremely difficult for two people to compare the degree of satisfaction received by each from taking the same action, such as eating a slice of pizza. However, a person can compare the degree of satisfaction that the person receives from different actions or purchases from which that person can choose. You, for example, know whether you enjoy a popular recording more, much more, or not as much as Mahler's Seventh Symphony. Try the exercise in Table 11.1 to reinforce this point.

Opportunity Cost
The cost of acquiring a good or service or taking an action measured in terms of the value of the opportunity or alternative forgone.

An individual usually measures the cost of an item by the dollars paid for it. As discussed in Chapter 1, however, cost can also be measured in terms of the alternative or opportunity forgone to acquire an item or take an action. That is, the cost of something can be measured in terms of its **opportunity cost**. For example, the cost of a $100 textbook could be measured by the dollars required to obtain it or by the football tickets, groceries, shirt, or whatever else would have otherwise been purchased.

---

[1]Alfred Lord Tennyson, "In Memoriam," in *The Poetic and Dramatic Works of Alfred Lord Tennyson*, W. J. Rolfe, ed. (Boston: Houghton Mifflin Co., 1898), p. 170.

TABLE 11.1	*Ranking Satisfaction*

People know what they like and dislike and are able to rank their preferences. The following lists various types of music that you may, or may not, enjoy. Find your favorite and give it 10 points of utility. Now compare all of the other types by giving each one points in comparison to your favorite. For example, if you like a type of music half as much as your favorite, give it 5 points; if you really dislike it, give it 0 points.

Type of Music	Number of Points
Blues	_____
Classical	_____
Country	_____
Jazz	_____
Salsa	_____
Gospel	_____
Opera	_____
Polka	_____
Rap	_____
Rock	_____

Everything one does has an opportunity cost. The cost of attending a class could be sleep, working out, watching a television program, or putting in an extra hour at a job. What is your opportunity cost of reading this chapter now?

We can relate opportunity costs to utility, or satisfaction, by measuring the points that would have been added to a Util-O-Meter had another course of action been chosen. For example, if by registering for next term you gave up 1 hour of running, which would have added 125 points to your total utility, then the opportunity cost of registering was 125 points.

Measuring Benefits and Costs

In the example that follows, we will show how individuals measure the benefits and costs of actions and how they apply some simple mathematical maximizing rules to their decision making. This example deals with a student who is planning to spend an evening at a concert on campus. The concert is lengthy and informal: People can come and go as they please. There is no admission charge, but the concert is not free because someone who attends has an opportunity cost in terms of time.

Remember that people try to maximize their satisfaction in taking actions. In this case, the individual going to the concert is attempting to maximize the satisfaction from the time spent during the course of the evening. This means that our concertgoer may spend the entire evening at the concert or may at some point have something else preferable to do and leave the concert. In this example, we will determine whether satisfaction is maximized by attending the entire concert, which lasts for 5 hours, or by leaving after the first, second, third, or fourth hour.

Measuring Benefits   By attending the concert, our student receives satisfaction, or utility: The concert adds points to the student's Util-O-Meter. Each additional hour spent at the concert adds a certain number of points to total satisfaction. The *change* in

Marginal Benefit (Marginal Utility)
The change in total satisfaction from consuming an additional unit of a good, service, or activity.

Total Benefit (Total Utility)
The total amount of satisfaction received from consuming a specified number of units of a good, service, or activity.

total satisfaction from attending each additional hour is called **marginal benefit**, or **marginal utility**. The *total* satisfaction received by attending the concert for a specified number of hours is called **total benefit**, or **total utility**.

Let's assume that our student's Util-O-Meter registers zero before the concert. Let us further assume that by the end of the first hour, 400 points of utility have clicked onto the meter. This means that the total benefit, or utility, from spending 1 hour at the concert is 400 points. At the end of the second hour, 700 points are registered on the meter; or we can say that the total benefit from spending 2 hours at the concert is 700 points. At the end of 3 hours, 900 points are registered; at the end of 4 hours, the total utility received is 1,000 points; and after 5 hours, the meter still registers 1,000 points. This information is given in Table 11.2 in the column labeled Total Benefit (Utility).

Marginal benefit, or utility, is the *change* in total benefit that results from attending the concert for each *additional* hour. Because the Util-O-Meter registered zero before the concert and 400 points at the end of 1 hour, the marginal benefit from the first hour is 400 points. At the end of the second hour, 700 points of total benefit are registered, which means that 300 points of utility are added during the second hour (700 points in total utility at the end of the second hour minus 400 points at the end of the first). Thus, the marginal utility, or benefit, of the second hour is 300 points. During the third hour, 200 points of marginal benefit are added (total benefit increases from 700 to 900 points). The marginal benefit of the fourth hour is 100 points; and the marginal benefit of the fifth hour is zero points because total benefit does not increase from the end of the fourth to the end of the fifth hour. These measures are given in Table 11.2 in the column labeled Marginal Benefit (Utility).

You may have noticed that the marginal benefit points given in Table 11.2 are listed midway between the hours. This is done because marginal values refer to *changes* in total values. When showing a change in total value, or marginal value, in a table like 11.2, the common practice is to place the number for the marginal value between the start point and end point of what is being measured.

TABLE 11.2   *Utility Points from Attending a Concert*

Total benefit, or utility, is the total satisfaction from consuming a particular amount of a good, service, or activity; marginal benefit, or utility, is the change in total satisfaction from consuming an additional unit of a good, service, or activity.

Number of Hours Attended	Total Benefit (Utility)	Marginal Benefit (Utility)
0	0 points	
		400 points
1	400 points	
		300 points
2	700 points	
		200 points
3	900 points	
		100 points
4	1,000 points	
		0 points
5	1,000 points	

Notice that the marginal benefit points decrease with each additional hour spent at the concert. In this example, this individual really enjoys the first hour, finds the second hour slightly less satisfying, and finds each successive hour less enjoyable than the previous one. By the fifth hour no additional satisfaction is received. This result is consistent with a principle in economics called the **Law of Diminishing Marginal Utility**. This law states that, as additional units of an item are consumed, *beyond some point* each successive unit consumed adds less to total utility than was added by the unit consumed just before it. In other words, as an individual consumes a good or service, there is some point beyond which he or she enjoys each additional unit of the item less.[2]

Food provides excellent examples of the Law of Diminishing Marginal Utility. If you are eating pizza, tacos, doughnuts, or anything else, there is some point beyond which each additional piece of pizza or taco or doughnut gives you less satisfaction than the one before it. Do you generally enjoy the fourth doughnut as much as the first? Also, would you enjoy a second bike or cell phone as much as the first, and do you find the third hour of a 3-hour lecture class as satisfying and stimulating as the second or first hour? And sometimes even a concert by a musician or group that we really like gets tiresome after awhile.

Measuring Costs   In our concertgoer example, the student faces costs as well as receiving benefits from attending the concert. These costs are opportunity costs based on forgone uses of the student's time, such as studying or watching television, which would have also given the student satisfaction, or would have added points to the student's Util-O-Meter. Thus, the costs of the concert can be measured by the number of forgone utility points from alternative opportunities.

Table 11.3 gives the total and marginal costs, measured in forgone satisfaction points, of spending the evening at the concert. **Total cost** is the cost of spending a specified number of hours at the concert. **Marginal cost** is the change in total cost from each additional hour spent at the concert. As before, the marginal measurements are given at the midpoints between the hours.

Our student has many alternatives to attending the concert. Assume that one alternative to attending the concert for 1 hour is doing laundry. This action would give our concertgoer 25 Util-O-Meter points, thereby making the marginal opportunity cost of the first hour at the concert 25 points. These 25 marginal cost points equal the total cost for attending the concert for 1 hour because no previous total cost points have been accumulated.

To attend the second hour of the concert, assume that the student in our example gives up socializing with a friend that would have yielded 50 additional points of satisfaction, thereby making the marginal cost of the second hour 50 points. When these 50 marginal points are added to the total cost of 25 points for the first hour, the total cost of 2 hours at the concert becomes 75 points. The marginal cost of the third hour is 100 points of satisfaction that our student would have received from working out at the rec center. When these 100 marginal points are added to the 75 total cost points for 2 hours spent at the concert, the total cost of 3 hours at the concert becomes 175 points.

Law of Diminishing Marginal Utility

As additional units of an item are consumed, beyond some point each successive unit of the item consumed will add less to total utility than was added by the unit consumed just before it.

Total Cost

The cost of producing a specified number of units of a good, service, or activity.

Marginal Cost

The change in total cost from each additional unit of a good, service, or activity produced.

---

[2]We are not suggesting that the second unit consumed of an item *will always* add less satisfaction than the first or that the third unit *will always* add less satisfaction than the second. Rather, as successive units of an item are consumed, *eventually* a point will be reached where each additional unit consumed will add less to total satisfaction than was added by the previous unit. This point may arrive early on, as in the case of our concertgoer, or after the consumption of a large amount of an item.

TABLE 11.3	*Total and Marginal Costs of Attending a Concert*

Both the total and marginal costs of an activity, such as attending a concert, can be measured in terms of the utility points that are given up by forgoing an alternative use of time.

Number of Hours Attended	Total Cost	Marginal Cost
0	0 points	
		25 points
1	25 points	
		50 points
2	75 points	
		100 points
3	175 points	
		200 points
4	375 points	
		625 points
5	1,000 points	

The alternative to the fourth hour at the concert is studying for an economics quiz that must be taken the following morning. The marginal cost of this hour is the 200 points that would be added to total satisfaction by working for a good grade on the quiz. These points, when added to the 175 points for 3 hours, make the total cost of 4 hours at the concert 375 points. The marginal cost of the fifth hour is 625 points, which is the satisfaction that would be received by putting the finishing touches on an application for law school admission that has to go out the following morning. These 625 marginal cost points bring the total cost of attending the entire 5-hour concert to 1,000 points.

Notice that the marginal cost of attending each additional hour of the concert rises with the number of hours attended. The individual first gives up those alternatives that cost the least, and, as the evening goes on, the alternatives become more and more expensive.

Maximizing Satisfaction

So far we have measured the benefits and costs for a student spending an evening at a concert. Remembering that the goal of any action is to maximize satisfaction, we will now evaluate these benefits and costs to determine the number of hours that the student would spend at the concert to accomplish this objective.

Table 11.4 lists the concertgoer's total and marginal benefits as well as the total and marginal costs that were given in Tables 11.2 and 11.3. Table 11.4 also includes a measure of the net benefit received from spending a specified number of hours at the concert. Net benefit is what the concertgoer is trying to maximize. Table 11.4 indicates that the net benefit of 1 hour at the concert is 375 points, the net benefit of 2 hours is 625 points, and so on.

The net benefit points given in Table 11.4 show that satisfaction from the concert is maximized by attending for 3 hours. At the end of 3 hours, 725 net benefit points, the most that our student can get from this concert, have been realized. Attending the concert for just 1 or 2 hours or staying for 4 or 5 hours will yield less satisfaction than 725 points.

TABLE 11.4		*Benefits and Costs of Attending a Concert (In Utility Points)*				

Net benefit is maximized at the point where total benefit exceeds total cost by the greatest amount. Net benefit increases as long as marginal benefit is greater than marginal cost and decreases when marginal cost is greater than marginal benefit.

Number of Hours Attended	Net Benefit	Total Benefit	Total Cost	Marginal Benefit	Marginal Cost
0	0	0	0		
				400	25
1	375	400	25		
				300	50
2	625	700	75		
				200	100
3	725	900	175		
				100	200
4	625	1,000	375		
				0	625
5	0	1,000	1,000		

Net Benefit
The result when total cost is subtracted from total benefit.

How is net benefit calculated? The **net benefit** for a specified number of hours at the concert is simply the result when the total cost of those hours is subtracted from the total benefit. For example, as shown in Table 11.4, the total benefit from attending the concert for 1 hour is 400 points and the total cost is 25 points, leaving a net benefit of 375 points; the total benefit from attending for 2 hours is 700 points and the total cost is 75 points, leaving a net benefit of 625 points; and so on.

Net Benefit Maximizing Rules
Net benefit is maximized where total benefit exceeds total cost by the greatest amount or where marginal benefit equals marginal cost.

Net Benefit Maximizing Rules   There are two **net benefit maximizing rules** with each rule providing the same answer.

♦ Net benefit is maximized where total benefit exceeds total cost by the greatest amount.
♦ Net benefit is maximized where marginal benefit equals marginal cost.

For our student, net benefit is maximized at 3 hours. It is easy to apply the first rule and see this result. But the second rule, the marginal benefit equals marginal cost rule, is not so easy to see. Let's go back to Table 11.4.

For the first hour of the concert, the marginal benefit is 400 points and the marginal cost is 25 points. If you think of marginal benefit as adding points to a Util-O-Meter and marginal cost as subtracting points, then 400 points are added and 25 are subtracted during the first hour, leaving a gain in satisfaction, or gain in net benefit, of 375 points.

During the second hour, 300 more points, the marginal benefit, are added and 50 points, the marginal cost, are subtracted. The result is a gain in net benefit of 250 points to be added to the gain from the first hour. Thus, the net benefit after 2 hours is 625 points (375 points from the first hour plus 250 points from the second hour). During the third hour, 200 marginal benefit points are added and only 100 marginal cost points are subtracted, increasing the net benefit registered by 100 points and bringing it to 725 on the Util-O-Meter.

Notice that for each of these 3 hours, marginal benefit is greater than marginal cost, causing net benefit to increase. But also notice that marginal benefit is shrinking and marginal cost is growing. At some point they will be equal.

During the fourth hour, the marginal benefit is only 100 points, but the marginal cost is 200 points, causing more to be subtracted from total satisfaction than is added. Because of this, net benefit falls from 725 points to 625 points. If our student stayed at the concert for a fourth hour, that fourth hour would cost more satisfaction than it would give. During the fifth hour no points are added, but 625 are subtracted, causing net benefit again to fall.

We can see that our student is increasing satisfaction, or net benefit, by attending the concert as long as more utility points are added from the concert than would be added from the alternatives. Once the alternatives become more attractive, it is to the student's advantage to switch from the concert to an alternative.

Clearly, using the marginal cost–marginal benefit approach, net benefit is maximized by attending the concert for 3 hours. During the third hour, more marginal benefit points are added than marginal cost points are subtracted, but during the fourth hour more marginal cost points are subtracted than marginal benefit points are added. The concertgoer should leave at the end of 3 hours because at this point marginal cost equals marginal benefit. This equality will be easy to see when this relationship is graphed in the next section.

From this we can conclude that

- net benefit increases as long as marginal benefit is greater than marginal cost, no matter how small the difference;
- net benefit decreases when marginal cost becomes greater than marginal benefit because more is subtracted than is added to satisfaction; and
- net benefit is maximized at the point where marginal cost equals marginal benefit.

In summary, this example illustrates the two rules for maximizing net benefit, both yielding the same result. These rules are so important that we will restate them one more time. Maximization occurs where total benefit exceeds total cost by the greatest amount or where marginal benefit equals marginal cost.

Would you act as the student in our example did? Most likely you would. Have you ever returned early from a date, movie, or shopping because an important test or job interview was scheduled early the next morning? You have applied the maximizing rules in countless situations where you, perhaps subconsciously, weighed the marginal cost and marginal benefit of an action. For example, the decision of whether to eat one more chocolate chip cookie involves balancing the additional cost of the extra calories against the additional enjoyment from the cookie. Other decisions, such as which route to take to work on a snowy day, or whether to access online student tutorials that accompany a textbook, or whether to purchase an expensive or cheap pair of boots, all involve an application of the maximizing rules. What are some of the marginal costs and marginal benefits that might be considered in deciding whether to break the speed limit to arrive at work on time? Application 11.1, "Do It Yourself," gives some additional examples of the application of cost–benefit principles. Do you recognize yourself or someone you know in this application?

APPLICATION 11.1

DO IT YOURSELF

Let's face it—economists generally do not have a reputation for being exciting, wild, and zingy. Perhaps it is their preoccupation with analysis that makes the average person think of adjectives like *staid* and *serious* when generalizing about economists.

So, what about your authors? You will have spent an entire course reading this text, perhaps thinking that the writers are somber individuals who don't think about much except economics. You might be surprised.

Your authors, like "regular" people, think about painting, home repair, the lawn, the old pipes and wiring, and all the other things that require attention in a 90-year-old house. And they balance off the costs and benefits of getting work done by the local painter or lawn care service or doing it themselves. Like everyone else, they are fully aware of the promotion of do-it-yourself projects by stores like Lowe's and Home Depot.

Since the biggest commitment for any do-it-yourself project is time, the authors, like anyone else, figure out whether investing the time is worth it. Some of it comes down to alternatives and some down to sheer satisfaction. Like the student who would like to paint her apartment and can afford the few gallons of paint, but thinks twice about it because of the need to spend some time studying, the authors think about the alternative uses of their time.

While there are the demands of teaching and writing and community service that are time consuming, there are also the demands of everyday life. And how they are addressed and how much time is devoted to them depends on the degree of satisfaction they bring. For some people (like one of your authors) there is little satisfaction in working around the house. For others (like the other author) there is great satisfaction. And here is where the rubber meets the road.

Patrick professes that there is little time to do home projects and jokes that his favorite tool is the checkbook. While you might think that he is too busy reading and enjoying economics articles, the real reason is his love of music. Playing out with his jazz quartet and taking in a set at a jazz club yield untold utility points or satisfaction for him. Home projects are way down on his list. On the other hand, Gerry is happiest with a shovel, loads of compost, wallpaper paste, and frequent visits to Home Depot and Lowe's. To her, that checkbook is best used for plants, tools, and repair of her favorite piece of equipment, the tiller. Home and garden projects are laden with satisfaction for her.

Sooner or later, we all realize that our lives and our decisions are pretty basic and really do come down to a cost–benefit analysis. Understanding that balance between costs and benefits makes us smarter—but, importantly, it also makes us thoughtful in our relationships with family members and friends who may not share our "loves" in life. Understanding this economics stuff actually makes life easier to negotiate.

Graphing Costs, Benefits, and Net Benefit

The relationships that were just introduced can be illustrated graphically. Our student's total cost and total benefit from attending the concert are shown in the upper graph of Figure 11.1, marginal cost and marginal benefit are given in the middle graph, and net benefit is shown in the lower graph. These figures are plotted from the information in Table 11.4.

As long as total benefit is greater than total cost, there is a positive net benefit. As can be seen in the upper graph of Figure 11.1, net benefit is equal to the vertical distance between total benefit and total cost for any given number of hours spent attending the concert. Thus, maximum net benefit occurs where the vertical distance between total benefit and total cost is the greatest in the upper graph and at the highest point on the net benefit curve in the lower graph. This occurs at 3 hours.

Notice also that as long as marginal benefit is greater than marginal cost in the middle graph, net benefit increases in the lower graph, and when marginal cost is greater than marginal benefit, net benefit falls. Net benefit reaches its maximum where marginal cost equals marginal benefit. This again occurs at 3 hours. You might also notice that marginal cost and marginal benefit are plotted at the midpoints, just as they were given at the midpoints in the tables.

| FIGURE 11.1 | *Total Cost and Benefit, Marginal Cost and Benefit, and Net Benefit* |

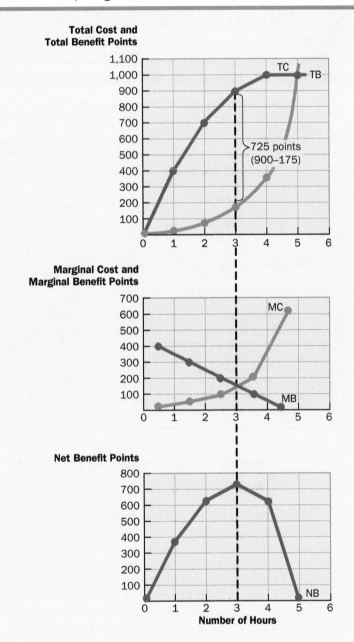

Graphically, net benefit is equal to the vertical distance between the total benefit and total cost curves; it is at its maximum where total benefit exceeds total cost by the greatest amount. Net benefit is increasing when marginal benefit is greater than marginal cost, at its maximum when marginal benefit equals marginal cost, and decreasing when marginal benefit is less than marginal cost.

BALANCING BENEFITS AND COSTS: THE BUSINESS

Defining Benefits and Costs

Just like individuals, businesses are constantly making decisions. These range from deciding among candidates to fill a part-time job to advertising budgets to possible mergers. While it may appear that business decision making is quite different from individual decision making, it is actually similar in several respects. Like individuals, businesses try to maximize their economic well-being. And, just like individuals, maximizing by a business requires balancing the costs and benefits of different courses of action to find the one most in its interest.

But a business differs from an individual in that its economic well-being is generally measured in terms of profit rather than utility, or satisfaction. So the goal of a business is to weigh its benefits, which are measured by the revenue it receives from selling a product, against its costs of producing the product to find the output level that maximizes its profit.

In economics, we categorize the various costs of producing a firm's good or service into two groups: explicit and implicit costs. **Explicit costs** are direct payments, or actual dollar outlays, made by a business for a workforce, materials, machinery, equipment, and so forth. The monthly paychecks that a company issues to its employees, liability insurance payments, and checks to the local paper for an ad are all examples of explicit costs. Explicit costs are sometimes called accounting costs.

Implicit costs are not direct payments for inputs but are opportunity costs to the owner(s) of a business that must be recovered through profit in order for the business to continue. Implicit costs could be forgone interest from money the owners have invested in the business rather than in securities, rental payments that could have been earned if a building that houses the business were leased to another company, income the owners could have received by using their talents and efforts in an alternative enterprise, or any other returns that have been given up by the owners.

The profit that the owners of a business expect to earn to cover their implicit costs is called **normal profit**. Normal profit is necessary to keep a business in operation because its owners will use their time, money, or talents in an alternative if they cannot receive the gain necessary to compensate for these inputs. In simple terms, normal profit is the profit necessary to keep a business going.

Because a business will shut down if its owners do not earn a normal profit, normal profit is considered to be an economic cost of production. The **economic cost of production** of a good or service is equal to the business's explicit costs plus its implicit costs, or normal profit to its owners.

Any profit beyond normal profit is called **excess profit**, or **economic profit**. For example, if an owner needed $80,000 of normal profit to remain in business and the actual profit were $92,000, then $12,000 would be economic, or excess, profit. Economic, or excess, profit is not a cost, because the owner would remain with the business if it were not earned. Review Question 5 at the end of this chapter provides a good opportunity for you to test your understanding of normal and economic profits.

Application 11.2, "You Need an Economist," provides some additional thoughts about the value of understanding the need to cover implicit costs in operating a business. Do you know anyone who has not succeeded in business because of the inability to cover implicit costs and earn a normal profit?

Explicit Costs

Payments that a business makes to acquire factors of production, such as labor, raw materials, and machinery.

Implicit Costs

The opportunity costs to business owners from using their resources in the business rather than in an alternative opportunity; must be recovered to keep the business in operation; normal profit.

Normal Profit

Profit necessary to recover implicit costs and keep a business in operation; considered to be an economic cost of production.

Economic Cost of Production

Includes all explicit and implicit costs of producing a good or service.

Excess Profit (Economic Profit)

Profit beyond normal profit; not considered a cost of production.

TABLE 11.5		*Revenues from Selling Chairs*		

The total revenue from selling an item is calculated by multiplying the price of the item times the quantity demanded at that price. Marginal revenue is the change in total revenue from selling one more unit of an item.

Price	Quantity Demanded	Total Revenue	Marginal Revenue
$450	0	$0	
			$400
400	1	400	
			300
350	2	700	
			200
300	3	900	
			100
250	4	1,000	
			0
200	5	1,000	

Measuring Revenues and Costs

The mechanics for determining profit maximization are the same as those for maximizing satisfaction. The only difference is what is being balanced and what is being maximized. For a business, revenues and costs from operations are being balanced to maximize profit. So the example we are about to work through introduces no new principles. Rather, it shows how the principles already learned for an individual can be applied to a business.

Measuring Revenues   Arts and crafts shows are abundant in communities across the country. Suppose that a metal craftsperson who produces all sorts of outdoor work—from yard art to iron gates—has also designed a unique rocking chair. This chair appeals to people looking for a piece of useful art for a porch or patio. The craftsperson's problem is to determine how many chairs to produce and haul for sale at each fair. It is important to put just the right number of rockers in the truck for any given fair to maximize profit.

The solution to how many chairs to haul off to a fair is found by balancing the costs from producing different quantities of the chair against the benefits, which in this example are the revenues, from different levels of sales. The revenues that the craftsperson could earn from selling different quantities of the chair at different prices are shown in Table 11.5.

The first two columns of the table give the demand for this chair by showing quantities of the chair demanded at different prices. At a price of $450, no chairs would be demanded. But if the price were lowered to $400, one chair would be demanded; if it were $350, two chairs would be demanded; and so on. Thus, the first two columns of Table 11.5 show how the Law of Demand operates for potential chair buyers.

The Total Revenue column in Table 11.5 shows how much revenue would be generated at each level of demand. **Total revenue** is calculated by multiplying the price of an item by the quantity demanded at that price. For example, two chairs demanded at $350 each would generate $700 in total revenue.

Total Revenue

Revenue received from selling a certain quantity of an item; calculated by multiplying the price of an item by the quantity demanded at that price.

APPLICATION 11.2

You Need an Economist

While small businesses, from the retail shop to specialty manufacturing to landscape design consulting, exemplify the entrepreneurial spirit that is so valued in the United States, it is a known fact that the life of many small businesses is short. About 25 percent of small businesses have employees; the rest do not. About half of new small businesses survive for five or more years and only one-third for ten or more years.[a]

We propose that economics needs to play a bigger role in helping small businesses succeed, especially in the early start-up of the business. It is the economic cost of production that needs to take center stage in making business decisions as a small business takes off. The accounting cost of production, which is the focus of most small businesses, needs to play a smaller role.

In today's world, many young, talented entrepreneurs are entering the food and wellness arena. These folks are being driven by passions for baking bread, pies, and cakes, producing organic cheeses and jams, making soap and lotions, and more. As they go into business, there are the typical questions. Can I make enough money to cover the rent? Can I borrow enough for and make the payments on equipment, inventory, and furnishings? Can I cover my costs?

That last question, can I cover my costs, is frequently at the root of the demise of a small business. So often, a small business counts on the labor of the owner, and sometimes the owner's family and friends, to keep the business running. The bread baker's spouse tends the shop while the passionate baker is at the oven, the aunt helps her niece with the soap shop, and the family-owned restaurant uses lots of relatives to serve and clear the tables. The issue is—how long can this last. When do family members and friends bail? When does the owner realize that 60-hour weeks are yielding very little return? When is the decision made to end the business and go to work somewhere else with decent hours and a steady salary?

It's all about that economic cost of production—the viewpoint that considers implicit costs in calculating the "real" cost of production. The entrepreneur needs to make decisions that allow enough profit to ensure that the business continues. The economic cost of production reminds the owner that an adequate return for that "free" labor and those entrepreneurial efforts is a necessary cost to cover.

The moral of the story is that the economic view of production costs should be a part of all small business endeavors.

[a]Small Business Administration, Office of Advocacy, "Frequently Asked Questions," March 2014, www.sba.gov/advocacy.

Marginal Revenue

The change in total revenue when one more (or additional) unit of an item is demanded.

The change in total revenue when one more (or additional) unit of output is demanded is termed **marginal revenue**. In Table 11.5, the Marginal Revenue column gives the change in total revenue with each additional chair demanded. For example, when the number of chairs demanded goes from zero to one, total revenue changes from $0 to $400, making the marginal revenue from the first chair equal to $400; when the number of chairs demanded goes from one to two, total revenue increases from $400 to $700, making the marginal revenue from the second chair $300; and so on. As was done with marginal benefits and marginal costs in the previous example, the marginal revenues in Table 11.5 are listed at the midpoints between the quantities demanded. (If you are interested in understanding why marginal revenue is less than price for the second, third, fourth, and fifth chairs sold, see footnote 3.)[3]

[3]You might have noticed that when the quantity demanded is two, three, four, or five chairs, marginal revenue is less than the price of the chair. For example, when two chairs are demanded at a price of $350, only $300 is added to total revenue by selling the second chair. Why is this so?

If the craftsperson sells only one chair, $400 in revenue is generated. However, in order to sell two chairs, the price must be lowered to $350. This means that the seller is going to charge $350 to the first buyer as well as the second buyer. Rather than receiving $400 from the first buyer, the craftsperson will have to give the first buyer a $50 discount. Because of this, what is added to total revenue from the sale of the second chair is not its price. Rather, the marginal revenue from the second unit sold is the price of the second unit minus the discount given to the first buyer, or $350 − $50 = $300.

Likewise, if the craftsperson wants to sell three chairs, the price must be lowered to $300. But if the third buyer pays only $300, $300 must also be charged to each of the other two buyers who would have otherwise paid $350. Thus, the marginal revenue from the third unit sold is not equal to the $300 price. Instead, it equals the $300 price minus the two $50 discounts given to the other two buyers, or $300 − $100 = $200. To test your understanding of this principle, see if you can explain why the marginal revenue from the fourth unit is $100, while its price is $250.

TABLE 11.6	*Costs of Producing Chairs*

Total cost is the cost of producing a specified number of units of output, and marginal cost measures the change in total cost from producing each additional unit of output.

Quantity	Total Cost	Marginal Cost
0	$0	
		$250
1	250	
		250
2	500	
		250
3	750	
		250
4	1,000	
		250
5	1,250	

Measuring Costs   The craftsperson's costs are shown in Table 11.6. To keep matters simple, let us say that these costs, which include implicit costs, or normal profit, come to $250 for each rocking chair.

Table 11.6 shows the craftsperson's total cost, which is the cost per chair times the quantity of chairs produced, at various levels of output. At a cost of $250 per chair, total cost would be zero if none were produced, $250 if one chair were produced, $500 ($250 × 2) if two were produced, and so on.

Marginal cost measures how much total cost changes as each additional unit of an item is produced. The Marginal Cost column of Table 11.6 shows the additional cost of producing one more chair. For example, when the quantity goes from zero to one, total cost goes from $0 to $250, making the marginal cost of the first chair equal to $250. When the quantity changes from one to two, total cost goes from $250 to $500, and the marginal cost of the second chair is again $250. As was done with the previous marginal values, the marginal costs in Table 11.6 are listed between the quantities produced.

Maximizing Profit

The number of chairs that the craftsperson should produce and sell to maximize profit can be shown by combining the information from Tables 11.5 and 11.6, as is done in Table 11.7. But before analyzing the numbers in the table, let us review what we should expect to find.

Remember that both the individual at the concert and the craftsperson are trying to maximize net benefit by weighing costs and benefits and that the only difference between them is how benefits and costs are measured and what they are looking to maximize. Given these similarities, we should expect that the rules for maximizing are the same. So, for the craftsperson, profit should be at a maximum where total revenue exceeds total cost by the greatest amount, or where marginal revenue equals marginal cost. Table 11.7 lets us check this out.

| TABLE 11.7 | | *Revenues, Costs, and Profit on Chairs* |

The maximum profit that can be obtained from producing and selling chairs occurs at two units. At this output level, total revenue exceeds total cost by the greatest amount and marginal revenue equals marginal cost.

Price	Quantity	Profit	Total Revenue	Total Cost	Marginal Revenue	Marginal Cost
$450	0	$0	$0	$0		
					$400	$250
400	1	150	400	250		
					300	250
350	2	200	700	500		
					200	250
300	3	150	900	750		
					100	250
250	4	0	1,000	1,000		
					0	250
200	5	−250	1,000	1,250		

Profit or Loss

The results when a business subtracts its total cost from its total revenue.

The Profit column in Table 11.7 shows that a maximum profit of $200 occurs at two units of output. How does this relate to total revenue and total cost? **Profit or loss** is found by subtracting total cost from total revenue at each level of output. For example, if the seller were to produce and sell three chairs, total revenue minus total cost would be $900 – $750, or $150. As indicated in this table, maximum profit for a business occurs where total revenue exceeds total cost by the greatest amount.

What is the relationship between marginal revenue and marginal cost where profit is maximized? Reading down the last two columns in Table 11.7, we can see that from zero to one, and from one to two units of output, marginal revenue is greater than marginal cost: Each chair adds more to total revenue than to total cost, causing profit to increase. This can be verified by noticing that the numbers in the Profit column increase as output and sales go from zero to two units.

In Table 11.7 marginal cost is greater than marginal revenue as output goes from two to three, from three to four, and from four to five units. In this case, the third, fourth, and fifth units are adding more to total cost than to total revenue, causing profit to fall. This is confirmed by the figures in the Profit column.

Profit-Maximizing Rules

Profit is maximized at the output level where total revenue exceeds total cost by the greatest amount, or where marginal revenue equals marginal cost.

Because marginal revenue is greater than marginal cost up to two units of output, and less than marginal cost beyond two units of output, marginal revenue and marginal cost must be equal at two units. Thus, the two **profit-maximizing rules** are satisfied at an output level of two units. Again, these rules state that profit is maximized at the output level where

♦ total revenue exceeds total cost by the greatest amount, and
♦ marginal revenue equals marginal cost.

Graphing Costs, Revenues, and Profit

The relationships among marginal revenue, marginal cost, and profit as well as among total revenue, total cost, and profit that were set out in Table 11.7 are illustrated in Figure 11.2. The bottom graph in Figure 11.2 shows that profit, or net benefit, is at its maximum where two chairs are produced and sold.

The middle graph in Figure 11.2 shows that marginal revenue and marginal cost are equal at exactly two units of output. For smaller output levels, marginal revenue is greater than marginal cost, which causes profit in the lower graph to increase. For output levels larger than two units, marginal revenue is less than marginal cost, causing profit to fall.

Finally, in the upper graph in Figure 11.2, the vertical distance by which the total revenue curve exceeds the total cost curve is at its maximum at two units of output, which, of course, is the output level where profit is maximized in the lower graph.

In summary, regardless of whether an individual, business, or government unit is being considered, the net benefit to the decision-making unit from an activity will be maximized if it operates where total benefit exceeds total cost by the greatest amount. This is also where marginal benefit and marginal cost are equal. The main difference between the decision-making units is not that they follow different rules. Rather, the difference is in what is maximized and how costs and benefits are measured. Working through Test Your Understanding, "Maximizing Profit," will allow you to master the maximizing rules.

SOCIAL BENEFITS AND COSTS

In the cases just discussed, any concern over whether, how, or to what extent others might be affected by an individual's or a business's decision was absent. People generally choose courses of action after considering the factors that affect them directly, even though sometimes what they do will benefit or impose a cost on others. Because of this, the costs and benefits to individuals and businesses of their actions may differ from the costs and benefits to society of those same actions.

Externality
The effect of an action on a person or thing that was not one of the parties involved in the action.

Positive Externality
An externality that creates a benefit for others.

Negative Externality
An externality that creates a cost for others.

The effects that decisions and actions have on persons or things that are not involved in the decisions or actions are called **externalities**. Externalities may be either positive and benefit others, or negative and costly to others. For example, getting a flu shot may benefit not only you but also those who could have caught the flu from you. Maintaining your car benefits you and also all the people who could have been delayed if you broke down on the road. In these cases your actions have worked to the advantage of others and have created **positive externalities**.

On the other hand, a factory that pollutes the air or water or individuals who buy alcohol and then drive while intoxicated contribute to the detriment of others and create **negative externalities**. Because of pollution, residents of a community could incur health problems and additional medical bills or have their property values decrease. For example, in one small town in southeastern Missouri, the dust particles from a lead smelter created some health issues for the community's children and left some homes virtually impossible to sell.

Application 11.3, "The Cost of Smoking," deals with recent reports by the Centers for Disease Control and Prevention and others on the costs of smoking, many of which are externalities.

FIGURE 11.2   *Total Revenue and Cost, Marginal Revenue and Cost, and Profit*

Graphically, profit is maximized at the output level where the total revenue curve exceeds the total cost curve by the greatest amount, or where the marginal revenue curve crosses the marginal cost curve.

MAXIMIZING PROFIT

Pete Casso has been invited to exhibit two of his works in the annual student art show and sale. Although those who are invited to participate in the show receive a great deal of personal satisfaction, or "psychic income," from having been selected, the show also presents an opportunity for the exhibitors to earn some money. Pete is concerned about making as much money as he can from this sale to help defray tuition costs for next semester. Because he studied economics last year, he realizes the importance of pricing his works of art correctly in order to maximize profit.

Pete has chosen to include a pen-and-ink drawing of a house and a colorful lithograph in the show because both of these items can bring multiple sales. The house drawing will serve as a sample of Pete's custom work in this area. That is, he produces pen-and-ink drawings of individual homes from photographs and, based on the sam-

ple, can take orders for these custom drawings. The lithograph that he has chosen can be easily reproduced many times without losing its design and color, so he can sell multiples of this work.

Table 1 gives the demand schedule that Pete thinks to be true for custom house drawings. He calculates his cost for each house drawing at $50, which accounts for his time and materials. Complete Table 1 to determine the price Pete should charge and the number of drawings he should sell to maximize his profit from the drawings. Why is his roommate not correct in advising him to go for volume and charge $58 per drawing?

Table 2 gives the demand schedule for Pete's lithograph. The cost of producing the first lithograph is high—$200—but the marginal cost for each additional print is only $15. Complete this table and indicate the price Pete should charge for his lithograph. What is the maximum profit that he can expect to make from the sale of his lithograph?

Answers can be found at the back of the book.

TABLE 1   *Demand, Revenue, and Cost Information for Custom-Drawn Houses*

Price per Drawing	Number of Drawings Demanded	Total Revenue	Marginal Revenue	Marginal Cost	Total Cost	Profit
$138	0	_____			_____	_____
128	1	_____	_____	_____	_____	_____
118	2	_____	_____	_____	_____	_____
108	3	_____	_____	_____	_____	_____
98	4	_____	_____	_____	_____	_____
88	5	_____	_____	_____	_____	_____
78	6	_____	_____	_____	_____	_____
68	7	_____	_____	_____	_____	_____
58	8	_____	_____	_____	_____	_____

TABLE 2   *Demand, Revenue, and Cost Information for Lithographs*

Price per Lithograph	Number of Lithographs Demanded	Total Revenue	Marginal Revenue	Marginal Cost	Total Cost	Profit or Loss
$180	0	_____		$200	_____	
170	1	_____	_____		$200	_____
160	2	_____	_____	_____	_____	_____
150	3	_____	_____	_____	_____	_____
140	4	_____	_____	_____	_____	_____
130	5	_____	_____	_____	_____	_____
120	6	_____	_____	_____	_____	_____
110	7	_____	_____	_____	_____	_____
100	8	_____	_____	_____	_____	_____
90	9	_____	_____	_____	_____	_____
80	10	_____	_____	_____	_____	_____

APPLICATION 11.3

THE REAL COST OF SMOKING

While the cost of smoking is high—an average of $6.36 per pack in the United States—or over $2,300 per year for the pack-a-day smoker, it is the external costs that can be shocking.

It has been well publicized that smoking results in significant health and medical costs as it causes damage throughout the body. "Tobacco use remains the single largest preventable cause of disease and premature death in the U.S.," says the American Cancer Society. Smoking risks include lung cancer, heart disease, chronic obstructive pulmonary disease, and other health issues such as cancers of the mouth and throat, and more. It has been estimated that health costs amount to $35 per pack of cigarettes smoked.

Secondhand smoke exposure also brings medical costs. Children who are exposed tend to have lung issues and more frequent and severe asthma attacks. There have been studies that indicate a lessening of heart attacks in communities that go smoke-free.

And there are so many other external costs. The productivity of smokers is reduced by illness and absence from work, and from the more frequent breaks taken by smokers. The money that is spent on cigarettes has opportunity costs: The one-pack-a-day smoker could save those thousands of dollars a year and build a nice savings account.

Smokers have higher life and health insurance costs. They have larger bills for dry-cleaning services, dental care, and perfumes. Smokers' cars and houses are either worth less or require expenditures to remove smells before selling them. New carpet and paint might be necessary to obtain a market price for a smoker's house that is for sale.

But one of the biggest costs is the lower lifetime retirement benefits received by smokers because they die, on average, at least ten years younger than non-smokers. A person might pay into the Social Security system for decades only to experience an early death and just a few years of Social Security benefits.

So, how do we deal with the costs and damage caused by smoking? How do we reduce the significant medical and other bills for smokers? We can spread the word that premature aging, stained fingers, a diminished ability to do physical activity, increased infections, and more come from smoking. Or we can increase the price of a pack of cigarettes through taxing, which some states have done. There are studies to indicate that increased prices do bring about a decrease in the consumption of cigarettes.

Sources: "Is Smoking Dragging You Down," www.webmd.com; "Tobacco: The True Cost of Smoking," www.cancer.org; "How Much Does Smoking Really Cost?" www.costofsmoking.com; "Health Costs," therealcost.betobaccofree.hhs.gov; "10 Reasons to Quite Smoking," www.webmd.com.

Maximizing Society's Net Benefit

Externalities must be added to individual or business cost–benefit calculations to determine how society is affected by an action. The total effect on society of the private benefits and costs plus the externalities of an action are the action's **social benefits** and **social costs**. So,

Social Benefits and Costs
The total effect on society from the private benefits, private costs, and externalities of an action.

♦   private benefits + positive externalities = social benefits;

♦   private costs + negative externalities = social costs; and

♦   social benefits − social costs = net benefits to society.

Net benefit for society is calculated in exactly the same way as for businesses and individuals. The only difference is that now we are concerned with social rather than private benefits and costs. Thus, the net benefit to society from an activity is maximized where its total social benefit exceeds its total social cost by the greatest amount, or where marginal social benefit equals marginal social cost.

How do externalities affect the relationship between what is best for the individual or business and what is best for society? If an action of an individual or business has no effect on others, there will be no externalities, and the level of activity that maximizes the net benefit of the individual or business will also maximize the net benefit of society. Where private actions impose costs on others and cause negative externalities, the level of activity that maximizes society's net benefit will be less than the level where private net benefit is maximized. For example, if the profit-maximizing output for a business results in costly pollution problems, society would be better off if the firm produced a lower level of output and less pollution. The evidence in Application 11.3 that smoking imposes significant external costs on society strongly suggests that society would be better off with less smoking.

When the actions of an individual or business benefit others and cause positive externalities, the level of activity that maximizes society's net benefit will be greater than the level that maximizes private net benefit. For example, some people maximize private net benefit by not spending money for a college education. But society is clearly better off with an educated population. Cities with a highly educated workforce tend to be more vibrant and economically healthy.

Relationship between Private and Social Net Benefits   The relationship between private and social net benefits is shown in Figure 11.3. Figure 11.3a illustrates production with negative but no positive externalities. Here the private marginal costs and benefits from producing this product are represented by PMC and PMB. Private net benefit (in this case, profit) would be maximized where PMB = PMC, which occurs at the output level shown by point Y on the horizontal axis.

Now let's add negative externalities, or costs to society (such as from air pollution), to determine social costs and, from that, the best output level for society. When the negative externalities are added to the private costs, society's marginal cost is represented by SMC in Figure 11.3a. And since there are no positive externalities, society's marginal benefit, SMB, is the same as private marginal benefit (shown by the line PMB = SMB). Now, from society's perspective, the best level of output is shown by point X on the horizontal axis of Figure 11.3a because here society's marginal benefit, SMB, equals society's marginal cost, SMC. In this case, it would be in the interest of society to cut back production from point Y to point X.

Production that yields positive externalities (such as creating jobs in a depressed area) and no negative externalities is shown in Figure 11.3b. In this case, private net benefit would be maximized by producing where private marginal benefit, PMB, and private marginal cost, PMC, are equal, or at point Y on the horizontal axis. But when the positive externalities are added to the private benefit, social marginal benefit, shown by SMB, results. In this case, where no costs are imposed on society (so that PMC = SMC), the best position for society would be at output level Z, where SMB = SMC. Here it would be in society's interest to increase production from point Y to point Z.

In very simple terms, too many goods and services are produced in markets with negative externalities and too few goods and services are produced in markets with positive externalities. If this is the case, how can society induce individuals and businesses to decrease undesirable and increase desirable activities? Activities that produce negative externalities can be reduced through fines, taxes, outright prohibition, or other penalties. Such methods have been used in the United States to control air and water pollution, drunk driving, and crime. To encourage activities that yield positive externalities, government can provide tax breaks, direct grants of money, subsidies, or other inducements. For example, at times local governments have given tax breaks to businesses for locating in their communities, thereby creating new jobs; and the federal government gives various types of financial assistance to students to help them complete their educations.

Up for Debate, "Should Drivers Be Banned from Using Cell Phones While Operating a Vehicle?" gives two sides of a hotly contested issue. On one side are those who think that the negative externalities created by driving and using a cell phone are

| FIGURE 11.3 | *Maximizing Social Net Benefit with Negative and Positive Externalities* |

When production generates negative externalities, society's net benefit is maximized by cutting back on the output level. When production generates positive externalities, society's net benefit is maximized by increasing the output level.

so serious that this action should be banned. On the other side are those who think that cell phone usage in cars is part of our lifestyles and that government should not regulate the use. What is your opinion, and how has your assessment of social costs and benefits led you to this position?

PUBLIC CHOICE

The goal of maximizing economic well-being and the principles of cost–benefit analysis are easily understood in the context of individual and business decision making. In our economic system, however, many important decisions are made collectively—that is, by a group. Collective decision making occurs primarily through the government sector. As a group we make choices about how many municipal police cars and dump trucks to purchase, whether to provide more funds for our schools, and how much money to allocate to national defense.

How do individuals participate in collective decision making? In the United States, voting is the root of collective choice. Individuals elect officials at the federal, state, and local government levels who receive the power and authority to act on behalf of the group. Thus, voting provides the link that transforms individual decision making into collective choice.

The term used to describe the set of economic theories that explains the motives and attitudes of voters and public officials in collective decision making is **public choice**. The basic idea behind public choice is that people try to maximize their own well-being in making collective choices. Thus, the fundamental rules of decision making do not change when a group is involved.

Public Choice

The study of the economic motives and attitudes of voters and public officials in collective decision making.

UP FOR DEBATE

SHOULD DRIVERS BE BANNED FROM USING CELL PHONES WHILE OPERATING A VEHICLE?

Issue *Cell phone usage is enormous, not only in the United States but around the globe. This reliance on cell phones to communicate by voice and by text has brought increasing concern about using cell phones while driving. While the private benefit of buying and using a cell phone while driving may bring an individual maximum satisfaction, there is concern for the negative externalities that are being generated by this action. There is evidence that accidents which cause harm to others are the result of cell phone usage while driving. The question that arises is: Should drivers be banned from using cell phones while operating a vehicle?*

Yes There are many studies which link cell phone usage while driving to accidents. One study at the University of Utah compared driving while drunk (using a simulator of course) and driving while using a cell phone. "We found that people are as impaired when they drive and talk on a cell phone as they are when they drive intoxicated at the legal blood-alcohol limit," said an assistant professor of psychology.

People are inattentive to their surroundings when they are engaged in conversation—sometimes a heated conversation fraught with emotion. The use of a cell phone to text means that eyes are taken off the road, sometimes for fairly long distances. Recognizing these impairments as well as the accident data associated with cell phones, many states have passed laws banning cell phone usage while driving or at least banning text messaging. As of 2015, 14 states have banned handheld cell phones, 44 have banned text messaging for all drivers, 38 states have banned cell phone usage by novice drivers, and 20 states prohibit school bus drivers from using cell phones.

There is also increased attention to making drivers aware of other distractions, from eating to conversations with passengers. These behaviors certainly put other drivers, bikers, and pedestrians at risk. Substantial negative externalities are created.

No Cell phones provide a huge convenience in a hectic world where multitasking has become the expected way of life. Cell phones allow families to keep connected and even travelers to be easily met at an airport. Friendships are extended and enriched by easy and frequent communication. Moreover, in a vehicle, a cell phone can mean security in the event of a car problem or dangerous road condition, and may even calm stressed drivers who can relay that they may be late for an important appointment.

While there are some studies that link cell phone usage to accidents, the real problem is driver inattention. This can occur when reaching for a drink, using GPS, or changing a CD. There are many other reasons for accidents, like driving while intoxicated or while impaired by health or other conditions. If there are such dire consequences from driving and talking on a cell phone, wouldn't there be a national ban against it?

It is a right of individuals to be able to buy and use cell phones when they want. We have enough government regulation and do not need for government to interfere with our right to communicate.

Sources: "Cell Phone Driving Laws," www.ghsa.org/html/stateinfo/laws/cellphone_laws.html; Robert Roy Britt, "Cell Phones Make Drivers as Bad as Drunks," LiveScience, http://www.livescience.com/health/060629_cell_phones.html; "Cellphones and Driving," Insurance Information Institute, http://www.iii.org/media/hottopics/insurance/cellphones/; Governors Highway Safety Association, "Cell Phone and Texting Laws," www.ghsa.org, 3/3/2012; "Distracted Driving Laws", February 2015, www.ghsa.org/html/stateinfo/laws/cellphone_laws.html.

Maximizing Behavior and the Voting Process

A look at the voting process helps to illustrate public choice theory. For an election, people make some basic decisions: whether to vote or not; how much information to seek about candidates and issues; and for whom to vote. Each of these choices carries costs and benefits.

The act of voting gives individuals varying degrees of satisfaction: If people believe that their votes make a difference, voting gives them more satisfaction than if they feel that their votes have no impact. Voting also imposes costs, especially the opportunity cost of time. Thus, a person's decision about whether or not to vote in an election depends on the marginal benefit and marginal cost of voting. If marginal benefit is greater than marginal cost, a person will vote in an election; if marginal cost is greater than marginal benefit, a person will not vote.

A second consideration in voting involves the amount of information about candidates and issues that a voter has when making a decision at the polls. Generally, when individuals make private decisions about spending large sums of money, they attempt to gather as much information as possible. Someone who is about to buy a car is probably visiting websites that rate automobiles, taking test drives, and asking car owners about particular models. Many people will pay as much in taxes this year as they do in car payments or even as much as the cost of a new car. Yet, are they investing as much time and energy in gathering information about the elected officials to whom they are entrusting these tax dollars? Probably not.

Information seeking about candidates and issues takes time. As a result, the opportunity cost of becoming an informed voter can be high, causing a person to be **rationally ignorant**. That is, a rational voter may perceive that the marginal benefit from becoming better acquainted with a candidate's record and position is less than the marginal cost of becoming enlightened. Because of this, voters often make choices based on limited information that comes from brief advertisements and "sound bites" designed to sell a candidate.

Which candidate does a voter choose? Again, the principles of cost–benefit analysis apply. A voter will select the candidate perceived to bring the greatest net benefit to the voter. This decision could be based on the candidate's record, the position of the candidate on an issue important to the voter, or any other consideration.

Public choice theory, with its emphasis on self-interest, helps to explain many of the problems that result from collective decision making. For example, **special-interest groups** often cause the will of a minority to be imposed on the majority. Public choice theory explains that members of special-interest groups actively promote their positions through letters, ads, campaign contributions, and other means because of the benefits they expect to receive. The response to these issues from the rest of the population may be weak because of lack of interest or because the opportunity cost of responding is too high. Elected officials are sometimes sensitive to the pleas of special-interest-group members because of the message that they hear or because the group members' support or opposition can impact an official's reelection.

Rational Ignorance
Choosing to remain uninformed because the marginal cost of obtaining the information is higher than the marginal benefit from knowing it.

Special-Interest Group
People who share a common position on a particular issue and actively promote that position.

Summary

1.   There are general rules for maximizing economic well-being that can be applied to any decision-making unit: an individual, a business, or society. These rules involve the balancing of costs and benefits from different courses of action in order to select the one that contributes most to economic well-being. The formal study of these rules and the balancing of costs and benefits is called cost–benefit analysis. These rules can be applied to many more areas of human endeavor than those traditionally studied in economics courses.

2.   For an individual, the benefits of an activity can be measured in terms of the satisfaction, or utility, received from the action. Costs can be measured by the opportunity forgone in accomplishing that action.

3.   For a business, benefits are measured by the total revenue received, which is calculated by multiplying the price of an item times the quantity sold. The economic cost of producing a good or service includes explicit costs, which are

direct payments for factors of production, and implicit costs, which are returns required by the owner(s) to keep the business in operation. Normal profit is what the owner(s) must earn to recover implicit costs. Economic profit is not a cost of production; it is that profit in excess of normal profit.

4.   Total benefit or revenue and total cost are, respectively, the benefit or revenue received and the cost incurred from producing a particular amount of an activity or output. Marginal benefit or revenue is the change in total benefit or revenue resulting from each additional unit of an activity performed or output sold. Marginal cost is the change in total cost from producing one more unit of activity or output.

5.   Maximum net benefit (or profit) occurs where total benefit (revenue) exceeds total cost by the greatest amount, or where marginal benefit (revenue) equals marginal cost. Both rules are satisfied at exactly the same level of activity. When marginal benefit (revenue) exceeds marginal cost, net benefit (profit) rises, and when marginal benefit (revenue) is less than marginal cost, net benefit (profit) falls. The main difference in how these rules are applied to various decision-making units is in what is maximized and how benefits and costs are measured.

6.   Activities by individuals or businesses may help or hurt others. These effects are called positive and negative externalities. Because of externalities, the level of an activity that maximizes an individual's or a business's net benefit may differ from the level that would maximize society's net benefit.

7.   Net benefit is calculated for society in the same way as for individuals and businesses. Society measures its net benefit in terms of social costs and social benefits. Social costs are private costs plus any negative external effects. Social benefits are private benefits plus any positive external effects. When negative externalities are present, society's net benefit is maximized at a lower level of activity than is private net benefit; when positive externalities are present, society's net benefit is maximized at a higher level of activity.

8.   Public choice deals with the economic theories behind collective decision making, much of which is carried out through the voting process. Individuals participate in the voting process based on the costs and benefits from the acts of voting, information seeking, and candidate selection. Problems that arise from collective decision making, such as the impact of special-interest groups, can be explained using cost–benefit analysis.

Key Terms and Concepts		
	Cost–benefit analysis	Total cost
	Utility	Marginal cost
	Opportunity cost	Net benefit
	Marginal benefit (marginal utility)	Net benefit maximizing rules
	Total benefit (total utility)	Explicit costs
	Law of Diminishing Marginal Utility	Implicit costs
		Normal profit

Economic cost of production
Excess profit (economic profit)
Total revenue
Marginal revenue
Profit or loss
Profit-maximizing rules
Externality

Positive externality
Negative externality
Social benefits and costs
Public choice
Rational ignorance
Special-interest group

Review Questions

1. In this chapter, you have been introduced to marginal benefit, marginal utility, marginal revenue, social marginal benefit, marginal cost, and social marginal cost. To what specifically does each term refer and what concept is common to all of these terms?

2. Explain why: (a) net benefit increases when marginal benefit exceeds marginal cost; (b) net benefit is at a maximum when marginal benefit equals marginal cost; and (c) net benefit falls when marginal benefit is less than marginal cost.

3. In what respects are the following maximizing decisions similar to each other and in what respects are they different?
   a. The decision by a person about how much cake to eat
   b. The decision by a community about how many resources to devote to law enforcement
   c. The decision by a business about how much of its product to produce and sell
   d. The decision by a person about how many hours to work per week

4. The following table gives the utility points received by a person from each additional hour of exercise per week, as well as the points that each additional hour costs. Using this table, answer the questions below.

Hours of Exercise	Marginal Benefit	Total Benefit	Marginal Cost	Total Cost	Net Benefit
0		0		0	_____
	60		5		
1		_____		_____	_____
	40		10		
2		_____		_____	_____
	30		20		
3		_____		_____	_____
	20		30		
4		_____		_____	_____
	10		40		
5		_____		_____	_____
	0		55		
6		_____		_____	_____

a. Calculate the total benefit and the total cost of exercising for each of the hours in the table.
b. Calculate the net benefit of exercising for each of the hours in the table.
c. How many hours per week should this person exercise to maximize satisfaction? What is the maximum number of net benefit points that can be earned from exercising?
d. Graph total benefit and total cost, marginal benefit and marginal cost, and net benefit on the graphs below. (Remember to plot marginal benefit and marginal cost at the midpoints between the hours.) Explain how these graphs illustrate the maximizing rules.

5. Suppose that your neighbor has just closed her books from her first year in the retail flower business and is ecstatic with the profit her accountant says that she has earned. The store grossed $250,000 in sales over the year, and its explicit costs for rent, plants and flowers, electricity, and the like were $175,000. Her husband is not quite as elated but can't figure out exactly why. In discussing the situation with you, he offers the following information. The two of them invested $200,000 of their savings, which was earning an 8 percent return, to go into this business. She gave up her job, which was paying her $64,000 a year, at a local corporation. He worked every evening and most weekends at the store—giving up the opportunity to take on additional clients or to work overtime. In addition to being tired, he figures that he lost $25,000 in additional income. What was their economic cost of production? How much normal profit should they have expected to receive? Have they made any economic profit? What kind of advice would you give them?

6. Use public choice theory to explain the following.
a. Low voter turnout for the election of a few candidates for minor offices
b. Voting along party lines instead of judging each candidate's individual merits
c. A change before an election in a candidate's position on an issue
d. Voting according to the recommendations given in a local newspaper
e. Low voter turnout when the weather is bad

7. Using the following cost and revenue information, answer the questions below the table.

Units of Output	Total Revenue	Marginal Revenue	Total Cost	Marginal Cost	Profit
0	$0		$0		___
		___		___	
1	50		25		___
		___		___	
2	90		35		___
		___		___	
3	120		40		___
		___		___	
4	140		50		___
		___		___	
5	150		70		___
		___		___	
6	150		100		___
		___		___	
7	140		140		___
		___		___	
8	120		200		___

a. What are the marginal revenue and marginal cost of each additional unit of output?
b. What is the profit-maximizing level of output?
c. What is total profit at the profit-maximizing level of output?

Discussion Questions

1. In each of the following situations, determine what the decision maker might be seeking to maximize and indicate (1) some factors that should be included in the calculation of costs and (2) some factors that should be included in the calculation of benefits.
   a. The decision to get a college education
   b. The decision to shoplift a coat
   c. The decision by voters to increase property taxes
   d. The decision by a business to drop a product line
   e. The decision to adopt a child
   f. The decision to lie
   g. The decision to stop smoking cigarettes
   h. The decision to text while driving

2. What could be opportunity costs of each of the following actions?
   a. Moving from a smaller home that takes 40 percent of your income to own and maintain to a larger "home of your dreams" that takes 60 percent of your income
   b. Working overtime during the next 2 months in the hope of getting a promotion

c. Deciding to stop seeing someone because you are not right for each other

d. Cutting back on certain foods to lose weight

3. Some cities have extensive codes regulating property use, from the types and sizes of fences and signs that are permitted to maintenance standards that require grass to be cut and yards to be free of derelict vehicles. Is this type of regulation justifiable to prohibit negative externalities that affect the property values of neighbors?

4. The emission of toxins into the air is a well-known example of a negative externality. What are some of the costs imposed on society by these emissions? In answering this question, be sure to consider possible effects from pollution on climate, health, maintenance of buildings and other property, and taxes.

5. Because pesticides and herbicides used by farmers are increasingly poisoning groundwater and streams, would you back a proposal to ban their use? Why?

6. Cost–benefit analysis can be applied to a wide range of economic and noneconomic decisions. Give five examples of noneconomic situations where the cost–benefit analysis developed in this chapter would be useful in arriving at a decision.

7. The pesticide DDT has been banned in the United States and many other countries world-wide. However, it is used in some nations to curb malaria caused by mosquito bites. In some parts of the world, malaria is a serious public health threat that causes severe symptoms and can cause death. Despite the problems created by extensive use of DDT, many countries find this the least expensive and most effective method for attacking malaria and mosquitoes. Using cost–benefit analysis, explain why you would favor or disapprove of the continued use of DDT in some countries.

Critical Thinking Case 11

A SPOONFUL OF SUGAR

Critical Thinking Skills

Tying values to decision making

Assessing arguments for a position

Economic Concepts

Social costs and benefits

Identifying externalities

There is no doubt that former New York City Mayor Michael Bloomberg was passionate about healthy living and healthy food. During his tenure as mayor he was in the forefront of successfully advocating for regulations that limit smoking and fat and sugar in foods and drinks offered for sale at some venues in New York City. It seems that Bloomberg's dream has always been a world of healthy people, especially children, enjoying life without food-induced disease.

On Bloomberg's urging, the New York City Board of Health in September 2012 approved a ban on sugary beverages, like soda, in sizes larger than 16 ounces (two cups) at restaurants, concession stands, and other venues. This meant that folks who might stop for that big gulp of their favorite sugary soda before they hit the subway or a bench in Central Park would be faced with buying a smaller size than they might want. Even to wash down a big burger, they would have to do with a smaller soda. But, if someone was really thirsty, a supersized diet soda or milk or fruit juice, or even a big bottle of water, could be purchased.

Why the proposed ban? Some studies suggest that the United States is in the throes of an obesity epidemic. The Centers for Disease Control and Prevention (CDC) point out that today 17 percent of kids aged 2–19 years are considered obese as are over one-third of adults.

The concern for these obesity rates is the medical issues and costs associated with carrying too much weight. The incidence of diabetes, heart disease, joint problems, the other medical concerns is raised by obesity. Add to these medical problems other issues like a lack of self-esteem, especially in children.

We know that sugary drinks loaded with calories contribute to obesity. But sugary drinks and fat-laden foods have always been part of the American diet. Today, the issue is that the portion sizes have greatly increased and we have not lost our propensity to eat everything in front of us. A generation ago, a plain McDonald's burger and an 8-ounce coke sufficed for lunch as did a ½ can of soup and a small glass of milk. Today we are supersizing everything—and we have gone from the 8-ounce drink to 32 and even 64 ounces.

There are many people who see obesity as a problem for society and, therefore, one that society must address. The link of obesity to diabetes and other chronic diseases means a rise in medical expenses. Since medical bills tend to be paid from health insurance, all of us experience an increase in insurance premiums as a result of these rising costs. Healthy people keep medical costs down—a benefit for all of us; chronic and severe diseases increase medical costs—a cost for all of us.

Not everyone agrees with regulations on food because they are viewed as an infringement on individual rights. There is a strong belief that we should be able to eat and drink whatever we want. And free markets should be able to sell whatever they want.

The ban on sugary drinks was struck down by a lower court and appealed to New York's highest state court which upheld the lower court ruling. While the New York ban is gone, it served to educate the public about obesity and its causes and costs. It also provided a model for other communities that want to enact this type of public health regulation. And, ultimately, it brought the issue of food regulation forward for debate. Did Mayor Bloomberg go too far in his beliefs that the social costs of large sodas are a valid basis for banning large sugary drinks?

Sources: Michael M. Grynbaum, "Health Panel Approves Restriction on Sale of Large Sugary Drinks," *The New York Times*, September 13, 2012; Reuters, "State High Court Rules NYC Ban on Large Sodas Is Illegal," *The New York Times*, June 26, 2014; www.cdc.gov, 02/19/2015.

Questions

1. Do you agree with Mayor Bloomberg's viewpoint and policy direction about banning sugar-laden drinks or do you agree with the court ruling that overturned the ban? What reasons can you provide for your position?
2. We have rules that, in essence, limit the consumption of alcohol when someone is driving because of the social costs of drinking and driving. Is the issue of limiting the consumption of sugary sodas the same as limiting the consumption of alcohol? How are these two situations the same and how are they different?
3. The line that is drawn between the philosophical positions on individual versus collective rights is different for everyone. Some are closer to supporting individual rights and some closer to supporting societal rights. Where do you stand in this debate? What has influenced your thinking?
4. If you had a magic wand, are there other bans you would place on consumer goods? Or would you use your magic wand to erase some bans away?

Production and the Costs of Production

CHAPTER OBJECTIVES

Explore some production basics: categories for productive activity, production methods, and technology and creative destruction.

Differentiate between the time frames in which production occurs and identify various types of costs.

Identify the types of costs associated with the short-run and explain their behavior patterns.

Identify long-run costs and their behavior patterns.

Provide a more detailed understanding of short-run average costs.

We engage in many productive activities. Students produce papers and projects; families wash cars and clothes and make meals; businesses produce computers, office buildings, and financial advice; and governments provide police and fire protection. Production is a process: It involves taking resources, like labor and materials, and using them to make goods and services.

This chapter is concerned with the microeconomic aspects of production. While all of the areas of the economy engage in production, the vast majority of measured production is done by businesses. So, while many of the concepts in this chapter can be applied to other areas, the focus is on goods and services produced by business firms and their costs of production.

There is an important connection between a firm's production, its costs of production, and its objective to maximize profit. Remember from the previous chapters that profit is what remains after costs are subtracted from revenue. All other things remaining unchanged, the lower the cost of producing a product, the greater the firm's profit from selling that product.

PRODUCTION BASICS

In 2014, the U.S. economy produced more than $17 trillion of goods and services.[1] Trying to sort through this huge macroeconomic number in order to explore production at a microeconomic level is a formidable task. Let's look at several ways in which the micro perspective is organized.

Sectors and Industries

To help us understand and analyze production, classification systems have been developed for grouping similar types of goods and services. Two widely used classifications are producing sectors and industries.

Producing Sectors

A broad classification system for grouping goods and services, and the firms that produce them.

Producing Sectors   The broadest classification system for grouping goods and services, and the firms that produce them, is called **producing sectors**. This enables us to lump some production together, track a type of production over time, and evaluate a group's size. Table 12.1 lists the major producing sectors of the U.S. economy, and the percentage of total output accounted for by each sector in 2014.

While different types of productive activities are in different sectors, these sectors are closely knit in the production and distribution of goods and services. For example, crops produced in the agricultural sector become food products in the manufacturing sector, and then move to households through the wholesale and retail trade sectors, with the assistance of the transportation sector.

Over time the importance of the different sectors changes. For example, from 1930 through 1988, manufacturing was unchallenged as the dominant producing sector, providing many jobs in companies that produced chemicals, cars, clothing, and other goods. But in 1989 manufacturing was surpassed by service areas, which

TABLE 12.1   *Sample Producing Sectors of the Economy*

Goods and services produced by businesses can be categorized into producing sectors of the economy. Service-related sectors are the largest sectors.

Sector	Percentage of Output in 2014
Manufacturing	12.0%
Finance, insurance, real estate, rental, and leasing	20.3
Professional and business services	12.1
Agriculture, forestry, fishing, and hunting	1.2
Arts, entertainment, recreation, accommodation, and food services	3.8
Health care and social assistance	7.2
Government	12.8
Information	4.6
Transportation and warehousing	2.9

Source: Bureau of Economic Analysis, Table 5a. Value Added by Industry as a Percentage of Gross Domestic Product, April 23, 2015, www.bea.gov.

[1]See Table 4.8.

| TABLE 12.2 | *Sample Industries and Products in the Manufacturing Sector* |

Firms producing similar products or using similar processes are grouped into the same industry.

Industry	Industry Product Examples
Dairy products	Frozen custard, ice cream, juice pops, tofu, frozen desserts
Books	Publishing and/or printing of books, pamphlets, textbooks
Dolls, toys, games, and sporting and athletic	Baseballs, basketballs, fishing tackle, skateboards, treadmills, playground equipment, boomerangs
Roasted coffee	Coffee extracts, roasting, instant coffee
Drugs	Antibiotics, cough remedies, lip balms, pills
Carpets and rugs	Carpets, door mats, rugs, sisal floor coverings

Source: United States Department of Labor, OSHA, www.osha.gov. Based on the *Standard Industrial Classification Manual*.

continue to be the largest. Today, college graduates are more likely to find employment in health care, law, and other service areas than in manufacturing.

Industries   A very useful, and narrower, classification is to put firms into industries. An **industry** is a group of firms producing similar products or using similar processes. Examples of industries include aircraft, health care, soft drinks, greeting cards, and food processing. Table 12.2 gives several industries in the manufacturing sector and examples of their products. Although the firms in each of these industries are listed in the manufacturing sector, the products they produce differ significantly from industry to industry.

It is common to find large, multiproduct corporations operating in several industries. Corporate giant General Electric, for example, through its divisions and subsidiaries produces appliances, jet engines, credit and loan services, health care, and water treatment systems.[2]

Methods of Production

Whether a huge company such as Boeing is producing commercial jetliners or a small family-owned company is producing carpet-cleaning services, there are usually many different ways, or methods, that a business can choose to produce a good or service. The method of production actually chosen is dependent on many considerations. It is important, however, to understand that whatever that method is, it underlies the firm's cost of production.

The Production Function   A **production function** shows the type and amount of output that results when a particular group of inputs is processed in a certain way. Production functions exist for every good and service: tomatoes, backhoes, economics courses, rain gardens, football helmets, hamburgers, and everything else that can be produced. For most types of goods and services, such as gasoline or automobiles, production functions can be clearly defined. But we do find that for some productive activities, such as learning, the functions are not as well understood.

Industry
A group of firms producing similar products or using similar processes.

Production Function
Shows the type and amount of output that results from a particular group of inputs when those inputs are combined in a certain way.

[2]www.ge.com, 06/19/2015.

TABLE 12.3	*A Production Function*

A recipe is a simple example of a production function because it gives the types and amounts of inputs and the processes needed to produce a particular output.

This dip was created by a Seton Hill University alumni from Pittsburgh, Pennsylvania. It has been a huge party hit, always bringing many compliments and an empty dish.

Jeannie's Warm Taco Dip

8 ounce cream cheese

15 ounce can chili—no beans

4 green onions sliced thin

½ tiny can chopped black olives—about 2½ ounces.

¾–1 lb. shredded Monterey Jack cheese with Jalapeno peppers (mild)

1 bag corn-type chips

Using a 9 × 12 pan (glass works nicely) layer: cream cheese, chili, green onion, olives, and shredded cheese. Bake at 350 degrees for 15–20 minutes.

Serve with chips.

A recipe, such as the one in Table 12.3, provides an easy way to understand a production function. In this production function, the output is a warm taco dip. The inputs include the ingredients listed at the top of the recipe—cheese, chili, and so forth—as well as kitchen equipment and the labor provided by the person preparing the dip. The process for combining these inputs is explained in the text of the recipe and involves such operations as layering the ingredients. All production functions are similar to this recipe in that they specify a type and amount of output, the numbers and types of inputs, and how the inputs are combined.

Usually, there are several production functions to choose from when producing a good or service. For example, a painting contractor could paint the exterior of a house with brushes or spraying equipment, a pie baker could make crust from scratch or frozen dough, and a city could provide for recycling with curbside pickup or a community drop-off facility. Because a business often can choose among several methods to produce an output, it is helpful to understand the factors that underlie this choice.

Choosing a Production Function   What causes a firm to choose a particular production function? This is easy to answer when we recall that the objective of a firm is to maximize profit and that profit is what remains after costs are subtracted from revenue. Every production function has a cost associated with it, and a business will use the production method that results in the type and quality of product it wants at the lowest cost. This is not much different from the way people operate: We look for the least-cost way to accomplish something. Whether our intention is to cook a gourmet meal or a simple supper, we will try to find the production method that yields our intended result at the lowest cost. When a good or service is produced at the lowest cost, an **efficient method of production** and the efficient use of resources occur.

Efficient Method of Production
The least-cost method of production.

The choice of the production function that leads to the lowest cost for a business differs from firm to firm, even when the firms are in the same industry. Sometimes the size of an operation influences the way a business produces. Take surveillance in retail stores. It could be more cost effective for a large store to prevent shoplifting by hiring security personnel and for a small store to use cameras.

Production Functions and Technology   Technological change has a significant influence on production functions. We can think of **technology** as the knowledge that we possess about production processes. Technology drives how we "do things" and it constantly changes. It affects the design of processes and machinery and equipment, and it influences inventory control, packaging, human relations, purchasing, and just about every other part of production. Technological change is leading the way to breakthroughs in the testing and treatment of medical problems, to solving crime through forensics, to advanced information systems that make e-mail and cell phones routine, and to more efficient ways to produce and distribute everything from pickup trucks to fresh herbs.

Technology defines the range of production methods from which a business can choose: from old methods to the latest advances. Even though the most technologically advanced production functions are usually the most efficient, some businesses cannot afford the transition to the latest design. Business profit may be maximized by keeping older equipment and methods. Over time, however, updated processes do become the norm.

Technology plays a major role in driving growth and change in an economy. As technology grows and new ideas are advanced, some processes and equipment become obsolete. The economist Joseph Schumpeter referred to this as **creative destruction**: New machinery, production processes, and other results of technological change frequently replace the old, causing one area of the economy to grow and prosper and another to shrink and perhaps ultimately disappear. For example, the introduction of robotics into assembly lines has not only affected the demand for labor but has also caused much machinery and equipment in automobile plants to become obsolete.

Creative destruction also occurs at the international level when firms in a country's industry lag because of technological advances adopted by competing firms in another country. For example, the U.S. steel and consumer electronics industries were hurt by the development of advanced production techniques for these products in Japan and elsewhere. Application 12.1, "Do You Know a Modern-Day Luddite?" looks at the positive and negative sides of advances in technology and production that come with creative destruction.

ECONOMIC TIME, PRODUCTION, AND THE COSTS OF PRODUCTION

The production function that a firm chooses is influenced by the time frame in which it views or plans its operations. Generally, production may be regarded as taking place over a short-run or a long-run period of time. These time periods are not defined in terms of hours, months, or years (the usual custom for measuring time). Rather, they are defined in a more abstract way.

The **short run** is the time frame in which production takes place using some factors that can be varied in amount and some that cannot as the level of output increases or decreases. Factors of production that can be varied in amount, such as hourly labor,

Technology
The body of knowledge that exists about production and its processes.

Creative Destruction
New, technologically advanced machinery and production methods cause the disappearance of old machinery and methods.

Short Run
A production time frame in which some factors of production are variable in amount and some are fixed.

DO YOU KNOW A MODERN-DAY LUDDITE?

When Joseph Schumpeter introduced the idea of creative destruction, he probably never thought that this expression would have as much relevance today as it had when he wrote in the early 1940s.

The expression itself has conflicting imagery as each word has a powerful, but different, connotation. Creative is a positive, bright, hopeful word. Destruction is a negative, dark, harmful word. And that is what creative destruction brings: positive and negative results.

On the bright side, creative destruction can be the foundation for economic growth and opportunity as new products, jobs, and advances in efficient production techniques lead to an improved quality of life and to changes that we thought were beyond our reach. Fifty years ago, the ability to talk every day to family members in other cities without spending a month's salary on long-distance phone charges was a dream. Today, the cell phone makes that dream a possibility.

On the dark side, creative destruction brings losses, sometimes profound, to businesses and employees that have a major stake in a product that is disappearing. The end of the run for many people is the fact that their products, jobs, and incomes are permanently disappearing and their lifestyles are in serious jeopardy. Think about the jobs lost with all of the online capabilities for travel, research, banking, and shopping, and the corporate losses for companies like Polaroid, Kodak, and Borders.

We sometimes use the expression "Luddite" to describe an opponent to the change that creative destruction brings. This classic expression comes from the early nineteenth century when the Luddites, a group of English weavers, were losing their jobs to newly designed stocking frames and power looms being introduced into clothing factories. This new technology was such a threat to the Luddites that they would storm factories in an effort to destroy the frames and looms that threatened their livelihood. Their aggression caused the passage of the Frame Breaking Act in 1812 that allowed the execution of those convicted of breaking weaving machines.

What would today's modern Luddite oppose? Certainly the Internet has brought a revolution to the way we communicate and work and the types of jobs that have been created in the past few decades. Maybe the modern Luddite experienced a job loss in the publishing or newspaper industry, or worked in a closed "record" shop that once had customers for cassette tapes and then CDs, or had a hardware store that was replaced by a big box store in a small rural town, or had a good job with a telephone company.

On the other hand, there are the employed who have benefitted from all of these changes with new jobs as computer engineers, software designers, medical technicians, and chemists and pharmacists. You might even say that the advent of cable television channels has brought professional and Olympic sports to a new level with a growth in athletes in all sorts of sports from women's basketball to curling.

Creative destruction will always be with us. It's about how we respond: Some will see the bright side and prepare themselves to move on and some will fight it.

Variable Factors
Factors of production that change in amount as the level of output changes.

Variable Costs
Costs of using variable factors.

Fixed Factors
Factors of production that do not change in amount as the level of output changes.

Fixed Costs
Costs of using fixed factors.

Long Run
A production time frame in which all factors of production are variable in amount.

raw materials, and replacement parts on machinery, are **variable factors**. Because the amount of variable factors used changes as the level of output changes, the costs of these factors to a business also change as the level of output changes. The costs for a business's variable factors are called **variable costs** and include, for example, hourly wages and payments for raw materials and machine parts.

Factors of production that cannot be changed in amount as the level of output changes are called **fixed factors**. Fixed factors might include a building, key personnel, some machinery, and insurance. Because the amounts of fixed factors remain unchanged as the level of production increases or decreases, their costs do not change. For example, a business might sign a lease to pay a specified rent over several years. The costs of fixed factors are called **fixed costs**. Importantly, fixed factors must be paid for regardless of whether the firm produces anything or not. In essence, the short run is the time period in which fixed factors form a boundary within which production takes place.

The **long run** is the time frame in which all factors are regarded as variable: There are no fixed factors to limit production. In the long run, a much wider range of production choices is available because all resources, including buildings and other production facilities, are regarded as alterable.

Suppose that the owners of a restaurant are trying to evaluate the production functions and associated costs of producing meals. If they can alter the number of servers, tables, and menu selections but not the size of the dining or kitchen area, they are planning in the short run. These same owners are planning in the long run when they analyze the methods and costs of producing meals as their facilities are expanded, or as they add new restaurants, or, more generally, when they no longer regard any of their factors as fixed.

This concept of planning in different time frames is easily applied to a student's production of a college education. The long run is the period in which general plans for earning a degree are made. In this long-run period, all factors can be altered: the selection of a college, the course of study to be followed, the number of hours to be taken each semester, and the commitment to a part-time job. Once some of these decisions are made and the student is enrolled in particular courses, producing a college education can be viewed in the short run. Each semester could represent a short-run time frame because the student is producing an education within boundaries set by the school attended, the semester's scheduled classes, and other factors to which the student is obligated.

UP FOR DEBATE

SHOULD THE SAME COST MEASURES USED BY BUSINESSES APPLY TO GOVERNMENT AND NONPROFITS?

Issue   *There is a tendency to think of cost calculations as applying solely to the business sector because of the profit motive. Should all individuals and organizations seek to measure costs in the same way that businesses measure them, or are the goals of nonbusiness entities so different that they should not focus on cost measurements in the same way?*

Yes   Costs are costs—they measure the value of resources used to produce "something" whether it is an SUV by an automobile company or snow plowing by a local government or a theater production by a nonprofit. All entities are well served by being data driven and reflective about how they use their scarce resources.

The basic problem of scarcity applies to all individuals and all organizations, business or otherwise. If people do not take care in calculating what costs go into a decision and take the time to evaluate those costs, they might be "missing the boat."

Take the example of a city that provides trash collection. That city should know precisely what it costs to pick up the trash in its neighborhoods and its business districts. What is the total cost of the operation? What does it cost per household? Are costs different for residential neighborhoods than they are for business areas? Unless the city gathers and evaluates these data, it is unable to determine whether it is more efficient for the city itself to collect trash or if it is better to negotiate a contract with a private firm.

Governments and nonprofits use funds provided through taxes and contributions and other private sources. When a nonprofit has a larger than necessary administrative staff or a county government has more park rangers than it needs, resources are used inefficiently and everyone pays for this. Nonprofits and governments produce services vital to communities and the effective evaluation of costs is necessary in this service provision.

No   The very basic goals of government and of nonprofits are quite different from those of a business. Businesses are created to produce profit for their owners, and governments and nonprofits exist to provide needed services for society. While it is useful to have an understanding of costs, the driving factor behind these nonbusiness entities is different because they address societal needs.

Take the example of emergency medical services. Many communities run their own EMT or ambulance services. They do so because their citizens demand a quick response time and the best qualified technicians available in the area. The service might not be as cost effective as it could be when provided by a private company, but the residents feel more secure with their own people and equipment. Without a profit motive, a community might choose to spend more for a better service and respond to the wishes of its members.

The same might apply to many nonprofits whose function is to serve the needy or homeless in a region, or to foster the arts through theater and music, or to provide an education in a needed field. A community college, for example, might encounter very high costs to provide a nursing program, yet it does so because it fulfills a community need.

Some of the functions performed by government and nonprofits take a different, sometimes longer, view of societal needs rather than being solely profit driven. In these cases, constantly evaluating costs might not result in the best service to their communities.

In order to make production decisions in either the short run or the long run, a business needs to determine the costs associated with producing various amounts of its output. Because production is planned differently in each time frame, we will examine costs in the short run and long run separately.

Up for Debate, "Should the Same Cost Measures Used by Businesses Apply to Government and Nonprofits?" provides an interesting issue to consider as you work through the rest of this chapter. Come back at the end of your reading of Chapter 12 and determine what your position is on this issue.

SHORT-RUN COSTS

Again, in the short run, all factors used in the production of a good or service can be classified as either variable or fixed. Variable factors and costs change as the level of output changes; fixed factors and costs do not. A hypothetical example follows in which the short-run costs of operating a lawn and grounds maintenance company to service housing complexes are calculated and analyzed. The costs given in this example are those for the weekly maintenance of small apartment and condominium complex lawns and grounds.

Total Costs

Total Fixed Cost (TFC)

The cost of all fixed factors; does not change as the level of output changes and must be paid even when output is zero.

Let's begin the calculation of the costs of operating this service by adding together the bills where a specific amount must be paid regardless of the number of complex grounds maintained: that is, by determining **total fixed cost (TFC)**. This could include payments on a loan for mowers and a truck as well as payments for a storage facility and insurance. Assume that total fixed cost is $400 per week.

Table 12.4, which illustrates the weekly total costs to the business of maintaining from zero through nine complexes, gives the total fixed cost for the firm's operations in the second column. Notice that the $400 fixed cost does not change as more or fewer complex grounds are maintained and that it must be paid even if none are serviced. This is because, regardless of how many lawns and grounds are cared for, the fixed factors, and thus the costs of the fixed factors, remain unchanged.

| **TABLE 12.4** | **Weekly Total Costs of Maintaining Lawns and Grounds** |

Total fixed cost does not change as the level of output changes and must be paid even if nothing is produced. Total variable cost is zero when nothing is produced and increases with the level of output. Because total cost is equal to total fixed cost plus total variable cost, it also increases as output increases.

Number of Sites Maintained	Total Fixed Cost (TFC)	Total Variable Cost (TVC)	Total Cost (TC)
0	$400	$0	$400
1	400	200	600
2	400	225	625
3	400	275	675
4	400	350	750
5	400	475	875
6	400	650	1,050
7	400	895	1,295
8	400	1,220	1,620
9	400	1,670	2,070

Total Variable Cost (TVC)
The cost of all variable factors of production; increases as the level of output increases but is zero when output is zero.

Next, we will calculate the firm's **total variable costs (TVC)**. Because these are costs of variable factors that change in amount as the number of sites maintained changes, variable costs could include expenditures for labor, gasoline, fertilizer and other chemicals, repair of the truck and mowing equipment, small hand tools, and such. The third column of Table 12.4 gives the company's total variable costs for servicing from zero through nine complexes. For example, if this firm were to service four a week, it would face a total variable cost of $350. Notice that the variable costs are zero if the firm services no grounds, they continually increase as more are maintained, and they increase significantly with a large number of complex grounds maintained. An explanation for this pattern of variable cost increases will be given shortly.

Total Cost (TC)
The cost of acquiring and using all factors of production; total fixed cost plus total variable cost.

The **total cost (TC)** of maintaining from zero through nine sites is given in the last column of Table 12.4. The total cost for a particular level of output is all fixed costs plus all variable costs at that level of production. For example, the total cost of maintaining five lawns and grounds is $875: $400 in fixed costs plus $475 in variable costs.

Unit Costs

In addition to its total costs, a business usually finds it essential to determine per unit costs at each level of output. The cost per unit at a particular level of output is called **average total cost (ATC)**. Average total cost is found by dividing total cost by the number of units produced.

Average Total Cost (ATC)
The cost per unit of output produced; total cost divided by the number of units produced.

Table 12.5 gives the total cost of maintaining grounds from Table 12.4 and the average total cost for each individual complex when a specified number is maintained.

TABLE 12.5   *Weekly Total, Average Total, and Marginal Costs of Maintaining Lawns and Grounds*

Average total cost measures the per unit cost at a specific production level, and marginal cost measures the change in total cost from producing an additional unit of output.

Number of Sites Maintained	Total Cost (TC)	Average Total Cost (ATC)	Marginal Cost (MC)
0	$400.00	—	
			$200.00
1	600.00	$600.00	
			25.00
2	625.00	312.50	
			50.00
3	675.00	225.00	
			75.00
4	750.00	187.50	
			125.00
5	875.00	175.00	
			175.00
6	1,050.00	175.00	
			245.00
7	1,295.00	185.00	
			325.00
8	1,620.00	202.50	
			450.00
9	2,070.00	230.00	

For example, the average total cost of servicing each site when three are maintained is $225. This is found by dividing the total cost of $675 by 3. The average total cost of $185 when seven sites are maintained is found by dividing the total cost of $1,295 by 7.[3]

Marginal Cost (MC)
The change in total cost when one more unit of output is produced.

Table 12.5 also gives the marginal cost of maintaining lawns and grounds. As explained in the previous chapter, **marginal cost (MC)** is the change in total cost from producing one more unit of output—in this case, caring for one more site. For example, if no sites are maintained, the total cost given in Table 12.5 is $400; if one is maintained, total cost increases to $600. Thus, the marginal cost of the first complex is $200($600 – $400). As in the previous chapter, marginal cost is listed midway between the units of output. Table 12.6 summarizes the characteristics of short-run total, average, and marginal costs.

A business could analyze its unit costs in even greater detail. It could, for example, determine its fixed costs per unit (average fixed cost) and variable costs per unit (average variable cost). More detailed cost calculations such as these appear in the appendix to this chapter.

The Pattern of Short-Run Costs

There are patterns to the way total cost, average total cost, and marginal cost behave in the short run. We can observe these patterns in tables of cost figures, such as those listed in Tables 12.4 and 12.5. But they can be more easily observed when the short-run costs are graphed.

TABLE 12.6	*Summary of Short-Run Costs*

Total, average, and marginal costs are different ways of looking at costs as the level of output changes.

Total Fixed Cost (TFC)

✓ Cost of all fixed factors; does not change as the level of output changes; must be paid even if nothing is produced.

Total Variable Cost (TVC)

✓ Cost of all variable factors; varies directly with the level of output; zero if nothing is produced.

Total Cost (TC)

✓ Total fixed cost plus total variable cost; equals TFC at zero production; increases with increases in output.

Average Total Cost (ATC)

✓ Cost per unit of output; total cost divided by the number of units of output; decreases then increases as production increases.

Marginal Cost (MC)

✓ Change in total cost per additional unit of output; decreases then increases as production increases.

[3]The average total cost of maintaining zero lawns is not given because any number divided by zero is undefined.

FIGURE 12.1   *Total Cost of Maintaining Lawns and Grounds*

Total cost increases slowly when just a few sites are maintained because few variable factors are needed with the fixed factors. At higher levels of output, total cost increases quickly as more variable factors are needed to compensate for the limitations imposed by the fixed factors.

Total Cost Pattern   Figure 12.1 plots the total cost, given in Table 12.5, of maintaining from zero through nine sites per week. Notice in Figure 12.1 that total cost is $400 when output is zero. This, of course, is due to the firm's fixed costs, which must be paid regardless of whether or not production occurs. Notice also that total cost continually increases as more places are serviced. Because the fixed cost of maintaining these grounds never changes, this increase is due solely to the increase in total variable costs.

A closer analysis of total cost shows that in the early stage of production, when few sites are maintained, total cost increases slowly. But in the latter stage of production, when many sites are maintained, total cost increases quickly. Why does total cost follow this pattern?

If this company plans to service just a few places, it might manage by hiring one employee (variable factor) to use the truck and equipment (fixed factors). For each site maintained, the company would also need to provide other variable factors, such as bags for the grass clippings and gasoline for the truck and mowing equipment. However, once labor is hired, the company will not encounter significant increases in the other variable costs to care for each additional site if just a few are maintained. Thus, total cost increases slowly for the first few units of output because the increase in variable factors needed to accompany the fixed factors is small.

After a while, maintaining more sites necessitates more than just an increase in bags and gasoline. Labor costs increase as more workers are needed or as the existing employees are paid overtime. As the truck and mowing equipment are used more often, breakdowns occur, causing the cost of repairs to increase. Also, the owner of the firm may expect a higher normal profit in return for the effort and responsibility of increasing production. At some point, these increases in variable costs cause total cost to increase more quickly as production grows.

As production increases to even higher levels, the number of places serviced will begin to seriously strain the capabilities of the fixed factors, and variable costs will increase substantially as the firm tries to compensate for the limits of the fixed factors. Perhaps, with the existing mowers and truck, the company might reasonably expect to maintain only six or seven sites. If it tries to service eight or nine, many variable factors will be needed to fill in for the limitations of the fixed factors. At this point, the company may encounter considerably higher variable costs as it rents another truck and more mowers, leases additional storage space, and hires a manager.

In short, total cost increases slowly at first because, with a given amount of fixed factors, few variable factors can increase production significantly. As output levels become larger, total cost increases more rapidly because more variable factors are needed with the fixed factors to increase production. At high levels of production, costs increase very quickly because the fixed factors are approaching or reaching the limits of their productivity, and many variable factors are needed to compensate for the fixed factor boundary.

Marginal Cost and Average Total Cost Patterns   Let us next examine the marginal cost (MC) and average total cost (ATC) patterns as production increases. The marginal cost and average total cost data given in Table 12.5 are graphed in Figure 12.2.

Notice that marginal cost, or the change in total cost from maintaining one more site, decreases at first and then increases. As with total cost, this drop and rise are due to the behavior of the variable factors as reflected in variable costs. With this in mind, the same reasoning that applies to the explanation of the total cost pattern applies to the explanation of the marginal cost pattern.

To service the first site, the marginal cost is $200. If you refer to Table 12.4, you can confirm that this equals the change in variable cost (and total cost) associated with maintaining one rather than no sites. Much of this $200 marginal cost is probably due to the hiring of labor. To maintain a second site, the marginal cost is only $25. This decrease in marginal cost occurs because the additional variable factors needed to maintain the second site cost the firm only $25. As explained earlier, at this point there will be only a slight increase in the use of some variable inputs, such as gasoline and grass bags.

When a third site is maintained, marginal cost begins to rise because of the increase in variable factors needed to increase production. And as more and more places are cared for, marginal cost rises more rapidly. This more rapid rise is due to the increasing amounts of variable factors that are required to compensate for the limits placed on production by the fixed factors.

Return to Figure 12.2 and observe the average total cost curve. Average total cost decreases and then increases with more production. Why is this so?

The cost per unit falls initially because marginal cost is lower than average total cost. When marginal cost is less than average total cost, it pulls average total cost down. When marginal cost becomes greater than average total cost, it pulls average total cost up. Figure 12.2 also shows that because of these relationships between average and marginal costs, marginal cost must cross, or equal, average total cost at minimum average total cost. Thus, average total cost behaves the way it does because of the behavior of marginal cost.

FIGURE 12.2 — *Marginal Cost and Average Total Cost of Maintaining Lawns and Grounds*

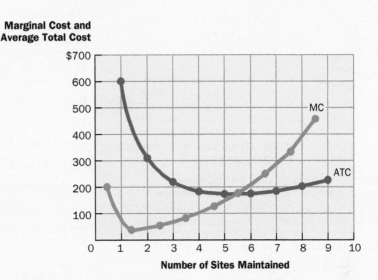

Both marginal cost and average total cost fall and then rise as production increases. When marginal cost is less than average total cost, it pulls average total cost down; when marginal cost is greater than average total cost, it pulls average total cost up.

You encounter this relationship between marginal and average values in determining your average in a course as you take additional exams. If you make a grade on your next exam (remember that each additional exam that you take is a marginal exam) that is lower than your average, that grade will pull your average down. If, on the next exam, you make a grade higher than your average, your average will increase. For example, if you have an average of 93 percent in this economics course and you earn a grade of 80 percent on your next exam, your average will fall; if you earn a grade of 98 percent on your next exam, your average will rise. Test Your Understanding, "Calculating Costs and Averages," gives you an opportunity to further explore the average–marginal relationship and to calculate some short-run costs.

The Law of Diminishing Returns

Law of Diminishing Returns

As additional units of a variable factor are added to a fixed factor, beyond some point the additional product from each additional unit of the variable factor decreases.

Underlying all the short-run cost patterns is a basic principle, which you may likely have heard, called the **Law of Diminishing Returns**. This law states that as additional units of a variable factor are added to a fixed factor, beyond some point (not necessarily right away) the *additional* product from each additional unit of the variable factor decreases. Put another way, the Law of Diminishing Returns says that, after some point, each additional unit of a variable factor used will add less to output than was added by the unit used just before it. This is easily illustrated with an example.

Assume that you own a small restaurant and plan to begin hiring people to prepare and serve meals. The dining room, outfitted with tables and other restaurant furniture, and a fully equipped kitchen are the fixed factors, and the labor used to work in the restaurant is a variable factor.

TEST YOUR UNDERSTANDING

CALCULATING COSTS AND AVERAGES

1. A student's grade in a psychology class at a state university is determined by averaging the percentage scores of four equally weighted exams. One of the students in the class earns a grade of 92 percent on the first exam, 79 percent on the second, 80 percent on the third, and 93 percent on the fourth.

The student's average after the first exam is _____ percent. After the second exam, the student's average will _____ (rise or fall) because the marginal score from the second exam is _____ (higher or lower) than the average after the first exam. After two exams, the student's average is _____ percent.

The student's average after the third exam will _____ (rise or fall) because the marginal score from the third exam is _____ (higher or lower) than the average. After three exams, the student's average is _____ percent.

The student's average after the fourth exam will _____ (rise or fall) because the marginal score from the fourth exam is _____ (higher or lower) than the average. After four exams, the student's average for the course is _____ percent.

2. Bert's Trash Company specializes in emptying large commercial recycling containers and delivering the material to a regional single-stream sorting facility. Bert has figured that his total fixed cost per business day is $100. He has also calculated that the total variable cost for one pickup is $250 per day, the total cost for three pickups per day is $400, the marginal cost of the second pickup as well as the fourth pickup is $50, and the average total cost with five pickups is $105. Fill in the following table for Bert's costs.

Pickups per Business Day	Total Fixed Cost	Total Variable Cost	Total Cost	Average Total Cost	Marginal Cost
0	$___	$___	$___	$___	
					$___
1	___	___	___	___	
					___
2	___	___	___	___	
					___
3	___	___	___	___	
					___
4	___	___	___	___	
					___
5	___	___	___	___	

3. The manager of a college food service has determined that the daily fixed cost of operation is $855. She has also calculated that the total variable cost for preparing 900 meals is $1,170; for preparing 1,800 meals, it is $2,565; and when 2,700 meals are prepared, total variable cost equals $5,328.

Given this information,

the total cost for 900 meals is $____,

the total cost for 1,800 meals is $____,

the total cost for 2,700 meals is $____,

the ATC per meal with 900 meals is $____,

the ATC per meal with 1,800 meals is $____, and

the ATC per meal with 2,700 meals is $____.

4. Assume that the following table applies to the costs of completing the short-form federal income tax return for students by a small accounting service. Fill in this table.

Output	Total Fixed Cost	Total Variable Cost	Total Cost	Average Cost	Marginal Cost
0	$80	$0	$___	–	
					$___
1	___	40	___	$___	
					___
2	___	60	___	___	
					___
3	___	70	___	___	
					___
4	___	100	___	___	
					___
5	___	150	___	___	
					___
6	___	220	___	___	
					___
7	___	340	___	___	
					___
8	___	520	___	___	

Answers can be found at the back of the book.

If one person is hired to work in the restaurant, that person working alone will need to prepare, serve, and clean up after a certain number of meals per day. If a second person is hired, the two together can divide up some of the tasks and work more efficiently. One person can work the kitchen and the other can work the dining room. Together the two will more than double the number of meals that can be prepared and served by one person alone. If you hire a third person, work can be further divided, and the number of meals may again significantly increase. As long as each worker hired adds more to output than was added by the worker hired just before, or as long as diminishing returns don't set in, the marginal cost of each additional meal falls.

At some point, assume when the fourth person is hired, the number of meals that can be prepared and served per day will no longer increase as rapidly with additional workers. That is, the number of *additional* meals prepared and served by hiring the fourth worker will not be as great as the number of *additional* meals prepared and served by hiring the third worker. Four workers cannot operate as efficiently as three because the fixed facility is becoming crowded. In other words, the boundary imposed by the fixed factors begins to limit the productivity of the variable factor. When this occurs, and the additional output from hiring an additional worker begins to fall, diminishing returns have set in. This causes the marginal cost of each additional meal to rise.

Beyond this point, as more (five, six, seven) people are hired, the *additional* work accomplished by each will further diminish. They will become less efficient as the fixed factors more severely limit their full use, and marginal cost will rise at a faster rate. It would, incidentally, be possible to hire so many restaurant workers that they would get in each other's way, causing output to fall.[4]

The Law of Diminishing Returns governs all production in the short run. For example, when a student tries to produce enough knowledge to pass an exam by studying for an extended and uninterrupted period of time, the Law of Diminishing Returns takes effect. During the first few hours of reading and reviewing, each hour will produce more additional knowledge than the hour before it as the material is comprehended. After a while, however, as the student becomes tired and fixed physical and mental factors approach their limit, diminishing returns take effect, and each additional hour of study is less productive than the one before it. Can you use the Law of Diminishing Returns to explain why it is better to study on a consistent basis for shorter periods of time than it is to cram the night before an exam?

While the Law of Diminishing Returns and the resulting pattern of costs given here are common to all production in the short run, the point at which diminishing returns set in differs from product to product. But these differences do not undermine the fact that all short-run production can be explained in terms of these patterns: The limitation of the fixed factors, which gives the short run its definition, causes diminishing returns to occur and thus causes marginal, average total, and total costs to rise in the latter stages of production.

Businesses are always trying to find ways to lower their costs, often by making their inputs more productive. Application 12.2, "Are Wellness Programs Cost Effective?," discusses the argument that employer-provided opportunities to create a healthier lifestyle for employees helps to reduce costs. If wellness programs work, how could they influence the Law of Diminishing Returns?

---

[4]This means that a point can be reached where more would be produced if some of the workers would quit.

ARE WELLNESS PROGRAMS COST EFFECTIVE?

Many organizations provide wellness programs for their employees. These range from fitness centers and weight-loss programs and contests to flu shots. While the purpose of these programs is to help employees live longer, healthier lives, there seem to be benefits for an organization that pursues them.

There are costs for providing wellness programs: expenditures to develop them, staff time to administer them, and lost work hours for employees who participate. But these costs must be balanced against the benefits that can be realized from staffing with a healthier workforce.

Healthier employees have lower absentee rates resulting in less overtime for other employees who need to cover for someone who is absent or for the loss of service that can occur. There is positive evidence of this in all types of organizations from restaurants to fire departments to banks.

Healthier employees reduce costly turnover in an organization. Turnovers mean more staff time devoted to hiring and increased expenditures for training. In many job situations, turnover is expensive. Consider the costs to do a search for and hire a new college president, a corporate CEO, or a university faculty member. Training costs are high for new police officers and firefighters.

One of the most important benefits to wellness programs is the reduced cost in health and life insurance premiums that an organization can experience. Today, employers wrestle with the cost of providing health care benefits which in many cases add thousands of dollars a year to the cost of each employee. When fewer health care claims are made, premiums tend to be lower.

Not everyone agrees that it is the obligation of an employer to provide wellness programs and opportunities, and some do not believe that it lowers costs. There are those who think that the decisions involved in leading a healthier life—getting flu shots, exercising, not smoking—are made by individuals who will invest their efforts and personal funds in pursuing wellness regardless of whether an employer provides them or not. People on this side of the argument might even think that an employer is unnecessarily raising its costs by providing wellness opportunities. They believe that health is a lifestyle choice regardless of where a person works.

As debates about wellness programs continue, it is interesting to look around at college campuses and community recreation centers. These centers have become almost as important as a library and, in many cases, have far more visitors than the library. This may be making a statement about how much we value exercise and physical activity. Does this focus on campus and community fitness replace the need for employers to provide wellness programs or does it make their provision more important?

LONG-RUN COSTS

The long run is the time frame long enough for a business to regard all its factors of production as variable and none as fixed. Calculating the cost of production in the long run means determining the cost of a given level of output when a business can alter the amounts of any and all of its resources. In the long run, production costs are not divided between fixed and variable because all factors, and therefore all costs, are variable.

Table 12.7 gives the long-run costs of constructing from zero through 10 houses by a hypothetical home builder. The second column of Table 12.7 gives the **long-run total cost** of constructing these houses. Notice that long-run total cost increases as more houses are produced and that, because there are no fixed factors or costs, it is zero when no houses are produced.

Long-run total cost is used to calculate **long-run average total cost**, which is determined in the same way as short-run average total cost: Total cost is divided by the quantity of output produced. Long-run average total cost is shown in the third column of Table 12.7. **Long-run marginal cost** can also be calculated from long-run total cost: It is the change in long-run total cost as one more unit of output is produced.

Economists like to focus on the pattern of long-run average total cost when analyzing the behavior of production and its costs in the long run. Figure 12.3 plots the long-run average total cost from Table 12.7. Notice that, at first, long-run average total cost decreases as the level of output increases. With an ability to vary inputs that were fixed in the short run, the company finds that, initially, the cost per unit of output

Long-Run Total Cost, Average Total Cost, and Marginal Cost
Total cost, per unit cost, and cost per additional unit of output, respectively; calculated for production when all inputs are regarded as variable.

TABLE 12.7	Long-Run Total Cost, Average Total Cost, and Marginal Cost

Long-run total cost is the total expenditure for each level of output in the long run. Long-run average total cost measures the per unit cost; and long-run marginal cost measures the cost of producing an additional unit of output.

Number of Houses	Long-Run Total Cost (LRTC)	Long-Run Average Total Cost (LRATC)	Long-Run Marginal Cost (LRMC)
0	$ 0	—	
			$400,000
1	400,000	$400,000	
			100,000
2	500,000	250,000	
			100,000
3	600,000	200,000	
			100,000
4	700,000	175,000	
			175,000
5	875,000	175,000	
			175,000
6	1,050,000	175,000	
			350,000
7	1,400,000	200,000	
			600,000
8	2,000,000	250,000	
			700,000
9	2,700,000	300,000	
			800,000
10	3,500,000	350,000	

drops. At some point long-run average total cost reaches a minimum and, in this example, stays at that level for a while as output continues to grow. But at some point, as production increases even further, the cost per unit of output increases. The explanation for this decreasing, constant, and increasing cost pattern, which is typical of the behavior of long-run average total cost, is based on economies of scale, constant returns to scale, and diseconomies of scale.

Economies of Scale, Diseconomies of Scale, and Constant Returns to Scale

Economies of Scale
Occur when the increasing size of production in the long run causes the per unit cost of production to fall.

In the initial stages of long-run production there are typically **economies of scale** that cause long-run average total cost to decrease. This means that initially as the size, or scale, of the operation becomes larger, the cost per unit of output falls. What causes economies of scale to occur?

With a larger scale and output, a firm can use highly specialized and efficient labor and equipment that might be expensive to obtain, but because of the large output, can actually allow the firm to produce at a lower per unit cost. Economies of scale permit a company to hire professionals specialized in an area such as supply-chain management. A large company can use more advanced technology and equipment, receive quantity discounts, and negotiate lower interest rates. Think about fast-food restaurants and your local pub. The cost per unit of a machine-sized, prepackaged, and frozen burger is considerably less than one made with fresh ingredients from a local market.

| FIGURE 12.3 | *Long-Run Average Total Cost* |

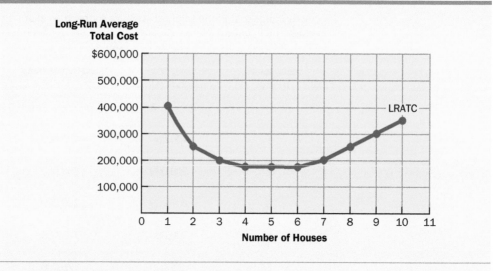

A typical long-run average total cost curve follows a pattern of decreasing, constant, and increasing per unit costs.

Unit cost savings, or efficiency gains, from economies of scale as a business becomes larger and produces higher levels of output have been a frequent argument in favor of allowing mergers between competing sellers in the same market. Mergers are covered in more detail in Chapter 14.

Diseconomies of Scale
Occur when the increasing size of production in the long run causes the per unit cost of production to rise.

When cost per unit increases in the latter stages of long-run production, there are **diseconomies of scale**. In this case, the size or scale of the operation has become so large and unwieldy that the cost per unit of output increases. Diseconomies of scale generally arise because the large size of a company makes control over its operations difficult. As the organization grows, the chain of command becomes more complex, and it is necessary to hire more managers at all levels. Authority and responsibility may become disjointed, causing wasted resources and poor communication, accountability, and control. Costs may also be affected by the amount of time required to pass information and commands through such a large organization. Many companies have restructured or reorganized in an effort to reduce diseconomies of scale created by layers of management.

Constant Returns to Scale
Occur in the range of production levels in which long-run average total cost is constant.

Between economies of scale and diseconomies of scale is a range of production where long-run average total cost neither decreases nor increases. Throughout this output range the firm experiences **constant returns to scale**, or operating levels that have become so large that economies of scale are exhausted but not large enough to encounter diseconomies of scale.

Many real-life examples attest to the existence of economies and diseconomies of scale. This does not mean, however, that every company faces a long-run average total cost curve that looks exactly like that in Figure 12.3. Instead, each firm's product curve differs in the length and strength of its decreasing, constant, and increasing ranges. A company producing automobiles will have a different curve than will a fast-food chain producing hamburgers. Figure 12.4 gives the three phases of long-run average production costs.

| FIGURE 12.4 | *The Three Phases of the Long-Run Average Total Cost Curve* |

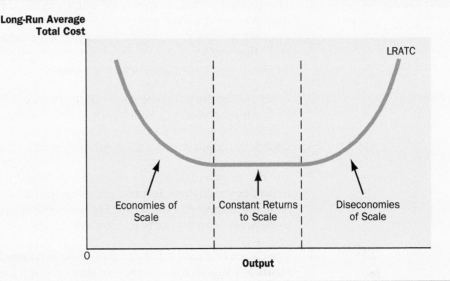

The long-run average total cost curve goes through three phases: a decreasing per unit cost phase caused by economies of scale; a phase of constant returns to scale where per unit costs neither decrease nor increase; and a phase where per unit costs increase due to diseconomies of scale.

Application 12.3 "Too Big to Help," offers a perspective on an issue experienced by many of us that could result from diseconomies of scale. After you read this application about poor customer service, think about how that service could be improved.

APPLICATION 12.3

TOO BIG TO HELP

Can poor customer service by a large company be the result of diseconomies of scale or is it something else?

We have all experienced the "contact for customer service" provided by so many entities and received what many of us might call useless help. It might have been a call to an 800 phone number or a note to an e-mail address that we used to deal with an issue or problem with a product or service.

Customer service contact information comes from banks, credit card companies, appliance and electronics manufacturers, insurance agents, packaged food sellers, and more. And, as we use this information to resolve an issue with a company, the response that we get varies with the company contacted and the person at the end of the line or e-mail.

So what accounts for differing responses and sometimes for the lack of useful information? Why might it be necessary to spend an hour or two on the phone to deal with a clog in the refrigerator's ice maker? Why might there never be a response? Or why after investing a lot of time do we get a response that doesn't solve our problem?

Could diseconomies of scale play a role in customer service? In a small locally owned business, there is usually a person with whom a customer can have direct access. The local bike shop owner, for example, is generally around and can provide direct contact for product issues. But many companies are huge entities with tens of thousands of employees. Their customer service representatives are likely far removed from any line of authority or decision-making ability, and may simply be a small cog in a large organization.

Perhaps we see this in government. At the local level where mayors and council members are friends and neighbors and easily accessible, pot holes get fixed and trash gets picked up. At the federal level, the response to an issue takes a much longer time as people wind their way through bureaucracy—and may never get a response.

Summary

1. The greatest portion of measured output in the U.S. economy comes through the business sector. Categories have been developed for classifying production. Producing sectors is a broad category that includes the services, manufacturing, and other sectors; industry is a narrower category that includes firms producing similar products or using similar processes.

2. A production function shows the output that results when a particular group of inputs is processed in a certain way. Firms have a choice of production functions and seek the least-cost, or efficient, method for producing a desired quantity and quality of output in order to maximize profit.

3. The development of new productive inputs and techniques can come from technological change. Technological change can also lead to creative destruction: New inputs and processes cause those currently in use to become obsolete and some areas of an economy to grow while others decline.

4. The choice of a method of production is influenced by the time frame in which a business plans its operations. The short run is a time period in which some factors of production are variable in amount and some are fixed. The capabilities of the fixed factors, because they cannot be changed, serve as a boundary within which production takes place. The long run is a time period in which all factors are regarded as variable.

5. In the short run, the total cost of producing a certain level of output is found by adding total fixed cost and total variable cost. Total fixed cost is the same regardless of how much is produced; total variable cost increases as output increases. Average total cost is the cost per unit of output at a given level of production and is found by dividing total cost by the number of units of output produced. Marginal cost is the change in total cost resulting from the production of an additional unit of output.

6. In the short run, total cost increases slowly at low levels of output and rapidly at high levels of output. Average total cost decreases and then increases, as does marginal cost. These patterns are the result of the way in which variable factor usage increases as production increases. At low levels of output, small amounts of variable factors are needed with the fixed factors, and at high levels of output, large amounts of variable factors are needed to compensate for the limits imposed by the fixed factors.

7. Underlying the patterns of short-run costs is the Law of Diminishing Returns, which says that as a variable factor of production is added to fixed factors, beyond some point the additional product from each additional unit of the variable factor will decrease.

8. Long-run average total cost illustrates the pattern of costs in the long run. The shape of the long-run average total cost curve is the result of economies of scale that occur in the early stages of long-run production and cause the cost per unit of output to drop, constant returns to scale where average total cost stays the same, and diseconomies of scale that occur in the late stages of long-run production and cause the cost per unit of output to increase.

Key Terms and Concepts

Producing sectors

Industry

Production function

Efficient method of production

Technology

Creative destruction

Short run

Variable factors

Variable costs

Fixed factors

Fixed costs

Long run

Total fixed cost (TFC)

Total variable cost (TVC)

Total cost (TC)

Average total cost (ATC)

Marginal cost (MC)

Law of Diminishing Returns

Long-run total cost, average total cost, and marginal cost

Economies of scale

Diseconomies of scale

Constant returns to scale

Review Questions

1. What is a producing sector? Give some examples. How does this differ from the industry classification?

2. A friend believes that, as far as the costs of operating a business are concerned, short-run costs are the costs that are incurred within the current year and long-run costs are those spread over more than a year. As a student of economics, how would you explain these costs differently to your friend?

3. The short-run average total cost curve and the long-run average total cost curve are similarly shaped. What causes the short-run average total cost curve to slope down and then up? What causes the long-run average total cost curve to slope down and then up?

4. When marginal cost is less than average total cost, average total cost decreases. When marginal cost is greater than average total cost, average total cost increases. Why is this so?

5. Why does a firm incur fixed costs over the short run when its output is zero, and why do fixed costs not change as the level of output changes? Why does a firm's short-run total variable cost increase slowly at smaller levels of output and rapidly at larger levels of output?

6. What is the Law of Diminishing Returns and why does it affect short-run but not long-run production? How will the Law of Diminishing Returns affect the productivity of each additional student who is washing cars at a local church parking lot to raise money for a charity?

7. Complete the following table of short-run costs. From the information in the completed table, plot a total cost curve on the left-hand graph that follows the table and an average total cost curve and a marginal cost curve on the right-hand graph. Remember to plot marginal cost at the midpoint.

Output	Total Fixed Cost	Total Variable Cost	Total Cost	Average Total Cost	Marginal Cost
0	$ ___	$ ___	$100	___	
					$ ___
1	___	___	150	$ ___	
					___
2	___	___	180	___	
					___
3	___	___	210	___	
					___
4	___	___	280	___	
					___
5	___	___	400	___	
					___
6	___	___	600	___	

8. Identify the three phases of a long-run average total cost curve. What is the reason for the behavior of long-run average total cost in each phase?

1. Can you construct a production function for earning an A in this course?
   a. What are the necessary inputs?
   b. How much of each input is required?
   c. How are the inputs combined?
   Does the production function for producing an A in a course differ by course?

2. List some possible explanations for the differences in production techniques used by two pizza restaurants: One is an independent mom-and-pop operation and the other is part of a national chain.

3. Technological change can cause creative destruction. Give a recent example of the process of creative destruction. What products and jobs were affected in your example?

4. The Law of Diminishing Returns was introduced in this chapter and the Law of Diminishing Marginal Utility was introduced in Chapter 11. Are there any similarities between these two Laws?

5. Indicate whether each of the following is probably a fixed factor or a variable factor in the short run.
   a. Fertilizer used to grow crops on a farm
   b. The heat required to keep the pipes in a warehouse from freezing
   c. Electricity used to run machinery and equipment
   d. The only person in a company who knows the trade secret formula to a highly profitable product
   e. A companywide computer-based software accounting system

6. Suppose a proposal is offered to consolidate the more than 75 towns surrounding a large city into a few larger towns. What economies of scale affecting fire, police, administrative, and other services might result from the consolidation? What diseconomies of scale might result from the consolidation? From an economic point of view, would you favor this proposal?

7. How might a business's ability to take advantage of economies of scale affect the price it charges for its product, its profitability, and its competitiveness with rival sellers? What concerns could diseconomies of scale create for pricing, profitability, and competitiveness?

8. We have all been in situations where we see or experience employees standing around and chatting and seemingly not working at their jobs. Discuss an example you have encountered. Do you believe this was due to diseconomies of scale?

Critical Thinking Case 12

THE HUMAN FACTOR

Critical Thinking Skills

Appreciation for a broad perspective

Understanding behavioral considerations

Economic Concepts

The Law of Diminishing Returns

Short- and long-run costs

Creative destruction

Too often there is a sterile, robotic view of factors of production, their costs, and cost-cutting for a business. Workers and managers, while recognized for the important roles they play, can be regarded like machines or buildings or any other resource needed to produce a good or service. But people are complex creatures with personal objectives, needs, and feelings. To neglect this personal side of employees is not smart: It can lead to underutilization of employees, stand in the way of solving problems, and ultimately affect costs.

In a perfect world, a manager would staff an operation with the right number of employees: that is, the number that would keep costs down. But a manager could have other objectives, like empire building. That is, a manager could think that having a large staff moves one up in the ranks and increases power, visibility, and influence. This type of manager might want to increase the size of an operating area for career reasons that could be costly to the business.

Or an organization that is struggling with its costs might need to lay off a few employees. In working through a reduction in force, a company could simply let those with the least seniority go—an easy way to address an often-difficult process. But there may be employees with good potential to improve production and increase the profitability of the organization in the future among this group. Again, a sterile view of workers does not recognize the unique abilities of employees who are valuable contributors to an employer.

The human factor is also related to the communication that occurs within an organization. With growth in the ability to rapidly communicate through methods such as text messaging and e-mail, it is easy to be in touch with virtually everyone in an organization and beyond. But how does a person decide what is necessary communication to do an effective job and what is extraneous, time consuming, and unnecessary? Answering those 200 e-mail messages a day takes time away from real production and raises costs.

We might also consider the sense of interconnectedness with one another that seems to be disappearing as, more and more, employees communicate electronically and spend less time meeting face-to-face. Today's workplace puts less emphasis on conversation and collegiality and more on sitting alone behind a desk and looking at a screen. This can lead to an increased sense of isolation and loss of commitment to an organization, which may lead to higher costs.

Questions

1. In addition to empire building and self-promotion, what other managerial traits have you seen that may not necessarily reduce costs?

2. How do today's communication systems lead to cost savings? How do they lead to increased costs? In your opinion, do the savings outweigh the increased costs?

3. How would you go about measuring whether the decreasing interconnectedness among people at work raises or lowers costs? Are there any strategies to improve this situation?

CHAPTER *13*

Competition and Market Structures

CHAPTER OBJECTIVES

Define how a market's boundaries are determined.

Give the basic characteristics of the four market structures: pure competition, monopolistic competition, oligopoly, and monopoly.

Describe the pricing behavior and long-run position of firms in the purely competitive market structure.

Discuss the behavior of firms in monopolistic competition including the effect of nonprice competition as well as the long-run performance of firms.

Explain the characteristics of the oligopoly market structure and several oligopoly pricing behavior theories.

Discuss the pricing behavior and long-run performance of a firm in a monopoly market.

Evaluate how consumers fare and how efficiency is achieved by firms in each of the four market structures.

Explain how a firm determines its profit-maximizing price and output level.

We interface with many businesses, ranging from the local sandwich shop to big box stores to huge insurance companies. Each of these businesses, like the other 30-plus million businesses in the United States, behaves differently. Some businesses have great control over the prices they charge for their products, while others have little or no control. Some spend millions of dollars on social media, advertising, and public relations, while others spend nothing. And the bottom line for some firms yields continuous economic profit, while other firms, no matter how well they are managed, have no such prospect.[1] Think about the different pricing, advertising, and profit behaviors of a farmer, your bank, a sports franchise, a favorite restaurant, a major oil company, and the owner of the concessions at a stadium.

The greatest influence over the price and nonprice decisions of a firm and its ability to earn economic profit over the long run is the competition it faces in its market. All other things being equal, the greater the competition in a market, the less control a business in that market has over the price it charges, and the less likely the firm is to earn economic profit on an ongoing basis. The less the competition in a market, the greater the control a business has over the price it charges, and the more likely the firm is to earn economic profit over the long run. Think again about a business that has the sole rights to concessions at a stadium. With no competition, that business has strong control over the pricing of whatever it sells. People will likely pay more for a drink and burger at a stadium than at one of several local pubs.

DEFINING A MARKET

Industry
A group of firms producing similar products or using similar processes.

Market
Includes firms that sell similar products and compete for the same buyers.

We know from Chapter 12 that an **industry** is a group of firms that produce similar products or use similar processes. How does this differ from a market where firms sell similar products?

Businesses are in the same **market** when they sell similar products and compete with one another for the same buyers. For example, a movie theater in Chicago and one in Manhattan are in the same industry because they sell similar products, but because they do not compete with each other for the same buyers, they are not in the same market. The movie theater in Chicago and the one in Manhattan are in different markets with different competitors and different customers. In simple terms, a market defines a firm's competitive environment.

Geographic Boundary of a Market
Defined by the geographic area in which sellers compete for buyers.

Product Boundary of a Market
Defined by product substitutability as seen by buyers.

The boundaries of a market are determined along two lines: geography and product substitutability. The **geographic boundary of a market** depends on the size of the area in which sellers compete for buyers. Markets may be local, regional, national, or international. A bagel shop that competes for customers from a particular neighborhood or town is in a local market, whereas a top-notch university graduate program in business is in an international market because it competes for buyers all over the world.

The **product boundary of a market** is defined by product substitutability. Sellers are in the same market when buyers view their products as substitutes. If movies are seen as substitutable for live theater, then they compete in the same market. If buyers think that movie rentals, band concerts, opera theater, and ballet are substitutes for movies, then all of these are in the same market.

Trying to identify the boundaries of a market and determine which products and geographic areas are included is important because the size of a market significantly affects the degree of competition that a firm faces: The larger the market, the greater the number of sellers and the greater the competition. However, the definition of a market can be debated because its boundaries are uncertain, and different perspectives yield different opinions as to what constitute the geographic and product dimensions of a market. For example, if you ask several friends to define the market that your local

---

[1] Remember that there are two types of profit: Normal profit is a return for implicit costs and necessary for a business to continue; economic profit is not a cost of production and is the profit that exceeds normal profit.

movie theater is in, you may get several different responses. One person might define the market in a very narrow sense and include only local movie theaters. Another person might regard the relevant market as entertainment and include all theatrical, sporting, musical, and other such events within 50 miles.

One place where the controversy about the boundaries of a market becomes important is in courts of law hearing cases on alleged violations of the antitrust laws. The antitrust laws are designed to protect competition in markets and will be more fully discussed in Chapter 14. One type of antitrust case heard by the courts involves a firm or other organization accused of taking over, or monopolizing, a market. In these cases, the definition of the boundaries of the market is critical because how broadly or narrowly the market is defined impacts the court's decision. In an antitrust case, the accused will likely present one definition of its market's boundaries, and the accuser another. The court must then determine which definition is correct and, partly on that basis, decide on the guilt or innocence of the accused.

THE MARKET STRUCTURES

Market Structures
A system for grouping and analyzing markets according to the degree and type of competition among sellers.

We know that the degree of competition that a business faces in a market influences its behavior with regard to the prices it charges, the profit it makes, and the nonprice competition it uses. Economists have created four models of market situations, called **market structures**, to represent degrees of competition and study their effects: pure competition, monopolistic competition, oligopoly, and monopoly.

The four market structures represent a spectrum of competitive conditions. At one end of the spectrum is pure competition, where the competitive pressure is the strongest, and at the other end is monopoly, where there is no direct competition. In between are monopolistic competition, which is closer to pure competition, and oligopoly, which is closer to monopoly.

Each of these market models has a set of characteristics that differentiates it from the other market models and is important for determining the type and amount of competition a firm faces. For example, certain features are associated with a monopoly structure and others with oligopoly. The distinguishing characteristics of each of the market models center around three areas.

♦ **Number of sellers.** The number of sellers in the market is important to the amount of competition. A market may have one seller, thousands of sellers, or some number in between.
♦ **Product type.** The product sold in the market can be identical from seller to seller or be differentiated. If a firm can distinguish its product from those of its competitors through size, color, or any other attribute, then nonprice competition can arise.
♦ **Entry and exit.** The ease or difficulty with which firms can enter or leave the market affects competition. It may be extremely easy for new firms to begin selling in the market, or it may be virtually impossible.

The remainder of this chapter describes the four market structures and analyzes the behavior of firms in each structure. For each structure we will evaluate the control that a business has over the price it charges, the influence and effect of nonprice competition, and whether firms tend to make an economic profit and operate efficiently in the long run.

PURE COMPETITION

Characteristics of Pure Competition

The following characteristics define a **purely competitive market**:

♦ There is a very large number of sellers acting independently of each other.
♦ The products offered for sale are identical: Buyers cannot distinguish the product of one seller from that of another.
♦ Entry by business firms into a purely competitive market is easy, as is exit from the market. There are no legal restrictions, fees, impossibly high capital requirements, patents, or other **barriers to entry**.

The markets for crops such as corn, oats, and wheat provide classic examples of pure competition. In each of these markets there are thousands of independent sellers, and the output of any one seller is indistinguishable from the output of any other. Entry into these markets is easy because not much is required to grow these crops.

The market in which a corporation's common stock is traded may also provide an example of pure competition. With companies such as Starbucks, millions of shares of stock are held by thousands of owners. Each share is identical to each other share, and it is easy to enter and exit the market to buy and sell.

Behavior of a Firm in Pure Competition

Pure competition is the market structure to which other markets are compared. As will be shown, it is the ideal from the buyer's point of view because of the prices, costs, profit levels, and efficiency gains that result from the competition.

Control over Price   One of the most important aspects of the behavior of purely competitive sellers is that the firms are **price takers**: No individual firm has any control over the price it receives for its product. Price is determined solely through the market's competitive forces; that is, price is determined by the interaction of market supply and market demand. The price that a firm gets is a result of the decisions of all buyers and all sellers in the market.

Figure 13.1 illustrates the market for a grain crop (such as wheat) and allows us to review the market price–setting process covered in Chapter 3. D is the market demand curve showing the different amounts of grain that all buyers together plan to purchase at different prices. As expected, the curve is downward sloping, indicating that the lower the price, the greater the quantity demanded in the market. S is the upward-sloping market supply curve, showing that all sellers (grain farmers) together offer more of the product for sale at a higher price. The actual price that emerges in this market is $3 per bushel. This is the equilibrium price that equates market demand and supply.

In this example, an individual purely competitive firm can sell as much or as little as it wants at the price of $3 per bushel. It cannot charge more than $3 and will not charge less than $3. Why is this so?

Due to the large number of independently acting sellers in the market, the entire output of any one seller represents a "drop in the bucket" compared to the total available output. A seller that would charge a price higher than the market price would sell nothing because buyers can choose from thousands of alternative sellers. Because one seller's product is identical to that of all other sellers, it makes no difference with whom a buyer deals.

FIGURE 13.1	*Market Demand and Supply for a Grain Crop*

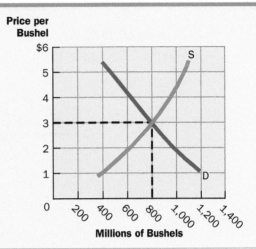

In a purely competitive market, market demand and supply determine the equilibrium price and quantity of a product.

It would also be pointless for a single seller to offer output at less than the market price. A grain farmer would not sell grain at $2, $2.50, or even $2.99 per bushel, knowing that the entire crop can be sold at the market price of $3 per bushel. The same pricing behavior exists with regard to common stock. If the market price of a share is $19.50, a person cannot sell shares for more than $19.50 and would not sell them for less.

Because of large numbers of independent sellers supplying identical products, purely competitive firms have neither the willingness nor the ability to deviate from the price set in the market.

Demand for an Individual Firm's Product   For any product sold, regardless of the market structure, there is a downward-sloping **market demand curve** such as that shown in Figure 13.1. In addition to the market demand curve, each individual seller also has a demand curve for its own product. This represents the amounts of the seller's product that buyers are willing and able to purchase at certain prices. Thus, an **individual firm's demand curve** dictates the price a firm will receive when it chooses an output to sell.

Remember that in pure competition the price an individual firm receives for its product is set by the forces of supply and demand in the market, and each firm supplies a minute fraction of the market. Since the firm's output is negligible when compared to the total, it can offer as much or as little as it chooses *at the market price*. Thus, the demand curve for any single purely competitive seller's product is graphed as a straight, horizontal line at the equilibrium market price.

The grain example in Figure 13.1 can be used to illustrate this concept. At an equilibrium price of $3 in the market, the demand curve for a single seller's grain output would be like that shown in Figure 13.2. At $3 per bushel, buyers are willing to purchase 1,000 bushels, 5,000 bushels, or whatever output the seller wants to offer. If the seller were to charge more, say, even $3.01, sales would drop to zero. There would also be no incentive to sell for less than $3 per bushel, since that is the price buyers will pay.

Market Demand Curve
The demand curve for all buyers in the market together.

Individual Firm's Demand Curve
Shows the amounts of an individual firm's product that buyers are willing and able to purchase at particular prices.

FIGURE 13.2   *Demand Curve for the Output of a Purely Competitive Seller*

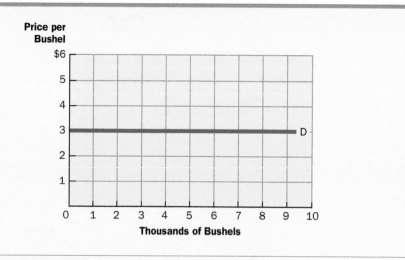

A firm in a purely competitive market can sell as much or as little as it wants at the market price.

The graphs enable us to better see the relationship between the equilibrium market price and the individual firm's demand curve as well as how changes in the market affect the individual seller. If the equilibrium price in the market increases or decreases, the individual firm's demand curve will also increase (shift upward) or decrease (shift downward). If a large number of new buyers enter the market for the grain in our example, the market demand curve will shift to the right. As a consequence, the equilibrium price in the market rises, and the individual firm's demand curve shifts upward. This is shown in Figure 13.3, where the price increases from $3 to $4 after market demand increases from D1 to D2. What would be the effect on an individual firm's demand curve from an increase in market supply?[2]

Application 13.1, "The Farmers' Almanac: It's a Necessity," takes a closer look at what it is like to be a seller in a purely competitive market. After reading the application, do you think that simply having to accept the price set in the market clears away a large amount of the uncertainty, risk, and complexity that we think accompanies the management of a business?

Pricing, Profit, and Loss   Given that the purely competitive firm has no control over price, can it make a profit? It is possible in the short run that a business could make an economic profit, operate at a loss, or break even with a normal profit. (Remember that normal profit is the profit necessary to stay in business and is included in the economic cost of production. Economic profit is that profit earned beyond normal profit.) To determine its profit or loss position, a firm will compare the price it receives for a product and the cost of producing it.

---

[2]An increase in market supply would cause the market supply curve to shift to the right. The resulting fall in equilibrium price would cause the individual seller's demand curve to shift downward.

FIGURE 13.3   *Effect on the Individual Purely Competitive Firm of an Increase in Market Demand*

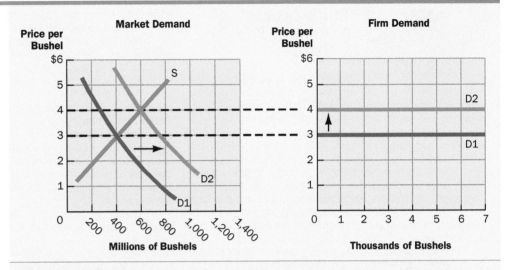

An increase in the market demand for a product will increase its equilibrium price and cause the individual firm's demand curve to shift upward.

Economic Profit, Loss, or Breaking Even
Occurs when price is greater than, less than, or equal to average total cost, respectively.

It is easy to see the profit or loss position of a firm by graphically comparing the firm's demand curve and its average total cost curve. The firm's demand curve gives the price it will receive for each unit of output sold, and the average total cost (ATC) curve gives the cost for producing each unit of output.

Figure 13.4a shows a firm in pure competition that is operating with an **economic profit**. Economic profit results because the firm's demand curve is above the average total cost curve or price is higher than average total cost. Figure 13.4b illustrates a firm

---

FIGURE 13.4   *A Purely Competitive Seller Operating with an Economic Profit, a Loss, or Breaking Even*

A seller will operate with an economic profit, a loss, or break even, depending on whether price is greater than, less than, or equal to average total cost, respectively.

APPLICATION 13.1

THE FARMERS' ALMANAC: IT'S A NECESSITY

What's it like to be a farmer selling corn in a purely competitive market? Take the case of Doug, a farmer in central Illinois. His harvest is in, and he has a few hundred acres of his corn crop stored in the local grain elevator—a place that holds grain until its owners are ready to sell.

Today Doug called the grain elevator to get a quote on the price per bushel for corn. Whatever it is, the price is completely beyond his control to change and is not a matter for argument. With the quote, Doug is left with a take-it-or-leave-it decision: sell all or some of the corn crop or not sell anything and continue to pay the storage fee.

Doug's decision rests largely on two factors: how badly he needs the money and where he thinks corn prices are heading. Most importantly, there are bills to be paid that can limit Doug's ability to hold out for higher prices. Planting and growing corn requires substantial outlays for seed, chemicals, and production equipment. Then there are family expenditures: college tuition, a mortgage, groceries, and everything else. When bills need to be paid, crops might need to be sold.

The question of where corn prices are headed is not easy to assess. While corn and other grain prices change frequently over the course of a single day, Doug is likely evaluating where they will be in a week, a month, or more. How much higher or lower will they go? Doug can check out some data and predictions about corn prices, but this will not lead him to clear and precise answers about direction.

For one thing, weather is unpredictable. Good weather can lead to high yields on crops, which will increase supply and drive corn prices down. Bad weather such as heavy rains can reduce supply and drive corn prices up. This is further complicated by the time of the year in which Doug is trying to make a decision. Is it immediately after a healthy harvest, when many farmers need to sell crops for the money? Is it February in the year following a poor harvest, when a new crop with weather uncertainty is about to be planted? The weather complications make us understand why the Old Farmers' Almanac, with its weather predictions, has been a necessity in a farm family's home.

There are other price-influencing factors beyond Doug's control. The market for grains is clearly international, causing the price to be influenced by what is produced elsewhere in the world. A bumper crop in Brazil can have a huge impact on farmers in central Illinois.

And then there is the whole debate surrounding ethanol. Certainly the prospect of converting corn into fuel has helped to increase prices. But with questions raised about the amount of water required to make ethanol and other issues, what will happen in the market for corn and its price in the future?

Here is the simple fact. While a farmer has no control over the prices for a crop, there are still many price-related decisions to be made. And there just might be more concern over prices in a purely competitive market than in other markets, where businesses can better influence the prices they get.

---

in pure competition operating with a **loss**. This loss occurs because the demand curve is below the average total cost curve or price is lower than average total cost, regardless of the level of output produced. In Figure 13.4c a firm is just **breaking even** (earning a normal profit) if it produces and sells Qx units of output because price is equal to average total cost at that level of output.

An appendix to this chapter explains in greater detail how a firm in pure competition determines its profit-maximizing or loss-minimizing level of output.

Nonprice Competition

Firms focus on a feature other than price to attract buyers to their products.

Nonprice Competition   Firms in pure competition have no need to engage in **nonprice competition**. A purely competitive seller makes no expenditures on advertising, public relations, or other efforts to bring its product to a buyer's attention. With so many firms selling identical products efforts at creating buyer awareness of a particular firm's product would be a waste of time and money.[3]

The benefit to consumers from this lack of nonprice competition is that, with no promotional expenditures, firms' costs are lower than they would otherwise be. This in turn means that over the long run, buyers pay less for products.

---

[3]Sometimes trade associations to which firms in an industry or market belong will advertise the product itself. Promotions for beef, eggs, and milk are good examples of product—not firm—advertising.

Long-Run Costs, Profit, and Efficiency   As we examine the four market models, one of the most important aspects of our study is the long-run behavior of firms. In pure competition, firms operate at the lowest possible cost, charge the lowest price that they can without going out of business, and earn no economic profit in the long run. All of these conditions are ideal for the consumer and result from competition among sellers.

The long-run position of a purely competitive seller is illustrated in Figure 13.5. This figure shows a simple long-run average total cost (LRATC) curve exhibiting economies and diseconomies of scale as well as the firm's demand curve. In the long run, an individual purely competitive seller's position is such that its demand curve just brushes the bottom of its long-run average total cost curve. A firm operating under the conditions given in Figure 13.5 would sell 4,000 units of output at $3 per unit or would operate at point A. Any other output level would result in a loss because the long-run average total cost curve would be above the demand curve.

Notice that point A is the lowest point on the firm's long-run average total cost curve. This means that the firm is producing at the lowest possible cost per unit of output in the long run or is operating at the most efficient level of output. **Efficient production** is an important goal for an economy because of the basic problem of scarcity.

Efficient Production

A good or service is produced at the lowest cost possible.

Notice also that at point A price equals average total cost, causing the seller to earn only normal and no excess profit. Also, the $3 price is the lowest price at which the firm can sell and still remain in business. Any price less than $3 would be less than the firm's long-run average total cost, causing it to go out of business.

So, in the long run in pure competition,

♦   the cost of production is as low as it can possibly be so firms are operating efficiently;
♦   the price of the product is as low as it can possibly be; and
♦   the consumer pays no economic profit.

| **FIGURE 13.5** | *Long-Run Position of a Purely Competitive Seller* |

In the long run, a purely competitive seller operates where price equals minimum average total cost, which allows just a normal profit.

Why does this long-run condition occur in pure competition? Easy entry into and exit from the market are the basis for the position of the purely competitive firm in the long run. When firms in a purely competitive market earn excess profits, potential sellers recognize the opportunity to also earn such profits and, because of easy entry, come into the market. As additional sellers enter the market, the market supply increases, causing the equilibrium market price to fall. As the equilibrium price falls, each individual seller's excess profit begins to disappear. This process of entry and reduction in both the market price and excess profit continues until sellers operate where price equals minimum long-run average total cost or with just a normal profit.

The mechanics of this process are illustrated in Figure 13.6a. With market price P_1 and the individual firm's demand curve D1 (right-hand graph), the firm is making an economic profit because its long-run average total cost curve lies below D1. As other firms attracted by this economic profit enter the market, the market supply curve (left-hand graph) increases from S1 to S2, market price falls to P_2, and the individual seller's demand curve falls to D2, which allows no economic profit.

If firms are losing money and experiencing less than normal profits, some sellers will close their operations and leave the market. As sellers leave, the market supply decreases, causing the equilibrium price to increase. As the price increases, the losses to remaining sellers get smaller and smaller. This process continues until, again, price equals minimum long-run average total cost.

Figure 13.6b illustrates the effect on an individual firm of an exodus of other firms from the market. At market price P_1, the individual firm is operating at a loss because the cost of producing each unit is greater than the price. As firms leave the market, the market supply curve shifts to the left, from S1 to S2, causing market price and the individual firm's demand curve to rise. When the price rises to P_2, the firm is just breaking even and earning a normal profit.

The description of precise movements toward the long run in pure competition should be tempered to reflect reality. These graphs and the explanation of how entry and exit affect the long run give us a way to think about where purely competitive markets move with time. To assume that all firms in a purely competitive market are exactly alike, have the same cost curves, and march together in lockstep doesn't paint a picture of reality. In short, this model, like others, gives us a framework within which to think about patterns of behavior, given some basic assumptions.

Is There Pure Competition?

The extent to which pure competition is found in the real world is open for discussion. The markets for grain and other agricultural products are generally regarded to be close examples of pure competition because these markets have large numbers of independent sellers supplying identical products. However, several factors need to be considered in labeling them as purely competitive.

There is the question of entry into and exit from agricultural markets. Substantial outlays for land, equipment, seed, fertilizer, and other factors may be barriers to entry to anything other than small-scale farming. In some instances, large-scale, efficient operation requires expensive capital for harvesting grain or caring for livestock. Exit from farming can also be difficult; the land or its location may not be well suited for an

| FIGURE 13.6 | *Effect of Entry and Exit of Sellers in a Purely Competitive Market* |

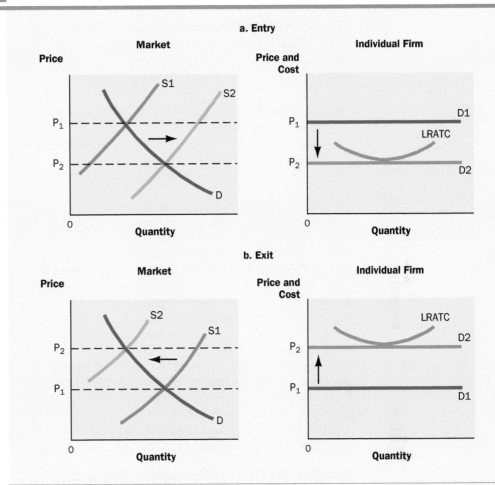

When individual firms in pure competition make an economic profit, new firms are attracted to the market in the long run, causing market supply to increase and equilibrium price to fall. When individual firms operate with a loss, some drop out of the market in the long run, causing market supply to decrease and equilibrium price to rise. Eventually, the price that each firm receives is equal to the firm's minimum long-run average total cost.

alternative use, and tax laws may make it difficult to sell a farm or pass it on to other family members.

With considerations such as these, of what value is the study of pure competition? The purely competitive model helps us better understand the behavior of firms in certain markets. It also provides an ideal against which all real-world markets can be judged. We cannot understand the extent to which markets are working well or poorly without the ideal of pure competition for comparison.

MONOPOLISTIC COMPETITION

Characteristics of Monopolistic Competition

The market structure closest to pure competition, and where we can find many real-world examples, is **monopolistic competition**. A monopolistically competitive market has

Monopolistic Competition
Market structure characterized by a large number of sellers with differentiated products and fairly easy entry and exit.

Differentiated Products
Products of competing firms are different and recognized as such by buyers.

- a large number of sellers—not as many as in pure competition, but a large number nonetheless;
- **differentiated products**—buyers can distinguish among the products of different sellers; and
- fairly easy entry into and exit from the market.

We frequently find ourselves as buyers in monopolistically competitive markets: coffee shops, restaurants, mall clothing stores, and other retailers where a large number of small shops compete with one another. In these markets each seller's product is somewhat different: It might be location, parking, service, image, or a variety of other things. Think about your local coffee shops, where the quality of the coffee used to make a latte, or even the crowd that frequents the shop, differentiates one place from another. It is relatively easy to open a small store or shop. A place can be leased; no highly trained workers are needed; and there are minimal capital equipment requirements. The small cupcake shops that are springing up all over the country exemplify these characteristics.

Another slightly different example of a monopolistically competitive market is the labor market for college graduates with a particular major, such as accounting. Each year a large number of accounting majors graduate from colleges and universities. Each of these graduates is unique in terms of grades, background, experience, courses completed, college attended, and initiative. Entry into this market is relatively easy: The major expenditure is the cost of a college degree.

Behavior of a Firm in Monopolistic Competition

Because of differences in the characteristics of monopolistically competitive and purely competitive markets, there are differences in the behavior of firms in these structures. Notably, unlike pure competitors, monopolistic competitors have some control over the prices they receive for their products, and they engage in nonprice competition.

Control over Price   With a large number of firms selling identical products, the individual purely competitive firm has no control over the price it can get for its product. In monopolistic competition there is also a large number of sellers, but because the sellers' products are differentiated, buyers do not view the product of one seller as a perfect substitute for the product of another. For this reason, when a monopolistically competitive firm raises its price, it will lose some, but not all, of its buyers. Some buyers will continue to purchase the product from the firm at a higher price because they see the firm's product as different from and preferable to those of its competitors. Thus, product differentiation allows a firm to carve out a little niche of its own within the larger market.

However, even with product differentiation, there is a limit to the amount of control a monopolistically competitive seller has over price. Since many other firms produce similar products, a firm that raises its price too much risks losing many of its buyers. Some buyers may be willing to pay a little extra for better service or a distinctive style, but if they have to pay a lot more, the alternatives become more attractive. For example, you and your friends may continue to eat lunch at a favorite restaurant even if it raises its prices somewhat. However, if the prices are raised too high, you may go somewhere else.

In short, a business selling in a monopolistically competitive market is in an interesting position: It has some control over price because of its ability to differentiate its product, but that control is limited by the presence of many other firms selling similar products.

Demand for an Individual Firm's Product   Because of product differentiation, the demand curve faced by an individual monopolistic competitor is downward sloping, like that in Figure 13.7.[4] This demand curve shows that if the firm raises its price, it will lose some, but not all, of its buyers. For example, in Figure 13.7, when the seller raises the price from $2.50 to $3.00, the quantity demanded falls from 500 to 200 units, not from 500 units to zero as would happen if the seller were a pure competitor.[5]

| **FIGURE 13.7** | *Demand Curve for the Output of a Monopolistically Competitive Seller* |

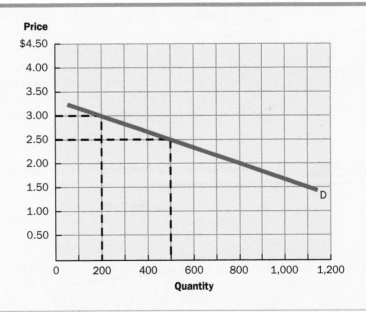

Because of product differentiation, a seller in monopolistic competition will lose some, but not all, of its buyers if it raises its price.

[4]Here we need to stress that we are talking about the demand curve for an individual seller's product, not the market demand curve.

[5]Generally, in monopolistic competition the response to a price change is elastic; that is, over the broadest range of the demand curve, buyers respond strongly to price changes. In Figure 13.7, when the price increases from $2.50 to $3.00, or by 20 percent, the quantity demanded decreases from 500 to 200 units, or by 60 percent. Since the percentage change in the quantity demanded is greater than the percentage change in price, the response is characterized as elastic. (The exact price elasticity is 60%/20% = 3%. You can refer to Chapter 3 to refresh your memory about elasticity.)

Pricing, Profit, and Loss   Just like other firms, the profit or loss position of a seller in a monopolistically competitive market can be determined by comparing the demand curve and average total cost curve for its product. If the average total cost curve lies below the demand curve or the cost per unit of output is less than the price, an economic profit is earned. This is shown in Figure 13.8a. If the average total cost curve is above the demand curve or the cost per unit of output is greater than the price, a loss occurs. This is shown in Figure 13.8b.

Nonprice Competition   Obviously, sellers in monopolistically competitive markets can compete with one another for buyers by lowering prices. But because their products are differentiated, rivalry through nonprice competition is also an option.

Nonprice competition takes all kinds of forms from packaging to service to location to name a few. A cafe, for example, can attract customers because of its reputation for outstanding food and service, hours open, or access to parking.

We can gauge the importance of nonprice competition by simply noticing how much advertising is based on nonprice factors. Notice how infrequently advertisements on television or on the Internet stress price as the selling feature.

Business firms are attracted to nonprice competition for two reasons. First, it provides a way for a firm to increase the demand for its product. By increasing buyer interest through service, packaging, and other features, a firm can shift the demand curve for its product to the right—thereby selling more at each price. Second, by highlighting differences and playing down similarities, nonprice competition helps an individual firm make its product appear unique. As this occurs, the seller becomes less sensitive to the presence of rivals. Uniqueness allows a seller to raise prices without losing as many buyers as would otherwise be the case.

Controversy exists over how much nonprice competition is appropriate. Some people argue that nonprice competition raises the cost of doing business and, therefore, brings higher prices for consumers. Others think that nonprice

---

FIGURE 13.8   *A Monopolistically Competitive Seller Operating with an Economic Profit or a Loss*

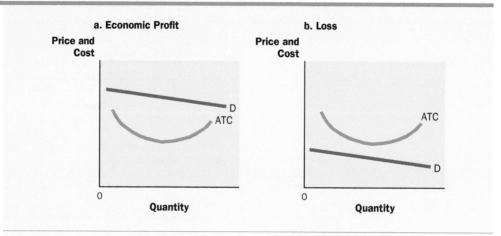

Economic profit is earned when the price of a product is greater than its average total cost or the demand curve is above the average total cost curve. A loss occurs when price is less than average total cost or the demand curve is below the average total cost curve.

competition benefits consumers with variety and better quality. Up for Debate, "Does Nonprice Competition Waste Resources?," adds an additional twist to this controversy by looking at its potential impact on sustainability of the world's resources.

Long-Run Costs, Profit, and Efficiency   Over the long run, sellers in monopolistically competitive markets earn only normal profits, just like firms in purely competitive markets. This occurs because, like purely competitive markets, monopolistically competitive markets are easy to enter and exit. Easy entry and exit cause the long-run position of a monopolistically competitive seller to look like that in Figure 13.9. The seller in Figure 13.9 can earn a normal profit by selling 500 units of output at $2.50 each. At any smaller or larger output, the long-run average total cost curve is above the demand curve, causing the firm to operate at a loss.

If sellers are earning economic, or excess, profit (like the firm shown in Figure 13.8a), new sellers enter the market and take some demand away from the existing sellers. This causes the demand curves of the existing sellers to shift to the left until they reach a position like that shown in Figure 13.9, where economic profit is competed away and only normal profit remains. If sellers are sustaining losses (like the firm shown in Figure 13.8b), some leave the market, causing the demand curves of the remaining sellers to shift to the right until they reach a position like that shown in Figure 13.9, and the remaining firms operate at a normal profit.

While purely competitive and monopolistically competitive sellers both earn only a normal profit over the long run, the two types of sellers differ in an important

FIGURE 13.9   *Long-Run Position of a Monopolistically Competitive Seller*

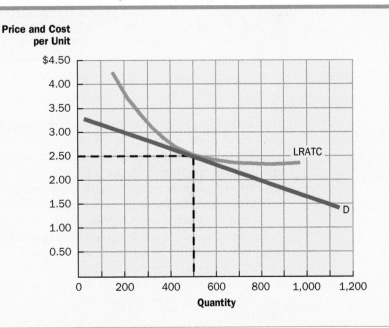

A monopolistically competitive seller earns no excess profit over the long run and operates at a long-run average total cost that is greater than the minimum.

Does Nonprice Competition Waste Resources?

Today there is great concern for the sustainability of our world in a time of diminishing nonrenew- able resources as well as the inability to keep renewable resources growing at a pace that matches their use. With this concern comes an important question: Does nonprice competition have an impact on sustainability by wasting resources?

Yes   There is just one answer to this question, and it is a loud and clear yes. There are several features that come with nonprice competition that certainly foster a waste of our resources.

Consider packaging. One of the popular ways in which producers distinguish their products is through packaging. Think about all of the cardboard boxes, many larger than they need to be, with their markings and colors that induce us to buy so many things housed in them— from toothpaste to cake mix to shoes. Then there are individually wrapped items: For example, there are ever-increasing numbers of snack foods packaged separately in 100-calorie snack bags. And there are water bottles and large, hard plastic shells with tiny items inside and detergent bottles, to name just a few. Can't we package in a way that requires fewer resources?

Another nonprice competitive feature is parking. Businesses like to have parking close by for their patrons, which can result in more paved surfaces. Increased impervious surfaces affect water runoff and the return of this important resource to the ground.

Finally, there is the expenditure of money for developing marketing strategies that focus on nonprice competition to increase sales. Wouldn't we be better off putting these funds into expenditures that focus on sustainability practices?

No   Nonprice competition leads to better products and increases the standard of living for consumers. It better satisfies buyers through closer attention to their wants and needs. Just because resources are diverted to buyer satisfaction is no reason to believe that they are "wasted."

One just needs to think about the areas in which nonprice competition has resulted in better products. Consider food. Today there is a greater abundance of choices, new and different products, and better quality. Individual foil-wrapped tea bags, small bite-sized candy, great one-cup coffee servings, and individual pouches of cat and dog food make life better. Even the 100-calorie snack bags have helped countless people keep their weight under control and fight an obesity problem. Plus, so many of these boxes, bottles, and bags can be recycled.

Nonprice competition has made many products more convenient and safer. With durable, small packages and bottled water and soft drinks, life is much easier for the average person to negotiate. And safety has been increased. The hard shell that encases many products, including medications, ensures a tamper-proof product. Finally, wouldn't it be a really dull world without nonprice competition and the features it brings?

way. A firm in a purely competitive market operates at minimum average total cost in the long run and is, therefore, efficient, whereas a firm in a monopolistically competitive market does not operate at minimum average total cost and is, therefore, not as efficient. For the firm in Figure 13.9, the long-run price and per unit cost are $2.50. If the firm were a pure competitor, its price and per unit cost would be about $2.35—the minimum point on the long-run average total cost curve.

It is impossible for a monopolistic competitor to operate in the long run with price equal to minimum long-run average total cost because of product differentiation, which results in a downward-sloping demand curve. This difference gives rise to a criticism of monopolistic competition: Even though price equals long-run average total cost and the firm is earning only a normal profit, the cost and price are higher than they would be in pure competition, and some efficiency is sacrificed.

Test Your Understanding, "Purely Competitive and Monopolistically Competitive Markets," helps to reinforce some of the behavioral characteristics of firms in these two market structures, including the long-run positions of firms in each structure.

OLIGOPOLY

Oligopoly is further removed from pure competition than is monopolistic competition. In fact, it is so far removed that it makes more sense to discuss how oligopoly and pure competition differ than to discuss what they have in common. While pure competition may be the ideal market structure, oligopoly is the dominant market structure in the U.S. economy. More business is transacted in oligopolistic markets than in any of the three other market structures.

Characteristics of Oligopoly

Oligopoly
A market dominated by a few large sellers; products are differentiated or identical; entry into the market is difficult.

In an **oligopoly,**

♦ the market is dominated by a few large sellers, but there may also be small fringe sellers in the market;
♦ the products of the sellers may be differentiated or identical; and
♦ entry of firms into the market is difficult because of barriers to entry such as the financing needed to enter the market or the large size needed to compete.

The cell phone service market is a good example of an oligopoly with differentiated products. At the time of this writing, there were several large providers—Verizon, Sprint, AT&T, and T-mobile—with a variety of smaller providers. The services of these companies are differentiated by plans and the availability of different types of free or low-cost phones. In the markets for some basic metals like aluminum, there are a few large firms that dominate the market. These products, like aluminum ingot, tend to be undifferentiated, and the product of one seller is like another. In the cases of cell phone providers and basic metals, new entrants to the market would require substantial money to rival the big firms.[6]

Examples of oligopoly are everywhere. Notice how few firms are in the market when you shop for a car, or a computer, or even breakfast cereal. You can find oligopolies in the markets for light bulbs, gasoline, credit cards, commercial television broadcasting, and even soap and toothpaste.

Behavior of a Firm in an Oligopolistic Market

Control over Price   With few sellers in an oligopoly, each of the dominant firms has a large share of the market. A large market share allows the firm some control over its price—more so than a monopolistic competitor who also has some control because of a differentiated product but faces a large number of rivals.

Having just a few competing sellers introduces an interesting twist to oligopoly that has an important effect on a firm's behavior. With so few rivals, the price, output, advertising, and other policies of one firm can have a significant impact on the other firms in the market, causing, in turn, those other firms to react. For example, if a credit card company offers a low interest rate or reward points for merchandise, this may reduce the use of competing credit cards, causing those companies to respond with programs of their own.

In the oligopolistic market structure, sellers are constantly watching and weighing the actions and reactions of their competitors. This phenomenon is called

[6]Some question whether there really are undifferentiated oligopolies. While the physical products of the sellers in the market might be the same, there can be differences among the sellers' delivery systems, financing options, and other arrangements.

TEST YOUR UNDERSTANDING

PURELY COMPETITIVE AND MONOPOLISTICALLY COMPETITIVE MARKETS

1. The following graphs represent a purely competitive market for a type of wheat and the demand for an individual seller in this market.

Market   Individual Seller

a. In the above, draw the individual seller's demand curve in this market.

b. Illustrate in both graphs the effect of a severe drought in the regions that grow this crop. Show the impact on the market and on the individual seller of the drought.

2. The following graphs illustrate the market and the short-run position for a seller in a purely competitive market.

Market   Individual Seller

a. What will happen in the long run in this market?

b. Illustrate the changes that lead to the long-run position in both graphs.

c. What is the long-run position in terms of price and long-run average total cost?

3. Illustrate the long-run position of a purely competitive firm in the left-hand graph and the long-run position of a monopolistically competitive firm in the right-hand graph.

Seller in Pure Competition   Seller in Monopolistic Competition

a. What is the difference between the long-run positions of the firms in these two different market structures? Why does the monopolistically competitive firm not operate at the lowest long-run average total cost and the purely competitive firm does operate at the lowest long-run average total cost?

Answers can be found at the back of the book.

Mutual Interdependence
So few sellers exist in the market that each seller weighs the actions and reactions of rivals in its decision making.

mutual interdependence. Because of mutual interdependence, sellers must consider not only the effects of their pricing and other policies on buyers but the effects on their rivals and their rivals' reactions as well. Mutual interdependence is unique to oligopoly.

Price of an Individual Firm's Product   Because mutual interdependence is manifested in so many different ways, there is no single explanation for oligopoly pricing. Rather, several theories have been developed to accommodate different types of interdependence. Two of the best-known theories are leadership pricing and the kinked demand curve model.

Leadership Pricing
One firm in a market sets a price that the other firms in the market then adopt.

Leadership pricing occurs when one firm in a market sets a price that is then adopted by other sellers. The firm that sets the price is called the price leader, and the firms that respond are the followers. Leadership pricing is not uncommon: Often firms in markets such as commercial airlines and banking follow suit when a price change is announced by one of their competitors. The price changes by the followers often come within a few hours or days after the leader's announcement.

Price leadership occurs for several reasons. When the largest firm in the market changes its prices, rivals choose to follow the changes rather than begin a price war. A price leader could be followed because of changing market conditions. The price leader may be the first to exhibit a sensitivity to these changes that the others will also experience. All banks, for example, face the same changes in money market conditions that cause a price leadership pattern to emerge with regard to interest rates. And sometimes price leadership is the result of tradition and expectations. Firms respond to a particular seller's price changes because over the years this has been a traditional pattern and firms expect that pattern to continue.

Kinked Demand Curve
Assumes that rivals will not follow price increases but will follow price decreases; illustrates that as a seller's price rises, the amount of its product demanded decreases substantially, but as its price falls, the amount demanded increases only slightly.

The second theory, the **kinked demand curve** model, is based on the assumption that rivals do not follow a seller's price increases but do follow its price decreases. The theory gets its name from the unusual shape of the individual oligopolist's demand curve under this assumption. A kinked demand curve is illustrated in Figure 13.10.

The price currently charged and the corresponding output sold by the firm are shown at the kink, or bend, in the demand curve. For the firm in Figure 13.10, the current price is $3 and sales are 400,000 units. If the firm raises its price above $3 and its rivals do not follow, it stands to lose a large number of buyers to those other sellers. For example, when it increases its price from $3 to $4, its sales fall by 200,000 units, from 400,000 to 200,000. But, when the firm lowers its price from $3 to $2, its sales increase by only 50,000 units, from 400,000 to 450,000.

The relatively flat portion of the kinked demand curve above the current price shows that a firm increasing its price stands to lose a large number of sales if its rivals do not follow its lead. The steep portion of the curve below the current price illustrates

FIGURE 13.10   *Kinked Demand Curve for the Output of an Oligopolist*

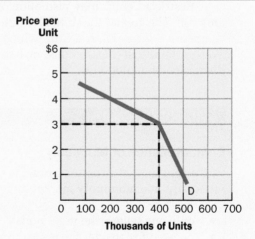

The kinked demand curve of an oligopolist is based on the assumption that the firm's rivals will follow a price decrease but not a price increase.

that with rivals following price cuts, sales increase only slightly. The conclusion to be drawn from this model is that prices are relatively stable in this type of oligopoly market because the fear of rivals' reactions gives little or no incentive to either raise or lower price. In other words, there is not much price competition.

Nonprice Competition   The degree of nonprice competition found in an oligopoly market depends on the extent to which the products are identical or differentiated. Where competitors sell largely identical products, spending money on product promotion could end up benefiting all firms in the market, rather than just the individual firm that makes the expenditure. On the other hand, a strong promotional campaign emphasizing a seller's product makes sense when the products are clearly differentiable on the basis of quality or some other characteristic. Think about all of the beer ads that want you to buy beer for its taste or its image.

Nonprice competition could be important if a seller's price cuts do not lead to large increases in sales. In this case, nonprice competition may provide a nice alternative to price competition. However, mutual interdependence also exists with regard to nonprice competition. Watch food companies. They respond quickly to new flavors of ice cream, the introduction of new types of chips, and the creation of new bottled drinks. Even the fast-food restaurants react to each other. And, when a textbook publisher offers a web-based tutorial for students in a course, the other publishers do the same.

Long-Run Costs, Profit, and Efficiency   Over the long run, purely competitive and monopolistically competitive sellers earn only normal profit: Easy entry allows new firms to come into the market and compete economic profit away. But with oligopoly, entry is not easy. Therefore, oligopolists can continue to earn economic profit over the long run because new sellers cannot readily enter the market.

The ability to earn economic profit over the long run affects the price buyers pay for a product. With pure competition, easy entry ensures that price is equal to long-run average total cost and is as low as possible. But the ability of an oligopolist to earn economic profit means that the firm's price can be greater than its cost. Thus, over the long run, restricted entry may result in economic profit for the firm and in higher prices for the buyer.

Restricted entry may also allow an oligopolist to operate inefficiently over the long run. The greater the difficulty potential rivals face entering a market, the less the competitive pressure on a firm, which can weaken its incentive to operate at lowest average total cost. Restrictions, or barriers to entry, are more fully explained in our discussion of monopolies.

MONOPOLY

Characteristics of Monopoly

Of the four market structures, none is further removed from pure competition than is monopoly. In a **monopoly** market there is

Monopoly
A market with one seller that maintains its position because entry of new sellers is impossible.

- only one seller—the monopolist;
- no need to consider the issue of product differentiation since there is just one seller; and
- no possibility of entry of new sellers.

There are a number of barriers to entry that can create a monopolized market. Significant economies of scale in the production of a good or service that cause long-run average total cost to fall as output expands can keep out competitors.[7] In this case, it may be cheaper and more efficient for one large firm to service the entire market by producing all the output at a lower average total cost than to have several firms each produce smaller amounts of output at a higher average total cost. This situation, called a **natural monopoly**, will be further discussed in Chapter 14.

If a monopoly is a public utility—the only firm providing natural gas, electricity, or some other essential service to a community—entry of a new seller may be blocked by its inability to receive permission to operate from a regulatory authority. For example, a start-up electric company cannot provide service in an area unless it obtains a license from the state commission that regulates utilities, and usually just one license is granted in an area.

The ownership of a patent on a product or a process may give a firm monopoly power in a market. In the United States, patents give the patent owner exclusive rights over it for 20 years. Anyone who uses the patented process or produces the patented product without the monopolist's permission can be sued. Patents have given many pharmaceutical companies exclusive rights to particular drugs until the patent expires.

A firm may be a monopolist because it is the sole owner of a factor necessary for production, such as the franchise for a professional sports team in a city. It may also have gained its monopoly position because it engaged in illegal practices involving prices and contracts that keep potential rivals out of the market.

Related to monopoly is an arrangement in which several sellers formally join together with the intention of acting as if they were a single-firm monopoly. The organization they form is called a **cartel**, and its purpose is to obtain more profit and other benefits for its members than they would receive if they competed with one another. A well-known example of a cartel is the Organization of Petroleum Exporting Countries (OPEC). Other organizations such as some professional sports associations carry out cartel-type activities.

Behavior of a Monopolist

Control over Price   Because it is the only seller in its market, there are two important points to consider about a monopolist's pricing. First, all other things being equal, a monopolist has more control over its price than does a firm in any other market structure. There are no direct competitors to take buyers away when a monopolist raises its price. Second, because the monopolist is the only seller in its market, its demand curve is the market demand curve: All buyers demanding the product demand it from the monopolist.

Demand for a Monopolist's Product   Since market demand curves are downward sloping and since the monopolist's demand is identical to the market demand, the monopolist's demand curve is the downward-sloping market demand curve.

Unlike the pure competitor, a price taker who must accept the price dictated by market supply and demand, the monopolist is a **price searcher** who will assess the costs and revenues from operating at different levels of output, or different points on the demand curve, and select the one price and output combination that maximizes profit. For example, the monopolist facing the demand curve in Figure 13.11 will assess revenues and costs at different levels of output and apply the profit-maximizing rules

Natural Monopoly
It is more efficient (less costly) to have the entire output of a product come from one large producer rather than from several smaller producers.

Cartel
An arrangement whereby sellers formally join together in a market to make decisions as a group on matters such as pricing.

Price Searcher
A firm that searches its downward-sloping demand curve to find the price–output combination that maximizes its profit.

[7]See Chapter 12 for a review of economies of scale.

FIGURE 13.11   *Demand Curve for the Output of a Monopolist*

A monopolist will search its downward-sloping demand curve and choose the one price and output combination that will maximize its profit. The monopolist's demand curve and the market demand curve are the same.

to find the one price–quantity combination that yields maximum profit. Depending on the behavior of costs, this combination could be shown by point A, B, C, or any other point on the demand curve in Figure 13.11. (The appendix to this chapter fully develops revenue and cost information to show how a monopolist locates the profit-maximizing point on its demand curve.)

One of the significant features about pricing in a monopoly market structure is that, since the monopolist's demand and the market demand are the same, the monopolist is establishing the price and output level for the whole market. In other words, one firm makes all the supply decisions. In addition, once the monopolist chooses a price, there are no competitors to force it down. The monopolist also has no immediate threat of entry by new firms.

Application 13.2, "Take Me Out to the Ball Game," gives the 2015 Major League Baseball Fan Cost Index for attending major league games in the league ballparks. The Fan Cost Index includes four average price tickets, some food and drinks, parking, programs, and caps. If the market is defined as live major league baseball and other forms of sports activities or entertainment are not regarded as substitutes, then buying tickets and spending time at a game could be regarded as participation in a monopoly market.

Nonprice Competition   Because monopolists face no direct competitors, they use nonprice competition differently from oligopolists or monopolistic competitors, who use it to attract buyers to a particular brand of a product. For example, in the hybrid market, nonprice competition encourages buyers toward a Ford Fusion, Toyota Prius, Honda Civic, or other hybrid. But with monopoly there are no competing brands; there is simply the product. As a result, a monopolist's messages may be designed to make people aware of the good or service itself, not the seller. For example, "A Diamond is Forever" is the advertising slogan used since 1947 by De Beers, the dominant force in the diamond industry for most of the twentieth century. Since De Beers supplied most of the world's diamonds, there was no need to advertise the company—just diamonds.

APPLICATION 13.2

TAKE ME OUT TO THE BALL GAME

Is buying major league baseball tickets and food and drink in the stadium a purchase in a monopoly market? Is there a lack of competition that accounts for the costs given in the table? Are there competitors to baseball, like alternative sports or entertainment?

Team Marketing Report's Major League Baseball Fan Cost Index

Team	2015 Fan Cost Index[a]
Boston Red Sox	$350.86
New York Yankees	337.20
Chicago Cubs	300.73
Philadelphia Phillies	252.18
San Francisco Giants	241.13
St. Louis Cardinals	236.81
Washington Nationals	232.08
Minnesota Twins	229.36
Miami Marlins	224.83
Houston Astros	220.28
New York Mets	219.68

Team	2015 Fan Cost Index[a]
Los Angeles Dodgers	$218.94
Detroit Tigers	213.03
Kansas City Royals	212.04
Seattle Mariners	212.00
Toronto Blue Jays	208.28
Chicago White Sox	208.18
Colorado Rockies	196.60
Oakland Athletics	195.00
Texas Rangers	190.54
Los Angeles Angels	190.16
Milwaukee Brewers	182.28
Pittsburgh Pirates	175.95
Atlanta Braves	174.06
Cincinnati Reds	166.62
Cleveland Indians	166.52
Baltimore Orioles	163.39
Tampa Bay Rays	157.60
San Diego Padres	153.45
Arizona Diamondbacks	126.89

[a]The Major League Baseball Fan Cost Index includes the price of four adult average-priced tickets (no premium or luxury included), two small beers, four small soft drinks, four hot dogs, parking for one car, and two caps.

Source: Team Marketing Report, "2015 mlb fan cost index," www. teammarketing.com.

Long-Run Costs, Profit, and Efficiency   The monopolist enjoys its position as sole seller in its market because of barriers to entry that keep potential rivals out. Those same barriers allow the monopolist to make an economic profit over the long run. With barriers to entry blocking new competitors, no seller can come into the market, force the monopoly firm to lower its price, and compete economic profit away. The monopolist can protect its economic profit as long as its monopoly position can be maintained. Also, with no competition, the monopolist can operate inefficiently or at higher than minimum average cost.

However, even with the monopolist's exclusive position in the market, some restraints may exist. Although it faces no direct competition in its own market, the monopolist must be concerned with competition from products in other closely related markets. While a natural gas utility may have no direct competition, it is aware of suppliers of other types of energy. For example, home builders and home owners have choices about energy sources and will think about installing electric, oil, or solar energy for heating if gas prices get too high.

The monopolist is also restrained in its profit-making ability when it is a public utility. With public utilities, state regulatory commissions or other public authorities oversee the prices they charge. For example, privately held water companies are subject to rates and standards set by a state commission. Typically, prices are set in such a way that the utility's ability to earn excess profit is limited.

APPLICATION 13.3

Patents Work–For a While

The names of large pharmaceutical companies in the United States, like Pfizer, Eli Lilly, and GlaxoSmithKline, are as familiar to us as are the names of many of the drugs that they produce. These companies are part of the substantial pharmaceutical industry that provides relief from headaches and pain, helps to reduce anxiety and depression, treats a variety of conditions like heart disease, and prolongs life for people who have serious illnesses.

The large pharmaceuticals (pharms) spend considerable sums of money on the research and development of drugs. In doing so, they typically apply for a patent on a proposed drug, usually when they begin its development. In the United States, a patent is granted for 20 years; however, by the time a drug is developed and tested and marketed, many of those patent years are used. So when a drug "hits" the market, it may provide the company monopoly protection over the drug for fewer than 20 years. For example, Pfizer's Lipitor hit the market in 1997 and its patent expired in 2011, giving Pfizer a 14-year window.

Patent protection sets up a monopoly over a particular drug for its company and becomes a barrier to entry of other sellers. Until it loses that protection and generics come onto the market, the company maintains complete control over the drug's price and availability. This monopoly protection comes with some controversy. Drug firms say that they need to price high enough to cover their costs, fund additional research and development of new products, and provide a profit to their stockholders. Those in opposition to this monopoly position believe that a high price keeps people who need the medication from having access to it. They cite examples of people who do not take needed medications or skimp on dosage because they cannot afford the drugs.

In 2011 and 2012, several well-known, highly prescribed drugs that were major sellers for their pharmaceutical companies went off patent coverage: cholesterol-busting Lipitor, the antipsychotic Zyprexa, asthma-fighting Advair, and the antibiotic Levaquin, to name a few. An upstate New York pharmacy officer for a major insurance company said, "My estimation is at least 15 percent of the population is currently using one of the drugs whose patents will expire in 2011 or 2012."

When generics enter the market, the monopoly position of a large pharm's drug is gone, and the price seriously declines. Generics are said to cost 20 to 80 percent less than name brands: There is no cost for development and marketing, and frequently the drug is produced in another country where the costs of production are lower. How do generics impact the pharmaceutical that loses its patent?

Take Lipitor, which has been the most prescribed name-brand drug in the United States and is said to have earned Pfizer $81 billion. It was anticipated that its generic, atorvastatin, when it became available in November 2011, would cause Pfizer to lose a substantial share of that market. However, rather than handing the market over to a generic, Pfizer went on a campaign to keep its users, including lowering the price of Lipitor to compete with the generic.

It is always interesting to watch the reaction by the big pharms to major drugs going generic. For those who study the market structures, it is watching the result of a transformation of a monopoly market to one of the other structures. Perhaps like Pfizer and Lipitor, it may not be a total exit from the market but entry into one with competition.

Sources: "Drug prices will fall sharply as patents expire," http://articles.boston.com/2011-07-25; Lisa Zamosky, "Lipitor patent ends; generic available: What now?" *Los Angeles Times*, http://articles.latimes.com/print/2012; "6 Drug Companies with Expiring Patents in 2011," www.investopedia.com, 3/19/2012.

Application 13.3, "Patents Work–For a While," discusses the coming changes in the monopoly markets for certain drugs as their patents expire. How do you think the large pharmaceutical companies plan for this sudden loss in a monopoly position?

MARKET STRUCTURES, THE CONSUMER, AND EFFICIENCY

Let's review what we have learned about competition and the behavior of a business in a market. We are particularly concerned with the effects on consumers of buying from sellers in each of the four market structures and the levels of efficiency achieved by firms in these structures.

Buyers fare best when facing purely competitive sellers because the market, not the individual seller, determines the price. In the long run, price is equal to average total cost, and average total cost is as low as possible. This means that over the long run, no economic profit goes to sellers (again, no more profit than is necessary for production to continue), consumers get the good or service at the lowest possible price, and these firms operate efficiently.

In monopolistic competition, price is again equal to average total cost in the long run. But because the demand curve for an individual seller's product is downward sloping, the long-run average total cost of the product is not at its lowest possible level. Thus, even though buyers pay no economic profit to the seller, they do not get the good or service at the minimum possible cost. Since firms do not operate at their lowest average total costs, they are less efficient than purely competitive firms. But, in this structure, consumers enjoy a differentiation in products among sellers.

In oligopoly and monopoly, the price of a product can remain above its average total cost over the long run; that is, in these market structures the prices buyers pay may regularly include an economic profit to the seller. These market structures may also lack the forces that cause firms to produce as efficiently as possible. Because of these and other manifestations of the market power of oligopolists and monopolists, the government has taken steps from time to time to modify their behaviors. Some of those measures are taken up in Chapter 14. Table 13.1 summarizes the characteristics and resulting behaviors of firms in each of the four market structures.

TABLE 13.1   *Characteristics and Behaviors of Firms in the Market Structures*

Consumers fare best in purely competitive markets: Sellers have no control over price, and over the long run, average total cost and price are as low as they can get, and sellers earn no economic profit.

Characteristics	Behavior
Pure Competition	
Very large number of sellers →	Price determined by market supply and demand
Identical products →	No nonprice competition
Easy entry and exit →	In the long run, price equals minimum ATC and firms operate efficiently with no economic profit
Monopolistic Competition	
Large number of sellers →	Firms have limited control over price
Differentiated products →	Firms engage in nonprice competition
Fairly easy entry and exit →	In the long run, price equals ATC, but not minimum ATC, and firms operate with no economic profit
Oligopoly	
Few sellers →	Firms have control over price
Mutual interdependence →	Firms assess rivals' reactions in setting strategies
Barriers to entry →	In the long run, firms can operate with economic profit and not at minimum ATC
Monopoly	
One seller →	Firm has most control over price
Impassable barriers to entry →	In the long run, seller can operate with economic profit and not at minimum ATC

Summary

1. A market is composed of firms selling similar products and competing for the same group of buyers. The boundaries of a market are determined by product substitutability and geographic considerations.

2. The degree of competition in a market influences a firm's pricing and nonprice policies as well as its ability to earn economic profit in the long run. To analyze competition and its effects, markets can be classified into four structures: pure competition, monopolistic competition, oligopoly, and monopoly.

3. Pure competition is characterized by a large number of independent firms selling identical products in a market that is easy to enter and exit. Individual purely competitive firms have no control over price, which is set by the forces of supply and demand in the market. An individual firm's demand curve is a straight, horizontal line at the market price. Nonprice competition doesn't occur in purely competitive markets since sellers' products are identical.

4. Due to easy entry and exit, in the long run a purely competitive seller's price is equal to minimum long-run average total cost. This results in efficient production, the lowest possible price that can be charged in the market, and no economic profit for the firm. For the buyer, pure competition is the ideal market structure. In the real world, there are few purely competitive markets.

5. Monopolistic competition is characterized by a large number of sellers with differentiated products in a market that is fairly easy to enter and exit. Because of product differentiation, each seller has a downward-sloping demand curve and exercises some control over its price. This control, however, is limited by the large number of sellers offering buyers similar products. Nonprice competition is important in these markets.

6. Since entry into and exit from the market are fairly easy, over the long run monopolistic competitors operate where price equals long-run average total cost, resulting in no economic profits. These firms do not produce at the lowest point on their long-run average total cost curves, so their prices and costs are higher and the firms are less efficient than pure competitors.

7. Oligopoly is characterized by a few sellers producing identical or differentiated products in a market that is difficult to enter. By virtue of their relatively large size in the market, oligopolists have some control over their prices. But large size also causes the competitive decisions of one firm to affect other firms in its market, giving rise to mutual interdependence among the sellers.

8. Since mutual interdependence can assume different forms, there are several explanations for oligopoly pricing. Two explanations are leadership pricing, which occurs when one firm changes its price and others follow, and the kinked demand curve model, which is based on the assumption that rivals follow a firm's price decreases but not price increases. With the entry of potential rivals into the market impeded, oligopolists may be able to charge prices greater than average total cost, earn economic profits over the long run, and not operate efficiently.

9. Monopoly is characterized by a single seller facing no direct competition in a market that is impossible to enter. A monopolist has more control over its price than a firm in any other market structure. As the only seller in its market, the market demand curve is the monopolist's demand curve, and the monopolist searches for the one price and output combination on the demand curve that maximizes its profit. With the entry of new rivals blocked, the monopolist can charge a price greater than its average total cost, earn economic profit over the long run, and not operate efficiently.

Key Terms and Concepts

Market structures	Nonprice competition
Industry	Efficient production
Market	Monopolistic competition
Geographic boundary of a market	Differentiated products
Product boundary of a market	Oligopoly
Purely competitive market	Mutual interdependence
Barriers to entry	Leadership pricing
Price taker	Kinked demand curve
Market demand curve	Monopoly
Individual firm's demand curve	Natural monopoly
Economic profit, loss, or breaking even	Cartel
	Price searcher

Review Questions

1. Into which of the four market structures would you place each of the following? Why would you make this classification?
   a. A small organic farm growing herbs, arugula, and tomatoes on 5 acres
   b. A large grain farm producing wheat on 2,500 acres
   c. A major airline
   d. A community college
   e. The water company for a region
   f. A small retail shoe store in a large mall
   g. A big box discount shoe store in a large city
   h. A college food service
   i. The only long-term parking facility at an airport
   j. Passenger travel on Amtrak
   k. The best bakery in town
   l. The local small town newspaper
   m. A coffee shop that sells a well-known global brand

2. How do firms in each of the four market structures differ in terms of their number of rivals, control over price, product differentiation, ability to earn economic profit over the long run, and efficiency?

3. What is the relationship between price and average total cost when a firm operates with an economic profit, takes a loss, or breaks even? Illustrate, in the accompanying graphs, the relationship between an individual firm's demand curve and average total cost curve in each of the following situations.
    a. A purely competitive firm in the long run
    b. A monopolist earning an economic profit
    c. A purely competitive firm operating with a loss
    d. A monopolistically competitive firm in the long run
    e. A monopolistically competitive firm operating with a loss
    f. An oligopolist pricing at the kink in its demand curve and earning an economic profit

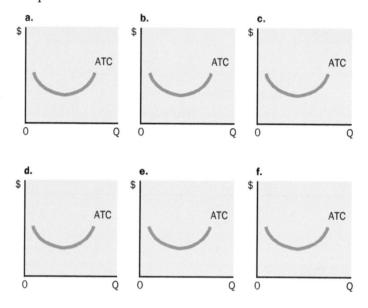

4. Explain the process that drives purely competitive firms to operate efficiently, receive a price equal to lowest average cost, and earn no economic profit in the long run.

5. Why does a firm in pure competition operate efficiently in the long run, while firms in the other three market structures do not? Why is it important to consumers that a firm operate efficiently?

6. Monopolistically competitive sellers face downward-sloping demand curves, and pure competitors face perfectly horizontal demand curves. What is the difference in the competitive environments of these two market structures that causes this difference in the behavior of the individual firm's demand curve?

7. Identify some important barriers to entry that keep firms out of a market.

8. Firms in monopoly and oligopoly markets are protected in varying degrees by barriers to entry and can earn excess profits in the long run. How do these barriers relate to a firm's ability to earn excess profits in the long run?

9. Explain what is meant by mutual interdependence and how it relates to the price leadership and the kinked demand curve models.

10. Explain why a monopolist is labeled as a price searcher and not a price taker.

Discussion Questions

1. Pure competition is said to be the most competitive of all the market structures. If this is true, why is it that no one firm is concerned with what any other firm does in a purely competitive market?

2. Your friend thinks the market for automobiles should be changed from oligopolistic to monopolistically competitive by breaking the existing firms into smaller firms. Do you agree or disagree with your friend's idea?

3. A market is defined according to the geographic area in which sellers compete for buyers and the extent to which buyers view sellers' products as substitutes. What, in your opinion, would be the substitutes and relevant geographic market for each of the following? Be able to defend your answers.
   a. Beer from a small microbrewery in central Pennsylvania
   b. A four-door Swedish automobile for sale at a U.S. dealership
   c. A ski resort in the Rocky Mountains
   d. A major state university
   e. Frozen pizza

4. In the United States, people keep increasing their purchases over the Internet. Does this growth in Internet shopping increase competition for retail stores, or are these different markets? Explain your reasoning.

5. Why might a seller in an oligopoly market where mutual interdependence and rivals' responses are important choose to increase its sales through an advertising campaign rather than by lowering the price of its product?

6. Certain vehicles are basically the same but are marketed under different brand names. The cars, sometimes built on the same assembly lines, may have different standard equipment, styling, accessories, and prices. The Ford Expedition and the Lincoln Navigator, for example, are largely the same. It is understandable why one automobile company would want recognizable differences between its cars and those of a rival, but what does the company gain by creating differences among its own products? What costs and benefits do automobile buyers experience from this differentiation strategy?

7. Why are economists so concerned with efficiency? Would the world be a better place to live if all goods and services were produced efficiently and sold in purely competitive markets?

8. In economics courses, students learn that there is value in competition in markets and that competition should be encouraged. In some business courses, students learn strategies for reducing competition. What accounts for the difference in the view of competition in these two areas of study?

Critical Thinking Case 13

THE $800 HAIRCUT

Critical Thinking Skills

Using criteria for grouping

Analyzing the unobvious

Economic Concepts

Market definitions

Market structures

$800 for a haircut? No way!

Well, not so fast. There are stories out there about people paying that much for a haircut. Just go to the Internet and type in $800 haircut, and you might be surprised at the number of hits you get.

It seems unlikely that the average person would pay such an outrageous price for a haircut. Most of us would like to eat a few meals a day, pay the cell phone bill, and put gas in our cars to get to work and the fitness center. But what will people pay for a haircut?

Some folks are willing to "do" the local cheapcuts hair salon. The $10 special on Thursday is okay and serves the purpose. Others search out the best in the area—which might mean a cool $200 rather than $10. In some places, the cheap joints are on almost every corner; in some places, there are independent hairdressers in malls, storefronts, home basements, and garages; and in some places, there are integrated hair salons and spas.

All of this brings us to market structures and pricing. At first glance, we might think that haircutting is a good example of a monopolistically competitive market. But spending $800, or even $200, for a haircut when you could spend $10 doesn't seem to conform to what people typically think of when describing monopolistic competition.

So what's the story? Are some of these haircutters monopolists? Have they risen so far above the competition and established such a name for themselves that no one can compete with them? If this is the case, can this happen with chefs? With surgeons? With college professors? With any career or profession?

Questions

1. In what market structure do haircuts generally belong? Does this differ by location?

2. Can a service seemingly in a monopolistically competitive market become so unique that it leaves that market? Could some sellers become oligopolists or monopolists? How do you explain this phenomenon?

3. What other markets can you identify that have behaviors similar to the haircut market described in this case?

4. Do you think a heart surgeon could ever be a monopolist? Why?

CHAPTER 14

Government and the Markets

CHAPTER OBJECTIVES

Identify the major federal antitrust statutes and the anticompetitive practices they address.

Identify the forms and organization of government regulation and distinguish between industry regulation and social regulation.

In the last chapter, we saw that a seller's price, output, promotional strategy, profit, and efficiency are all influenced by the type of market it is in and degree of competition it faces. Obviously, markets and competition play an important role in economic decision making and in determining the well-being of businesses and households.

Economies where decisions are made primarily by individual businesses and households are built on the philosophy that free markets and competition should be at the foundation of economic activity. Although the U.S. economy is based on this philosophy, historically government has intervened in the operation of markets in several important ways. In this chapter, we discuss government intervention and focus on the two essential ways government influences competition and market forces in the United States: antitrust enforcement and regulation.

We typically find a wide range of views on the appropriateness of government intervention. Some people feel that current intervention is too extensive; others feel that it is inadequate. Some people hold that government intervention is not achieving its intended results or that it creates an unjustified administrative or financial burden on businesses; others are satisfied with its effects and comfortable with the requirements it imposes.

Why would people who basically favor free markets seek government intervention in the operation of those markets? It might be sought where the number of firms in a market is so small that strong competition is unlikely to occur or where one firm is so large that it significantly weakens competitive forces. Government intervention might also be sought in the public interest: The public might be better served by a single large, efficient seller that answers to a public authority than by several less efficient, smaller sellers competing with one another. This is often the case with the distribution of gas, electric, and water services.

Another reason for seeking government intervention is security. As the economist John Maurice Clark wrote:

> [C]ompetition has two opposites: which we may call monopoly and security. . . . Nearly everyone favors competition as against monopoly, and nearly everyone wants it limited in the interest of security. And hardly anyone pays much attention to the question where one leaves off and the other begins.[1]

Finally, government may be called in to intervene when consumers or workers can be hurt by dangerous products or working conditions. Protection may be sought when people believe that the market does not provide it.

Competition introduces some risks for businesses, and the desire to reduce these risks may inspire support for some government intervention. For example, antitrust laws specifying the ground rules about allowable competitive practices may reduce the risk of failure for smaller sellers in a market. Laws that regulate monopolies, such as gas or electric suppliers, increase security for consumers by ensuring that these firms continue to supply the market at prices that are regulated.

ANTITRUST ENFORCEMENT

Antitrust Laws
Laws prohibiting certain practices that reduce competition.

Antitrust enforcement centers on a series of laws designed to promote the operation of market forces by limiting certain practices that reduce competition. Specifically, **antitrust laws** are aimed at two broad categories of practices.

Monopolization and Attempts to Monopolize
A firm acquires or attempts to acquire a monopoly share of its market through unreasonable means.

The first is **monopolization and attempts to monopolize**, which occur when a firm, through unreasonable means, acquires or attempts to acquire such a large share of its market that it does not feel strong competitive pressure from its rivals. The effect that a firm with a great deal of market power can have on competition has been compared by the economist Walter Adams to a poker game where one player brings much more money to the table than the others.

> [I]n a poker game with unlimited stakes, the player who commands disproportionately large funds is likely to emerge victorious. If I have $100 while my opponents have no more than $5 each, I am likely to win regardless of my ability, my virtue, or my luck.[2]

Combinations and Conspiracies in Restraint of Trade
Practices carried out jointly by two or more firms that unreasonably restrict competition.

The second category of practices at which antitrust laws are aimed is **combinations and conspiracies in restraint of trade**. This includes acts carried out jointly by two or more firms that unreasonably limit competition, such as price fixing and the division of sales territories. Monopolization and attempts to monopolize, and combinations and conspiracies in restraint of trade, are explained more fully as we review the major antitrust statutes.

Antitrust enforcement is carried out by both the federal and state governments, with the main responsibility falling on the Department of Justice and the Federal Trade Commission (FTC) at the federal level. In addition to federal and state enforcement, private parties such as businesses can bring charges that other companies and/or individuals have violated the laws.

---

[1] John Maurice Clark, *Alternative to Serfdom* (New York: Alfred A. Knopf, 1948), p. 61.
[2] Quoted in Estes Kefauver, *In a Few Hands* (New York: Pantheon Books, 1965), p. 196.

Administration of the antitrust laws depends heavily on the courts and is carried out on a case-by-case basis, where each violation is treated separately. In some instances a suit may be dropped because it is judged to have insufficient merit to go to trial, or a pretrial settlement may be reached where the accused firm promises to discontinue a practice or arrives at some other agreement with the opposing side. In other instances, a trial may be required before the issue is resolved. Antitrust disputes can become long, costly, and complicated.

The Antitrust Laws

At the federal level, there are five main antitrust laws: the Sherman Act (1890), the Federal Trade Commission Act (1914), the Clayton Act (1914), the Robinson–Patman Act (1936), and the Celler–Kefauver Act (1950). The Robinson–Patman and Celler–Kefauver acts both amend the Clayton Act.

The Sherman Act (1890)   The original and most broadly worded federal antitrust statute is the **Sherman Act**. When people speak of this act, they tend to refer to it by sections:

- Section 1 condemns combinations and conspiracies in restraint of trade, and
- Section 2 attacks monopolization and attempts to monopolize.

Combinations and conspiracies condemned by Section 1 of the Sherman Act are either per se or rule of reason violations. **Per se violations** are agreements between firms where proof of the agreement is sufficient to establish guilt: There is no defense for a per se violation. Price fixing, division of sales territories among competitors, tying arrangements, and exclusive dealing arrangements are included in this category.[3]

Price fixing occurs when sellers take joint action to influence prices. An agreement between competing sellers about the prices they will charge their buyers or the price below which they will not sell would be price fixing, as would be an agreement on a system for determining who will submit the lowest offer when pricing is done with sealed bids. With price fixing, competition is diminished and sellers act more like monopolists.

Territorial division occurs when competing firms divide a sales area among themselves. For example, two firms competing in a national market might agree that one takes the territory east, and the other takes the territory west, of the Mississippi River. As with price fixing, territorial division diminishes competition.

A **tying arrangement** occurs when a firm will sell its product to a buyer only if the buyer agrees to also purchase different products from the seller. For example, Firm A will sell its piece of advanced computer hardware to Firm B only as long as Firm B also buys other types of hardware from Firm A. This can hurt competition between Firm A and the other firms that produce and sell the other types of hardware.[4]

Sherman Act
Original and most broadly worded federal antitrust statute; condemns combinations and conspiracies in restraint of trade, and monopolization and attempts to monopolize.

Per Se Violations
Anticompetitive agreements between firms where proof of the agreement is sufficient to establish guilt; includes price fixing and division of sales territories.

Price Fixing
Joint action by sellers to influence their product prices; considered anticompetitive.

Territorial Division
Joint action by sellers to divide sales territories among themselves; considered anticompetitive.

Tying Arrangement
A buyer can obtain a good from a seller only by purchasing another good from the same seller.

---

[3] One explanation for the per se rule is that the court's time is a scarce resource, and the likelihood of society benefiting from acts such as price fixing or territorial division is so remote that it would be a waste of time to require a court to listen to a defense for these acts.

[4] Until fairly recently, all price fixing agreements and tying arrangements were classified as per se violations of the Sherman Act. But recent Supreme Court decisions such as *Leegan Creative Leather Products, Inc. v. PSKS, Inc.* (2006) and *Illinois Tool Works, Inc. et al. v. Independent Ink, Inc.* (2005) in Application 14.1 have opened the door for price fixing and tying arrangements to be seen as being either per se or rule of reason violations, depending on the facts and matters under consideration.

Exclusive Dealing Arrangement
A firm will sell its product to another firm if the buying firm gets this product only from the selling firm.

An **exclusive dealing arrangement** occurs when a firm will sell its product to another firm only if the buying firm agrees to not get a comparable product from another supplier. For example, suppose that Firm C makes a widely recognized piece of high-quality electronic equipment that goes into large-scale communications systems. Suppose also that there are several other firms that make similar equipment and compete with Firm C. To get an advantage over its competitors, Firm C will sell its equipment to businesses producing these communications systems only if the businesses agree to not purchase similar equipment from any of Firm C's competitors. This can hurt competition between Firm C and its competitors.

Both tying and exclusive dealing arrangements can be tried under the Sherman Act and the Clayton Act.

Rule of Reason Violations
Actions that may or may not be unreasonable restraints of trade.

Rule of reason violations occur when firms come together in a way that may or may not unreasonably restrain trade. With the rule of reason, there is no blanket condemnation of business practices like there is with price fixing and territorial division. Rather, each challenged practice must be examined to see whether *in this particular case* the restraint is unreasonable.

Trade Association
An organization representing firms in a particular industry that performs functions to benefit those firms.

Activities of industry trade associations and joint ventures fall under the rule of reason umbrella. A **trade association** is an organization of firms in a particular industry, such as construction or furniture manufacturing, that performs certain functions to benefit its members. If a trade association collects data on overall industry trends and general information on supply conditions or buyer behavior and reports it to all its members, the trade association may enhance competition by improving the general state of knowledge in the industry. But if the information gives specific details on the terms of each firm's sales and the names of its buyers, or if the information is not equally available to all interested parties, the trade association's information gathering might help to foster a price-fixing agreement or division of buyers among sellers and would therefore be subject to condemnation under Section 1 of the Sherman Act.

Joint Venture
A cooperative effort by two or more firms that is limited in scope.

A **joint venture** is a cooperative effort by two or more firms that is limited in scope. The operation of an automobile plant by a U.S. and a Japanese manufacturer or the drilling for oil in a remote part of the world by several firms acting together would be examples of joint ventures. As with trade association activities, the legality of joint ventures must be judged on a case-by-case basis to determine whether competition has been unreasonably restricted. For example, in one case, a joint venture might allow two firms to have the resources needed to succeed in a new market that neither of them alone would have been able to enter and survive, and in another case, a joint venture would give the two firms sufficient resources and power to drive smaller competitors out of the market.

Cases involving Sherman Act Section 2 violations of monopolization and attempts to monopolize rest largely on two issues:

♦ the specific actions taken by a firm that demonstrate its intent to monopolize its market, and
♦ the firm's share of its market.

Where the firm's market share is small and it is clearly not a monopolist, an attempt to monopolize may be inferred from such actions as pricing below cost to drive rivals out of the market or contracting with critical suppliers or distributors to foreclose their services to the firm's rivals.

For firms with larger market shares, monopolization may be inferred less from what the firm does and more from its relative size in comparison to its rivals. For example, in *United States v. Aluminum Company of America,* a leading monopolization case, the court enunciated a rough guide for analyzing Sherman Act monopolization questions known as the "30-60-90 rule": "[A greater than ninety per cent share of the market] is enough to constitute a monopoly; it is doubtful whether sixty or sixty-four per cent would be enough; and certainly thirty-three per cent is not."[5]

An extremely important aspect of monopolization cases is the definition of the relevant market, which was discussed in Chapter 13. Ordinarily, the broader a market is defined in terms of its geographic boundaries and/or number of substitute products, the smaller will be the share of that market taken by any one firm. The narrower a market is defined, the larger will be the share taken by the firm. Thus, it may be to the advantage of a firm accused of monopolizing a market to define that market as broadly as possible.

Application 14.1, "Cases Involving the Sherman Act," gives excerpts from the court records of some important and influential antitrust cases dealing with price fixing, tying arrangements, and exclusive dealing arrangements that were brought under the Sherman Act. The decision of the court in each case is also provided. Can you explain how competition would have been injured in each case?

We might warn you before reading Applications 14.1 and 14.2, both of which deal with court rulings, that you will be getting a first-hand opportunity to see the complexity in the writing of court documents. They are not always easy to read.

The Federal Trade Commission Act (1914)   The Federal Trade Commission (FTC) was created by the **Federal Trade Commission Act** and granted power to "prevent persons, partnerships, or corporations, . . . from using unfair methods of competition in commerce."[6] Included among unfair methods of competition are antitrust violations.

When the FTC thinks that a business is engaged in unfair competition, it can issue a complaint and arrange a hearing to determine whether the practice should be prohibited. If it is found that the practice is unfair competition, the FTC can issue a "cease and desist order" requiring the firm to stop the activity. If the firm fails to follow the order, or if it thinks the order is incorrect, either the FTC or the firm can have the order brought before a court for a ruling.[7]

The Clayton Act (1914)   Unlike the Sherman Act and the Federal Trade Commission Act, which are not specific as to the practices they condemn, the **Clayton Act** is directed toward several particular activities that "substantially lessen competition or tend to create a monopoly."[8] These include tying and exclusive dealing arrangements, also subject to the Sherman Act, interlocking directorates, price discrimination, and mergers and acquisitions.

Interlocking directorates occur where the same person sits on the boards of directors of different corporations: For example, the same person is on the boards of a health care group and a banking corporation. Interlocking directorates are not necessarily anticompetitive, but injury to competition could occur if, for example, a person sitting on the boards of two firms competing in the same market enables them to

Federal Trade Commission Act
Created the Federal Trade Commission and empowered it to prevent unfair methods of competition, which include antitrust violations.

Clayton Act
Federal antitrust statute prohibiting specific activities that substantially reduce competition or tend to create a monopoly.

Interlocking Directorates
The same person sits on the boards of directors of different corporations.

---

[5] *United States v. Aluminum Company of America,* 148 F. 2d 416 (1945), p. 424.
[6] *United States Statutes at Large,* vol. 38, part 1 (Washington, DC: U.S. Government Printing Office, 1915), p. 719.
[7] Ibid., pp. 719, 720.
[8] Ibid., p. 730.

APPLICATION 14.1

CASES INVOLVING THE SHERMAN ACT

Price Fixing: *F. Hoffmann-La Roche Ltd et al. v. Empagran S. A. et al.* **(2004)**   The Foreign Trade Antitrust Improvements Act of 1982 (FTAIA) . . . provides that the Sherman Act "shall not apply to conduct involving trade or commerce . . . with foreign nations," . . . but creates exceptions for conduct that significantly harms imports, domestic commerce, or American exporters. In this case, vitamin purchasers filed a class action [suit] alleging that vitamin manufacturers and distributors had engaged in a price fixing conspiracy, raising vitamin prices in the United States and foreign countries, in violation of the Sherman Act. As relevant here, defendants moved to dismiss the suit as to the . . . foreign companies located abroad, who had purchased vitamins only outside United States commerce. . . .

Ruling Where the price-fixing conduct significantly and adversely affects both customers outside and within the United States, but the adverse foreign effect is independent of any adverse domestic effect, the FTAIA exception does not apply, and thus, neither does the Sherman Act, to a claim based solely on the foreign effect.

Vertical Price Fixing: *Leegin Creative Leather Products, Inc. v. PSKS, Inc., DBA Kay's Kloset . . . Kay's Shoes* **(2006)**   Given its policy of refusing to sell to retailers that discount its goods below suggested prices, [Leegin, Inc.] stopped selling to [PSKS's] store. PSKS filed suit, alleging . . . that Leegin violated the antitrust laws by entering into vertical agreements with its retailers to set minimum resale prices. The District Court [where the case was first heard] excluded expert testimony about Leegin's pricing policy's precompetitive effects on the grounds that [the landmark 1911 Case] *Dr. Miles Medical Co. v. John D. Parks & Sons, Co.*, 220 U.S. 373, makes it per se illegal under of the Sherman Act for a manufacturer and its distributor to agree on the minimum price the distributor can charge for the manufacturer's goods. At trial, PSKS alleged that Leegin and its retailers had agreed to fix prices, but Leegin argued that its pricing policy was lawful under §1.

Ruling [The Supreme Court held that] *Dr. Miles* is overruled, and vertical price restraints are to be judged by the rule of reason.

Tying Arrangements: *Illinois Tool Works, Inc. et al. v. Independent Ink, Inc.* **(2005)**   [Illinois Tool Works and other adjoined companies] . . . manufacture and market printing systems that include a patented printhead and ink container and unpatented ink, which they sell to original equipment manufacturers who agree that they will purchase ink exclusively from [Illinois Tool and the other companies] and that neither they nor their customers will refill the patented containers with ink of any kind. [Independent Ink, Inc.] developed ink with the same chemical composition as [Illinois Tool and the other companies'] ink. After . . . Trident's [one of the companies with Illinois Tool, patent] infringement action [against Independent Ink] was dismissed, [Independent Ink] filed suit seeking a judgment of noninfringement and invalidity of Trident's patents on the grounds that [Trident, Illinois Tool Works and the other companies] are engaged in illegal "tying" and monopolization in violation of § 1 and § 2 of the Sherman Act.

Ruling Because a patent does not necessarily confer market power upon the patentee, in all cases involving a tying arrangement, the plaintiff must prove that the defendant has market power in the tying product [in this case the printhead and ink container].

Exclusive Dealing Arrangements: *American Needle, Inc. v. National Football League et al.* **(2010)**   Respondent National Football League (NFL) is an unincorporated association of 32 separately owned professional football teams, also [defendants] here. The teams, each of which owns its own name, colors, logo, trademarks, and related intellectual property, formed [defendant] National Football League Properties (NFLP) to develop, license, and market that property. At first, NFLP granted nonexclusive licenses to [American Needle] and other vendors to manufacture and sell team-labeled apparel. In December 2000, however, the teams authorized NFLP to grant exclusive licenses. NFLP granted an exclusive license to respondent Reebok International Ltd. to produce and sell trademarked headware for all 32 teams. When [American Needle's] license was not renewed, it filed this action alleging that the agreements between respondents violated the Sherman Act, §1 of which makes "[e]very contract, combination . . . or, conspiracy, in restraint of trade" illegal. Respondents answered that they were incapable of conspiring within §1's meaning because the NFL and its teams are, in antitrust law jargon, a single entity with respect to the conduct challenged.

Ruling The alleged conduct related to licensing of intellectual property constitutes concerted action that is not categorically beyond §1's coverage.

Sources: *F. Hoffmann-La Roche Ltd et al. v. Empagran S.A. et al.* 542 U.S. 155 (2004), p. 155; *Leegin Creative Leather Products, Inc. v. PSKS, Inc., DBA Kay's Kloset . . . Kay's Shoes*, 551 U.S. 877 (2006), p. 877; *Illinois Tool Works, Inc. et al. v. Independent Ink, Inc.*, 547 U.S. 28 (2005), p. 28; *American Needle, Inc. v. National Football League et al.*, 130 S. Ct. (2010), p. 2201; supremecourt. gov/opinions/09pdf/08-661.pdf.

communicate about prices, or a person on the boards of corporations in a buyer–seller relationship gives the seller an unfair advantage over its rivals with regard to major purchases by the buyer.

In each of the activities addressed by the Clayton Act, as well as those included under its amendments, the practices themselves do not automatically constitute violations of the antitrust laws. They become violations only when the activities tend to significantly reduce competition or create a monopoly.

Robinson–Patman Act

Federal antitrust statute concerned with anticompetitive price discrimination; amends Section 2 of the Clayton Act.

Price Discrimination

Different buyers acquire the same product from the same seller with the same treatment and service but pay different prices.

The Robinson–Patman Act (1936)

Section 2 of the Clayton Act condemns price discrimination when it weakens competition or leads to a monopoly. The **Robinson–Patman Act** elaborates further on that condemnation. **Price discrimination** occurs when a seller charges different buyers different prices for the same product. If a firm sells an item at a particular price to one buyer and sells exactly the same item with exactly the same treatment and service to another buyer at a lower price, price discrimination has occurred.

Price discrimination can injure competition between a seller and its rivals. Through price discrimination, a seller can lower its price to buyers where there is intense competition from a rival, while keeping the price unchanged, or even raising it, for customers where it is not facing competition. If the rival is unable to meet these price cuts, it may lose sales and perhaps be driven from the market.

A buyer's market position, particularly at the wholesale level, can be injured when it pays a higher price than its rivals. The difference in price paid by the discriminated-against firm raises its costs, causing it, in turn, to charge a higher price or absorb the higher costs through forgone profit, either of which damages its competitive position.

The Robinson–Patman Act attacks outright price discrimination as well as several types of "indirect" price discrimination, such as granting quantity discounts on terms that only a few large buyers can meet, paying purchasers for services that have not been rendered, and treating buyers unequally in providing sales facilities.[9]

Celler–Kefauver Act

Federal antitrust statute concerned with anticompetitive mergers and acquisitions of firms; amends Section 7 of the Clayton Act.

Horizontal Merger

A merger between two sellers competing in the same market.

The Celler–Kefauver Act (1950)

Section 7 of the Clayton Act deals with anticompetitive mergers and acquisitions, and is amended by the **Celler–Kefauver Act**. A business can be acquired or merged with another in two ways: by the purchase of a controlling number of shares of stock or by the outright purchase of assets. The Clayton Act condemned anticompetitive acquisitions through stock purchases but said nothing about the purchase of assets. This loophole was closed by the Celler–Kefauver Act.[10]

As we learned in Chapter 10, there are three main types of mergers: horizontal, vertical, and conglomerate. Each type of merger can have potentially anticompetitive effects. A **horizontal merger** occurs where two sellers competing in the same market join together. When two extremely small sellers in a market merge, the consequence may not be noticeable: A small dairy farmer buying a second farm will have no effect on the dairy market. But where the acquiring and/or acquired firm has a substantial market share, their joining may have an anticompetitive effect by creating a larger organization with an even greater share of the market.

---

[9] *United States Statutes at Large*, vol. 49, part 1 (Washington, DC: U.S. Government Printing Office, 1936), pp. 1526–1527.
[10] *United States Statutes at Large*, vol. 38, part 1 (1915), pp. 731–732; *United States Statutes at Large*, vol. 64, part 1 (1952), pp. 1125–1126.

Vertical Merger

A merger between a firm and a supplier or distributor.

Conglomerate Merger

A merger between a firm and another firm that is not a competitor, supplier, or distributor.

A **vertical merger** involves the joining of a firm with a supplier or a distributor; it may be anticompetitive if it forecloses the firm's rivals from key suppliers or distributors. If a major developer/builder were to acquire both of the existing lumber yards in an area, the local supply of building materials could be foreclosed to rival developers and cause them additional expenses or perhaps even force them out of business. If competition is injured, a vertical merger can also cause antitrust concerns.

A **conglomerate merger** occurs when one firm joins with another that is not a competitor, supplier, or distributor. The joining of a steel wire manufacturer and a large beverage company would be a conglomerate merger, as would be the combining of a publishing company and a chain of retail clothing outlets.

Conglomerate mergers can have anticompetitive effects because of what is known as the "deep pocket." For example, a large, profitable hotel chain might acquire one of several small competing candy companies. As a result of the acquisition, the candy company could receive financial help from the hotel chain's deep pocket full of money for spending on such things as advertising, expansion of facilities, and a larger sales staff. With the help of this money, the candy company could increase its sales and share of the market at the expense of its rivals who do not have comparable financial resources with which to compete.

In the spring of 2002, Sears purchased Lands' End, the mail-order retailer, giving Sears the right to sell Lands' End clothing in its stores. Lands' End had been one of the largest catalog retailers in the country, along with J.C. Penney and L.L. Bean. In your opinion, was this merger horizontal, vertical, or conglomerate?

Application 14.2, "Cases Involving the Clayton Act and Its Amendments," presents facts and rulings from classic, landmark court cases on tying arrangements, price discrimination, and mergers. Can you explain how competition would have been injured in each of these cases?

Antitrust Penalties   Violations of the antitrust laws can result in one or more of four types of penalties, depending on the offense and who is bringing the suit. The penalties include imprisonment for up to 10 years, fines as large as $1 million per offense for individuals and $100 million per offense for corporations, structural remedies, and triple damages.

Structural remedies involve preventing two or more firms from merging, or breaking an offending firm into two or more unrelated units. Preventing firms from merging is appropriate where a proposed merger would significantly reduce competition in violation of the antitrust laws. In this situation, competition can be promoted by disallowing the merger and requiring the companies to remain separate. Breaking up an offending firm might be used where a single firm has been found guilty of monopolizing a market. Here the monopoly could be ended by separating one or more of the company's divisions into independent units. At one point in the highly publicized government antitrust suit against Microsoft in 1999, breaking the company into two separate entities was given serious consideration.

With triple damages, an injured party can, under certain conditions, collect three times its damages from the offending firm. Suppose it was proven in a court suit that over the last three years Company B lost $90 million in profit because of an antitrust violation committed by Company A. On the basis of this, the court could require Company A to pay Company B three times $90 million, or $270 million, in damages.

APPLICATION 14.2

CASES INVOLVING THE CLAYTON ACT AND ITS AMENDMENTS

Tying Arrangements: *International Business Machines Corp. v. United States* (1936) This is an appeal . . . of a decree of a District Court [enjoining IBM] from leasing its tabulating and other machines upon the condition that the lessees shall use with such machines only tabulating cards manufactured by [IBM], as a violation of §3 of the Clayton Act. . . .

[IBM's] machines and those of Remington Rand, Inc., are now the only ones on the market which perform certain mechanical tabulations and computations . . . by the use in them of cards upon which are recorded data. . . .

To insure satisfactory performance by [IBM's] machines it is necessary that the cards used in them conform to precise specifications as to size and thickness, and that they be free from defects . . . which cause unintended electrical contacts and consequent inaccurate results. The cards manufactured by [IBM] are electrically tested for such defects.

[IBM] leases its machines for a specified rental and period, upon condition that the lease shall terminate in case any cards not manufactured by [IBM] are used in the leased machine. . . .

[IBM's] contentions are that its leases are lawful [partly because their] purpose and effect are only to preserve to [IBM] the good will of its patrons by preventing the use of unsuitable cards which would interfere with the successful performance of its machines. . . .

[It appears] that others are capable of manufacturing cards suitable for use in [IBM's] machines. . . .

Ruling [IBM] is not prevented from proclaiming the virtues of its own cards or warning against the danger of using, in its machines, cards which do not conform to the necessary specifications, or even from making its leases conditional upon the use of cards which conform to them. [S]uch measures would protect its good will, without the creation of monopoly or resort to the suppression of competition. [Case decided against IBM.]

Price Discrimination: *Volvo Trucks North America, Inc. v. Reeder-Simco GMC, Inc.* (2006) Reeder-Simco GMC, Inc. (Reeder), an authorized dealer of heavy-duty trucks manufactured by Volvo Trucks North America, Inc. (Volvo), generally sold those trucks through an industry-wide competitive bidding process, whereby the retail customer describes its specific product requirements and invites bids from dealers it selects based on such factors as an existing relationship, geography, and reputation. Once a Volvo dealer receives the customer's specifications, it requests from Volvo a discount or "concession" off the wholesale price. Volvo decides on a case-by-case basis whether to offer a concession. The dealer then uses its Volvo discount in preparing its bid; it purchases trucks from Volvo only if and when the retail customer accepts its bid. Reeder was one of many regional Volvo dealers. . . . In the atypical case in which a retail customer solicited a bid from more than one Volvo dealer, Volvo's stated policy was to provide the same price concession to each dealer. In 1997 . . . Reeder learned that Volvo had given another dealer a price concession greater than the discounts Reeder typically received.

Reeder, suspecting it was . . . [a dealer] Volvo sought to eliminate, filed this suit under . . . § 2 of the Clayton Act, as amended by the Robinson–Patman Act . . . alleging that its sales and profits declined because Volvo offered other dealers more favorable price concessions.

Ruling A manufacturer may not be held liable for . . . price discrimination under the Robinson–Patman Act in the absence of a showing that the manufacturer discriminated between dealers competing to resell its product to the same retail customer. The act does not reach the case Reeder presents. It centrally addresses price discrimination in cases involving competition between different purchasers for resale of the purchased product. Competition of that character ordinarily is not involved when a product subject to special order is sold through a customer-specified competitive bidding process.

Horizontal Mergers: *United States v. Philadelphia National Bank et al.* (1963) [The Philadelphia National Bank and Girard Trust Corn Exchange Bank] are the second and third largest of the 42 commercial banks in the metropolitan area consisting of Philadelphia and its three contiguous counties, and they have branches throughout that area. [The banks'] boards of directors approved an agreement for their consolidation. . . . After obtaining reports, as required by the Bank Merger Act of 1960, from the Board of Governors of the Federal Reserve System, the Federal Deposit Insurance Corporation and the Attorney General, all of whom advised that the proposed merger would substantially lessen competition in the area, the Comptroller of the Currency approved it. The United States sued to enjoin consummation of the proposed consolidation, on the ground . . . that it would violate §7 of the Clayton Act.

Ruling . . . The proposed consolidation . . . would violate §7 of the Clayton Act. . . . The consolidated bank would control such an undue percentage share of the relevant market . . . and the consolidation would result in such a significant increase in the concentration of commercial banking facilities in the area . . . that the result would be inherently likely to lessen competition substantially. . . .

Sources: *International Business Machines Corp. v. United States*, 298 U.S. 131 (1936), pp. 132–134, 139, 140; *Volvo Trucks North America, Inc. v. Reeder-Simco GMC, Inc.*, 546 U.S. 164 (2006), pp. 164, 165; *United States v. Philadelphia National Bank et al.*, 374 U.S. 321 (1963), pp. 321, 322.

Application 14.3, "Antitrust Enforcement Up Close and Personal," looks at how the possibility of being named a defendant in an antitrust suit can have a significant impact on a person's life.

GOVERNMENT REGULATION

Government Regulation
Government participation, through agencies and commissions, in business decision making; may be industry regulation or social regulation.

In our daily lives, we are much more likely to be affected by government regulation, another way in which government plays a role in the market process, than by the antitrust laws. **Government regulation** refers to participation by the federal and state governments, through agencies and commissions, in business decision making. Actions of the Securities and Exchange Commission (SEC), Federal Communications Commission (FCC), Food and Drug Administration (FDA), and state utility commissions are just a few examples of government regulation.

In some cases, government regulation involves direct participation in specific aspects of a company's operations: The company's product price, the markets it serves, and other decisions must be approved by a regulatory commission before they can be implemented. In other cases, government regulation involves indirect participation in business operations through setting standards for firms to follow. These standards could apply to safety, health, the environment, and other areas. The FDA for example, sets purity and safety standards for food and drugs, and the Environmental Protection Agency (EPA) sets pollution standards.

While the antitrust laws are directed at the relationships between businesses and the degree of competition in specific markets, regulation is concerned with the interests of particular groups in the economy. For example, some regulation is aimed at protecting the consumer, some at labor, and some at the general public.

Government regulation can be divided into two basic types: industry regulation and social regulation. The first type involves regulation of businesses in a particular industry. In the United States, the railroad, electric power, gas distribution, and other industries have been subject to this type of regulation. Generally, industry regulation is direct: Government plays an important role in determining price, profit, and other aspects of the firms' operations.

With social regulation, a regulatory body deals with a particular problem common to businesses in different industries. The commissions with authority over job discrimination (Equal Employment Opportunity Commission), consumer product safety (Consumer Product Safety Commission), and protection of workers' safety and health (Occupational Safety and Health Administration) are examples of agencies that carry out this type of regulation. Much social regulation is indirect and involves setting standards for businesses to follow. Social regulation is often more familiar to us than industry regulation because more resources are devoted by the federal government to social regulation. Estimated federal spending on social regulation in 2013 was $46.1 billion, as compared to $9.5 billion for industry regulation.[11]

Approximately 80 regulatory agencies exist at the federal level. Table 14.1 lists these in chronological order. Notice that a large number of regulatory agencies was created in the early 1970s. Although historically we associate the Great Depression and the New Deal era with the growth of regulation, the number of federal agencies that originated in the 1970s was nearly double the number created during the 1930s.

APPLICATION 14.3

ANTITRUST ENFORCEMENT UP CLOSE AND PERSONAL

There's a story told about Bob, a sales representative, who was having dinner at an annual business convention with several friends who work for companies that compete with his company. Shortly into the meal, one of the diners mentioned that his company was about to drop the price on a product that all the companies represented at the table sell. On hearing this, another diner said that her company was also going to drop its price. Discussion about the potential price drops began to lead the conversation to potential "spot" dropping, which is where companies stay away from dropping prices in each other's largest sales territories.

This turn in the conversation is when Bob, reaching for a roll, knocked over his full glass of water—soaking his shirt and pants. Everyone at the table laughed, Bob waved his hands in feigned embarrassment, said good night to everyone as he got up, and left. As it turns out, Bob knocked the water over on purpose because he saw that the conversation at the table was turning to price fixing, which is an unquestionable antitrust violation. Bob wanted it very clear in everyone's memory that he was not there as the conversation went on.

Anyone who has been involved in an antitrust proceeding would likely say that Bob did exactly the right thing because the stress created by an antitrust violation accusation can be personally devastating. First, there is the financial stress: If found guilty, a person could face a fine of $1 million *per offense*—not per suit filed. So if, for example, there were four charges listed in a suit, a person found guilty of each of the charges might face a fine of $4 million. Here, we're talking about an individual, not a company. In addition to fines, there is the cost of retaining defense counsel. And there is reason to expect that an employer might not come to an employee's aid; it might be in the employer's best interest to fire an employee, saying, "Wait, he did this, not us."

Another added stress of an antitrust accusation is the possibility of a prison sentence and all that an incarceration implies. A guilty individual could be looking at up to 10 years in either a minimum or maximum security prison, depending on where the prison system sends the guilty person.

Even if a person is not named as a defendant, the mere possibility of being named a defendant in an antitrust suit can take over one's life. The government typically never tells a target when its investigation has concluded, so a person can live under a cloud of stress and suspicion whether or not he or she is actively under investigation.

There is also the reality that once an indictment is issued, the ongoing investigation and litigation can last for years. Over this time, the accused's friends and coworkers might be interviewed, and there may be requests for mountains of documents by, say, the Antitrust Division of the Department of Justice.

The long and short of it is that the antitrust laws should be taken seriously. Violations have the potential to affect personal finances and emotional and physical stress with additional destructive effects on a defendant's family and friends.

The Structure of Regulation

How does regulation come about? First of all, a particular industry or a specific problem is under federal or state regulation depending on whether interstate or intrastate commerce is involved. Federal agencies have jurisdiction over interstate commerce, and state commissions regulate intrastate commerce. For example, the rates charged by utility companies, such as your electric power company, that serve customers within a particular state are under the regulatory jurisdiction of a state public utility commission. Federal regulatory agencies, such as the Occupational Safety and Health Administration (OSHA), are established by Congress to regulate activities that cross state lines.

[11] Susan Dudley and Melinda Warren, *Sequester's Impact on Regulatory Agencies Modest: An Analysis of the U.S. Budget for Fiscal Years 2013 and 2014*, Weidenbaum Center on the Economy, Government, and Public Policy, Washington University, St. Louis, 2013, p. 5.

| TABLE 14.1 | *Chronology of Federal Regulatory Agencies* |

Regulatory agencies have been formed throughout the history of the economy, with a large number created in the 1930s and 1970s.

Year	Agency	Department Association[a]
1789	Customs Service	Treasury
1836	Patent and Trademark Office	Commerce
1863	Comptroller of the Currency	Treasury
1870	Copyright Office	Library of Congress
1887	Interstate Commerce Commission [Transferred to Department of Transportation in 1996]	
1899	Army Corps of Engineers [Regulatory duties from this date; established 1824]	Defense
1903	Antitrust Division	Justice
1913	Federal Reserve System	
1914	Federal Trade Commission	
1915	Coast Guard [Transferred to Homeland Security in 2002]	Transportation
1916	Tariff Commission [Became International Trade Commission in 1974]	
1920	Federal Power Commission [Became Federal Energy Regulatory Commission in 1977]	
1922	Commodity Exchange Authority [Became Commodity Futures Trading Commission in 1974]	Agriculture
1927	Bureau of Customs [Became Customs Service in 1973]	Treasury
1931	Food and Drug Administration	Health and Human Services
1932	Federal Home Loan Bank Board	
1933	Farm Credit Administration	
1933	Federal Deposit Insurance Corporation	
1934	Federal Savings and Loan Insurance Corporation [Abolished in 1989]	
1934	Federal Communications Commission	
1934	National Mediation Board	
1934	Securities and Exchange Commission	
1935	National Labor Relations Board	
1936	Maritime Administration [Transferred to Federal Maritime Commission in 1961]	Commerce
1937	Agricultural Marketing Service and Other Agencies [Transferred to other services in 1972 and 1977]	Agriculture
1938	Civil Aeronautics Authority [Became Civil Aeronautics Board in 1940; abolished in 1984]	
1940	Fish and Wildlife Service [Established as Bureau of Fisheries in 1871]	Interior
1946	Atomic Energy Commission [Transferred to Nuclear Regulatory Commission and Energy Research and Development Administration in 1975]	
1951	Renegotiation Board [Abolished in 1979]	
1953	Foreign Agricultural Service	Agriculture
1953	Small Business Administration	
1958	Federal Aviation Agency [Became Federal Aviation Administration in 1967]	Transportation
1961	Agricultural Stabilization and Conservation Service [Reorganized into the Farm Services Agency in 1994]	Agriculture
1963	Labor-Management Services Administration	Labor
1964	Equal Employment Opportunity Commission	

TABLE 14.1	Chronology of Federal Regulatory Agencies

Year	Agency	Department Association[a]
1966	Federal Highway Administration	Transportation
1966	National Transportation Safety Board [Reestablished as independent agency in 1974]	Transportation
1966	Federal Railroad Administration	Transportation
1969	Council on Environmental Quality	
1970	Cost Accounting Standards Board [Abolished in 1980]	
1970	Environmental Protection Agency	
1970	National Credit Union Administration	
1970	National Highway Traffic Safety Administration	Transportation
1970	Occupational Safety and Health Administration	Labor
1971	Employment Standards Administration	Labor
1971	Farm Credit Administration	
1971	Occupational Safety and Health Review Commission	
1972	Bureau of Alcohol, Tobacco, Firearms and Explosives [Previously part of Internal Revenue Service]	Justice
1972	Consumer Product Safety Commission	
1972	Domestic and International Business Administration [Became International Trade Administration in 1980]	Commerce
1973	Drug Enforcement Administration	Justice
1973	Mining Enforcement and Safety Administration [Became Mine Safety and Health Administration in 1977, Department of Labor]	Interior
1973	Architectural and Transportation Barriers Compliance Board	
1974	Federal Energy Administration [Became Economic Regulatory Administration in 1977, Department of Energy]	
1974	Council on Wage and Price Stability [Abolished in 1981]	
1974	Federal Election Commission	
1975	Materials Transportation Board	Transportation
1976	Federal Grain Inspection Service [Merged with Packers and Stockyards Administration in 1994 to create the Grain Inspection, Packers, and Stockyards Administration]	Agriculture
1977	Office of Neighborhoods, Voluntary Associations and Consumer Protection [Abolished in 1981; functions transferred to HUD]	Housing and Urban Development
1977	Office of Surface Mining Reclamation and Enforcement	Interior
1979	Office of the Federal Inspector of the Alaska Natural Gas Transportation System	Agriculture
1979	Federal Emergency Management Agency	
1982	Packers and Stockyards Administration	
1985	Office of Environment, Safety and Health [Renamed Office of Health, Safety and Security in 2006]	Energy
1986	Pension and Welfare Benefits Administration [Renamed Employee Benefits and Security Administration in 2003]	Labor
1987	Bureau of Export Administration [Renamed Bureau of Industry and Security in 2002]	Commerce
1989	Office of Environmental Management	Energy
1989	Resolution Trust Corporation [Terminated in 1995]	

TABLE 14.1   *(Continued)*

Year	Agency	Department Association[a]
1989	Office of Thrift Supervision	Treasury
1995	Chemical Safety and Hazard Investigation Board	Treasury
1997	Mine Safety and Health Administration	Labor
2000	Federal Motor Carrier Safety Administration	Transportation
2001	Transportation Security Administration	Transportation
2002	Election Assistance Commission	
2003	Alcohol and Tobacco Tax and Trade Bureau *[Authority previously in Bureau of Alcohol, Tobacco, and Firearms]*	Treasury
2003	Bureau of Customs and Border Protection	Homeland Security
2003	Bureau of U. S. Citizenship and Immigration Security	Homeland Security
2004	Research and Innovation Technology Administration	Transportation
2005	Pipeline and Hazardous Materials Administration	Transportation
2006	Postal Regulatory Commission *[Former Postal Rate Commission]*	
2008	Federal Housing Finance Agency	

[a] Not all agencies are associated with a department.

Sources: Ronald J. Penoyer, *Directory of Federal Regulatory Agencies—1982 Update*, Center for the Study of American Business, Formal Publication Number 47 (St. Louis: Washington University, June 1982); Paul N. Tramontozzi and Kenneth W. Chilton, *U.S. Regulatory Agencies under Reagan: 1980–1988*, Center for the Study of American Business, OP 64 (St. Louis: Washington University, May 1987); Melinda Warren and Kenneth W. Chilton, *Regulation's Rebound: Bush Budget Gives Regulation a Boost*, Center for the Study of American Business, OP 81 (St. Louis: Washington University, May 1990); Melinda Warren, *Mixed Message: An Analysis of the 1994 Regulatory Budget*, Center for the Study of American Business, OP 128 (St. Louis: Washington University, August 1993); Melinda Warren and Barry Jones, *Reinventing the Regulatory System: No Downsizing in Administration Plan*, Center for the Study of American Business, OP 155 (St. Louis: Washington University, July 1995); *Federal Regulatory Directory*, 6th ed. (Washington, DC: Congressional Quarterly, 1990); 10th ed., 2001; 11th ed., 2003; 13th ed., 2008; 14th ed., 2010; U.S. Department of Labor, http://www.dol.gov/dol/pwba.

There are several interesting points to understand about these agencies:

♦ The enabling legislation (legislation that creates the agency) is general. It contains an overall mandate and specifies the structure of the agency and other important information pertaining to its operation.

♦ When a regulatory agency is established, it is given the power to carry out the general mandates stated in the enabling legislation and can make detailed rules and regulations to be followed. For example, if the mandate is airline safety, the agency can establish rules regarding air personnel qualifications, airplane inspections, equipment, and such.

♦ An agency has the power to enforce its own rules and regulations and to punish those who do not comply. Companies that choose to dispute their treatment by an agency may appeal their case to a court of law.

Some regulatory agencies are established as independent bodies governed by commissioners who are appointed to oversee the operations of the agency, while others are created as part of an existing department (such as the Department of Commerce) and are headed by an administrator within that department. For example, the Federal Reserve system is an independent body headed by an appointed board of seven governors, whereas the Mine Safety and Health Administration is within the Department of Labor and headed by one of its Administrators. State public utility commissions are usually headed by commissioners who are either elected or appointed by the governor.

Industry Regulation

Industry Regulation
Regulation affecting several aspects (such as pricing, entry of new sellers, and conditions of service) of the operations of firms in a particular industry.

Firms in certain industries, such as the railroad, natural gas, and electric power industries, are subject to **industry regulation**. This type of regulation deals with pricing, entry of new sellers into the market, extension of service by existing sellers, the quality of service, and other matters. Some of the decision-making ability of a business in a free market does not exist for this type of regulated firm.

In some regulated industries, the firm itself is not free to independently choose or alter the price it charges for its product and must seek approval from its regulatory agency to change its price. For example, privately owned water companies generally must obtain state government approval to change their rates. Also, in many regulated industries, new firms cannot begin operation unless they receive permission or a license from that industry's regulatory body. Sewer, water, electric, and other utility companies cannot be initiated at will.

Firms already in existence may need to get permission to abandon service or to extend or alter current services. For years, the railroads were not permitted to drop unprofitable passenger routes, and a water company cannot simply cut off service when it wants. These firms may also be subject to a host of other regulations, such as on the quality and safety of the product offered for sale.

Justifications for Industry Regulation

Two reasons are frequently cited for industry regulation: an economic justification, and the public interest.

Efficiency considerations underlie the economic justification for regulation. For some products it is more efficient (less costly) to have the entire output in a market come from one large producer rather than from several smaller producers. In these cases, a **natural monopoly** exists in the market.[12] Water companies are good examples of natural monopolies: It would be inefficient and complicated to have several water companies, each with its own pipes and valves running under streets, serving an area.

Natural Monopoly
A market situation where it is more efficient (less costly) to have the entire output of a product come from one large producer rather than from several smaller producers.

Natural monopolies are the result of strong economies of scale in production and distribution. With economies of scale, which were introduced in Chapter 12, a seller's long-run unit or average total cost falls as its output increases. Economies of scale enable a firm to take advantage of cost-reducing benefits due to size.

The benefits of a natural monopoly are illustrated in Figure 14.1. Here we have the downward-sloping region of a long-run average total cost (LRATC) curve, which shows that, because of economies of scale, as the level of output increases, the unit or average cost of producing that output falls. Suppose that 10 million units of the output in Figure 14.1 would serve the whole market. If one firm produced the entire amount, the cost per unit would be $1; if two firms each supplied half of the market, or 5 million units, the cost per unit would be $2.25.

Some industries have significant economies of scale, particularly electric power, water, and others where firms depend on large costly plants and equipment (generators, power plants, and so forth) to be efficient. By having one large company that can spread these high capital costs over a larger output, the cost per unit is considerably less.

---

[12] Natural monopoly was introduced in Chapter 13.

FIGURE 14.1   *Economies of Scale and Long-Run Average Total Cost*

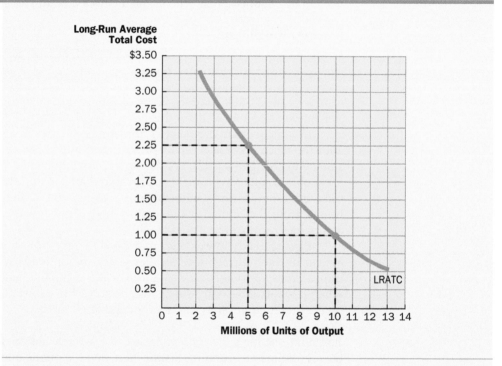

A natural monopoly exists when economies of scale and the size of the market make the long-run average total cost of production lower with one seller in the market.

Unfortunately, natural monopolies create a dilemma. On the one hand, because of economies of scale, buyers benefit from lower unit costs when dealing with one seller. But on the other hand, as the only seller in the market the firm could abuse its monopoly power. Regulation that allows only one firm in the market, while at the same time placing the firm's operations under detailed scrutiny by a public authority, resolves this dilemma.

Natural monopoly may explain regulation in certain areas of the economy where there are advantages to having only one seller in a market. But what justifies the regulation of firms that produce in industries where there is more than one seller in a market? This regulation is based on the public interest justification.

Public Interest Justification for Regulation

A good or service is so important to the public well-being that its production and distribution should be regulated.

According to the **public interest justification**, certain types of businesses provide goods or services so important to the public well-being that the public has a right to be assured of their proper operation through regulation. Examples include radio and television companies whose programming can influence public opinion, and transportation firms such as railroads, motor and water carriers, and airlines, which are necessary to keep goods, services, and resources moving.

The public interest justification can be applied in many more situations than the natural monopoly justification. If the argument can be made that the welfare of the public is so affected by the operation of a business that it is desirable to regulate that business, then the public interest justification might be used for regulation. The breadth of this justification was defined in 1934 in one of the most important court decisions on regulation, *Nebbia v. New York*. In this case, which dealt with the regulation of milk prices, the Supreme Court stated:

> *It is clear that there is no closed class or category of businesses affected with a public interest. . . . [A] state is free to adopt whatever economic policy may reasonably be deemed to promote public welfare, and to enforce that policy by legislation adapted to its purpose. . . .*[13]

Simply, this case said that states are allowed to regulate a broad range of businesses in a number of ways in the name of the public interest, provided certain conditions of fairness are met.

Cost-Plus Pricing
Prices are set to generate enough revenue to cover operating costs plus a fair return to stockholders.

Price Regulation   One important aspect of industry regulation is the oversight of prices, or rates, charged by a regulated company. In many cases a regulated firm, such as a gas or electric company, that seeks to raise or lower its rates must appeal to its regulatory commission for permission to do so. And the commission can approve, deny, or modify the request. Typically, rate changes involve formal filings, investigations, and hearings before the request is approved or denied.

Regulated firms have two concerns in making rate requests: They must cover their costs, and they must earn enough profit to attract and retain stockholders. Because of these, pricing by regulated firms has traditionally been carried out on a cost-plus basis. With **cost-plus pricing**, the rates buyers pay are designed to generate revenues sufficient to cover the costs of operation plus a fair return to those who invest in the business.

Incentive Regulation
A regulatory philosophy that provides incentives for regulated firms to operate efficiently.

But cost-plus pricing may not promote economic efficiency. Permission to collect revenues to cover costs plus a fair return to investors may not provide sufficient incentive to keep costs down, as would happen with competition. As a result, there has been a movement toward **incentive regulation**, which allows firms subject to price regulation to profit by improving the efficiency of their operations.

Price Caps
An incentive system allowing regulated firms to price up to a pre-set maximum and retain additional profit from operating more efficiently.

A popular form of incentive regulation is **price caps**, where a maximum is set by a regulatory authority on the price a regulated firm can charge for its product. The company can charge what it wants up to that maximum and, more importantly, retain any additional profit it earns by operating more efficiently.

Social Regulation
Regulation aimed at correcting a problem or protecting a group; not limited to a specific industry.

Social Regulation

The type of regulation that generates the most discussion and controversy because it is closest to our lives is **social regulation**. Social regulation is aimed at correcting a problem, such as pollution, or at protecting a group in the economy, such as workers or consumers. Rather than focusing on a single industry, social regulation applies to all firms that are affected by the mandate of the regulatory body, regardless of the industry.

Social regulation does not directly intervene into a company's price, profit, and other related decisions (although complying with social regulation can raise a firm's costs and affect its prices and profit). Instead, it focuses on setting and enforcing standards concerning products, employees' working conditions, and other matters that could be harmful to the general public. The OSHA is concerned with worker safety and working conditions and is a good example of an agency dealing with social regulation.

[13] *Nebbia v. New York*, 291 U.S. 502 (1934), pp. 536, 537.

Table 14.2 lists some of the federal agencies responsible for social regulation, categorized according to the group each protects (the consumer, the worker, the environment). Notice that some of the agencies listed in the table affect a broader range of firms and industries than do others. For example, how many industries might be affected by a National Highway Traffic Safety Administration ruling? How does this compare with the number that could be affected by an EPA ruling?

It is more difficult to summarize the functions of social regulation than industry regulation because social regulation is so diverse: Consider the differences between the Consumer Product Safety Commission and the National Labor Relations Board. However, some generalizations can be made about social regulation. First, as we noted earlier, much more is spent at the federal level on social regulation than on industry regulation: Approximately 80 percent of the expenditures of the major federal regulatory agencies in 2014 were expected to go to social regulation. Second, the direction of social regulatory spending has changed over the years. In 2000, 37 percent of all federal social regulatory spending went to homeland security and 32 percent went to the environment and energy. In 2014, 52 percent of social regulatory spending was expected to go to homeland security and 17 percent to the environment and energy.[14]

Test Your Understanding, "Government and Business," lets you practice distinguishing among activities that might call for antitrust enforcement, industry regulation, social regulation, or no government intervention at all.

TABLE 14.2	*Some Social Regulatory Agencies*

Much of the effort of agencies concerned with social regulation is directed toward protecting consumers, workers, and the environment.

Protecting Consumers

Consumer Product Safety Commission	National Transportation Safety Board
Food and Drug Administration	Bureau of Alcohol, Tobacco, Firearms, and
Drug Enforcement Administration	Explosives
Food Safety and Inspection Service	Federal Aviation Administration
	National Highway Traffic Safety Administration

Protecting Workers

Mine Safety and Health Administration	Employment and Training Administration
National Labor Relations Board	Equal Employment Opportunity Commission
Occupational Safety and Health	Employee Benefits Security Administration
Administration	

Protecting the Environment

Environmental Protection Agency	Army Corps of Engineers
Office of Surface Mining Reclamation	Forest Service
and Enforcement	Council on Environmental Quality

Source: Melinda Warren and Barry Jones, *Reinventing the Regulatory System: No Downsizing in Administration Plans*, Center for the Study of American Business, OP 155 (St. Louis: Washington University, July 1995), pp. 23–24; *Federal Regulatory Directory*, 16th ed. (Washington, DC: Congressional Quarterly, 2014), pp. 964–1001.

[14] Dudley and Warren, *Sequester's Impact*; Regulatory Studies Center, The George Washington University, and Weidenbaum Center, Washington University, St. Louis, 2013, p. 5.

GOVERNMENT AND BUSINESS

Below are 10 hypothetical situations concerning business practices. Determine in each situation whether the practice would likely:

a. violate the antitrust laws, and if so, which one,
b. be subject to industry regulation,
c. call for social regulation, and if so, by which federal agency, or
d. call for no government intervention at all.

1. Several firms located along a major river find that the river provides an easy method for disposing of toxic chemicals from production.
2. The purchaser of a large amount of carpeting that has been specially cut by the seller for installation in an office complex is demanding a refund after the purchaser mistakenly ordered the wrong color.
3. The purchaser of a home appliance is injured when properly using the product because it was poorly designed.
4. Two competing manufacturers of a popular consumer product that currently sells for $14 per unit agree that their prices will never fall below $10.
5. After discussing developments in the world grain market, two small farmers agree that now is the time to sell their corn if they want to get the best price.
6. A regional electric company would like to eliminate its service to a small village of 300 people because the service is losing money.
7. The theater chain showing 60 percent of the films in a major city wants to acquire the second largest chain, which shows 20 percent of the films in the city.
8. A manufacturer charges $30 per unit to buyers who purchase directly from its warehouse and $35 per unit to buyers who want to pay the additional cost of having the product packaged and shipped to them.
9. A local natural gas distribution company decides to double its charge to residential users in order to increase its profits.
10. A major supermarket chain cuts prices below cost in three cities until some of its smaller competitors go out of business.

Answers can be found at the back of the book.

The Performance of Regulation

The spectacular growth of regulation in the 1970s came to an end toward the end of that decade. Concern over the performance of regulation and its effects on business costs and the economy in general brought about an interest in **deregulation**. Deregulation of the airline, trucking, natural gas, banking, telephone, and other industries came quickly.

Deregulation
A reduction in government regulatory control of the economy.

Proponents of deregulation, then as well as now, believe that in many instances the costs of regulation outweigh its benefits to society. Supporters of regulation hold the opposite view. Up for Debate, "Is Government Intervention Reaching Too Far?" concerns a case where regulation is proposed for new, more stringent fuel efficiency standards for medium and large vehicles. What is your assessment of the argument on each side in this case?

The growth in global markets and international economic activity is also an important area of regulatory discomfort. Regulation and antitrust policies tend to be national in scope. Barring a special international agreement, U.S. policies usually will not affect foreign firms doing business in foreign markets. As a result, some believe that U.S. firms are at a disadvantage when competing with foreign firms that face less or little regulation at home or are not subject to the antitrust laws that firms in the United States face. For example, one issue that repeatedly surfaces is the U.S. labor laws that forbid child labor and protect U.S. workers from potential harm at work. While these regulations clearly protect children and workers, they can also raise costs for U.S. businesses. Countries that permit child labor and have few laws protecting their workers can produce and sell goods at a lower price.

IS GOVERNMENT INTERVENTION REACHING TOO FAR?

Issue   *In 2015, the U.S. EPA and the Department of Transportation's National Highway Traffic Safety Administration proposed standards that would increase fuel efficiency and reduce climate/health-endangering carbon pollution in medium and large vehicles like semi trucks, large pickup trucks, vans, and all sizes of busses and work trucks. The standards would apply to these vehicles that will be produced from 2021 through 2027. At the time this proposal was put forward, other standards were already in place for trucks and lighter vehicles. Are all of these standards reaching too far with government intervention?*

Yes   To go ahead with this is moving too far and too fast in the wrong direction. When new standards are put in place, there is always an issue of the costs of production. They could rise and buyers of these vehicles would be forced to pay higher prices for them. So the consumer could be hurt when government imposes new costs on businesses. Also, if these standards apply to vehicles that will not be produced until 2021, how can we be comfortable thinking these standards will coordinate with the best ways of producing in the future?

Are we asking Americans to bear the brunt of emissions problems? It has been argued that perhaps by 2018 China, India, and other developing countries will be generating more emissions than industrialized countries like the United States. Shouldn't our focus be global and based on remedies that go beyond national borders and do not put such costs on U.S. businesses and consumers?

No   The government would be following a highly beneficial course of action for its citizens and the environment. Over time such standards reportedly could cut fuel costs by $170 billion and reduce oil consumption by as much as 1.8 billion barrels over the life of the vehicles that meet the standards of the program. By way of comparison, the oil saved would be greater than one year's worth of oil imported from the Organization of Petroleum Exporting Countries. Also, the vehicles at which the proposal is directed currently create about 20 percent of greenhouse gas emissions while they account for approximately 5 percent of all vehicles. Focusing attention on these vehicles would have a good positive effect.

While these emissions are a global problem, the United States should be taking a lead in trying to control them. Not only would this be a model change for other countries, but it is simply the right thing to do.

Based on: "EPA, DOT Propose Greenhouse Gas and Fuel Efficiency Standards for Heavy-Duty Trucks," http://yosemite.epa.gov/opa/admpress.nsf, 6/19/2015, National Energy Information Center (NEIC), www.eia.gov.

The questions created by nationally focused antitrust and regulatory policies are becoming increasingly important as economic activity becomes more global. And the debates over the costs and benefits of government intervention are becoming more complicated as a wider array of values and traditions from different cultures are brought forward.

Summary

1. Government intervenes in the operation of markets in the U.S. economy in two ways: antitrust enforcement and regulation. Intervention occurs to ensure competition in markets, efficiencies from large-scale operations, and security for specific groups.

2. Antitrust laws are concerned with the relationships between firms and competition in markets. They promote market forces by attacking monopolization and combinations and conspiracies in restraint of trade. Government intervention is carried out at the federal and state levels.

3. There are five major federal antitrust laws: the Sherman, Federal Trade Commission, Clayton, Robinson–Patman, and Celler–Kefauver acts. The Sherman Act Section 1 condemns combinations and conspiracies in restraint of trade, and Section 2 condemns monopolization. Combinations and conspiracies in restraint of trade may be either per se or rule of reason violations. Monopolization cases depend largely on the actions and market share of the accused firm.

4. The Federal Trade Commission is empowered to prevent unfair methods of competition. The Clayton Act condemns several anticompetitive practices. Price discrimination and merger provisions of the Clayton Act were amended by the Robinson–Patman and Celler–Kefauver acts.

5. Penalties facing those found guilty of violating the antitrust laws include imprisonment, fines, structural remedies, and triple damages.

6. Regulation is participation by federal and state government agencies and commissions in business decision making. Regulatory authority is under federal jurisdiction for interstate commerce and under a state agency for intrastate commerce.

7. There are two types of regulation: industry and social regulation. Industry regulation involves direct government participation in pricing, output, profit, and other decisions of firms in certain industries. Social regulation focuses on protecting certain groups and on setting and enforcing standards. It is not limited to firms in any single industry.

8. Industry regulation can occur because of a natural monopoly due to economies of scale or effects on the public interest from the operation of certain businesses. One aspect of industry regulation is rate or price setting. Prices can be set on a cost-plus basis, where they are designed to cover expected costs plus a fair return to investors. There are also incentive pricing schemes, such as price caps.

9. Social regulation focuses mainly on protecting consumers, workers, and the environment. Much more is spent on social regulation than industry regulation.

Key Terms and Concepts

Antitrust laws	Rule of reason violations
Monopolization and attempts to monopolize	Trade association
	Joint venture
Combinations and conspiracies in restraint of trade	Federal Trade Commission Act
	Clayton Act
Sherman Act	Interlocking directorates
Per se violations	Robinson–Patman Act
Price fixing	Price discrimination
Territorial division	Celler–Kefauver Act
Tying arrangement	Horizontal, vertical, and conglomerate merger
Exclusive dealing arrangement	

Government regulation   Cost-plus pricing
Industry regulation   Incentive regulation
Natural monopoly   Price caps
Public interest justification   Social regulation
   for regulation   Deregulation

Review Questions

1. What do Section 1 and Section 2 of the Sherman Act condemn? What specific acts could be considered violations of Section 1? What are the main factors the courts consider when judging whether a firm has committed a Section 2 violation?

2. What is the difference between a per se violation of the antitrust laws and a rule of reason violation? Why are some business practices considered per se violations while others are not?

3. What activities are prohibited by the Clayton Act, the Robinson–Patman Act, and the Celler–Kefauver Act?

4. In what respects are industry and social regulation similar and in what respects are they different?

5. What is a natural monopoly and how is it related to economies of scale? What sort of dilemma does the combination of efficiency and monopoly power create for the consumer and the policymaker?

6. Explain the difference between the natural monopoly justification for regulation and the public interest justification. Why is the public interest justification applicable to a wider range of firms than the natural monopoly justification?

7. What is cost-plus pricing and how can it lead to inefficient performance by a regulated firm? What are price caps and how can they improve efficiency?

8. Provide some examples of social regulatory agencies and identify the main groups or areas that each protects.

Discussion Questions

1. Horizontal mergers, vertical mergers, conglomerate mergers, price discrimination, and interlocking directorates may or may not be anticompetitive. For each of these five activities, describe a set of circumstances where you think the effect would be anticompetitive and where it would not be anticompetitive.

2. The antitrust laws are designed to control the growth of monopoly power in specific markets. What are some economic reasons for concern over monopoly power? Are there any noneconomic reasons for wanting to control this power?

3. Antitrust laws reinforce the operation of free markets, while regulation replaces free market forces with an authoritative body. How do you explain that certain economic problems are dealt with by strengthening market forces while others are dealt with by replacing the market mechanism with regulatory authority?

4. Suppose legislation is passed to repeal the major federal antitrust statutes. How do you think such a repeal would affect competition? Would competition between sellers continue much the same as before the repeal? Would there be a blossoming of monopoly power? Would something else occur?

5. Assume that the production of a particular good is accompanied by significant economies of scale. Would you recommend vigorous enforcement of the antitrust laws to ensure that no one firm could monopolize the production of this product, or would you allow a monopoly to form and then subject it to industry regulation? Justify your answer.

6. There is concern about the costs and benefits of regulation. What costs and benefits might be created if the Equal Employment Opportunity Commission were abolished? In your opinion would we be better off without the agency than with it?

7. What complications are created for businesses and the economy in general as a result of the administration of regulatory and antitrust policies in an increasingly global environment?

Critical Thinking Case 14

EMINENT DOMAIN: IN THE PUBLIC INTEREST OR NOT?

Critical Thinking Skills

Weighing the merits of competing arguments

Identifying consequences of policy choices

Economic Concepts

Social regulation

Public interest justification for regulation

Cost–benefit analysis

In July 2005 the U.S. Supreme Court, in a closely watched 5-to-4 decision, ruled that a local government can condemn and seize someone's property and turn it over to a private contractor to build a development that will strengthen the local economy. The case, *Kelo v. New London,* was brought by a New London, Connecticut, homeowner whose property was to be condemned and transferred by the city to a developer, who would take it and other adjacent properties, tear down the houses and other buildings, and construct a hotel and office complex in their place.

The issue at the foundation of this court decision is a long-standing practice called "eminent domain," where a government unit buys someone's property (often against the seller's wishes) and then uses it in the public interest. Usually, "using property in the public interest" is understood to mean invoking eminent domain for a public project like a highway or flood protection. But in this case, the property was to go to a private developer who would benefit from the project.

The reaction to this court decision was quick and furious. Within a few weeks, bills were introduced in the U.S. House and Senate and over half the state legislatures to limit the use of eminent domain for the benefit of private developers.

Arguments can be made both in support of and opposition to the Supreme Court's decision. In support of the decision, eminent domain might be necessary to encourage private developers to restore declining, at-risk urban areas to healthy, productive places. In addition to the benefit of a revitalized area, construction-related jobs would be created, leading to more spending that benefits everybody. And if handing the property to a private developer leads to more tax revenue for the city than before the property was condemned, then the public interest is further served.

On the other side is the fear that all private property will now be fair game for seizure in behalf of a developer if it can be argued that the developer will contribute more to the area's economic growth than the current owner. There is also the issue of who benefits and who loses from this broader freedom to seize property. Can developers with more money and influence than homeowners of average or lower-than-average income come out on top?

There are other concerns: This expanded power to condemn could be abused by local governments desperate to increase economic development. And there is concern also that the strong and growing resistance to the Supreme Court's decision could lead to the canceling of projects and losses to contractors.

Questions

1. The Supreme Court's ruling stretches "improving the public good" to increasing overall economic wealth. Is this an appropriate measure?

2. Suppose a law is passed condemning the use of eminent domain to benefit private developers. How could this affect economic renewal in urban areas?

3. Is it possible to have any social regulation that benefits one group without hurting another? What criteria should be used in balancing competing interests?

Labor Markets, Unions, and the Distribution of Income

CHAPTER OBJECTIVES

Understand the behavior of the demand for labor and the factors determining that demand.

Examine the factors that determine the supply of labor.

Explain how changes in demand and supply and other modifications in labor markets influence wages and the quantity of labor employed.

Describe the types and structure of unions, collective bargaining, and major legislation affecting labor.

Examine the distribution of income in the United States, and discuss some explanations for that distribution.

Define poverty, identify the poverty population in the United States, and discuss some government programs for alleviating poverty.

When we think about markets, we frequently think only of the markets in which goods and services are bought and sold: the discount malls we visit, our grocery stores, and the local shops that provide haircuts. But in a market economy, factors of production, like labor and capital equipment, are also bought and sold in markets. There are markets for nurses, book editors, high school math teachers, plumbers, architects, CEOs, and unskilled labor. As in product markets, substitutability and geography play an important role in defining factor markets. For example, an electrician in Denver will likely not compete with one in Houston for a job, but when a large corporation searches for a CEO, it will likely do an international search and consider people with a range of skills and experiences. And prices of factors, such as wages for labor, are the result of the degree of competitiveness in each factor market.

While there are markets for all of the factors of production, we will focus on labor markets in this chapter. The income from the sale of labor—wages, salaries, and such—is the largest single source of income in the U.S. economy: In 2015, labor income accounted for about 63 percent of all income.[1]

[1] See Table 10.1.

Since most of us will spend a lifetime in labor markets, learning about how they function is useful information. We begin this chapter with a look at a simple demand and supply model for wage determination and then explore the factors that cause many labor markets to deviate from this model. We will also learn in this chapter some basics about labor unions, income distribution, how much people earn, and how we measure poverty in the United States.

LABOR MARKETS: DEMAND

In a market system, labor is bought and sold in the same way as goods and services: through the interaction of demand and supply. In the case of labor, however, businesses (and governments and nonprofits) are the buyers and individuals are the sellers.

Wage
The price of labor.

The price of labor is called its **wage**. If someone works for a wage of $20 an hour, this is the price of that person's labor as well as the price the buyer is willing to pay.[2]

Figure 15.1 gives a basic supply and demand model for determining the wage in a competitive labor market for workers who produce a particular service. The vertical axis of the figure gives wages per hour and the horizontal axis gives the quantity of labor demanded and supplied. In this particular market, the equilibrium wage is $15 an hour, and the number of workers employed is 800.

| **FIGURE 15.1** | *A Competitive Labor Market* |

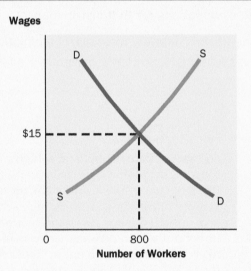

There is a downward-sloping demand curve and an upward-sloping supply curve in a competitive market for labor.

---

[2] Workers often receive a fringe benefit package from an employer, which includes such features as health and life insurance, vacation days, and pension contributions. These benefits can be a substantial cost for the employer and an important financial consideration for an employee. Although this additional compensation package affects labor demand and supply decisions, we will confine our analysis to money wages for the sake of simplicity. Including fringe benefits would not affect our analysis of labor markets in this chapter in a significant way.

According to Figure 15.1, the demand curve for labor is downward sloping and the supply curve of labor is upward sloping: Buyers are willing to hire more labor as the wage falls, and more labor is offered in the market as the wage increases.

The Demand for Labor

Derived Demand

The demand for a factor of production depends on the demand for the good or service the factor produces.

The demand for labor, or any other factor of production, is a **derived demand**: It is derived from, or depends on, the demand for the good or service the factor produces. Autoworkers have jobs because cars are demanded; grocery clerks are employed because people buy groceries; and the professors who teach your courses do so because students enroll in them.

The wage that a firm is willing to pay for a unit of labor is based on the dollar value of the labor's productivity to the firm. An employee whose daily product is valued at $150 will not be paid $175 per day. In fact, the company will not be willing to pay the employee over $150 a day. No firm can afford to hire at a wage rate greater than the employee's dollar contribution to the company. Baseball players with contracts in the tens of millions of dollars command this kind of money largely because of their expected contributions to their teams' earnings. Outstanding players attract fans who purchase tickets to games and increase revenues for the clubs.

As seen in Figure 15.1, the typical market demand curve for labor is downward sloping. This is because each individual firm's demand curve for labor is downward sloping: A firm is willing to hire more labor when the wage rate falls and less labor when the wage rate increases.[3] If the amount a firm is willing to pay for labor is based on the dollar value of workers' productivity, then the downward-sloping demand curve indicates that the dollar value of workers' productivity falls as more labor is hired.

The declining value of labor's productivity as more labor is hired occurs for two reasons: (1) decreasing marginal productivity, and (2) the need to lower product price in order to sell more of a good or service.

Law of Diminishing Returns

As additional units of a variable factor are added to a fixed factor, beyond some point the product from each additional unit of the variable factor decreases.

Marginal Product

The change in total product when one more unit of a variable resource, such as labor, is utilized.

Labor Demand and Productivity   In discussing the pattern of short-run production costs in Chapter 12, the **Law of Diminishing Returns** was introduced. This law says that, beyond some point, the extra (marginal) product from adding successive units of a variable factor to a fixed factor falls. This concept applies to labor.

Table 15.1 provides an example of a hypothetical company varying the amount of labor it utilizes to produce good X. The second column of the table shows the total product that results when a specific number of workers is employed: For example, four workers together with the fixed factors produce 280 units of good X. The third column lists **marginal product**, which is the change in total product when one more unit of labor (the variable factor) is used. In Table 15.1, for example, the second worker has a marginal product of 80 units of good X (total product goes from 100 to 180 when the second worker is used), and the fifth worker has a marginal product of 20 units (total product goes from 280 to 300 when the fifth worker is used).

The most important point to observe in Table 15.1 is that marginal product declines as more workers are used.[4] This decline is significant to the company employing the labor because it shows that, due to the Law of Diminishing Returns, each additional unit of labor produces less than the previous unit and is therefore worth less to the firm. This declining marginal productivity is reflected in the downward-sloping demand curve for labor.

[3] Recall from Chapter 3 that market demand curves are found by adding together individual demand curves.
[4] In this example diminishing returns set in after the first worker. This is not always the case; a firm may employ several workers before diminishing returns set in.

| TABLE 15.1 | | *Total Product and Marginal Product of Labor for a Producer of Good X* |

As more workers are hired, after some point the Law of Diminishing Returns causes each additional worker's marginal product to decline.

Number of Workers	Total Product	Marginal Product
0	0	
		100
1	100	
		80
2	180	
		60
3	240	
		40
4	280	
		20
5	300	
		0
6	300	

Declining marginal productivity can be found in all work situations. Imagine the limited productivity of a baseball team's third, fourth, or fifth catcher. A restaurant will find that at some point the marginal productivity of its additional servers declines as more are employed, and a high school that hires several assistant principals may find each successive one adding less to total product than the one before.

Labor Demand and Product Price   The second reason for the declining value of labor's productivity and the resulting downward-sloping labor demand curve is the demand for the good or service the labor is producing. In all market situations except pure competition, firms face downward-sloping demand curves for their products: Consumers will increase their purchases of a company's product only if its price falls. This downward-sloping demand curve for the good or service that labor produces causes the value of labor's productivity to decrease, since the increased output resulting from employing more workers can only be sold at lower prices. Thus, additional units of labor are worth less to the company because the product they produce is sold for less.

To illustrate this point, Table 15.2 gives the total product information from Table 15.1 for the producer of good X and adds a third column listing the prices at which good X can be sold. The price and total product columns reflect the inverse

| TABLE 15.2 | | *A Good X Producer's Total Product and Price per Unit* |

A firm facing a downward-sloping demand curve for its product can sell the increased output that results from hiring more workers only if it lowers the price.

Number of Workers	Total Product	Price per Unit
0	0	$6.25
1	100	6.00
2	180	5.75
3	240	5.50
4	280	5.25
5	300	5.00
6	300	5.00

relationship between price and quantity demanded: If the company intends to sell more of its product, it must lower the price. However, lowering the product's price decreases the value of what labor produces.

Combining Declining Marginal Productivity and Declining Product Price   The demand curve for labor is downward sloping because the marginal productivity of additional units of labor decreases and because the value of additional production is lowered by the decline in price necessary to sell the product. In other words, *the Law of Diminishing Returns and the Law of Demand combine to determine the value of labor.*

The effects of declining marginal productivity and decreasing product price can be combined to determine what each unit of labor is worth to a firm. This in turn determines the wage rate a firm is willing to pay. Returning to the good X example, Table 15.3 adds two columns to those given in Table 15.2 in order to determine the wage rate the producer of good X is willing to pay.

The fourth column of Table 15.3 gives the total revenue when various amounts of good X are sold. (Remember: Total revenue is price times quantity.) For example, with a total production of 240 units that can be sold for $5.50 each, total revenue is $1,320 (240 × $5.50).

The last column of Table 15.3 gives **marginal revenue product**, which is the change in total revenue that results from the sale of output produced when one more unit of *labor* is utilized.[5] When one worker is hired, 100 units of good X are produced and sold for $6 each, bringing in $600 for the company. Since the total revenue with no workers is $0, the marginal revenue product of the first worker is $600. When a second worker is employed, 180 units of output are produced and sold for $5.75 each, creating a total revenue of $1,035. Thus, when the second worker is utilized, the company's total revenue increases from $600 to $1,035, or the marginal revenue product of the second worker is $435. For the third unit of labor, the marginal revenue product is $285 because total revenue increases from $1,035 to $1,320. The marginal revenue product of the fourth worker is $150 and of the fifth worker is $30.

Marginal revenue product is important because it establishes the firm's demand curve for labor. In the example in Table 15.3, this firm would not hire any labor if the wages were above $600. In this case, the wage paid would be greater than the extra

Marginal Revenue Product

The change in total revenue that results from the sale of output produced when one more unit of a variable factor, such as labor, is utilized.

TABLE 15.3   *A Good X Producer's Total Product, Price, Total Revenue, and Marginal Revenue Product*

Marginal revenue product is the change in total revenue that results from the sale of output produced when one more unit of a variable factor, such as labor, is utilized.

Number of Workers	Total Product	Price per Unit	Total Revenue	Marginal Revenue Product
0	0	$6.25	$ 0	$600
1	100	6.00	600	435
2	180	5.75	1,035	285
3	240	5.50	1,320	150
4	280	5.25	1,470	30
5	300	5.00	1,500	0
6	300	5.00	1,500	

[5]Be careful not to confuse this with marginal revenue, which is the change in total revenue when one more unit of *output* is sold.

| FIGURE 15.2 | *A Firm's Demand Curve for Good X Workers* |

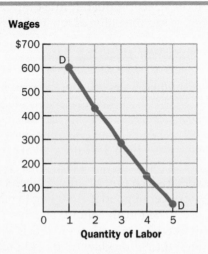

A firm's demand curve for labor is based on the marginal revenue product of labor, which declines as additional workers are hired.

revenue created by the production of any worker. The producer would, however, be willing to hire one worker at a wage of $600. At $600, the first worker's contribution (marginal revenue product) equals the wage.

The wage would need to fall to $435, the marginal revenue product of the second worker, before the producer would hire two units of labor. At any wage higher than $435, the second worker's contribution to the firm's revenue would be less than the wage. For three units of labor to be employed, the wage would have to fall to $285, the marginal revenue product of the third worker. Four workers would be demanded at a wage of $150 and five at $30.[6]

Demand Curve for Labor
Downward-sloping curve showing the amount of labor demanded at different wage rates; based on the marginal revenue product of labor.

When the wages and the amount of labor the good X producer is willing to hire at each of those wages are plotted in a graph, the firm's **demand curve for labor** results. This is given in Figure 15.2. Notice that the wage is equal to the marginal revenue product of labor at each point on the demand curve. Test Your Understanding, "A Small Business Determines Its Demand for Employees," provides an opportunity to calculate some of these demand-related numbers and to derive a labor demand curve.

LABOR MARKETS: SUPPLY

Supply Curve of Labor
Upward-sloping curve showing the amount of labor supplied at different wage rates.

In a typical labor market there is a direct relationship between wages and the quantity of labor supplied, causing the **supply curve of labor** to slope upward like that given in Figure 15.3. This relationship implies that less labor will be attracted to a market at a lower wage than at a higher wage. In Figure 15.3, for example, 300 people are willing to work in this labor market for $11.00 per hour, but 700 want to work for $14.50 per hour.

[6] When this firm demands four workers at $150, it does not mean that the firm hires one worker for $600, a second for $435, a third for $285, and a fourth for $150. Instead, the firm pays the same wage rate to all four workers. Since the firm will pay no worker more than the worker is worth and since all workers are paid the same, the wage is based on the marginal revenue product of the last worker.

FIGURE 15.3   *Supply Curve of Labor*

A typical upward-sloping labor supply curve indicates that a direct relationship exists between wage rates and the quantity of labor supplied in a market.

In labor markets, money may be only part of the consideration in seeking a job. Many important factors other than wage or salary influence the supply of labor: location preferences, psychological rewards, long-term work objectives, and other nonwage considerations. Think about your current job or one you have held in the past. What nonwage factors influenced you in taking this job? How do nonwage factors contribute to the lack of job applicants to pick up trash in July in cities with extremely high temperatures? Or what might cause a teenager to want a job at Starbucks or Macy's while not even considering a job at a fast-food restaurant that pays the same wage?

Location is an important nonwage influence on the supply of labor in some markets, particularly small towns with few employers where workers face limited job choices. Rather than relocate, some people choose to stay in their familiar surroundings and work at a lower wage. When there are many job opportunities in an area, workers can be more selective and sensitive to wage rates. National chain stores, such as Wal-Mart, may be able to pay lower wages in areas with little competition for unskilled labor than in large, populated metropolitan areas.

Many people seek a job that is psychologically rewarding or that gives them "psychic" income: Prestige, a sense of accomplishment, or freedom from supervision may induce a person to work for a lower wage. Someone with an advanced degree in international management, for example, might prefer to teach and receive a smaller salary from a prestigious university than to work for a higher salary from a large corporation. A freelance writer might sell an essay for little money to a highly regarded magazine because of the sense of accomplishment from having an article in that particular publication.

The possibility of long-term gain can also influence the supply of labor. A college graduate may take a position with an employer at a lower salary than that offered by other employers because the potential for future advancement is great or because the

TEST YOUR UNDERSTANDING

A SMALL BUSINESS DETERMINES ITS DEMAND FOR EMPLOYEES

Suppose you plan to start a small business that will label and stuff envelopes for other small businesses, charitable fund raisers, and political candidates. Since your biggest cost will be for employees to do the actual labeling and stuffing, you are very concerned about determining the hourly wage you would be willing to pay.

Assume that the information given in the following tables is from a study done for a company similar to the one you plan to start. This information serves as the basis for determining the wages you would be willing to pay and how many employees you would be willing to hire at each wage rate.

Table 1

Number of Workers	Hourly Total Product	Hourly Marginal Product
0	0	_____
1	500	_____
2	1,000	_____
3	1,500	_____
4	1,900	_____
5	2,200	_____

The hourly total product (envelopes) that can be produced with different numbers of workers is shown in Table 1. Determine the hourly marginal product of each additional worker.

1. At what number of workers does the Law of Diminishing Returns take effect? _____

Table 2 gives the price for stuffing and labeling each quantity of envelopes: If your output is 1,500 envelopes per hour, you can charge 4¢ ($0.04) per envelope and sell that output. But if you raise your output to 2,250 per hour, you must lower your price to 3¢ ($0.03) per envelope to sell your services to more buyers.

Table 2

Number of Workers	Hourly Total Product	Charge per Envelope
0	0	$0.055
1	500	0.05
2	1,000	0.045
3	1,500	0.04
4	1,900	0.035
5	2,250	0.03

Determine the hourly total revenue and the hourly marginal revenue product per worker from the information in Table 2. Put these numbers in Table 3 and answer Questions 2 through 4.

---

job will look good on a resume. Other factors affecting supply include job security; the safety, cleanliness, and working conditions on a job; the degree of skill or formal training required; and flexibility in scheduling work.

CHANGES AND MODIFICATIONS IN LABOR MARKETS

Changes in Labor Demand and Supply

In any labor market, changes can occur that will cause labor demand and/or supply to increase or decrease and the demand and/or supply curves for labor to shift to the right or left. When these changes occur, the equilibrium wage and amount of labor hired are affected in the same way that equilibrium price and quantity are affected when demand and/or supply shift in an output market. An increase in the demand for labor, for example, causes the demand curve to shift to the right, resulting in an increase in both the equilibrium wage rate and the number of workers employed. This

Table 3

Number of Workers	Hourly Total Revenue	Hourly Marginal Revenue Product
0	$_____	
1	_____	$_____
2	_____	_____
3	_____	_____
4	_____	_____
5	_____	_____

Table 4

Number of Workers Demanded	Wage Rate
1	$_____
2	_____
3	_____
4	_____
5	_____

2. What is the highest hourly wage that you would be willing to pay? _____
3. What wage would you be willing to pay to hire enough workers to label and stuff 1,500 envelopes per hour? _____
4. Suppose you have enough demand for your services to label and stuff 2,250 envelopes per hour at 3¢ each, but the minimum wage is $7.50. Would you lower your price to 3¢? _____

Based on the numbers in Table 3, complete the demand schedule for employees in Table 4 and draw the resulting demand curve for labor in the graph provided.

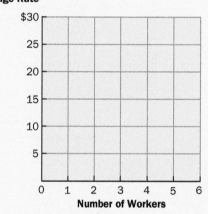

Answers can be found at the back of the book.

is illustrated in Figure 15.4, which demonstrates graphically the effect of an increase in the demand for labor from D1 to D2 in a competitive labor market. As demand increases, the equilibrium wage rate rises from W_1 to W_2, and the number of workers employed increases from Q_1 to Q_2.

Changes in Labor Demand   There are many factors that can cause a demand curve for labor to shift to the right or left: changes in the prices of substitute inputs, technological change, and changes in the demand for the good or service the labor is producing are just a few. Let's consider each of these.

Businesses are always looking for cheaper methods of production to improve profits. If they can find and use a cheaper input, the demand for the more expensive input will decrease and its demand curve will shift to the left while the demand for the cheaper input will increase and its demand curve will shift to the right. The search for cheaper inputs has affected many labor markets. Automobile companies have turned to robotics in their plants, causing the demand for labor to fall, and lower labor costs in many foreign countries have led to the closing of U.S. manufacturing plants for clothing, electronics, and more.

FIGURE 15.4   *Effect of an Increase In Demand In a Labor Market*

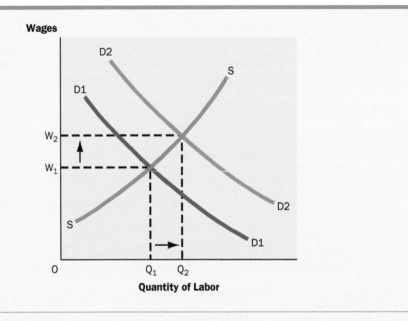

An increase in the demand for labor causes both the equilibrium wage rate and quantity of workers employed to increase.

Technological change has an important impact on the demand for labor. The widening use of computer-based information, programs, and storage systems has increased the demand for people with technology-related skills, while at the same time decreasing the demand for many other types of labor. Today many organizations employ a staff of skilled computer technicians. The emergence of programs that allow individuals to prepare and file income taxes online has influenced jobs in accounting. Grocery stores are eliminating jobs because of computerized self-checkouts, and trash trucks need fewer workers because of mechanized lifts.

Finally, a change in the demand for the good or service that a type of labor is producing may change the demand for that labor. When the demand for new single-family housing increases, home builders increase their production, causing the demand curve for construction workers to shift to the right. In 2008 and 2009, as the economy fell into a serious recession, the demand for cars and trucks took a serious hit. Automobile companies were shutting down production lines and the demand for auto workers went on the decline. The decline was so severe that several U.S. auto companies sought a government bailout to survive.

Application 15.1, "Go Green," deals with the rise in new jobs and careers coming from the emphasis on creating products and services associated with sustainability of the earth's limited resources. The movement toward "greening" is affecting a large number of labor markets from various types of engineers to environmental consultants.

Changes in Labor Supply   We can identify a number of factors that cause the supply of workers in a labor market to change and the supply curve to shift to the right or left.

APPLICATION 15.1

Go Green

Today the concern over sustainability is a strong and clear acknowledgement of the basic principle of scarcity at the root of economics: scarce resources with unlimited wants and needs. Apprehension over the limits of basic resources necessary to sustain life—clean air and water and energy sources—has given rise to a movement that focuses on policies and actions to address these concerns.

Our language now includes words and phrases that have a different meaning than they did in our parents' and grandparents' generations: sustainability, recycling, wind farms, and hybrids to name a few. And, adding to that lexicon is the new usage of green—green products, green building, green jobs, and more.

There is focus today on a new green economy with its positive impact on the creation of green jobs and green careers. Job seekers are being directed toward employment opportunities that are arising from our concerns for sustainability.

So what exactly is a green job? How do we define that sector of the economy? Recently, the U.S. Department of Labor's Bureau of Labor Statistics (BLS) began to collect data on green jobs in order to analyze the impact that sustainability concerns are having on economic activity. In doing so, the BLS has developed an "official" definition. Green jobs are:

♦ jobs in businesses that produce goods or provide services that benefit the environment or conserve natural resources; and

♦ jobs in which workers' duties involve making their establishment's production processes more environmentally friendly or use fewer natural resources.

According to the BLS, green jobs range from those associated with producing energy from sources like wind and solid waste to those that reduce the release of toxic compounds to jobs that increase public awareness of environmental issues or introduce technologies that conserve natural resources.

While we struggle to assess and measure the strength of the green economy and the jobs it is creating, we continue to aspire toward the goals of a cleaner, better, healthier world. And those aspirations show up in the continued emphasis on green activities whether they are formally measured or not. All one needs to do is google "green jobs" and a plethora of websites that direct job seekers toward a variety of positions pops up.

Experienced workers and new college graduates will find firms looking for environmental engineers, landscape designers who can create rain gardens, energy consultants, solar sales representatives, urban farmers, and more. Even in traditional fields like marketing and communications, there are jobs with a green emphasis. And, the LEED certification (Leadership in Energy and Environmental Design) developed by the U.S. Green Building Council is encouraging professionals in architecture and construction to incorporate the knowledge and practice of green design and building into their projects.

Sources: Jacquelyn Smith, U.S. Green Building Council, "What LEED is," www.usgbc.org; U.S. Department of Labor, Bureau of Labor Statistics, "Measuring Green Jobs," www.bls.gov/green/.

These include, among others, changes in economic conditions, demographic trends, expectations, and immigration.

Some labor markets are affected by the state of the economy. Consider markets for low-paying, unskilled jobs in businesses like fast food, retail, and lawn care. With a healthy economy, the supply of workers in these labor markets decreases as people find better-paying jobs. When the economy falls into a recession and workers are laid off—especially for long periods of time—laid-off workers, as well as those who now need to supplement household income, enter these labor markets and increase supply.

Demographic trends also affect labor supply. For example, when the teenage population increases, firms that typically hire from this age group experience an increase in labor supply. With the trend toward early retirement there is a drop in supply in some labor markets with full-time jobs and a movement of workers into labor markets where part-time employment is available.

The expectation of future job prospects influences the supply in some labor markets. College students, for example, tend to select majors that are perceived as providing good employment opportunities. When the number of teaching positions in secondary and elementary schools increases, for example, the supply of new teachers increases as more students major in education, and when getting a good job in investment banking or other financial services appears less likely, the supply of students with majors in finance decreases.

Many other factors cause labor supply to increase or decrease. For example, changes in immigration laws and the extent to which illegal immigrants are returned to their home countries affect several labor markets, and the number of students accepted into medical and law schools influences the supply of labor in those markets.

Changes in Labor Demand and Supply, and Changes in Quantity Demanded and Supplied   The distinction made in Chapter 3 between a change in demand or supply and a change in quantity demanded or supplied applies to labor demand and supply. A **change in labor demand or supply** refers to a *shift* of the entire labor demand or supply curve to the right or left as a result of changes in nonwage factors, such as the prices of substitute inputs, technology, product demand, economic conditions, and expectations about future job prospects. A **change in the quantity of labor demanded or supplied** occurs only as a result of a change in the price (wage) of labor. A change in quantity demanded or supplied is represented by a movement from one wage–quantity combination to another *along* a labor demand or supply curve: The curve itself does not change.

Change in Labor Demand or Supply

A shift in the demand or supply curve for labor caused by changes in nonwage factors.

Change in the Quantity of Labor Demanded or Supplied

A change in the amount of labor demanded or supplied that occurs when wages change; a movement along the demand or supply curve.

Modifications of the Labor Demand and Supply Model

The labor market model introduced in Figure 15.1 at the beginning of the chapter is a useful starting point for analyzing how wages are determined through the forces of supply and demand. But, just as there are imperfections in output markets, there are certain factors at work in real-world labor markets that go beyond what is explained in the simple supply and demand model and that impact the determination of wages and the amount of labor employed. Three of these factors—wage rigidities, legal considerations, and unequal bargaining power—merit consideration.

Wage Rigidities   In a labor market such as that in Figure 15.1, a decrease in the demand for labor would shift the demand curve to the left, causing fewer workers to be hired and the equilibrium wage to fall. In reality, a decrease in the demand for labor will most likely cause employment to drop but not money wages.[7] Firms with a need for fewer workers usually respond by laying off workers rather than by lowering their wages. On the supply side, contrary to the operation of the simple model, an increase in the number of workers in a market (a shift of the supply curve to the right) will also likely not lower the money wage. Thus, money wages tend to adjust upward but not downward to changing labor market conditions.

There are several reasons why money wages tend not to fall: Some workers are earning the minimum wage and by law can be paid no less; an employer may be bound by a labor agreement that sets wages; and it may be in the worker's best interest to be laid off rather than take a cut in pay. A laid-off worker may become eligible for

---

[7]Notice that the expression *money wages* is used. Money wages are wages stated in current dollars, such as $12 per hour or $45,000 per year. Real wages, a different measure, are money wages adjusted for inflation, or what money wages can buy. In labor markets, money wages tend not to fall, but real wages may fall over time. This occurs when money wage increases do not keep up with inflation, or with increases in the general level of prices. The model in this chapter uses money wages, not real wages. Money and real income are explained more fully in Chapter 4.

unemployment compensation, can use the idle time to find another job, and will not be acknowledging a willingness to work for less. Also, an employer might believe that better long-term employee relationships can be maintained by laying off workers for a short period of time rather than by asking workers to accept a lower wage.

Legal Considerations   Labor markets are affected by legislation that influences wages and the demand for and supply of labor. The most obvious legislation is the **minimum wage law**. By setting minimum hourly earnings, this law can override supply and demand by not allowing wages to fall to equilibrium. Figure 15.5 gives the federal minimum wage over time from $0.25 per hour when established in 1938 to $7.25 per hour set in 2009.

Minimum Wage Law
Legislation specifying the lowest hourly earnings that an employee can be paid.

Figure 15.6 shows the influence of the minimum wage law on a labor market. The equilibrium wage in Figure 15.6 is $6.00 per hour, and the equilibrium employment is 2,200 workers. If the government establishes a minimum wage above the equilibrium—say, $7.25 per hour—employers will want to hire only 1,800 workers, but 2,400 workers will be available. As a result, a surplus of 600 workers will develop in the market. Many critics of minimum wage legislation point out that it causes unemployment in some labor markets. The graphics in Figure 15.6 suggest this may be so.

Some legislation can change the demand for labor. For example, the minimum wage law may reduce the demand for a type of labor if the increased wage makes it cheaper to use a piece of machinery to do the job. Rules, such as those of the

| FIGURE 15.5 | *The Federal Minimum Wage* |

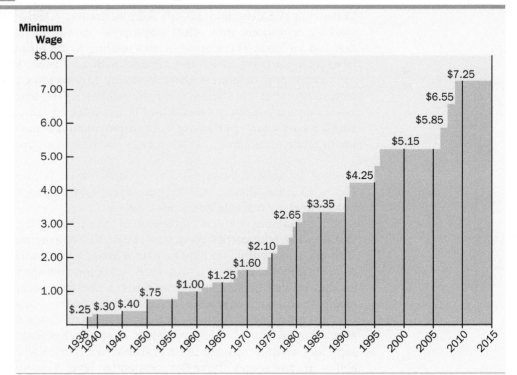

Over the years, the minimum wage has been raised many times from its original $0.25.

FIGURE 15.6   *Effect of a Minimum Wage on a Labor Market*

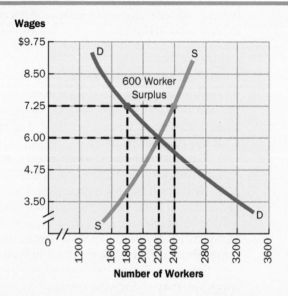

When the equilibrium wage in a labor market is lower than the minimum wage, the minimum wage prevails, and a surplus of workers results in that market.

Occupational Safety and Health Administration (OSHA) that specify safety and working conditions, may affect employers' costs of using labor and, in turn, their demand for labor. There are also laws relating to the hiring of specific groups in the labor force, such as women and minorities, that influence labor demand.

The supply of labor is also affected by various laws. Licensing and certification requirements for physicians, occupational therapists, teachers, and others have an impact on the supply of labor. Laws limiting the amount people can earn while on Social Security, laws pertaining to unemployment compensation, laws that influence immigration levels, and child labor laws also affect the supply of labor.

Unequal Bargaining Power   The equilibrium wage of $15 in the labor market in Figure 15.1 was determined by employers and employees with equal bargaining power. In many markets this is not the case.

If bargaining power is on the side of the employer, the wage will likely be below that set when both parties are of equal strength. For example, workers living in a town with one major employer may be paid a lower wage than if there were several firms competing for their services. And, years ago before free agency status for athletes, studies showed that their salaries were much lower. In general, the fewer the alternative employers from which workers can choose, the weaker the workers' bargaining power.

If bargaining strength is on the side of labor suppliers, the wage will likely be above that set when buyers and sellers have equal power. In general, the greater the suppliers' control over the labor available to a particular employer, the greater their ability to raise wages above the competitive level. One method used by workers to raise wages has been unionization. In addition, exceptional abilities and skills, such as those of some network news anchors or sports personalities, provide greater control over their supply of labor.

LABOR UNIONS

Labor Union
An organization of workers that bargains in its members' behalf with management on wages, working conditions, fringe benefits, and other work-related issues.

A **labor union** is an organization of workers that bargains with management on its members' behalf. Usually unions represent their members in negotiations for wages, working conditions, fringe benefits, and other matters. Unions in the United States are primarily economic in their focus, although they may engage in some political activity.

Types of Unions and Union Membership

The percent of the labor force belonging to unions has not been stable over the years, and in recent decades the power and influence of unions have declined. In 1983, 20.1 percent of all wage and salary employees belonged to unions, but since then membership has fallen. By 2014, only 11.1 percent of these workers were unionized. And, perhaps surprisingly, a much larger percentage of public sector workers are unionized than are private sector workers: About 35.7 percent of government workers were unionized in 2014 as compared to 6.6 percent of private sector workers.[8]

The erosion of union membership and power has stemmed from many sources: an antiunion political climate, growth in service sector jobs where unionism has not been strong, the decline in blue-collar manufacturing jobs where unions have been active, expanded government regulation of working conditions, and retirements of union workers who were strong advocates for the union movement.

Craft Union
A union that represents workers with a specific skill or craft.

Labor unions fall into two categories: craft unions and industrial unions. **Craft union** membership is made up of workers who have specific skills, such as bricklaying or plumbing. A craft union may restrict membership through setting conditions like completing an apprenticeship program. This gives the union some control over the supply of workers, which helps raise its members' wages and fringe benefits. A simple supply and demand model for wage determination indicates that any action that restricts supply (shifts the supply curve to the left) results in a higher wage rate. Figure 15.7 shows that a decrease in the supply of labor from S1 to S2 leads to an increase in the wage rate from W_1 to W_2. Notice also another important result. This action reduces employment: in this case from Q_1 to Q_2.

Industrial Union
A union that represents all workers in a specific industry, regardless of the type of job performed.

An **industrial union** represents all workers in a specific industry. For example, workers performing different jobs in the automobile industry may be represented by the United Auto Workers, and communications workers performing different jobs may be represented by a single union. When it comes to membership, industrial unions are broader in their focus than craft unions.

A union, whether craft or industrial, is typically headed by a national or international organization that operates on behalf of all the members. Below this headquarters organization are individual "locals" to which the members belong. In some cases, such as a musicians' union, members who work for different employers in an area belong to the same local. In other cases, such as an industrial union, a local represents members working in a single plant or for a single employer.

Collective Bargaining

With unions, the process of wage determination is more complicated than the simple interaction of market supply and demand since a union represents the suppliers of labor and management represents the buyer of labor. Here the impersonal forces of the market are replaced by negotiations between union and management representatives seeking to reach an agreement on wages and other aspects of a labor contract. This

---

[8]U.S. Department of Labor, Bureau of Labor Statistics, "News Release: Union Members-2014," www.bls.gov, January 23, 2015.

| **FIGURE 15.7** | *Restricting Supply in a Labor Market* |

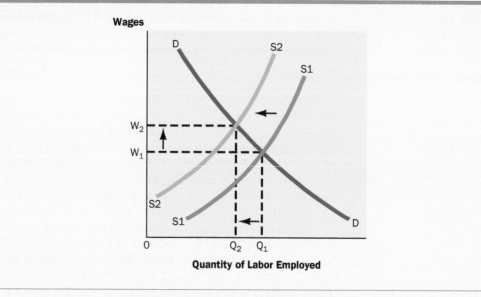

A craft union can obtain higher wages for its members by limiting the supply of labor, which is shown by a shift of the supply curve to the left from S1 to S2.

Collective Bargaining

The process through which a union and management negotiate a labor contract.

Strike

Work stoppage by union members.

National Labor Relations Act (Wagner Act)

Legislation supportive of unions; permits and strengthens collective bargaining.

process in which a union negotiates a contract on behalf of its members is referred to as **collective bargaining**.

Union and management negotiations are primarily about economic issues: wages, job security, payments for insurance, and such. But the actual bargaining process itself is largely political where each side tries to gain the most of what it seeks while giving up the least. The terms of a negotiated contract depend in large part on the relative bargaining ability and strength of the participating parties.

If the parties to a negotiation fail to agree on the terms of a contract, a union may go on strike against the employer. When on **strike**, union members stop working and often set up a picket line that other workers may refuse to cross. The purpose of the strike is to bring economic pressure on the employer to return to the bargaining table and draft an agreement acceptable to the union. In recent years little labor time has been lost due to strikes. In 2014, for example, less than 0.005 percent of estimated working time was lost because of work stoppages.[9]

Collective Bargaining and the Law

Over the years, we have created a large body of laws concerning the rights and responsibilities of labor unions in collective bargaining and related matters. Two laws have been especially important: the National Labor Relations Act of 1935 and the Labor Management Relations Act, better known as the Taft–Hartley Act, of 1947.

Passed in the depths of the Depression, the **National Labor Relations Act** (also called the **Wagner Act**) specifically gives workers the right to organize and bargain collectively, to choose who will represent them in their collective bargaining, and to

[9] Ibid., Table 15.1, Work Stoppages.

carry out "concerted activities" for prolabor purposes. The law also defines certain actions by employers, such as discrimination against employees because they belong to a union, as unfair labor practices. The **National Labor Relations Board (NLRB)**, which hears complaints about unfair labor practices and can order that those practices cease and be remedied, was also established by the act.[10]

National Labor Relations Board (NLRB)
Hears complaints on unfair labor practices and orders remedies where appropriate.

The **Taft–Hartley Act** of 1947, which became law in a troublesome year for work stoppages, is generally less supportive of organized labor. Under certain circumstances the Taft–Hartley Act gives workers the right to not join a union or otherwise engage in organized labor activities. Section 14(b) of the law says that union membership cannot be a condition of employment in states that have passed laws to that effect. This is better known as the "right to work" issue, and state laws prohibiting union membership as a condition of employment are called **right to work laws**. With right to work laws, a union's ability to control the supply of labor is diminished, and the union's bargaining strength is weakened. In 2014, 24 states had right to work laws.[11]

Taft–Hartley Act
Legislation that contains several provisions limiting union activities.

The Taft–Hartley Act also allows the president of the United States to impose an 80-day "cooling-off period" during which a particular strike or lockout (where an employer prevents laborers from entering a work site) cannot occur if, in the president's opinion, the work stoppage is a threat to the national interest. If, after 80 days, the situation leading to the strike or lockout is not corrected, the ban is lifted, and the work stoppage can continue.[12]

Right to Work Laws
State laws prohibiting union membership as a condition of employment.

THE DISTRIBUTION OF INCOME

In any economy there are always questions about income. How much does the average person make? How is income divided—are there many or a few rich or poor? The **distribution of income** refers to the way income is divided among the members of society. If the distribution of income to individuals were perfectly equal, everyone would receive the same amount. But income is not divided equally: Some households are better or worse off than others; and at the extremes, some are very rich and others are very poor.

Distribution of Income
The way income is divided among the members of society.

We can see how income is distributed in the United States in Table 15.4. The left-hand column of the table divides households into five groups—each representing 20 percent of all households—ranked according to the amount of income each group received. The lowest group represents the 20 percent of all households that received the lowest incomes, and the highest group is the 20 percent that received the largest incomes. The right-hand column of the table gives the percentage of total income that went to each of the five groups in 2013.

With an equal distribution of income among households, each of the five groups would receive 20 percent of the total. However, in 2013, the lowest 20 percent received 3.2 percent of total income, while the highest 20 percent of households claimed 51.0 percent. Not shown in the table, the top 5 percent received 22.2 percent of total income.[13]

---

[10] *United States Statutes at Large*, vol. 49, part 1 (Washington, DC: U.S. Government Printing Office, 1936), pp. 452–454.
[11] National Right to Work Legal Defense Foundation, www.nrtw.org. The 24 states that have passed Right to Work laws are: Alabama, Arizona, Arkansas, Florida, Georgia, Idaho, Indiana, Iowa, Kansas, Louisiana, Michigan, Mississippi, Nebraska, Nevada, North Carolina, North Dakota, Oklahoma, South Carolina, South Dakota, Tennessee, Texas, Utah, Virginia, and Wyoming.
[12] *United States Statutes at Large*, vol. 61, part 1 (1948), pp. 136, 140–142, 151, 155–156.
[13] See source for Table 15.4.

TABLE 15.4	*Income Distribution among Households*

Income is not distributed evenly among households in the United States. In 2013 the poorest one-fifth of U.S. households received 3.2 percent of total income while the richest one-fifth received 51.0 percent of the total.

Percent of Households	Percent of Total Income In 2013
Lowest 20%	3.2%
Second 20%	8.4
Middle 20%	14.4
Fourth 20%	23.0
Highest 20%	51.0
Total	100.0

Source: U.S. Census Bureau, "Income and Poverty in the United States: 2013," p. 30, www.census.gov.

Over the years, journalists and others have watched the release of these annual quintile data to determine the direction shares of income are going. Since 1970 there has been a slow and gradual change in the shares: The rich are getting richer, the poor are getting poorer, and the middle class is slowly shrinking.[14] With the recession and financial crisis that began in 2008, a spotlight has been put on these data. Notice now that the top 20 percent of households earn over 50 percent of the income generated and that the lowest 60 percent of all households earn just 26 percent of all income generated. Interest has also been sparked in knowing just how much money top income earners make, and the salaries of corporate CEOs are popular public information. Today there is reference to the amount of income generated by the top 1 percent and an interest in the mega-rich.

Some members of society are more likely than others to be at the lower or higher end of the distribution of income. In Chapter 10, it was noted that, on average, households with certain characteristics tend to earn more than other households. For example, households headed by a married couple typically earn more than households headed by a single female.[15]

Differences in Income

Why is income in the United States distributed as it is? Why do some people receive a large annual income while others do not? Several explanations merit discussion.

Resource Ownership   Most income depends on the quality and quantity of productive resources that individuals own and the uses to which those resources are put. People with highly productive or many resources stand to earn more money than those who own less productive or fewer resources. An outstanding athlete or top-rated chef earns more than others with less impressive performances; the owners of fertile farmland in the heart of Illinois earn more income per acre from the production of

[14] In 1970, the share going to the poorest 20 percent was 4.1 percent, and the share going to the richest 20 percent was 43.3 percent. U. S. Census Bureau, Table H-2, "Share of Aggregate Income Received by Each Fifth and Top 5 Percent of Households, All Races, 1967 to 2010," www.census.gov.
[15] See Table 10.2.

TABLE 15.5	*Levels of Education and Income*

Education has a strong positive influence on a person's income.

Education Level	Average Weekly Earnings in 2014
Professional degree	$1,639
Doctoral degree	1,591
Master's degree	1,326
Bachelor's degree	1,101
Associate degree	792
Some college, no degree	741
High school graduate	668
Less than high school diploma	488

Source: U.S. Bureau of Labor Statistics, Employment Projections, "Earning and unemployment rates by educational attainment," http://data.bls.gov.

crops than the owners of less fertile farmland in the hills of western Pennsylvania; and a family with a ranch, an apartment complex, and a fleet of rental trucks is going to have a higher income than one whose sole income source is the labor of an unskilled household head.

Sometimes resource ownership comes from inheritance. Income generated from the ownership of real estate, securities, or other assets can be passed on through a will or trust.

Education and Experience   The case can be made that nothing beats education as a way of improving a person's lifetime earnings. We saw the data in Chapter 10 that show a direct relationship between annual household income and years of education. Table 15.5 provides more detailed information about average weekly incomes for people whose education levels range from less than a high school diploma through a professional degree like an MD or a law degree. The data in the table strikingly demonstrate the importance of education: In 2014, a person with a professional degree was earning about 3.4 times as much as a person with less than a high school diploma.

There is also a case to be made for experience, training, additional coursework, and other work-related opportunities to learn. The expenditures of time, effort, and money to gain an education and improve a person's productivity are called **human capital investments**. Just as a business can invest in machinery and equipment, human beings can invest money and time in improving their own productive capabilities. Human capital investments include not only learning-related expenditures but also spending on health care, fitness, and other related programs.

Human Capital Investments
An expenditure to improve a person's productivity.

As the world becomes "flatter" and we compete in a more global environment, there is increased recognition that knowledge-based economies are important for sustained economic growth.

Application 15.2, "Making the Most of Intellectual Capital," discusses the transition in the United States from an economy that was focused on industrial work and skills to a more sophisticated economy dependent on brain power or intellectual capital.

APPLICATION 15.2

MAKING THE MOST OF INTELLECTUAL CAPITAL

Knowledge didn't fuel America's economy in the past. The Industrial Age thrived on man's mastery over machine. Most work required steady hands to operate factory equipment and minds geared to such repetitive tasks as measuring and counting. . . . Over the course of workers' careers, jobs changed little, so talents acquired in youth often served until retirement. Lifetime learning didn't matter all that much.

America has left the Industrial Age behind. Factory work is increasingly being performed in other countries; much of what remains in the United States is highly technical, relying more on sharp minds than nimble hands.

Postindustrial nations are shifting workers to more sophisticated jobs that require analytical intelligence, imagination and creativity, and the ability to interact with others. The work relies on brains rather than brawn. . . . Equally important, these skills have to be kept sharp in a world of rapidly changing tastes and technology. We can't just get a good education while young and expect it to suffice for an entire career.

The transformation of the way we work gives intellectual capital precedence over the physical capital that once drove the U.S. economy. Both kinds of capital make us richer, but they differ in important ways.

Physical capital grows when businesses invest in buildings, machinery, and other productive assets. These are largely management decisions, and the process usually takes just a few months or years. To expand intellectual capital, we invest in human beings over decades—from learning the ABCs in preschool to mastering the latest computer programs at the office.

Companies make important contributions to creating intellectual capital, but workers must assume a large part of the responsibility. No one can learn for us. We have to supply the effort to develop our skills.

Knowledge is ultimately the property of the employee. . . . Workers take it with them when they switch jobs, a factor that limits companies' ability to capture the benefits of investing in human capital. As a result, workers can't count on employers to provide all the training they'll need. They must be active participants in their own education, engaging in lifetime learning on their own.

Source: "Making the Most of Intellectual Capital," Federal Reserve Bank of Dallas, 2004 Annual Report, pp. 13–14.

Discrimination

Unequal treatment in a labor market because of an employer's perception of a category to which a worker belongs.

Discrimination   Workers experience **discrimination** when they are treated unequally in a labor market because they are placed in a category and judged on the perception of that category, rather than on their skills or merit. In the United States, concern over discrimination has centered mainly on the labor market experiences of nonwhite as compared to white workers and female as compared to male workers. But discrimination can be based on religion, political preference, ethnic origin, or any other categorical distinction. Discriminated-against workers may receive lower wages or have fewer job choices or advancement opportunities. Discrimination that leads to unequal access to good housing, medical care, or education can lead to small, less productive human capital investments, which can result in lower incomes.

POVERTY

The income distribution data in Table 15.4 show that, in 2013, the lowest 20 percent of all households received only 3.2 percent of total income, and the next lowest 20 percent received only 8.4 percent. Are these households considered to be the "poor" in our society?

Each of us has a different concept of poverty or what is meant by poor. Someone living in luxury likely considers poor differently from the average income earner. Someone who drives an expensive new car may think a person who drives an old,

TABLE 15.6	*Poverty Levels for Families and Individuals*

Poverty levels vary according to family size. They indicate the annual money income that must be received to be considered *not* poor by the federal government.

Size of Unit	Income Level in 2013[a]
1 person	$11,888
2 persons	15,142
3 persons	18,552
4 persons	23,834
5 persons	28,265
6 persons	31,925
7 persons	36,384
8 persons	40,484
9 persons or more	48,065

[a]Thresholds vary with the number of related children under 18. Shown are weighted average thresholds.

Source: Ibid., Table 15.4, p. 43.

obviously used car is poor. Someone who drives an old, used car may view as poor a person who cannot afford a car at all. In general, poverty is based on a person's income and material possessions such as housing, cars, and clothing.

Government Measures of Poverty   In order to calculate an "official" measure of poverty in the United States, the federal government has created income measures called **poverty levels**. They indicate the amount of annual money income that must be received to be considered *not* poor, and are based on family size. Any individual or family receiving an income below its designated level is classified as poor and is included in government poverty statistics.

Poverty levels
Government-designated levels of income that must be received to be considered *not* poor.

Table 15.6 gives the average poverty levels for families and individuals in 2013. The poverty level increases as the number of persons in a family increases. In 2013, 45.3 million people, or 14.5 percent of the total population, lived in poverty—that is, in households where the money income fell below the poverty levels.

Table 15.7 provides information about poverty levels for some groups in 2013. For example, there was a high incidence of poverty among female-headed families: About one-third lived below the poverty levels. Notice that almost 20 percent of children lived below the poverty levels and that the incidence was higher for high school dropouts—24.3 percent—than for persons with a four-year college degree or higher—5.4 percent. Many of the poor had jobs, and the incidence of poverty differed among the states.

There has been some disagreement over the official definitions of the poverty levels. Many argue that the levels are too low and do not represent a true measure of poverty. For example, according to Table 15.6, in 2013 the poverty level for a family of three was $18,552—far below the median income of $51,939 for a household.[16] Also, according to the poverty levels in Table 15.6, a family of four persons earning

[16] Ibid., Table 15.4, p. 23.

TABLE 15.7	*Groups Living Below the Poverty Level in 2013*

Many children, elderly, poorly educated persons, and people in female-headed households live below the poverty levels.

Group	Number of Persons in Group Below the Poverty Level	Percentage of Group Below the Poverty Level
Total population	45.3 million	14.5%
People in female-headed families	15.6 million	33.2
Children under 18	14.7 million	19.9
Persons 65 years and older	4.2 million	9.5
Persons employed full time, year round	2.8 million	2.7
Persons employed less than full time, year round	8.2 million	15.8
Persons with no high school diploma	10.2 million	24.3
Persons with a four-year college degree or higher	3.8 million	5.4
Persons living in New Mexico	347 thousand	22.9
Persons living in Vermont	128 thousand	8.5

Source: U.S. Census Bureau, Current Population Survey (CPS), Tables POV01, POV02, POV22, POV29, POV46, 2014, www.census.gov.

$23,835 in 2013 would not have been "poor" because its income was $1 above the poverty line.

Some people argue that the plight of the poor is overstated because the income levels used to measure poverty do not account for in-kind benefits, such as government noncash aid for food, housing, and medical care, that improve one's standard of living. If these were added to money incomes, then a smaller percentage of the population would fall below the poverty levels.

The opinion is sometimes expressed that the poor live well on public support and that poverty is largely due to an unwillingness to work. Unfortunately, poverty is a complicated problem that may not be eliminated by simply insisting that people work. In some instances, the poverty we see is a symptom of deeper human suffering. A federal task force study reported that one out of every three of the homeless in the United States suffers serious mental illness.[17] Application 15.3, "Young and Homeless," deals with another area of poverty that is of major concern.

Government Programs and Poverty   There are several government programs that provide cash transfer payments and in-kind benefits. These include Social Security, unemployment compensation, housing assistance, food stamps, medical care, vocational rehabilitation, and others. Among these, there is no single program aimed specifically and exclusively at persons living below the poverty levels. Each federal and state program has its own eligibility requirements under which a poor person may qualify. For example, a poverty-level retired couple could be eligible for Social Security

[17] Task Force on Homelessness and Severe Mental Illness, *Outcasts on Main Street: Report of the Federal Task Force on Homelessness and Severe Mental Illness* (Washington, DC: U.S. Department of Health and Human Services, 1992), pp. 1–2.

APPLICATION 15.3

YOUNG AND HOMELESS

It was estimated that in 2013 in the United States, approximately 2.5 million children, or about 1 in every 30 children, experienced homelessness. This is a large number of children facing hunger and sickness and emotional distress, sometimes on a daily basis. Many think about whether or not there will be a roof over their heads at night and whether there will be something to eat. Most of these children are in families that live in poverty.

The lack of affordable housing that comes with poverty is the obvious cause of family and child homelessness. A full-time worker that earns the minimum wage cannot afford a two-bedroom apartment at fair market rent. One would need to earn over $18 an hour to do so.

Homelessness severely impacts the health and well being of all family members. Children without a home are in fair or poor health twice as often as other children and have higher rates of asthma, ear infections, stomach problems, and speech problems. Homeless children also experience more mental health problems, such as anxiety, depression, and withdrawal. They are twice as likely to experience hunger, and four times as likely to have delayed development. These illnesses have potentially devastating consequences if not treated early.

Deep poverty and housing instability are especially harmful during the earliest years of childhood; alarmingly, it is estimated that almost half of children in shelter are under the age of five. School-age homeless children face barriers to enrolling and attending school, including transportation problems, residency requirements, inability to obtain previous school records, and lack of clothing and school supplies.

Homelessness frequently breaks up families. Families may be separated as a result of shelter policies, which deny access to older boys or fathers. Separations may also be caused by placement of children into foster care when their parents become homeless.

Source: National Coalition for the Homeless, "Homeless Families with Children," February 21, 2012, http://www.nationalhomeless.org; The National Center on Family Homelessness, www.familyhomelessness.com.

UP FOR DEBATE

SHOULD THERE BE A WORK REQUIREMENT FOR THOSE SEEKING PUBLIC ASSISTANCE?

Issue Since 1996, many families have relied on a government assistance program with training and work requirements—TANF (Temporary Assistance for Needy Families). Many have touted this program with its work requirement as successful since the number of assistance recipients has dropped. Given this apparent success, should we place even more demands on those seeking public assistance by instituting a stronger work requirement?

Yes We should place more demands on those seeking public assistance. Certainly we have an obligation to those around us who are in need, but at the same time, we are not doing either taxpayers or those receiving assistance a favor by sending the message that public support will always be there for the asking.

Concern is often expressed about creating a permanent underclass of citizens who spend their lives in a culture of poverty with no serious expectation, or attempt, to raise themselves out of poverty. The necessity to work might urge public assistance recipients to attend school and training and to take advantage of other opportunities to improve their economic status.

Responsibility is something we learn, and if the assurance that public assistance will always be available dulls people's sense of responsibility and makes them dependent on others for their day-to-day maintenance, then public assistance is not serving its intended purpose. And, there is a sense of satisfaction from work that people receive: It can be a very positive experience.

No We should not place any more demands on those seeking public assistance. As a society, without a clear picture of how many people really are in a position to work, we could make some serious mistakes by making assistance more difficult to obtain and instituting a stronger work requirement.

By acting on a belief that all adults should work, we neglect to acknowledge the difficult positions of caring for a chronically ill child or of the person with poor health or limited talent, or mental illness.

We must also acknowledge the costs of working. In addition to clothing, transportation costs may be prohibitive, especially if public transportation is not accessible. The cost of a car, insurance, maintenance, and gas may be impossible to pay. Then there is child care, which may not be available or may be too costly. It is possible that the costs of working may be greater than the salary of a low-income earner.

Finally, are the restrictions imposed because of concern that all adults should engage in productive work, or is this group a good target for spending cuts because it is significantly underrepresented in the political process?

if they made payments into the system, or a low income could entitle a household to food stamps.

Many government programs, such as Social Security or unemployment compensation, are closed to those who have no regular employment. As a result, some government benefits may not be available to poverty-level families. In addition, many of the homeless in the United States receive no government aid because they do not qualify for specific programs, have no address, or do not sign up for benefits.

Welfare reform has occurred with several aid programs. The maximum time for receipt of certain kinds of aid is limited, and there is a work requirement to qualify for some types of aid. Welfare reform brings into focus a controversy that has simmered for years: Should there be a limit to how much aid is given to the out-of-work poor? Two opposing views on this question are presented in Up for Debate, "Should There Be a Work Requirement For Those Seeking Public Assistance?"

Summary

1. The prices of land, labor, capital, and entrepreneurship are determined basically by the forces of supply and demand. Businesses, governments, and nonprofits are the primary buyers, and their demands for labor and all other inputs are derived from the demands for the goods or services the inputs produce.

2. A demand curve for labor is downward sloping because of diminishing marginal productivity (the Law of Diminishing Returns) and the need to lower output prices to increase sales in all but purely competitive markets (the Law of Demand). A buyer's labor demand curve is based on the marginal revenue product of its labor. A market demand curve for labor is the sum of the labor demand curves of all individual buyers in the market.

3. A market supply curve of labor is upward sloping, indicating a direct relationship between the wage rate and the amount of labor offered in the market. The supply of labor is affected by the wage rate and by other factors, such as job satisfaction and locational preference.

4. A change in labor demand or supply, shown by a shift of the demand or supply curve to the right or left, results from changes in nonwage factors, such as the prices of substitute inputs, technology, and future job prospects. A change in the quantity of labor demanded or supplied results from a change in the wage rate.

5. The simple supply and demand approach to a market for labor can be modified to account for certain real-world considerations. Wage rigidities, legislation, and unequal bargaining power all influence the determination of wages.

6. A labor union is a workers' organization that bargains in its members' behalf with management on matters such as wages, fringe benefits, and job security. A craft union represents workers who have a particular skill; an industrial union represents workers who perform different jobs in a particular industry.

7. The process through which union contracts are negotiated is called collective bargaining. Two important laws affect collective bargaining: the National Labor Relations Act (Wagner Act) of 1935, which is basically supportive of unionism, and the Labor Management Relations Act (Taft–Hartley Act) of 1947, which is a limiting force on unionism.

8. Income distribution refers to how income is divided among the members of society. In the United States, households with the lowest incomes receive less than a proportional share of the total, while those with the highest incomes receive more. There are several explanations for this income distribution pattern.

9. The U.S. government has created an official measure of poverty in the United States based on annual money income levels, which vary according to the size of the family. Many of the poor in the United States are children or in a household headed by a woman.

Key Terms and Concepts

Wage
Derived demand
Law of Diminishing Returns
Marginal product
Marginal revenue product
Demand curve for labor
Supply curve of labor
Change in labor demand or supply
Change in the quantity of labor demanded or supplied
Minimum wage law
Labor union
Craft union

Industrial union
Collective bargaining
Strike
National Labor Relations Act (Wagner Act)
National Labor Relations Board (NLRB)
Taft–Hartley Act
Right to work laws
Distribution of income
Human capital investments
Discrimination
Poverty level

Review Questions

1. What would be the effect of each of the following on Company X's demand for labor? (Remember the distinction between a change in demand and a change in quantity demanded.)
   a. An increase in the price of Company X's major competitor's product
   b. A decrease in the price of an input that can be substituted for Company X's workforce
   c. A decrease in the number of buyers in Company X's product market
   d. A decrease in the price of Company X's product
   e. An increase in the wage paid to Company X's workers

2. Explain fully how the Law of Diminishing Returns and the Law of Demand cause a demand curve for labor to be downward sloping.

3. Given the following table for a hypothetical company, fill in the columns for Total Revenue and Marginal Revenue Product. Based on this information, complete the company's demand schedule for labor and illustrate the schedule in the accompanying graph that follows.

Units of Labor	Total Product	Price per Unit	Total Revenue	Marginal Revenue Product
0	0	$13	$_____	
				$_____
1	100	12	_____	
				_____
2	170	11	_____	
				_____
3	230	10	_____	
				_____
4	280	9	_____	
				_____
5	320	8	_____	
				_____
6	350	7	_____	

Wages	Quantity of Labor Demanded
$_____	1
_____	2
_____	3
_____	4
_____	5
_____	6

4. Explain how wage rigidities, the minimum wage law, and unequal bargaining power modify the basic labor supply and demand model.

5. What is the difference between a craft union and an industrial union? How can a craft union keep its members' wages high?

6. What was the intent of the National Labor Relations Act and the Taft–Hartley Act? Generally, what is the impact of each act on collective bargaining and organized labor in the United States?

7. What is meant by the expression income distribution? What are some of the explanations as to why incomes are unequally distributed?

8. What groups in society are most likely to be included among the poor, and why is there controversy over the official definition of the poverty levels?

Discussion Questions

1. Match each occupation with what you think is the correct salary, and explain why you think each match is correct. Salaries are averages for 2013. (Answers and source are on page 412.)

Occupation		Salary
1. Air traffic controller	_____ a.	$ 18,870
2. Chemical engineer	_____ b.	$ 38,040
3. Commercial airline pilot	_____ c.	$ 41,800
4. Computer programmer	_____ d.	$ 80,800
5. Court judge	_____ e.	$ 80,930
6. Fast-food cook	_____ f.	$ 82,180
7. Petroleum engineer	_____ g.	$ 96,140
8. Physical therapist	_____ h.	$104,340
9. Preschool teacher	_____ i.	$105,380
10. Radio and television announcer	_____ j.	$118,650
11. Surgeon	_____ k.	$149,180
12. Veterinarian	_____ l.	$233,150

2. Assume that the leaders of a local union seek your advice on actions that could be taken to stem the decline of unionism in the United States. What would you suggest to reverse this trend? Do you think that the labor movement will ever return to the status and strength it had during its peak years?

3. Two laws that affect the operations of labor markets are the minimum wage law and the right to work law. Who benefits and who loses from each of these laws?

4. Sometimes a business makes investments in machinery and equipment, and those investments do not pay off—the business does not recover its costs plus something more. Is it possible for an individual to make a human capital investment that does not pay off? In making an informed human capital decision on, say, a college major, what sorts of information would you want to know and why?

5. You have a friend who argues that poverty is really not a problem in this country because the poor are better off than millions of people in other parts of the world. Evaluate this position.

6. There is much criticism that the poverty levels are not an accurate method for determining who is poor in the United States. Do you think these levels are too high or too low? How would you redefine poverty for statistical purposes?

7. What are the eligibility requirements in your state for a family to receive TANF (Temporary Assistance for Needy Families)? What are the requirements to receive food stamps? What is the monthly TANF benefit? What is the monthly allotment of food stamps? If the qualifications for these two programs are different, explain how and why.

Critical Thinking Case 15

INCOME DISTRIBUTION: ARE THE SHARES OF THE PIE FAIR?

Critical Thinking Skills

Weighing arguments in support of different sides of an issue

Tying philosophy and values to positions on an issue

Economic Concepts

Distribution of income

Equity

The data in Table 15.4, which shows the distribution of income among household quintile groups, provides a basis for serious thought and conversation. The table is simple and straightforward: It shows that over 50 percent of income goes to the highest income earners, while 3.2 percent goes to the lowest. Put in plain language, about half the income pie goes to 20 percent of households, and the other half of the pie is shared by about 80 percent of households.

As noted in the text, journalists and others who follow income distribution numbers watch these data closely because of the trend in changes, as well as the social and economic implications, of the numbers.

And, the trend has been a general move toward "the rich getting richer" and the "poor getting poorer."

You might want to share this table with your family and friends and provoke some conversation around the data. Here are some questions to guide that discussion.

Questions

1. Is this income distribution pattern "okay"? Is the trend toward richer and poorer "okay"? How do these data fit with the basic philosophy of a market economy where people are rewarded for their contributions to production?

2. What, if any, are the social, economic, cultural, and political implications for an economy that moves in this direction from a more even distribution of income?

3. For people who want to alter the income distribution pattern, what policy recommendations might they make to do so? Might they support any of the following?

- Raise taxes on the highest income earners.
- Raise the minimum wage to a higher level.
- Increase public assistance to provide every person with a minimum base amount of income on which to live.
- Cap salaries and earnings at $1 million.
- Provide free tuition to guarantee that every person can attend college. (Remember: Higher incomes are associated with higher levels of education.)

Answers and Source for Discussion Question 1
Answers: 1. j, 2. h, 3. d, 4. e, 5. i, 6. a, 7. k, 8. f, 9. b, 10. c, 11. l, 12. g

Source: U.S. Department of Labor, Bureau of Labor Statistics, *Occupational Employment and Wages*, May 2013, www.bls.gov.

International Trade

CHAPTER OBJECTIVES

Present an overview of U.S. international trade by highlighting major U.S. exports and imports as well as major U.S. trading partners.

Explain the principle of comparative advantage.

Discuss free trade and protectionism and explore some arguments in their favor.

Examine possible trade policies and some key trade agreements.

Economic activity is highly globalized. In today's world, it is not unusual to hop a plane to do business in Singapore; for a middle-level corporate manager to work closely with subsidiaries around the world; or to furnish our homes with rugs, art, and furniture from Africa, South America, or Asia. One way to quickly see how globalized economic activity has become is to open your closet and scan the labels on your clothes showing where they were manufactured.

International economics is about the movement of goods and services as well as financial transactions among nations. Medical and disaster aid, military activity, overseas investments, and the import and export of goods such as oil, wine, grain, and automobiles are all relevant to international economics.

This chapter introduces some important topics that relate to international trade or the movement of goods and services between nations. It begins with an overview of U.S. international trade, including major traded products and important trading partners. Comparative advantage, a basic theory that underlies international trade, the great debate in international economics over free trade versus protectionism, trade policies for stimulating exports, and important agreements affecting trade among nations are then covered. Chapter 17 deals with the financial aspects of international economics.

Trade and financial relationships among nations are growing in importance as the world becomes more globally connected or "flatter." These relationships affect jobs available to us, our national security, international relations, and social understanding.

Today we are much more aware of the conditions in which people in many countries work, the use of child labor, and the lack of access to safe drinking water in some parts of the world.

AN OVERVIEW OF U.S. INTERNATIONAL TRADE

International Trade

The buying and selling of goods and services among different countries.

An important aspect of international economics is **international trade**: the buying and selling of goods and services among different countries. International trade affects the availability of goods and services as well as the levels of production, employment, and prices in the trading countries. Sales in overseas markets can increase employment among a nation's workers. But international trade can also bring in strong foreign competitors and lead to a drop in sales for a nation's businesses, which in turn could lower production and employment for the nation. Also, the presence of foreign goods in a market increases competition, which in turn influences product prices. And for a country that is dependent on a major foreign product, increases in the price of that product can influence the country's inflation rate.

The Size and Composition of U.S. Trade

Exports

Goods and services that are sold abroad.

Imports

Goods and services purchased from abroad.

The Size of U.S. Trade   The importance of international trade to the U.S. economy is illustrated in Table 16.1, which lists data on **exports** and **imports** of goods and services for selected years. The middle columns, Exports and Imports, show that in recent years, U.S. transactions have resulted in the movement of over $2 trillion in goods and services annually. For example, in 2014 exports and imports amounted to approximately $2.3 and $2.9 trillion, respectively. Notice also that, not surprisingly, the dollar values of exports and imports have grown over the years.

TABLE 16.1					
U.S. Exports and Imports of Goods and Services (Billions of Dollars)					

Both the dollar amount of exports and imports, and exports and imports as a percentage of GDP, have increased over the years.

Year	Gross Domestic Product	Exports	Imports	Exports as a Percentage of GDP	Imports as a Percentage of GDP
1970	$1,038.3	$59.7	$55.8	5.7%	5.4%
1975	1,637.7	138.7	122.7	8.5	7.5
1980	2,788.1	280.8	293.8	10.1	10.5
1985	4,217.5	302.0	417.2	7.2	9.9
1990	5,800.5	552.1	629.7	9.5	10.9
1995	7,414.7	811.9	902.6	10.9	12.2
2000	10,284.8	1,096.8	1,472.6	10.7	14.3
2005	13,093.7	1,308.9	2,030.1	10.0	15.5
2010	14,964.4	1,852.3	2,365.1	12.4	15.8
2014	17,420.7	2,334.2	2,872.3	13.4	16.5

Source: *Economic Report of the President* (Washington, DC: U.S. Government Printing Office), 2012: data from 1970–1995; 2015: data from 2000–2014; Tables B-1, B-2. The figures for 2014 are preliminary.

The last two columns of Table 16.1 list exports and imports of goods and services as percentages of gross domestic product (GDP) for each of the selected years. Notice that both exports and imports have generally grown in relative importance when compared to GDP. In 1970, exports were 5.7 percent and imports were 5.4 percent of GDP. By 2014 exports were 13.4 percent of GDP and imports were 16.5 percent. One can conclude from Table 16.1 that foreign trade has become an increasingly important part of the U.S. economy over the years. Notice also the increasing difference between exports and imports as a percentage of GDP.

The Composition of U.S. Trade   What types of goods and services does the United States export and import? Table 16.2 shows the distribution of U.S. merchandise exports and imports by broad product group for selected years. A broad product group is composed of several related types of goods. For example, the foods, feeds, and beverages group includes grains, meat products, vegetables, fish, and wine.[1]

The upper half of the table shows that the most important class of exports has been capital goods, followed by industrial supplies and materials. The capital goods category includes products ranging from oil drilling and metalworking machinery to hospital equipment and civilian aircraft. Industrial supplies and materials include such things as iron and steel products, fuels and petroleum products, and building materials.[2]

TABLE 16.2	*Percentage Distribution of U.S. Merchandise Exports and Imports by Broad Product Categories*

U.S. exporting and importing activity primarily involves capital goods and industrial supplies and materials.

Exports				
Product Group	**1995**	**2005**	**2010**	**2013**
Foods, feeds, and beverages	8.6%	6.5%	8.4%	8.7%
Industrial supplies and materials	25.0	25.9	30.6	31.6
Capital goods, except automotive	39.8	39.8	34.9	34.3
Automotive vehicles, parts, and engines	10.6	11.0	8.8	9.8
Nonfood consumer goods, except automotive	11.0	12.8	13.0	12.1
Other	5.0	4.0	4.3	3.5

Imports				
Product Group	**1995**	**2005**	**2010**	**2013**
Foods, feeds, and beverages	4.5%	4.1%	4.8%	5.1%
Industrial supplies and materials	24.5	31.3	31.5	30.2
Capital goods, except automotive	29.8	22.7	23.5	24.5
Automotive vehicles, parts, and engines	16.7	14.3	11.8	13.6
Nonfood consumer goods, except automotive	21.5	24.3	25.3	23.5
Other	3.0	3.3	3.1	3.2

Sources: *Economic Report of the President* (Washington, DC: U.S. Government Printing Office, 2012), p. 440, data for 1995–2010; ProQuest Statistical Abstract of the U.S. 2015 Online Edition, Table 1300, data for 2013.

[1] U.S. Census Bureau, U.S. Bureau of Economic Analysis, *News*, January 12, 2006, p. 10.
[2] Ibid., pp. 10–11.

Imports by broad product group are shown in the lower half of Table 16.2. The table shows that three import categories are significant: capital goods, industrial supplies, and nonfood consumer goods. More specific significant imports to the United States in recent years have been electrical machinery, televisions and related electronics, data equipment, crude oil, vehicles, chemicals, and clothing.[3] Notice that capital goods and industrial supplies and materials are important both as exports and imports. Why do you think this is the case?

The Geographic Distribution of U.S. Trade The percentages of U.S. exports to and imports from major U.S. trading partners in 2014 are given in Table 16.3. The majority of U.S. trade is with developed nations in North America, Europe, and Asia, although trade with less developed nations has grown in relative importance over the years.

In terms of specific countries, Canada, Mexico, China, and Japan are the four most important trading partners of the United States. However, several of the other countries listed in the table are part of the European Union or EU. The 27 member countries of the EU are joined into a single market area and, in many ways, act like a single trading partner. The United Kingdom, Germany, France, Italy, Netherlands,

---

TABLE 16.3   *Fifteen Largest U. S. Export and Import Trading Partners In 2014*

Most of the largest trading partners with the United States are developed nations in North America, Europe, and Asia.

Exports		Imports	
Country	**Percent of Total Exports**	**Country**	**Percent of Total Imports**
Canada	19.3%	China	19.6%
Mexico	14.9	Canada	14.8
China	7.4	Mexico	12.6
Japan	4.1	Japan	5.7
United Kingdom	3.3	Germany	5.2
Germany	3.1	South Korea	2.9
South Korea	2.7	United Kingdom	2.3
Brazil	2.7	Saudi Arabia	2.1
Netherlands	2.7	France	2.0
Hong Kong	2.5	India	2.0
Belgium	2.2	Italy	1.8
France	1.9	Taiwan	1.7
Singapore	1.9	Ireland	1.4
Australia	1.7	Venezuela	1.4
Taiwan	1.6	Switzerland	1.3
Total, Top 15 Partners	72.1%	Total, Top 15 Partners	76.8%

Source: U.S. Census Bureau, "Top Trading Partners—October 2014," http://www.census.gov/foreign-trade/statistics.

---

[3] U.S. Bureau of the Census, *Statistical Abstract of the United States*: 2012, 131st ed. (Washington, DC: U.S. Government Printing Office, 2011), p. 812.

APPLICATION 16.1

A SAD STORY

More and more, goods and services sold by U.S. companies are produced outside of the United States: from Nike shoes produced in factories around the world to help with your computer problems from a technician in India. But as foreign-produced goods account for more of our purchases, there is concern over the working conditions endured by many of those producing these goods. When reading about these conditions, one frequently comes across terms such as sweatshop and human trafficking.

There have been many accusations of child labor and deplorable working conditions, especially in factories and mills producing footwear and apparel. And, many U.S. companies, including Apple and Walmart, have faced media coverage of alleged violations with products they have sold.

In 2007, an accusation against the retailer Gap brought special attention to the child labor problem and made many U.S. consumers aware of child labor used in the production of clothing. In this case, Gap found that one of its products—some hand-stitched blouses—was being sewn by child labor in a New Delhi, India, sweatshop with squalid conditions. A British newspaper reported that some of the children were as young as 10, worked for 16 hours a day, and were punished with hits from a rubber pipe or by having oily rags stuffed in their mouths.

One young boy said, "I was bought from my parents' village in [the northern state of] Bihar and taken to New Delhi by train. The men came looking for us in July. They had loudspeakers in the back of a car and told my parents that if they sent me to work in the city, they won't have to work in the farms. My father was paid a fee for me, and I was brought down with 40 other children."

U.S. companies that subcontract work to foreign vendors have tried to monitor operations. In this case, the work was further subcontracted in violation of Gap's policies.

Gap was obviously concerned, and its response to this situation was immediate. It promised that none of the garments would ever be sold, ensured that the children were cared for and reunited with their families, reduced the contract of the vendor responsible for the subcontract, made a grant toward improving working conditions in India, and partnered with other organizations to help monitor the kind of work done in more informal settings, such as beadwork.

In its Social & Environmental Responsibility Report 2011/2012, Gap has reiterated its work to combat child labor. "Child labor is an unacceptable practice that violates our Code of Vendor Conduct and Human Rights Policy. However, taking a stand on child labor is the easier part of the equation. The more difficult part is creating solutions that not only remediate occurrences, but also help address their underlying causes."

Sources: Gap Inc., Update: Combating Child Labor in the Garment Industry, June 12, 2008, www.Gapinc.com; "Gap: Report of Kids' Sweatshop 'Deeply Disturbing'," October 29, 2007, http://www.cnn.com/2007/ WORLD/asiapcf/10/29/gap.labor/index.html; "The Gap Caps Work with Child Labor Vendor," November, 15, 2007, http://www.cbsnews.com/stories/2007/11/15/business/main3505020.shtml?source=RSSattr . . . ; "The Gap Falls Into Child Labor Controversy," October, 29, 2007, http://www.cbsnews.com; Gap Inc., Social & Environmental Responsibility Report 2011/2012, www.gapinc.com.

Ireland, and Belgium—all listed on the table—are part of the EU. As a unit, the EU is a leading exporter and importer.[4]

As the globalization of trade expands, more buyers of shoes, shirts, electronics, pharmaceutical drugs, vitamins, food, and other products are becoming aware of another side of importing low-cost goods to the United States. It has become clear that safety, quality, and labor standards adopted by the United States are not being applied in many cases by foreign producers. In recent years, we have been faced with a pet food scare due to contaminants in ingredients, lead in toys and other consumer products, impurities in drugs, and the use of child labor in many of the factories that produce these cheap goods. Application 16.1, "A Sad Story," deals with one case where a retailer, Gap, discovered the use of child labor in a factory subcontracted through one of its vendors.

---

[4] The 27 member countries of the EU are Austria, Belgium, Bulgaria, Cyprus, the Czech Republic, Denmark, Estonia, Finland, France, Germany, Greece, Hungary, Ireland, Italy, Latvia, Lithuania, Luxembourg, Malta, Netherlands, Poland, Portugal, Romania, Slovakia, Slovenia, Spain, Sweden, and the United Kingdom. In 1992, 12 of these countries formed the European Community or EC. The name was later changed to the European Union. See http://www.state.gov/p/eur/rt/eu/c12191.htm.

COMPARATIVE ADVANTAGE AND INTERNATIONAL TRADE

Scarcity and Specialization

As we have seen from the very beginning, the study of economics is rooted in scarcity: The resources necessary to produce goods and services are scarce relative to the material wants and needs those goods and services satisfy. One way to lessen the scarcity problem is through increases in production gained by specialization.

Specialization
Productive resources concentrate on a narrow range of tasks or the production of a limited variety of goods and services.

Specialization occurs when productive resources concentrate on a narrow range of tasks or on the production of a limited variety of goods and services. The concept applies to all factors of production but is most often associated with individuals and locations. For example, a doctor may specialize in cardiovascular surgery, a student may select economics as his or her major, and northern California is known for its wine production.

Specialization permits greater levels of production than would be attained without it. By concentrating on one productive activity, a resource can be used more efficiently—and greater efficiency results in greater output without raising costs. Specialization, however, depends on the ability to sell what one produces and buy what one needs from someone else or on the ability to trade. Thus, access to appropriate markets where trade can take place is a prerequisite to specialization.

Specialization occurs on an international level when countries concentrate their productive efforts on the goods and services they are best at producing and trade for the goods and services that are most costly to produce. A country that has a relatively inexpensive labor force might specialize in producing goods requiring substantial labor inputs, a country with good agricultural resources might concentrate on growing crops or on livestock, and a country possessing technologically advanced equipment and production methods might use these to its benefit. When each country concentrates on what it does more efficiently than other countries, international specialization increases total production and lessens the scarcity problem on a global level.

The Principle of Comparative Advantage

Comparative Advantage
One country has a lower opportunity cost when producing a good or service than does another country.

International trade can lessen the scarcity problem if each country produces and trades on the basis of its comparative advantage. **Comparative advantage** is practiced when a country produces those goods and services for which it has a cost advantage in comparison to other countries and trades for what it is less adept at producing. If countries produce and trade on the basis of their comparative advantages, the world will have more goods and services than it otherwise would. In essence, the principle of comparative advantage is a restatement of the benefits of international specialization.

A country has a comparative advantage in the production of a good or service when the opportunity cost of producing that item is less in that country than in another country. Fewer goods or services are given up to produce a unit of a particular item in the country with the comparative advantage than in another country.

To illustrate how comparative advantage works and how it results in overall gains in output, let us examine a simple hypothetical production and trade relationship between the United States and Japan.

Assume that with 1 unit of resources (where 1 unit is equal to a defined combination of land, labor, capital, and entrepreneurship), the United States can produce either 10 tons of corn or 1 high-definition television set (HDTV). Assume further that with 1 unit of resources, Japan can produce either 1 ton of corn or 10 high-definition television sets. Table 16.4 illustrates these production possibilities.

TABLE 16.4	*Production Possibilities from 1 Unit of Resources*

The United States and Japan have a choice of producing either corn or high-definition television sets when employing 1 unit of resources.

Country	Production Possibilities
United States	10 tons of corn or 1 HDTV
Japan	1 ton of corn or 10 HDTVs

The comparative advantage of each country in this example is obvious: The United States has the advantage in corn, and Japan in television sets. This can be verified by comparing the opportunity costs in each country.

The opportunity cost (measured in forgone television sets) of producing 10 tons of corn in the United States is just 1 television set, while the opportunity cost of producing 10 tons of corn in Japan is 100 television sets. This gives the United States the comparative advantage in corn because its opportunity cost of producing corn is lower. The opportunity cost of producing 1 television set in the United States is 10 tons of corn, whereas in Japan producing 1 television set would mean giving up only one-tenth of a ton of corn. The opportunity cost of producing a television set is lower in Japan, giving Japan the comparative advantage in television sets.

Gains from Specialization and Trade   Let us continue the corn and television example to illustrate why the world would be better off in terms of the amounts of goods and services produced if comparative advantage and trade were exercised. Assume now that the United States has 2 units of resources to employ and uses 1 unit for the production of corn and 1 unit for the production of television sets. In this case, the United States will produce 10 tons of corn and 1 television set. Assume further that Japan also has 2 units of resources to employ and also uses 1 unit for the production of corn and 1 unit for television sets. In this case, Japan will produce 1 ton of corn and 10 television sets. With resources employed in this way, total production of these items by these two countries is 11 tons of corn and 11 television sets. This is shown in Table 16.5.

Now assume that Japan and the United States each decides to devote its productive resources to the good in which it has the comparative advantage and to engage in international trade. The United States will now devote its 2 units of resources to corn production, resulting in 20 tons of corn instead of 10 tons of corn and 1 television set. With Japan's 2 units of resources, it will now produce 20 television sets instead of 10 television sets and 1 ton of corn. Table 16.6 summarizes the resulting production when each country specializes its production based on its comparative advantage.

TABLE 16.5	*Production from 2 Units of Resources per Country without Specialization*

When the United States and Japan both produce corn and high-definition television sets with 2 units of resources each, 11 tons of corn and 11 television sets can be produced.

Item	Amount of Production
Corn	10 tons (U.S.) + 1 ton (Japan) = 11 tons total production
Television sets	1 HDTV (U.S.) + 10 HDTVs (Japan) = 11 HDTVs total production

TABLE 16.6	*Production from 2 Units of Resources per Country with Specialization*

When countries devote their resources to producing goods in which they have a comparative advantage, the total production of these goods increases.

Item	Amount of Production
Corn	20 tons (U.S.) + 0 ton (Japan) = 20 tons total production
Television sets	0 HDTVs (U.S.) + 20 HDTVs (Japan) = 20 HDTVs total production

The increased total production registered in Table 16.6 (as compared to the numbers in Table 16.5) demonstrates the benefits of specialization and trade. Without international specialization, a total of 11 tons of corn and 11 television sets can be produced by both countries together. With production based on comparative advantage, Japan and the United States can together produce a total of 20 tons of corn and 20 television sets using the same amount of resources. Clearly, the scarcity problem can be lessened through the exercise of comparative advantage and trade.

Does the principle of comparative advantage work in the real world? How closely is it followed? In order to fully exercise comparative advantage and reap its benefits, an environment of free trade is necessary. **Free trade** occurs when goods and services can be bought and sold by anyone in any country with no restrictions. Everyone is free to choose with whom he or she deals, regardless of location, and there are no barriers to trade. Import taxes are not imposed to artificially raise prices and discourage purchases of foreign-made goods, and limits are not set on the amounts that can be bought and sold. This free flow of trade permits specialization to work to its fullest. You can check your grasp of the material in this section by answering the questions in Test Your Understanding, "Comparative Advantage."

Free Trade
Goods and services can be exported and imported by anyone in any country with no restrictions.

FREE TRADE AND PROTECTIONISM

In practice, countries often impose restrictions that impede the international flow of goods and services. Such policies, despite the fact that they may reduce a country's ability to fully exploit its various comparative advantages, are generally justified on the grounds that they are in the best interest of the nation that is imposing them.

The philosophy that it is in a country's best interest to restrict free trade is known as **protectionism**. According to the protectionist viewpoint, unrestricted importing and/or exporting may lead to economic and noneconomic consequences injurious to the economy as a whole, to certain groups within the economy such as workers in particular industries, and/or to national security. Because of these potentially adverse effects, protectionists argue for restrictions on international trade.

Protectionism
The philosophy that it is in the best interest of a country to restrict free trade.

Protectionist policies can be employed in varying degrees: A nation may choose to have detailed regulations or loose restrictions. Also, a nation may alter the degree to which it relies on protectionist policies as economic and noneconomic conditions change.

The merits of free trade and protectionism have been debated for hundreds of years. (See the Critical Thinking Case at the end of this chapter, "A Petition (By Frederic Bastiat, 1801–1850)," which excerpts a satirical protectionist plea from the early 1800s.) In light of this debate, it is useful to know some arguments on both sides of the issue in order to better form your own opinions. But before introducing the cases for free

COMPARATIVE ADVANTAGE

1. Assume that Canada can produce 8 tons of wheat or 4 tons of soybeans with 1 unit of resources and that Brazil can produce 4 tons of wheat or 8 tons of soybeans with 1 unit of resources.
    a. The opportunity cost to Canada of producing 1 ton of wheat is _____ tons of soybeans, and the opportunity cost to Brazil of producing 1 ton of wheat is _____ tons of soybeans. The country with the comparative advantage in wheat is _____.
    b. The opportunity cost to Canada of producing 1 ton of soybeans is _____ tons of wheat, and the opportunity cost to Brazil of producing 1 ton of soybeans is _____ tons of wheat. The country with the comparative advantage in soybeans is _____.
    c. If Canada and Brazil each has 2 units of resources and each uses 1 unit for the production of wheat and the other for the production of soybeans, together they will produce _____ tons of wheat and _____ tons of soybeans.
    d. If each country uses its 2 units of resources to produce the crop in which it has the comparative advantage, Canada will produce _____ tons of _____ and Brazil will produce _____ tons of _____.
    e. If, for political or other reasons, each country uses its 2 units of resources to produce the crop in which it does *not* have the comparative advantage, together they will produce _____ tons of wheat and _____ tons of soybeans.

2. Assume that Mexico can produce 500 lamps or 100 gallons of gasoline with 1 unit of resources and that Venezuela can produce 25 lamps or 100 gallons of gasoline with 1 unit of resources.
    a. The opportunity cost to Mexico of producing 1 lamp is _____ gallons of gasoline, and the opportunity cost to Venezuela of producing 1 lamp is _____ gallons of gasoline. The country with the comparative advantage in lamps is _____.
    b. The opportunity cost to Mexico of producing 1 gallon of gasoline is _____ lamps, and the opportunity cost to Venezuela of producing 1 gallon of gasoline is _____ lamps. The country with the comparative advantage in gasoline is _____.
    c. If Mexico and Venezuela each has 2 units of resources, and each uses 1 unit for the production of lamps and the other for the production of gasoline, together they will produce _____ lamps and _____ gallons of gasoline.
    d. If each country uses its 2 units of resources to produce the good in which it has the comparative advantage, Mexico will produce _____ (of) _____ and Venezuela will produce _____ (of) _____.
    e. If, for political or other reasons, each country uses its 2 units of resources to produce the good in which it does *not* have the comparative advantage, together they will produce _____ lamps and _____ gallons of gasoline.

Answers can be found at the back of the book.

trade and for protectionism, we will examine the different types of trade-restricting policies that a country may employ.

Trade-Restricting Policies

Three basic policies have traditionally been used to restrict trade: tariffs, quotas, and embargoes. In addition to these, some countries have developed more subtle measures to discourage trade, such as setting very high product standards or an overwhelming number of bureaucratic steps to import a product.

Tariff
A tax on an import.

A **tariff** is a tax placed on an import. Tariffs have the effect of raising import prices to domestic buyers, thereby making foreign goods less attractive. This reduces the quantities of imports demanded and makes it easier for domestic producers to sell their own products.

Examples of tariffs on goods entering the United States are given in Table 16.7. The columns to the right classify nations into three categories for tariff purposes. The

TABLE 16.7   *Tariffs for Selected Goods*

Tariffs, which raise the prices of imported goods to domestic buyers, can be expressed in dollar terms or as a percentage of the value of the imported good.

	Tariff		
Item	General	Special	Designated Countries
Smoked salmon	5.0% of value	Free	25.0% of value
Cheddar cheese	10.0% of value	Free	35.0% of value
Oranges	$0.019 per kilo	Free	$0.025 per kilo
Men's wool suits	7.5% of value	Free	65.0% of value
Women's wool dresses	7.20% of value	Free	90.0% of value
Footwear incorporating protective metal toecaps	37.5% of value	Free	75.0% of value
Drums	4.8% of value	Free	40.0% of value
Pistols designed to fire only blank ammunition	4.2% of value	Free	105.0% of value
Cotton bedspreads	12.0% of value	Free	90.0% of value

Source: U.S. International Trade Commission, *Harmonized Tariff Schedule of the United States*, 2014 (Washington, DC: U.S. Government Printing Office, 2014), pp. 3–23, 4–37, 8–6, 62–16, 62–42, 63–14, 64–3, 92–3, 93–3; www.usitc.gov.

column headed General is for nations whose products are not imported under any preferential tariff treatment. Countries such as England, France, and Japan fall into this category. The column headed Special is for nations whose products are imported at reduced tariff rates under special programs, and the rates differ with each program. For example, products from Mexico are imported under the North American Free Trade Agreement (NAFTA). Other examples of special programs are the Automotive Products Trade Act and the Generalized System of Preferences, which allow developing nations such as Belize and Nepal to sell to the United States at reduced tariff rates or tariff-free. Finally, the column headed Designated Countries is for a short list of nations such as Laos and North Korea.[5]

Table 16.7 illustrates that tariffs can be expressed in dollar terms or as a percentage of the value of the imported product and that they differ according to the three country categories. Designated countries pay the highest tariffs, while countries that receive special treatment pay the lowest or, in some cases, no tariff at all.

Quota
A restriction on the quantity of an item that can be imported into a country.

Quotas are restrictions on the quantities of various goods that can be imported into a country. For example, a country may impose a quota allowing only 10 million bushels of wheat to be imported from another country over a one-year period. Once that amount is reached, no more wheat can flow in from the other country for the remainder of the year. A quota, like a tariff, restricts the ability of foreign goods to compete with domestic goods.

[5]U.S. International Trade Commission, *Harmonized Tariff Schedule of the United States* (Washington, DC: U.S. Government Printing Office, 2012), General Notes, pp. GN 3, 6.

Embargo
A ban on trade in a particular commodity or with a particular country.

An **embargo** is an outright ban on trade in a particular commodity or with a particular nation. These embargoes are often imposed for noneconomic reasons such as sanctioning a government. Trade sanctions have been imposed on Libya, North Korea, Iraq, and Sudan.[6]

Free Trade Arguments

Arguments favoring unrestricted international trade center on the ability of free trade to increase economic efficiency, provide a source of competition, and increase the availability of goods while lowering their prices. Free trade benefits the consumer.

Trade, Specialization, and Efficiency   Free trade permits the markets in which goods and services are bought and sold to expand, and the possibility of additional sales from expanded markets makes it feasible for resources to specialize in narrower ranges of tasks. In turn, this specialization allows resources to be used more efficiently than would otherwise be the case.

By using resources more efficiently, more goods and services can be produced, lessening the scarcity problem. This was illustrated earlier in the corn and television set example used to explain the principle of comparative advantage.

Increased Competition, Availability of Goods, and Lower Prices   Another argument in favor of free trade is that it increases competition in markets. Competition leads to benefits for consumers: There are larger quantities of goods from which to choose, and prices tend to be lower.

Recall the material in Chapter 3 that deals with supply and demand. An increase in supply will lower prices in a competitive market. And, in Chapter 13 we learned that as the number of sellers increases in a market, the ability of an individual firm to exercise control over price and output decreases, and price moves more toward cost. Thus, with foreign competitors in a market, more products are available and domestic sellers are in less of a position to extract excessive profits.

With free trade, the absence of tariffs benefits the consumers by making foreign goods available at lower prices. In addition, removing quotas has the obvious effect of increasing the amounts of goods available for sale.

Protectionist Arguments

The main thrust of the **protectionist arguments** is that, for either economic or noneconomic reasons, it is in the best interest of a nation to place restrictions on imports. The major protectionist arguments center on protection of industries and employment, diversification, and national security.

Infant Industry
An industry in the early stage of its development.

Protection of Infant Industries and Domestic Employment and Output   An **infant industry** is one in the early stage of its development. Technology, new resources, or innovations, for example, can spawn an industry new to an economy. In the early stages of a new industry, strong competitive pressures from established foreign producers might destroy a prospect for growth. Protectionists argue that it is appropriate to impose trade restrictions to allow the newly forming domestic industry to establish itself.

Protectionists also argue that it is appropriate to protect a domestic industry when the availability of foreign goods would lead to lower domestic output and higher

[6]U.S. State Department, "Country Policies and Embargoes," www.pmddtc.state.gov, 07/07/15.

domestic unemployment. In this case, the protectionist point of view is to impose trade restrictions that would make it difficult, or impossible, for foreign goods to compete. Support for this argument frequently comes from both manufacturers and labor organizations in specific industries facing strong foreign competition.

Diversification   The protectionist argument for diversification is based on the potential risks from developing a dependency on foreign-produced goods rather than home-produced goods because changes in the prices or availabilities of those foreign goods could lead to serious economic disruptions at home. A striking example of this problem is the continuing concern over the U.S. dependency on foreign oil. Huge price increases from time to time have caused some issues in the economy.

Protectionists argue that a country should not specialize to the point where it develops critical dependencies on foreign products. Instead, domestic production should be diversified so that there are feasible alternatives to foreign-produced goods.

National Security   For a variety of reasons, arguments have been put forward to impose tariffs, quotas, and embargoes in the name of national security. These reasons include the need to develop strong domestic defense-related industries and the need to diversify in anticipation of interruptions of foreign supplies resulting from military or economic aggression or some other type of international hostility.

It is up to you to decide which of these free-trade and protectionist arguments has greater merit than the others. Application 16.2, "Gloria Flunks the Professor," is a classic writing concerning the free-trade and protectionism debate. How many of the arguments that were just introduced can you find? How does the application illustrate that a person's position on this issue can be colored by both philosophical commitment and personal interest?

THE REAL WORLD OF INTERNATIONAL TRADE: POLICIES AND AGREEMENTS

Most countries do not choose a strict free trade or protectionist philosophy and then adhere only to policies aligned with that philosophy. Instead, these two philosophies are the extremes toward which a country may lean. A country may adopt a comprehensive trade policy based on the principles of free trade or protectionism, or it may adopt more liberal terms of trade with some of its favored trading partners and restrict trade with other countries. Recall from Table 16.7 that the United States gives preferential tariff treatment to goods imported from Mexico and other countries with special trade agreements and imposes higher-than-average tariffs on goods coming in from North Korea.

A country's policies concerning international trade tend to shift with changing political and economic conditions. During a recession or economic downswing, a country's mood tends to become protectionist, resulting in a greater tendency to raise tariff barriers than is the case during a period of economic growth. The Smoot–Hawley Tariff, which was passed in 1930 at the beginning of the Great Depression, raised U.S. tariff rates to some of their highest levels.

Trade Subsidy
A government payment to the domestic producer of an exported good.

Instead of restricting trade, a country will sometimes adopt policies, such as **trade subsidies**, to promote the export of a domestically produced good. For example, if the United States decided that it wanted to encourage foreign purchases of its domestically produced pianos, it could offer domestic piano manufacturers a subsidy, or

APPLICATION 16.2

GLORIA FLUNKS THE PROFESSOR

It's not easy to be an economist these days. It used to be enough to have a theory with a good, positive name: like Free Trade. Now people actually expect you to understand the real world. . . .

Take last night. I'm having a quiet drink with Professor Dyzmil. He teaches economics at our local university. In sails Larry [who] announces that he just bought a new Honda—top of the line, all the extras. People around the bar mutter, "Wow," "Great," and so forth. Gloria [the bartender] just keeps pouring drinks.

Finally she says: "I think it's a shame to buy a foreign car when there's so much unemployment in our own auto industry."

"Hey," says Larry, "What am I supposed to buy? . . . Anyway, one car isn't going to make all that much difference to Detroit."

"I know" Gloria sighs, "but it seems like somebody ought to be doing something to protect our people from all these imports."

"Protect *our* people? *Your* people maybe," says Larry. "I think it's awfully nationalistic to worry about protecting American autoworkers. My lifestyle is international. Whoever makes the most interesting, least expensive products gets my business." . . .

["Besides,] protectionism is bad for the economy. Isn't that right, professor?"

"Absolutely," says Dyzmil, solemnly. "Quotas and tariffs and other devices to keep out foreign goods raise domestic prices. As a result, the consumer pays more."

"So what?" says Gloria. "Wouldn't it be worth it if it saved jobs here? . . . "

Seems like a good point, but the professor isn't impressed. "Very superficial analysis," he says sternly. "The real problem is that protecting U.S. industries will make them less competitive. Having to compete with foreign goods keeps you on your toes, makes you more conscious of quality and price, more responsive to the needs of the customer. Protectionism makes an industry lazy and inefficient." . . .

"By that logic," muses Gloria, "the answer to Japanese imports is to open up our markets to even more imports so our industries will be more efficient. That doesn't make sense."

"It's true that the U.S. is already pretty much of an open market," says the professor. "What we need to do is to get other countries to open their economies to free trade."

"Like?"

"Like Japan," the professor replies. "Japan is notoriously protectionist. They have an intricate system of rules and regulations and quotas that keep foreign goods out." . . .

"But if free trade makes a country more competitive and protectionism makes a country less competitive . . . "

"Yes," he nods encouragingly.

"And the Japanese markets are protected and ours are open. . . . Then how come the Japanese are so competitive and we're so uncompetitive?"

"Well . . . uh . . .," stammers Dyzmil, "it's very complicated. For one thing, there are cultural differences. . . . [T]he Japanese work together better. They work more as a unit, as a community. . . ."

"Doesn't sound bad," says Gloria. "Maybe we ought to try some of that here."

"No, my dear," Dyzmil says, shaking his head. "Americans don't like to do things collectively. We thrive on the excitement of competition between individuals."

"Real exciting to be out of work," says Gloria, dryly. "A lot of people *aren't* exactly thriving."

"Not to worry," the professor says. "Our old industries are adjusting. And free trade is helping. . . . Old jobs have to die, Gloria. Just like old people. It's a law of economic nature. Jobs will open up in new industries."

"But aren't imports also taking over the new industries? VCRs are the hottest new item around. I read somewhere that the Japanese made 27 million last year and we made zero."

"Not to worry," Dyzmil assures her. "Even if they do take our manufacturing, Americans excel at services."

"Like laundry?"

"No. Like banking, advertising, computer software."

"But it stands to reason that Japanese businesses will use *Japanese* banks and advertising agencies. So as they expand their industry, they'll expand their services too. If they make the computers, won't they eventually make the software?". . . "Anyway," she continues, "how many laid off autoworkers are going to get a job in a bank or advertising?". . .

I can see that the professor is getting annoyed at having to defend free trade. . . . After all, in the hierarchy of economic principles, free trade ranks above the law of gravity.

"Look, Gloria," says the exasperated scholar, "there are plenty of other places Americans can work. In bars and restaurants, for example. Granted, the jobs pay less.". . .

"Ok," says Gloria suddenly, "You've convinced me, but I don't think you've gone far enough with your free trade idea."

"How's that?"

"Why not extend free trade to economics professors? Maybe the reason that the Japanese economy is better is because Japanese *economists* are better. So if we got rid of tenure in our universities, we might import some Japanese economists who could show us how to create more jobs by working together."

"My dear Gloria," says the stunned professor, . . . "if America exported its economists, who would be left to defend free trade?"

Source: Jeff Faux, "Gloria Flunks the Professor," *Mother Jones* (October, 1985), pp. 50–51, © 1985, Foundation for National Progress.

payment, for each piano sold abroad—which would allow the manufacturers to lower their prices on the pianos and still make a profit. This policy, which might be considered unfair by foreign piano makers, would be useful if the United States wanted to increase its share of the world piano market.

On occasion a country has been accused of **dumping** its products in foreign markets. This occurs when a good is sold in a foreign market below its actual cost or below the price at which it is sold in its own domestic market. Countries pursue this policy to eliminate excess production or to gain a greater share of a foreign market.

In the interdependent world of foreign trade, a change in a country's trade philosophy, tariffs, quotas, embargoes, subsidies, or dumping may cause retaliation by a trading partner. And there is always the danger that changing policies and retaliations will result in a trade war. When a trade war breaks out, the benefits of specialization on an international basis are jeopardized. No one seems to benefit.

Trade Agreements among Nations   Since World War II, world trade has been carried out in a relatively liberal environment, thanks to greater international cooperation to reduce tariffs and the work of organizations that facilitate the trading process. For example, the **International Monetary Fund (IMF)**, which began operations in 1947, provides loans and other financial assistance to nations seeking to improve their competitiveness in world trade. Tariff reductions have occurred in large part as a result of the **General Agreement on Tariffs and Trade (GATT)**, under which countries held their first round of talks in 1947. Since then, there have been several rounds of negotiations, each leading to lower tariff rates.

Three landmark trade agreements were negotiated in the early 1990s. In 1992, 12 Western European nations formally joined together as the European Community, or EC. This alliance now includes 27 members with others seeking admission and is called the **European Union (EU)** which was introduced earlier in the chapter. The goal of the EU is to create a trading area within which no national barriers slow the movement of people, capital, or goods and services. The EU represents a major world trading power: While less than one-half the size of the United States, in 2015 the combined population of its member countries was about 60 percent larger than the population of the United States.[7]

In 1994, the **North American Free Trade Agreement (NAFTA)** was put in place. This trade agreement among the United States, Canada, and Mexico removed many barriers to trade and investment in these three countries. One of the effects of NAFTA has been the establishment of businesses in Mexico along the border with the United States that tend to import inputs from the United States, process them with cheaper labor, and return the finished products to the United States as exports. While there is evidence that the Mexican economy has benefited from this trade agreement, NAFTA continues to be a source of debate over many issues such as labor conditions and rights, the environment, and impacts on labor in the United States.[8]

The third important agreement was the approval in 1993 of the Uruguay Round of GATT negotiations. This treaty reduced tariffs and other trade barriers, involved more than 100 nations, and took years to complete. The trade rules agreed to at the Uruguay Round are implemented by the **World Trade Organization (WTO)**, which was founded in 1995 to take over the responsibilities of GATT.

Dumping
Selling a product in a foreign market below cost or below its price in its own domestic market.

International Monetary Fund (IMF)
An international organization that provides loans and other financial assistance to countries.

General Agreement on Tariffs and Trade (GATT)
An international forum for negotiating tariffs.

European Union (EU)
The single unified market formed by the majority of Western European nations; a major trading power.

North American Free Trade Agreement (NAFTA)
Treaty creating a unified market involving the United States, Canada, and Mexico.

World Trade Organization (WTO)
An organization founded in 1995 to take over responsibilities of GATT.

---

[7]www.europa.eu
[8]Jeff Fugate, "A Recipe for Success," *Yale Economic Review*, http://www.yaleeconomicreview.com/spring2005/nafta.php.

UP FOR DEBATE

SHOULD TRADE BE RESTRICTED IF IT RESULTS IN ENVIRONMENTAL DAMAGE?

Issue   *During the past few decades, we have become quite aware of the impact on the global environment from the production and consumption of goods and services by people throughout the world. We know that overharvesting trees, emitting carbon in the air and toxins in streams, and even pursuing some fishing practices can destroy air and water quality, tilt our delicate ecological balance, and ruin habitats and species. Global warming, a serious environmental concern, is a relatively new phrase in our vocabulary.*

It is apparent that some environmental destruction occurs because of international trade: The ability to partici- pate in a large global market can spur production habits that are unfriendly to the environment. The capacity to sell cheap wood, clothing, and food all over the globe, rather than solely in home markets, contributes to these destruc- tive practices. So, the question to ponder is: Should trade in a particular product be restricted if its production causes environmental damage?

Yes   We are more aware than ever that responsibility for the environment is a global concern that requires global action. Air and water quality destruction isn't isolated to a single country: The practices of one country can affect another half a globe away. It is appropriate and necessary that sustainability of the planet be a key component of international trading relationships.

International trade agreements can be vehicles for creating environmental standards of production. They are powerful tools to mandate countries to adopt environmen- tally safe production practices. If countries like China had to cut toxic air emissions or had to find production meth- ods that ensure safe water quality to be able to trade glob- ally, you can be sure that this would get done.

Furthermore, economic development can be an additional positive impact from agreements that force countries to adopt "green" practices. New technology, industries, and jobs can and do come with new environ- mental practices.

NO   Restricting trade because of environmental issues would be just another excuse to move toward protection- ism. Restricting trade hurts consumers because of less competition, fewer products, and higher prices. Just think about the higher prices on clothing in the United States that would result if some of the global factories that pro- duce it were closed.

There are already about 200 international agree- ments dealing with environmental issues—called multilat- eral environmental agreements (MEAs)—now in place.[a] These are more effective and expedient ways for nations to deal with one another than creating a wholesale ban on a product.

Trade agreements can be difficult to create and enforce. The environment is just another feature to add to the difficulty. And, countries differ in their standards. The United States, for example, might want to set standards so high that they hurt employment and production in another country. Can countries really dictate environmental stand- ards for other countries?

[a]World Trade Organization, "Understanding the WTO—The environment: a new high profile," http://www.wto.org/english/thewto_e/whatis_e/ tif_e/bey2_e.htm.

The WTO is a forum for countries to sort out trade issues and negotiate trade rules. These trade rules, or WTO agreements, provide some legal ground rules for international commerce. The WTO also works to settle trade disputes. In 2014, there were more than 160 members of the WTO. In addition to trade in goods, the WTO cov- ers trade in services, inventions, and designs.[9]

In 2004, another regional trade agreement, the Dominican Republic–Central America–United States Free Trade Agreement, or CAFTA-DR, was signed. The seven CAFTA partners—Costa Rica, Dominican Republic, El Salvador, Guatemala, Honduras, Nicaragua, and the United States—have worked to eliminate trade barriers and expand trade opportunities among themselves. In 2013, U.S. exports to these countries had increased by 96 percent over their 2003 value.[10]

[9]World Trade Organization, www.wto.org.
[10]Office of the United States Trade Representative, "CAFTA-DR (Dominican Republic-Central America FTA)," www. ustr.gov/trade-agreements/free-trade-agreements/cafta-dr-dominican-republic-central-america-fta.

Gaining consensus on a unified trading program like the EU, NAFTA, or WTO is not easy. Controversy is to be expected when a new treaty changes the economic relations among countries and the economic security of individuals and groups within those countries. In addition, as the world becomes more aware of threats to the environment from the production and consumption of goods and services, there is an added dimension to trade relationships: the issue of whether environmental protection should become part of future trade negotiations. Up for Debate, "Should Trade Be Restricted if It Results in Environmental Damage?," briefly tackles this thorny and complicated issue. What is your position in this debate?

Summary

1. International economics deals with the economic relationships among countries. International trade is concerned with the exporting and importing of goods and services and is important because it affects production, employment, and prices in the trading countries.

2. In the United States, international trade has grown over the years. Important classes of U.S. exports and imports are capital goods and industrial supplies and materials. Most U.S. trade is with developed countries in Asia, Europe, and North America, particularly China, Japan, Canada, Mexico, and the European Union.

3. Specialization occurs when resources concentrate on a narrow range of tasks or on the production of a limited variety of goods and services. This permits greater efficiency and larger levels of output than would otherwise be the case.

4. Specialization on an international scale is based on the principle of comparative advantage. A country has a comparative advantage when the opportunity cost of producing a good or service is less in that country than in another. Specialization based on comparative advantage and international trade can increase overall production levels and lessen the scarcity problem. An environment of free trade is necessary for comparative advantage to be fully exercised.

5. Free trade occurs when there are no restrictions on the flow of international trade. The alternative to free trade is protectionism, which is based on the argument that restricted trade is in the best interest of a country. Protectionist policies include tariffs, which are taxes on imports; quotas, which are quantity limits on imports; and embargoes, which are outright bans on trading a product or on trade in general.

6. The arguments for free trade center on the production gains and efficiencies to be obtained from comparative advantage, the increased availability of goods and services for consumers, and the lower prices and other benefits resulting from more competition in markets.

7. The protectionist arguments for trade restrictions include the need to protect infant industries and domestic output and employment, to diversify in case of economic disruptions, and to protect national security. The United States has reverted to protectionist policies at different times in its history.

8. In addition to trade-restricting policies, a nation can seek to increase its foreign sales through the use of subsidies and dumping. International agreements, such as the General Agreement on Tariffs and Trade, the agreements creating the European Union, and the North American Free Trade Agreement, have a significant effect on world trade.

Key Terms and Concepts

International trade

Exports

Imports

U.S. trading partners

Specialization

Comparative advantage

Free trade

Protectionism

Tariff

Quota

Embargo

Free trade arguments

Protectionist arguments

Infant industry

Trade subsidy

Dumping

International Monetary Fund (IMF)

General Agreement on Tariffs and Trade (GATT)

European Union (EU)

North American Free Trade Agreement (NAFTA)

World Trade Organization (WTO)

Review Questions

1. Explain how international trade can affect a country's levels of production, employment, and prices.

2. What have been the main export and import categories for the United States in recent years, and who are the primary trading partners of the United States?

3. "Comparative advantage is the application of specialization on an international level." What is meant by this statement? Define comparative advantage and explain how it lessens the basic scarcity problem.

4. With 1 unit of resources, China could produce either 2 tons of wheat or 4 tons of rice and Hungary could produce either 4 tons of wheat or 4 tons of rice. What is China's opportunity cost of 1 ton of wheat and of 1 ton of rice? What is Hungary's opportunity cost of 1 ton of wheat and of 1 ton of rice? Which country has the comparative advantage in wheat? Which country has the comparative advantage in rice?

5. Given the information in Question 4, how much wheat and rice would be produced if each country had 2 units of resources and devoted 1 unit to the production of wheat and 1 unit to the production of rice? If each country used both units to produce the item in which it has a comparative advantage, how much wheat and rice would be produced?

6. Differentiate among a tariff, a quota, an embargo, a subsidy, and dumping. Explain how each affects trade.

7. Summarize the arguments for free trade and for protectionism.

8. What are the International Monetary Fund (IMF), General Agreement on Tariffs and Trade (GATT), European Union (EU), North American Free Trade Agreement (NAFTA), and World Trade Organization (WTO)? What are the EU and NAFTA countries trying to accomplish?

Discussion Questions

1. Over the past few decades, both exports and imports have grown as a percentage of GDP in the United States.
    a. What effect would an increase in exports have on the level of unemployment and the level of prices in the United States if the economy were operating far below full employment?
    b. What effect would an increase in imports have on the level of unemployment and the level of prices in the United States if the economy were operating at full employment?
    c. What effect would dumping a U.S.-produced good in a foreign country have on employment in the United States if that country responded by dumping one of its goods in U.S. markets?

2. International trade must occur in free markets if countries' comparative advantages are to be fully exploited. Why is this so? If the United States produced according to its comparative advantage, in what goods and services do you think it would specialize?

3. The level of tariffs on foreign-produced cars is a source of continual debate in the United States. What is the current tariff status of automobiles imported from Japan, Germany, and South Korea? Would you favor increasing or decreasing these tariffs? Why?

4. Some people favor free trade, while others favor protectionism. This suggests that some groups gain from free trade, while others gain from protectionism. Who gains and who loses from free trade and from protectionism? What is your position on free trade and protectionism, and why do you hold this point of view?

5. Protectionists argue that putting a tariff on a good protects a domestic industry's output and employment. Others argue that a country hurt by the tariff may retaliate by restricting trade from the country imposing the tariff. The result could be a loss of output and employment in an exporting industry of the country that initiated the tariff action. Comment.

6. There were strong opinions supporting and opposing the passage of NAFTA. What groups would you expect to favor an agreement such as this, and what groups would you expect to oppose it?

7. The EU, NAFTA, and CAFTA have eased trade among European countries; among the United States, Mexico, and Canada; and among the United States and Central American countries, respectively. Do you see these developments easing trade worldwide or leading to the growth of "trade blocs" that make it virtually impossible for traders from other countries to enter markets?

Critical Thinking Case 16

A Petition (By Frederic Bastiat, 1801–1850)

Critical Thinking Skills

Using satire to make a point

Identifying flaws in arguments

Economic Concepts

Free trade

Protectionism and protectionist arguments

From the Manufacturers of Candles, Tapers, Lanterns, Candlesticks, Street Lamps, Snuffers, and Extinguishers, and from the Producers of Tallow, Oil, Resin, Alcohol, and Generally of Everything Connected with Lighting.

To the Honorable Members of the Chamber of Deputies. Gentlemen: . . .

We are suffering from the ruinous competition of a foreign rival who apparently works under conditions so far superior to our own for the production of light that he is *flooding* the *domestic market* with it at an incredibly low price; for the moment he appears, our sales cease, all the consumers turn to him, and a branch of French industry whose ramifications are innumerable is all at once reduced to complete stagnation. This rival, which is none other than the sun, is waging war on us . . . mercilessly. . . .

We ask you to be so good as to pass a law requiring the closing of all windows, dormers, skylights, inside and outside shutters, curtains . . . and blinds—in short, all openings, holes, chinks, and fissures through which the light of the sun is wont to enter houses. . . .

Be good enough, honorable deputies, to take our request seriously, and do not reject it without at least hearing the reasons that we have to advance in its support.

First, if you shut off as much as possible all access to natural light, and thereby create a need for artificial light, what industry in France will not ultimately be encouraged?

If France consumes more tallow, there will have to be more cattle and sheep, and consequently, we shall see an increase in cleared fields, meat, wool, [and] leather. . . .

If France consumes more oil, we shall see an expansion in the cultivation of the poppy, the olive, and rapeseed. . . .

Our moors will be covered with resinous trees. . . . Thus, there is not one branch of agriculture that would not undergo a great expansion. . . .

It needs but a little reflection, gentlemen, to be convinced that there is perhaps not one Frenchman, from the wealthy stockholder . . . to the humblest vendor of matches, whose condition would not be improved by the success of our petition.

We anticipate your objections, gentlemen, but there is not a single one of them that you have not picked up from the musty old books of the advocates of free trade. . . .

Will you tell us that, though we may gain by this protection, France will not gain at all, because the consumer will bear the expense?

We have our answer ready:

You no longer have the right to invoke the interests of the consumer. You have sacrificed him whenever you have found his interests opposed to those of the producer. You have done so in order *to encourage industry and to increase employment*. For the same reason you ought to do so this time too. . . .

Questions

1. What protectionist arguments are presented by the petitioners?
2. Why is this petition absurd?
3. Can a country develop a trade policy that simultaneously benefits domestic producers and consumers?

Source: Frederic Bastiat, "A Petition," Arthur Goddard, trans. and ed., *Economic Sophisms* (Irvington-on-Hudson, NY: The Foundation for Economic Education, Inc., 1964), pp. 57–60.

CHAPTER 17

International Finance

CHAPTER OBJECTIVES

Explain how exchange rates are determined, how foreign exchange markets work, and how some factors can cause exchange rates to fluctuate.

Identify the major categories into which international financial transactions can be placed and discuss the balance of trade and its performance over the past few decades.

Introduce the debt problem faced by some countries and issues in unifying monetary systems.

Chapter 16 focused primarily on the exporting and importing of goods and services. But many other types of international transactions are important to an economy: the buying and selling of foreign stocks, bonds, and other assets; foreign assistance; and private gifts to foreigners.

Most international transactions involve payment flows between countries, making it necessary to have a mechanism for determining the values of foreign currencies and for exchanging domestic money for foreign money. The value of an economy's currency in foreign exchange markets is especially important because it affects the prices of the country's exports, imports, and foreign investments. The value of the dollar in relation to the yen, euro, and other foreign currencies is so important to U.S. international transactions and to the economy that it is quoted daily in many news broadcasts, in most major newspapers, and is easily found on the Internet.

The first part of this chapter deals with exchange rates between countries' currencies, how exchange rates are determined, and how foreign exchange markets operate. The second section of the chapter explains how different types of international financial transactions affect payment flows between countries and how these transactions are classified in the United States for analysis purposes. A discussion of the balance of trade, an important and often-referred-to transactions classification, is included in this section. The chapter closes with a discussion of two current problems in international finance: the external debt crisis caused by the inability of some countries that have borrowed heavily from foreign lenders to repay their loans and issues encountered in forming a unified monetary system among countries.

EXCHANGING CURRENCIES

Exchange Rates

U.S. goods, services, and investment opportunities—such as stocks, bonds, and real estate—carry price tags that are expressed in dollars. You can buy a particular car for, say, $30,000, or invest in a piece of farmland for, say, $8,000 per acre. Regardless of whether the individual who buys U.S. goods, services, or assets is from the United States, Poland, Indonesia, or some other nation, payment for these items is usually made in dollars. Similarly, buyers and investors, regardless of their nationality, typically pay pounds for British goods and yen for Japanese goods. Thus, importing from or investing in another country requires converting one's money into the money of the nation with which one is dealing. An importer in the United States who buys Japanese cars will need to convert dollars to yen to transact business with the Japanese auto manufacturer, and a Chinese student with yuans from home will need to convert them to dollars before paying U.S. tuition.

Importers and investors need to know how much foreign goods, services, and investment opportunities cost in terms of their own money. The U.S. importer of Japanese automobiles must know not only how many yen each car will cost, but also, and perhaps more importantly, how many *dollars* that price represents. To determine the dollar cost of a car purchased from Japan, the U.S. importer must know the exchange rate between the U.S. dollar and the Japanese yen.

Exchange Rate

The number of units of a nation's currency that is equal to one unit of another nation's currency.

The **exchange rate** between two nations' currencies is the number of units of one nation's currency that is equal to one unit of the other nation's currency. For example, the exchange rate between the Swedish krona and the dollar might be 10 krona to $1, or 1 krona to $0.10. At this exchange rate, a product selling for 400 krona in Stockholm could be purchased by a U.S. tourist for the equivalent of $40. If the exchange rate were 5 krona to the dollar, then each krona would be equal in value to $0.20, and the same 400-krona product would cost the tourist the equivalent of $80.

Exchange rates between the U.S. dollar and several foreign currencies are given in Table 17.1. Using the British pound as an example, Table 17.1 shows that on July 21, 2015, one pound was worth $1.5549 or 0.643101 pounds would have exchanged for $1 ($1/1.5549 = 0.643101).

Notice in Table 17.1 that there is a listing for the European Union. This is because EU member countries, such as France and Germany, went to a common currency called the euro. Notice also the differences in the exchange rates between different countries' currencies and the dollar. For example, about 16 Mexican pesos were needed to exchange for $1, while more than 1,149 South Korean won were needed to exchange for $1. Put differently, one peso was worth about 6 cents while a Korean won was worth about 8 one-hundredths of a penny.

The exchange rate quotations in Table 17.1 are for one day only. This is because exchange rates between nations' monies are continually changing in response to economic and noneconomic factors. How and why these rates change will be discussed shortly.

The Determination of Exchange Rates

Today most nations are on a flexible, or floating, exchange rate system. In the past, however, many countries, including the United States, operated under a system of fixed exchange rates. While the United States abandoned this system in late 1971, the terms and mechanics associated with a fixed system are worth understanding. From time to time, the topic of fixing rates resurfaces.

TABLE 17.1		

Exchange Rates between the U.S. Dollar and Selected Foreign Currencies (July 21, 2015)

The exchange rates between nations' currencies are constantly changing as economic and noneconomic conditions change.

Nation	Amount of Dollars Equal to One Unit of Foreign Money	Amount of Foreign Money Equal to One Dollar
Brazil	$0.3151 = 1 real	3.173306 reals = $1.00
Britain	$1.5549 = 1 pound	0.643101 pounds = $1.00
Canada	$0.7715 = 1 Canadian dollar	1.296045 Canadian dollars = $1.00
China	$0.1609 = 1 yuan	6.211318 yuans = $1.00
European Union	$1.0927 = 1 euro	0.915121 euros = $1.00
Japan	$0.0080 = 1 yen	123.936401 yen = $1.00
Mexico	$0.0626 = 1 peso	15.957983 pesos = $1.00
Russia	$0.0175 = 1 ruble	56.911627 rubles = $1.00
South Korea	$0.0008 = 1 won	1149.431185 won = $1.00

Source: "Currency Exchange Table," X-Rates, www.x-rates.com, 07/21/2015.

Fixed Exchange Rates Before adoption of a flexible exchange rate system, exchange rates between the dollar and many other currencies were based primarily on gold; that is, the value of the dollar and other currencies was expressed in terms of the amount of gold one unit of each country's currency would command. For example, if $1 was worth 1/35 of an ounce of gold, and if 4 German marks were worth 1/35 of an ounce of gold, then the exchange rate between the dollar and the mark would have been $1 equals 4 marks, or 1 mark equals $0.25.

Because the values of their currencies were based on gold, nations were on a **fixed exchange rate** system. As a result, the exchange rates between their monies generally did not change or changed through a very narrow range. The only way a major change could occur in exchange rates was if one nation redefined the value of its money in terms of gold.

When a country declared that its monetary unit would be backed by less gold than previously, that country devalued its money. **Devaluation** of a nation's money constituted an important international economic policy tool because it changed all exchange rates between the devaluing nation's money and all other monies. This in turn had an effect on international trade, investments, and other transactions.

Flexible Exchange Rates Today, economies are typically on a system of **flexible,** or **floating, exchange rates**, where the rates at which nations' monies exchange are determined by the forces of demand and supply. As demand and supply conditions change, exchange rates change. In the United States as elsewhere, people who are planning trips to another country or planning to make foreign investments watch the movement of exchange rates as they make decisions. When supply and demand result in a strong dollar, for example, people in the United States take more trips to Europe to shop and sightsee.

The process of determining exchange rates under this system can be illustrated with a hypothetical example involving the U.S. dollar and the Brazilian real. A hypothetical

Fixed Exchange Rates
Exchange rates fluctuate little, if at all, because the values of nations' monies are defined in terms of gold.

Devaluation
The amount of gold backing a nation's monetary unit is reduced.

Flexible (Floating) Exchange Rates
Exchange rates that fluctuate because they are determined by the forces of demand and supply.

FIGURE 17.1   *Demand and Supply Curves for Brazilian Reals*

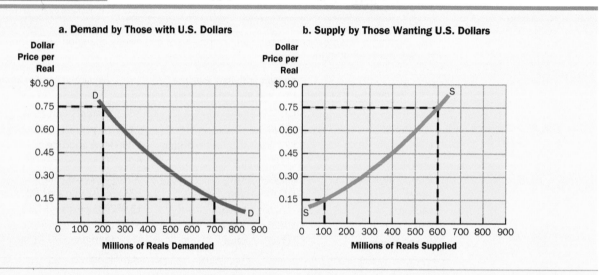

A demand curve for foreign money is downward sloping, indicating that less of the money is demanded as its price increases. A supply curve of foreign money is upward sloping, indicating that more of the money is made available as its price increases.

demand curve for Brazilian reals by those with U.S. dollars who want to import Brazilian goods, take advantage of Brazilian investment opportunities, or travel to Brazil on vacation is illustrated in Figure 17.1a. The horizontal axis indicates the quantity of reals demanded, while the vertical axis shows the price *in U.S. dollars* that must be paid per real. As expected, the demand curve is downward sloping: At a price of $0.75 per real, 200 million reals are demanded, while at a price of $0.15 per real, 700 million are demanded.

The reason for the inverse relationship between the price and quantity demanded of Brazilian reals is that as the dollar price of reals goes up, the prices of Brazilian goods, services, and investment opportunities also increase for buyers wanting to convert their dollars to reals. With Brazilian goods, services, and investment opportunities becoming more expensive for these buyers, they want to purchase less, causing the quantity of reals demanded to be lower.

For example, suppose that a Brazilian travel agency has a vacation package with a price tag of 8,000 reals. At an exchange rate of $0.30 = 1 real, the cost of the vacation would be $2,400. If the price of reals to U.S. buyers were to rise to $0.45 each, the same 8,000-real vacation would cost $3,600. This higher dollar price would cause fewer U.S. buyers to want to purchase this package, which in turn would lower the quantity of reals demanded.

The supply curve for Brazilian reals is given in Figure 17.1b. This curve shows the amount of reals available at various dollar prices in this foreign exchange market. The supply curve is upward sloping: At a price of $0.15 per real, 100 million reals would be supplied, and at a price of $0.75 per real, 600 million reals would be supplied. The supply of reals in this market comes from individuals, businesses, and governments that want to purchase U.S. dollars with reals. For example, a Brazilian investor who wants to buy stock listed on the New York Stock Exchange will need to

FIGURE 17.2 | **FIGURE 17.2**   *Supply of and Demand for Brazilian Reals*

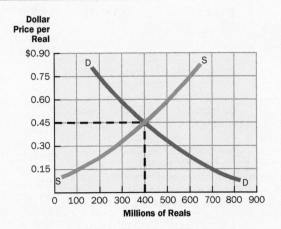

In a flexible exchange rate system, supply and demand determine the exchange rate for a nation's money.

convert reals to dollars in order to complete the stock transaction. The curve slopes upward because as the dollar price of reals increases, the real is worth more in terms of the U.S. goods, services, and financial assets that it can purchase, causing those holding reals to want to convert more of them to dollars.

The rate of exchange between the U.S. dollar and the Brazilian real can now be determined by combining the supply and demand curves, as is done in Figure 17.2. Given these supply and demand conditions, the exchange rate that emerges is shown at the intersection of the two curves: $0.45 = 1 real. At this rate, the number of reals supplied by sellers and demanded by buyers who want to convert U.S. dollars and reals is 400 million.

Understanding Foreign Exchange Markets

Foreign Exchange Market

A market for the trading of two nations' monies.

A **foreign exchange market** is one in which the currencies of two nations are traded. With a flexible exchange rate system, it is the mechanism through which the values of two nations' monies are determined by supply and demand and by which the exchange of those monies is carried out. The Canadian dollar and the U.S. dollar, the Canadian dollar and the British pound, and the Japanese yen and the British pound are traded in three different foreign exchange markets. Foreign exchange markets involve buyers and sellers all over the world who are linked together by sophisticated communications networks. Application 17.1, "Foreign Exchange Markets," provides some detail about these markets.

Changes in Exchange Rates   Since exchange rates are determined by the forces of supply and demand in foreign exchange markets, any factor that causes a change in the supply and/or demand of a nation's currency in one of these markets will cause a change in the currency's exchange rate and the amount traded in that market. For example, referring to Figure 17.2, if the demand for Brazilian reals by those with U.S. dollars increases, the demand curve for reals will shift to the right, causing the dollar price of reals as well as the amount exchanged to increase. At an exchange rate

APPLICATION 17.1

FOREIGN EXCHANGE MARKETS

Foreign exchange markets (known also as forex markets) and the amounts of nations' currencies traded in these markets do not get nearly the media attention that is given to the New York Stock Exchange and stock price movements. This is something of a surprise since, in the aggregate, the market for foreign currencies is the largest and most active financial market in the world. In 2013, the average daily exchange was over $5 trillion. One reason the daily dollar figures are so big is that in many cases hundreds of millions of dollars are spent on a single trade.

In addition to being big, the markets for foreign currencies are very active. Price quotes on a single currency can change every few seconds. And if the currency is actively traded, the quoted rate might change more than 15,000 times over the course of a day.

Not all currencies are actively traded because there is not as much demand for some currencies as there is for others. In fact, a distinction is made between "hard" and "soft" currencies. Hard currencies are from advanced industrialized countries like the United States, England, European Union members, and Japan. These currencies are widely demanded and easily converted to other currencies. A very large percentage of foreign exchange trades involves the dollar, pound, euro, or yen. Soft currencies are typically from less developed countries. There is not a strong demand for these currencies, partly because various controls might make it difficult to trade them for other currencies.

Foreign exchange markets are best understood as networks of traders. Unlike the New York Stock Exchange, which is a hub through which listed stock transactions flow, there is no central or base location through which foreign currency transactions are made. Rather, trades are done largely—but not only—in the United States, United Kingdom, and Japan.

Because primary trading locations are spread around the world, trade goes on 24 hours a day. A New York trader coming to work in the morning can contact a trader in London, where it is early afternoon, and late in the day a trader in Los Angeles can contact a trader in Japan, where it is early the next day.

Who are the main participants in foreign exchange markets? The largest group is banks and other financial institutions. There are also intermediaries, called brokers, who conduct trades for banks. While banks can directly deal with one another, sometimes there is a preference to remain anonymous. Going through a broker allows the buyer or seller to keep its identity a secret. Nations' central banks also participate in foreign exchange markets. In the case of these banks, participation might be to support a national economic policy objective. And private businesses and individuals might trade one currency for another in order to expand sales, make an investment, travel, or simply make a purchase.

Finally, we need to acknowledge the role that technology is playing in encouraging more participation in these markets by making it easier to trade.

Based on: "Foreign Currency Exchange," Federal Reserve Bank of New York, 2001, http://www.ny.frb.org/education/fx/foreign.html; Sam Y. Cross, "All about . . . the Foreign Exchange Market in the United States," Federal Reserve Bank of New York, 1998, http://www.ny.frb.org/education/addpub/usfxm; http://www.gocurrency.com/articles/stories-fx-market.htm; Simon Pottes, "Trends in Foreign Exchange Markets and the Challenges Ahead," Remarks at the 2015 FX Week Conference, July 14, 2015, www.newyorkfed.org.

of $0.45 = 1 real in Figure 17.2, $4.50 will buy 10 reals. If, because of an increase in the demand for reals, the exchange rate becomes $0.60 = 1 real, the dollar is worth less compared to the real, and $4.50 will buy only 7.5 reals. Can you graphically determine the results of an increase in supply?[1]

When an exchange rate changes, the value of one nation's money changes compared to the value of the other nation's money. One becomes worth more compared to the other, and one becomes worth less. Expressions that are heard in the media such as "the declining value of the dollar in world trade" refer to the fact that the exchange rate is changing in favor of other nations' currencies and against the U.S. dollar.

It is important to understand some of the major factors that cause supply and demand to change and exchange rates to fluctuate in foreign exchange markets, because a change in the value of a nation's currency in international exchange markets can have significant economic consequences. As exchange rates rise and fall, the international

[1]The supply curve of reals will shift to the right, causing the dollar price of reals to fall and the amount exchanged to rise.

APPLICATION 17.2

Does a Lower-Valued Dollar Help the Economy?

Suppose that over the course of a year the value of the U.S. dollar falls by over 15 percent in relation to the Japanese yen and the Canadian dollar. Since a drop in the value of the dollar on foreign exchange markets effectively puts the U.S. economy on sale, this would make purchases of U.S. goods and services cheaper for these foreign buyers. People with yen or Canadian dollars would be able to buy tuition at U.S. colleges and universities, a trip to Disney World, and even U.S.-manufactured jeans for less of their own money.

At first glance this looks like a good deal for the U.S. economy because a drop in the dollar's value should lead to more spending on U.S.-produced goods and services, which in turn should increase U.S. production and employment. But it just isn't that simple. There are some downsides to a devalued dollar.

While a lower-valued dollar makes U.S. goods cheaper to foreign buyers, it makes imports more expensive for U.S. consumers. A drop in the value of the dollar on foreign exchange markets forces U.S. consumers to pay more for the lumber, automobiles, metals, electronics, and other products they purchase from Canada and Japan, as well as the coffee, bananas, gloves, violins, and other items purchased from other countries.

These changes in the price of exports and imports give rise to important questions that come with the lower-valued dollar. Will we face a problem with demand-pull inflation from more foreign purchases of U.S. goods as well as increased spending on U.S. goods by U.S. consumers who want to avoid the rise in prices of foreign goods? Could there be a problem with cost-push inflation if U.S. firms, having to pay more for imported inputs, are forced to raise prices on their finished products?

We should also consider that a devaluation of the dollar can hurt a vulnerable part of the U.S. population: immigrants who come to the United States to work and support their families living in poverty in their home countries. When the value of the dollar drops, $1,000 sent home exchanges for fewer units of the home money—which means less food, shelter, and other needs for the family.

Based on: Roberto Perez Betancourt, "Devaluation of Dollar Hurts U.S. Consumers," Radio Habana Cuba, May 4, 2005, http://www.radiohc.cu/ingles/especiales/abril05/especiales05abril.htm.

---

prices of a country's goods and services rise and fall as well. For example, when the value of the dollar drops in foreign exchange markets, goods produced in the United States become cheaper for foreign buyers and foreign-made products become more expensive for U.S. buyers. In addition, an increase or decrease in the value of a country's money may discourage or encourage foreign ownership of real assets in the country.

Application 17.2, "Does a Lower-Valued Dollar Help the Economy?," explores the effect on the U.S. economy when the value of the dollar falls in foreign exchange markets. Because a lower-valued dollar makes U.S. exports cheaper to foreign buyers and foreign imports to the United States more expensive, it is entirely reasonable to presume that it helps the U.S. economy while hurting foreign economies. But Application 17.2 points out that a drop in the dollar's value can, in fact, hurt the U.S. economy.

Factors Influencing Demand and Supply in Foreign Exchange Markets   Several factors can cause a change in the demand and/or supply of a nation's money in foreign exchange markets. One important factor that causes the demand for foreign currencies to shift is a change in the taste for foreign products: As a country's products become more popular, demand for that country's money increases, and as they become less popular, demand falls. The demand for foreign-made goods has increased in the United States in recent years. This may be due to real or imagined perceptions of the quality of foreign products, a larger array of foreign goods that are now available, or other factors. Consider, for example, the increased popularity of Australian wines, bike trips through France and Vietnam, and Belgian chocolates.

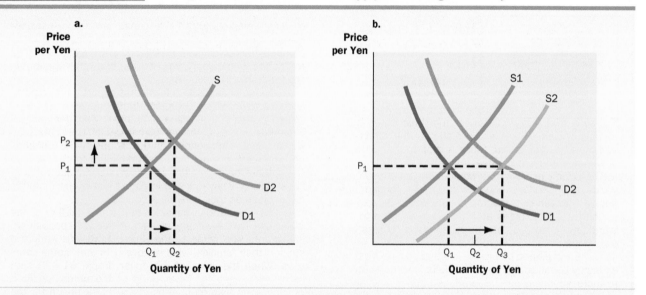

FIGURE 17.3   *Changes in the Demand for and Supply of a Foreign Currency*

An increase in the demand for a nation's currency will increase the price of its currency. If an increase in the demand for the currency is matched by an increase in supply, the exchange rate will remain unchanged.

Figure 17.3a illustrates the impact on exchange rates of an increase in the demand for a nation's currency caused by an increase in the demand for its products. Using the U.S. dollar and the Japanese yen as an example, an increase in the U.S. demand for Japanese products will increase the demand for yen and shift the demand curve to the right from D1 to D2. This causes the dollar price of yen to rise from P_1 to P_2 and the value of the dollar to decline. Can this decline in the value of the dollar be stopped?

An increase in the supply of yen could cause the exchange rate to return to its original level. This is shown in Figure 17.3b, where the supply curve shifts to the right from S1 to S2 following the shift in demand from D1 to D2, which brings the price per yen back to P_1. This increase in the supply of yen could occur if there were an increase in the Japanese demand for U.S. products or investment opportunities: A larger quantity of yen would appear on the market as the Japanese sought dollars to buy U.S. products or invest in U.S. assets.

A second factor that can cause a change in the demand or supply of a nation's currency and its exchange rate is a change in economic conditions in either the demanding or supplying country. Consider the effect of inflation on the demand for Canadian dollars by U.S. importers and investors. If the inflation occurs in the United States, it will make the price tags on Canadian goods relatively lower for U.S. importers and investors, thereby causing the U.S. demand curve for Canadian dollars to increase, or shift to the right. As a result, the price of Canadian dollars will rise, as will the number of Canadian dollars exchanged. If the inflation occurs in Canada, it will make the cost of Canadian goods relatively higher for U.S. investors and importers and lead to a decrease, or leftward shift, in the demand curve for Canadian dollars. As a result, the price of Canadian dollars will fall and so will the amount exchanged.

A third factor that influences exchange rates is the rate of interest that can be earned on securities issued by private and government borrowers in different countries.

TEST YOUR UNDERSTANDING

CHANGES IN EXCHANGE RATES

Each of the following hypothetical situations could affect the exchange rate between the U.S. dollar and another country's money. For each situation, indicate how supply or demand and the equilibrium price and quantity in that particular foreign exchange market would change and whether the value of the U.S. dollar would rise or fall in that market.

1. A report is issued that certain wines produced in Argentina could contain chemicals that are harmful to a person's health. As a result, the U.S. demand for pesos would _____, the dollar price of pesos would _____, the equilibrium quantity of dollars traded for pesos would _____, and the value of the dollar in relation to the peso would _____.

2. Rates of interest in the United States move above rates in Britain. As a result, the supply of British pounds to the United States would _____, the dollar price of pounds would _____, the equilibrium quantity of pounds traded for dollars would _____, and the value of the dollar in relation to the pound would _____.

3. Japan introduces a newly designed hybrid car that is an immediate hit with U.S. automobile buyers. As a result, the U.S. demand for Japanese yen would _____, the dollar price of yen would _____, the equilibrium quantity of dollars traded for yen would _____, and the value of the dollar in relation to the yen would _____.

4. The rate of inflation in the United States rises above the rate of inflation in Switzerland. As a result, the supply of Swiss francs to the United States would _____, the dollar price of francs would _____, the equilibrium quantity of francs traded for dollars would _____, and the value of the dollar in relation to the Swiss franc would _____.

5. More U.S. citizens travel to Israel as airlines offer substantial discounts on fares. As a result, the U.S. demand for shekels would _____, the dollar price of shekels would _____, the equilibrium quantity of dollars traded for shekels would _____, and the value of the dollar in relation to the shekel would _____.

6. Political unrest develops in Bahrain. As a result, the U.S. demand for Bahrain dinars would _____, the supply of dinars to the United States would _____, the dollar price of dinars would _____, the equilibrium quantity of dinars traded for dollars would _____, and the value of the dollar in relation to the dinar would _____.

Answers can be found at the back of the book.

If investment opportunities in another country yield a higher return than is available domestically, some individuals and corporations with global investment strategies will want to purchase the higher-yielding foreign securities. To do so increases the demand for the currency of the nation with the higher interest rates, thereby causing a change in its exchange rate. The increased buying and selling of financial instruments on a global level in recent years has had an important effect on exchange rate determination.

Fourth, the supply and demand of a nation's money in foreign exchange markets may be influenced by government and central bank policies. For example, in an effort to keep the value of a country's money from falling, its government or central bank might intervene in a foreign exchange market to restrict the supply of its currency. Government intervention in foreign exchange markets occurs from time to time, despite the fact that they are considered to be basically free markets.

Changes in exchange rates will also cause buyers and sellers of foreign currencies to enter or leave the market if they regard foreign goods, services, and assets as substitutes for domestic items. For example, when the value of the peso falls, travel to Mexico by residents of the United States becomes a desirable alternative to travel at home. This increase in foreign travel, considered by itself, would cause the demand curve for pesos to shift to the right and the value of the peso to increase. Finally, other factors such as political climates, expectations, and trade restrictions can cause the demand and/or supply curves for a nation's money to shift and the exchange rate to change. Test Your Understanding, "Changes in Exchange Rates," lets you practice evaluating how changes in economic and noneconomic conditions in two countries would affect exchange rates between their monies.

INTERNATIONAL FINANCIAL TRANSACTIONS AND BALANCES

A wide variety of international transactions requires payment flows from one country to another. These include importing and exporting goods and services, buying and selling financial instruments and real assets, military and foreign assistance, gifts, grants, and travel. Some of these transactions involve major outlays for real estate, production equipment, and corporate stock; some involve small sums for gifts to relatives back home.

To analyze the many and varied types of financial transactions that occur between the United States and other nations, these transactions are grouped into major categories. Through the use of these categories, the accounting process for international transactions is simplified and, more importantly, transactions that could cause problems for the economy can be more readily identified. The two major transactions categories are the current account and the financial account.

The Current Account

Current Account

A category of international transactions that records figures for exports and imports of merchandise, services, unilateral transfers, and other foreign dealings.

The **current account** records payments for exports and imports of goods; payments for military transactions, foreign travel, transportation, and other services; income from investments; and unilateral transfers (gifts). The major components of the current account and their dollar values for 2014 are shown at the top of Table 17.2. In presenting these figures, dollar payment outflows to other countries are indicated by negative numbers and dollar payment inflows from other countries by positive numbers. For example, the value of U.S. exports of goods in 2014 was over $1.6 trillion, a positive

| **TABLE 17.2** | *U.S. International Financial Transactions* |

Type of Transaction		Amount in 2014 (billions of dollars)
Current Account Balance		−$389,526
Balance on goods and services		−$508,324
Exports of goods	$1,632,639	
Imports of goods	−2,851,529	
Exports of services	710,565	
Imports of services	−477,428	
Balance on primary income (investments)		237,984
Balance on secondary income (unilateral transfers)		−119,185
Financial Account		
New U.S. acquisition of financial assets		$792,145
Net U.S. incurrence of liabilities to foreigners		−977,421
Net financial derivatives		−56,585
Net lending/borrowing from financial account transactions		−239,648

Source: Bureau of Economic Analysis, Table 17.1. U.S. International Transactions, June 18, 2015, www.bea.gov.

| FIGURE 17.4 | U.S. Balance of Trade: 1970–2014 |

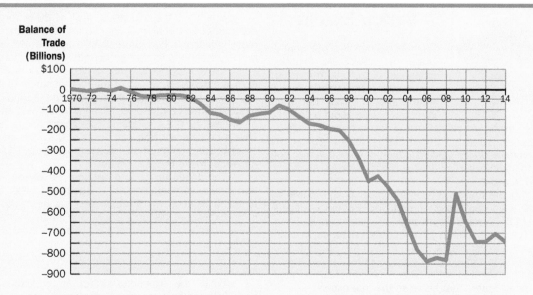

Since the mid-1970s, and especially since the mid-2000s, the United States has run significant balance of trade deficits as the value of merchandise imports has exceeded the value of exports.

Sources: *Economic Report of the President* (Washington, DC: U.S. Government Printing Office, 2012), p. 436; Bureau of Economic Analysis, Table 1. U.S. International Trade in Goods and Services, 07/07/2015, www.bea.gov.

Balance of Trade

The figure that results when merchandise imports are subtracted from exports.

Balance of Trade Surplus (Deficit)

The value of a country's merchandise exports is greater (less) than the value of its imports.

number because exports bring payment inflows, while the value of imports of merchandise in 2014 was –$2.85 trillion, a negative number because dollars flow out when foreign goods are purchased.

When goods imports are subtracted from goods exports, a net figure called the **balance of trade** results. The balance of trade is significant because it involves a large flow of money, reflects the results of a nation's international trade activity, and is frequently cited in studies and discussions of international transactions. When the value of a country's exports of goods is greater than the value of its imports, a **balance of trade surplus** occurs; when the value of a country's imports of goods is greater than the value of its exports, a **balance of trade deficit** arises.[2]

Figure 17.4 charts the annual balance of trade for the United States from 1970 through 2014. In recent decades, sizeable trade deficits have occurred, especially in the mid-2000s, and the trade deficits are so large that they are a matter of concern. Factors such as the popularity of foreign goods like automobiles and home electronics equipment, the availability of inexpensive shoes and clothing, strong foreign rivals in markets for U.S. export products, the rise in the price of oil, and changes in the value of the dollar have contributed to the significant deficits of recent years.

The dollar figures for some other current account classifications in Table 17.2 are given as net amounts; that is, unlike merchandise exports and imports, the payment

[2] Be careful to notice that the term *balance of trade* is different from the term *net exports*, which was discussed in Chapter 5. The balance of trade is calculated on the basis of exports and imports of goods, whereas net exports uses both goods and services.

APPLICATION 17.3

A PRIZED EXPORT

When people think about what it is that the United States exports, items like aircraft, farm machinery, soybeans, and even California wine come to mind. But they don't often think about a growing and prized export: an education and degree from a college or university located in the United States. At first glance, an education for a foreign student in the United States may not appear to be an export, but it clearly brings foreign spending on a U.S. product.

There are and have been a number of U.S. universities that have campuses abroad, like Boston College's campus in Brussels, Belgium, and St. Louis-based Webster University's campuses in six countries, which serve both U.S. and foreign students. While these offer students the opportunities to experience another culture, it is the actual arrival and study of foreign students on campuses located in the United States that serve as the true export.

The number of foreign students now attending colleges and universities in the United States is significant. The Institute of International Education reported that 886,052 attended during the 2013–2014 academic year. An appreciation for the size of this number can be gained from a comment by Michael K. Young, President of the University of Washington, who noted that in 2012 there were more foreign students in the state of Washington than there were students from the other 49 states.

Where are the home countries of foreign students coming to the United States? In 2014, the largest group of students—274,439—came from China, followed by students from South Korea, India, Saudi Arabia, and Canada. Together the students from these five countries accounted for more than 50 percent of the foreign students in the United States.

How does the education of all of these foreign students affect international finance and the balance of payments for the United States? Like anyone who wants to purchase an item in another country, "home" money must be converted to the currency of the country in which the item is purchased. So, all of the foreign students purchasing tuition, books, fast food, and more in the United States need to convert their home currency from China, India, and elsewhere to U.S. dollars in foreign exchange markets. This is no different from the buyer of U.S. farm machinery or soybeans who must also convert home currency to U.S. dollars to make the purchases.

The Institute of International Education reported that foreign students contribute about $21 billion per year to the U.S. economy through their payments for tuition, living expenses, transportation, and other expenditures. These sizeable expenditures help to add a positive number to the U.S. current account by increasing exports which helps to counter the outflow of dollars for spending on imports.

While the expenditures for an education in the United States by a foreign student may not be thought of as an "export" since no good or service leaves the country, the service each student receives behaves like an export. Perhaps the U.S. higher education system should be regarded as something in which the United States has a strong comparative advantage. We may not recognize the value of one of our most prized U.S. products.

Based on: Mary Beth Marklein, "More Foreign Students Studying in USA," *USA Today*, November 13, http://usatoday30.usatoday.com/news/education/story/2011-11-13/foreign-students-boost-usa-economy/51188560/1; Tamar Lewin, "Taking More Seats on Campus, Foreigners Also Pay the Freight," *The New York Times*, February 4, 2012, http://www.nytimes.com/2012/02/05/education/international-students-pay-top-dollar-at-us-colleges.html; "International Students in the United States," www.iie.org/services/project-atlas.

---

outflows have already been subtracted from the inflows and are not given separately. For example, on primary income (investments) more payment inflows than outflows occurred, resulting in a net figure of $238 billion. On the other hand, the unilateral transfer number of –$119.2 billion indicates that, for that category, more payments flowed out of than into the United States.

The balance of trade, net services, net income, and unilateral transfers are added together to arrive at the current account balance, which was –$389.5 billion in 2014. This figure means that transactions from the current account components caused 389.5 billion more U.S. dollars to flow out for payments than the value of money that flowed in. This is referred to as a **current account deficit**. Had the figure been a positive number, there would have been a **current account surplus**.

Current Account Deficit (Surplus)

A negative (positive) figure results when all current account transactions are added together.

Application 17.3, "A Prized Export," looks at one group of expenditures that positively impacts the current account: the spending by foreign students getting an education and earning degrees at colleges and universities in the United States.

The Financial Account

Financial Account
A category of international transactions that records the purchase and sale of financial and real assets between the United States and other nations.

The **financial account**, which is listed in the lower part of Table 17.2, records payment flows for investment purchases such as stocks, bonds, government securities, and real estate. When U.S. individuals, businesses, and governments buy foreign-owned financial or real assets, there are payment flows from the United States. These flows are recorded in the account component as negative numbers since payments are flowing out of the country. When corporate financial instruments, government securities, and real estate owned by U.S. entities are purchased by foreign buyers, there are payment flows to the United States. These are recorded in the account as positive numbers, indicating payment inflows.

CHALLENGES TO THE INTERNATIONAL FINANCIAL SYSTEM

The globalization of economic activity has created both opportunities and challenges for the international financial system. Two challenges have been particularly important: the debt issues faced by a number of countries as a result of large-scale borrowing from foreign lenders and efforts to integrate the monetary systems of the countries in the European Union.

External Debt Issues

One important type of international financial transaction is loan making. Many governments and businesses, including those in developing nations, borrow from lenders, such as banks, governments, and individuals, in other countries to help finance investments and other activities. For example, a U.S. bank could lend money to the government of Greece, a South African could buy U.S. Treasury bonds, or Canadian and U.S. investors could buy corporate bonds in companies of each other's countries. This type of borrowing results in **external debt** because it is owed to lenders outside of, or external to, the borrowing country.

External Debt
Money owed by borrowers in one country to lenders in other countries.

External debt has been a mounting problem for some countries. The external debt of some nations has become so large that they are unable to repay the interest on their loans, much less the loans themselves.

The Opportunity Cost of External Debt   There are substantial opportunity costs for borrowing nations that seek to service and repay their large external debts and substantial opportunity costs for lending nations if they do not.

To honor their financial obligations to foreign lenders, borrowing nations must cut back on spending by their households, businesses, and governments in order to send money to their debt holders. (This is the same situation that a family faces when it falls deeply into debt: It must cut back on current consumption in order to pay lenders.) In developing nations where incomes are low, the harsh austerity measures needed to cut back spending to repay the debt may not be tolerable or even possible. In some cases, government programs that provide income to individuals may need to be reduced or even eliminated. In addition, payment of a debt of a large magnitude causes the postponement of spending on investment goods, which hampers future economic growth. In short, the opportunity cost of external debt repayment is substantial: The decline in current spending could send the economy into a recession, making payments even more difficult and sacrificing future economic growth. To these economic costs can be added the political unrest that could well result from such serious economic disruptions.

Failure by countries to meet external debt interest payments or repay loan principals in a timely manner creates problems for lending institutions, especially commercial banks. When countries can no longer meet their loan obligations, millions of dollars of interest income are at risk for these banks, in addition to possible default on the principal. The unacceptably high risk associated with loan making to developing countries has reduced the flow of funds from banks to these countries.

Brady Plan

A proposal to restructure and reduce developing country indebtedness to commercial banks.

Highly Indebted Poor Countries (HIPC) Initiative

A joint initiative by the World Bank and International Monetary Fund to help heavily indebted developing countries manage their external debt.

Dealing with External Debt Issues   An early attempt to alleviate an external debt crisis was the **Brady Plan**. This 1989 proposal, which was used in several countries, aimed to restructure and reduce the debts owed to commercial banks by developing countries, provided the countries implemented policies to strengthen their economies.[3] In 1996 the World Bank and International Monetary Fund, in conjunction with several governments and international financial organizations, launched the **Heavily Indebted Poor Countries (HIPC) Initiative** to ease the external debt burden of highly indebted developing countries that carried out economic reforms to improve educational attainment, health care, and other social conditions. Prior to the Initiative, eligible countries were spending more on debt service than on health and education. By 2004, they were spending almost four times as much on health, education, and other social services than on debt service. By 2015, 36 countries had been approved for debt reduction under the HIPC Initiative.[4]

Monetary Integration in Europe

As indicated in Chapter 16, an important development in the 1980s and 1990s was the formation of the European Community (EC), which later became the European Union (EU), a single trading entity larger in population and economic size than the United States. Most of the countries that comprise this large and closely knit trading bloc integrated their monetary systems in 2002.

European Monetary System (EMS)

An agreement to limit the variability of exchange rates between European nations' currencies.

Maastricht Treaty

Called for a common currency and central bank to oversee a single monetary policy for countries belonging to Europe's Economic and Monetary Union.

The first step toward monetary integration occurred in 1979, when the **European Monetary System (EMS)** was formed to limit the variability of exchange rates between European nations' currencies. Rates were aligned using a mechanism that allowed exchange rates to fluctuate by only a small percentage around a central value. The German mark was the keystone currency on which the EMS was built.

The next major step toward monetary unification was the **Maastricht Treaty** of 1991, which was ratified by the EC members in 1993. Under the terms of the treaty, the EMS would be replaced by an Economic and Monetary Union, or EMU, and there would be a common currency and a European Central Bank to oversee a single monetary policy for the member countries. The Maastricht Treaty, in effect, called for a fixed exchange rate system to apply to member countries' currencies.[5]

In 1999, a monetary union of 11 countries was formed, and the euro, a common European currency, was launched. By 2002, the euro replaced the currencies of

---

[3] See John Clark and Elliot Kalter, "Recent Innovations in Debt Restructuring," *Finance & Development*, September 1992, p. 6; William R. Rhodes, "The Disaster That Didn't Happen," *The Economist*, September 12, 1992, pp. 22–23.

[4] International Monetary Fund, "Debt Relief under the Heavily Indebted Poor Countries (HIPC) Initiative," May 29, 2015, http://www.imf.org.

[5] Craig R. Whitney, "Worry over the Euro Sweeps Europe," *The New York Times*, April 19, 1997, p. 4.

UP FOR DEBATE

EURO-DREAMS

Issue   *Imagine the place in history that awaits the person who persuaded the leaders of nations whose past relations were largely uneasy alliances or hostilities that sometimes degenerated into all-out war to come together, abandon their sovereign currencies and the autonomy of their central banks, and accept a common currency called the euro. Is the dream and reality of a single currency among the member countries of the European Union realistic in the long term?*

Yes   It is realistic to expect the countries of the European Union to accept the euro. The world that European nations face today is vastly different from the world where European relations were marked by distrust and highly focused nationalism. With economic activity crossing national borders on a huge scale, countries that want to be an "island fortress" insulated against all outside interests are painfully out-of-step with the times.

By acting as one economic unit rather than separately, European nations will be better able to specialize and flex their muscle in the global arena. Surely it is obvious to the leaders in Europe's capitals that if they are to join together and seek a common outcome, their solidarity will be enhanced by adopting a common currency.

No   It is not realistic to expect the countries of the European Union to wholeheartedly accept the euro. Centuries of deep and abiding nationalism cannot be erased with the stroke of a pen. The unified monetary system may well surpass expectations—until a serious crisis occurs. When this happens, member countries may be slow to support policies that benefit the EU and stabilize the euro at the expense of national objectives. Further, even if the countries are willing to act as one and put EU interests above national interests, the fact is they face different problems that may require conflicting responses, not a single central bank policy. Finally, should we really expect member countries to always be willing and able to follow stringent government tax and expenditure policies in order to stabilize the euro?

most EU member countries. This became the world's largest currency transformation. With time, new countries have joined the EU, and 19 of the members have adopted the euro.

From the beginning there were supporters and skeptics of this union, and many concerns—either real or perceived. One concern has been that as the member countries experience different economic problems, a single monetary policy may not be able to address all of their needs at one time. One country might face inflation while another faces unemployment, leading to advocacy for different types of economic policies to follow. Furthermore, some of the smaller countries in the EU may have less capacity to strengthen their economies in a time of severe economic conditions, and they may feel that their economies are of less concern than those of the larger, more powerful members.

The mobility of resources and protection of tradition are other issues. Because of differences in language and tradition, Europeans are less mobile than individuals in the United States. It may be more difficult to relocate from Copenhagen with its Danish language to Madrid with its Spanish language than it would be from Seattle to Boston. The strong attachment to culture and tradition can also be extended to the currency in many countries. There are stories of small towns and villages that have clung to their native currency rather than adopt the euro.

Approaching two decades of experience with the euro, time will tell whether the original intentions of the EU and the euro, such as improved trade among euro countries, are successful. Up for Debate, "Euro-Dreams," takes a look at some of the arguments for and against the continued success of the euro. What do you think will be the long-term reality of the euro?

Summary

1. An exchange rate is the number of units of one country's money that is equal to one unit of another country's money. In the past, exchange rates were often fixed, or tied to the value of the gold backing a country's money. When the gold backing was reduced, devaluation occurred.

2. Most exchange rates are flexible and continually changing because they are determined by supply and demand. The demand curve for a country's money by those holding another country's money is downward sloping, and the supply curve for a country's money is upward sloping.

3. Foreign exchange markets are the mechanisms through which the monies of different nations are traded and exchange rates are determined. When an exchange rate between two nations' monies changes, one nation's money becomes worth more in terms of the other nation's money. Changes in exchange rates affect economic conditions through their effects on the prices of exports, imports, and financial and real assets.

4. Any factor that causes demand and/or supply in a foreign exchange market to change will alter the exchange rate, as well as the amount of money traded. Some important factors affecting the demand for and/or supply of a foreign money include the popularity of imports and exports, economic conditions in either the importing or exporting nation, interest rates that can be earned on investments in other countries, and intervention in foreign exchange markets by governments or central banks.

5. All international transactions that cause payment outflows or inflows are of economic importance. For accounting and analysis purposes, these transactions are placed into different categories, the most important of which are the current account and the financial account.

6. The current account includes the balance of trade, as well as figures for invest-ment income, unilateral transfers, and the like. When the U.S. current account balance is a negative number, more dollars have flowed out of the United States than foreign payments have flowed in, and a current account deficit exists. When the current account balance is a positive number, more foreign payments have flowed in than dollars have flowed out, resulting in a current account surplus. In recent years, substantial balance of trade deficits have contributed to negative current account balances and caused serious concern in the United States.

7. The financial account records payment flows for financial and real assets including purchases of stocks, bonds, and real estate.

8. Several nations have accumulated large external debts that may be beyond their abilities to repay. External debt presents problems for both lending and borrowing countries. Significant opportunity costs exist whether the debt is repaid or not, and actions have been taken to reduce many developing countries' external debts.

9. Most nations in the European Union have integrated their currencies. There are ongoing questions about the costs and benefits of having several nations use a single, common currency.

Key Terms and Concepts

Exchange rate

Fixed exchange rate

Devaluation

Flexible (floating) exchange rates

Foreign exchange market

Exchange rate determination

Current account

Balance of trade

Balance of trade surplus (deficit)

Current account deficit (surplus)

Financial account

External debt

Brady Plan

Highly Indebted Poor Countries (HIPC) Initiative

European Monetary System (EMS)

Maastricht Treaty

Review Questions

1. Would the value of the dollar, compared to the Swiss franc, increase or decrease if the exchange rate went from 1.3 francs = $1.00 to 1.2 francs = $1.00? Why?

2. Explain why devaluation of a nation's currency could increase the demand for that nation's exports and decrease the demand by that nation for imports.

3. Why is the demand curve for a nation's money in a foreign exchange market downward sloping, and why is the supply curve upward sloping?

4. Illustrate graphically how the exchange rate for a nation's money is determined in a flexible exchange rate system, and show how the rate would be affected by an increase and a decrease in demand and by an increase and a decrease in supply.

5. How would each of the following transactions affect payment flows into or out of the United States?
   a. The purchase of U.S. Treasury securities by a Canadian bank
   b. The sale of U.S. grain to China
   c. A gift of cash from a family in Pennsylvania to relatives in Poland
   d. The purchase of a condo in Paris by a family in New York
   e. The purchase of stock in an Indonesian company by an economics professor in Chicago
   f. A student from Indonesia comes to study at a university in St. Louis

6. What are the major components of the current account? Give some examples of international transactions that would cause positive and negative dollar amounts to register in the current account.

7. What is an external debt and what opportunity costs does its repayment impose on a highly indebted country?

8. Summarize the steps Europeans have taken toward a monetary union. What problems could stand in the way of sustaining that union in the long run?

Discussion Questions

1. Locate a recent listing of foreign exchange rates. Compare the recent rates with those given in Table 17.1. Are there any instances in which the rate has changed substantially? If so, give your opinion as to what factors might have caused such a change.

2. Answer each of the following.
   a. How many Japanese yen would have to be converted to dollars for a person in Japan to purchase a $40,000 U.S. SUV if the exchange rate were 125 yen = $1.00?
   b. How many yen would have to be converted to dollars to purchase the $40,000 SUV after the exchange rate changed to 110 yen = $1.00?
   c. How many dollars would have to be converted to yen for a person in Los Angeles to purchase a 4,000,000-yen Japanese automobile if the exchange rate were 125 yen = $1.00?
   d. How many dollars would have to be converted to yen to purchase the 4,000,000-yen auto after the exchange rate changed to 110 yen = $1.00?

3. What are some advantages and disadvantages of a fixed exchange rate system and of a flexible exchange rate system?

4. Explain how each of the following developments, taken alone, would affect the value of the dollar in foreign exchange markets. Use supply and demand analysis in your answer.
   a. The perception in other countries that the quality of goods produced in the United States is improving
   b. A large federal government budget deficit that raises interest rates in the United States
   c. Intervention by the Federal Reserve in foreign exchange markets that results in dollars moving into those markets
   d. A poor harvest in most of the grain-producing countries of the world except the United States
   e. The expectation of war among several African countries

5. The United States has primarily experienced balance of trade deficits since the late 1970s and serious deficits since the mid-2000s. What could be the short-term and long-term effects if this condition persists? What policy actions would you recommend to reverse this trend?

6. What problems would arise if a country defaulted on its external debt? Who would be hurt? What policies would you recommend to ease external debt problems, and what would be the effects of these policies on borrowing countries?

7. Do you expect that in the long term the euro will be successful as a currency?

Critical Thinking Case 17

HELPING POOR COUNTRIES

Critical Thinking Skills

Examining cause-and-effect relationships

Identifying criteria for appropriate policies

Economic Concepts

External debt

Balance of payments

The IMF provides low-income countries with policy advice, technical assistance, and financial support. Low-income countries receive more than half of the technical assistance provided by the Fund, and financial support is extended at low interest rates and over relatively long time horizons. Low-income countries with high external debt burdens are also eligible for debt relief.

Despite progress in recent decades, the extreme poverty prevalent in low-income countries is a critical problem facing the global community. At present, more than a billion people are living on less than $1 a day. More than three-quarters of a billion people are malnourished—about a fifth of them children. One-hundred and sixteen of every 1,000 children born in low-income countries die before reaching the age of five, the majority from malnutrition or disease that is readily preventable in high-income countries.

[The United Nations has set goals] centered on halving poverty between 1990 and 2015. There is little dispute that a sustained, rapid rate of growth in average per capita incomes is essential for meaningful poverty reduction. The factors that have been shown to promote such growth include openness to international trade, sound economic policies, strong institutions and legal frameworks, and good governance.

[In March 2002, strategies were adopted to meet the United Nations' goals.] The first is the pursuit of sound policies and good governance by the low-income countries themselves. The second is larger and more effective international support, including official development assistance and opening markets to developing country exports.

The IMF is helping low-income countries make progress [toward these goals] through each of the Fund's three key functions—lending, technical assistance, and surveillance.

Questions

1. How might a loan by the IMF to help a developing country meet its obligations to foreign lenders reduce malnutrition, illness, and premature death among its population?

2. The IMF requires that in order to get IMF aid, developing countries must accept technical assistance to help manage their economic affairs and surveillance of some policies. Is this an appropriate intrusion into how those countries manage their affairs?

3. What criteria would you recommend for determining whether a country qualifies for financial support by the IMF?

Source: International Monetary Fund, "How the IMF Helps Poor Countries," October 2007, http://www.imf.org/External/np/exr/facts/poor.htm.

GLOSSARY

Actual reserves A financial depository institution's reserve account plus its vault cash.

Antitrust laws Laws prohibiting certain practices that reduce competition.

Asset Something that an individual or business owns; can be used to cover liabilities.

Assumptions Conditions held to be true within a model.

Automatic fiscal policy (automatic stabilization) Changes in government expenditures and/or taxes that occur automatically as the level of economic activity changes; helps to control unemployment or demand-pull inflation.

Average fixed cost Fixed cost per unit produced; total fixed cost divided by the number of units produced.

Average total cost The cost per unit of output produced; total cost divided by the number of units produced.

Average variable cost Variable cost per unit produced; total variable cost divided by the number of units produced.

Balance of trade surplus (deficit) The value of a country's merchandise exports is greater (less) than the value of its imports.

Balanced budget A government's total expenditures equal its total revenues.

Bank holding company Corporation formed for the purpose of owning, or holding, the controlling shares of stock in a bank or banks.

Barriers to entry Factors that keep firms from entering a market; can be financial, legal, technical, or other barriers.

Barter (barter system) Goods and services are exchanged for each other rather than for money.

Base year The year against which prices in other years are compared in a price index; given the index number 100.0.

Basic economic decisions The choices that must be made in any society regarding what to produce, how to produce, and to whom production is distributed.

Board of Governors Seven-member board heading the Federal Reserve system; develops policies concerning money, banking, and other financial institution practices.

Bond A financial instrument through which a corporation can borrow funds and repay them over the long run.

Business An organization established to produce and/or sell goods and services.

Business cycles Recurring periods of growth and decline (or expansion and contraction) in an economy's real output or real GDP.

Capital (goods) Goods, such as machinery and equipment, used in the production of other goods and services.

Capitalism An economic system with free enterprise and private property rights; economic decision making occurs in a market environment.

Celler–Kefauver Act (1950) Federal antitrust statute concerned with anticompetitive mergers and acquisitions of firms; amends Section Seven of the Clayton Act.

Change in demand A change in the demand schedule and curve for a product caused by a change in a nonprice factor influencing the product's demand; the demand curve shifts to the right or left.

Change in labor demand or supply A shift in the demand or supply curve for labor caused by changes in nonwage factors.

Change in quantity demanded and quantity supplied A change in the amount of a product demanded or supplied that is caused by a change in its price; represented by a movement along a demand or supply curve from one price–quantity point to another.

Change in supply A change in the supply schedule and curve for a product caused by a change in a nonprice factor influencing the product's supply; the supply curve shifts to the right or left.

Change in the quantity of labor demanded or supplied A change in the amount of labor demanded or supplied that occurs when wages change; a movement along the demand or supply curve.

Circular flow model A diagram showing the real and money flows between households and businesses in output, or product, markets and input, or resource, markets.

Classical economics Popularly accepted theory prior to the Great Depression of the 1930s; says the economy will automatically adjust to full employment.

Clayton Act (1914) Federal antitrust statute prohibiting specific activities that substantially reduce competition or tend to create a monopoly.

Collective bargaining The process through which a union and management negotiate a labor contract.

Commercial bank Institution that holds and maintains checking accounts (demand deposits) for its customers, makes commercial (business) and other loans, and performs other functions.

Comparative advantage One country has a lower opportunity cost when producing a good or service than does another country.

Conglomerate merger A merger between firms that are not competitors, suppliers, or distributors.

Constant returns to scale Occur in the range of production levels in which long-run average total cost is constant.

Consumer Price Index (CPI) Measures changes in the prices of goods and services that consumers typically purchase, such as food, shelter, clothing, and medical care.

Corporation A legal entity, owned by stockholders; can carry on in its own name business functions normally performed by individuals.

Correspondent banking Interbank relationship involving deposits and various services.

Cost of living adjustment (COLA) An arrangement whereby an individual's wages automatically increase with inflation.

Cost–benefit analysis Weighing the costs and benefits of an action in order to maximize the net benefit from the action.

Cost-push inflation Pressure on prices from the sellers' side of the market, particularly from increases in costs of production.

Creative destruction New, technologically advanced machinery and production methods cause the disappearance of old machinery and methods.

Crowding out Occurs when borrowing by the federal government increases the interest rate and reduces borrowing by households and businesses.

Currency Coins and paper money.

Current account A category of international transactions that records figures for imports and exports of merchandise, unilateral transfers, and other foreign dealings.

Cyclical unemployment Involuntary unemployment that results from a downswing in a business cycle or a recession.

Debt service The cost of maintaining a debt; generally measured in interest costs.

Decrease in demand A change in a nonprice influence on demand causes less of a product to be demanded at each price; the demand curve shifts to the left.

Decrease in supply A change in a nonprice influence on supply causes less of a product to be supplied at each price; the supply curve shifts to the left.

Deficit budget A government's expenditures are greater than its revenues.

Deflation A sustained decrease in the general level of prices.

Demand The different amounts of a product that a buyer would purchase at different prices in a defined time period when all nonprice factors are held constant.

Demand curve A line on a graph that illustrates a demand schedule; slopes downward because of the inverse relationship between price and quantity demanded.

Demand curve for labor Downward-sloping curve showing the amount of labor demanded at different wage rates; based on the marginal revenue product of labor.

Demand deposits Checking account balances kept primarily at commercial banks.

Demand-pull inflation Pressure on prices from the buyers' side of the market; tends to occur when buyers' demands (or spending) are greater than the productive capability of the economy.

Depository Institutions Deregulation and Monetary Control Act (1980) Legislation that increased the similarity among many financial institutions and increased the control of the Federal Reserve system.

Deregulation A reduction in government regulatory control of the economy.

Derived demand The demand for a factor of production depends on the demand for the good or service the factor produces.

Devaluation The amount of gold backing a nation's monetary unit is reduced.

Direct relationship Two variables move in the same direction: when one increases, so does the other; graphs as an upward-sloping line.

Discount rate Interest rate that a Federal Reserve bank charges a financial depository institution for borrowing reserves.

Discouraged workers Persons who drop out of the labor force because they have been unsuccessful for a long period of time in finding a job.

Discretionary fiscal policy Deliberate changes in government expenditures and/or taxes to control unemployment or demand-pull inflation.

Diseconomies of scale Occur when the increasing size of production in the long run causes the per unit cost of production to rise.

Disinflation A slowing of the inflation rate.

Distribution of income The way income is divided among the members of society.

Dodd–Frank Legislation passed in 2010 to increase accountability in and regulation over financial institutions and the instruments and products they provide.

Dual banking system Label given to the U.S. banking system because both the federal and state governments have the right to charter banks.

Durable good A good that has a useful lifetime of more than one year.

Easy money policy Policy by the Federal Reserve to increase excess reserves and decrease interest rates to increase spending.

Econometrics The use of statistical techniques to describe the relationships between economic variables.

Economic cost of production Includes all explicit and implicit costs of producing a good or service.

Economic growth An increase in an economy's full production (full employment) output level over time.

Economic policy A guide for a course of action.

Economic profit (excess profit) Profit beyond normal profit; not considered a cost of production.

Economic profit, loss, breaking even Occurs when price is greater than, less than, or equal to average total cost, respectively.

Economic system The way in which an economy is organized to make the basic economic decisions.

Economic theory A formal explanation of the relationship between economic variables.

Economics The study of how scarce, or limited, resources are used to satisfy unlimited material wants and needs; the study of decision making in a world of scarcity.

Economies of scale Occur when the increasing size of production in the long run causes the per unit cost of production to fall.

Efficiency Producing a given good or service at the lowest possible cost; getting the most output from resources.

Elasticity coefficient The absolute value of the percentage change in quantity demanded or supplied divided by the absolute value of the percentage change in price; greater or less than one when demand or supply is price elastic or inelastic, respectively.

Elastic price change and total revenue Total revenue moves in the opposite direction of a price change when consumers react strongly or elastically.

Embargo A ban on trade in a particular commodity or with a particular country.

Employment Act of 1946 Legislation giving the federal government the right and responsibility to provide an environment for the achievement of full employment, full production, and stable prices.

Entrepreneurship The function of organizing resources for production and taking the risk of success or failure in a productive enterprise.

Equation of exchange $MV = PQ$; illustrates how changes in the supply of money (M) influence the level of prices (P) and/or the total output of goods and services (Q).

Equilibrium price and equilibrium quantity The price and quantity where demand equals supply; price and quantity toward which a free market automatically moves.

Equity Justice or fairness in the distribution of goods and services.

European Union (EU) The single unified market formed by the majority of Western European nations; a major trading power.

Excess profit (economic profit) Profit beyond normal profit; not considered a cost of production.

Excess reserves Reserves of a financial depository institution over the amount it is required to maintain in actual reserves; actual reserves minus required reserves.

Exchange rate The number of units of a nation's currency that is equal to one unit of another nation's currency.

Expectations Anticipations of future events; can affect current actions by households and businesses and the likelihood that the future events will occur.

Explicit costs Payments that a business makes to acquire factors of production, such as labor, raw materials, and machinery.

Exports Goods and services that are sold abroad.

External debt Money owed by borrowers in one country to lenders in other countries.

Externality The effect of an action on a person or thing that was not one of the parties involved in the action.

Federal Deposit Insurance Corporation (FDIC) Government agency established in 1933 to insure deposits in commercial banks up to a specified amount.

Federal Funds market Market in which banks borrow reserves from other banks.

Federal Funds rate The interest rate banks charge to lend reserves to other banks for a short period of time, usually overnight.

Federal Reserve banks Twelve banks that deal with commercial banks and other financial institutions.

Federal Reserve notes Paper money issued by the Federal Reserve banks; includes almost all paper money in circulation.

Federal Reserve system Coordinates commercial banking operations, regulates some aspects of all depository institutions, and oversees the U.S. money supply.

Federal Trade Commission Act (1914) Created the Federal Trade Commission and empowered it to prevent unfair methods of competition, which include antitrust violations.

Financial account A category of international transactions that records the purchase and sale of financial and real assets between the United States and other nations.

Financial depository institution Institution that accepts and maintains deposits, and makes loans; can create and destroy money.

Financial institutions Organizations such as banks, savings associations, and insurance companies that provide a means for saving and borrowing.

Fiscal policy Influencing the levels of aggregate output and employment or prices through changes in federal government purchases, transfer payments, and/or taxes.

Fixed costs Costs of using fixed factors.

Fixed exchange rates Exchange rates fluctuate little, if at all, because the values of nations' monies are defined in terms of gold.

Fixed factors Factors of production that do not change in amount as the level of output changes.

Flexible (floating) exchange rates Exchange rates that fluctuate because they are determined by the forces of demand and supply.

Foreign exchange market A market for the trading of two nations' monies.

Free enterprise The right of a business to make its own decisions and to operate with a profit motive.

Free trade Goods and services can be exported and imported by anyone in any country with no restrictions.

Frictional unemployment Occurs when people are voluntarily out of work for a short period of time while searching for a job.

Full employment Occurs when only those voluntarily out of work are unemployed or the unemployment rate includes only frictional unemployment.

Full production Occurs when an economy is producing at its maximum capacity or at full employment.

GDP price index The price index used when calculating price changes for the entire economy.

General Agreement on Tariffs and Trade (GATT) An international forum for negotiating tariffs.

General partner An owner in a partnership who is subject to unlimited liability.

Government purchases of goods and services Government spending on new goods and services; nonincome-determined spending.

Government regulation Government participation, through agencies and commissions, in business decision making; may be industry regulation or social regulation.

Gramm–Leach–Bliley Act Passed in 1999 to allow bank holding companies to become financial holding companies and engage in securities and insurance activities.

Gross domestic product (GDP) A dollar figure that measures the value of all finished goods and services produced in an economy in one year.

Holding company A corporation formed for the purpose of owning or holding stock in other corporations.

Horizontal merger A merger between two sellers competing in the same market.

Household A person living alone or a group of related or unrelated persons who occupy a house, an apartment, or other housing units.

Human capital investments Investments, such as formal education, that increase the productivity of people.

Implicit costs The opportunity costs to business owners from using their resources in the business rather than in an alternative opportunity; must be recovered to keep a business in operation; normal profit.

Imports Goods and services purchased from abroad.

Income-determined spending Household spending on new goods and services that comes from income earned from providing resources to producers.

Increase in demand A change in a nonprice influence on demand causes more of a product to be demanded at each price; the demand curve shifts to the right.

Increase in supply A change in a nonprice influence on supply causes more of a product to be supplied at each price; the supply curve shifts to the right.

Individual firm's demand curve Shows the amounts of an individual firm's product that buyers are willing and able to purchase at particular prices.

Industrial Revolution A time period during which an economy becomes industrialized; characterized by such social and technological changes as the growth and development of factories.

Industry regulation Regulation affecting several aspects (such as pricing, entry of new sellers, and conditions of service) of the operations of firms in a particular industry.

Industry A group of firms producing similar products or using similar processes.

Inelastic price change and total revenue Total revenue moves in the same direction of the price change when consumers react weakly or inelastically.

Inferior good (or service) Changes in the demand for a good or service relate inversely to changes in income.

Inflation An increase in the general level of prices.

Injections into the spending stream Spending that comes from a source other than household earned income; nonincome-determined spending.

Input markets (resource markets) Markets in which households are sellers and businesses are buyers; factors of production are bought and sold.

Interest Income return to owners of capital.

Interest rate The price of money; determines the return to savers and lenders of money and the cost to borrowers; a percentage of the amount borrowed.

Interest rate effect The interest rate moves with changes in overall prices; there is an inverse relationship between the interest rate and the amount people borrow and spend.

International Monetary Fund (IMF) An international organization that provides loans and other financial assistance to countries.

International trade The buying and selling of goods and services among different countries.

Inventories Stocks of goods on hand; can be intentional or unintentional.

Inverse relationship Two variables move in opposite directions: when one increases, the other decreases; graphs as a downward-sloping line.

Investment spending Business spending on new goods, such as machinery, equipment, buildings, and inventories; nonincome-determined spending.

Invisible hand doctrine Adam Smith's concept that producers acting in their own self-interest will provide buyers with what they want and thus advance the interests of society.

Keynesian economics Based on the work of John Maynard Keynes (1883-1946), who focused on the role of aggregate spending in determining the level of macroeconomic activity.

Kinked demand curve Assumes that rivals will not follow price increases but will follow price decreases; illustrates that as a seller's price rises, the amount of its product demanded decreases substantially, but as its price falls, the amount demanded increases only slightly.

Labor Physical and mental human effort used to produce goods and services.

Labor force All persons 16 years of age and older who are working or actively seeking work.

Laissez-faire capitalism Capitalism with a strong emphasis on individual decision making; little or no government interference.

Land Productive inputs that originate in nature, such as coal and fertile soil.

Law of Demand There is an inverse relationship between the price of a product and the quantity demanded.

Law of Diminishing Marginal Utility As additional units of an item are consumed, beyond some point each successive unit of the item consumed will add less to total utility than was added by the unit consumed just before it.

Law of Diminishing Returns As additional units of a variable factor are added to a fixed factor, beyond some point the product from each additional unit of the variable factor decreases.

Law of Supply There is a direct relationship between the price of a product and the quantity supplied.

Leadership pricing One firm in a market sets a price that the other firms in the market then adopt.

Leakages from the spending stream Uses for earned income other than spending, such as paying taxes and saving.

Liability A claim on assets; an obligation or a debt of an individual or a business.

Liquidity Ease of converting an asset to its value in cash or spendable funds.

Long run A production time frame in which all factors of production are variable in amount.

Long-run total cost, average total cost, and marginal cost Total cost, per unit cost, and cost per additional unit of output, respectively; calculated for production when all inputs are regarded as variable.

M1 Narrower definition of the U.S. money supply; includes coins and paper money in circulation, some traveler's checks, most demand deposits, and other checkable deposits.

M2 M1 plus savings and small-denomination time deposit accounts and other financial instruments.

Macroeconomics The study of the operation of the economy as a whole.

Macroeconomic equilibrium Occurs when the amount of total planned spending on new goods and services equals total output in the economy.

Marginal benefit (marginal utility) The change in total satisfaction from consuming each additional unit of a good, service, or activity.

Marginal cost The change in total cost when one more unit of output is produced.

Marginal product The change in total product when one more unit of a variable resource, such as labor, is utilized.

Marginal revenue The change in total revenue when one more (or additional) unit of an item is demanded.

Marginal revenue product The change in total revenue that results from the sale of output produced when one more unit of a variable resource, such as labor, is utilized.

Market Place or situation in which the buyers and sellers of a product interact for the purpose of exchange; includes firms that sell similar products and compete for the same buyers.

Market clearing price Equilibrium price; price at which the quantity demanded equals the quantity supplied.

Market demand and market supply The demand of all buyers and supply of all sellers in a market for a good or service; found by adding together all individual demand or supply schedules.

Market economy An economy in which the basic economic decisions are made by individual buyers and sellers in markets using the language of price.

Market failure A market system creates a problem for a society or fails to achieve a society's goals.

Market structures A classification system for grouping markets according to the degree and type of competition among sellers.

Maximizing economic well-being Obtaining the greatest possible satisfaction, or return, from an economic decision.

Measure of value A function of money; the value of every good, service, and resource can be expressed in terms of an economy's base unit of money.

Medium of exchange Something that is generally accepted as payment for goods, services, and resources; the primary function of money.

Mercantilism An economic system or philosophy that subordinates individual interests and decisions to those of the state.

Microeconomics The study of individual decision-making units and markets within the economy.

Mixed economy An economy in which the basic economic choices are made through a combination of market and centralized decision making.

Model The setting within which an economic theory is presented; includes variables, assumptions, data collection, and conclusions.

Monetarism School of thought that favors stabilizing the economy through controlling the money supply.

Monetary policy Influencing the levels of aggregate output and employment or prices through changes in interest rates and the money supply.

Monetizing the debt Increasing the money supply by the Federal Reserve to accommodate federal government borrowing and reduce upward pressure on the interest rate.

Money Anything that is generally accepted as a medium of exchange.

Money (nominal) income Income measured in terms of current dollars.

Money GDP (current, or nominal, GDP) Measures the value of production in terms of prices at the time of production.

Money multiplier Multiple by which an initial change in excess reserves in the system can change the money supply.

Monopolistic competition Market structure characterized by a large number of sellers with differentiated outputs and fairly easy entry and exit.

Monopolization and attempts to monopolize A firm acquires or attempts to acquire a monopoly share of its market through unreasonable means.

Monopoly market A market with one seller that maintains its position because entry by new sellers is impossible.

Multiplier effect The change in total output and income generated by a change in nonincome-determined spending is larger than, or a multiple of, the spending change itself.

Multiplier effect (money) An initial change in excess reserves in the depository institutions system causes a larger change in the money supply.

Mutual interdependence So few sellers exist in the market that each seller weighs the actions and reactions of rivals in its decision making.

National bank Commercial bank incorporated under a federal rather than a state charter.

National debt The accumulated total debt of the federal government due to deficit spending.

National Labor Relations Act (Wagner Act) Legislation supportive of unions; permits and strengthens collective bargaining.

National Labor Relations Board (NLRB) Hears complaints on unfair labor practices and orders remedies where appropriate.

Natural monopoly A market situation where it is more efficient (less costly) to have the entire output of a product come from one large producer rather than from several smaller producers.

Natural rate hypothesis Over the long run, unemployment will tend toward its natural rate, and policies to reduce unemployment below that level will be ineffective.

Natural rate of unemployment The unemployment rate that includes the frictionally and structurally unemployed; occurs when cyclical unemployment is eliminated.

Negative externality An externality that creates a cost for others.

Net benefit The result when total cost is subtracted from total benefit.

Net benefit maximizing rules Net benefit is maximized where total benefit exceeds total cost by the greatest amount, or where marginal benefit equals marginal cost.

Net exports Exports minus imports; is positive when exports exceed imports and negative when imports exceed exports.

New classical economics A return to the basic classical premise that free markets automatically stabilize themselves and that government intervention in the macroeconomy is not advisable.

New Deal A series of programs and legislative reforms instituted during the administration of Franklin D. Roosevelt in the Great Depression of the 1930s.

New Keynesian economics Builds on the Keynesian view that the economy does not automatically return to full employment; emphasizes downward sticky prices and individual decision making in the microeconomy.

Nondurable good A good that has a short useful lifetime.

Nonincome-determined spending Spending that is generated from sources other than household earned income.

Nonprice competition Firms focus on a feature other than price to attract buyers to their products.

Nonprice factors influencing demand Nonprice factors such as income, taste, and expectations that help to determine the demand for a product.

Nonprice factors influencing supply Nonprice factors such as the cost of production and the number of sellers that help to determine the supply of a product.

Normal good (or service) Changes in the demand for a good or service relate directly to changes in income.

Normal profit Profit necessary to recover implicit costs and keep a business in operation; considered to be an economic cost of production.

Oligopoly A market dominated by a few large sellers; products are differentiated or identical; entry into the market is difficult.

On budget/off budget Categories of the unified budget established by Congress; generally refers to programs that have immediately controllable and noncontrollable receipts and expenses, respectively.

Open Market Committee Determines the general policy on the buying and selling of government securities by the Federal Reserve.

Open market operations The buying and selling of securities, primarily U.S. government securities, on the open market by the Federal Reserve.

Opportunity cost The cost of acquiring a good or service or taking an action measured in terms of the value of the opportunity or alternative forgone.

Other checkable deposits Interest-bearing accounts similar to demand deposits offered by financial depository institutions.

Output markets (product markets) Markets in which businesses are sellers and households are buyers; consumer goods and services are exchanged.

Paper monetary standard An economy's money is not backed by anything of tangible value such as gold or silver.

Participation rate The percentage of some specified group that is in the labor force.

Partnership The legal organization of a business that is similar to a proprietorship but has two or more owners.

Per se violations Anticompetitive agreements between firms where proof of the agreement is sufficient to establish guilt; includes price fixing and division of sales territories.

Personal consumption expenditures Household spending on new goods and services.

Personal income Household gross, or pretax, income; used to pay taxes, spend, and save.

Planned economy (command economy) An economy in which the basic economic decisions are made by planners rather than by private individuals and businesses.

Positive externality An externality that creates a benefit for others.

Poverty levels Government-designated levels of income that must be received to be considered *not* poor.

Price ceiling (upper price limit) A government-set maximum price that can be charged for a good or service; if the equilibrium price is above the price ceiling, a shortage will develop.

Price elastic A strong response to a price change; occurs when the percentage change in the quantity demanded or supplied is greater than the percentage change in price.

Price elasticity A measure of the strength of a buyer's or seller's response to a price change.

Price fixing Joint action by sellers to influence their product prices; considered to be highly anticompetitive.

Price floor (lower price limit) A government-set minimum price that can be charged for a good or service; if the equilibrium price is below the price floor, a surplus will develop.

Price index Measures changes in the price of an item or a group of items using a percentage scale.

Price inelastic A weak response to a price change; occurs when the percentage change in the quantity demanded or supplied is less than the percentage change in price.

Price searcher A firm that searches its downward-sloping demand curve to find the price-output combination that maximizes its profit.

Price taker A seller with no control over the price of its product; takes the market price.

Producer Price Index (PPI) Measures changes in the prices of goods and services that businesses buy, either for further processing or for sale to a consumer.

Production function Shows the type and amount of output that results from a particular group of inputs when those inputs are combined in a certain way.

Production possibilities table (or curve) Gives the various amounts of two goods that an economy can produce with full employment and fixed resources and technology.

Productivity Concept of assessing the amount of output produced by an economy's resources; often measured specifically by output per worker.

Profit maximizing rules Profit is maximized at the output level where total revenue exceeds total cost by the greatest amount, or where marginal revenue equals marginal cost.

Profit Income return to those performing the entrepreneurial function.

Profit or loss What results when a business subtracts its total costs from its total revenue.

Progressive tax A tax reflecting a direct relationship between the percentage of income taxed and the size of the income.

Proportional tax (flat tax) A tax equal to the same percentage of income regardless of the size of the income.

Proprietorship A one-owner business.

Protectionism The philosophy that it is in the best interest of a country to restrict free trade.

Public choice The study of the economic motives and attitudes of voters and public officials in collective decision making.

Public good A good (or service) provided for all of society; no one is excluded from use of a public good.

Purely competitive market A market with a large number of independent firms selling identical products, and with easy entry into and exit from the market.

Rational expectations Households and businesses base their expectations of future policies on how they think they will be affected by those policies.

Rational ignorance Choosing to remain uninformed because the marginal cost of obtaining the information is higher than the marginal benefit from knowing it.

Real GDP (constant GDP) Money GDP adjusted to eliminate inflation; measures real production.

Real income Income measured in terms of the goods and services that can be purchased with a particular amount of money income.

Real rate of interest The nominal, or stated, rate of interest minus the inflation rate; a nominal interest rate adjusted for inflation.

Recovery, peak, recession, trough The phases of the business cycle during which real GDP, or output, increases, reaches its maximum, falls, and reaches its minimum, respectively.

Regressive tax A tax reflecting an inverse relationship between the percentage of income taxed and the size of the income.

Rent Income return to owners of land resources.

Required reserves The amount of actual reserves that a financial depository institution must keep to back its deposits.

Reserve account Deposit in the name of a financial institution held at a Federal Reserve bank or other designated place.

Reserve requirement Specific percentage of deposits that a financial depository institution must keep as actual reserves.

Resources (factors of production) Persons and things used to produce goods and services; limited in amount; categorized as labor, capital, land, and entrepreneurship.

Retained earnings The portion of a business's accumulated profits that has been retained for investment or other purposes.

Revenue Money or income that a company receives from selling its product.

Right to work laws State laws prohibiting union membership as a condition of employment.

Robinson–Patman Act (1936) Federal antitrust statute concerned with anticompetitive price discrimination; amends Section Two of the Clayton Act.

Rule of Reason violations Actions that may or may not be unreasonable restraints of trade.

Saving–borrowing relationship The relationship between the amount saved by households and businesses and the amount returned to the spending stream through investment and household borrowing.

Scarcity Too few goods and services to satisfy all wants and needs.

Shadow banking The institutions and markets that engage in some traditional banking functions but operate outside of traditional banking regulations.

Sherman Act (1890) Original and most broadly worded federal antitrust statute; condemns combinations and conspiracies in restraint of trade and monopolization and attempts to monopolize.

Short run A production time frame in which some factors of production are variable in amount and some are fixed.

Shortage Occurs in a market when the quantity demanded is greater than the quantity supplied or when the product's price is below the equilibrium price.

Social benefits and costs The total effect on society from the private benefits, private costs, and externalities of an action.

Social insurance program Contributions from an individual's earnings are made to a fund from which that individual may draw when eligible for benefits.

Social regulation Regulation aimed at correcting a problem or protecting a group; not limited to a specific industry.

Socialism An economic system in which many of the factors of production are collectively owned, and an attempt is made to equalize the distribution of income.

Specialization Productive resources concentrate on a narrow range of tasks or the production of a limited variety of goods and services.

Stagflation Occurs when an economy experiences high rates of both inflation and unemployment.

Strike Work stoppage by union members.

Structural unemployment Involuntary unemployment that results when a worker's job is no longer part of the production structure of the economy.

Subprime mortgages Borrowers have lower credit ratings and a greater risk of default; interest rates tend to be higher than prime mortgages.

Supply The different amounts of a product that a seller would make available for sale at different prices in a defined time period when all nonprice factors are held constant.

Supply curve A line on a graph that illustrates a supply schedule; slopes upward because of the direct relationship between price and quantity supplied.

Supply curve of labor Upward-sloping curve showing the amount of labor supplied at different wage rates.

Supply-side economics Policies to achieve macroeconomic goals by stimulating the supply side of the market; popular in the 1980s.

Surplus Occurs in a market when the quantity supplied exceeds the quantity demanded, or when the product's price is above the equilibrium price.

Surplus budget A government's revenues are greater than its expenditures.

Taft–Hartley Act Legislation that contains several provisions limiting union activities.

Tariff A tax on an import.

Tax abatement A policy of reducing or eliminating a tax that would normally be charged.

Tax base The particular thing on which a tax is levied.

Tax rate The amount that is levied on a tax base.

Tax reform Changes in tax policies and structures.

Technology The body of knowledge that exists about production and its processes.

Tight money policy Policy by the Federal Reserve to reduce excess reserves and raise interest rates to reduce spending.

Total benefit (total utility) The total amount of satisfaction received from consuming a specified number of units of a good, service, or activity.

Total cost The cost of producing a specified number of units of a good, service, or activity; total fixed cost plus total variable cost.

Total fixed cost The cost of all fixed factors; does not change as the level of output changes and must be paid even when output is zero.

Total revenue Revenue received from selling a certain quantity of an item; calculated by multiplying the price of an item by the quantity demanded at that price.

Total, or aggregate, spending The total combined spending of all units in the economy (households plus businesses plus government plus foreign) for new goods and services.

Total utility Total satisfaction from consuming a particular combination of goods and services.

Total variable cost The cost of all variable factors of production; increases as the level of output increases, but is zero when output is zero.

Traditional economy An economy that relies on tradition, custom, or ritual to decide what to produce, how to produce it, and to whom to distribute the results.

Transfer payments Money from the government for which no direct work is performed in return.

Trust fund A restricted fund; payments from this fund are specified as to recipients and/or uses.

U.S. Treasury security Issued by the federal government in return for funds lent to it.

Underemployment A resource is employed in a way that does not fully use its capabilities; intensifies the scarcity problem.

Unemployment Resources available for production are not being used.

Unemployment rate The percentage of the labor force that is unemployed and actively seeking work.

Unified budget A budget that assembles all federal government receipts and outlays, and the resulting overall deficit or surplus, in one report.

Unitary price elastic The percentage change in quantity demanded or supplied equals the percentage change in price; elasticity coefficient equals one.

Unlimited liability A business owner's personal assets are subject to use as payment for business debts.

Utility Satisfaction realized from consuming a good or service, or taking an action.

Value judgment The relative importance one assigns to an action or alternative.

Value of money Measured by the goods, services, and resources that money can purchase.

Variable costs Costs of using variable factors.

Variable factors Factors of production that change in amount as the level of output changes.

Velocity of money Average number of times the money supply is turned over in a year in relationship to GDP.

Vertical merger A merger between a firm and a supplier or distributor.

Wage The price of labor; income return to labor.

Wealth A measure of the value of tangible assets; includes such items as real estate and corporate securities.

Wealth effect In order to maintain the same amount of accumulated wealth, people spend less when prices rise and more when prices fall.

Chapter 1

The economy's production possibilities curve is shown by the solid line in the figure accompanying these answers.

1. Twelve million units of capital goods (capital goods decreased from 32 to 20 million units); 10 million units of consumer goods (consumer goods decreased from 10 million units to zero).
2. Point A is slightly to the left of the production possibilities curve, and point B is further to the left than point A.
3. The location of point C depends on how one views the relative importance of capital goods and consumer goods. Point C will be closer to the horizontal axis if capital goods are considered to be relatively more important and closer to the vertical axis if consumer goods are considered to be relatively more important. Students put point C on the curve based on their opinions about the relative importance of capital goods and consumer goods.
4. If only consumer goods were produced, no machinery or equipment would be produced to replace what is currently being used, and future production would be adversely affected. If only capital goods were produced, there would be nothing to sustain people currently.
5. The production possibilities curve would shift to the right as illustrated by the lighter line in the accompanying figure.

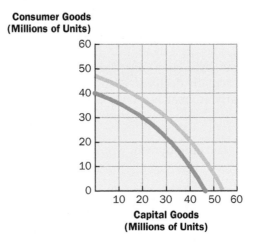

Chapter 2

1. a. pure market; b. pure planned; c. mixed; d. pure market; e. pure planned; f. mixed
2. a. Flow of money from households to businesses and flow of goods and services from businesses to households; saving more and spending less reduce the money flow and the goods and services flow.
   b. Flow of factors of production from households to businesses and flow of income from businesses to households; reducing the flows on the bottom half reduces the flows on the top half.
   c. Saving more and spending less decrease the production of goods and services which, in turn, decreases employment of resources and income.

Chapter 3

1. d; supply curve shifts to the left; increase; decrease
2. a; demand curve shifts to the right; increase; increase
3. d; supply curve shifts to the left; increase; decrease
4. e; no shifts; none; none (changes price, not a nonprice factor)
5. b; demand curve shifts to the left; decrease; decrease
6. a; demand curve shifts to the right; increase; increase
7. c; supply curve shifts to the right; decrease; increase
8. b; demand curve shifts to the left; decrease; decrease
9. a; demand curve shifts to the right; increase; increase
10. e; no shifts; none; none (changes price, not a nonprice factor)
11. b; demand curve shifts to the left; decrease; decrease
12. c; supply curve shifts to the right; decrease; increase
13. e; no shifts; none; none (changes price, not a nonprice factor)
14. c; supply curve shifts to the right; decrease; increase

Chapter 4

1. Price Index	Price Index		2. Money GDP	GDP Price Index	Real GDP
80.0	64.0		$5,000,000	100.0	$5,000,000
100.0	80.0		6,050,000	110.0	5,500,000
110.0	88.0		6,250,000	125.0	5,000,000
125.0	100.0		5,850,000	130.0	4,500,000
130.0	104.0		9,000,000	150.0	6,000,000
150.0	120.0		9,300,000	155.0	6,000,000

3. Real GDP 2006: $1,000; 2007: $1,000; 2008: $1,200; 2009: $1,250; 2010: $1,250; 2011: $1,200; 2012: $1,250.
   a. The economy's output did not grow from 2006 to 2007, grew from 2007 through 2009, did not grow in 2010, decreased in 2011, and grew again in 2012.
   b. Unlike the impression given by money GDP, the economy's real GDP, or output, did not grow every year, and in 2011 it actually declined. Also, the overall growth rate in output from 2006 through 2012 was not nearly as great as money GDP would lead one to believe.

Chapter 5

From each action taken alone, output and employment would change as follows:

1. increase
2. decrease
3. increase
4. increase
5. decrease
6. no change (demand-pull inflation would result)
7. decrease
8. increase
9. increase
10. no change (demand-pull inflation would result)
11. decrease
12. decrease
13. no change (demand-pull inflation would result)
14. increase
15. decrease

From each of these actions, total output and income would change as follows:

16. increase by $200 million
17. decrease by $87.5 billion
18. increase by $400 million

19. decrease by $12 billion
20. decrease by $12.5 million ($20 million export injection − $25 million import leakage ÷ 0.40 = −$12.5 million)
21. increase by $400 million (80 percent of $100 million transfer payment = $80 million in spending; $80 million ÷ 0.20 = $400 million)

Chapter 6

1. output and employment increase
2. output and employment will decrease (some portion of the Social Security will be saved and not spent, while all of the government purchases amount will be a decrease in spending)
3. price levels increase
4. output and employment increase
5. output and employment decrease
6. output and employment decrease
7. output and employment decrease
8. output and employment increase
9. price levels increase
10. price levels increase
11. output and employment decrease
12. output and employment decrease
13. output and employment increase
14. output and employment decrease

Chapter 7

1. $18,871,340
2. $38,014,440
3. $11,956,741
4. $14,840,000

Chapter 8

1. required reserves = $1,350,000; actual reserves = $6,000,000; excess reserves = $4,650,000
2. new loans = $9,700,000
3. new borrowing = $50,000
4. money multiplier = 12.5; money supply increase = $625,000,000
5. decrease in excess reserves = $335,000
6. new excess reserves = $2,000,000
7. new excess reserves by Carolina Coast = $0; new excess reserves by Inland Bank = $4,000,000
8. money supply increase = $280,000,000

Chapter 9

1. Draw a vertical supply curve (S) at full employment output and a downward-sloping demand curve (D). a. Label their intersection as P_0W_0. b. Draw a demand curve (D1) that has shifted to the left. c. Label the intersection of D1 and S as P_1W_1. d. The economy arrived at this new position because prices and wages are flexible downward. See the following graph.

2.

Total Output	Economic Condition
$0	Expansion
$200	Expansion
$400	Expansion
$600	Equilibrium
$800	Contraction
$1,000	Contraction

3.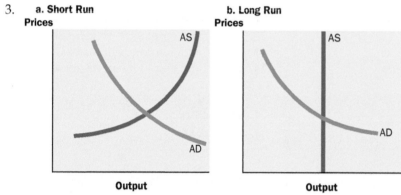

a.   In the short run, a decrease in demand would bring a slight decrease in prices and a decrease in output. In the long run, a decrease in demand brings a decrease in prices, but no change in output.

Chapter 10

1. increase in supply causing equilibrium price to fall
2. increase in demand and a possible decrease in supply causing equilibrium price to rise
3. decrease in demand and a possible increase in supply causing equilibrium price to fall
4. decrease in demand and increase in supply causing equilibrium price to fall
5. increase in supply causing equilibrium price to fall
6. decrease in demand and increase in supply causing equilibrium price to fall

Chapter 11

According to Table 1, Pete should charge $98 and complete four drawings to maximize his profit from the drawings. In going for volume, as suggested by his roommate, his total profit would be $128 less than that received from producing and selling four drawings.

As for the lithographs, Pete should charge $100 each and sell eight earning a total profit of $495. This is indicated in Table 2.

TABLE 1 *Custom-Drawn Houses*

Price per Drawing	Number of Drawings Demanded	Total Revenue	Marginal Revenue	Marginal Cost	Total Cost	Profit
$138	0	$0			$0	$0
128	1	128	$128	$50	50	78
118	2	236	108	50	100	136
108	3	324	88	50	150	174
98	4	392	68	50	200	192
88	5	440	48	50	250	190
78	6	468	28	50	300	168
68	7	476	8	50	350	126
58	8	464	−12	50	400	64

TABLE 2 *Lithographs*

Price per Lithograph	Number of Lithographs Demanded	Total Revenue	Marginal Revenue	Marginal Cost	Total Cost	Profit or Loss
$180	0	$0			$0	$0
170	1	170	$170	$200	200	−30
160	2	320	150	15	215	105
150	3	450	130	15	230	220
140	4	560	110	15	245	315
130	5	650	90	15	260	390
120	6	720	70	15	275	445
110	7	770	50	15	290	480
100	8	800	30	15	305	495
90	9	810	10	15	320	490
80	10	800	−10	15	335	465

Chapter 12

1. 92 percent, fall, lower, 85.5 percent
   fall, lower, 83.7 percent
   rise, higher, 86 percent

2.

Pickups per Business Day	TFC	TVC	TC	ATC	MC
0	$100	$0	$100	—	
					$250
1	100	250	350	$350	
					50
2	100	300	400	200	
					0
3	100	300	400	133.33	
					50
4	100	350	450	112.50	
					75
5	100	425	525	105	

3. $2,025; $3,420; $6,183; $2.25; $1.90; $2.29

4.

Output	TFC	TVC	TC	ATC	MC
0	$80	$0	$80	—	
1	80	40	120	$120	$40
2	80	60	140	70	20
3	80	70	150	50	10
4	80	100	180	45	30
5	80	150	230	46	50
6	80	220	300	50	70
7	80	340	420	60	120
8	80	520	600	75	180

Chapter 13

1. a.

b. The drought will decrease supply raising market price and shifting the individual seller's demand curve upward. See the above graph.

2. a. In the long run, supply will decrease as sellers that are losing money leave the market, price will increase, and the individual demand curve will shift upward until sellers are just breaking even or operating where price equals lowest average total cost.

b.

c. In the long run, price will equal lowest average total cost.

3.

4. In pure competition, the monopolistically competitive firm does not operate at lowest average total cost because product differentiation causes the individual firm's demand curve to be downward sloping. In pure competition where the individual firm's demand curve is a horizontal line at the market price and there is no product differentiation, firms can operate at lowest average total cost.

Chapter 13 Appendix

1. The total revenue values in the table are $0, $2, $4, $2,000, $2,002, $2,004, $20,000, $20,002, and $20,004. All marginal revenue values are $2.00.
   a. Draw a perfectly horizontal line at $2.00 and mark it D = MR
   b. 7,000 bushels
   c. $2.50; loss $0.50; loss $3,500
   d. Draw a perfectly horizontal line at $3.50 and mark it D = MR
   e. 9,000 bushels
   f. $2.50; profit $1.00; profit $9,000
2. 5,000 units; $9.00; $5.00; profit $4.00; profit $20,000

Chapter 14

1. social regulation—Environmental Protection Agency
2. no government intervention
3. social regulation—Consumer Product Safety Commission
4. antitrust enforcement—Sherman Act Section 1 price fixing violation
5. no government intervention—the sellers are pure competitors responding to the price rather than fixing it
6. industry regulation
7. antitrust enforcement—Celler–Kefauver Act
8. no government intervention
9. industry regulation
10. antitrust enforcement—Sherman Act Section 2 monopolization violation

Chapter 15

In Table 1, marginal product is 500, 500, 500, 400, and 300.
1. the fourth worker
In Table 3, total revenue is $0, $25, $45, $60, $66.50, and $67.50. Marginal revenue product is $25, $20, $15, $6.50, and $1.00.
2. $25 per hour
3. $15 per hour
4. no, the MRP of the fifth worker is just $1
In Table 4, the quantity of workers demanded with each wage rate is 1—$25; 2—$20; 3—$15; 4—$6.50; 5—$1.00. These numbers are used to plot the demand curve in the figure.

Chapter 16

1. a. 1/2, 2, Canada
   b. 2, 1/2, Brazil
   c. 12, 12
   d. 16 of wheat, 16 of soybeans
   e. 8, 8

2. a. 1/5, 4, Mexico
   b. 5, 1/4, Venezuela
   c. 525, 200
   d. 1,000 lamps, 200 gallons of gasoline
   e. 50, 200

Chapter 17

1. decrease, decrease, decrease, increase
2. increase, decrease, increase, increase
3. increase, increase, increase, decrease
4. decrease, increase, decrease, decrease
5. increase, increase, increase, decrease
6. decrease, increase, decrease, decrease or increase depending on whether the effect of the change in demand was greater or less than the effect of the change in supply, increase

INDEX